SYMBOLISM

Exposition of the Doctrinal Differences
Between Catholics and Protestants
as Evidenced by Their Symbolical Writings

SYMBOLISM

EXPOSITION OF THE DOCTRINAL DIFFERENCES
BETWEEN CATHOLICS AND PROTESTANTS
AS EVIDENCED BY THEIR SYMBOLICAL WRITINGS

JOHANN ADAM MÖHLER

TRANSLATED BY
JAMES BURTON ROBERTSON

INTRODUCTION BY
MICHAEL J. HIMES

A Crossroad Herder Book
THE CROSSROAD PUBLISHING COMPANY   NEW YORK

The Crossroad Publishing Company
370 Lexington Avenue, New York, NY 10017

Introduction Copyright © 1997 by Michael J. Himes

All rights reserved. No part of this introduction may be reproduced, stored in a retrieval system, or transmitted, in any form or by any means, electronic, mechanical, photocopying, recording, or otherwise, without the written permission of The Crossroad Publishing Company.

Imprimatur
GULIELMUS PRAEPOSITUS JOHNSON
Vicarius Generalis

WESTMONASTERII
die 24 Augusti 1905

Library of Congress Cataloging-in-Publication Data

Möhler, Johann Adam, 1796-1838.
 [Symbolik, oder, Darstellung der dogmatischen Gegensätze Katholiken und Protestanten nach ihren öffentlichen Bekenntnisschriften. English]
 Symbolism : exposition of the doctrinal differences between Catholics and Protestants as evidenced by their symbolical writings / Johann Adam Möhler; translated by James Burton Robertson; introduction by Michael J. Himes.
  p. cm.
 "A Crossroad Herder book"
 Includes bibliographical references.
 ISBN 978-0-8245-1665-9 (pbk.)
  1. Creeds—Comparative studies. 2. Catholic Church—Doctrinal and controversial works—Catholic authors. Protestantism.
 I. Robertson, James Burton, 1800-1877. II. Title.
 BT990. M5513 1997
 238—dc21   96-51962
                                                           CIP

CONTENTS

Introduction to the 1997 Edition *by Michael J. Himes* . . . xi
Preface xxiii

INTRODUCTION

Nature, extent, and sources of Symbolism 1
    SYMBOLICAL WRITINGS OF CATHOLICS AND PROTESTANTS
The Catholic formularies 11
The Lutheran formularies 15
The Calvinistic and Zwinglian formularies 17

BOOK I

CHAPTER I

DIFFERENCES IN DOCTRINE RESPECTING THE PRIMITIVE STATE OF MAN AND THE ORIGIN OF EVIL

SECTION
I. Primitive state of man, according to the Catholic doctrine . 23
II. The Lutheran doctrine on man's original state . . . 29
III. The Calvinistic doctrine on the primitive state of man . 33
IV. On the Cause of moral evil 37

CHAPTER II

ON ORIGINAL SIN AND ITS CONSEQUENCES

V. The Catholic doctrine of original sin 45
VI. Doctrine of the Lutherans respecting original sin . . 54
VII. Considerations on Heathenism, in reference to the doctrines controverted between the two Churches . . . 66
VIII. Doctrine of the Calvinists on original sin . . . 73
IX. Zwingle's view of original sin 79

CHAPTER III

OPPOSITE VIEWS ON THE DOCTRINE OF JUSTIFICATION

X. General statement of the mode in which, according to the different confessions, man becomes justified . . 82
XI. Of the relation of the operation of God to that of man, in the work of regeneration, according to the Catholic and the Lutheran systems 86

CONTENTS

SECTION		PAGE
XII.	Doctrine of the Calvinists on the relation of grace to freedom, and human co-operation—Predestination	96
XIII.	Of the Catholic notion of justification	101
XIV.	Doctrine of the Protestants on justification and sanctification	110

ON JUSTIFYING FAITH

XV.	Catholic view of this subject	118
XVI.	Lutheran and Calvinistic view of faith	124

APPRECIATION OF THE THEORETIC AND PRACTICAL GROUNDS, WHICH THE PROTESTANTS ALLEGE FOR THEIR VIEW OF FAITH

XVII.	Appreciation of the theoretic grounds	132
XVIII.	Appreciation of the practical grounds	138
XIX.	Survey of the differences in the doctrine of faith	149
XX.	On the assurance of justification and eternal felicity	152

OF GOOD WORKS

XXI.	Doctrine of Catholics respecting good works	157
XXII.	Doctrine of the Protestants respecting good works	161
XXIII.	The doctrine of purgatory in its connection with the Catholic doctrine of justification	170
XXIV.	Opposition between the communions in their general conception of Christianity	175
XXV.	The culminating point of inquiry—Luther maintains an inward and essential opposition between religion and morality, and assigns to the former an eternal, to the latter a mere temporal value	184
XXVI.	Analysis of the elements of truth and of error in the Protestant doctrine of faith, as hitherto stated	191
XXVII.	Affinity of Protestantism with Gnosticism, and some Pantheistic systems of the Middle Age—More accurate determination of the difference between Zwingle's and Luther's principles	194

CHAPTER IV

DIFFERENCES IN THE DOCTRINE OF THE SACRAMENTS

XXVIII.	Doctrine of Catholics on the sacraments in general	202
XXIX.	Lutheran doctrine of the sacraments in general—Consequences of this doctrine	205
XXX.	Further consequences of the original Lutheran view of the essence of a sacrament	213
XXXI.	Zuinglius and Calvin on the Sacraments	216
XXXII.	Baptism and penance	218
XXXIII.	Continuation of the doctrine of penance	223

CONTENTS

SECTION		PAGE
XXXIV.	Doctrine of the Catholics on the most Holy Sacrament of the Altar, and on the Mass	235
XXXV.	Doctrine of the Lutherans, Zwinglians, and Calvinists, on the Eucharist	249

CHAPTER V

DIFFERENCES IN RESPECT TO THE DOCTRINE ON THE CHURCH

XXXVI.	Notion of the Church—Combination of divine and human elements in her—Infallibility of the Church	255
XXXVII.	More detailed exposition of the Catholic view of the Church	260
XXXVIII.	The Church as teacher and instructress—Tradition—The Church as judge in matters of faith	277
XXXIX.	The Church as interpreter of Holy Writ, and the doctrine on tradition continued	282
XL.	Formal distinction between scriptural and ecclesiastical doctrine	288
XLI.	Tradition in a more limited sense—The canon of the Scriptures	292
XLII.	On the relation of the ecclesiastical interpretation of Holy Writ to the learned and scientific exegesis—Patristic authority and free investigation	295
XLIII.	The Hierarchy	304

LUTHERAN DOCTRINE ON THE CHURCH

XLIV.	The Bible the only source and arbitress in matters of faith	310
XLV.	Continuation—Internal ordination—Every Christian a priest and teacher, and consequently independent of all ecclesiastical communion—Notion of ecclesiastical freedom	318
XLVI.	Continuation—Invisible Church	323
XLVII.	Continuation—Rise of the visible Church according to Luther—Ultimate reasons for the truth of an article of faith	326
XLVIII.	Continuation—Divergences in the doctrine on the Church, shortly expressed	330
XLIX.	The truth and the falsehood in Luther's doctrine on the Church	334
L.	Negative doctrines of the Lutherans in regard to the Church	337
LI.	Doctrine of the Calvinists on the Church	340

CHAPTER VI

THE CHURCH IN THE NEXT WORLD, AND ITS CONNECTION WITH THE CHURCH MILITANT

LII.	Doctrine of Catholics on this matter	349
LIII.	Doctrine of Protestants on this subject	354

CONTENTS

BOOK II

THE SMALLER PROTESTANT SECTS

SECTION		PAGE
LIV.	Introduction	359

CHAPTER I

THE ANABAPTISTS OR MENNONITES

FIRST PERIOD OF THE ANABAPTISTS

LV.	Fundamental principle of the Anabaptists	363
LVI.	Initiation into the sect—Signs and confirmation of covenant	367
LVII.	These sectaries assail the Protestant doctrine of justification	370
LVIII.	Continuation—Concurrence of the most various errors in the sect	372
LIX.	Continuation—Relation of Scripture to the inward spirit—The Church	375
LX.	Hatred against all outward institutions for promoting edification—Ecclesiastical discipline—Manners and customs	378
LXI.	The Anabaptists in the form of Mennonites; their second period	379
LXII.	Peculiar doctrines of the Mennonites—Their Church discipline	381
LXIII.	Conclusion—Special controversies	384

CHAPTER II

THE QUAKERS

LXIV.	Some historical preliminary remarks	387
LXV.	Religious system of the Quakers—The inward light	390
LXVI.	Continuation of the same subject—Effects of the inward light	393
LXVII.	Continuation of the same subject—Of justification and sanctification—Perfect fulfilment of the law	396
LXVIII.	Continuation of the same subject—Doctrine on the Sacraments	400
LXIX.	Continuation of the same subject—Rejection of a distinct order of ministry—Preaching—Public worship	401
LXX.	Peculiar manners and customs of the Quakers	405
LXXI.	Remarks on the doctrinal peculiarities of the Quakers	407

CHAPTER III

THE HERRNHUTTERS, OR THE COMMUNITY OF BROTHERS, AND THE METHODISTS

| LXXII. | Historical remarks—The Moravian Brethren | 422 |
| LXXIII. | Continuation of the same subject—Spener and the Pietists | 425 |

CONTENTS

SECTION
LXXIV. Combination of the doctrinal peculiarities of the Moravians and the Pietists 430
LXXV. The Methodists—Religious state of England at the beginning of the eighteenth century—Profound degradation of public morals — The Methodists wish to bring about a reform—Comparison between the reforming efforts of Catholics and of Protestants at similar epochs 434
LXXVI. Peculiar doctrines of the Methodists—Marks of distinction between them and the Herrnhutters—Division of the sect into Wesleyans and Whitfieldites . . . 438

CHAPTER IV

THE DOCTRINE OF SWEDENBORG

LXXVII. Some preliminary historical remarks . . . 445
LXXVIII. Practical tendency of Swedenborg—His judgment on the Reformers, and his account of their destiny in the next life 447
LXXIX. Swedenborg's doctrine on the Trinity—His motive for assailing that of the Church 450
LXXX. Swedenborg denies the fall of man in Adam—Contradictions in his theory on this matter . . 454
LXXXI. Incarnation of the Divinity—Objects of the incarnation —Relation between grace and free-will . . 456
LXXXII. Swedenborg's doctrine relative to the sacraments . 462
LXXXIII. Swedenborg's revelations from the other world . 464
LXXXIV. Biblical canon of Swedenborg—Allegorico-mystical exegesis 466
LXXXV. Swedenborg's place in history 469
LXXXVI. Concluding remarks 476

CHAPTER V

THE SOCINIANS

LXXXVII. Relation of the Socinians to the Reformers, Historical remarks 478
LXXXVIII. Principles of the Socinians, as to the relation between reason and revelation, and the functions of the former in the interpretation of Holy Writ . . . 482
LXXXIX. Doctrine of the Socinians respecting God and the person of Christ 484
XC. On the fall and the regeneration of man . . 490
XCI. On the sacraments 496

CHAPTER VI

THE ARMINIANS, OR REMONSTRANTS

SECTION
- XCII. Some historical preliminary remarks . . . 497
- XCIII. Doctrine of the Arminians . . . 499
- XCIV. Doctrine of the Arminians on the sacraments . . 504

APPENDIX

Note A, referred to at page 232 507
Note B, referred to at page 238 508

INTRODUCTION TO THE 1997 EDITION

For most of the 165 years since its first publication, *Symbolik*[1] was far and away the best-known and most influential work by Johann Adam Möhler (1796-1838). After its appearance in 1832, responses to Möhler's comparison of Catholic and Protestant doctrinal positions on the basis of the official credal statements of the various churches came from several distinguished theologians of the time.[2] The most notable was a book-length attack by Ferdinand Christian Baur, a member of the Protestant theology faculty at Tübingen, the university where Möhler taught on the Catholic faculty.[3] This provoked from Möhler a book-length defense of *Symbolik* to which Baur replied with a long article which in turn led to Möhler's issuing a second and longer edition of his defense.[4] The controversy surrounding his book led Möhler to issue in rapid succession a number of expanded and considerably revised editions of *Symbolik* in the five years following its first publication. The need for these new editions is an indication of the interest that the book excited. By 1843, when the English translation appeared, *Symbolik* had appeared in French, Italian, Dutch, and Swedish, and a Polish translation was to follow later in the century. Möhler, who taught what we today would describe as historical theology, came to be remembered as first and foremost a *Symboliker*, a "symbolist" or student of credal statements.[5] For new readers of *Symbolik* or *Symbolism*, as the English translation is called,[6] it may be useful to offer a brief note about the author, the book, and the translation.

THE AUTHOR

Johann Adam Möhler was born on May 6, 1796, in the little town of Igersheim in Württemberg (southwestern Germany), the son of the local baker. He studied first at the Latin school in nearby Mergentheim and then at the *Lyzeum* at Ellwangen. In 1815 he began the study of theology at the seminary there.

The Ellwangen seminary had been founded three years before Möhler became a student. Ellwangen proved too remote from intellectual centers to be a suitable location for the new theological faculty, and in

1817 the faculty was moved to Tübingen and incorporated into the university. This was an unusual decision because Tübingen already boasted a distinguished Protestant theological faculty whose recent students had included Schelling, Hegel, and Hölderlin. Möhler moved with his teachers and fellow students to Tübingen. Several members of the Catholic faculty were interested in the new currents at work in German romanticism and idealist philosophy. The most influential of these was Johann Sebastian Drey, Möhler's teacher and subsequently his colleague on the faculty. Drey was eager to replace the combination of rationalism and scholasticism that served as the philosophical base for much of Catholic theology with the more "scientific" (i.e., methodologically rigorous) and historically conscious philosophy best represented by Schelling.[7] Drey was a prime mover in the Catholic Tübingen faculty's founding of the *Theologische Quartalschrift*, a journal that remains today one of the most important organs of Catholic theology in the German-speaking world.

After some hesitation about whether he should seek ordination, Möhler entered the major seminary in Rottenburg in 1818 and was ordained a priest the next year. Following a year of pastoral ministry, he was chosen to continue his studies at Tübingen in preparation for teaching at a Catholic *Gymnasium*. His education had prepared him for a career in classical philology, but when the need arose in the Catholic theology faculty for a teacher of church history, the young priest's knowledge of Greek and Latin made him a suitable candidate. In 1821 he was appointed as a tutor and the next year a lecturer in church history at Tübingen. To prepare himself to teach he began a seven-month tour of the major German theological faculties, both Protestant and Catholic. Berlin proved to be the highlight of his trip; there Möhler heard Schleiermacher and was especially impressed by church historian August Neander.

At Tübingen Möhler initially concentrated his teaching on patristics. This interest in the early church combined with the desire to fulfil the need that he and his colleagues such as Drey saw for a new theological and ecclesiastical vision found expression in his first book *Einheit in der Kirche*, published in 1825. Although the book claimed to be a study of ante-Nicene patristic theology, it was in fact far more concerned with the nineteenth century than the first three Christian centuries. The book inspired many young Catholic intellectuals and alarmed some church leaders. Möhler himself came to think that he had overstated some things in the book but refused to disavow *Einheit* even when it cost him a professorship at the university of Bonn. In 1827 he published

Athanasius der Grosse und der Kirche seiner Zeit, a study of the Arian controversy in the fourth century centering on the role of Athanasius of Alexandria. Once again, however, theological issues of his own time played through the supposedly patristic study. In it Möhler distanced himself from Schleiermacher, who had been a very important influence on *Einheit*, by a careful critique of the latter's teaching on the Trinity.[8] In the next five years he wrote a number of important articles for the *Theologische Quartalschrift*, most notably two lengthy pieces on Anselm of Canterbury in which he began to pay closer attention to medieval theology.[9] Then in 1832 came *Symbolik*. Its subsequent revised editions and his responses to F. C. Baur occupied most of the rest of Möhler's life. By 1834 his health, always somewhat precarious, was clearly failing; the underlying cause was probably tuberculosis. The atmosphere at Tübingen was acrimonious; his chief critic, Baur, was a member of the faculty there. A change of scene seemed necessary, and so in 1835 he accepted a call to a professorship at Munich which was engineered by his young admirer, Ignaz von Döllinger, who was destined for a long, distinguished, and—after Vatican I—tragic career in German Catholic theology. But Möhler's health continued to deteriorate. When early in 1838 it became clear that his failing strength could no longer bear the strain of teaching, he was appointed a canon of the cathedral of Würzburg, in effect, an early retirement. But before he could leave Munich, he died on April 12, 1838, a few weeks before his forty-second birthday.

Möhler has remained the best known of the group of theologians frequently described as the Catholic Tübingen school, although increased attention is now deservedly being given to Drey and to Möhler's student, Johannes Evangelist Kuhn. The triumph of neo-scholasticism later in the century and the fact that the Tübingen theologians were not ardent supporters of the definition of papal infallibility as it was formulated at Vatican I led to an eclipse of the kind of theology associated with the Catholic faculty at Tübingen. *Symbolik*'s portrayal of Protestant doctrinal positions remained part of the standard Catholic polemical arsenal, but its positive presentation of the Catholic tradition was less regarded. Möhler's other work, especially *Einheit*, went largely unread. The Tübingen theologians stood apart from much of the rest of Catholic theology in the nineteenth century by their criticism of the regnant neo-scholasticism, openness to modern philosophical thought, and emphasis on the importance of critical historical research. In a church whose theology tended to be ultramontanist, ahistorical, and intensely hostile to modern philosophy, the Tübingen school was suspect. Early in the twentieth century some even tried to trace the roots of Modernism to

Tübingen.[10] In the middle years of the twentieth century, the work of scholars like Stefan Lösch[11] and especially Joseph Rupert Geiselmann[12] contributed to a great revival of interest in the work of Möhler and his colleagues and students. The ecclesiological work of Yves Congar and Henri de Lubac among others reawakened interest particularly in Möhler's first book *Einheit in der Kirche*.[13] Since Vatican II more and more attention has been paid to that earlier work with its Spirit-centered understanding of the church, its insistence on the charismatic basis of church leadership, and its profoundly organic model of the community so typical of German romantic thought. But the fact that it had to wait 170 years to be translated into English, whereas *Symbolik* appeared in English eleven years after its first edition in German and five years after its author's death, is testimony to how much Möhler's reputation has rested on the latter book, especially among English-speaking readers.[14]

THE BOOK

In the six years between its first publication in 1832 and its author's death, *Symbolik* was something of a work in progress. Möhler issued a second edition in 1833, a third in 1834, a fourth in 1835, and was working on a fifth at the time of his death in 1838. Each of these editions contains significant revisions and expansions of the previous edition. The text as we have it is that of the fifth edition which Möhler had revised to section 25 (the middle of his discussion of "good works"); from section 26 on the text is the same as that of the fourth edition.[15]

Why did Möhler write the book? Like his teacher Drey, he was convinced that theology has to be "of the age," i.e., it must reflect the intellectual spirit of its time, whether that reflection is an embrace or a rejection. The spirit of his age was a growing reaction against the Enlightenment's attempt to discern abstract rational truths behind historical forms. The idea that one could disengage a "timeless" truth from its husk, the way it was expressed at a particular time and place, and then discard that husk was being challenged by the celebration of the historical and the particular in German romantic thought. Hegel's insistence that consciousness is embodied in concrete, historically conditioned forms and that it is by the study of those forms that consciousness unfolds is paralleled by Möhler's claim that one gains insight into a particular religious confession only by recovering the living perception expressed in doctrinal formulae.[16] Thus in *Symbolik* Möhler attempted to uncover the inner religious vision expressed by the doctrinal positions of Catholicism and Protestantism.

We may gain insight into the book by considering what Möhler understood as the task of symbolics. He addresses this issue in the introduction to *Symbolik*, and much of what he writes accords with the position assigned to this field of study by his teacher Drey in his outline of the areas of theology and their methods.

Drey had described "symbolics" as the study of what is "closed" in doctrine, i.e., what has reached mature formulation and is accordingly "fixed." Symbolics

> stands necessarily in close relation to particular forms of church—ecclesiastical sects—each of which possesses its own peculiar confession and so its own creed. In consequence, each sect compares its creed with those of others. Thus symbolics serves an ecclesial purpose. In a still narrower sense, although one derived from this same purpose, symbolics is also called the study of *doctrinal differences* among the various Christian confessions.[17]

This certainly describes part of what Möhler does in *Symbolik*. But the even more important part of his work is what Drey describes as "the system of Christian doctrine":

> The task of this branch of scientific theology is to study the doctrine of Christianity in the development which it has undergone up until now and in its relation to the Christian confession, whose tradition one shares, by constructing the whole from its idea with systematic coherence.[18]

Thus *Symbolik* was not primarily a historical study. First and foremost, it was designed by its author to be a work of systematic theology.

What made *Symbolik* such a *cause célèbre* when it appeared? Of the many factors that made the book important to Möhler's contemporaries two may be especially noted: its method and its structure. The structure of *Symbolik* flows from Möhler's "scientific," *wissenschaftlich*, method. Möhler received this notion of science from Schelling through Drey. Science is, in this sense, a body of knowledge rigorously organized in accord with basic principles. The basic principle is that of "construction," which Schelling had described as "the representation of the universal and the particular in their unity,"[19] i.e., the conscious and deliberate attempt to render the whole and the part intelligible in terms of one another, a method closely related to Hegel's claim that the true cannot be grasped except through its concrete manifestations. The romantic metaphor for this was the organism in which the parts are the outgrowth of the whole to which they contribute and the whole is the living interplay of the parts. Truly to know something, to understand it, to grasp its reality, is to see its organic unfolding. And that is precisely what Möhler set out to do in *Symbolik*: to show how a fundamental religious insight into the relation of the divine and the human develops into a coherent doctrinal system — and how a fundamentally mistaken and inadequate religious insight of this sort inevitably leads to a destructive and irrational doctrinal system such as he believed the Protestant theology of his time to be. He wanted his readers to see the doctrinal formulae related to one another like the unfolding petals of a flower, each distinct, each an intrinsic part of the whole. This method determined the arrangement of topics in the book.

Critics of *Symbolik* complained that the order of the topics treated was incomprehensible. The author, they suggested, should have followed either a historical presentation and begun with a discussion of the leading idea of the Reformation which Luther first put forth, the doctrine of justification by faith, or a doctrinal organization and started with scripture and church authority as different norms of faith for Protestants and Catholics.[20] Instead, Möhler begins with what we might today term theological anthropology. He starts with a discussion of the differing views contained in Protestant and Catholic pronouncements on the state of humanity prior to the fall and the effects of original sin. In doing so, although he does not seem to have been aware of it, he was adopting and inverting a claim first put forward at the time of the Reformation by Erasmus. In his debate with Luther in 1524 Erasmus maintained that Luther's positions on sin and justification necessarily implied a rejection of any meaningful freedom of the will. In other words, Erasmus saw that Luther's doctrine of grace entailed a vision of the human person that belittled human freedom.[21] Three centuries later Möhler urged that what he regarded as Luther's distorted vision of the human person found expression in an inevitably inadequate understanding of sin, grace, and justification. The core problem with Protestantism according to Möhler is that it fundamentally misunderstands the human being. And so it is with differing Catholic and Protestant views on the human nature and its capacities that he begins his study of symbolics.

Möhler's contemporaries were most interested in—and, in some cases, outraged by—the polemical aspect of *Symbolik*, its depiction of classical Protestantism as rooted in a distorted view of the human person and its charge that nineteenth-century Protestant theologies, however different they might look from those of the Reformers, were inevitable outgrowths of the original flawed anthropology. That argument may remain of considerable historical interest to students of eighteenth- and nineteenth-century theology. But readers at the end of the twentieth-century will probably find the primary importance of *Symbolik* to be its attempt to understand the Catholic tradition as a coherent, systematic world-view responding to human beings' deepest needs and capacities. It remains an extraordinary work of modern Catholic systematic theology.

THE TRANSLATION

The English translator of *Symbolik*, James Burton Robinson (1800-1877), managed in the course of his life to touch directly or indirectly many of the most influential Catholic figures of his century. He was a friend of a friend of Möhler's, Franz Georg Benkert, who succeeded to the canonry at Würzburg to which Möhler had been appointed just before his death. But Robertson was familiar with the work of Möhler and his Catholic colleagues at Tübingen apart from this personal connection. Born in London, raised in the West Indies, he began studies at St. Edmond's College in Cambridge and then lived and studied for years in France, Belgium, and Germany. He read philosophy with Lamenais and in 1836 translated Friedrich Schlegel's history of philosophy into English. For nearly twenty years he was a regular contributor to *The Dublin Review* and so had contact with Nicholas Wiseman (later the first cardinal archbishop of Westminster) and Daniel O'Connell. His 1843 translation of *Symbolik* made an important stream of continental Catholic thought available to interested English readers, not least members of the Oxford movement within the Anglican community. In 1855 John Henry Newman, then rector of the fledgling Catholic University in Dublin, appointed Robertson professor of modern history and geography. Later he defended the doctrine of papal infallibility in the wake of Vatican I but without following the ultramontane line of W. G. Ward who had taken over the editorship of *The Dublin Review*. Before his death he was the recipient of honors from both the papacy and the English government under Gladstone.

Robertson's translation has the supreme virtues of accuracy and fluency. His early Victorian English has a slightly distancing effect now which is probably all to the good, since Möhler's German with its touches of romanticism and idealism has much the same effect in the original. One infelicity in the translation should be noted, however, although the reader of this brief introduction has undoubtedly already noticed it. The title *"Symbolism"* can be misunderstood in English. (This is why I have referred throughout this introduction to *Symbolik*.) "Symbol," from *symbolon*, for Möhler has the classic patristic meaning of an explanatory statement of belief, the sense in which we find it used by Augustine in his *De fide et symbolo*, often translated as "On Faith and the Creed." *Symbolik* might better have been rendered *"Symbolics,"* an odd word in English which would have alerted the reader to the peculiar meaning of "symbol" that Möhler intended. That cavil aside, Robertson's translation remains an excellent rendering in English of Möhler's by no means easy German. After several reprintings in the nineteenth century, it last appeared in 1906 and has long been difficult to find. Its republication following the appearance of the translation of *Einheit in der Kirche* marks the first time that English-speaking readers have had available to them the two principal works of one of the originators of modern Catholic theology.

Michael J. Himes
Boston College

[1] The excellent critical edition and commentary are by Josef Rupert Geiselmann, *Symbolik oder Darstellung der dogmatischen Gegensätze der Katholiken und Protestanten nach ihren öffentlichen Bekenntnisschriften*, 2 vols. (Köln: Jakob Hegner, 1960-61).

[2] For example, Philipp Konrad Marheineke, *Über Dr. J. A. Möhlers Symbolik oder Darstellung der Lehrgegensätze zwischen Katholiken und Protestanten* (Berlin, 1833), and Karl Immanuel Nitzsch, *Eine protestantische Beantwortung der Symbolik von Dr. Möhler* (Hamburg, 1835). Marheineke was the most distinguished of the "right-wing Hegelians" at the university of Berlin; Nitzsch was an influential Lutheran theologian who became a principal representative of Schleiermacher's theology.

[3] Ferdinand Christian Baur, *Der Gegensatz des Katholicismus und Protestantismus nach den Principien und Hauptdogmen der beiden Lehrbegriffe mit besonderer Rücksicht auf Herrn. Dr. Möhler's Symbolik* (Tübingen, 1834). There is a very fine study of the Möhler-Baur debate by Joseph Fitzer, *Moehler and Baur in Controversy, 1832-38: Romantic-Idealist Assessment of*

the Reformation and Counter-reformation (Tallahassee, Florida: American Academy of Religion, 1974).

[4] Möhler's defense was *Neue Untersuchungen der Lehrgegensätze zwischen den Katholiken und Protestanten. Eine Vertheidigung meiner Symbolik gegen die Kritik des Herrn Professors Dr. Baur in Tübingen* (Mainz, 1834; 2nd expanded edition, Mainz, 1835). Baur's reply to the first edition was "Erwiederung auf Herrn Dr. Möhler's neueste Polemik gegen die protestantische Lehre und Kirche in der Schrift: *Neue Untersuchungen...*," *Tübinger Zeitschrift für Theologie* 8 (1834): 127-248.

[5] For example, by Anton Günther, *Der letzte Symboliker. Eine durch die symbolischen Werke Doctor J. A. Möhlers und Doctor F. C. Baurs veranlasste Schrift in Briefen* (Wien, 1834), and by Johann Friedrich, *Johann Adam Möhler, der Symboliker. Ein Beitrag zu seinem Leben und zu seiner Lehre aus eigenen und anderen ungedruckten Papieren* (München, 1894).

[6] *Symbolism or Exposition of the Doctrinal Differences between Catholics and Protestants as Evidenced by Their Symbolical Writings: Translated from the German, with a Memoir of the Author, Preceded by a Historical Sketch of the State of Protestantism and Catholicism in Germany for the Last Hundred Years by J. B. Robertson*, 2 vols. (London, 1843).

[7] The best and fullest statement of Drey's aims is his *Brief Introduction to the Study of Theology with Reference to the Scientific Standpoint and the Catholic System*, trans. Michael J. Himes (Notre Dame: University of Notre Dame Press, 1994); this 1819 book can almost serve as a groundplan for what came to be known as "the Catholic Tübingen school." Drey wrote a shorter statement of his criticism of previous Catholic theology in 1812, the year of the founding of the Catholic faculty at Ellwangen: "Toward the Revision of the Present State of Theology," trans. by Joseph Fitzer in his *Romance and the Rock: Nineteenth-Century Catholics on Faith and Reason* (Minneapolis: Fortress Press, 1989), pp. 62-73.

[8] For a discussion of this critique of Schleiermacher and its significance in Möhler's development, see Michael J. Himes, "'A Great Theologian of Our Time': Möhler on Schleiermacher," *The Heythrop Journal* 37 (1996): 24-46.

[9] "Anselm als Erzbischof von Canterbury," *Theologische Quartalschrift* 9 (1827): 435-97 and 585-664, and "Die Scholastik des Anselmus," *Theologische Quartalschrift* 10 (1828): 62-130.

[10] For the most elaborate attempt to make the connection between the Catholic Tübingen school and Modernism, see Edmond Vermeil, *Jean-Adam Möhler et l'École catholique de Tubingue (1815-1840). Étude sur la théologie romantique en Wurtemberg et les origines germaniques du modernisme* (Paris: Librairie Armand Colin, 1913).

[11] See especially Stefan Lösch, *Die Anfänge der Tübinger Theologischen Quartalschrift (1819-1831). Gedenkgabe zum 100. Todestag Joh. Ad. Möhlers* (Rottenburg: Bader, 1938), and "J. A. Möhler und die Lehre von der

Entwicklung des Dogmas," *Theologische Quartalschrift* 99 (1917/1918): 28-59, 129-52. Lösch also edited *Johann Adam Möhler. Bd. 1: Gesammelte Aktenstücke und Briefe* (München: Beck, 1928), the first volume of a projected collection of Möhler's shorter works, unfortunately never completed; it remains, however, a valuable edition of his correspondence.

¹² The list of Geiselmann's books and articles on the Tübingen school is long. Most notable are *Die katholische Tübinger Schule. Ihre theologische Eigenart* (Freiburg: Herder, 1964); *Lebendiger Glaube aus geheiligter Überlieferung. Der Grundgedanke der Theologie Johann Adam Möhlers und der katholischen Tübinger Schule*, 2nd ed. (Freiburg: Herder, 1966); and *Die theologische Anthropologie Johann Adam Möhlers. Ihr geschichtlicher Wandel* (Freiburg: Herder, 1955). Specifically on *Symbolik*, see his "Der gefallenen Mensch. Die Wandlungen des Erbsündebegriffs in der Symbolik Joh. Adam Möhlers," *Theologische Quartalschrift* 124 (1943): 73-98, and "Wandlungen des Erbsündebegriffs in der Symbolik Möhlers," *Theologische Quartalschrift* 126 (1946): 19-42.

¹³ Again the critical edition and commentary are by Josef Rupert Geiselmann, *Die Einheit in der Kirche oder das Prinzip des Katholizismus. Dargestellt im Geiste der Kirchenväter der drei ersten Jahrhunderte* (Köln: Jakob Hegner, 1956).

¹⁴ The translation of *Einheit* is Johann Adam Möhler, *Unity in the Church or The Principle of Catholicism Presented in the Spirit of the Church Fathers of the First Three Centuries*, ed. and trans. Peter C. Erb (Washington, D.C.: The Catholic University of America Press, 1996). Prior to this, apart from *Symbolism*, the only English translations of any of Möhler's writings were two exceedingly hard-to-come-by pieces: *The Life of St. Anselm, Archbishop of Canterbury*, trans. Henry Rymer (London, 1842), and an article, "On the Relation of Islam to the Gospel," trans. J. P. Menge, in *The Calcutta Christian Intelligencer*, 1847.

¹⁵ See the careful discussion of the changes Möhler made from one edition to another in volume two of Geiselmann's critical edition. The import of some of these changes, especially in theological anthropology and ecclesiology, is discussed at length in Michael J. Himes, *Ongoing Incarnation: Johann Adam Möhler and the Beginnings of Modern Ecclesiology* (New York: Crossroad, 1997), chapters 6-9.

¹⁶ In his introduction to the critical edition of *Symbolik*, Geiselmann notes that it is clear in the manuscript of the book that Hegel's "theory of objective spirit" led Möhler to his position on the proper way to understand symbolical statements; Johann Adam Möhler, *Symbolik*, 1:[69].

¹⁷ Drey, *Brief Introduction to the Study of Theology*, p. 119, #262.

¹⁸ Ibid., p. 116, #255.

¹⁹ F. W. J. Schelling, *Vorlesungen über die Methode des akademischen Studiums*, ed. by Otto Weiss with additional notes by Walter E. Ehrhardt (Ham-

burg: Felix Meiner Verlag, 1974), p. 46; the book was originally published in Tübingen in 1803.

[20] These were respectively the criticisms of Baur pp. 304-8 n, and Nitszch, pp. 24-25.

[21] Erasmus, "The Free Will," in *Erasmus - Luther: Discourse on Free Will*, trans. and ed. Ernst F. Winter (New York: Frederick Ungar Publishing Co., 1961), pp. 3-94, esp. at p. 85.

PREFACE TO THE FIRST EDITION

EVERY book has a two-fold history; a history before, and a history after its publication. The first can be described only by the author himself; and respecting this, the public imposes on him the duty to make no mystery, and, accordingly, to relate to it partly the outward occasions that induced him to undertake the composition of his work; and partly to assign the more intrinsic reasons, by which he was determined to the undertaking. Hereupon I have now to communicate to the indulgent reader the following remarks.

The present work has arisen out of a course of lectures, that for several years I have delivered on the doctrinal differences between Catholics and Protestants. On this subject it has been the custom for years, in all the Lutheran and Calvinistic universities of Germany, to deliver lectures to the students of theology; and highly approving of this custom, I resolved to transplant it to the Catholic soil, for the following reasons. Certainly those, who are called to take the lead in theological learning, may be justly expected to acquire a solid and comprehensive knowledge of the tenets of the religious communities, that for so long a time have stood opposed to each other in mutual rivalry, and still endeavour to maintain this their position. Justly are they required not to rest satisfied by any means with mere general, uncertain, obscure, vague, and unconnected notions upon the great vital question, which has not only, for three hundred years, continually agitated the religious life of Europe, but has in part so deeply and mightily convulsed it.

If the very notion of scientific culture makes it the duty of the theologian to enter with the utmost possible precision and depth into the nature of the differences that divide religious parties; if it imperiously requires him to set himself in a condition to render account of and assign the grounds for, the doctrinal peculiarities of the different communions; so regard for his own personal dignity and satisfaction of mind, presses the matter on him, nay, on every well-instructed Christian, with a still more imperious claim. For what is less consistent with our own self-respect than to neglect instituting the most careful and accurate inquiry into the grounds and foundation of our own religious belief; and convincing ourselves whether, and how far, we stand on a firm footing, or whether we have not placed ourselves on some treacherous covering, that conceals beneath it an enormous abyss? How is it possible to enjoy a true and solid peace of the soul, when in the midst of great ecclesiastical communities, that all pretend alike to the possession of the pure and unmutilated truth, we stand almost without reflection, and without possessing any adequate instruction? There is, indeed, in this respect, a quiet, such as they possess, in relation to a future life, who are utterly heedless whether there be such a state. This is a quiet that casts deep, indelible disgrace on any being endowed with reason. Every man accordingly owes it to himself to acquire the clearest conception of the doctrinal peculiarities, the inward power and strength, or the inward weakness and untenableness of the religious community, whereof he acknowledges himself a member; a conception which entirely depends on a very accurate and precise knowledge of the opposite system of belief. There can even be no solid acquisition nor confident use of the arguments for any communion, unless they be conceived in relation to the antagonist system. Nay, solid acquaintance with any Confession must necessarily include its apology, if at least that confession make any pretensions to truth. For every educated Christian possesses such general notions of religion and Christianity—he possesses such general acquaintance with Holy Writ—that so soon as any proposition be presented to him in its true light, and in its general bearings, he can form a judgment as to its truth, and immediately discern its conformity or its repugnance to the fundamental doctrines of Christianity.

We are also at a loss to discover how a practical theologian, especially in countries where conflicting communions prevail, can adequately discharge his functions, when he is unable to characterise the distinctive doctrines of those communions. For public homilies, indeed, on matters of religious controversy, the cycle of Catholic festivals, conformably to the origin and the nature of our Church, happily gives no occasion. All the festivals established by her have reference only to facts in the life of Jesus Christ, and to those truths whereon all our faith and all our hopes depend; as well as to the commemoration of those highly meritorious servants of God who hold a distinguished place in the history of the Church, such, in particular, as were instrumental in the general propagation and consolidation of Christianity, and in its special introduction into certain countries. For the office of preaching, accordingly, the Catholic pastor, with the exception of some very rare and peculiar cases, can make no immediate use of his knowledge of other creeds. On the other hand, we may hope that his discourses on the doctrines of the Catholic faith, will be rendered more solid, more comprehensive, more animated, and more impressive, when those doctrines have been studied by him, in their opposition to the antagonist confessions in the strict sense of that word. That the highest class of catechumens should receive solid instruction, nay, a far more solid one than has hitherto been given, on the dogmas controverted between Christians; nay, that in this instruction the doctrinal differences should be explicitly, and as fully as possible attended to, is a matter on which I entertain not the slightest doubt. Whence proceeds the deplorable helplessness of many Catholics, when in their intercourse with Protestants, the concerns of religious faith come under discussion? Whence the indifference of so many among them towards their own religion? From what other cause, but from their almost total ignorance of the doctrinal peculiarities of their Church in respect to other religious communities? Whence comes it, that whole Catholic parishes are so easily seduced by the false mysticism of their curates, when these happen to be secretly averse to the doctrines of the Church? Whence even the fact that many curates are so open to the Pietistic errors, but because both, priest and congregation, have never received the adequate, nay, any instruction at all, respecting the doctrinal differences between the Churches? How much are Catholics put to shame by the very great activity which Protestants display in this matter! It is of course to be understood, that instruction on these points of controversy must be imparted with the utmost charity, conciliation, and mildness, with a sincere love of truth, and without any exaggeration, and with constantly impressing on the minds of men, that however we be bound to reject errors (for the pure doctrine of Jesus Christ and the Gospel truth is the most sacred property of man), yet are we required by our Church to embrace all men with love for Christ's sake, and to evince in their regard all the abundance of Christian virtues. Lastly, it is clear that opportune and inopportune questions, consultations, and conferences on the doctrines controverted between the Churches will never fail to occur; but most assuredly the appropriate reply, the wished-for counsel, and the instructive refutation will be wanting, in case the pastor be not solidly grounded in a knowledge of the respective formularies of the Christian communities.

But if what I have said justifies the delivery of academic courses on the doctrinal peculiarities of the different communions, yet it proves not the necessity of their publication, at least as regards their essential substance. On this subject I will take the liberty of making the following remarks. In the Protestant Church, for many years, a series of manuals on Symbolism have been published. The elder Plank, Marheineke (in two works, a larger and a smaller), Winer, Clausen, and others, have tried their efforts in this department. The Catholics, indeed, on their part, have put forth a great multitude of apologetic and such like works, having for their object to correct the misrepresentation of our doctrines as set forth by non-Catholics. But any book containing a scientific discussion of all the doctrinal peculiarities of the Protestant Churches, has not fallen within my knowledge. Accordingly, in communicating to the public the substance of my lectures, I conceived I should fill up a very perceptible void in Catholic literature.

During my researches into the authorities required by the subject of my lectures, I thought I had further occasion to observe, that the territory I had begun to explore, had not by any means received a sufficiently careful cultivation, and that it was yet capable of offering much useful and desirable produce. This holds good even when we regard the matter from the mere historical point of view. But it cannot fail to occur, that by bringing to light data not sufficiently used, because they were not thoroughly understood, or had been consigned again to oblivion; the higher scientific judgment, on the mutual relations of the Christian communities, will be rendered more mature and circumspect. Whether my inquiries, in either respect, have been attended with any success, it is for competent judges to decide. Thus much, at least, I believe I may assert, that my labours will offer to Catholic theologians especially, many a hint, that their industry would not be unrepaid, if in this department they were to devote themselves to solid researches. For several decades, the most splendid talents spend their leisure, nay, give up their lives, to inquiries into the primitive religions and mythologies, so remote from us both as to space and time; but the efforts to make us better acquainted with ourselves, have evidently been more rare and less perseverant, in proportion as this problem is a matter of nearer concern than the former. There are not, indeed, wanting a countless multitude of writings, that dilate in prolix dissertations on the relations between the different Churches. But alas! their authors too often possess scarcely the most superficial knowledge of the real state of facts; and hereby it not unfrequently comes to pass, that treatises, which would even perhaps merit the epithet of ingenious, tend only to render the age more superficial, and to cause the most important questions that can engage the human mind and heart, to be most frivolously overlooked. Such sort of writings are entitled 'Considerations'; while, in truth, nothing (objective) was at all *considered;* but mere phantoms of the brain that passed before the writer.

Pacific objects, also, induced me to commit this work to the press; and these objects I conceived I should be able to attain, by giving the most precise and the most unreserved description of the doctrinal differences. I did not, indeed, dream of any peace between the Churches, deserving the name of a true reunion, as being about to be established in the present time. For such a peace cannot be looked for in an age, which is so deeply degraded, that even the guides of the people have oftentimes so utterly lost sight of the very essence of faith, that they define it as the adoption of what appears to them probable, or most probable; whereas its nature consists in embracing, with undoubting certainty, the revealed truth, which can be only one. As many men now believe, the heathens also believed; for they were by no means devoid of opinions respecting divine things. When in so many quarters there is no faith, a reunion in faith is inconceivable. Hence, only an union in unbelief could be attained; that is to say, such a one wherein the right is mutually conceded to think what one will, and wherein there is therefore a mutual tacit understanding, that the question regards mere human opinions, and that it is a matter left undecided, whether in Christianity God have really revealed Himself or not. For with the belief in Christ, as a true envoy of the Father of light, it is by no means consistent, that those who have been taught by him, should be unable to define in what his revelations on divine things consist, and what, on the other hand, is in contradiction to his word and his ordinances. All things, not this or that in particular, appear, accordingly, opposed to a religious union. A real removal, therefore, of the differences existing between the Christian communities, appears to me to be still remote. But in the age in which we live, I flattered myself that I might do something towards bringing about a religious peace, by revealing a true knowledge of the great dispute ; in so far as by this knowledge men must come to perceive that that contest sprang out of the most earnest endeavours of both parties to uphold the truth—the pure and genuine Christianity in all its integrity. I have made it therefore my duty to define, with the utmost possible precision, the points of religious difference, and nowhere, and at no time, to cloak and disguise them. The opinion sometimes entertained, that the differences are not of importance, and affect not the vitals of Christianity, can conduce only to mutual contempt ; for opponents, who are conscious of not having adequate grounds for opposing each other and yet do so, must despise one another. And, certainly, it is this vague feeling of being an adversary of this stamp that has in modern times given rise to violent sallies on the part of many Protestants against Catholics, and *vice versa ;* for many, by a sort of self-deception, think by these sallies to stifle the inward reproaches of their conscience, and mistake the forced irritation against an opposite communion, for a true pain on account of the rejection of truth on the part of its adherents. Even the circumstance is not rare that an ignorance of the true points of difference leads to the invention of false ones. And this certainly keeps up a hostile, uncharitable spirit of opposition between parties, far more than a just and accurate knowledge of the distinctive doctrines could do ; for nothing wounds and embitters more than unfounded charges. From the same cause it so frequently happens, that men on both sides charge each other with obduracy of will, and with a selfish regard to mere personal and transitory interests, and ascribe to these alone the divisions in religious life. Protestants are uncommonly apt, without hesitation, to ascribe to what they denominate hierarchical arrogance and the plan of obscuration, any resistance in the Catholic Church to the full influx of Protestant light. Many Catholics, on the other hand, are of opinion that, in the same way as at the commencement of the Reformation, political interests, and the desire to exercise over the Church an absolute domination, were the sole inducements that engaged princes to embrace and encourage the Protestant doctrines ; and domestic ease, sensual gratifications, hollow arrogance, and a frivolous love of independence, were the only motives that brought over Churchmen to the new opinions; so this is for the most part the case, even at the present day. These charges indeed of pride, arrogance, and the rest, which parties bring against each other, cannot, alas! be entirely disputed. We know, moreover, from experience, that everywhere there are very zealous men, who, in their conduct towards opposite communions, are not actuated by quite base motives, yet have immediately in view only the interests of a party, a faction, or a system, and not the cause of Divine truth, especially in its living manifestation in Christ Jesus, who should alone be the object of our love, and all else should be so, only in so far as it is nearly or remotely connected with that love. All this, indeed, is unquestionably true. Yet it would betoken a very great narrowness of mind if the duration of the mighty religious contest were not sought for in deeper causes than in those assigned. Under these circumstances, I conceived it were no small gain if I should succeed in drawing back attention entirely to the matter itself, and in establishing the conviction, that in the conflict between Catholicism and Protestantism, moral interests are defended; a conviction which, as it implies in the adversaries earnestness and sincerity, must lead to more conciliatory results, and is alone calculated to advance the plan, which, in the permission of so fearful a strife, Divine Providence had in view.

Lastly, I must mention also a phenomenon of the age, which, if I remember right, first inspired me with the thought of committing to the press my treatises on the distinctive doctrines of the Christian communions. For a long time Lutheranism seemed to have entirely disappeared from Germany—at least to possess no voice in public opinion; in fact, it was scarcely represented in literature by a single theologian of any name. In our thoughtful Germany, the gloomier Calvinism never found itself really at home; and when it penetrated into some of its provinces, it was almost always with considerable modifications. Its real home has always been a part of Switzerland and of France; next Holland, England, and Scotland.

Through the great revolution in public affairs during our times, the old orthodox Protestantism has again assumed new life, and not only finds many adherents among the clergy and laity, but in the number of its partisans can reckon very able theologians. As was naturally to be expected, it immediately marked out its position relatively to the Catholic Church, and assailed the latter with all the resources it could command. The more this party visibly increases, and, partly by its junction with the Pietistic movement that had previously existed, partly by the encouragement of one of the most influential cabinets in Germany,[1] begins again to constitute a power; the more must Catholics feel the necessity of taking up their right position in respect to it, and of clearly discerning the true nature of the relation wherein they stand towards it. This, however, is not so easy, as we might at the first view imagine. For when from Rationalism and Naturalism we must turn our thoughts to the old Protestantism as represented in the symbolical books, we are required to transport ourselves into a totally different religious world. For while for the last fifty years Catholics have been called upon to defend only the Divine elements in Christianity, the point of combat is now changed, and they are required to uphold the human element in the Christian religion. We must now march precisely from one extreme to the other. Yet the Catholic has this advantage, that his religious system embraces as well what constitutes an object of one-sided or exclusive reverence with the Rationalist, as what the orthodox Protestant, with an equally one-sided or exclusive veneration, adheres to in Christianity. In fact, these two contrarieties are in the Catholic system adjusted, and perfectly reconciled. The Catholic faith is as much akin to one principle, as to the other; and the Catholic can comprehend the two, because his religious system constitutes the unity of both.

The Protestant rationalists are indebted to Luther, only in so far as he acquired for them the right to profess completely the reverse of what he himself, and the religious community he founded, maintained. And the orthodox Protestants have with the rationalists no tie of connection, save the saddening conviction, that Luther established a Church, the very nature whereof must compel it to bear such adversaries with patience in its bosom, and not even to possess the power of 'turning them away.' The Catholic, on the other hand, has with either party a moral affinity, inherent in his very doctrines: he stands higher than either, and therefore overlooks them both. He has alike what distinguishes the two, and is therefore free from their one-sided failings. His religious system is no loose, mechanical, patchwork combination of the two others, for it was anterior to

---

[1] Prussia is here alluded to.—*Trans.*

either; and when it was first revealed to the Church, organically united the truth, which in the other two is separated. The adverse parties seceded from the Catholic Church, breaking up and dividing its doctrine—the one appropriating the human, the other the divine principle in Christianity, just as if the indivisible could be at pleasure divided!

I have further to observe, that German solidity, or German pedantry, or German distrustfulness, call it by what name we will, appeared to me to require that I should give the passages I quoted at full length. The reader is thus enabled to form his own judgment by the materials brought before him, or at least is furnished with the means for testing the judgment of the author. I was bound to suppose that to by far the greater number of my readers the symbolical books of the Protestants, the writings of Luther, Zuinglius, and Calvin were inaccessible; and if I were unable to preserve the true medium between an excess and a deficiency in quotations, I preferred to offend by the former. He who is unable to read the quotations, which are for the most part thrown into the notes, can easily pass them over. On the other hand, it cannot be said that he who would feel desirous to make himself acquainted with the passages cited, could have easily collected these himself.

TÜBINGEN, 1832.

PREFACE TO THE SECOND EDITION

From the attention with which the theological public have been pleased to favour this work, I have conceived it my duty to endeavour, as much as the small space of time that intervened between the first and the second edition allowed, to improve and even to enlarge it. In the first part, there are few sections which, whether in the language, or whether by additions or omissions in the text, or in the notes, have not undergone changes advantageous, as I trust, to the work. Under the article of faith, the seventeenth section has been newly inserted; and the twenty-seventh section, which contains a more precise definition of the real distinctive points in the theological systems of Luther and of Zuinglius, was not found in the first edition. The article on the Church has undergone considerable changes; the addition of the thirty-seventh section appeared to be peculiarly calculated to render more clear the theory of the Catholic Church.

In the second part, the article on the Methodists has been entirely recast, as I have now been able to procure Dr Southey's 'Life of Wesley.' Clarkson's 'Portraiture of Quakerism,' which, in despite of many endeavours, I had been unable to obtain in time for the first edition, but which has since come to hand, has been less useful for my purpose than I had expected.

In the Introduction, it has appeared to me expedient to enter into more particulars as to the use which, in a work like the *Symbolism*, is to be made of the private writings of the Reformers. I have deemed it useful also to point out there the important distinction, which, in all Symbolical researches, should be observed between the use of the private writings of the Reformers, and that of the works of Catholic theologians.

PREFACE TO THE THIRD EDITION

The information of my publisher, that the second edition is out of print, was too sudden to allow me to bestow on this third edition those improvements which I would fain have made, and whereof it stood in so much need. There is but one article I can name, which has undergone an important amelioration; it is the eighth section, on original sin; for in the former editions, there were some historical notices, touching the Catholic views of that doctrine, that much needed correction.

The very ponderous criticism on my *Symbolism*, which in the meanwhile Professor Baur has put forth, I will leave unnoticed in the present work; for the necessary discussions would occupy proportionally too great a space, to find insertion either in the notes or in the text. I have therefore prepared to write a separate reply, which, please God, will soon be sent to press.

PREFACE TO THE FOURTH EDITION

After the publication of the third edition, which appeared at the beginning of the year 1834, I saw myself compelled to compose a defence of the *Symbolism*. It has already appeared under the title *New Investigations*, etc. (*Neue Untersuchungen*). In this work many subjects, having reference to the controversy and which, in the *Symbolism*, had been only lightly, or not at all touched upon, were more fully treated; while not a few articles have been investigated under a new point of view, others more precisely defined, and several more fully established. From this book nothing has been transferred to the fourth edition of the *Symbolism*. I held it to be my duty to make no essential alteration in the form, under which the present work was originally presented to the public, and under which it has been favoured with their indulgent attention. To notice in the body of the work the various writings, treatises, and reviews, that have been directed against it, I conceived to be in every way unsuitable; independent even of the fact that I was unwilling to see the pacific tone of the *Symbolism* converted into an angry and warlike tone. Yet some things have been amended in this fourth edition; others have been added. These are changes which could be made without any external provocation, and without any alteration of my original plan, and as have formerly been made in every new edition.

By God's providence the *Symbolism* has hitherto produced much good fruit, as from many quarters has been related to me, partly by word of mouth, and partly by writing. Even Protestant periodicals, as, for example, the *Evangelical Church Gazette* (*Evangelische Kirchen Zeitung*) of October, 1834, do not in their peculiar way call this fact in question. May it be still further attended with the blessing of the Saviour, who from the beginning hath ever chosen weak and imperfect things for the instruments of his glorification!

PREFACE OF THE GERMAN EDITOR TO THE FIFTH EDITION

While the fifth edition of this work was in the press, the Catholic Church of Germany had the affliction to see its illustrious author snatched away from her by an untimely death. If his loss for Catholic literature be an event so deeply to be deplored, it is so especially in reference to the *Symbolism*. The lamented author had intended to introduce many amendments into this new edition, and so to render it more complete,—partly by transferring into it several things from his work, entitled, *New Investigations of Doctrinal Differences*—partly by incorporating with it the results of new researches. As regards a very considerable part of the work, his intention he has happily been able to carry into effect. Many articles and sections—as, for example, that on original sin—have received from him extension or greater precision, or have been entirely recast. The like he had designed in respect to the articles on the doctrine of the sacraments, and the following sections. Down to the close of his life, this concern of his heart ever occupied him; but the final execution of his design was not permitted by Divine Providence.

May this new edition produce those blessed effects, which had ever been intended by the author, and that have doubtless gained a rich recompense for him before the throne of God!

MUNICH, 21st *June*, 1838.

INTRODUCTION

PART I

NATURE, EXTENT, AND SOURCES OF SYMBOLISM

By Symbolism we understand the scientific exposition of the doctrinal differences among the various religious parties opposed to each other, in consequence of the ecclesiastical revolution of the sixteenth century, as these doctrinal differences are evidenced by the public confessions or symbolical books of those parties. From this definition it follows:

First, that Symbolism has directly and immediately neither a polemical nor an apologetic aim. It has only to give a statement, to furnish a solid and impartial account, of the differences which divide the above-mentioned Christian communities. This exposition, doubtless, will indirectly assume, partly a defensive, partly an offensive, character; for the personal conviction of the writer will involuntarily appear, and be heard, sometimes in the tone of adhesion and commendation, sometimes in the tone of reproof and contradiction. Still, the mere explanatory and narrative character of Symbolism is thereby as little impaired, as that of the historical relation, in which the historian conceals not his own personal opinion respecting the personages brought forward and the facts recounted. The claims of a deeper science, especially, cannot be satisfied unless the exposition occasionally assume, in part a polemical, in part an apologetical, character. A bare narrative of facts, even when accompanied with the most impartial and most solid historical research, will not suffice; nay, the individual proportions of a system of doctrine must be set forth, in their mutual concatenation and their organic connection. Here, it will be necessary to decompose a dogma into the elements out of which it has been formed, and to reduce it to the ultimate principles whereby its author had been determined; there, it will be expedient to trace the manifold changes which have occurred in the dogma: but at all times must the parts of the system be viewed in their relation to the whole, and be referred to the fundamental and all-pervading idea. During this analytic process,—without which a true, profound, and vivid apprehension of the essential nature of the different confessions is absolutely impossible,—the relation of these to the gospel, and to Christian reason, must necessarily be brought out, and the conformity of the one, and the opposition of the other, to universally acknowledged truths, must follow as a matter of course. In this way, indeed, Symbolism becomes the most cogent apology, or allusive refutation, without designing to be, in itself, either the one or the other.

Secondly, in the definition we have given, the limits and extent of our course of Symbolism have been expressed. For, as they are only those ecclesiastical differences that sprang out of the convulsions of the sixteenth century, that form the subject of our investigations; so all those religious communities that have arisen out of earlier exclusion or voluntary secession from the Church, even though they may have protracted their existence down to our times, will necessarily be excluded from the range of our inquiries. Hence, the course of doctrinal disputes in the Oriental Church will not engage our attention. The religious ferment of the sixteenth century, and the ecclesiastical controversies which it produced, are of a totally different nature from the contest which divides the Western and Eastern Churches. The controversy, agitated in the West, regards exclusively Christian anthropology; for it will be shown, that, whatever other things may be connected with this, they are all mere necessary deductions from the answer given to the anthropological question mooted by the Reformers. The controversy, on the other hand, agitated in the East, has reference to Christology; for it would be strange indeed, if the orthodox Greek Church, whose dispute with the Catholic regards no doctrine of faith, were alone to claim attention; while the Nestorians and the Monophysites, who are separated from Catholics, orthodox Greeks, and Protestants, by real doctrinal differences, were to be excluded from the inquiry. But the special objects of our undertaking neither occasion nor justify so extended a discussion. An account of these doctrinal differences has, moreover, appeared to us uncalled for; since even the most abridged ecclesiastical history furnishes, respecting all these phenomena, more information than is requisite for practical purposes. In fact, no present interest conducts us to the Oriental Church and its various subdivisions; for, although the ancient disagreement of these communities with the Catholic and Protestant Churches still continues, it is at present without real and vital influence.

On the other hand, the doctrinal peculiarities of the Lutheran and Reformed Churches, in opposition to the Catholic Church, as well as to each other, must be set forth with the utmost precision, and in every possible bearing, as must also be the positions of the Catholic Church, against the negations of the two former. It might, indeed, appear proper to presuppose a general acquaintance with the Catholic dogmas, as asserted and maintained against the Reformers, in the same way as Plank, in his ' Comparative View of the Churches,' has presupposed the knowledge of the Lutheran system of doctrine. But, as the tenets of Protestants have sprung only out of opposition to Catholic doctrine, they can be understood only in this opposition : and, therefore, the Catholic thesis must be paralleled with the Protestant anti-thesis, and compared with it in all its bearings, if the latter would be duly appreciated. On the other hand, the Catholic doctrine will then only appear in its true light, when confronted with the Protestant. The present comparative view of the differences between the Christian confessions, is besides, as indicated in the Preface, destined for Protestant readers also ; but that these on an average possess more than a superficial acquaintance with Catholic doctrine, we cannot here reasonably suppose.

The various sects which have grown out of the Protestant Church, like the Anabaptists or Mennonites, the Quakers, Methodists, and Swedenborgians, could the less pass unnoticed by us, as they only further developed the original Protestantism, and have in part alone consistently carried out its principles, and pushed them to the farthest length. Hence, although all these sects did not spring up in the sixteenth century, we still regard them, as in their inward purport, belonging to that age.

The Socinians and Arminians, also, will claim our attention. These appear, indeed, as the opposite extreme to primitive Protestantism. For, while the latter sprang out of a strong but one-sided excitement of feelings, the former, as in the case of the Socinians, either originated in a one-sided direction of the understanding ; or, as in the case of the Arminians, terminated in such a course, completely rejecting the fundamental doctrines of the Reformation ; so that in them one extreme was replaced by the other, while Catholicism holds the just medium between the two. Whether, moreover, the Socinians are to be numbered among Protestant sects, is a matter of dispute among the Protestants themselves. It is, however, really unquestionable, that Socinianism ought not to be looked upon as an appendage to orthodox Protestantism, as was strongly pointed out by us, when we just now called the Socinian conception of Christianity, the precise opposite to the old Protestant view. But, as the Protestants have not yet succeeded in dismissing the Rationalists from their community (to use the language of Mr Hahn), we do not see why they should now, at least, refuse admittance to the Socinians. Nay, everyone who abandons the Catholic Church, who only ceases to be a Catholic, whatever in other respects may be the doctrines which he believes, or refuses to believe, though his creed may stand ever so low beneath that of the Socinians, is sure to find the portals of the Protestant Church thrown open to him with joy. It would, therefore, not be praiseworthy on our parts, if in the name of Protestants we were to exercise an act of intolerance, and deny to the Socinians the gratification of seeing, in one writing, at least, the object of their ancient desire attained. On the other hand, the doctrines of the Rationalists cannot be matter of investigation here, because they form no separate ecclesiastical community; and we should have to set forth only the views of a thousand different individuals, not the tenets of a church or sect. They have no symbol, and therefore can claim no place in our Symbolism. Röhr has, indeed, put forth such a one, and Bretschneider has passed on it no unfavourable judgment; but that it has been in any place adopted by any one community, we have not learned.

Still less could any notice be taken of the Saint-Simonians, for they are not even to be numbered among Christian sects. In order that a religious party may be deemed worthy of that place of honour, it is at least requisite that it should revere Christ, as Him through whom mankind have attained to their highest degree of religious culture; so that all which, from Him downwards, has been thought or felt in a religious spirit, should be regarded only as the further expansion of what, in germ at least, He had imparted to His followers. Hence, the Carpocratians are by no means to be included in the class of Christian sects, because they placed Christ merely on a level with Orpheus, Pythagoras, Socrates, and Plato. The same honour must be refused to the Mohammedans also, because they exalt the Arabian prophet above Christ. Although the latter they still revere as a Divine envoy. The same now holds good of the Saint-Simonians. According to them, Christianity, like heathenism, comprises only a one-sided conception of the religious idea. It is, indeed, according to their principles a necessary point of transition, but still *only* a point of transition, to attain to what they please to term absolute religion; in which every preceding form, as a mere transitory phase, is abolished. As they have thus exalted themselves above Christianity, they have thereby absolutely excluded themselves from her pale.

Thirdly, the definition we have given establishes the limits, within which the characterisation of the different ecclesiastical communities, that fall within the compass of the present work, must be confined. Treating only of doctrinal differences, it is the object of the present work solely to unfold the distinctive articles of belief, and to exclude all liturgical and disciplinary matters, and, in general, all the non-essential ecclesiastical and political points of difference; although, even thus, the peculiarities of the communities to be described must find a general explanation in our Symbolism. In this respect, Symbolism is distinguished from the science of comparative liturgy, ecclesiastical statistics, etc. It is only in a few cases that an exception from this principle has appeared admissible.

Fourthly and lastly, the sources are here pointed out from which Symbolism must draw. It is evident that the public confessions, or symbols, of the ecclesiastical communities in question, must, above all, be attended to, and hence hath the science itself derived its name. Other sources, meanwhile, which offer any desirable explanations, or more accurate decisions, in reference to the matters in hand, must not be neglected. To liturgies, prayers, and hymns, also, which are publicly used, and are recognised by authority, Symbolism may accordingly appeal; for in these the public faith is expressed. In appealing to hymns, however, great prudence is necessary, as in these the feeling and the imagination exert a too exclusive sway, and speak a peculiar language, which has nothing in common with dogmatic precision. Hence, even from the Lutheran church-songs, although they comprise much very serviceable to our purpose, and some peculiar Protestant doctrines are very accurately expressed in them, as also from Catholic lays, hymns, and the like, we have refrained from adducing any proofs.

That even those writings of the Reformers, which have not obtained the character of public confessions, are of great importance to our inquiries into Symbolism, must be perfectly clear. Reference must especially be made to these, when the internal signification and the worth of Protestant dogmas is to be apprehended. In the same way, Catholic theologians of acknowledged orthodoxy, and, above all, the history of the Council of Trent, offer many satisfactory and fuller elucidations of particular decisions in the Catholic formularies. Yet the individual opinion of one or more teachers belonging to any confession must not be confounded with the doctrine of the confession itself; a principle which must be extended even to the Reformers, so that opinions which may be found in their writings, but have not received any express public sanction, must not be noted down as general Protestant tenets. Between the use, however, of Catholic writers and of the Reformers, for the purpose of proof and illustration in this Symbolism, a very observable difference exists. The importance of the matter will render deeper insight into this difference necessary. The relation, namely, wherein the Reformers stand to the religious belief of their followers, is of a very peculiar nature, and totally different from that of Catholic teachers to Catholic doctrine. Luther, Zwingle, and Calvin, are *the creators* of those religious opinions prevalent among their disciples; while no Catholic dogma can be referred to any theologian as its author. As in Luther the circle of doctrines, which constitute the peculiar moral life of the Protestant communities, was produced with the most independent originality; as all who stand to him in a spiritual relation, like children to their parents, and on that account bear his name, draw from him their moral nurture, and live on his fulness; so it is from him we must derive the most vivid, profound, and certain knowledge of his doctrines. The peculiar emotions of his spirit, out of which his system gradually arose, or which accompanied its rise; the higher views, wherein often, though only in passing, he embraced all its details, as well as traced the living germ out of which the whole had by degrees grown up; the rational construction of his doctrine by the exhibition of his feelings; all this is of high significancy to one, who will obtain a genuine scientific apprehension of Protestantism, as a doctrinal system, and who will master its leading, fundamental principle. The Protestant articles of faith are so livingly interwoven with the nature of their original production in the mind of Luther, and with the whole succession of views which filled his soul, that it is utterly impossible to sever them. The dogma is equally subjective with the causes, which cooperated in its production, and has no other stay nor value than what they afford. Doubtless, as we have before said, we shall never ascribe to the Protestant party, as such, what has not been received into their symbolical writings. But although we must never abandon this principle, yet we cannot confine ourselves to it. For this religious party was generally satisfied with the results of that process of intellectual generation whereby its doctrines had been produced; and, separating by degrees those results from their living and deepest root, it rendered them thereby for the most part unintelligible to science; as the bulk of mankind are almost always contented with broken, unsubstantial, and airy theories. But it is for science to restore the connection between cause and effect, between the basis and the superstructure of the edifice; and, to discharge this task, the writings of Luther, and in a relative degree, of the other Reformers, are to be sedulously consulted.

It is otherwise with individual Catholic theologians. As they found the dogmas, on which they enlarge, which they explain, or illustrate, *already pre-existing*, we must in their labours accurately discriminate between their special and peculiar opinions, and the common doctrines declared by the Church, and received from Christ and the apostles. As these doctrines existed *prior* to those opinions, so they can exist *after* them, and can therefore be scientifically treated *without* them, and quite *independently* of them. This distinction between individual opinion and common doctrine presupposes a very strongly constituted community, based at once on history, on life, on tradition, and is only possible in the Catholic Church. But, as it is possible, so also it is necessary; for unity in its essence is not identity. In science as in life, such scope is to be afforded to the free expansion of individual exertion, as is compatible with the existence of the common weal; that is to say, so far as it is not in opposition to it, nor threatens it with danger and destruction. According to these principles the Catholic Church ever acted; and by that standard we may estimate not only the oft-repeated charge, that, amid all their vaunts of unity, Catholics ever had divisions and various disputes among themselves, but also the Protestant habit of ascribing to the whole Church the opinions of one or more individuals. Thus, for instance, it would argue a very defective insight into the nature of Catholicism, if any one were to give out, as the doctrine of the Church, Augustine's and Anselm's exposition of original sin, or the theory of the latter respecting the vicarious atonement of Christ, or Anthony Günther's speculative inquiries on those dogmas. These are all very laudable and acute endeavours to apprehend, as a conception of reason, the revealed doctrine, which alone is binding upon all; but it is clear that it would be gross ignorance to confound them with the teaching of the Church itself. For a time, even *a conception of dogma*, or an opinion, may be tolerably general, without, however, becoming an integral portion of a dogma, or a dogma itself. There are here eternally changing individual forms of an universal principle, which may serve this or that person, or a particular period for mastering that universal principle by way of reflection and speculation—forms which may possess more or less of truth, but whereon the Church pronounces no judgment; for the data for such a decision are wanting in tradition, and she abandons them entirely to the award of theological criticism.

From what has been said, it follows that such a distinction as we speak of between dogma and opinion must be extremely difficult for Protestants. As their whole original system is only an individuality exalted into a generality; as the way in which the Reformers conceived certain dogmas, and personally thought and lived in them, perfectly coincided, in their opinion, with those dogmas themselves; so their followers have inherited of them an irresistible propensity everywhere to identify the two things. In Luther, it was the inordinate pretension of an individuality which wished to constitute itself the arbitrary centre, round which all should gather—an individuality which exhibited itself as the universal man, in whom everyone was to be reflected,—in short, it was the formal usurpation of the place of Christ, who undoubtedly, as individual represents also redeemed humanity—a prerogative which is absolutely proper to Him, and, after Him, to the Universal Church, as supported by Him. In modern times, when the other opposite extreme to the original Reformation has in many tendencies found favour with the Protestants, not only are all the conceivable individualities and peculiarities, which can attach themselves to dogma, willingly tolerated, but even all the peculiar Christian dogmas are considered only as doctrines, which we must tolerate, and leave to individuals who may need them for their own personal wants; so that, if Luther raised his own individuality to the dignity of a generality, the generality is now debased into a mere individuality, and thus the true relation of the one to the other can never be established. In the consistent progress of things, everyone considered himself, in a wider circle, the representative of humanity, redeemed from error at least—as a sort of microcosmic Christ. But in order that this phenomenon might not appear too strange, for it is no easy matter to reconcile one Christ with the other, an expedient of compromise was discovered, by leaving to each one his own—that is to say, by permitting him to be his own Redeemer, and to represent himself, as also to consider the extreme points, wherein all individuals concur, as representing redeemed humanity. The common property of Protestants could only now consist of some abstract formulas, which must be acceptable to very many non-Christians. As everyone wished to pass for a Christ, the true Christian, the real scandal to the world, necessarily vanished; for as each one redeemed himself, there was no longer a common Redeemer.

To this we may add the following circumstances, whereby was formed that peculiar kind of individuality, which the Protestants would fain confound with the universal principles of the Catholic Church. Protestantism arose partly out of the opposition to much that was undeniably bad and defective in the Church; and therein consists the good it has achieved, although this was by no means peculiar to it, since hostility to evil upon Church principles existed before it, and has never ceased to exist beside it. Protestantism, too, sprang partly out of the struggle against peculiar scientific expositions of doctrine, and against certain institutions in ecclesiastical life, which we may comprehend under the expression of a mediæval individuality; but a change in this respect was the object of many zealous churchmen since the latter half of the fourteenth century. As the contest grew in vehemence, it came to pass, as passion views everything in a perverse light, that matters took such a shape in the eyes of the Reformers, as if the whole pre-existing Church *consisted* of those elements of evil, and of those individual peculiarities—as if both constituted the *essence* of the Church. This opinion having now been formed, the two things were further set forth in the strongest colours of exaggeration; for in this course of proceeding there was a manifest advantage, since with such weapons the Catholic Church was most easily combated. Accordingly, among the Reformers, we very frequently find (if we except some rare but gratifying avowals in Luther's writings), not only the necessary distinction between the dogmas of the Church, and the individual views or conceptions of particular writers and periods of time, entirely overlooked, but the latter so pointedly brought forward, that the former not seldom sink totally into the background. The nature of the origin of any institution determines in general its duration. If, accordingly, Protestants would enter into the distinction in question; if, in their estimate of Catholicism, they would look only to what was universally received, what was laid down in her public formularies, and leave all the rest to history; then as their first rise would have been impossible, their separate existence even now would be essentially endangered. The complaint here adverted to, a complaint which has so often been made by Catholics, appears, therefore, to be so intimately interwoven with their whole opposition against Protestantism, that it is only by the cessation of that opposition the complaint will ever be set aside.

Though from this it will be evident, that, in the course of our symbolical inquiries, an use is to be made of the works of the Reformers, which cannot be made of those of any Catholic writer, we must nevertheless now draw attention to some peculiar difficulties attending the use of Luther's and Melancthon's writings. Luther is very variable in his assertions. He too often brings forward the very reverse of his own declarations, and is, in a surprising degree, the sport of momentary impressions and transient moods of mind. He delights in exaggerations also, willingly runs into extremes, and likes what are called energetic expressions, in which oftentimes, when taken by themselves, his true meaning is certainly not easy to be discovered. The most advisable course, under these circumstances, is, by a careful study of his writings, to learn the key-note which pervades the whole: individual passages can in no case be considered as decisive in themselves; and a sort of average estimate, therefore, naturally commends itself to our adoption. With Melancthon we have fewer difficulties to encounter. He, indeed, is involved in contradictions of greater moment than Luther, but, for that very reason, he lightens for us the task of separating in his works the genuine Protestant elements from their opposites. In this respect, his reforming career may be accurately divided into two distinct parts. In the first, being yet a young man, little familiar with theological studies, and versed only in classical literature, he was by degrees so subjugated in religious matters by the personal influence of Luther, as to embrace without any qualification his way of thinking; and it was in this period that the first edition of his most celebrated work, the *Loci Theologici*, appeared. When his ripening talents, his more extended theological learning, and a more enlarged experience of life, had pointed out to him the abyss before which he had been conducted, he receded by degrees, but yet was never able to attain to a decided independence of mind; for, in the flower of his years, he had given himself up to foreign influences that confined and deadened his spirit. He now, on one side, vacillated without a compass between Catholicism and Lutheranism; on another side, between Lutheran and Calvinistic opinions. Hence, we have felt no difficulty in making use only of his abovementioned work in the edition described: and in opposition to those, who may be of another opinion, we appeal to the controversies that have been agitated among the Lutherans respecting the *Corpus Philippicum*, and to the final settlement of the question. In respect to Zwingle and Calvin, there are no such difficulties; as the former for the most part has only an historical importance, and the latter is ever uniform with himself.

PART II

SYMBOLIC WRITINGS OF CATHOLICS AND PROTESTANTS

I—THE CATHOLIC FORMULARIES

BEFORE we proceed to the treatment of our subject, we must inquire into the public confessions of Catholics as well as of Protestants. It is a matter of course that those formularies only are here understood, wherein the peculiar and opposite doctrines of the two confessions are set forth, and not by any means those wherein the elder class of Protestants, in accordance with Catholics, have expressed a common belief. The Apostolic, Nicene, and Athanasian Creeds, and in general all the doctrinal decrees, which the first four general councils have laid down in respect to the Trinity, and to the Person of Christ, those Protestants, who are faithful to their Church, recognise in common with Catholics; and on this point the Lutherans, at the commencement of the Augsburg Confession, as well as in the Smalcald Articles, solemnly declared their belief. Not less explicit and public were the declarations of the Reformed. These formularies constitute the common property of the separate Churches—the precious dowry which the overwise daughters carried away with them from the maternal house to their new settlements: they cannot accordingly be matter of discussion here, where we have only to speak of the disputes which occasioned the separation, but not of those remaining bonds of union, to which the severed yet cling. We shall first speak of those writings, wherein, at the springing up of dissensions, the Catholic Church declared her primitive domestic laws.

1. *The Council of Trent.* Soon after the commencement of the controversies, of which Luther was the author, but whereof the cause lay hidden in the whole spirit of that age, the desire from many quarters was expressed and by the Emperor Charles V warmly represented to the Papal court, that a general council should undertake the settlement of these disputes. But the very complicated nature of the matters themselves, as well as numerous obstacles of a peculiar kind, which have seldom been impartially appreciated, did not permit the opening of the council earlier than the year 1545, under Pope Paul III. After several long interruptions, one of which lasted ten years, the council, in the year 1563, under the pontificate of Pius IV, was, on the close of the twenty-fifth session, happily concluded. The decrees regard dogma and discipline. Those regarding the former are set forth, partly in the form of treatises, separately entitled *decretum* or *doctrina*, partly in the form of short propositions, called *canones*. The former describe, sometimes very circumstantially, the Catholic doctrine; the latter declare in terse and pithy terms against the prevailing errors in doctrine. The disciplinary ordinances, with the title *Decretum de Reformatione*, will but rarely engage our attention.

2. The second writing, which we must here name, is the Tridentine or Roman catechism, with the title *Catechismus Romanus ex Decreto Concilii Tridentini*. The fathers of the Church, assembled at Trent, felt, themselves, the want of a good catechism for general use, although very serviceable works of that kind were then not altogether wanting. These, even during the celebration of the council, increased to a great

quantity. None, however, gave perfect satisfaction; and it was resolved, that one should be composed and published by the council itself. In fact, the council examined the outline of one prepared by a committee; but this, for want of practical utility and general intelligibleness, it was compelled to reject. At length, when the august assembly was on the point of being dissolved, it saw the necessity of renouncing the publication of a catechism, and of concurring in the proposal of the Papal legates, to leave to the Holy See the preparation of such a work. The Holy Father selected for this important task three distinguished theologians, namely, Leonardo Marino, archbishop of Lanciano; Egidio Foscarari, bishop of Modena; and Francisco Fureiro, a Portuguese Dominican. They were assisted by three cardinals, and the celebrated philologist, Paulus Manutius, who was to give the last finish to the Latin diction and style of the work.

It appeared in the year 1566, under Pope Pius IV, and as a proof of its excellence, the various provinces of the Church—some even by numerous synodal decrees—hastened publicly to introduce it. This favourable reception, in fact, it fully deserved, from the pure evangelical spirit which was found to pervade it; from the unction and clearness with which it was written, and from that happy exclusion of scholastic opinions, and avoidance of scholastic forms, which was generally desired. It was, nevertheless, designed merely as a manual for pastors in the ministry, and not to be a substitute for children's catechisms, although the originally continuous form of its exposition was afterwards broken up into questions and answers.

But now it may be asked, whether it possess really a symbolical authority and symbolical character? This question cannot be answered precisely in the affirmative; for, in the first place, it was neither published nor sanctioned, but only occasioned, by the Council of Trent. Secondly, according to the destination prescribed by the Council of Trent, it was not, like regular formularies, to be made to oppose any theological error, but only to apply to practical use the symbol of faith already put forth. Hence, it answers other wants, and is accordingly constructed in a manner far different from public confessions of faith. This work, also, does not confine itself to those points of belief merely which, in opposition to the Protestant communities, the Catholic Church holds; but it embraces all the doctrines of the Gospel; and hence it might be named (if the usage of speech and the peculiar objects of all formularies were compatible with such a denomination), a confession of the Christian Church in opposition to all non-Christian creeds. If, for the reason first stated, the Roman catechism be devoid of a formal universal sanction of the Church, so it wants, for the second reason assigned, all the internal qualities and the special aim which formularies are wont to have. In the third place, it is worthy of notice, that on one occasion, in a controversy touching the relation of grace to freedom, the Jesuits asserted before the supreme authorities of the Church, that the catechism possessed not a Symbolical character; and no declaration in contradiction to their opinion was pronounced.

But, if we refuse to the Roman catechism the character of a public confession, we by no means deny it a great authority, which, even from the very circumstance that it was composed by order of the Council of Trent, undoubtedly belongs to it. In the next place, as we have said, it enjoys a very general approbation from the teaching Church, and can especially exhibit the many recommendations, which on various occasions the sovereign pontiffs have bestowed on it. We shall accordingly often refer to it, and use it as a very important voucher for Catholic doctrine; particularly where the declarations of the Council of Trent are not sufficiently ample and detailed.

3. The *Professio Fidei Tridentina* stands in a similar relation.

4 Shortly after the times of the Council of Trent, and in part during its celebration, there arose within the Catholic Church doctrinal controversies, referring mostly to the relation between grace and freedom, and to subjects of a kindred nature; and hence, even for our purposes, they are not without importance. For the settlement of the dispute, the Apostolic See saw itself forced to issue several constitutions, wherein it was obliged to enter into the examination of the matter in debate. To these constitutions belong especially the bulls, published by Innocent X, against the five propositions of Jansenius, and the bull *Unigenitus*, by Clement XI. We may undoubtedly say of these constitutions, that they possess no symbolical character, for they only note certain propositions as erroneous, and do not set forth the doctrine opposed to the error, but suppose it to be already known. But a formulary of faith must not merely reject error; it must state doctrine. As the aforesaid bulls, however, rigidly adhere to the decisions of Trent, and are composed quite in their

spirit; as they, moreover, have reference to many important questions, and settle, though only in a negative way, these questions in the sense of the above-named decrees; we shall occasionally recur to them, and illustrate by their aid many a Catholic dogma.

It is evident from what has been said, that the Catholic Church, in fact, has, in the matters in question, but one writing of a symbolical authority. All that, in any respect, may bear such a title, is only a deduction from this formulary, or a nearer definition, illustration, or application of its contents, or is in part only regulated by it, or in any case obtains a value only by agreement with it, and hence cannot, in point of dignity, bear a comparison with the original itself.

II—THE LUTHERAN FORMULARIES

The first symbolical book of the Lutherans is the Augsburg Confession: it owes its rise to the following circumstances. The schism in the Church, which had proceeded from Wittenberg, had already engaged the attention of several diets; but the decrees, framed against it at Worms, in the year 1521, appeared impracticable at Spires, in the year 1526, and three years later led to a very critical dissension, in the assembly of princes which, in March 1529, was again convoked at the last-mentioned place. Those states of the empire, which had protested against the demand to give no further extension to Luther's Reformation, and had expressed a decided repugnance to tolerate, as the Catholic party proposed, those Catholic peculiarities of doctrine and practice yet subsisting in their dominions, now formed close leagues with each other; and nineteen articles, framed at Schwabach, composed the doctrinal basis of the association, without the recognition whereof no one could become a member. At Torgau, the above-mentioned articles were confirmed. Out of these elements was formed the Augsburg Confession.

Charles V summoned a diet to be held at Augsburg, in the year 1530, which, after an impartial and earnest examination of the doctrines of either party, was to secure peace to the Church and the empire. This laudable object was in no other way to be attained, than by letting the Protestant states set forth their doctrinal views, and allege what they found offensive in the rites and discipline of the Church, as hitherto practised.

Melancthon received a commission to state in a brief essay, afterwards called the *Augsburg Confession*, the opinions of his party; for Luther was generally deemed unfit for the office of pacification.

Although the author of this confession had altered, in many respects, the articles of Schwabach and Torgau, and on the whole had very much softened down, and really improved, the assertions of Luther, yet much was still wanting to make it acceptable to Catholics. Hence, a refutation of the Protestant confession, that had been read out, was composed, and in like manner delivered before the assembly of the princes. But this also failing to carry conviction to the minds of the Lutheran states, Melancthon wrote an apology for his confession, which, although no public use could be made of it at the diet, was yet subsequently honoured as the second symbolical writing of the Lutherans.

The object of the emperor to restore peace and concord in Germany was not attained, although special conferences between the most pacific and moderate theologians of the two parties were still instituted at Augsburg. On several articles, indeed, they came to an understanding; but, as the conciliation had been forced by circumstances, it remained merely outward and apparent. All hope, meanwhile, had long been fixed on a general council, and such a one was now convoked for Mantua, by Pope Paul III. Even the Protestant states received an invitation to attend it; and in the year 1537, Smalcald was selected by them, in order, among other things, to confer with each other, and with the imperial and Papal deputies, Held and Vorstius. Luther had previously been charged with drawing up the propositions, which were to express the Protestant sentiments, form the basis of some subsequent reunion, and note down the points, which might perhaps be conceded to the Catholics. At Smalcald, these propositions received the sanction of the Protestant princes, as well as of several theologians, summoned for advice. These propositions were, indeed, never employed for the purpose designed; for, from a concurrence of obstacles, occasioned by the circumstances of the time, the council was not assembled. The Lutherans, however, had thus another opportunity of expressing their opinions in regard to the Catholic Church; and, under the name of the Smalcald articles, a place among the Protestant symbolical books was conceded to this essay of Luther's.

Already, during these manifestoes against the Catholics, the seeds of a great inward conflict were laid among those to whom Luther had given his name and his doctrine; yet it was only after his death that these seeds were really brought to maturity. The subject of the dispute, and the persons engaged in it, will be noticed in the course of the present work; but we cannot here refrain from observing, that, after long and stormy dissensions, it was Andrew, chancellor of Tubingen, to whom the honour eminently belongs of discovering a formulary, which, in opposition to the attempted innovations, so expressed itself in favour of the genuine orthodoxy, as to be everywhere received for the only correct exposition of the Lutheran faith—which consolidated concord for ever, and secured the orthodox doctrine against future falsifications. After long and very doubtful efforts, which taxed his patience to the severest lengths, this person at last succeeded, with the aid of Chemnitz (a highly respectable theologian of Brunswick), in establishing, in the year 1577, the intended formulary. It is commonly called the *Formulary of Concord*, or sometimes the *Bergen Book*, from the monastery of Bergen, in the vicinity of Magdeburg, where the above-mentioned theologians, aided by Sellnecker, put the finishing hand to the work. This confession consists of two pieces —a short outline of the orthodox doctrine, called the *Epitome*, and a very diffuse exposition of the same, which is commonly cited under the name of the *Solida Declaratio*. Moreover, this writing, however much conceived in the spirit of Luther's original doctrines, and singularly enough, even because it was so conceived, was by no means universally accepted.

Lastly, to the aforesaid symbolical writings must be added the larger and the smaller catechism of Luther—called, by the Epitome, *the Bible of the Laity*. These two catechisms in themselves, though, as we may conceive, they comprise the contents of the Lutheran formularies, were not intended to be symbolical books; yet it has pleased the Lutheran Church so to revere them.

III—THE CALVINISTIC AND ZWINGLIAN FORMULARIES

If the symbolical books of the Lutheran confession were adopted by all the particular churches that embraced the views of the Wittenberg Reformers—a fact which only in regard to the Formulary of Concord admits of an exception—the Reformed communities, on the other hand, possess no confessions received with the like general respect. The reason is to be sought, partly in Zwingle's conception of the doctrine of the holy Eucharist, which too deeply wounded the profounder religious feelings of the sixteenth century, to gain a permanent, or even a very extensive, reception, and partly in Calvin's doctrine of predestination, which, revolting as it was to the sense of Christians, could not in like manner penetrate into all the Reformed Churches. Hence, as no general harmony existed among the Reformed communities, no such general harmony could possibly be expressed in a common formulary. Add to this the peculiar circumstances of the Anglican Church, wherein the divine institution of episcopacy was asserted against the Presbyterian system of the other partisans of Zwingle and Calvin, and wherein consequently, in accordance with this view, a liturgy more approximating to that of the Catholic Church was introduced.

Thus it happened that nearly every Reformed national church had its own formulary, or even several formularies differing from each other. The more remarkable are the following:

1. *The Confessio Tetrapolitana*, which was presented by the four cities—Strasburg, Constance, Memmingen, and Lindau—to the diet of Augsburg, in the year 1530, but was not attended to by that assembly, because the Protestant states refused these cities, on account of their leaning to the Zwinglian view of the Lord's supper, admission into their league. The abovementioned cities having, some years later, out of pure political motives, subscribed the Augsburg Confession, the *Confessio Tetrapolitana* was, in a short time, abandoned by everyone.

2. *The Three Helvetic Confessions.* The Helvetic Confession, that stands at the head of the collection of the Reformed symbolic writings (accordingly the first), was, in the year 1536, composed by Henry Bullinger and Leo Judas, Myconius and Simon Grynæus; but, in the year 1566, was revised and published in the name of all the Helvetic Churches, those of Basle and Neufchatel excepted. The second confession is the first we have named, but in its original form. The third is the Confession of Mühlhausen, published by Oswald Myconius, in the year 1532; it is also denominated the Confession of Basle.

3. *The Thirty-nine Articles*—the formulary of the Anglican Church. In the year 1553, under king Edward VI, forty-two articles had been composed, probably by Cranmer, archbishop of Canterbury, and Ridley, bishop of London, as the Confession

of the English Church. But under Elizabeth they were, in the year 1562, reduced to thirty-nine articles, and were confirmed by a London synod.

4. The French Calvinists framed their confession of faith in a synod at Paris, which Antoine de Chantieu, a Calvinistic preacher at Paris, had, on a bidding to that effect, convoked.

5. The disciples of Calvin in the Netherlands received, in the year 1562, a confession of faith, composed in the French tongue by Guy de Bres and Hadrian Saravia, with the aid of several co-operators, and which was soon after translated into Flemish. But these men not having been publicly charged with this undertaking, this formulary obtained only by degrees a symbolical authority; which (especially after the synod held at Dort, in the year 1574, had, with the exception of a few unimportant particulars, given it their sanction), could not fail to occur.

6. Far more celebrated and more notorious, however, were the decrees of another Calvinistic synod, held likewise at Dort, in the years 1618 and 1619. Calvin's rigid theory of predestination could not long be maintained, without encountering opposition even in the bosom of the Reformed. This lay in the very nature of things. But the majority of Calvinists showed themselves as little inclined to suffer one of the fundamental dogmas of their Church to be called in question, as did the Lutherans in Germany. Hence, when Arminius, a preacher in Amsterdam, and, after the year 1603, a professor in Leyden, together with other men of a similar way of thinking, called in doubt Calvin's opinions (and these again were vehemently defended by his colleague Gomar), a very eventful contest arose —the settlement whereof the above-mentioned synod attempted, while in reality it only confirmed the dissension. The Arminians, or Remonstrants, though very much persecuted, maintained themselves as a distinct sect. Meanwhile, the decrees of Dort met with a very favourable reception out of Holland, even in Switzerland, among the Calvinists in France, and in other parts; while in England they were formally rejected, and in other countries were not approved of.

7. Frederick III, Count Palatine on the Rhine, who renounced the Lutheran for the Calvinistic creed, and forced upon his subjects his own cherished opinions, caused, in the year 1562, a catechism to be composed, which has also been included in the number of Calvinistic symbolical books. It is commonly

called the *Heidelberg* or *Palatine Catechism*, and has met with so much approval, that many Reformed communities have adopted it as a school-book.

8. The Protestant princes mostly entertained the same view of their prerogative as the Count Palatine Frederick, and thought they were bound to decide for their subjects all religious controversies, and to make their own individual opinions the property of all. On his death this prince was succeeded, in the year 1576, by his son Lewis, who in his turn expelled the Calvinistic preachers, and, together with the Lutheran creed, re-established the Lutheran service; until his successor, Frederick IV, in the year 1582, a second time restored the peculiar doctrines and practices of Calvinism, and inflicted on the ministers and professors of the again outlawed confession the same fate, which, under his predecessor, those of Calvinism had sustained. Even the decrees of Dort were obliged to be believed in the Palatinate. The like occurred in the principality of Anhalt. John George, from the year 1586, Prince of Anhalt-Dessau, believed it his duty to purge his land from Luther's opinions and institutions, and to enforce the introduction of Calvinism. In the year 1597, appeared a formulary, comprised in twenty-eight articles; and no other alternative was left to the preachers, but subscription, or banishment from the country. When, however, prince John, in the year 1644, assumed the reins of government, he re-established by as violent means the Lutheran confession. In Hesse-Cassel, after the Landgrave Maurice had changed his creed, the Calvinistic confession, indeed, was enforced, and the preachers of Lutheran orthodoxy were deposed; yet (a circumstance which must excite great astonishment) no special symbolical book was proposed to the acceptance of believers. Perhaps such a formulary would not have failed to appear, had not belief in the doctrinal decisions of Dort been, shortly afterwards, ordained.

9. On the other hand, the Margrave of Brandenburg, John Sigismund, on abandoning the Lutheran for the Calvinistic Church, was unable to refrain from the pleasure of publishing a special formulary. It is known under the name of the *Confession of the Marches*.

10. Lastly, we must observe, that the altered confession of Augsburg not only possesses a symbolical authority in German Calvinistic Churches, but it is in general highly esteemed by all Calvinists. Melancthon, in fact, approximated in his latter

years to the Calvinistic view of the Lord's supper; and, for that reason, introduced into the editions of this confession, revised by him from the year 1540, certain alterations, which must the more recommend it to Calvinists, as uninstructed persons, at least, might be led to suppose, that Calvin's opinion was favoured by the primitive orthodoxy of the Lutheran Church. More details on this subject hereafter. On the confessions of Poland, Hungary, Thorn, and other places, as we learn nothing of a peculiar nature from them, it is unnecessary here to dwell at any length.

The symbolical writings of the smaller Protestant sects, or those other books whence their system of belief can be derived, it will be more proper to notice in the chapters devoted to the consideration of those sects.

BOOK I

THE DOCTRINAL DIFFERENCES AMONG CATHOLICS, LUTHERANS, AND THE REFORMED

CHAPTER I

DIFFERENCES IN DOCTRINE RESPECTING THE PRIMITIVE STATE OF MAN AND THE ORIGIN OF EVIL

§ I—PRIMITIVE STATE OF MAN ACCORDING TO THE CATHOLIC DOCTRINE

IN proportion as we consider the history of mankind, or even of individual man, from the Catholic or the Protestant point of view, very different conclusions will in part be formed respecting our common progenitor — conclusions which will affect the destinies of his whole race, even to their passage into the next life : and even the first degrees of that life take a very different form, according as we regard them in the light either of Catholic or of Protestant doctrine.

The parties, indeed, originally were not conscious of the full extent of their divisions ; for ecclesiastical, like political, revolutions, are not conducted according to a preconcerted, fully completed system : but, on the contrary, their fundamental principles are wont to be consistently unfolded only in and by practical life, and their heterogeneous parts to be thereby only gradually transformed. Hence, at the commencement of the ecclesiastical revolution of the sixteenth century, reflection was not immediately directed towards the origin of our kind, nor even to its passage into eternity ; for a more minute explanation of these articles of doctrine appeared in part to possess but a very subordinate interest, and many points seemed only brought forward to fill up the breaches in the general system of belief. The great contest, which now engages our attention, had rather its rise in the inmost and deepest centre of human history, as it turned upon the mode whereby fallen man can regain fellowship with Christ, and become a partaker of the fruits of redemption. But from this centre the opposition spread backward and forward, and reached the two terms of human history which where necessarily viewed in accordance with the changes introduced in the central point. The more consistently a system is carried out and the more harmoniously it is framed, the more will any modification in its fundamental principle shake all its parts. Whoever, therefore, in its centre assailed Catholicism, whose doctrines are all most intimately intertwined, was forced by degrees to attack many other points, also, whose connection with those first combated, was in the beginning scarcely imagined.

We could now have started from the real centre of all these disputes, and have shown how all doctrines have been seized and drawn into its circle; and undoubtedly the commencement of our work would have much more excited the interest of the reader, had we immediately placed him in the midst of the contest, and enabled him to survey the entire field, which the battle commands. But we conceive that the controverted doctrines may be stated in a simpler and more intelligible manner, when we pursue the contrary course, and, by following the clue presented by the natural progress of human history, bring under notice these doctrinal differences. Hence, we begin with the original state of man, speak next of his fall, and the consequences thereof, and then enter on the very central ground of the controversy, as we proceed to consider the doctrine of the restoration of man from his fall through Christ Jesus. We shall afterwards point out the influence of the conflicting doctrines, respecting the origin and nature of the internal life of those united with Christ, on their external union and communion with each other, and thus be led to enlarge on the theory and essence of this outward communion, according to the views of the different confessions; and we shall conclude with the passage of individuals from this communion, existing on earth, to that of the next world, as well as with the lasting mutual intercourse between the two.

The first point, accordingly, which will engage our attention is the primitive state of man.

Fallen man, as such, is able, in no otherwise, save by the teaching of divine revelation, to attain to the true and pure knowledge of his original condition: for it was a portion of the destiny of man, when alienated from his God, to be likewise alienated from himself, and to know with certainty, neither what he originally was, nor what he became. In determining his original state, we must especially direct our view to the renewal of the fallen creature in Christ Jesus; because, as regeneration consists in the re-establishment of our primeval condition, and this transformation and renewal is only the primitive creation restored, the insight into what Christ hath given us back affords us the desired knowledge of what in the origin was imparted to us.

This course has been at all times and by all parties pursued, when the original condition of man was to be traced.

As regards the Catholic dogma, this embraces the whole spiritual as well as corporeal existence of the Paradisaic man, extending not only to his pre-eminent endowments of soul and body, but to those gifts which he possessed in common with all men, so far at least as the doctrinal controversies of the sixteenth century required a special explanation, on this latter point. Accordingly, in the higher portion of his nature, he is described as the image of God, that is to say, as a spiritual being, endowed with freedom, capable of knowing and loving God, and of viewing everything in him.[1] As Adam had this divine similitude in common with the whole human race, the distinction, which he enjoyed herein, consisted in his being what the simple expression of the Council of Trent denominates, *just and holy;* in other words, completely acceptable to God.[2] Or as the school says, in language, however, not quite expressive enough, ' His inferior faculties of soul, and bodily impulses, acted unresistingly under the guidance of his reason, and therefore everything in him was in obedience to reason, as his reason was in obedience to God;' and accordingly he lived in blessed harmony with himself and with his Maker. The action of the faculties and impulses of the body was in perfect accord with a reason devoted to God, and shunned all conflict with it: it was, moreover, coupled with the great gift of immortality, even in man's earthly part, as well as with an exemption from all the evils and all the maladies, which are now the ordinary preludes to death.[3]

---

[1] Catechism. ex decret. Concil. Trident. ed. Col. 1565, p. 33. ' Quod ad animam pertinet, eam ad imaginem et similitudinem suam formavit (Deus), liberumque ei tribuit arbitrium : omnes præterea motus animi atque appetitiones ita in ea temperavit, ut rationis imperio nunquam non parerent. Tum originalis justitiæ admirabile donum addidit,' etc.

[2] Concil. Trident. Sess. v. decret. de peccat. origin. The council says only, ' Justitiam et sanctitatem, in qua constitutus fuerat.'

[3] Catechism. ex decret. Concil. Trident. p. 33. ' Sic corpore effectum et constitutum effinxit, ut non quidem naturæ ipsius vi, sed divino beneficio immortalis esset et impassibilis.' Very well observes St Augustine (de

The ideal moral state, in which Adam existed in paradise, the theologians of antiquity knew by the name of 'original justice'; on the notion and nature whereof it will be proper to make some other remarks, partly of an historical kind, in order to explain the opposition, which, in this article of doctrine, the Catholic Church has had to encounter from the Protestants.

The essential and universal interest of the Christian religion, in determining the original condition of our common progenitor, is by the above-stated brief doctrine of the Church amply satisfied. Herein consists the interest—on one hand to guard against evil in the world being attributed to a Divine cause, and the dogma of the supreme *holiness* of God, the creator of the world, being disfigured;—and on the other hand, to establish on a solid basis the principle of a totally unmerited redemption from the fall— that practical fundamental doctrine of Christianity—by most earnestly inculcating, that God had endowed the first man with the noblest gifts, and that thus it was only through his own deep self-guiltiness he fell. Upon both points, however, there exist more stringent, and by no means superfluous, definitions of the Church. Theologians, likewise, taking as their standard the ecclesiastical doctrine, clearly based as it is on Scripture and Tradition, and following certain hints which particular passages of Holy Writ, and some dogmas appear to furnish, having endeavoured to fathom more deeply the nature of original justice; and the Church has viewed with pleasure the attention and love bestowed on the consideration of the holy work, and permitted, within the determined limits which revelation itself has marked out, the freest scope to speculation.

When the Church attributes to Adam, in his original state, *holiness* and justice, she by no means merely means, that he was unpolluted with any alloy adverse to God or contrary to his natural impulse and bearing to God, but, what is far more, that he stood in the most interior and the closest communion with his Maker. Now, it is an universal truth, holding good of all, even the highest orders and circles of intellectual creatures, that such a relation to God, as that of the paradisaic man, is no wise to be attained and upheld by natural powers; that consequently a special condescension of the Almighty is required thereto; in short, that no finite being is holy, save by the holy and sanctifying spirit; that no finite being can exist in a living moral com-

Genes, ad lit. vi, c. 25), ' Aliud est, non posse mori, aliud posse non mori,' etc.

munion with the Deity, save by the communion of the self-same holy spirit. This relation of Adam to God, as it exalted him above human nature, and made him participate in that of God, is hence termed (as indeed such a denomination is involved in the very idea of such an exaltation) a supernatural gift of divine grace, superadded to the endowments of nature. Moreover, this more minute explanation of the dogma, concerning the original holiness and justice of Adam, is not merely a private opinion of theologians, but an integral part of that dogma, and hence, itself a dogma.[1]

The following observation will not, perhaps, appear unimportant. So often as from a mere philosophical point of view —we mean to say, so often as without regard to, or knowledge of, revealed truth—the relation of the human spirit to God hath been more deeply investigated, men have seen themselves forced to the adoption of a *homousia*, or equality of essence between the divine and the human nature ; in other words, to embrace pantheism, and, with it, the most arrogant deification of man. How, on the other hand, the doctrinal system of the Catholic Church obviates the objections of pantheism, and, while filled with the spirit of humility, satisfies those cravings after a more profound science, which a profane pantheistic philosophy vainly endeavours to supply, is apparent from what has been above stated. What man, as a creature, by the energy of his own nature abandoned to itself, was unable to attain, is conferred on him as a grace from his Creator. So exceedingly great is the goodness and love of God!

The blessing above described, which knit the bonds of an exalted, holy, and happy communion between God and the paradisaic man, is founded on the supposition that a struggle would by degrees have naturally arisen between the sensual and the spiritual nature of man, characterised by many theologians as that power, whereby the sensual and super-sensual parts of Adam were maintained in undisturbed harmony. The

---

[1] Popes Pius V and Gregory XIII have condemned the following propositions : ' Art. xxi. Humanæ naturæ sublimatio et exaltatio in consortium divinæ naturæ debita fuit integritati primæ conditionis, ac proinde naturalis dicenda est, non supernaturalis. Art. xxvi. Integritas conditionis non fuit indebita naturæ humanæ exaltatio, sed naturalis ejus conditio.'

The opinion put forth in the earlier editions of this work, that the doctrine of the *donum supernaturale primi hominis*, though generally received among theologians, and grounded in the whole Catholic system, had not, however, received a formal sanction from the Church, must now be corrected.

same divines necessarily suppose, that on Adam the supernatural gifts were bestowed simultaneously with his natural endowments; that is to say, that both were conferred at the moment of his creation.[1]

Other theologians, on the other hand, distinguishing undoubtedly between justice and holiness, prefer the opinion that Adam was created as a sound, pure, unpolluted nature (with the harmonious relation of all his parts); and that he was favoured with the supernatural gift of a holy and blessed communion with God at a later period only: to wit, when he had prepared for its reception, and by his own efforts had rendered himself worthy of its participation. This latter opinion possesses the advantage of more accurately distinguishing between the two orders of nature and grace, and is moreover recommended by the fact, that what nature is in itself, and what it is enabled to accomplish of itself, is pointed out with great clearness. That the spiritual nature of man, as being in its essence the image of God, hath the faculty and the aptitude to know and to love Him; nay that, to a certain extent, it is of itself really capable of loving Him, and that the desire after the full union with the Deity is a want inherent in his very nature, are truths very well pointed out in this theory. Thus the natural and necessary points of contact for the higher communications of grace are here very finely brought out. The same opinion also distinguishes Adam's original justice from his *internal* sanctity and acceptance before God, considering the former to be the attribute of pure nature, as it came from the hand of the Creator; the latter to be only the gift of supernatural grace. The advocates of this opinion are thus in a condition successfully to prove, that it was not the creation as such, which gave occasion to any incongruity in the relation of man to God—any interruption of the former's freedom; but that every such incongruity, every

---

[1] Thom. Summa, P. I, q. 95, art. 1. 'Manifestum est, quod illa subjectio corporis ad animam, et inferiorum virium ad rationem, non erat naturalis; alioquin post peccatum mansisset, cum etiam in dæmonibus data naturalia post peccatum manserint. Ex quo datur intelligi, si deserente gratia soluta est obedientia carnis ad animam, quod per gratiam in anima existentem inferiora ei subdebantur.' Bellarmine (de grat. primi hom. c. v) adds: ' Ex hoc loco aperte discimus, hominem in puris naturalibus conditum habiturum fuisse rebellionem illam carnis ad spiritum, quam nunc post amissum justitiæ originalis donum omnes experimur. Quandoquidem obedientia carnis ad spiritum non fuit in primo homine naturalis et gratuita. Proinde justitia originalis divinitus homini collata non conservavit solum, sed attulit et fecit rectitudinem partis inferioris.'

such disturbance, had its rise only in the abuse of freedom. (Compare sect. v.) Further, this theory significantly implies, that without any antagonism of evil, man could yet have attained to the consciousness of his own nature and the wants extending beyond it, as well as of the manifestations of Divine favour and grace—a doctrine which is of the highest importance. Lastly, the·possible condition of man after his fall, and the course of his conversion and regeneration are here prefigured.

Moreover, both these opinions regard the justice and sanctity of Adam as accidental qualities. The Council of Trent has not pronounced itself either for or against either of them, but has employed such expressions, that both may co-exist within the pale of the Church. The first declaration of the council, regarding our great progenitor, was couched in the following terms: 'the justice and sanctity, wherein he (Adam) was *created*' (*conditus*). This form was afterwards in so far modified, that, instead of the word 'created' that of 'established' (*constitutus*) was selected.[1]

§ II—THE LUTHERAN DOCTRINE ON MAN'S ORIGINAL STATE

Luther by no means called in question the fact that Adam was positively holy and just. On the contrary, he was totally unacquainted with the later negative conceptions of a state of mere innocency—an indifference between good and evil, wherein the paradisaic man is represented to have existed; and was accordingly far removed from those opinions, which make the doctrine of the fall a foolishness, and make the human race adopt a course, which is the necessary entrance into evil, in order to serve as a transition to a self-conscious return to good.[2] Un-

[1] Pallavic hist. Concil. Trident. lib. vii, c. 9, p. 275, ed. Antw. 1675. He says this change was made at the suggestion of Pacecus. 'Paceco monente, non esse citra controversiam, an Adamus interiorem sanctitatem obtinuerit primo quo creatus fuit momento; unde patet, quam infirma a quibusdam deducatur probatio ad id affirmandum ex verbis concilii, quæ nunc extant.'—Sess. v. decret. de peccat. origin.

[2] *A trial* of Adam was doubtless necessary, that man should make his own decision, and thereby attain to a complete self-consciousness of the good which he already possessed, and especially of his freedom; but the fall was by no means necessary. Undoubtedly the fall brought about the self-consciousness and free possession of truth and goodness, because, by God's grace, even evil must conduce towards the promotion of good. But the bare assertion that the fall was necessary, exalts evil itself into goodness.

happily he fell into other errors, which, considered in their consequences, outweigh at least those we have mentioned.

Respecting original justice, Luther brought no new and peculiar views into vogue. He only selected, out of the rich store of theories which the fruitfulness of scholasticism had produced, the one which seemed most favourable to his own opinions, handled it with no great dexterity, and, in the form which it assumed under his hands, interwove it in such a way into his whole system of doctrine, that the latter without it, cannot be at all understood. Hence, it is only later that its full importance in the whole Lutheran system will become perceptible. Against those theologians, who called Adam's acceptableness before God, supernatural, Luther asserted it to be natural; and in opposition to the schoolmen, who regarded it as accidental, he conceived it to be essential to human nature—an integral and constitutive part of the same; *esse de natura de essentia hominis.*[1] He meant to say the pure nature of man, as it sprang forth at the omnipotent word of the Creator, comprised absolutely in itself all the conditions to render it pleasing unto God; that the various parts of Adam's nature, by the peculiar energy inherent in them, were maintained in the most beautiful harmony, and the whole man preserved in his due relation to God. The religious faculty, especially of the first man, in virtue of an inborn fulness of energy, expanded itself in a way acceptable to the Deity, so that, without any supernatural aid, he truly knew God, believed in Him, loved Him perfectly, and was holy. The religious and moral disposition of Adam, together with its practical development, the Reformers called the image of God, without drawing any distinction between the bare faculty itself, and the exercise of that faculty in correspondency to the divine will. From the very fact that Adam possessed this faculty, he was, according to them, truly religious, truly pious, devoted in all things to God and His Holy will, and perfectly united with Him.[2] Catholic theologians, on the

[1] Luth. in Genes. c. iii, Op. ed. Jen. tom. i, p. 83. 'Quare statuamus, justitiam non esse quoddam donum, quod ab extra accederet, separatumque a natura hominis [so the schoolmen never expressed themselves], sed fuisse vere naturalem, ut natura Adæ esset diligere Deum, credere Deo, cognoscere Deum, etc.

[2] Apol. de peccat. origin. § 7, p. 56. 'Itaque justitia originalis habitura erat æquale temperamentum qualitatum corporis, sed etiam hæc dona: notitiam Dei certiorem, timorem Dei, fiduciam Dei, aut certe rectitudinem, et vim ista efficiendi. Idque testatur scriptura, cum inquit, hominem ad imaginem et similitudinem Dei conditum esse. Quod quid est aliud, nisi

other hand, distinguished very exactly between the one and the other; so that, to determine rightly the distinction, they commonly termed the religious faculty, ' the image of God'; but the pious exertion of that faculty, ' the likeness unto God.'[1] We shall later see what mighty consequences were involved in these, at the first view, trifling doctrinal differences, that seemed merely to concern the schools; and we must, in the meanwhile, prepare ourselves to expect, on the part of Luther, a most singular doctrine respecting original sin. Moreover, the non-distinction adverted to, had partly its foundation in the endeavour of the Reformers to be in their teaching very practical and generally intelligible. Hence, they avoided, with as much care as possible, all distinctions and abstract expressions, as a scholastic abuse, but thereby frequently fell into a strange and most pernicious confusion of ideas.

The second main point of difference between the two confessions, in the matter under discussion, is the doctrine of free-will. Luther asserted (and he would have this assertion maintained as an article of faith), that man is devoid of freedom; that every (pretended) free action is only apparent; that an irresistible divine necessity rules all things, and that every

in homine hanc sapientiam et justitiam effigiatum esse, quæ Deum apprehenderet, et in qua reluceret Deus, hoc est, homini dona esse data notitiam Dei, timorem Dei, fiduciam erga Deum et similia.' They thus understand by what God gave to Adam, as well real acts of the spirit (timorem Dei, fiduciam) as the faculty for these (vim ista efficiendi). Very remarkable is Gerhard's assertion, that according to the Lutheran doctrine the divine image in man is not anything substantial, but merely a condition of human substance, a quality of it. (Joann. Gerhard, loci theolog. ed. Cotta, 1765, tom. iv, p. 249 seq. Compare ejusdem Confess. Cathol. lib. ii, art. xx, c. 2, p. 349.) It is observable, he refutes himself by saying, that conscience in man is still a remnant of the divine image. As, he adds, conscience is not to be explained from any supernatural action of God on man, so it follows it must be a substantial faculty of the latter, and consequently such the image itself. But he says the latter is, ' concreata humanæ substantiæ integritas, perfectio ac rectitudo, et proinde in categoria qualitatis collocanda.' Loci theol. lib. c, p. 268. Comp. Chemnit, loc. theol. pt. i, p. 217, ed. 1615.

[1] Bellarm. de grat. prim. hom. c. ii, lib. c, p. 7. ' Imago, quæ est ipsa natura mentis et voluntatis, a solo Deo fieri potuit : similitudo autem, quæ in virtute et probitate consistit, a nobis quoque, Deo adjuvante, perficitur. God can give us no actions. Further on Bellarmine says : ' Ex his igitur tot patrum testamoniis cogimur admittere, non esse omnino idem imaginem et similitudinem, sed imaginem ad naturam, similitudinem ad virtutes pertinere.' The well known passage in Genesis may, or may not, bear such an interpretation ; but the distinction has a value in itself, independently of all scriptural interpretation.

human act is at bottom only the act of God.[1] Melancthon taught the same. He also comprised all things in the circle of an unavoidable necessity and predestination, declared the doctrine, that God is the sole agent, to be a necessary part of all Christian science, for thereby the wisdom and cunning of human reason were duly repressed and condemned, and he repeatedly insisted, that the word 'freedom of election' was unknown to Scripture, and that its meaning must be rejected by the judgment of the spiritual man. He added, that this expression, like the very pernicious word, 'reason,' to which he declared equal hostility, had been introduced through philosophy into the Christian Church. From no other cause did he deem himself so well justified in daring to apply to the professors of the theological faculties in the middle age—the so-called schoolmen—the terms sophists, theologues, and the like, as on account of their crime in having established among Christians the doctrine of human free-will so firmly, that, as he complained, it was scarcely any longer possible to root it out.[2] Perceiving, after more diversified experience and maturer reflection, especially after the controversy with the Catholics, the prodigious abyss into which such a doctrine must precipitate the Church, he subsequently

---

[1] Luther. de servo arbitrio adv. Erasm. Roterod. Opp. ed. Lat. Jen. tom. iii, f. 170. 'Est itaque et hoc imprimis necessarium et salutare Christiano nosse, quod Deus nihil Præscit contingenter, sed quod omnia incommutabili et æterna infallibilique voluntate et providet, et preponit, et facit. Hoc fulmine sternitur et conteritur penitus liberum arbitrium. Ideo qui liberum arbitrium. volunt assertum, debent hoc fulmen vel negare vel dissimulare, aut alia ratione a se abigere' (fol. 171). 'Ex quo sequitur irrefragabiliter, omnia quæ facimus, etsi nobis videntur mutabiliter et contingenter fieri et fiant, et ita etiam contingenter nobis fiant, revera tamen fiunt necessario et immutabiliter, si voluntatem Dei spectes' (fol. 177). 'Alterum paradoxon: quidquid fit a nobis, non libero arbitrio, sed mera necessitate fieri.' The book closes with these words (fol. 238), 'Ego vero hoc libro non contuli, sed asserui et assero, ac penes nullum volo esse judicium, sed omnibus sua deo, ut præstent obsequium.' The *Solida Declaratio* (ii, de libero arbitrio, p. 639) sanctions this book, and especially approves what it says 'de absoluta necessitate contra omnes sinistras suspiciones et corruptelas,' and thus concludes: 'Ea hic repetita esse volumus, et ut diligentur legantur, et expetantur omnes hortamur.'

[2] Melancth. loc. Theol. ed. August, 1821. 'Sensim irrepsit philosophia in Christianismum, et receptum est impium de libero arbitrio dogma. Usurpata est vox liberi arbitrii, a divinis literis, a sensu et judicio spiritus alienissima . . . additum est e Platonis philosophia *vocabulum rationis* æque *perniciosissimum* (p. 10). In quæstionem vocatur, sitne libera voluntas et quatenus libera sit? Respons. Quandoquidem omnia, quæ eveniunt *necessario* juxta divinam prædestinationem eveniunt, nulla est voluntatis nostræ libertas' (p. 12).

abandoned, and even combated it.[1] On the other hand we are unacquainted with any such recantation on the part of Luther; and the formulary of concord gives an express sanction to the writing of the latter against Erasmus. This doctrine of the servitude of the human will has had the greatest weight; and its influence, according to Melancthon's assurance, pervades even the whole religious system of the Lutherans.[2]

In regard to the original constitution of the human body, both confessions are agreed; and if the Lutheran formularies speak not expressly of that property of Adam's body, whereby, if he had never sinned, he would have remained exempt from death, this silence is to be ascribed to the total absence of all controversy on the matter.[3]

§ III—THE CALVINISTIC DOCTRINE ON THE PRIMITIVE STATE OF MAN

In enlarging on the spiritual condition of the paradisaic man, Calvin, by representing it, with Luther, as one devoid of supernatural graces, set himself up in opposition to the Catholic Church; but, by expressly ascribing to the first man the gift of free-will, he equally opposed the Lutherans.[4] In other

[1] This he did in the editions of the *Loci Theologici*, dating from the year 1535. It is a remarkable fact, that he now reproaches the schoolmen with having taught the doctrine of an absolute necessity, but observes a total silence respecting himself and Luther, while in the earlier editions of the same work he had charged these very schoolmen with an arrogant assertion of the tenet of free-will. ' Et quod asperior paulo sententia de prædestinatione vulgo videtur, debemus illi impiæ sophistarum theologiæ, quæ inculcavit nobis contingentiam et libertatem voluntatis nostræ, ut a veritate scripturæ molliculæ aures abhorreant.' This is the language of the first edition: but on the other hand in the editions from the year 1535 down to 1543, we read as follows: ' Valla et plerique alii non recte detrahunt voluntati hominis libertatem.' Who are then these *plerique*? A vast number of such indecencies do we meet with in the writings of the Reformers. In the editions dating from the year 1543, this doctrine is referred to the Stoics. ' Hæc imaginatio orta ex Stoicis disputationibus,' etc.

[2] Melancth. l. c, p. 13. ' In omnes disputationis nostræ partes incidet.'

[3] Cf. Gerhardi, loc. theolog. tom. iv, p. 268 (loc. ix, c. iv, § 99).

[4] Calvin. Institution. l. i, c. 15, § 8, fol. 55, ed. Gen. 1559. ' Animam hominis Deus mente instruxit, qua bonum a malo, justum ab injusto discerneret; ac quid sequendum vel fugiendum sit præcunte rationis luce videret; unde partem hanc directricem *to hegemonikon* dixerunt Philosophi. Huic adjunxit voluntatem, penes quam est electio. His præclaris dotibus excelluit prima hominis conditio, ut ratio, intelligentia, prudentia, judicium non mode ad terrenæ vitæ gubernationem suppeterent, sed quibus trans-

respects we find in this article no difference of doctrine; and the same remark will hold good of the confessions of the reformed Churches.[1] In respect to the injurious consequences produced by the sin of our first parent on his corporeal existence, and that of his posterity, most of the formularies of the reformed expressly teach, with Calvin, that death is the fruit of Adam's transgression.[2]

But the question here occurs, how Calvin could feel himself justified in attributing free-will to Adam, when, in common with Zwingle, he completely shared Luther's doctrine touching a divine necessity of all occurrences, and even pushed this opinion to the extremest verge. Conscious of this discrepancy, he observes undoubtedly, that the question as to the mysterious predestination of God is here unseasonably mooted; for the matter at issue is not what could have happened, but how man was originally constituted.[3] In despite of this express demand, to hold the two doctrines distinct,—that of a divine necessity, of an absolute eternal destiny, which enchains and holds all things together, and that of the freedom of man, prior to his fall, we are at a loss to discover how this claim can be satisfied; for these two doctrines are in fact incompatible; and with the adoption of the one, the other must be abandoned; unless to the word 'freedom' a notion be attached, which in reality destroys its very existence. And such is really the case; for, as we shall have occasion to show, Calvin evidently after Luther's example, makes, not inward necessity, but outward constraint, the opposite to freedom.[4] On the other hand, Melancthon has

cenderent usque ad Deum ad æternam felicitatem. In hac integritate libero arbitrio pollebat homo, quo si vellet adipisci posset æternam vitam.
[1] Helvet. i, c. vii (Corpus libr. symbol. eccles. reform. ad August. 1817), p. 16; ii, p. 95; iii, p. 103. Yet without any minuter definition they merely say, man was created after God's image, and except in the first Helvetic Confession, they make no mention of free-will. The Scottish Confession (art. ii, 1. c, p. 145) accords to Adam freedom: the Gallic and the Anglican are silent on the subject; and the Belgic again concedes this gift to the first man (c. xiv, p. 128). These are differences which may be easily accounted for.
[2] Helvet. i, c. viii, 1. c, p. 17; Belg, c. xiv, 178. 'Quo (peccato) se morti corporali et spirituali obnoxium reddidit.'
[3] Calvin. l. c, § 8. 'Hic enim intempestive quæstio ingeritur de occulta prædestinatione Dei: quia non agitur, quid *accidere* potuerit, necne, sed qualis fuerit hominis natura.'
[4] Luther. de servo arbitrio ad Erasm. Roterod. l. i, fol. 171. 'Optarim sane aliud melius vocabulum dari in hac disputatione, quam hoc, Necessitas, quod non recte dicitur, neque de divina, neque de humana voluntate: est enim nimis ingratæ et incongruæ significationis pro hoc loco, quandam

expressed himself openly and honestly on the mutual correlativeness of these two articles of doctrine, and declared that, from that very correlativeness, they should be simultaneously treated.[1]

We shall find, moreover, that Calvin even teaches an eternal, immutable predestination of the fall of the first man ; an opinion which is certainly quite incompatible with the proposition, that Adam was free, that is to say, could have avoided sinning. Hence it has happened that, though some symbolical writings of the Reformed communities have with Calvin expressly ascribed free-will to Adam, others have judged it more expedient, in what they teach respecting the paradisaic man, to pass this matter over in silence; and this was evidently the most consistent course.

We think it still proper to direct attention to the internal reasons, which Calvin alleged in behalf of the doctrine of an absolute necessity destructive of all human freedom partly because it will then follow, that it ought not, at least absolutely and immediately,[2] to be confounded with the Pagan *fatum*, and partly because a knowledge of this reasoning will be of importance in later investigations. If Melancthon, after indulging in harsh assertions, could assign no other practical ground for this doctrine, than that the relation of man towards God adverted to was very useful towards subduing[3] human

velut coactionem, et omnino id quod contrarium est voluntati, ingerens intellectui : cum tamen non hoc velit causa ista quæ agitur. Voluntas enim, sive divina sive humana nulla coactione, sed mera lubentia vel cupiditate quasi vere libera, facit quod facit, sive bonum sive malum. Sed tamen immutabilis et infallibilis est voluntas Dei quæ nostram voluntatem mutabilem gubernat, ut canit Boetius : " stabilisque manens das cuncta moveri." ' This is a very inappropriate citation, for Manlius Torquatus Boethius was no believer in Luther's doctrine of necessity.

[1] Melancth. loc. theolog. p. 13. ' Sed ineptus videar, qui statim initio operis de asperrimo loco, de prædestinatione disseram. Quamquam quid attinet in compendio, primo an postremo loco id agam, *quod in omnes disputationis nostræ partes incidet.*'

[2] Calvin (Instit. rel. Christ. lib. i, c. 16, n. 8) takes notice of this parallel, and observes as follows : ' Non enim cum stoicis necessitatem comminiscimur ex perpetuo causarum nexu et implicita quadam serie, quæ in natura contineatur : sed Deum constituimus arbitrum ac moderatorem omnium, qui pro sua sapientia ab ultima æternitate decrevit quod factorus esset, et nunc sua potentia, quod decrevit, exsequitur.' A special defence against the charge of fatalism, laid to Calvin's doctrine, was written by Beza. Abstersio calumniarum, quibus aspersus est Joan. Calvinus a Tillemanno Heshusio, a Lutheran professor in Heidelberg, p. 208, seq.

[3] Melanct. lib. c. ' Multum enim omnino refert ad premendam damnandamque humanæ rationis tum sapientiam, tum prudentiam, constanter credere, quod a Deo fiant omnia.'

arrogance, Calvin, on the other hand, observed, that the knowledge not merely that God guided the affairs of the world in small, as in great things, but that nothing whatever could occur without the express ordinance of God (*destinante Deo*), comprised a very abundant source of consolation ; for it is only in this way man feels himself secure in the hands of an all-wise, all-ruling, powerful, and indulgent Father.[1] Hence, the idea of a divine permission, and such a conduct of things, that ultimately everything, even evil, in the world, conduces to the benefit of those who serve God, did not satisfy him. He believed the elect insecure, and the notion of a divine providence not sufficiently defined, unless, for example, the assaults of the enemy on an elect were absolutely willed and ordained by God. Moreover, even the public confessions of the Reformed occasionally adopt this view, which Calvin here enforces, of the providential guidance of all things, mitigating considerably, however, this opinion, and evincing a very laudable dread of stamping on their articles the harsh spirit of Calvin.[2] By the latter, however, as well as by his disciple, Theodore Beza,[3] the opinions adverted to, respecting divine providence, were held with such tenacity, and carried out with such consistency, that they found it a matter of extreme difficulty to convince the world, nay, in despite of all their eloquence and dialectic art, they utterly failed to convince very many, that they did not in fact refer

---

[1] Calv. Instit. rel. Christ. lib. i, c. 17, § 3. Yet Luther, in this matter, had prepared the way for him with some hints. Luther. de servo arbitrio. Opp. tom. iii, fol. 171, b. ' Ultra dico, non modo quam ista sint vera, de quo infra latius ex scripturis, dicetur, verum etiam, quam religiosum, pium, et necessarium sit, ea nosse ; his enim ignoratis, neque fides, neque ullus Dei cultus consistere potest. Nam hoc esset vere Deum ignorare, cum qua ignorantia salus stare nequit, ut notum est. Si enim dubitas, aut contemnis nosse, quod Deus omnia, non contingenter, sed necessario et immutabiliter præsciat et velit, quomodo poteris ejus promissionibus credere, certo fidere, ac niti ? Cum enim promittit, certum oportet te esse, quod sciat, possit et velit præstare, quod promittit ; alioqui eum non veracem, nec fidelem æstimabis, quæ est incredulitas et summa impietas et negatio Dei altissimi.

[2] Confess. Belgic. c. xiii, in Augusti. Corp. libror. symbol. eccles. reform. p. 177 seq.

[3] Theod. Bezæ quæstionum et respons. christian. lib. ed. 4to, 1573, p. 105. (N.B. Place where printed is not named.) ' Quæso, expone, quid providentiam appellas ? Resp. Sic appello non illam modo vim inenarribilem, qua, fit, ut Deus omnia ab æterno prospexerit omnibusque futuris sapientissimi providerit, sed imprimis decretum illud æternum Dei sapientissimi simul et potentissimi, ex quo quicquid fuit, fuit ; quicquid est, est ; et quicquid futurum est, erit, *prout ipsi* ab æterno decernere libuit.

all evil to God. We are bound to enter more fully into the investigation of this subject.

§ IV—ON THE CAUSE OF MORAL EVIL

In all the more important doctrinal manuals and polemical writings of the sixteenth and seventeenth centuries—in the works of Bellarmine, Becanus, Chemnitz, Gerhard, and others, nay even in several public confessions, the reader meets with a special and copious chapter, bearing the title of the present section. As, in the second and third centuries of the Church, no writer could enlarge on the religious concerns of his times without entering upon the question, ' whence is evil ' ; so the same question was now again most anxiously investigated ; and it soon became apparent that the opposition between Catholicism and Protestantism could not be duly appreciated, and that the inmost essence of the latter would remain eternally misconceived, if the different replies which had been made to that question were not well considered.

No subject in the first times of the Reformation so embittered the Catholics against the authors of that revolution, as their doctrine respecting the relation wherein the Deity stands to moral evil. It was precisely on this account the Catholic Church laid down again, with so much earnestness and emphatic energy, the proposition, that man was created with the endowment of freedom, in order that, without any restriction and without subterfuge, the guilt of evil in the world might fall on the head of man. For the denial of free-will on the part of Luther, Melancthon, Zwingle, and Calvin was calculated to excite an apprehension, that, in consequence thereof, the Catholic doctrine of God's perfect sanctity, to whom sin is an abomination, would be thrown into the shade, and, on the other hand, that even the most vicious man would be thus sheltered from all responsibility. And, in fact, Melancthon, in his commentary on the epistle to the Romans, in the edition of the year 1525, had the hardihood to assert that God wrought all things, evil as well as good ; that He was the author of David's adultery, and the treason of Judas, as well as of Paul's conversion. Now, howsoever strange and prejudiced a notion an individual may have formed of the errors of the Catholic Church, we ask him, would he dare to assert, that all these errors put together can outweigh the single enormity here uttered by Melancthon ? And yet Chemnitz, to whom we are indebted for the original passages in question (for in the later editions of Melancthon's aforesaid work they have disappeared)—Chemnitz, we say, excuses his teacher, Melancthon. And how does he excuse him ? In so complicated a matter, he says among other things, all in the beginning could not be systematically and properly treated, more especially as, on the part of Catholics, the doctrine of free-will had been exaggerated.[1] Just as if the question 'whence is evil,' had only in the sixteenth century first excited attention ;—just as if Holy Writ left us at all in doubt how that question was to be answered ;—just as if in the second and third centuries the question had not been really settled by the Church ! However, in this matter, Melancthon merely spoke after Luther, as the writing of the latter against Erasmus will show. But it was Melancthon's assertion the Council of Trent had in view, when it anathematised the proposition, that God works evil as well as good, and that it is not in the power of man to abstain from wickedness.[2]

In proportion, however, as the notions, which the Saxon Reformers, especially Melancthon, had entertained respecting free-will, became purer, they abandoned the opinion that God was the author of evil ; and the last-named writer had even the courage to revoke in the Augsburg Confession his former doctrine.[3] The latter formularies of the Lutherans are in perfect accordance with this amelioration in opinion.[4] But it

[1] Martin. Chemnit. loc. theol. ed. Leyser. 1615. P. 1, p. 173. The words of Melancthon are : ' Hæc sit certa sententia a Deo fieri omnia, tam bona quam mala. Nos dicimus, non solum permittere Deum creaturis, ut operentur, sed ipsum omnia proprie agere, ut sicut fatentur, proprium Dei opus fuisse Pauli vocationem, ita fateantur, opera Dei propria esse, sive quæ media vocantur, ut comedere, sive quæ mala sunt, ut Davidis adulterium ; constat enim Deum omnia facere, non permissive, sed potenter, *i.e.* ut sit ejus proprium opus Judæ proditio, sicut Pauli vocatio.'

[2] Sess. vi. Can. vi. ' Si quis dixerit, non esse in potestate hominis, vias suas malas facere, sed mala opera ita ut bona Deum operari, non permissive solum, sed etiam proprie et per se, adeo ut sit proprium ejus opus non minus proditio Judæ, quam vocatio Pauli anathema sit.'

[3] Art. xix, p. 81. ' De causa peccati docent, quod tametsi Deus creat et conservat naturam, tamen causa peccati est voluntas malorum, videlicet diaboli et impriorum, quæ, non adjuvante Deo, avertit se a Deo, sicut Christus ait (Joan viii. 44) : cum loquitur mendacium, ex ipso loquitur.'

[4] Solid. declar. 1, § 5, p. 613. ' Hoc extra controversiam est positum, quod Deus non sit causa, creator, vel auctor peccati, sed quod opera et machinationibus satanæ per unum hominem (quod est diaboli) in mundum sit introductum.'

was quite otherwise with the Swiss Reformers, who remained obstinately addicted to their errors. The importance of the subject calls upon us to describe at greater length the nature of their opinions. In his writing on Providence, addressed to the Landgrave Philip of Hesse (anno 1530), Zwingle asserts, that God *is the author, mover, and impeller to sin ;* that also He makes the sinner; that by the instrumentality of the creature He produces injustice, and the like.[1] In numberless places Calvin uses the expression, man, at the instigation of God, doeth what it is unlawful to do; by a mysterious divine inspiration, the heart of man turneth to evil; man falleth, because the providence of God so ordaineth.[2] If these principles fill us with just detestation, they were pushed still further by Theodore Beza; although what he brought forward was only deduction, and indeed a necessary deduction, from the doctrines just adduced. This leader of the Reformed, after Calvin's death, is not satisfied with repeating that God incites, impels, and urges to evil; but he even adds that the Almighty creates a portion of men as His instruments, *with the intent* of working evil through them.[3]

[1] Zwingli de providentia c. vi, Opp. tom. i (without date or place), fol-365, b. 'Unum igitur atque idem facinus, puta adulterium aut homicidium, quantum Dei auctoris, motoris, impulsoris, opus est, crimen non est, quantum autem hominis est, crimen ac scelus est.' Fol. 366, a: 'Cum movet (Deus) ad opus aliquod, quod perficienti instrumento fraudi est, sibi tamen non est, ipse enim libere movet, neque instrumento facit injuriam, cum omnia sint magis sua, quam cujusque artificis sua instrumenta, quibus non facit injuriam, si nunc limam in malleum, et contra malleum in limam convertat. Movet ergo latronem ad occidendum innocentem, etiamsi imparatum ad mortem.'

[2] Calvin institut. lib. iv, c. 18, § 2 : 'Homo justo Dei impulsu agit quod sibi non licet.' Lib. iii, c. 23, § 8 : 'Cadit igitur homo, Dei providentia sic ordinante.' With this proposition Calvin found himself in a singular situation. On one hand, he held the maintenance of it as theoretically necessary, and practically useful; and, on the other, he was extremely incensed if anyone attempted to deduce from it the consequences which it involved. I have scarcely ever read any work clothed in coarser language, than the reply which Calvin made to an anonymous, but very learned, theologian, who in fourteen theses had condensed all contained in the doctrine of Calvin respecting the origin of evil, and then furnished copious illustrations on each article. We find the writing and the reply in 'Calumniæ nebulonis cujusdam, etc. Joannis Calvini ad easdem responsio.' Genev. 1558. Calvin concludes his reply with these words : 'Compescat te Deus, Satan. Amen.'

[3] Beza Aphorism. xxii. 'Sic autem agit (Deus) per illa instrumenta, ut non tantum sinat illa agere, nec tantum moderetur eventum, sed etiam incitet, impellat, moveat, regat, atque adeo, quod omnium est maximum, *et creat, ut per illa agat, quod constituit.*'

The reasoning attempted in support of these notions is quite of a character with them. In order to show that God, although he urged to wicked actions, doth nevertheless not sin, but only man, Zwingle observes: God, as the just one, is subject to no law; for it is written, the law is not given for the just! Thus, should God *make* an angel or a man transgress the law (*cum transgressorem facit*), He himself doth not transgress it; but the creatures, whom the law oppresses and accuses.[1] A more pitiable train of reasoning it would be impossible to invent, whether we consider the notion which Zwingle here gives of the just man (for, according to the meaning of the passage in St Paul adverted to, the just man is in himself, the living moral law, and therefore does not stand in a mere extraneous relation to its precepts, but bears them in himself and constantly fulfils them), or whether we look to the essence of the Deity, from whose wisdom and holiness the moral law is only an emanation, and which in pure and eternal glory he realises; or whether, lastly, we contemplate the moral law in itself alone, which Zwingle, however much he may incidentally exalt it, treats as an arbitrary, and merely positive code.[2]

The Reformer of Zurich completely destroys the objectiveness of evil, and has not a perception of a holy moral government of the world, even in those passages where he seems to speak in such a sense. For these reasons he did not perceive, that, if

[1] Zwingl. de providentia, c. v. 'Cum igitur Angelum transgressorem facit et hominum,' etc. C. vi, fol. 365, b: 'Quantum enim Deus facit, non est peccatum, quia non est contra legem; illi enim non est lex posita, utpote justo, nam justis non ponitur lex, juxta Pauli sententiam. Unum igitur atque idem facinus, puta adulterium aut homicidium, quantum Dei auctoris, motoris, ac impulsoris, opus est, crimen non est, quantum autem hominis est, crimen est ac scelus est. Ille enim lege non tenetur, hic autem lege etiam damnatur.'

[2] Zwingli. de provid. c. v, lib. i, p. 364, b. 'Duobus exemplis id fiet luculentius. Habet pater familiæ leges quasdam domesticas, quibus liberos a deliciis ac desidia avocet. Lecythum mellis qui tetigerit, vapulato: calceum qui non recte induxerit, aut inductum passim exuerit ac dimiserit, discalceatus incedito—et similes. Jam si mater familiæ, aut adulti liberi mel non tantum attre taverient, sed etiam insumpserint, non continuo vapulant, non enim tenentur lege. Sed pueri vapulant, si tetigerint, illis enim data est lex. Taurus si totum armentum ineat et impleat, laudi est. Herus tauri, si unam modo præter uxorem agnoscat, reus fit adulterii. Causa est, quia huic lex est posita, ne adulterium admittat; illum nulla lex coercet. Ut breviter, verissime, sicut omnia, Paulus summam hujus fundamenti pronuntiaverit, ubi non est lex, ibi non est prævaricatio. Deo, velut patri familiæ, non est lex posita, idcirco nec peccat, *dum hoc ipsum agit in homine*, quod homini peccatum est, sibi vero non est.'

God were to impel to the transgression of a moral law given by Himself, He would then be in contradiction with Himself, and would violate His own nature, and not merely an outward rule; that is to say, the Reformer did not see that his theory destroyed the very notion of the Deity. The injurious influence of this doctrine on public morality, is evident of itself, and was strongly represented to Calvin.[1]

Zwingle still endeavours to justify his unhappy doctrine by the pretence, that God is ever guided by pure intentions, that consequently the end sanctifies the means, and, in a somewhat strange connection with this matter, he adds, that David's adultery, whereof God was the author, could as little convict God of a bad action, as when a bull impregnates a whole herd of cows.[2] Here he only overlooks the circumstance, that man is no more a cow, than God is a bull; that, accordingly, if man had been instigated by God to adultery, this could not occur without a violation of man's moral nature, and consequently the guilt would revert to God. Zwingle's conception more nearly examined, consists herein, that God wrought on the sensuality of David, which by its power overmastered his will; that, in consequence, God performed only the outward work indifferent in itself, and not the evil in it—the work, which, in the nuptial union as well as in adultery, is identical. But how could he distinguish between the temptations of Satan, and such an agency as here described.

Reverting to the observation which Zwingle deemed calculated to justify the Deity, that, in alluring to bad actions, God had good objects in view, it must be said that this notion was shared by Calvin and Beza; though, by the latter, it was put forth with more acuteness. Hence it will be our duty to state the opinions of these two Reformers. Calvin admits, that the

[1] Calumniæ nebul. Calv. resp. p. 19. 'Hæc sunt, Calvine, quæ adversarii tui de doctrina tua perhibent, admonentque homines, ut de doctrina ista ex fructu judicent. Dicunt autem te et tuos discipulos ferre multos fructus Dei tui: esse enim plerosque litigatores, vindictæ cupidos, injuriæ tenaces et memores, cæterisque vitiis, quæ Deus suggerit præditos. . . . Jam vero doctrina Christi qui credebant, reddebantur meliores, sed tua doctrina aiunt, homines manifeste fieri deteriores. Præterea quum dicitis, vos habere sanam doctrinam, respondent, non esse vobis credendum. Si enim Deus vester sæpissime aliud cogitat et vult, metuendum esse, ne vos, Deum vestrum imitantes, idem faciatis, atque homines decipiatis.'

[2] L. c. 'Quod Deus facit, libere facit, alienus ab omni affectu noxio, igitur et absque peccato, ut adulterium David, quod ad auctorem Deum pertinet, non magis Deo sit peccatum, quam cum taurus totum armentum inscendit et implet.' What a comparison!

opinion, according to which God determines man to moral corruption and impels him to sin, is not compatible with the known will of the Deity. Hence, like Luther, in his book against Erasmus, he has recourse to a hidden will of God, whereby his mode of proceeding is indeed very just, though its equity be not obvious to our perception.[1] If this be the ordinary way wherein Calvin in his Institutions seeks to defend himself, in his instruction against the so-called libertines, who, evidently induced by his own and Zwingle's writings, had denied the distinction between good and evil, and placed redemption in the knowledge, obtained through Christ, that no distinction exists between the two ; he still labours to show the great difference existing between the act of God, and the act of the impious, in one and the same deed. So he says, God works to exercise justice while the wicked man is actuated by avarice, covetousness, etc.[2] God, for instance, instigates a man to murder, but from no other motive than to punish a crime committed. We leave it to the judgment of everyone, whether the employment of such means be compatible with the very notion of the Deity, and how extremely pernicious it would be, and subversive of all human morality, were men herein to imitate the Deity so represented ? But it is evident that the inquiry must here be carried back as far as the fall of man, and the question arises, what share is to be allotted to God in that event. Calvin never thinks of deducing

[1] Calvin. institut. lib. iii, c. 23, § 9. ' Nos vero inde negamus, rite excusari (homines), quandoquidem Dei ordinationi, qua se exitio destinatos queruntur, sua constet equitas, nobis quidem incognita, sed illi certissima.'

[2] Calvin instructio advers. libertinos, c. 14 (in Joan. Calvini opuscula omnia in unum vol. collecta. Genev. 1552, p. 528). ' Altera exceptio, cujus infelices isti nullam habent rationem, hæc est,—magnam esse differentiam inter opus Dei, et opus impii cum eo Deus vice instrumenti utitur. Impius enim sua avaritia aut ambitione, aut invidia, aut crudelitate incitatur ad facinus suum, nec alium finem spectat. Ideo ex radice illa, id est, ex animi affectione, et fine, quem spectat, opus qualitatem sumit, et merito malum judicatur. Sed Deus respectum omnino contrarium habet : nempe ut justitiam exerceat ad conservandos bonos,' etc.

Cf. de æterna prædest (Opusc. lib. 1, p. 946). ' Turpi quidem et illiberali calumnia nos gravant, qui Deum peccati auctorem fieri obtendunt, si omnium, quæ aguntur, causa est ejus voluntas. Nam quod homo injuste perpetrat, vel ambitione,' etc.

Beza (in his Quæst. et Respons. lib. i, p. 113) distinguishes between *in aliquo agere*, and *per aliquem agere*, and accordingly adds ' adjiciendum est, Deum agere quidem in bonis et per bonos : per malos vero agere, et non in malis.' Zwingle makes use of the expression *in aliquo agere*, when speaking of that act of God, whereby He produces evil. De Provid. c. v, p. 364.

the fall of Adam from the abuse of human freedom ; but, on the contrary, in perfect accordance with his own fundamental principles, he admits that God had ordained the fall, and by an eternal decree brought it about.[1]

In Beza, we find these monstrous errors pushed to still further length. The principal points of his reasoning are as follows : God wished on one hand to show mercy, and on the other to reveal His justice. Adam was created morally just and holy; for from God's hand nothing unclean can come forth. But how could God unfold His mercies, since the sinner only can be the subject of these ? How could He manifest His justice, if no one committed wrong, and thereby incurred punishment ? Hence, for the unfolding of these attributes, the Deity must prepare a channel which was found in ordaining the fall of the first man. These divine objects being perfectly just and holy, their quality is transmitted to the means also selected for their execution.[2] Here Beza does not speak of a mere co-operation

[1] Calvin. Institut. lib. iii. c. 23, § 4. ' Nonne ad eam, quæ pro damnationis causa obtenditur, corruptionem, Dei ordinatione prædestinati ante fuerant ? Cum ergo in sua corruptione pereant, nihil aliud quam pœnas luunt ejus calamitatis, in quam *ejus prædestinatione* lapsus est Adam, ac posteros præcipites secum traxit. § 7. Disertis verbis hoc exstare negant (sophistæ sc. papistici), decretum fuisse a Deo, ut sua defectione periret Adam, quasi vero, etc. § 8. Cadit igitur homo, Dei providentia sic ordinante.'

Beza (Quæst. et Respons. p. 117) deduces the sin of Adam from a spontaneo motu voluntatis, that is to say, from a natural impulse, the meaning whereof is, that God so formed human nature, that evil could not fail to arise, which He then makes use of for His own ends.

[2] Beza Absters. calum Heshus. adv. Calvin. (with the *kreophagia* sive Cyclops ; in one volume, Genev. 1561, p. 231). ' Superest, ut ostendamus, ita decretum esse a Deo Adami lapsum, ut tamen tota culpa penes Satanam et Adamum resideat. Hoc autem liquido apparebit, si, quemadmodum paulo ante Calvinus nos monuit, diversa atque adeo penitus contraria Dei, Satanæ, et hominis consilia, ac deinde etiam diversos agendi modos consideramus. Quid enim Deo propositum fuit, quum lapsum hominis ordinaret ? Nempe patefaciendæ suæ misericordiæ in electis gratuito servandis; itemque justo suo judicio in reproborum damnanda malitia viam sibi aperire. Nam nisi sibi et posteris suis lapsus esset Adam, nec ulla extaret in hominibus miseria, cujus misereretur Deus in filio suo, nec ulla malitia quam condemnaret : ac proinde neque appareret ejus misericordia neque etiam judicium. Hoc igitur quum molitur et exequitur Dominus, quis eum ullius injustitiæ coarguerit ? Quid autem moliebatur Satan, quamvis imprudens Dei consilio subserviret ? Nempe quia Deum odit, et totus invidia exæstuat, inimicitias serere voluit inter Deum et hominem. Quid autem cogitant Adamus et Heva simul atque se dociles Satanæ discipulos præbuerunt ? Nempe Deum ut invidum et mendacem coarguere, et eo invito sese in illius solio collocare.'

The outlines of Beza's reasoning may be seen in Zwingle (De Provid.

of the Deity in the performance of the mere outward part in an evil action; for God, whether to punish or to exercise mercy, has regard to the inward evil sentiment, since, without this, sin is not possible. It was thus the part of the Deity to call forth somehow an evil sentiment, in order to attain His ends; that is to say, he must annihilate His sanctity, in order on its ruins to attain to compassion and justice. Hence, Beza does not deny, that the first man, when he sinned, succumbed under an invincible destiny; that it was thus not left to his freedom to abstain from sin. But, like Luther and Calvin, distinguishing between necessity and compulsion, he says the latter does not occur in sin; that on the contrary, Adam sinned willingly, with an inward pleasure (*spontaneo motu*, in opposition to *libero* and *voluntario motu*), and although he was not able to avoid sinning, he did not wish to avoid it: and it was this very thing which constituted his criminality.[1]

It is by these principles, that passages in the Reformed confessions are to be estimated. They all assert, that God is not the author of sin, that is to say, in the sense wherein Zwingle, Calvin, and Beza, attempt to exculpate the Deity, after having denied man's free-will.[2]

cap. vi, p. 364). How little, moreover, the sound common-sense of the Christian, who, on one hand, upholds the idea of God's holiness and justice, and, on the other hand, clings to the doctrine of rewards and punishments according to man's works, could be led astray by such dialectic arts, the anonymous writer already very well points out, when he says: 'Equidem favi ego aliquando doctrinæ tuæ, Calvine, eamque, quamvis non satis mihi perspicuam, defendi, quod tantum tribuebam auctoritati tuæ, ut vel contra cogitare putarem nefas; sed nunc auditis adversariorum argumentis, non habeo quod respondeam. . . . *Nam tuæ rationes sunt obscuræ, et fere ejusmodi, ut statim, deposito de manu libro, excidant ex memoria, neque adversarios convincant. At adversariorum argumenta sunt aperta, acria, et quæ facile memoriæ mandentur, et ab illiteratis, quales fere erant qui Christum sectabantur, percipiantur.* Hinc fit ut tui discipuli fere magis authoritate tua nitantur, quam ratione. *Et quum adversarios vincere non possunt, habent eos pro hæreticis et pertinacibus, et ab eorum consortio abstinent, et omnes ubique monent, ut abstineant.*' And such doctrines were to be held as formal articles of faith!

[1] Beza Absters lib. i. 'Quærenda est vitii origo in instrumentorum spontaneo motu, quo fit ut Deus juste decreverit, quod illi injuste fecerant,' etc. A distinction very familiar to Beza! Compare his 'Quæst. et Respons.' lib. i, p. 120.

[2] Confess. Helv. cap. ix. (ed. August. p. 19). 'Ergo quoad malum sive peccatum, homo non *coactus* vel a Deo, vel a diabolo, sed *sua sponte* malum fecit, et hac parte liberrimi est arbitrii.' Cap. viii, p. 18. 'Damnamus præteria Florinum et Blastum, contra quos et Irenæus scripsit, ut omnes, qui Deum faciunt auctorem peccati.' Confess. Gallic. cap. viii, lib. c, p. 113. 'Negamus tamen illum (Deum) esse autorem mali, aut eorum, quæ

CHAPTER II

ON ORIGINAL SIN AND ITS CONSEQUENCE

§ V—THE CATHOLIC DOCTRINE OF ORIGINAL SIN

IT is one of the most remarkable phenomena in the history of the religious controversies of the last three centuries, that the Reformers, according to whose principles Adam in his fall only succumbed under a sentence of irresistible necessity pronounced upon him, should have represented the Deity as kindling into so fearful a wrath, and inflicting so frightful a chastisement for this *act* of the first man, which, according to their own views, should be called rather his pure misfortune. It is no easy task to explain how ideas so unconnected should have been associated in one and the same head. When we just now used the comprehensive word 'Reformers,' we did so advisedly; for even Luther and Melancthon had both completely framed their theory of original sin, when they were entangled in those opinions described in the preceding section—opinions which Zwingle and Calvin only took up and further developed. How could Adam be the subject of such fearful wrath, if he did only what he was obliged to do; if he perpetrated only what he could not avoid?[1] Hence arises a conception of original sin on the part of Protestants, which is in almost every respect (we trust we may be pardoned the expression) devoid of sense and reason. By the most exaggerated description of the effects of Adam's fall, they seem anxious to resuscitate the feeling of sin, and the consciousness

---

perperam fiunt, ullam culpam in ipsum transferri posse, quum ipsius voluntas sit summa et certissima omnis justitiæ norma. Habet autem ipse admirabiles potius quam explicabiles rationes, ex quibus sic utitur diabolis omnibus et peccantibus hominibus, tanquam instrumentis, ut quicquid illi male agunt, id ipse sicut juste ordinavit, sice tiam in bonum convertat.' The Belgic Confession (cap. xiii, lib. c, p. 177) speaks in the same way.

[1] Calvin (Instit. lib. iii, cap. i. sec. 4, fol. 77) very well enlarges on the magnitude of Adam's sin; but his whole description makes no impression, so soon as we remember the author's assertion, that Adam must needs sin. He shows acutely enough the unbelief, ingratitude, and pride of Adam; but it is only a pity that our first parent *was obliged* to lose faith, gratitude, and humility.

of guilt, which, by their view of God's relation to evil, they were on the point of utterly destroying. And yet they only aggravate the matter, as will appear in the course of the present chapter, which must, however, in the first instance, be devoted to an examination of the principles laid down by the Council of Trent.

The doctrine of the Catholic Church on original sin is extremely simple, and may be reduced to the following propositions. Adam, by sin, lost his original justice and holiness, drew down on himself by his disobedience the displeasure and the judgments of the Almighty, incurred the penalty of death, and thus, in all his parts, in his body as well as soul, became strangely deteriorated.[1] This his sinful condition is transmitted to all his posterity as descending from him, entailing the consequence that man is of himself incapable, even with the aid of the most perfect ethical law offered to him from without (not excepting even the one revealed in the old Covenant), to act in a manner agreeable to God, or in any other way to be justified before Him, save only by the merits of Jesus Christ, the sole mediator betwixt God and man.[2] If to this we add, that the fathers of Trent attribute to fallen man free-will, representing it, however, as very much weakened,[3] and in consequence teach, that not every religious and moral action of man is necessarily sinful, although it be never, in itself and by itself, acceptable to God, nor anywise

---

[1] Concil. Trid. sess. v. decret. de peccat. orig. 'Si quis non confitetur primum hominem Adam, cum mandatum Dei in paradiso fuisset transgressus, statim sanctitatem et justitiam, in qua constitutus fuerat, amisisse, incurrisseque per offensam prævaricationis hujusmodi iram et indignationem Dei, atque ideo mortem . . . totumque Adam . . . secundum corpus et animam in deterius commutatum fuisse, anathema sit.'

[2] Loc. cit. 'Si quis hoc Adæ peccatum, quod origine unum est, et propagatione, non imitatione, transfusum omnibus, inest unicuique proprium, vel per humanæ naturæ vires, vel per aliud remedium asserit tolli, quam per meritum unius mediatoris Domini nostri Jesu Christi, qui nos Deo reconciliavit sanguine suo, factus nobis justitia, sanctificatio, et redemptio, anathema sit.'

[3] Concil. Trid. sess. vi. cap. v. 'Si quis liberum hominis arbitrium post Adæ peccatum amissum et extinctum esse dixerit, aut rem esse de solo titulo, imo titulum sine re, figmentum denique a Satana invectum in ecclesiam, anathema sit.' Cap. i: 'Primum declarat sancta synodus, ad justificationis doctrinam probe et sincere intelligendam, oportere, ut unusquisque agnoscat, et fateatur, quod cum omnes homines in prævaricatione Adæ innocentiam perdidissent, facti immundi, et, ut Apostolus inquit, natura filii iræ . . . usque adeo servi erant peccati, et sub potestate diaboliac mortis, ut non modo gentes per vim naturæ, sed ne Judæi quidem per ipsam etiam literam legis Moysis, inde liberari, aut surgere possent, tametsi in eis liberum arbitrium minime extinctum esset, viribus scilicet attenuatum et inclinatum.'

perfect,[1] we then have stated all, which is to be held as strictly the doctrine of the Church. That, moreover, fallen man still bears the image of God (section 1) necessarily follows from what has been advanced.[2]

If, in reading these decrees of the Council of Trent, we call to mind all those questions, which, since the rise of the Pelagian heresy, and even much earlier, were, on the matter at issue, proposed to scientific investigation, we shall not fail to observe, that the assembled fathers found it expedient in their decision not to touch upon a considerable number of these questions, and to express themselves in regard to them with a certain generality. We say, in regard to these questions; for, on the matter itself, considered according to Scripture and ecclesiastical tradition, the council has pronounced very definite and full declarations. But, as in this doctrine the Lutherans were driven to the most pernicious exaggerations; and as, in the first years of the Reformation, some Catholic theologians—for example, Albertus Righius (as is often the case in the refutation of extreme opinions) approximated to the opposite extreme;[3] the decrees of Trent were received with feelings of very great prejudice by the Protestants, who, in their rash vehemence, charged them with Pelagianism.

As regards the deliberations of Trent, Payva ab Andrada, a Portuguese theologian who assisted at them, informs us in the third book of his defence of the council, that it purposely abstained from any minuter definitions. And Pallavicini says that the council has expressed itself more negatively, yet with such distinctness, that the errors on this matter then current were, as such, clearly and distinctly rejected. If the Church, he continues, be unable to give any accurate definition of original sin, it is sufficient for her to denote what original sin is not; and this she can do with as much propriety as one who, having no clear notion of heaven, could still assert with confidence, that it was not composed of linen adorned with gold paper! The

[1] Concil. Trid. sess. vi, cap. vii. 'Si quis dixerit, opera omnia quæ ante justificationem fiunt, quacumque ratione facta sint, vere esse peccata, vel odium Dei mereri, anathema sit.'

[2] Bellarmin de gratia primi hominis, cap ii. 'Imago ad naturam, similitudo ad virtutes pertinet; proinde Adam peccando non imaginem Dei, sed similitudinem perdidit.'

[3] To this Chemnitius (Exam. Concil. Trid. ed. Francof. 1599, Pt. i, p. 168) refers, when he exclaims: 'Ad perpetuam igitur rei memoriam notum sit toti orbi Christiano,' etc. See also his 'Loci. Theol.' P. i, p. 227. Gerhard loci theolog. tom. iv, p. 518 (loc. ix, sec. 58).

same celebrated historian also relates, that the papal legates reminded the assembled fathers not to decide on the nature of original sin itself, because Scripture and tradition are silent upon this matter; and he adds, the holy synod was not convoked to pronounce upon opinions, but to condemn errors. We shall soon be enabled to see the great propriety of this judgment of Pallavicini's.[1]

In order to point out more nearly the points whereon the various schools were united, and the points about which they were at variance, we shall lay before our readers a summary statement of the scholastic views respecting original sin, in so far at least as their relation to the Protestant errors may require. By showing their agreement, it will appear, that it was only the most envenomed prejudice which could venture to charge the schoolmen with a superficial Pelagianism; that is to say, with the denial of original sin, or at least, with the misapprehension of its magnitude. But while we mark the point at which the schoolmen diverge in opposite directions, we encounter the limit which a higher hand hath set to the investigations of human science. If their efforts to extend this boundary have been somewhat unsuccessful—if they explain nothing, or much less than they ought—it would still be unjust to regard what has been explained as the sole criterion of that which it was their task to have explained.

'All who descend from the seed of Adam,' says St Bonaventura, 'have a nature marred not only by punishment, but by guilt.' This is manifest in the want of God's intuition, in the ignominy which weighs upon reason, and in the preponderance of evil desire (*concupiscentia*). The want of the divine intuition evidently presupposes guilt; because no one can be deprived of eternal good, for the enjoyment whereof he has been created, unless there be in him something which renders him unworthy of standing in the presence of his God. In respect to the second, no one need be ashamed of anything which is the property of his nature; but is not reason ashamed of certain

---

[1] Loc. cit. p. 248, lib. vii, cap. x, p. 247: 'Hic vero admonuerunt (Legati) ne quid certi statuerent de natura ipsa originalis culpæ, de qua scholastici discordant: nec enim synodus collecta fuerat ad decidendas opiniones, sed ad errores recidendos.' Further on, it is said: 'Quoties damnantur hæritici, optimum consilium est, magis generalia, quippe magis indubitata complecti, quod a synodo peractum est. Quoties in eosdem scriptis agitur, prudentis est, nullam ipsis ansam præferre transferendæ disputationis a re ipsa, quæ certa est, ad modum, qui est incertus.'

motions of the flesh ? This, too, betokens an inherited guilt. The preponderance of evil lust is a matter of certainty also, because then only is the soul of man *well ordered*, when the spirit is in subjection to God, and the flesh and animal faculties are in subjection to the spirit.[1] But ill-ordered, and therefore perverted, is the soul of man, when its relation to God and the senses has been inverted. This is now the case ; and not only doth faith teach so, but philosophy herein concurs. The violence of wicked lust, and the law of the members, which each one hath from his birth, holds the spirit captive, and overmasters it. It is thus undeniable that the soul of each one is from his birth perverted (*perversa*) ; but if the right state of the soul be justice, its perverted state is guilt ; and as we are perverted from our birth, we bear about with us from our birth the stain of guilt. Of this no one doubts, except he who is ignorant of the power of evil desire, and doth not know in what way the rational spirit should be obedient unto God. For it is acknowledged, that, unless our spirit love God above all things, and for His own sake, it is not perfectly obedient unto Him. It is also acknowledged, that without the gift of grace no one in the state of corrupt nature loveth God above all things, and for His own sake ; nay, he is necessarily overcome by the force of wicked lust, so as to be more enamoured of himself and of some apparent good. Thus is every soul from its birth a sinner, because perverted and disordered. And hence the apostle, speaking in the person of fallen humanity, saith : ' I see another law in my members, which striveth against the law of the spirit, and holdeth me captive under the law of sin.' Then he exclaims : ' Unhappy man that I am, who shall deliver me from the body of this death ? ' And he replies : ' The grace of God through Jesus Christ.' Whoever pays attention to this law in the members, and to our false relation to God, will certainly not deny that man from his birth is sinful ; nay, he will clearly see that it is

[1] From this it is clear, in what estimation we should hold the objection made to the divines before the Reformation, that they merely admitted the soul to have fallen into *disorder*, in consequence of original sin. Such was the reply made to the following passage cited by me from Duns Scotus. 'Deordinut autem peccatum originale totam animam ; ergo si est aliqua una culpa, in illa potentia est, ad cujus deordinationem tota anima deordinatur. Illa sola est voluntas : quia ipsa ordinata ordinat alias, ita deordinata deordinat' (lib. ii, Sent. Dist. xxx, q. 2). To form a right judgment on this matter, men must understand the usus loquendi of the schoolmen ; but for this knowledge a study of their writings is requisite.

impossible to doubt the existence of original, any more than of actual, sin. If philosophers and some heretics have not acknowledged this, it is because they had no notion of the rectitude of the soul, of justice, nor how much the soul should turn to God. Thus all human nature is given up to corruption; and not only because it has incurred a penalty, but because it is in fact sinful.'[1] ' Original sin,' adds this great teacher of the Church, ' may be described as the want of original justice, whereby the perversity of nature and evil concupiscence hath arisen.'

Let us hear now St Thomas Aquinas, the head of another great school in the middle age. He thus enlarges on the subject of original sin : ' As between things opposite, there is an opposite relation, so from original justice its opposite, original sin, may be explained. But the whole order of original justice consisted therein, that the will of man was obedient to God—an obedience which in an eminent degree was practised by the will; for it is the province of the will to direct all other parts of the soul, in conformity to this its highest destination. Hence, when the will fell away from God, disorder in all other faculties of the soul ensued. Thus, in original sin the deprivation of original justice is the *formal part*, that is to say, the causal, determining, and essential part ; but every other disorder in the faculties of the soul is the *material* part of original sin, that is to say, the thing determined—the consequence—the manifestation of the essence. The disorder of the other powers of the soul shows itself in the perverted affection to transitory good,—a disorder which may be denoted by the well-known expression, wicked desire, *concupiscentia*. Thus in its essence (*forma*), original sin is the want of original justice; in its manifestation (*materia*) it is evil desire.'[2]

In another place he says : ' All the faculties of the soul have been, to a certain degree, displaced from their proper direction and destination—a displacement which is called the wound of nature. But there are four powers of the soul, which can become the conduits of virtue—namely, reason, wherein is recognition ; the will, wherein is justice ; the faculty of exertion, wherein is courage ; the faculty of desire, wherein is temperance. In so far as reason has been diverted from its bearing towards the

---

[1] J. Bonavent. ad lib. ii, Sent. Dist. xxx, q. 11, art. 1, Op. Lugd. 1668, t. vi, P. xi, p. 373.

[2] Thom. Aquin. I. P. ii, q. 82, art. iv. The words ' forma ' and ' materia ' cannot always be rendered into our language in the same way.

truth, has arisen the wound of ignorance ; inasmuch as the will has been diverted from its bearing towards good, has arisen the wound of wickedness ; inasmuch as the faculty of exertion has been diverted from its bearing towards the arduous, has arisen the wound of frailty ; lastly, inasmuch as the faculty of desire has been diverted from its course, as directed by reason, towards the term of pleasure, has arisen concupiscence.' [1]

As original sin was represented by Bonaventura in the more practical tone of eloquent complaint, and by Thomas, with more scientific accuracy and subtlety of distinction ; so we find the same generally expounded in the ecclesiastical schools prior to the period of the apostacy from the Church : so that anyone who judges the matter with sobriety, and with competent knowledge, will be utterly unable to discover in them any, even the slightest, traces of Pelagianism.

If we turn now to the differences of opinion which divide the schoolmen, the most important will be found to consist in the representation of the mode wherein the sin of Adam was transmitted to his descendants. It must be especially observed, that, for very weighty reasons, the schoolmen rejected as erroneous the opinion, that souls were transmitted through generation by the parents to their children (*traducianismus*) ; and on the other hand, held as alone true and orthodox, the doctrine that souls are ever created by God (*creatianismus*). If according to the first view, the transmission of original sin (from the principle, that like comes of its like, and so that a sinner will beget a sinner) is apparently easy to explain ; so, on the other hand, the doctrine of the successive creation of souls offers at the first view great difficulties, in the scientific treatment of the article of belief, which now engages our attention. For what happens to the soul created by God, and created in all soundness, purity, and integrity, that, at the moment of its union with the body, it should be deprived not only of all supernatural gifts, but so deeply wounded in all its natural faculties, and placed in so fearfully incongruous a relation to the Deity ?

The teachers of science have at all times found it a matter of difficulty to acknowledge their ignorance. The expectation of scholars, to be able to comprehend everything, is met by the presumptuous confidence of teachers to make all things comprehensible. The proposition is indeed defended, that in the

[1] Thom. Aquin. lib. i, q. 85, art. iii.

true religion there must be mysteries—there must be things incomprehensible. But instead thereof, it should be broadly maintained, that for us, in our present condition, the true religion is itself a mystery—that it is *the* mystery, and that, in consequence, all its particular parts must offer mysteries. Here is the whole mysterious—therefore its parts: not this or that only is mysterious, but all is so.

Yet there is within us an irrepressible longing after comprehension: it is the same which in its excess leads to the denial of everything above comprehension. This very longing to comprehend, like the fact, that we are surrounded by incomprehensible mysteries, points to the distraction which has convulsed our nature, to the wound inflicted on our reason—to a lost intuition, and, in so far, to an unhappy past. Yet it betokens, too, a happy futurity—an intuition for which we are destined, which beams upon us from afar, and for which, even in this life, we seek some sort of compensation. This desire to comprehend, is a meagre vital sign of a yet extant, but deeply concealed germ of future intuition, and a warranty, that that intuition will be one day imparted to us. So a well-regulated development ought not to be refused to this inborn desire. But full satisfaction here below, we may rest assured, it neither finds nor communicates. Shall then this very effort after comprehension, which is so closely connected with the original convulsion of our nature—with the night that has since spread over our spirit, be crowned with success in the attempt to dispel this darkness? We may be permitted to entertain a doubt. Who comprehends evil in itself? Whose eye has ever penetrated into the deep connection between moral and physical evil? Who has ever explored the mysterious ties which unite the soul and the body? Who knows the sexual relations, and comprehends what is life, and the generation of life?

Some schoolmen taught, that, by the fall of Adam, a destructive and infectious quality was introduced into the human body; and that this quality, propagated by generation, contaminated the soul at the moment of its union with the body, debased it, and communicated to it the disorder of the body. But even overlooking the fact, that the rise of a positive *bad* quality is itself an enigma, nay, is utterly inconceivable; still this theory takes a very material view of evil. And although it may appear to offer some satisfactory explanations as to bodily diseases, and as to death; yet in the spiritual regions it is utterly unavailing. How could the infusion of such a corporeal poison convey to the soul the germs of all which, in the most comprehensive sense, constitutes self-seeking—to wit, revolt against God—arrogance and envy toward our fellow men—vanity and complacency in regard to ourselves? If so disordered a spiritual condition, if so distempered a moral state could be engendered by the connection of the soul with the body, it would be then certainly very difficult to uphold the notion of moral evil.

This theory was in consequence rejected by most of the schoolmen; and, instead of this, another was adopted, namely, that, with the exception of his heritage of guilt, fallen man is born exactly like Adam, when considered without his supernatural graces—that is to say, with all the natural faculties, powers and properties of the paradisaic man, as well as without any quality, evil in itself. The conflict between reason and sensuality is caused by the two very heterogeneous essences, whereof man is composed; and therefore without the divine principle imparted to him, which held the inferior in subjection to the superior part, Adam would have gradually felt this combat within him (*vide* section 1), and indeed without incurring thereby the guilt of sin; for it is the nature of sensuality to be irrational. The conflict we speak of, would have been a natural event. The evil of that corrupt condition, wherein man is now born, consists in the fact, that, in Adam he has deserved to be deprived of the justice conferred by supernatural grace; that is to say, to feel the rebellion of the flesh against the spirit. What nature, without supernatural grace, would have been, is now, in consequence of the self-incurred loss of that divine gift, the penalty of all born of Adam.[1]

But as this theory doth not explain, and is unable to explain the perversity of the will, wherewith we are born, it also is

[1] Bellarmin de gr. primi hom. cap. v. ' Nos vero *existimamus* rectitudinem illam etiam partis inferioris fuisse donum supernaturale, et quidem per se, non per accidens, ita ut neque in naturæ principiis fluxerit, neque potuerit fluere. Et quia donum illud supernaturale erat, ut statim probaturi sumus, eo remoto natura humana, sibi relicta, pugnam illam experiri cœpit partis inferioris cum superiori, quæ naturalis futura erat, id est, ex conditione materiæ secutura nisi, Deus justitiæ donum homini addidisset. Quare non magis differt status hominis post lapsum Adæ a statu ejusdem in puris naturalibus, quam differat spoliatus a nudo, neque deterior est humana natura, si culpam originalem detrahas, neque magis ignorantia et infirmitate laborat, quam esset et laboraret in puris naturalibus condita. Proinde corruptio naturæ non ex alicujus doni naturalis carentia, neque ex alicujus malæ qualitatis accessu, sed ex sola doni supernaturalis ob Adæ peccatum amissione profluxit.'

insufficient. It speaks only of a conflict between the sensual and the rational principle, which without the divine aid would have arisen as a natural occurrence. But the question before every other is, to account for the wounds of the spirit, especially for the perversity of the will. Would the spirit of man, because it is an essence distinct from God, when considered in itself—that is to say, as void of the gift of supernatural grace, and as a bare finite being, be found in that attitude of opposition to God, and all things holy, wherein man is now born? Then man, as a finite being, would be of himself disposed to sin, and would not be so merely through abuse of his freedom. The supernatural, divine principle, can certainly not be destined merely to remove that inclination to opposition against his Creator existing in man as a creature, or rather only to prevent its outbreakings. It is not by the absence of this supernatural grace, without which all are now born, that man is perverted in his will; he may become so, and doubtless easily, but he is not yet so at the moment of his creation.

The inadequacy of this theory, to an explanation of the subject, has given rise to many objections against the Catholic doctrine of original sin. Men went on the supposition suggested by excited passions, that Catholic theologians would admit as notions of original sin, only what was really explained by the above-stated theory. Instead of accusing the weakness of speculation, they impeached the principle itself.[1]

§ VI—DOCTRINE OF THE LUTHERANS RESPECTING ORIGINAL SIN

The Augsburg Confession expresses itself in the following manner respecting original sin: 'They (the Protestants) teach, that, after Adam's fall, all men, who are engendered according

---

[1] Even Bellarmine, who defends, with great acuteness and subtlety, the last-stated opinion, says of original sin:

'Omnibus imputatur (peccatum Adæ) qui ex Adamo nascuntur, quia omnes in lumbis Adami existentes, in eo, et per eum peccavimus, cum ipse peccavit.... Præterea dicimus, quemadmodum in Adamo, præter actum illius peccati, fuit etiam perversio voluntatis et obliquitas ex actione relicta, per quam peccator proprie et formaliter dicebatur et erat... ita quoque in nobis omnibus, cum primum homines esse incipimus, præter imputationem inobedientiæ Adami, esse etiam similem perversionem et obliquitatem unicuique inhærentem, per quam peccatorse proprie et formaliter dicimur.'

to nature, are born in sin—that is to say, without fear of God, without confidence in Him, and with concupiscence.'[1] This article describes original sin as something at once privative and positive ; as the deprivation of good, and the establishment of evil. It is our duty, in the first instance, to determine more accurately the nature of the good withdrawn. The Catholic theologians at the Diet of Augsburg, Eck, Wimpina, and Cochlæus, who had prepared a refutation of the Lutheran confession there read, remarked in their essay, that the description of original sin, ' men *were born* without fear of God, and without confidence in Him,' was very unfitting and inadmissible ; because the fear of God and confidence in Him consisted in a succession of intellectual acts, which not anyone would think of demanding of the unconscious child. Hence, they said, the absence of such acts is by no means to be considered as constituting a sin in the new-born ; the non-existence of those virtues would establish guilt perpetrated with self-consciousness and with freedom, and would not, in consequence, denote the essence of original sin, because man is born therewith, and this sin exists in him prior to all self-consciousness.[2]

The author of the apology saw himself hereby forced to express himself on this subject with the scientific accuracy to be desired. The obscure meaning of the passage he elucidated with the remark, that, by it, nothing more was signified, than that man, engendered in the course of nature, wanted the *capacity or the gifts* for producing the fear of God, and confidence in Him.[3] Hereby, in fact, the tenet of the Protestants was stated with the utmost precision ; yet in a manner to be intelligible only to one, who knew its connection with other doctrines. The reader will remember, that, according to the views of Luther and his followers, man was originally endowed with only natural powers—an opinion which in the present matter exerts a very important influence. For as fallen man, as such, is evidently unable to exercise those virtues, which were possible to him in his state of

[1] Confess. August. art. ii, p. 12. ' Docent, quod post lapsum Adæ omnes homines, secundum naturam propagati, nascantur cum peccato, hoc est, sine metu Dei, sine fiducia erga Deum et cum concupiscentia.'

[2] Resp. theolog. Cath. ad art. ii. ' Declaratio articuli est omnino rejicienda, cum sit cuilibet Christiano manifestum, esse sine metu Dei, sine fiducia erga Deum, potius esse culpam actualem, quam noxam infantis recens nati, qui usu rationis adhuc non pollet.'

[3] Apol. ii, sect. 2, p. 54. ' Hic locus testatur, nos non solum actus, sed et potentiam seu dona efficiendi timorem et fiduciam erga Deum adimere propagatis secundum carnalem naturam.'

original purity; and as he is unable to do so, because the powers fail him; the Reformers saw themselves in a situation to put forth the doctrine, that certain *natural powers* man no longer possessed.[1]

But most insight into these lost natural powers is afforded us by the Formulary of Concord. In the synergistic controversies which agitated the Lutheran Church, Victorinus Strigel [2] (a leader of the heterodox party, an acute, well-informed thinker, who was very familiar with the Catholic points of defence,[3] and convinced of the incontrovertible character of the dogma of free-will), asserted, that even fallen man possesses at least the faculty, the capacity, the aptitude, to know God, and to will what is holy; although this faculty is completely paralysed, and, as it were, benumbed, and is not susceptible of any spontaneous exertion. The formulas, which he made use of, are these: fallen man possesses still the '*modum agendi, capacitatem, aptitudinem;*' that is to say, he still at least enjoys, in reference to spiritual things, the empty form of knowledge and of will, void, though that form be, of all real and essential purport.[4] Although Victorinus considered the consequences of the sin of Adam, in respect to his whole posterity as of a far more destructive character, than Catholics, by the decisions of Trent

[1] Luther (in c. iii, Genes.) says, after the above-cited passage, wherein he rejects the doctrine of Catholic theologians respecting the supernatural powers of Adam: ' Hæc probant, justitiam esse de natura hominis, *ea autem per peccatum amissa, non mansisse integra naturalia ut delirant scholastici.*'

[2] See Plank's ' History of the Rise, Changes, and Formation of our Protestant System of Doctrine' (in German), vol. iv, p. 584.

[3] He was a scholar versed in the old Christian Greek literature, and we are, as is well-known, indebted to him for some translations from that literature into the Latin language. But the Greek Church shows *only* advocates of the doctrine of free-will.

[4] Calvin (Instit. lib. ii, sect. 14, fol. 87) gives us the wished for explanation of the notion, which, in the sixteenth century, was attached to the word ' aptitudo.' We may compare with great utility this passage with one in St Thomas Aquinas. (See Summa tot. theolog. p. i, q. xciii, art. iv, ed. Cass. Lugd. 1580, vol i, p. 417.) St Thomas here inquires, wherefore the spirituality of man constitutes his similitude to God; and he then says, the divine image within us may be considered in a threefold point of view. ' Uno quidem modo secundum quod homo habet aptitudinem naturalem ad intelligendum et amandum Deum. Et hæc aptitudo consistit in ipsa natura mentis, quæ est communis omnibus hominibus. Alio modo secundum quod homo actu vel habitu Deum cognoscit et amat,' etc. *Aptitudo* accordingly signifies, in opposition to *actus*, the natural disposition—the faculty—and here, the moral and religious faculty. See more copious proofs of this in my work, ' New Inquiry,' etc., in reply to Dr Baur, p. 35, second edition.

at least, are immediately bound to regard them; still his view did not satisfy the orthodox party in his own Church. They called him a Pelagian, and asserted that even that bare faculty of knowledge and will—that mere empty form in the soul of man—had been utterly destroyed; and here they doubtless spoke quite in the sense of Luther. The Formulary of Concord likewise rejected the view of the synergist, and declared that fallen man no longer possessed even the mere natural faculty to understand God and His holy will, and, in conformity to that knowledge to direct his own will.[1] In one word, the faculty of knowledge and will, inasmuch as it has reference to divine things, or (if we prefer the expression) the rational aptitude, is denied to the mere natural man—the man as born of Adam. The truth of this mode of conceiving the Lutheran doctrine, on original sin, is not done away with, nay, is confirmed by the declaration of the Formulary of Concord, that it was not thereby intended to hold fallen man for an irrational creature.[2] For to that faculty of the human mind, which *it* terms reason, it assigns merely the finite world as the sphere of activity:[3] and thereby

---

[1] Solid. declar. ii. de lib. arb. sect. 44, p. 644: 'Eam ob causam etiam non recte dicitur, hominem in rebus spiritualibus habere modum agendi aliquid, quod sit bonum et salutare. Cum enim homo ante conversionem in peccatis mortuus sit, non potest in ipso aliqua vis ad bene agendum in rebus spiritualibus inesse; itaque non habet modum agendi seu operandi in rebus divinis.' I. Sect. 21, pp. 616, 617: 'Repudiantur, qui docent, hominem ex prima sua origine adhuc aliquid boni, quantulumcunque etiam et quam exiguum atque tenue id sit, reliquum habere; capacitatem videlicet et aptitudinem et vires aliquas in rebus spiritualibus,' etc.

[2] Solid. declar. ii, de lib. arbitr. sect. xvi, p. 633. 'Non tamen in eam sententiam sic loquuntur, quasi homo post lapsum non amplius sit creatura rationalis.'

[3] Solid. declar. i, de peccat. orig. sect. x, p. 614. 'In aliis enim externis et hujus mundi rebus, *quæ rationi subjectæ sunt*, relictum est homini adhuc aliquid intellectus, virium, et facultatum, etsi hæ etiam miseræ reliquiæ debiles, et quidem hæc ipsa quantulacunque per morbum illum hæreditarium infecta sunt atque contaminata, ut Deus abominetur ea.' Sect. xl, p. 644: 'Et verum quidem est, quod homo etiam ante conversionem sit creatura rationalis, quæ intellectum et voluntatem, habeat: *intellectum autem non in rebus divinis; et voluntatem, non ut aliquid boni et sani velit.*' Victorinus Strigel, in his commentary on the Psalms, which appeared in the year 1563, had adduced the following passage from St Augustine: 'Non Omnino deletum est in corde hominis per peccatum, quod ibi per imaginem Dei, cum crearetur, impressum fuerat, *neque adeo imago Dei detrita est illa labe, ut nulla in anima veluti lineamenta extrema remanserint, remansit enim quod homo non nisi rationalis esse possit.*' These words the theologians of Würtemberg note as reprehensible. See Plank's 'History of the Rise and Changes of the Protestant System of Doctrine' (in German), vol. iv, p. 682. We see that Victorinus Strigel attached a different meaning to the

clearly shows, that, in its opinion, Adam, rejected of God, and all his descendants, considered merely as such, have no longer preserved any spiritual aptitude for God and His kingdom.

We arrive at the same result by various ways. The first, presenting itself to our view, is the following. The Lutheran confessions, as was proved above (see section II), describe the image of God, as the natural capacity in man to know God, to fear Him, and to confide in Him. But it is precisely this capacity which we especially revere as rationality —the rational disposition in man. Yet of this very divine image the Lutherans repeatedly assert, that it has been utterly effaced by original sin, and thereby plucked from the posterity of Adam.[1] The second course which leads to the above-mentioned result, consists in the views entertained by the Lutherans respecting man's free-will subsequently to his fall. They hold that he possesses only a certain external freedom, but none at all in spiritual things; and that, in respect to the latter, he is no more than a stone or a stock (these are comparisons they frequently use).[2] In like manner, the Formulary of Concord observes, that fallen man can neither *think, believe, nor will*, any thing having reference to divine and spiritual concerns; that he is utterly dead to all good, and no longer possesses any, *even the least spark of spiritual* powers.[3] The expression word *reason*, from that which was attached to it by the Formulary of Concord. He considered it as the faculty for the apprehension of the super-sensual, as the principle of the Divine similitude in man; for as man appeared to him a being necessarily rational, he asserted, that remains of that faculty had survived his fall. This view, now, his adversaries rejected, and consequently regarded fallen man as really irrational, that is to say, as devoid of every faculty for the apprehension of the supermundane.

[1] Solid. declar. i, de pecc. or. sect. 9, p. 614. 'Docetur, quod peccatum originis sit horribilis *defectus* concreatæ in paradiso justitiæ originalis, et *amissio* seu *privatio* imaginis Dei.'

[2] Confess. Aug. art. xviii. 'De libero arbitrio docent, quod humana voluntas habeat *aliquam* libertatem ad efficiendam *civilem* justitiam, et diligendas res rationi subjectas.' Here is reason, the highest faculty in man, that has survived his fall, confined purely to the finite. Let the reader compare the *Solida Declaratio*, ii, de lib. arb. sect. 21, p. 635, ibidem: 'Antequam homo per Spiritum Sanctum illuminatur ... ex sese et propriis naturalibus suis viribus, in rebus spiritualibus nihil inchoare, operari, aut cooperari potest : non plus, quam lapis, truncus aut limus.'

[3] Solid. declar. ii, de lib. arb. sect. 7, p. 629. 'Credimus igitur, quod hominis non renati intellectus, cor, et voluntas in rebus spiritualibus et divinis prorsus nihil intelligere, credere, amplecti, cogitare, velle. inchoare, perficere, etc., possint. Et affirmamus, hominem ad bonum (vel cogitandum vel faciendum) prorsus corruptum et mortuum esse: ita quidem,

'spiritual powers' is here constantly employed as synonymous with 'the powers of free-will.' Yet we need no further investigation, for even Plank admits, ' Luther gave to the assertion, that man no longer possesses any will for good, so extensive a sense, that it would thence follow, that man, corrupted by original sin, no longer possesses *the power of will*, that is the faculty of will.'[1] Had Plank only added, 'and no longer possesses *the faculty of knowledge* for the supermundane' (for both are included *in liberum arbitrium*), he would then have stated with perfect accuracy the Lutheran doctrine.[2] Thus, according to Lutheran orthodoxy, did man lose, through Adam's fall (to express ourselves once more with comprehensive brevity), the most exalted and most subtle portion of this spiritual essence —the part of his substance kindred to divinity—the implanted organ for God, and for divine things inherent in his nature; so that, after its loss, he sank down into a mere earthly power, having henceforth organs only for the finite world, its laws, its ordinances, and its relations?

It is indeed absolutely inconceivable, how out of the organism of the human mind a link could be plucked out and destroyed; how any faculty of a simple essence, uncompounded of parts, whose faculties science only separates and distinguishes (for they in themselves are one in all, and all in one), should be loosed from the others, and be annihilated: but we have not yet done with the impenetrable obscurity of the Lutheran theory of original sin.[3] Of the positive part which supplied

ut in hominis natura, post lapsum et ante regenerationem, *ne scintillula quidem spiritualium virium reliqua sit.*'
We must remember that here the question is only respecting the *natural* powers of man, since, according to the P otestant theory, he had no *supernatural* powers to lose.

[1] Plank's History of Protestantism (in German), vol. vi, p. 715. But when the revered author adds, that every genuine follower of the theology of St Augustine is of this opinion, he certainly advances an assertion without proof, nay, very easy of refutation.

[2] Solid. declar. ii, de lib. arb. sect. 2, p. 628. ' Hic est verus et unicus controversiæ status, quid hominis nondum renati *intellectus* et *volunta* . . . ex propriis suis, et post lapsum reliquis, viribus præstare possit.'

[3] Beza (Quæst. et resp. p. 45) reproaches the Lutheran doctrine with leading to Epicurianism, since if it were consistently followed out, the immortality of the soul must be denied.

'Quæstio. Ais igitur in summa, corruptas esse animæ qualitates, non essentiam? Resp. Aio, et contrarium dogma dico esse certum et apertum ad Epicuræismum iter, id est, ad mortalitatem animæ adstruendam, quoniam posita essentiæ ipsius vel levissima corruptione, necesse sit, rem ipsam interitus obnoxiam confiteri,' etc.

the place of one withdrawn, it is as difficult to arrive at any sort of clear conception. In his commentary on the third chapter of Genesis, Luther institutes a comparison between original sin and original justice, and, from the essential character of original sin, draws conclusions as to the essential character of original justice.[1] If, accordingly, with Luther, original justice be the faculty to love and discern God, original sin must in his opinion be THE FACULTY not to love God and not to discern Him, or rather to hate Him, and to be in a state of darkness as to all things appertaining to Him. This is about the same, as if a man were to say, everyone possesses *the faculty* not only to have no property, but moreover to have debts! To Luther it was not only perfectly clear, that, through Adam's fall the whole human race had lost an integral portion of its spiritual existence; but also, that in man an opposite essence had been substituted in its room. And the latter occurrence he conceived to be so placed beyond the reach of doubt, that without the least hesitation he inferred from it, as a matter perfectly indisputable, and, as is were, self-evident, ulterior consequences! If it is inconceivable how the image of God can be utterly eradicated from the human spirit, it is still more inconceivable how a new essence could be inserted into the soul! And then evil was converted into something substantial! Such-like opinions, after indescribable efforts on the part of the Church, had, together with those of the Gnostics and the Manicheans, almost entirely disappeared; and now they again emerged, full of vigour and lofty pretension!

The substance which Luther found in original sin, was, moreover, according to him, implanted alike in the soul and body of man. The following passages, which are found in different books composed by him, may serve as proofs of what has been

[1] Luth. in Genes. c. iii. 'Vide, quid sequatur, ex illa sententia, si statuamus justitiam originalem non fuisse naturæ, sed donum quoddam superfluum (!), superadditum. Annon sicut ponis, justitiam non fuisse de essentia hominis, ita etiam sequitur, peccatum, quod successit, non esse de essentia hominis?' We know the reasons by which it may be alleged, that Luther's words are not to be so strictly construed. But if he meant, to assert nothing more than what was long customary, why did he not make use of the customary form of speech? The new language evidently betokens new conceptions. And how shall we account for the subsequent doctrines of Flacius, if Luther had given no occasion thereto? It is also said, *essentia* is very different from *substantia;* but let anyone consider the preceding note, and determine by it the *usus loquendi.*

stated, as well as set beyond doubt the nature of his opinions on this subject. His expressions are as follows: 'It is the nature of man to sin; sin constitutes the essence of man; the nature of man, since his fall, is become quite changed; original sin is that very thing which is born of father and mother.' Of like import are these forms of expression: 'The clay out of which we are formed is damnable; the fœtis in the maternal womb is sin.' He says likewise, 'Man, as he is born of his father and mother, together with his whole nature and essence, is not only a sinner, but sin itself.'[1] Melancthon also calls original sin 'an innate power,' and indeed the context would lead us to suppose, that he ascribed to this power something substantial.[2]

At last, Matthias Flacius arose, and broadly asserted that original sin was the very substance of fallen man! Error having now reached its highest pitch of extravagance, a retrogressive movement necessarily took place. The mere negative and primitive character of evil was anew understood, and men again more approximated towards the Catholic view of the subject,

[1] Quenstedt (Theologia didactico polemica, Wittenberg, 1669, par. ii, pp. 134, 135) has collected, and indeed excused, the above-cited formulas of doctrine. They run thus in the Latin language: 'Naturam hominis esse puram, hominis essentiam esse peccatum, hominis naturam post lapsum esse mutatam, peccatum originis esse id ipsum quod nascitur ex patre et matre; hominem esse ipsum peccatum,' etc. See also Bellarmine de statu peccati, lib. v, c. 1. The same Bellarmine said, it is inconceivable that the soul, which is created by God in the act of generation, should receive from its Creator, any bad ingredients, in the same way that a bad *material* power should pass into the soul, which is a *spiritual* essence. To this Gerhard replied: 'Contra nos, qui animæ corruptæ ex anima corrupta propagationem propugnamus, argumentum hoc non pugnat!' (Loci theol. tom. iv, p. 331, loc. x, sect. 88.) Hence the doctrine of Creationism, as well as the opinion of the schoolmen, that unbaptised children go not to hell, but are admitted into a third place, Gerhard declares to be Pelagianism (*oblique pelagianizare*). Bellarmine, moreover, blames the expre sion of the Lutheran divines, that original sin is a positive quality. Gerhard is very much offended with him at this: then he says, the expression is not to be taken in its metaphysical strictness; next he adds, no quality is really thereby meant. 'Quando pravam concupiscentiam dicimus esse qualitatem positivam, non intelligimus hoc secundum *akribeian* metaphysicam . . . non quasi aliqua vis agendi sit peccatum, sed quia illa vis agendi in homine est tantum ad peccatum prona atque prompta.' This may be listened to, but is by no means Luther's meaning, as Gerhard thinks, but an improvement on it. In the same way speaks Chemnitius. Exam. Concil. Trid. par. i, p. 162.

[2] Melancthon loci. theol. p. 19. 'Sicut in igne est genuina vis, qua sursum fertur, sicut in magnete est genuina vis, qua ad se ferrum trahit; ita est in homine nativa vis ad peccandum.'

without, however, rejecting the notion that a 'positive' evil power, accompanied with the inmost and deepest corruption of all human nature, particularly of the yet surviving higher energies of the soul, was transmitted by parents to their children.[1]

The positive evil now—the true image of the devil, which after the loss of the divine image is to be propagated by generation through the whole human race—constitutes the Lutheran notion of concupiscence, which the Reformers wished to enforce on the Christian world, as the sole scriptural, the sole just, accurate, and comprehensive view of original sin.[2] They understand by concupiscence a complete rise and setting of all the impulses, inclinations and efforts, of fallen and unregenerated man in evil, and indeed in virtue of a wicked energy transmitted to him from Adam.

Luther, it cannot be denied, here touched on the borders of Manicheism, if he did not actually overstep the frontier; and we are bound gratefully to acknowledge the fact, that his followers resisted with so much energy the intrusion of such monstrous errors. Yet the expressions which they ever employed respecting original sin, such as *congenita prava vis, positiva qualitas*, betray the original stamp of their master's doctrine. The Protestant belief, too, that so long as a man lives here below, original sin is not totally effaced from him even by regeneration, even by the power of God, presupposes that essential substance, which Luther discovered in the inborn evil:—a belief, which, as we shall have occasion later to show, constitutes an essential difference between Catholicism and Protestantism.

Moreover, when the first glimpses of his new theory respecting original sin flashed on his mind, Luther must have been in the most singular disposition of mind, and must have been agitated by the darkest, the gloomiest, and the most perplexed feelings.

---

[1] Solid. declar. i, § 10, p. 614. 'Præterea affirmatur, quod peccatum originale in humana natura non tantummodo sit talis, qualem diximus, horribilis defectus omnium bonarum virium in rebus spiritualibus ad Deum pertinentibus; sed quod etiam in locum imaginis Dei amissæ successerit intima, pessima, profundissima (instar cujusdam abyssi), inscrutabilis et ineffab corrili uptio totius naturæ et omnium virium, imprimis vero superiorum et principalium animæ facultatum, qua infixa sit penitus intellectui, cordi et voluntati hominis. Itaque jam, post lapsum, homo hæreditario a parentibus accipit congenitam pravem vim, immunditiam cordis, pravas concupiscentias et pravas inclinationes.'

[2] Apolog. ii, sect. 3 seq., p. 54 seq.

For if he then taught, with Melancthon, that God works evil in man, how could he ascribe to it any sort of essence, and speak of a sinful stuff, out of which we are formed ? The establishment of such a relation between God and evil—to wit, that God is the author of the latter, is not indeed in conformity to Manichean principles, but would conduct us (if we were to give the peculative notion of the Lutheran doctrine respecting original sin) to a quite special view, which, in the proper place, we shall lay before our readers, as soon as all the intermediate points, which may furnish a complete insight into the subject, shall have been stated.

Here we shall only point out some of the consequences, which the symbolical writings of the Lutherans deduce from the fundamental doctrines already set forth.

It is there taught, that in fallen man, not the slightest good, how paltry soever it may be conceived, has survived;[1] that corrupt nature, of itself, and by its own force, can do nought but sin before God ;[2] that fallen man is all evil.[3] After this, we are nowise surprised at the opinion, that all so-called actual or personal sins, committed in the self-consciousness of freedom are *only* the particular forms and manifestations of original sin —the boughs, as it were, and branches, and blossoms, and fruits of the wicked stem and its root.[4] The Catholics, on the other

---

[1] Solid. declar. i, de pecc, orig. sect. 21, p. 716, 717. Those are noted as heretics, who assert :—' Adhuc aliquid boni, quantulumcunque etiam, et quam exiguum atque tenue id sit reliquum habere.'

[2] Solid. declar. l, c. sect. 22. ' Insuper etiam asserunt, quod natura corrupta ex se viribus suis coram Deo nihil nisi peccare, possit.'

[3] Solid. declar. ii, de lib. arb. sect. 14, p. 632. ' Docent, ut ex ingenio et natura sua totus sit malus.'

[4] Melancthon loci, p. 19. ' Scriptura non vocat hoc originale, illud actuale, peccatum : est enim et originale peccatum plane actualis quædam prava cupiditas,' etc. Luther, Works, Wittenberg, Part II, 1551, p. 335. ' And original sin may be called the arch-sin or chief sin, because it is not a sin which is committed like any other, but it is the only sin, the one which commits and incites to other sins, from whieh all other sins are derived, and are nought else than *the mere* fruits of this hereditary * or arch-sin.' This writing was from the pen of Justus Menius, but the preface was composed by Luther. In the work entitled ' Fundamental Doctrines of Dogmatic Divinity,' by Dr Marheineke, the present professor of theology at Berlin, second edition, sect. 267, p. 158, we find quite the same principle laid down, at least quite the same form of speech. It is as great an error to identify the sin of nature with the sin of person, as to separate the latter from the former. There is here the same vice, as in the rude antagonism of Nominalism and Realism.

* In the German, original sin is called *erb-sünde*, hereditary sin. The play of words in the original of the above passage cannot be rendered in English.—*Trans.*

hand, believe that in fallen and unregenerated man, the transition from original to actual sin is determined by free-will, which possesses the power to resist the carnal propensity in a manner not totally unsuccessful, and not merely exterior: although abandoned to itself, it is unable to accomplish perfect actions, in their inward spirit morally good, and consequently acceptable to God.

On this Lutheran doctrine of original sin, we shall now take the liberty of indulging in the following remarks. It is not to be denied that the feeling which called forth this article of belief, was in itself very laudable. It evidently sprang out of a deep sense of human misery, of the universal sinfulness of mankind, and their need of redemption; and it would fain keep that sentiment alive. If we acknowledge this with pleasure, it is yet equally certain, that the doctrine in question attains this object only where thought does not exercise much sway, and we yield to the pressure of dark, unconscious feelings. It is forgotten that when God makes man the mere mechanical instrument of his activity—when there occurs in man a violent obliteration (so revolting to all rational, and still more to all Christian minds) of a natural spiritual faculty, and indeed the moral and religious faculty—(the prerogative which solely and truly distinguishes him from the brute—sin then, from Adam to Christ, must be a thing unknown, and all moral must be transformed into physical evil. How should man sin, when he has not even the faintest knowledge of God, and of his own destination; when he has not the faculty to will what is holy; when he is even devoid of freedom? He may rave—he may be furious—he may destroy; but his mode of acting cannot be considered other than that of a savage beast.

The second consideration which presses itself upon our attention, is this, that Luther's exaggeration, so soon as it was recognised as untenable by his disciples, necessarily led the way to another doctrinal excess. From the one extreme opinion, that through Adam's fall all germs of good were utterly, even to the last vestige, eradicated from the whole human race, men passed to the other extreme, that even now, man in every respect is as well conditioned, and the universe wears as good an aspect for him, as for the paradisaic man. As soon as the dam of vigorous but unenlightened feelings was broken through, nothing could prevent the whole doctrine of the fall being swept away; for this in fact was the offspring of the most confused feelings, and in its construction no scope had been conceded to the influence of the higher intellectual faculties.

Thirdly. When in the times of the primitive Church, the heathens so often put the question, Wherefore did God send the Redeemer only after thousands of years, which had elapsed since the fall, and deny him to so many generations ? the holy fathers (as, for instance, the author of the epistle to Diognetus and Saint Irenæus) were wont, viewing the subject from the pedagogic point of view, to make the following reply: The Almighty, by a long and severe experience, wished to teach the human race what, when abandoned to itself, it was capable of. He designed to bring it thus to self-knowledge, to consciousness of its sinfulness and guilt, to a likely feeling of its disorders, and to a sense of humiliation before Him, in order to awaken within it a more intense desire after supernal aid, and to cause that aid to be received with a clearer insight as to its absolute necessity for redemption. The theologians of the Middle Ages, also, frequently gave the same reply.[1]

But what reply could the Lutheran divines make? That man, without the faculty of knowledge and of will for divine things, must remain far from God and His kingdom, is very conceivable; it is as evident as that a man, having no feet, cannot walk. But to what end is this act of violence, that obliterated from the soul of man, all religious aptitude—the very image of the Creator? Who would, in such case, venture

[1] Bonav. Breviloq. p. iv, c. 4. Opp. ed. Lugd. 1668, p. 27. 'Ratio autem ad intelligentiam horum hæc est quia incarnatio est opus primi principii reparantis, juxta quod decet et convenit secundum libertatem arbitrii, secundum sublimitatem remedii, et secundum integritatem universi: nam sapientissimus artifex in agenod omnia hæc attendit. Quoniam ergo libertas arbitrii hoc requirit, ut ad nihil tradatur invita, sic debuit Deus genus humanum reparare, ut salutem inveniret, qui vellet quærere salvatorem; qui vero nollet quærere salvatorem, nec salutem per consequens inveniret. Nullus autem quærit medicum, nisi recognoscat morbum: nullus quærit adjutorem, nisi recognoscat se impotentem. Quia igitur homo in principio sui lapsus adhuc superbiebat de scientia et virtute; ideo præmisit Deus tempus legis naturæ, in quo convinceretur de ignorantia. Et post cognita ignorantia, sed permanente superbia de virtute, qua dicebant, non deest qui faciat, sed deest qui jubeat, addidit legem preceptis moralibus erudientem ceremonialibus aggravantem: ut habita scientia et cognita impotentia, confugeret homo ad divinam misericordiam et gratiam postulandam, quæ data est nobis in adventu Christi: ideo post legem naturæ et scripturæ subsequi debuit incarnatio Verbi.' We see how this whole theory, to which S. Paul in his epistle to the Galatians has furnished the first materials, is based on Freedom. Compare Alex. Halens. sum. theolog. p. 111, Q. L. V., art. II, Ed. Ven., 1575, p. 231, b. Also Hugh St Victor and others.

on a Theodicea? who, even in the slightest degree, would be bold enough to justify Providence in the drama of the world's history?

The Formulary of Concord attempts, moreover, to extract from its theory some grain of solace. It observes, that, if the Christian can discover in himself only a little spark of desire after eternal life, he may, by this feeling, convince himself, that God has commenced His operations within him; and he may joyfully look forward to the moment when He will consummate the work begun.[1]

From the opinion, that in fallen man all the higher spiritual faculties are utterly destroyed, it follows of course, that not the faintest or remotest longing after God could spring up in his bosom: but if such a desire exist in the Christian, then, in the opinion of the authors of the above-named symbolical writing, such a desire is the surest proof that the work of regeneration is begun. But from the belief, that in man after his fall, there still survives the religious aptitude, and that therefore the possibility of higher aspirations yet remains, no such consolation, according to these authors, can possibly flow! A dangerous self-delusion! for that even in the breast of the heathens such a divine spark beyond a doubt still glowed, is evident from a contemplation of their history, on which we shall now take the liberty of offering a few remarks.

§ VII—CONSIDERATIONS ON HEATHENISM, IN REFERENCE TO THE DOCTRINES CONTROVERTED BETWEEN THE TWO CHURCHES

We said above, that a very different representation would be formed of the entire history of mankind, according as we contemplated it from the Catholic, or from the orthodox Lutheran, point of view. We are now enabled to make good this assertion; but before entering on the proof, we wish to premise a few remarks, for which we beg to claim the indulgence of the reader, as he will meet with statements in part previously advanced.

Nothing more distressing for the Church could possibly occur,

---

[1] Solid. declar. ii, sect. 11, p. 631. 'Deus est, qui operatur in nobis velle et perficere pro bona voluntate; quæ Scripturæ dulcissima sententia omnibus piis mentibus, quæ scintillulam aliquam et desiderium gratiæ divinæ et vitæ æternæ in cordibus suis sentiunt, eximiam consolationem offert. Certi enim sunt, quod Deus ipse initium illud veræ pietatis tanquam flammulam in cordibus ipsorum accenderit,' etc.

than to see herself called upon to set a limit to the idea of the magnitude of original sin. For it becometh the Christian to give himself up with all his soul to an infinite grief at that alienation from God, and at that misery, wherein fallen humanity is sunk; and it is irksome, amid feelings of sorrow, which are boundless in themselves, to be obliged to think of a limitation to an error, that rushes with violence from an extraneous source. It is, however, consoling for the Church that this limitation should be made, in order to uphold the notion of moral evil, and thereby to impart to the sense of pain and sorrow a true and a solid basis, which, as has been stated above, is wanting in the system of her adversaries. It is only so long as an irregular excitement of the feelings and the imagination endures, that it can furnish any nurture to this sense of pain. But so soon as this ebullition of sentiment subsides, and calm, sober reflection awakes, the utter groundlessness of such feelings is discovered, and then they totally vanish, along with their empty motives. What man can grieve, on perceiving that his existence is not consecrated to God, so soon as he seriously reflects on the import of those words, that God had deprived him of all power for so doing? To recognise the evil in its true and entire magnitude, it should not be represented in such exaggerated colours, as we find it in the public formularies of the Lutheran faith. Hence, if in the following pages we lay before our readers a sketch of the religious and ethical life of the heathen nations—a sketch hitherto rarely or never completed from the Catholic point of view—we trust no one will imagine we are insensible to the enormity of that hereditary evil which afflicts our race, and thereby to the fulness of the blessings conferred by the Redeemer. It is precisely in order to give a firm basis to our feelings of thankfulness to Him, that we bring out the brighter side of the heathen world; and we can only regret to be obliged to give no more than a very imperfect account of the subject.

The extensive researches of our age in the ancient world, and in the remotest parts of the New Continent, have brilliantly corroborated the truth of the Catholic doctrine, respecting fallen man. No people has been found without a belief in God, and without sacrifices, whereby it rendered its homage to the Deity. Nowhere are the religious ideas found pure—nay, everywhere they are polluted with great errors; yet in superstition faith lies concealed; and this is the good element in the former. Even in the grossest Fetish-worship, the aspiration of the human soul towards God is not to be denied; it proves, that fallen man, to speak the language of the Lutheran formularies, is still in possession of *spiritual powers*.

Melancthon appears to have had a perception of the weight which this fact throws into the Catholic scale, for he endeavours to restore the equipoise, by observing, that these remnants of faith are to be ascribed to primitive traditions.[1] Without these traditions, doubtless (and this was ever the Catholic view), faith would have been lost; but had they not likewise found in the breast of man a point of contact and a hold, they could not possibly have been preserved. As things merely extraneous to man, they must have soon been entirely forgotten, and have perished.

The union of men in social life, and the formation of states, were certainly not possible without religion; and this truth is evidenced by the fact, that nations had their divinities, to whose protection they committed their commonwealth, to whom they erected temples, and sent up their supplications. The nations manifested thereby a sense of their dependence on a higher power, which, although it received no worthy adoration, yet really guided and protected the suppliants. This indestructible propensity in man to unite and to associate with his fellows is at bottom eminently religious, and is an indelible proof of surviving faculties of a higher kind. The man all evil (*totus malus*) would have felt no social inclinations, and he and his fellows must have annihilated each other in the savage conflict, had even, under such circumstances, a plurality of men by possibility come into existence. When Calvin imagined these societies—these types of the future Church—to have been formed without religion, and without faith, and to have sprung up solely out of the exercise of man's lower faculties, he proved himself utterly unacquainted with their nature.[2]

This is especially exemplified in China—that empire of the

[1] Melancth. loci. theol. p. 67. 'Ita tu mihi poene libeat vocare legem naturæ non aliquod congenitum judicium seu insitum et insculptum natura mentibus hominum, sed leges acceptas a patribus et quasi per manus traditas subinde posteritati. Ut de creatione rerum, de colendo Deo docuit posteros Adam : sic Cainum docuit, ne fratrem occideret.' The *Solida Declaratio* asserts still more (§ ix, p. 630); but in perfect contradiction with itself. It says, that human reason retains a little spark of the knowledge that there is a God ('notitiæ illius scintillulam, quod sit Deus'); but how is this possible without a spark of spiritual powers ('scintillula spiritualium virium')?

[2] Calvin. Instit. lib. ii, c. 2, sect. 13, p. 87.

Medium—which, according to the spirit of its primitive constitution, was destined to be a real theocracy. The emperor was to hearken to the voice of God, and be His organ in respect to the people, who formed the family of the prince. All evils and calamities, which afflict the citizens of this paternal empire, are, according to this principle, considered as divinely inflicted chastisements for disobedience to the invisible ruler; and *moral* improvement, and recurrence to pious ancestral simplicity, are looked upon as the condition for the renewal of the country's prosperity. Who could suppose the spiritual powers of man to be obliterated here, where the religious view of all existence is so consummate, and is interwoven with the inmost vitals of the constitution and administration of the state? Who has ever read any fragments of the writings of the Chinese sages, without admiring the earnest view of life, the excellent ethical precepts, and the often profound wisdom which they frequently exhibit? Doubtless, Melancthon would have passed on the virtues of Lao-tseu, Confucius, and Mang-tseu, the same sentence he pronounced on the fortitude of Socrates, the continence of Xenocrates, and the temperance of Zeno—to wit, that *only* selfish motives were at the bottom of these qualities, and that hence they should be accounted vices.[1] We undoubtedly are not disposed to revere these Chinese or Greek sages, as pure patterns of virtue, who, as far as they rested on themselves, could stand before the judgment-seat of God, or to assert that all their endeavours flowed from a source acceptable to God. But the question is not, whether anyone, who neither knows Christ nor is penetrated by His light, nor strengthened by His divine grace, be in and by himself pure and just in the eyes of God; but the question is, whether fallen man be entirely corrupted, whether all which he does and thinks be sin,[2] and be damnable,[3] whether he have lost all moral and religious qualities, whether those virtues ought to be considered as things merely extraneous, and in no more intimate relation to man, than wealth and corporeal beauty.[4] This we deny, and deny at the risk (not

---

[1] Melancth. loc. theolog. p. 22. 'Esto fuerit quædam in Socrate constantia, in Xenocrate castitas, in Zenone temperantia . . . non debent pro veris vertutibus, sed dro vitiis haberi.'

[2] Melancth. loc. cit. 'Negant tamen (Pelagiani) eam esse vim peccati originalis, ut *omnia* hominum opera, omnes hominum *conatus* sint peccata.'

[3] Calvin. Instit. lib. ii, c. 3, fol. 93. The title of the chapter runs even to the effect: 'Ex corrupta hominis natura nihil nisi *damnabile* prodire.'

[4] Melancth. loc. cit. 'Effundit autem hujusmodi virtutum umbras

indeed very great in our times), of this being imputed to us as a crime, and of our being held up as bad theologians, in the same way as Philip Melancthon reproached our noble ancestors for having introduced into the schools philosophic studies, and recommended the reading of Plato and Aristotle, the former full of presumption which he easily communicates to his admirers and the latter, in fact, teaching only the art of contention.[1] That those venerable men were yet capable of better conceptions and higher moral exertions, the Catholic deems a proof of the surviving faculties for good in the human breast. That those conceptions were not pure and those exertions not perfect, nay, very imperfect, and for the most part positively evil, he holds to be a necessary consequence of the fall.

Let us now turn from the Chinese to the Hindoos. The feeling of estrangement from God, and of the deep degradation of humanity, was so intense among the latter, that they conceived the infantine (and when we take into consideration the intellectual modes of conception in the youthful world, which in order to preserve the pure, eternal idea of man in God, ever imparted to it a concrete reality in time), they conceived the no less infantine and amiable, than earnest, doctrine of the pre-existence of spirits, who on account of their sins had been by God cast out on the earth. Hence, they looked on all human existence as a period graciously vouchsafed by God for purification and purgation, as this is so clearly and vividly expressed in the well-known fragment of Holwell, and is generally believed not only in Hindostan, but in Thibet, in the kingdom of the Burmese, by the Siamese, etc. This idea is also stamped on the civil life of the Hindoos, and is particularly perceptible in the mutual relations of the several castes.

Who can possibly, we ask, be so painfully alive to this alienation from God, without retaining in his bosom something kindred to divinity—the image of the Godhead ? Were the means, employed to attain to the reunion with the Deity, mistaken, they

Deus in gentes, in impios quosvis non aliter atque formam, opes, et similia dona largitur.' Thus in a manner purely mechanical, so that no higher spiritual activity was to be found. Moreover, such a view is doubtless consistent when man no longer possesses spiritual faculties for the exercise of virtue.

[1] 'Pseudotheologi nostri falsi cæco naturæ judicio commendarunt nobis philosophica studia. Quantum in Platone tumoris est et fastus ? Neque facile fieri mihi posse videtur, quin ab illa Platonica ambitione, contrahat aliquid vitii,' etc.

were so, only because no other name is given to us, whereby we can be just before God, save that of Christ Jesus alone. But in these oft convulsive, these most tragic efforts to be united again to God, lies the irrefragable evidence of the desire after eternal life never obliterated from the breast of man. Who can look at the temples of Elephanta and Salsette, and deny the Hindoos the capability of religious feeling? Who has ever reflected on their doctrine of the present period of humanity—the Cali-yuga, in its relation to anterior ages, and can refuse to acknowledge the deep sense of the evergrowing degeneracy of mankind, which this people hereby evinces? Who has ever examined their doctrines on the divine incarnations, and can fail to recognise in them the remote desire at least for a divine deliverance from the fall?—a desire, indeed, which is to be found in all antiquity. If the earlier Indian theism often degenerated into pantheism, we must seek the cause of this in the finite reason of man, more and more debilitated by the progress of sinfulness. But that no atheism—no consummate impiety—was openly avowed, we must ascribe to that indelible image of God stamped on the human soul.

What would a Luther and Melancthon, a Musæus and Wigand, a Flacius and Hesshuss, have replied to anyone, who had pointed to them the doctrine of the Parsees, who were so deeply impressed with a sense of the monstrosity of evil, that they were at a loss how to explain its existence in the good creation, otherwise than by supposing some self-existent wicked principle, who eternally counteracted the good one? Doth not a tenderer religious feeling lie here concealed, than in the above-stated opinion of Melancthon, Calvin, and Beza, that the good, holy God Himself instigates to evil, and needs the same for the execution of His designs? If the Parsees confounded moral and physical evil—if they did not at least duly separate them,—this by no means justifies an objection against the judgment we have pronounced; for we would have only invited the Reformers to reflect, whether their doctrine were better than that of the Parsees, who were so very differently circumstanced (for they were ignorant of the Christian doctrine), while the Reformers contended against the truth, which shone beside them in all its lustre.

In the whole ancient world we discern a seeking after truth. Let us but consider what that signifies! If none by their own faculties were enabled to discover it—for to every creature must it be communicated—still it was the object of desire. The man all evil—the man who hath been despoiled of all spiritual powers—in whom the likeness of God hath been utterly effaced—strives not after truth, and cannot so strive. Undoubtedly, truth was but too frequently sought for in the world of creatures; and it was only rarely that man could persuade himself to raise a look of joy upwards to heaven. But if we discover one such example only, it can then be no longer a matter of doubt, that man could do so when he wished—and the freedom, even of the fallen creature, is then fully established.

History makes us acquainted with endless gradations of moral character, and religious forms. From the most hideous depravity, up to an affecting piety, we find living examples in countless grades; and in all these do we find no evidence of moral freedom, but merely of an outward and civil liberty? Why was one individual, in exactly the same relations, other than his fellow-man, in a moral and religious point of view? In truth, if everything be conditionally referred to God—everything considered as His deed, and evil, as well as good, ascribed to Him, as the primary cause—then assuredly we shall find no evidence of the truth, that man, even in his fall, has retained his freedom, and is endowed with moral and religious faculties, the use whereof is left to himself: then we must cease to speak of good and of evil, and must class the opinion of an all-holy God, and of moral capabilities, among the dreams of fancy.

History, accordingly, confirms the Catholic doctrine of original sin, and incontrovertibly demonstrates, that, deep as his fall might have been, man lost not his freedom, nor was despoiled of the image of God; that not all which he thought and did, was necessarily sinful and damnable; and that he possessed something more than the 'mere liberty to sin'—as the Lutheran symbolical books assure us. Moreover, it is by no means astonishing, when we consider the extravagance of the view, as to the world before Christ, expressed in the Lutheran formularies, that in the course of time, it should have been opposed by another opinion equally extravagant—an opinion which regards the profoundest doctrines of the Gospel as mere heirlooms of heathenism; or even, in the mildest view, holds Christianity to be a natural result of the progress of our species, and consequently reveres paganism, independently of man's man's fall as a stage, *necessary in itself*, of human civilisation.

§ VIII—DOCTRINE OF THE CALVINISTS ON ORIGINAL SIN

In their account of original sin, and its consequences, the Calvinists did not proceed to near such lengths as the Lutherans. It may certainly be asserted in more than one respect, that the Reformed system of doctrine, as invented or arranged by Calvin, derived on many points undeniable advantages from the mistakes and errors of the earlier Reformers. Hence the more learned and scientific Calvin shows himself here and there more equitable towards the Catholics, presents their doctrine at times in a form not quite so disfigured as his predecessors, and on the whole proceeds with far more calmness and circumspection than Luther. Thus it happened, that, in the same way as Zwingle's cold and inane theory on the sacrament of the altar was by Calvin brought much nearer to the true Christian standard, so, in the doctrine which now engages our attention, only a slight deviation from the truth is perceptible. But this retrograde movement, when it occurred—for it did not often take place—was almost always brought about at the cost of clearness and distinctness of ideas, and if the mitigation of a too great severity afford pleasure, the uncertainty and fluctuation of notions that is substituted, is but the more perplexing.

Even Calvin expresses himself in various ways respecting original sin and its consequences. In some places, he says the image of God has been utterly effaced from the soul of man.[1] In other passages he expresses the same thing to the following effect: 'Man,' says he, 'has been so banished from the kingdom of God, that all in him which bears reference to the blessed life of the soul, is extinct;'[2] and he asserts, that man has received again organs for the divine kingdom only by the new creation in Christ Jesus.[3]

These assertions are, however, opposed by other passages, in which it is asserted, that the divine image stamped on the

---

[1] Calvin. Instit. lib. iii, c. 2, n. 12. 'Denique sicut primi hominis defectione deleri potuit ex ejus mente et anima imago Dei,' etc.

[2] Calvin. Instit. lib. ii, c. 2, sect. 12, p. 86. 'Unde sequitur, ita exulare a regno Dei, ut quæcumque ad beatam animæ vitam spectant, in eo extincta sint.'

[3] Calvin. Instit. lib. iii, c. 29, sect. 2, p. 355. 'Ac ne glorietur, quod vocanti et ultro se offerenti saltem responderit, nullas ad audiendum esse aures, nullos ad videndum oculos affirmat Deus, nisi quos ipse fecerit.'

human soul has never been totally destroyed and obliterated, but only fearfully disfigured, mutilated, and deformed.[1]

The same indistinctness, the same vacillation is apparent when Calvin investigates in detail the faculties yet belonging to the sinful and unregenerated man; or when he subjects to a most comprehensive examination the principle of freedom, which, according to the Catholic dogma, survives even in fallen man. He observes, that reason (*ratio, intellectus*), and the will (*voluntus*), could not be eradicated from man, for these faculties formed the characteristic distinction between man and the brute.[2] In the circle of social institutions, of the liberal and mechanical arts, of logic, dialectics, and mathematics, he accords to reason (he had better said understanding) the most glorious scope, even among the heathens; and takes occasion to indulge in a bitter sally against that contempt of philosophy, so prevalent among the Protestants of his day.[3] But when he comes to describe the religious and moral faculties of man, then the most singular indistinctness appears. As regards the knowledge of God, he by no means calls in question, that some truths were found scattered even among the nations unfavoured with a special divine revelation; and he seems on that account not to approve the opinion of a total destruction of the spiritual powers.[4] But, then, he destroys the hope which this concession offers, by adding, that the Almighty had granted such glimpses in the depth of night, in order to be able to condemn, out of their own mouth, the men whom they had been imparted to, or rather forced on; for then they could not excuse themselves as having been unacquainted with the ways of the Lord.[5]

[1] Calvin. Instit. lib. i, c. 15, sect. 4, p. 57. ' Etsi demus non prorsus exinanitam ac deletam in eo fuisse Dei imaginem, sic tamen corrupta fuit, ut quidquid superest, horrenda sit deformitas. Ergo quum Dei imago sit integra naturæ humanæ præstantia, quæ refulsit in Adam ante defectionem, postea sic vitiate ac prope deleta est, ut nihil ex ruina, nisi confusum, muti lum, labeque infectum supersit,' etc.

[2] Calvin. Instit. lib. ii, c. 2, sect. 22, p. 86.

[3] Calvin. Instit. lib. ii, sect. 15, fol. 88. ' Pudeat nos tante ingratitudinis, in quam non inciderunt ethnici poetæ qui et philosophiam, et leges, et bonas omnes artes Deorum inventa esse confessi sunt.'

[4] Loc. cit. sect. 12, fol. 86. ' Hoc sensu dicit Joannes, lucem adhuc tenebris lucere, sed a tenebris non comprehendi: quibus verbis utrumque clare exprimitur, in perversa et degenere hominis natura micare adhuc scintillas, quæ ostendant, rationale esse animal et a brutis differre.'

[5] Loc. cit. sect. 18, fol. 89. ' Præbuit quidem illis Deus exiguum divinitatis suæ gustum, ne ignorantiam impietati obtenderent: et eos interdum ad dicenda nonnulla impulit, quorum confessione ipsi convincerentur.'

Accordingly, he appears again indisposed to regard those traces of the true knowledge of God, as the result and property of higher human faculties co-operating with God. Nay, he seems to look upon them as the consequence of some strange and marvellous influence of the Deity upon certain men, for certain purposes; and this is the more remarkable, as he elsewhere deduces the anxiety for a good reputation from the feeling of shame, and this again from the innate sense of justice and virtue, wherein the germ of religion is already involved.[1] Thus we see throughout, a sound, excellent mind, struggling for the victory with disordered feelings, but, after a short vigorous onset for the mastery, compelled to succumb.

Nearly in the same way he treats the moral phenomena of the ancient world. The Catholics were wont at times to refer to men, like Camillus, and from their lives to demonstrate the moral freedom enjoyed even by the heathens, and the remnants of good to be found among them. They defended, moreover, the proposition, that God's special grace, communicated for the sake of Christ's merits, working retrospectively, and confirming the better surviving sentiments in the human breast, is undeniably to be traced in many phenomena.[2]

What course does Calvin now pursue to explain such phenomena? He observes, that it is very easy to let ourselves be deceived by the same, as to the true nature of corruption, and he does not precisely deny the finer traces of a moral spirit. But, he says, we should remember that the Divine grace here and there works as an impediment, not by its aid to strengthen and purify the interior of man, but mechanically to prevent the otherwise infallible outbreaks of evil.[3]

The conduct of the good Camillus he accordingly explains by the assumption, that it might have been purely exterior and hypocritical, or the result of the above-mentioned grace mechanically repressing evil in his breast, but in no wise rendering him better than his fellows.[4] By such more than mechanical

[1] Loc. cit. lib. i, c. 15, n. 8.
[2] Constitut. Unigenitus (Harduin. Concil. tom. xi, fol. 1635). This bull rejects, in consequence, the following Calvinistico-Jansenistical propositions: ' N. xxvi. Nullæ dantur gratiæ, nisi per fidem. N. xxix. Extra ecclesiam nulla conceditur gratia.' By *fides*, 'faith in Christ,' is to be understood.
[3] Calvin. Instit. lib. ii, c. 3, sect. 2, fol. 94. ' Exempla igitur ista monere nos videntur, ne hominis naturam in totum vitiosam putemus. . . . Sed hic succurrere nobis debet, inter illam naturæ corruptionem esse nonnullum Dei gratiæ locum, non quæ illam purget, sed quæ intus cohibeat.'
[4] Loc. cit. sect. 3, fol. 95. ' Quid autem, si animus pravus fuerit et

attempts at explanation, Calvin shows beyond doubt, that when he speaks of reason and the will as undestroyed and indestructible faculties of the soul, distinguishing man from the brute, he is far from thinking that man has preserved out of his unhappy catastrophe any moral and religious *powers whatever*.

Extravagant, however, as the judgment might be which Calvin formed of unregenerated man,[1] he yet did not forget himself so far as the Lutherans. When he teaches that the will and the reason exist even after the fall, he means thereby the *faculty* of faith, and of the higher will. Those passages, wherein he seems to deny this faculty to fallen man—and of these there are very many—must be corrected by others, wherein he expressly asserts, that, when he speaks of a destruction of the will, he understands only the really good will, and not the mere faculty of will;[2] so that the opinion of Victorinus Strigel, which was rejected by the Lutherans, appears to be precisely that of Calvin.

Of concupiscence, moreover, as is evident from the preceding account, Calvin entertains nearly the same notion as the Lutheran formularies profess,[3] only that he is unwilling to use this technical

contortus, qui aliud potius quidvis quam rectitudinem sectatus est ? . . . Quamquam hæc certissima est et facillima hujus quæstionis solutio, non esse istas communes naturæ dotes sed speciales Dei gratias, quas varie et in certum modum profanis alioqui hominibus dispensat.'

[1] Loc. cit. lib. ii, c. 5. n. 19. In this passage he says, in reference to the man who had fallen among robbers, whom the good Samaritan took pity on : ' Neque enim dimidiam homini vitam reliquit Dei verbum, sed penitus interiisse docet, quantum ad beatæ vitæ rationem.' The Catholics appealed to this parable to show that fallen man still retained some vital powers. Then Calvin proceeds : ' Stet ergo nobis indubia ista veritas, quæ nullis machinamentis quatefieri potest ; mentem hominis sic alienatam prorsus a Dei justitia, ut nihil non impium, contortum, fœdum, impurum, flagitiosum concipiat, concupiscat, moliatur : cor peccati veneno ita penitus delibutum, ut nihil quam corruptum fœtorem efflare queat.'

[2] Instit. lib. ii, c. 3, n. 6. ' Voluntatem dico aboleri, non quatenus est voluntas: quia in hominis conversione *integrum manet, quod primæ est naturæ : creari etiam novam dico, non ut voluntas esse incipiat, sed ut vertatur ex mala in bonum.* Hæc in solidum a Deo fieri affirmo.' Compare lib. i, c. 5, n. 16, where he allows, that the good which may happen through us, may be called our own, because the faculty of will is ours.

[3] Loc. cit. lib. ii, c. 1, n. 8. ' Neque enim natura nostra boni tantum inops et vacua est ; sed malorum omnium adeo fertilis et ferax, ut otiosa esse non possit. Qui dixerunt esse concupiscentiam, non nimis alieno verbo usi sunt, si modo adderetur (quod minime concideretur a plerisque, namely the Catholics) quidquid in homine est, peccatum est, ab intellectu ad voluntatem, ab anima ad carnem usque, hac concupiscentia inquinatum refertumque esse.'

word: and hence we can understand why in the confessions of the Calvinistic Churches it is but very rarely employed.[1]

As regards the Calvinistic formularies, they may be divided into several classes: since those which were framed under the immediate or remoter influence of Zwingle, are clearly distinguishable from those wherein the spirit of Calvin breathes. In the Tetrapolitana the doctrine of original sin is not specially treated, but is only incidentally touched on under the article of Justification: a fact, for the explanation whereof, we shall have occasion to notice later the doctrine of Zwingle on original sin.

The most ancient Helvetic Confessions (II and III) express themselves on this head with much caution and circumspection, and could we be only assured of their spirit—that is to say, were we but certain that this their boasted peculiarity did not proceed from the same motive which induced the Tetrapolitana to take no special notice of original sin—they might call forth from the Catholic expressions of perfect satisfaction.[2]

To the Helvetic Confessions we may add that of the Anglican Church, which on every point endeavours to avoid a tone of exaggeration.[3]

The first Helvetic Confession (which, however, is not the most ancient), the Gallic, Belgian, and Scotch Confessions on the other hand, unequivocally express Calvin's doctrine, that

---

[1] Except in Article IX of the thirty-nine articles of the Anglican Church, I do not remember to have read it anywhere.

[2] Confess. Helvet. ii, c. xiii, p. 95. 'Atque hæc lues quam originalem vocant, genus totum sic pervasit, ut nulla ope iræ filius inimicusque Dei, nisi divina per Christum curari potuerit. Nam si quid bonæ frugis superstes est, vitiis nostris assidue debilitatum in pejus vergit. Superest enim mali vis, et nec rationem persequi, nec mentis divinitatem excolere sinit.' What means *mentis divinitas*?

Confess. Helvet. iii, c. 2, p. 103. 'Confitemur, hominem ab initio, secundum Dei imaginem, et justitiam, et sanctitatem a Deo integre factum. Est autem sua sponte lapsus in peccatum, per quem lapsum totum humanum genus corruptum et damnationi obnoxium factum est. Hinc natura nostra vitiata est, ac in tantam propensionem ad peccatum devenit, ut nisi eadem per Spiritum Sanctum redintegretur, homo per se nihil boni faciat, aut velit.'

[3] Confess. Anglic. art. ix, p. 129. 'Peccatum originale non est, ut fabulantur Pelagiani, in imitatione situm, sed est vitium et depravatio naturæ cujuslibet hominis ex Adamo naturaliter propagati, qua fit, ut ab originali justitia quam longissime distet, ad malum sua natura propendeat, et caro semper adversus spiritum concupiscat, unde in quoque nascentium iram Dei atque damnationem meretur.'

man is thoroughly and entirely corrupted.[1] However, in these, as in the writings of Calvin, we meet with many indeterminate and wavering expressions. It is worthy of observation, moreover, that the first Helvetic formulary pronounces the Lutheran opinion, that fallen man no longer possesses the faculty of will and knowledge for the kingdom of God, to be Manichean.[2]

The following fact is worthy of our attention:—

Even the Confessions of the Reformed consider actual sins as *only* the manifestations of original sin—as the gradual revelation of the same in special determinate phenomena. According to them, also, Adam's sin is the *unique*, the *only* source, whence all sins flow, without ever exhausting it; the infinite source, ever active and stirring to find an outlet, and, when that outlet is found, impatient to find a new one.[3]

With reason, Catholics were able to reply that, according to this view, all sins would be necessarily equal, since, according to the maxims of a false realism, the person is considered as absorbed in nature, the individual in universal being; and the fact, that not all the unconverted are in a like degree rogues and villains, not all fractricides and parricides, robbers and poisoners, the Calvinists can by no means explain by the different use of freedom, since, according to their doctrine, no one possesses it. Thus, observe the Catholics, the primitive evil, according to the maxims of Calvin, progresses with a blind necessity, and finds in every man a ready, though servile, instrument for the perpetration of its most horrible deeds. It can, therefore, be regarded only as an accident, when one appears as a frightful criminal, the other as a moral man: the latter at bottom is as bad as the former; the sinfulness, alike in each, and repressible

---

[1] Confess. Helvet. l. c. viii-ix, p. 15; Gall. c. x-xi, p. 144; Scot. Art. iii, p. 146; Belg. c. xiv. p. 178. The Hungarian Confession speaks not at all of original sin, yet from motives different from the *Tetrapolitana*. In respect to the discrepancies noticed in the text, we find several in the first Helvetic Confession, which we cannot now enter into, as it would lead us into too many details. The Belgian Confession, for example, says that by original sin man hath been entirely severed from God, and yet in another place it leaves him some *vestigia exigua* of the earlier gifts of divine similitude.

[2] Confess. Helvet. i, c. ix. p. 19. 'Non sublatus est quidem homini intellectus, non erepta ei voluntas, et prorsus in lapidem vel truncum est commutatus.' P. 21: 'Manichæi spoliabant hominem omni actione, et veluti saxum et truncum faciebant:' words which by the employment of the peculiar Lutheran expressions, can refer only to the Lutheran opinions.

[3] Confess. Belg. c. xv, p. 179.

by none, manifests itself sometimes here, sometimes there, in more violent explosions. The first Helvetic Confession guards itself against these and such like consequences, and condemns the Jovinians, the Pelagians, and the Stoics, who taught the equality of all sins.[1] But it can establish no other difference of sins, than that of external manifestation, according to which, truly, not one sin perhaps is like to the other. However, we honour in this cautiousness a sound feeling—a welcome perception of that deep, indescribable abyss of error, out of which the Reformation sprang.

The doctrine of the Reformed Confessions respecting wicked lust (*concupiscentia*), we shall not set forth at length, since it does not materially differ from the view of the orthodox Lutherans. In respect to the bodily death, this is regarded, as in the Catholic Church, to be a consequence of original sin.[2]

§ IX—ZWINGLE'S VIEW OF ORIGINAL SIN

To explain some phenomena in the Formularies of the Reformed Churches, we annex the doctrine of Zwingle on original sin. This Reformer ventures on the attempt, not merely to determine according to Scriptural evidence the nature of man's hereditary evil, but to give a psychological explanation of the sin of Adam—an attempt for which he is utterly incompetent, and which is very inferior to preceding efforts for the illustration of this very obscure mystery, nay, in reality explains absolutely nothing, and presupposes original sin. In the first place, Zwingle troubles the serious reader with a very untimely jest, when he says, that it was a bad prognostic for the future married man, that Eve should have been formed out of a rib of the sleeping Adam; for, from observing that her husband, during this operation, was not awakened nor brought to consciousness, the thought naturally arose in her mind, that her mate might be easily deceived and circumvented! Satan now observed Eve's growing spirit of enterprise, and withal, her total inexperience in all intrigues. Aiding, therefore, her internal desire to play a trick, and her utter impotence to accomplish

---

[1] Confess. Helv. l. c. viii, p. 17.
[2] Confess. Belg. c. xiv, p. 178. 'Quo morti corporeæ et spirituali oɒnoxium reddidit.' Helvet. l. c. viii, p. 17. 'Per mortem itaque intelligimus non tantum corpoream mortem,' etc.

her purpose, he pointed out to her the way for deceiving her husband, and the result was the first sin. This man, sporting over sin, seriously observes, that from this whole process of Satanic seduction, and especially from the enticements offered, it is easy to conclude, that the self-love of Adam was the cause of his sin, and that consequently from self-love flows all human misery. But then, as, according to all the laws of the outward world, the like can only proceed from its like, so, since Adam's fall, all men were born with this self-love, the germ of all moral evil. Zwingle then proceeds to describe original sin, which in itself is not sin, but only a natural disposition to sin—a leaning propensity to sin; and endeavours to illustrate his meaning by the following comparison: A young wolf has in all respects the natural qualities of a wolf, that is to say, it is one, that, in virtue of its innate ferocity, would attack and devour the sheep, though yet it has not actually done so; and huntsmen, on discovering it, will treat it in the same manner as the old ones, for they feel convinced, that, on its growing up, it will, like others of its species, fall upon the flocks, and commit ravages. The natural disposition is the hereditary sin, or the hereditary fault; the special robbery is the actual sin growing out of the former; the latter is sin in the strict sense of the word, while the former ought not to be considered either as a sin or as a debt.[1]

This account, while it explains nothing, is withal of a genuine Protestant stamp. That it explains nothing, is evident from its representing self-love as the cause of Adam's sin, which accordingly before his fall lay concealed in him, and by the mediation of Satan was only introduced into the outward world. This self-love is represented as the effect of Adam's sin extending to all his posterity—as the natural disposition of all his sons; so that original sin appears as a corruption already innate in Adam; and it must be considered, not so much as inherited of

[1] Zwingli de peccato origin. declarat. op. tom. ii, fol. 1777. 'Quam ergo tandem causam tam imprudentis facti aliam esse putemus, quam amorem sui? etc. Habemus nunc prævaricationis fontem *philautian* scilicet, hoc est sui ipsius amorem: ex hoc manavit quicquid uspiam est malorum inter mortales. Hoc mortuus jam homo filios degeneres procreavisse neutiquam cogitandus est: non magis quam quod ovem lupus aut corvus cygnum pariat. . . . Est ergo ista ad peccandum amore sui propensio peccatum originale: quæ quidem propensio non est proprie peccatum, sed fons quidem et ingenium. Exemplum dedimus de lupo adhuc catulo. . . . Ingenium ergo est peccatum sive vitium originale: rapina vero peccatum, quod ex ingenio dimanat, id ipsum peccatum actu est, quod recentiores actuale vocant, quod et proprie peccatum est.'

Adam, but as implanted by God himself. But this explanation is also a genuine Protestant one, since it frankly and undisguisedly holds up God as the author of sin, and looks upon all particular actual sins as the necessary results—the outward manifestations of a natural disposition; a disposition which is well illustrated by that of the young wolf, that, devoid of freedom, is totally unable to resist the impulse of instinct. Hence, also, Zwingle with reason regards original sin, not as sin, but *only* as an evil, clinging to human nature : he is, however, chargeable with an inconsistency, in considering actual sins to be sins, for they are only the necessary growth of a natural disposition. It would have been also more in conformity with his abovementioned principles, as to the cause of evil, to have considered no moral transgression as contracting a debt.

CHAPTER III

OPPOSITE VIEWS ON THE DOCTRINE OF JUSTIFICATION

§ X—GENERAL STATEMENT OF THE MODE IN WHICH, ACCORDING TO THE DIFFERENT CONFESSIONS, MAN BECOMES JUSTIFIED

THE different views entertained respecting the fall of man must, necessarily, exert the most decisive influence on the doctrine of his regeneration. The treatment of this doctrine is of so much the more importance for us, and claims so much the more our attention, as it was in the pretended improvement on the Catholic view of man's justification, according to the special observation of the Smalcald articles, that the Reformers placed their principal merit. They call this subject not only the first, and the most important, but that, without the maintenance whereof,. the opponents of Protestantism would have been completely in the right, and have come victorious out of the struggle.[1]

In conformity with this, Luther says, very pithily, in his *Table-talk*, ' If *the doctrine* fall, it is all over with us.' We shall, in the first place, state generally the various accounts which the opposite Confessions give of the process of regeneration, and then enter, with the minutest accuracy, into details.

According to the Council of Trent, the course is as follows :— The sinner, alienated from God, is, without being able to show any merit of his own, without being able to put in any claim to grace, or to pardoning mercy, called back to the divine kingdom.[2]

---

[1] Pars ii, sect. 3. Cf. Sol. Declar. iii, p. 653.

[2] Concil. Trident. sess. vi, c. 5. 'Declarat præterea, ipsius justificationis exordium in adultis a Dei per Christum Jesum præveniente gratia sumendum esse, hoc est, ab ejus vocatione, qua, nullis eorum existentibus meritis, vocantur ; ut, qui per peccata a Deo aversi erant, per ejus excitantem atque adjuvantem gratiam ad convertendum se ad suam ipsorum justificationem, eidem gratiæ libere essentiendo et cooperando disponantur : ita ut tangente Deo cor hominis per Spiritus Sancti illuminationem, neque homo ipse omnino nihil agat, inspirationem illam recipiens, quippe qui illam et abjicere potest, neque sine gratia Dei movere se ad justiam coram illo libere sua voluntate possit. Unde in sacris literis, cum dicitur— convertimini ad me, et ege ad vos convertar, libertatis nostræ admonemur.

This divine call, sent to the sinner for Christ's sake, is expressed not only in an outward invitation, through the preaching of the Gospel, but also in an internal action of the Holy Spirit which rouses the slumbering energies of man, more or less sunk in the sleep of spiritual death, and urges him to unite himself with the power from above, in order to enter upon a new course of life, and in order to renew the communion with God (preventive grace). If the sinner hearkens to this call, then faith in God's Word is the first effect of divine and human activity, co-operating in the way described. The sinner perceives the existence of a higher order of things, and with entire, and till then unimagined, certainty, possesses the conviction of the same. The higher truths and promises which he hears, especially the tidings that God has so loved the world, as to give up his only-begotten Son for it, and has offered to all forgiveness of sins, for the sake of Christ's merits, shake the sinner. While he compares what he is, with what, according to the revealed will of God, he ought to be; while he learns, that so grievous is sin, and the world's corruption, that it is only through the mediation of the son of God it can be extirpated, he attains to true self-knowledge, and is filled with the fear of God's judgments. He now turns to the divine compassion in Christ Jesus, and conceives the confiding hope, that, for the sake of his Redeemer's merits, God may graciously vouchsafe to him the forgiveness of his sins. From this contemplation of God's love for man, a spark of divine love is enkindled in the human breast—hatred and detestation for sin arise, and man doth penance.[2]

Thus, by the mutual interworking of the Holy Spirit, and of the creature freely co-operating, justification really commences. If man remains faithful to the holy work thus begun, the Divine Spirit, at once sanctifying and forgiving sins, communicates all the fulness of his gifts—pours into the heart of man the love of

Cum respondemus—converte nos Domine ad te, et convertemur, Dei nos gratia præveniri confitemur.'

[1] Loc. cit. c. vi. 'Disponuntur ad ipsam justitiam, dum excitati divina gratia et adjuti, fidem ex auditu concipientes, libere moventur in Deum credentes vera esse, quæ divinitus revelata et promissa sunt, atque illud imprimis, a Deo justificari impium per gratiam ejus, per redemptionem quæ est in Christo Jesu, et dum peccatores, se intelligentes, a divinæ justitiæ timore, quo utiliter concutiuntur, ad considerandam Dei misericordiam se convertendo in spem eriguntur, fidentes Deum sibi propter Christum propitium fore, illumque, tanquam omnis justitiæ fontem diligere incipiunt, ac propterea moventur adversus peccata per odium aliquod et destationem,' etc.

God, so that he becomes disentangled from the inmost roots of sin, and, inwardly renewed, leads a new and virtuous life—that is to say, becometh really just in the sight of God—performeth truly good works—the fruits of a renovation of spirit, and sanctification of feeling—goeth from righteousness on to righteousness, and in consequence of his present religious and moral qualities, acquired through the infinite merits of Christ, and his Holy Spirit, he is rewarded with celestial happiness.[1] However, without a special revelation the just man possesses not the unerring certainty, that he belongs to the number of the elect.

The Lutheran view, on the other hand, is as follows: When the sinner has been intimidated by the preaching of the law, which he is conscious of not having fulfilled, and hath been brought to the brink of despair, the Gospel is announced to him, and with it the solace administered—that Christ is the Lamb of God, that taketh upon him the sins of the world. With a heart stricken with fear and terror, he grasps at the Redeemer's merits, through faith, which alone justifieth. God, on account of Christ's merits, declares the believer just, without his being so in fact; though released from debt and punishment, he is not delivered from sin (original sin); the inborn sinfulness still cleaves to the just, though no longer in its ancient virulence. If it be reserved to faith alone, to justify us before God, yet faith is not alone: on the contrary, sanctification is annexed to justification, and faith manifests itself in good works, which are its fruits. Justification before God, and sanctification, must not by any means, however, in despite of their close connection, be considered as one and the same thing; because this would render impossible the certainty of the forgiveness of sins, and of salvation, which is an essential property of Christian faith. Lastly, the whole work of regeneration is God's doing alone, and man acts a purely passive part therein. God's act doth not only precede the working of man, as if this could, or ought to follow; as if the latter co-operated with the former, and so both together; but the Holy Spirit is exclusively active, in order

---

[1] Loc. cit. c. vii. 'Hanc dispositionem, seu præparationem, justificatio ipsa consequitur, quæ non est sola peccatorum remissio, sed et sanctificatio et renovatio interioris hominis per voluntariam susceptionem gratiæ et donorum, unde homo ex injusto fit justus, et ex inimico amicus, ut sit hæres secundum spem vitæ æternæ. . . . Ejusdem sanctissimæ passionis merito per Spiritum sanctum caritas Dei diffunditur in cordibus eorum, qui justificantur,' etc.

that to God alone the glory may accrue, and all pretensions of human merit be rendered impossible.[1]

The Calvinists, though with some differences, agree in the main with the disciples of Luther. Calvin is dissatisfied with the Reformers of Wittenberg, for having ascribed to the law alone, the property of exciting a sense of sin, and a consciousness of guilt. He thinks, on the contrary, that the first place is due to the Gospel, and that it is by the enlargement of the divine mercy in Christ Jesus, that the sinner is made attentive to his reprobate state—so that repentance follows on faith.[2]

That the severe remark of Calvin at the passage, where he states the relation between faith and repentance, to wit, that those understood nothing of the essence of faith, who conceived this relation other than himself, is not entirely destitute of foundation, nor based on an empty spirit of controversy, we shall clearly prove later, when it will be shown, that, with Calvin, repentance bears a very different signification from the terror caused by sin, in the Lutheran system ; and that according to the former, justification and sanctification appear in a more vital connection.

---

[1] Solid. declar. v, de lege et Evang. sect. 6, p. 768. ' Peccatorum cognitio ex lege est. Ad salutarem vero conversionem illa pœnitentia, quæ tantum contritionem habet, non sufficit : sed necesse est, ut fides in Christum accedat, cujus meritum, per dulcissimam et consolationis plenam Evangelii doctrinam, omnibus resipiscentibus peccatoribus offertur, qui per leges doctrinam perterriti et prostrati sunt. Evangelion enim remissionem peccatorum non securis mentibus, sed perturbatis et vere pœnitentibus annuntiat. Et ne contritio et terrores legis in desperationem vertantur, opus est prædicatione Evangelii : ut sit pœnitentia ad salutem.' Apolog. iv, sect. 45, p. 87 : ' Fides illa, de qua loquimur, existit in pœnitentia, hoc est, concipitur in terroribus conscientiæ, quæ sentit iram Dei adversus nostra peccata et quærit remissionem peccatorum, et liberari a peccato.' Apolog. iv, de justit. sect. 26, p. 76 : ' Igitur sola fide justificamur, intelligendo justificationem, ex injusto justum effici seu regenerari.' Sect. 19, p. 72 : ' Nec possunt acquiescere perterrefacta corda, si sentire debent se propter opera propria, aut propriam dilectionem, aut legis impletionem placere, quia hæret in carne peccatum, quod semper accusat nos.' Sect. 25, p. 25 : ' Dilectio etiam et opera sequi fidem debent, quare non sic excluduntur, ne sequantur, sed fiducia meriti dilectionis aut operum in justificatione excluditur.'

[2] Calvin. Instit. lib. iii, c. 3, sect. 1, fol. 209. ' Proximus autem a fide ad pœnitentiam erit transitus : quia hoc capite, bene cognito, melius patebit, quomodo sola fide et mera venia justificetur homo, ne tamen a justitiæ imputatione separetur realis (ut ita loquar) vitæ sanctitas : pœnitentiam vero non modo fidem continuo subsequi, sed ex ea nasci extra controversiam esse debet. Quibus autem videtur, fidem potius præcedere pœnitentiæ, quam ab ipsa manari vel proferri, tanquam fructus ab arbore, nunquam ejus vis fuit cognita, et nimium levi argumento ad id sentiendum moventur.'

More important still is the departure of the Calvinists from the Lutheran formularies, by their assertion, that it is only in those elected from all eternity, that the Deity worketh to justification and to regeneration. On the other hand, the Lutherans, like the Catholics, reject the doctrine of absolute predestination. Finally, the Calvinists lay a still more violent stress on the certainty which the believer must have of his future happiness.

It follows, accordingly, that we must treat in succession, first, the distinctive doctrines in respect to the operation of God and of man in the affair of regeneration; secondly, the doctrine of predestination; thirdly, the differences in the notion of justification; fourthly, those respecting faith; fifthly, those touching works; and sixthly, those in respect to the certainty of salvation. When these points shall have been first gone through in detail, then comprehensive reflections on the nature and deeper significance of this opposition between the Confessions, in respect to the doctrine of justification, will follow in a more intelligible, as well as instructive form. Then he who, after a general view, would not have suspected any practical or theoretical differences, important enough to occasion an ecclesiastical schism, will clearly see that the Catholic Church could not possibly exchange her primitive doctrine for the new opinion; nay, could not, even by any possibility, tolerate in her bosom the two opposite views. The minute investigation of particulars will bring out, in the clearest light, those divergences of opinion, which in a general survey, may be easily overlooked; and in the considerations which we have announced, we will clearly establish the absolute incompatibility of the two doctrines in one and the same system; and will point out the momentous interests which the Catholics defended in the maintenance of their dogma.

§ XI—OF THE RELATION OF THE OPERATION OF GOD TO THAT OF MAN, IN THE WORK OF REGENERATION, ACCORDING TO THE CATHOLIC AND THE LUTHERAN SYSTEMS

According to Catholic principles, in the holy work of regeneration we find two operations concur—the Divine and the human; and when this work succeeds, they mutually pervade each other, so that this regeneration constitutes one theandric work. God's holy power precedes, awakening, exciting, vivifying :—man, the while, being utterly unable to merit, call forth, or even desire, that divine grace; yet he must let himself be excited, and follow with freedom.[1] God offers his aid to raise the sinner after his fall; yet it is for the sinner to consent, and to receive that aid. By accepting it, he is accepted by the Divine spirit; and through his faithful co-operation, he is exalted again gradually (though never completely in this life) to that height from which he was precipitated. The Divine Spirit worketh not by absolute necessity, though he is urgently active: His omnipotence suffers human freedom to set to it a bound, which it cannot break through, because an unconditional interference with that freedom would bring about the annihilation of the moral order of the world, which the Divine wisdom hath founded on liberty. With reason, therefore, and quite in conformity with her inmost essence, hath the Church rejected the Jansenistical proposition of Quesnel, that human freedom must yield to the omnipotence of God.[2] This proposition involves as an immediate consequence, the doctrine of God's absolute predestination; and asserts of those who attain not unto regeneration, that they are not the cause of their own reprobation, but that they have been absolutely cast off by the

[1] Concil. Trident. sess. vi, c. v. '. . . ut, qui per peccata a Deo aversi erant, per ejus excitantem atque adjuvantem gratiam ad convertendum se ad suam ipsorum justificationem, eidem gratiæ libere assentiendo et cooperando, disponantur, ita ut, tangente Deo cor hominis per Spiritus Sancti illuminationem, neque homo ipse omnino nihil agat, inspirationem illam recipiens quippe qui illam et abjicere potest, neque tamen sine gratia Dei movere se ad justitiam coram illo libera sua voluntate possit. Unde in sacris literis cum dicitur—convertimini ad me, et ego convertar ad vos, libertatis nostræ admonemur. Cum respondemus—converte nos Domine ad te, et convertemur, Dei nos gratia præveniri confitemur.' Can. iv. ' Si quis dixerit, liberum arbitrium a Deo motum et excitatum nihil cooperari assentiendo Deo excitanti atque vocanti, quo ad obtinendam justificationis gratiam se disponat ac præparet, neque posse dissentire, si velit, sed velut inanime quoddam nihil omnino agere, merique passive se habere, anathema sit.'
[2] The Constitution of Pope Innocent X (Apud Hard. Concil. tom. xi, fol. 143) rejects the proposition, No. ii. ' Interiori gratiæ in statu naturæ lapsæ nunquam resistitur;' and the Constitution Unigenitus (Hard. l. c. fol. 1634), No. xiii. ' Quando Deus vult animam salvam facere, et eam tangit interiori gratiæ suæ manu, nulla voluntas humana ei resistit.' No. xvi. ' Nullæ sunt illecebræ, quæ non cedant illecebris gratiæ: quia nihil resistit omnipotenti.' No. xix. ' Dei gratia nihil aliud est, quam ejus omnipotens voluntas: hæc est idea, quam Deus ipse nobis tradit in omnibus suis Scripturis.' No. xx. ' Vera gratiæ idea est, quod Deus vult sibi a nobis obediri et obeditur, imperat et omnia fiunt, loquitui tanquam dominus, et omnia sibi submissa sunt.'

Deity Himself; for a mere inspiration of the Divine Spirit would have moved their free-will to faith, and to holy obedience.

It is not difficult to see, that the above-stated doctrine of the Catholic Church, is determined by her view of original sin; for, had she asserted that an utter extirpation of all germs of good, a complete annihilation of freedom in man, had been the consequence of his fall, she then could not have spoken of any co-operation on his part, of any faculties in him, that could be excited, revivified, and supported. Man, who in this case would have lost all affinity, all likeness unto God, would no longer have been capable of receiving the Divine influences towards the consummation of a second birth; for the operation of God would then have found in him as little response, as in the irrational brute.

On the other hand, it is evident, from the Lutheran representation of original sin, that the Lutherans could not admit the co-operation of man; and the reason wherefore they could not, is equally obvious; namely, because, according to them, the hereditary evil consists in an obliteration of the Divine image from the human breast; and this is precisely the faculty capable of co-operating with God. Accordingly, they teach, that man remains quite passive, and God is exclusively active. Even so early as the celebrated disputation at Leipsig, Luther, defended this doctrine against Eck and compared man to a saw, that passively let itself be moved in the hand of the workman. Afterwards he delighted in comparing fallen man to a pillar of salt, a block, a clod of earth, incapable of working with God.[1] It may be conceived, that not only was such a doctrine necessarily revolting to Catholics, but that even among Luther's disciples, who, in the first unreflecting excitement of feelings, had followed him, a sound Christian sense, rallying by degrees, must offer resistance to such errors. In Melancthon's school, more enlightened opinions spread; and his followers, after Luther's death, had even the courage openly to defend them. Pfeffinger,[2] and after him, the above-named Victorinus Strigel[3] arose;

---

[1] Luther in Genes. c. xix. 'In spiritualibus et divinis rebus quæ ad animæ salutem spectant, homo est instar statuæ salis, in quam uxor patriarchæ Loth est conversa, imo est similis trunco et lapidi, statuæ vita carenti, quæ neque oculorum, oris, aut ullorum sensuum cordisque usum habet.'

[2] Pfeffinger propositiones de libero arbitrio. Lips. 1555. 4. Compare Plank, lib. cit. p. 567.

[3] Plank, lib. cit. p. 584.

but their power went no further than to occasion a struggle, wherein they succumbed. Luther's spirit gained so complete a victory, that his views, nay his very expressions, were adopted into the public formularies.[1]

I shall take the liberty of citing a passage from Plank, which states the opinion of Arnsdorf, on the nature of God's operation in respect to man—an opinion, which was put forth amid the synergistic controversies. Nicholas von Arnsdorf said: 'By his will and speech God worketh all things, with all creatures. When God wills, and speaks, stone and wood are carried, hewn, and laid, how, when, and where He will. Thus, if God wills, and speaks, man becomes converted, pious, and just. For, as stone and wood are in the hand and power of God, so, in like manner, are the understanding and the will of man in the hand and power of God; so that man can absolutely will and choose nothing, but what God wills and speaks, either in grace or in wrath.'[2] Who will not here see the remarkable influence which Luther's theory touching the mutual relation between the divine and the human operations, considered in themselves, and even independently of the fall, has exerted on this article of belief? God's wrath thought Nicholas von Arnsdorf, forces one person to evil, in the same way as His grace absolutely determines another to good. So much doth the human mind find itself constrained to reduce to general laws that special relation between God and man, which was revealed by the redemption of Christ Jesus.

Remarkable is the subterfuge, which the Formulary of Concord saw itself forced to adopt, in order to prevail upon men to hear preaching—a subterfuge which of itself should have convinced its authors, how erroneous was the doctrine which they inculcated. For as, according to their view, man on his part can contribute nought towards justification, as he possesses not even the faculty of receiving the Divine influences, and thus, in consequence of the loss of every trace of similitude to his Maker, is cut off from all possibility of union with God, what blame

---

[1] Solid. declar. ii, de lib. arbitr. sect. 43, p. 644, 'Ad conversionem suam prorsus nihil conferre potest.' Sect. 20, p. 635. 'Præterea sacræ literæ hominis conversionem, fidem in Christum, regenerationem, renovationem . . . simpliciter *soli*, divinæ operationi et Spiritui Sancto adscribunt.' On the comparison of man with a stone, and so forth, see sect. 16, p. 633, sect. 43, p. 644.

[2] Plank, 'History of the Rise, the Changes, and the Formation of the Protestant System of Doctrine,' vol. iv, p. 708.

could be uttered, and what reproaches made, if anyone remained obdurate, when it depended on God alone to remove that obduracy ? What blame was yet possible, when anyone was disinclined to read the Bible, or obstinately resisted hearing the evangelical sermon, which was laid down by the Reformers, as the condition for receiving the Divine Spirit ? To be asked to listen to a sermon, must certainly seem to one, devoid of all spiritual qualities and susceptibilities, as the most singular demand—not less singular than if he were asked to prepare for flying; nay, more singular, for in the latter case he could understand the purport of the demand, while, in default of every spiritual organ for understanding the sermon, he could not even comprehend what was the proposed design : he might conjecture, indeed, that it was intended to pass a joke on him! The Formulary of Concord can say naught else than, that man hath still the power to move from one place to another ; he still possesses outward, though no inward ears; his feet and his external ears he need only exert, *and the consequences he must attribute only to himself, if he fail to do so.* So must the feet supply the place of the will, which according to the Catholic doctrine, has yet survived the fall ; the ears discharge the functions of reason ; and the body undertake the responsibility of the mind.[1]

In general, the Reformers were unable to succeed in finding, in their system, a tenable position for the idea of human responsibility—an idea not to be effaced from the mind of man, and whereon Kant established what he deemed the only possible proof of the existence of God. They observe, indeed, as we have

[1] The Solida Declaratio ii (de lib. arbit. sect. 19, p. 636), allows man still the 'locomotivam potentiam' seu externa membra regere. Sect. 33, p. 640. ' Non ignoramus autem et enthusiastas et epicureos pia hac de impotentia et malitia naturalis liberi arbitrii doctrina, qua conversio et regeneratio nostra soli Deo, nequaquam autem nostris viribus, tribuitur, impie, turpiter et maligne abuti. Et multi impii illorum sermonibus offensi atque depravati, dissoluti et feri fiunt, atque omnia pietatis exercitia, orationem, sacram lectionem, pias meditationes remisse tractant aut prorsus negligunt, ac dicunt,—Quandoquidem propriis suis naturalibus viribus ad Deum sese convertere nequeant, perrecturos se in illa sua adversus Deum contumacia, aut expectaturos, donec a Deo violenter, et contra suam ipsorum voluntatem convertantur,' etc. Sect. 39, p. 642. ' Dei verbum homo etiam nondum ad Deum conversus, nec renatus, externis auribus audire aut legere potest. In ejusmodi enim externis rebus homo adhuc, etiam post lapsum, aliquo modo liberum arbitrium habet, ut in ipsius potestate sit ad coetus publicos ecclesiasticos accedere, verbum dei audire, vel non audire.'

seen, that man can repel the Divine influence, though he cannot co-operate with it; whereby, they think, his guilt is sufficiently established. But this solution of the difficulty in question is unsatisfactory, because every man can *only* resist; since all are in a like degree devoid of freedom, and of every vestige of spiritual faculties. The explication of the fact, that some become just, and others remain obdurate, can be sought for, not in man, but in God only—whom it pleases to remove in one case, and to let stand in another, the obstacle which is the same in all!

At least, we cannot at all see, how it would cost the Almighty a greater exertion of power, to supply among some, rather than among others, the spiritual faculties that are wanting; for, all are herein equally passive. In other words, the doctrine of the non-co-operation of man, which rests on the original theory of Luther and Melancthon touching the absolute passiveness of the created spirit towards its Creator, finds only in this theory its metaphysical basis, and presupposes, accordingly, absolute predestination, which, in the course of the synergistic controversies, was embraced by the most consistent Lutheran theologians, Flacius, Hesshuss, and others,[1] while the Formulary of Concord sacrificed to a better feeling the harmony of its own system.[2]

Proceeding, now, to the task of more nearly determining what is the work of regeneration, which the exclusively active Spirit of God hath to achieve, we can discover naught else but that the religious and moral qualities—the faculty of faith and of will, which had been lost through Adam's fall—must be inserted anew in the defective spiritual organisation; and, accordingly, the inward ears be replaced. While, therefore, according to the Catholic system, the first operation of God consists in the resuscitation, excitement, higher tuning, strengthening, and glorification of these faculties, it is, according to the Lutheran system, to exert itself in a new creation of the same. In this way, we can understand, in some degree, the remark in the Formulary of Concord, that, in the further progress of regeneration, man co-operates with God, not indeed, as to the integrity of his being, but only through his renovated parts

---

[1] Plank, loc. cit. vol. iv, p. 704, 707.
[2] Solid. declar. p. 644. 'Etsi autem Dominus hominem non cogit, ut convertatur (qui enim semper Spiritui Sancto resistunt . . . ii non convertuntur), attamen trahit Deus hominem, quem convertere decreverit.'

—through the new divine gift; the remaining portion of his being—the mere natural man, who had come down from that earlier state of alienation from God—being never active for the kingdom of God.[1] Moreover, by this doctrine, the identity of consciousness is destroyed; and we cannot see how the man, new-born or newly created, can recognise himself to be the same—at least, it is not easy for him to do so, unless he stands before the mirror, and perceives to his contentment, that he has ever the same nose, and consequently is the same person as heretofore. Nor can we conceive how repentance can be possible; for the new-created faculties will have difficulty to repent for what they have not perpetrated; and the old cannot repent, for the divine is not within their competence.

Here we may remark, that, by the Lutheran doctrine here stated, the reproach which its professors so perpetually urge against the Catholic tenet, to wit, that it is Pelagian, receives its explanation.[2] In truth, we discover everywhere, we might almost say, an intentional misrepresentation of the Catholic doctrine: and Melancthon, in this, surpasses Luther himself. Want of solid historical information had an undoubted share in this charge; and this becomes more evident, when we see the Thomists called Pelagian; nay, the views of Luther, on the relation of Grace and Nature, represented as containing the true old Catholic doctrine in opposition to Pelagianism; for *never* was it taught, not even by St Augustine, that, by original

---

[1] Solid. declar. ii, de lib. arbitr. sect. 45, p. 645. ' Ex his consequitur, quam primum Spiritus Sanctus, per verbum et sacramenta, opus suum regenerationis et renovationis in nobis inchoaverit, quod revera tunc per virtutem Spiritus Sancti cooperari possimus, ac debeamus, quamvis multa adhuc infirmitas concurrat. Hoc vero ipsum, quod cooperamur, non ex nostris carnalibus et naturalibus viribus est, sed ex novis illis viribus et donis, quæ Spiritus Sanctus in conversione in nobis inchoavit.' This decision, of necessity, presupposes the opinion, that the faculty lost through original sin, and recurring in regeneration, can be no mere quality of the human spirit. It is the higher faculty of will and of knowledge, if the passage cited is to bear any sort of sense.

[2] Calvin (Instit. lib. iii, c. 14, sect. 11, fol. 279) is far more just and equitable. ' De principio justificationis nihil inter nos et saniores scholasticos pugnæ est, quin peccator gratuito a damnatione liberatus justitiam obtineat, idque per remissionem peccatorum, nisi quod illi sub justificationis vocabulo renovationem comprehendunt, qua per Spiritum Sanctum renovamur in vitæ novitatem. Justitiam vero hominis regenerati sic describunt, quod homo per Christi fidem Deo semel conciliatus, bonis operibus justus censeatur et eorum merito sit acceptus.' In this there is something inaccurate, but how much more conscientious is Calvin here, than the *Solida Declaratio* ii, 52, p. 648.

sin, man was bereft of the moral and religious faculties. But in all this there evidently existed an internal obstacle to the full comprehension of the Catholic doctrine—an obstacle which we feel ourselves called upon to point out—while it makes the Lutheran view appear more pardonable, since it shows that it sprang out of a true Christian zeal, which, in this, as in almost every instance, was foolishly directed. The Catholic dogma, that even, in fallen man, moral and religious faculties exist— faculties which are not always sinful in themselves, and must be exercised even in the work of regeneration—led some to believe, that such an exercise of the faculties in question was the natural transition to grace, so as to suppose that, according to Catholic principles, a very good use of them was the medium of grace, or, in other words, merited it. Such an opinion were undoubtedly Pelagian; and in that case, not Christ, but man, would merit grace, or rather, grace would cease to be grace. To escape now the like errors, the Reformers supposed man was unable to achieve anything, and received only in regeneration itself those faculties which can be active in and for the kingdom of God. But the fine and delicate sense of the Catholic dogma, which very carefully distinguishes between nature and grace, totally escaped the perception of the Reformers. The finite, even when conceived as without sin, though it may stretch itself on every side, can never attain to the infinite, nor ever cling to it but with an illusive grasp.

Nature may honestly exert all her powers; she will never of herself, and by herself, reach a *supernatural* transfiguration; the human, by no strain of power, will become of itself the divine. There would remain an eternal gap betwixt the two, if it were not filled up by grace: the divinity must stoop to humanity, if humanity is to become divine. Hence did the Son of God become man, and not man become God in order to reconcile humanity with the Godhead. The like must typically recur in every believer. Thus the Church may look on the non-regenerated as endowed with the fairest faculties of nature, and as turning them to the best account. Yet it is not by the use of such faculties that they acquire life in grace, either its beginning, its middle, or its end. On the contrary, Divine grace must ever compassionately stoop to our lowliness, and impart to our sin-polluted faculties the first heavenly consecration, in order to prepare them for the kingdom of heaven, and the receiving of Christ's image. Here, accordingly, we see how important is the difference, which divides the Confessions in the view of man's original state. As in the finite, though yet unstained, faculties of the paradisaic man, Catholics deem the aid of a high supernatural power to have been absolutely necessary to preserve him in a living intimate communion with God; so they must necessarily look on the restoration of the fallen Adam to that communion, by means of his mere unaided natural powers, as a thing utterly impossible, or, in other words, as solely the result of grace. But while the Protestants, on the other hand, conceived that primeval man accomplished this union with God through his finite faculties alone, they necessarily considered the existence of a Divine similitude in the natural powers of fallen man, and still more, the exercise and expansion of such powers in the work of regeneration, as quite incompatible with the notion of grace, and as very derogatory to, if not utterly subversive of, the merits of Christ. That man should retain the possession of all his natural powers and faculties, signifies, according to the Protestant system, that he is able of himself to attain to the perfect knowledge and love of God. Thus, if the Protestants wished to maintain the notion of grace, they were obliged to exhibit man as absolutely passive in the work of regeneration, and as devoid of all powers acted on by grace. It was far otherwise in the Catholic system, which they were unwilling to probe.

When we endeavour to trace the cause which led the Reformers to the adoption of such a view, we must search for it in another quarter. They confounded, as it appears to us, what was objective, and subjective, in the matter of justification. In relation to the former, man is completely and entirely passive, but not so in respect to the latter. Fallen man cannot be justified, unless he confess before God, and to himself, that he is utterly incapable of discovering within him any means capable of reconciling him, sinner as he is, with his God. He must, with the most heartfelt confession of his own nothingness, with perfect humility give himself up to God—resign himself to His all-gracious disposal, acknowledging that he can only receive, and thus, is merely passive.

In this way only, doth man fall back into the natural relation of the creature to the Creator. But, should he wish to present to God anything—be they works, or aught else—in order thereby to exhibit the Almighty as his debtor, and to demand His grace, as his wages, and in this manner to display his activity—he would then be raising himself to an equality with God, and, if I may so speak, be placing himself on the same footing with the Deity, and, by such arrogance, would throw himself out of the relative sphere of the creature to the Creator. But, when man rests on the merits of Christ alone, and knows nothing of his own merits, he is then passive, and inactive, letting God alone work. But, when man coincides with these operations of God, he then becomes himself active, and co-operates with God; and the free acknowledgment, that in the sense above-mentioned, he can be in the relation only of a passive recipient, forms the very highest activity whereof he is capable. Now, the Reformers did not accurately distinguish between these two things, and, in the excess of a pious zeal, rejected all exertion, all energy, in every sense of the word, on the part of man. The Catholic recognises the necessity of a completely passive demeanour, since he rejects all merits that could earn the redemption; but he insists on the necessity likewise of an active demeanour, since he is convinced, that it is only by his free and faithful co-operation he can receive and appropriate to himself the workings of God. When man professes the first, he gives the glory to God; and when he declares the second, he gives thanks to God for his ability to render glory to Him; and this, without freedom, he were unable to do.[1]

---

[1] The Reformers, Luther, Melancthon, and others, and after them, all modern Protestant theologians, reproach *the Church* with admitting the opinion of ' meritum de congruo '; that is to say, an opinion that it is to be expected of God (*congruum esse*), that upon a heathen, who should make the best and most serious use of his natural faculties, He would bestow his grace, and admit him into His divine kingdom. This would be the admission of a quasi-merit, and consequently Pelagian. The Council of Trent knows nothing of such scholastic distinctions, that is to say, distinctions which were current in many schools, and therefore takes no notice of the above-mentioned *meritum de congruo*. Those schoolmen, who adopted this opinion, appealed particularly to the centurion Cornelius, in the Acts of the Apostles, c. x, 22-35; they might have also pointed to the fact, that so many Platonists became converts to Christianity, while no ancient document states the conversion of any Epicurean. We should be very desirous to hear an explanation of this phenomenon from an orthodox Lutheran. Such a man would undoubtedly pronounce as heretical one of the finest portions of Neander's *Church History*—the one wherein he points out those elements favourable to Christianity, or preparatory to it, in the ' Religious and philosophical systems of antiquity.' See more particularly vol. i, part i, p. 31. According to the orthodox Protestantism, no philosophy of history is possible. In fine, this Protestantism, should be made to observe, that it is one thing to assert that God will certainly have regard to the sincere seeking and desire of a heathen,

§ XII—DOCTRINE OF THE CALVINISTS ON THE RELATION OF GRACE TO FREEDOM, AND HUMAN CO-OPERATION—PREDESTINATION

The doctrine of the Calvinists, respecting original sin, which, according to them, commits fearful ravages on the human mind, without, however, eradicating the faculties of faith and will, extends its influence to the matter in question. They necessarily teach, that grace first determines, and, consequently, goes before, all the truly pious endeavours of man; so that on this subject we meet with a gratifying general uniformity between all the Confessions. On account of their milder and sounder view of original sin, the Calvinists are enabled, moreover, to uphold the doctrine of the active co-operation of man with God[1]; and

and another thing to maintain that all should *believe* that Divine grace is due to him, on account of this his seeking and desire.

Moreover, the German Reformers approached the theology of that day with teaching, that by his own powers man was enabled to love God above all things. But whoever has only the most superficial acquaintance with the theology of the Middle Age, must be astounded when he hears this; and that when the respected Professor Hahn lately referred to this subject, in his *Dogmatic Theology*, he should not have expressed his astonishment, would afford no favourable idea of his historical acquirements, did we not know the object he had in view. There were, doubtless, some obscure individuals, destitute of all consideration, who taught something of the like; and to these we may apply the following passage from the intellectual Pallavicini, though it is directed against a degenerate scholasticism in general:—' Si vitium aliquorum accusat, reminisci debuerat (Sarpi) in omnibus disciplinis, ac potissimum in nobilissimis, adeoque maxime arduis, tolerandos esse professorum plerosque vitiis laborantes: plurimis concedi, ut in illis ingenia exerceant, quo doctrinæ præstantia in paucis efflorescat. . . . Nulli datum reipublicæ est, ut in sua quisque arte præcellat: vel ipsa natura, quacunque solertia humana major, vitiosos partus, abortus, monstra præpedire non valet. Unicum superest remedium, ut videlicet eos artifices adhibeas, quos communis existimatio comprobat. Id usu venit scholasticæ theologiæ. Disciplinarum omnium præstantissima simulque difficillima ea est: ejus possessionem sibi multi arrogant, pauci obtinent: hoc constanter admiratur hominum consensio: alii processu temporis, qua neglecti, qua ignoti jacent, qua etiam derisi.'
—Hist. Concil. Trid. lib. vii, c. 14, p. 253.

[1] Calvin. Instit. lib. ii, c. 3, n. 6. ' Sed erunt forte, qui concedent, a bono suopte ingenio aversam, sola Dei virtute converti (voluntatem): sit tamen ut præparata suas deinde in agendo partes habeat. (Calvin here combats Peter Lombard.) ' Ego autem . . . contendo, quod et pravam nostram voluntatem corrigat Dominus, vel potius aboleat, et a seipso bonam submittat. Quatenus a gratia prævenitur, in eo ut pedissequam apelles, tibi permitto, sed quia reformata opus est domini.' Hereby Calvin appears to establish the distinction between the Catholic view and his own, in this point namely that God alone in the first place heals the will, without any

herein they again coincide with the Catholics, but oppose the Lutherans. By this power of co-operation, however, the Calvinists mean not to affirm, that it is in the power of man to receive, or to reject, the action of God. Where Divine grace knocks, the door *must* be opened; *it works quite invincibly,* and those who enter not into life are never touched by it. Here we immediately come to the doctrine of predestination.

By the side of many very shallow and sterile conceptions, there were ever agitated, in the bosom of the Catholic Church, the most manifold, profound, and speculative theories on divine predestination, and its relation to human freedom. To philosophical talent and acuteness, as well as to the imagination, a wide, and (according to the favourite turn of speculation in every age) a very enticing field is here opened, which constantly invites the hand of cultivation. The Church, however, has deemed it her duty to set certain limitations to this spirit. For God can be represented in such relations to man, as to make the latter entirely disappear; or man, again, may be conceived in such a position, *relatively* to God, as to subvert the notion of the Almighty, as the dispenser of grace. According to the first view, God appears acting with a cruel caprice, which cannot be conceived by man; according to the second, so ruled by the caprice of man, that He ceases to be who He is, and through whom all goodness *springs.* Accordingly, the Catholic Church alike rejects an over-ruling of God on the part of man, to impart sanctifying and saving grace; and an over-ruling of man on the part of God, to *compel the former to become this or that.* On the contrary, she teaches, in the former case, as is well known, that divine grace is unmerited; in the latter, that it is offered to all men, their condemnation depending on the free rejection of redeeming aid.[1]

co-operation on the part of man (how this is to come about, let him understand who can); and that next, the will (which is the natural faculty) co-operates: whereas the Catholic teaches that the human will must labour with God at its own improvement. But the difference between Calvin and Luther is this: that according to the latter, nothing of the old man is any longer fit for an active co-operation. Confess. Helvet. i, c. ix, p. 21: 'Duo observanda esse docemus; primum, regeneratos in boni electione et operatione, non tantum agere passive, sed active. Aguntur enim a Deo, ut agant ipsi, quod agant. Recte enim Augustinus adducit illud, quod Deus dicitur noster adjutor. Nequit enim adjuvari, nisi is, qui aliquid agit.'

[1] Concil. Trident. Sess. vi, c. 2. 'Hunc proposuit Deus propitiatorem per fidem in sanguine ipsius pro peccatis nostris, sed etiam pro totius mundi.' C. iii: 'Ille pro omnibus mortuus est.' Can. xvii: 'Si quis

The Lutheran formularies emancipated themselves, in this respect, from the authority of Luther ; and, in accordance with the Catholics, taught, not, indeed, as we before observed (§ XI), without detriment to the internal consistency of their system, that Christ died for all men, that he calleth all sinners to Himself, and earnestly willeth that all men should come to Him, and receive His proffered aid.[1]

It is otherwise with Calvin. He assures us, indeed, that he will move cautiously between two shoals, one consisting in the temerity of the believer, to scrutinise the unfathomable mysteries of God—the second consisting in the studious avoidance of the subject of predestination—speaking of it as a dangerous sandbank.[2] He finds, for his own part, a great practical interest in this doctrine. The sweet fruits (*suavissimus fructus*), which he discovered in the dogma of absolute predestination, and which tended to confirm him in his opinion, are thus noted by him. In the first place, men can have no firm and deep conviction of the truth, that it is only God's mercy which hath insured human salvation, unless the believer be assured, that not all are destined for happiness ; nay, that God grants to one, what He refuseth to another. In the second place, ignorance in this respect, obscures the glory of God—plucks humility up by the roots (*ipsam humilitatis radicem evellit*)— renders a sense of internal gratitude towards God impossible, and disturbs the quiet of conscience in the pious ; for the consciousness that, in respect to sins, no difference exists between

---

justificationis gratiam non nisi prædestinatis ad vitam contingere dixerit ; reliquos vero omnes, qui vocantur, vocari quidem, sed gratiam non accipere, utpote divina potestate prædestinatos ad malum ; anathema sit.' Pope Innocent X, in his constitution against Jansenius, rejected the proposition (n. v) : ' Semipelagianum est dicere, Christum pro omnibus omnino hominibus mortuum esse, aut sanguinem fudisse.'—Hardin. Concil., tom. xi, fol. 143.

[1] Solid. declar. xi, de æterna Dei prædestinat. sect. 28, p. 765. ' Si igitur æternam electionem ad salutem utiliter considerare voluerimus, firmissime et constanter illud retinendum est, quod non tantum prædicatio pœnitentiæ, verum etiam promissio Evangelii revera sit universalis, hoc est, quod ad omnes homines pertineat.' Here follow many Scripture texts. Sect. 29, p. 766 : ' Et hanc vocationem Dei, quæ per verbum Evangelii nobis offertur, non existimemus simulatam et fucatam : sed certo statuamus, Deum nobis per eam vocationem voluntatem suam revelare : quod videlicet in iis, quos ad eum modum vocat, per verbum efficax esse velit, ut illuminentur, convertantur, et salventur.' Sect. 38, p. 769 : ' Quod autem verbum Dei contemnitur, non est in causa Dei vel præscientia vel prædestinatio, sed perversa hominis voluntas.'

[2] Calvin. Instit. lib. iii. c. 21, fol. 336.

him and the reprobate, and that faith alone establishes the difference, comprises a source of the purest consolation.[1]

Calvin has left a warning example to those, who, from any subjective practical motives, think they are obliged to adopt any new or strange doctrine; an example that shows it to be the exclusive duty of the theologian to seek out with humility what the doctrine of the Church prescribes, for the promotion and excitement of religious and moral feelings; since the truth and objectivity of the Church doctrine imparts, likewise, to all the practical precepts it sanctions, the character of truth and objectivity. For the reasons above-stated—that is to say, in order to call forth a deep Christian piety, Calvin lays down the following notion of predestination: 'We call predestination that eternal decree of God, whereby He hath determined what the fate of every man should be. For not to the same destiny are all created: for, to some is allotted eternal life; to others eternal damnation. According as a man is made for one end or for the other, we call him predestined to life, or to death.'[2] The same idea the Reformer again expresses in the following way: 'We assert that, by an eternal and unchangeable decree, God hath determined whom He shall one day permit to have a share in eternal felicity, and whom He shall doom to destruction. In respect to the elect, this decree is founded in his unmerited mercy without any regard to human worthiness; but those, whom He delivers up to damnation, are, by a just and irreprehensible judgment, excluded from all access to eternal life.[3]

---

[1] Loc. cit. c. 21, sect. 2, fol. 336; c. 24, sect. 17, fol. 390: 'Nempe tutius piorum conscientiæ acquiescent, dum intelligunt, nullam esse peccatorum differentiam, modo adsit fides.' Calvin (de æterna Dei prædest. opusc. p. 883) goes still further: ' Inprimis rogatos velim lectores . . . non esse, ut quibusdam falso videtur, argutam hanc vel spinosam speculationem, quæ absque fructu ingenia fatiget: sed disputationem solidam et ad pietatis usum maxime accommodatam: nempe, quæ et fidem probe ædificet, et nos ad humilitatem erudiat, et in admirationem extollat immensæ erga nos Dei bonitatis, et ad hanc celebrandum excitet,' etc.

[2] Loc. cit. lib. iii, c. 21, n. 5, p. 337. ' Prædestinationem vocamus æternum Dei decretum, quo apud se constitutum habuit, quid de unoquoque homine fieri vellet. Non enim pari conditione creantur omnes: sed aliis vita æterna, aliis damnatio æterna præordinatur. Itaque prout inalterutrum finem quisque conditus est, ita vel ad vitam, vel ad mortem prædestinatum dicimus.'

[3] Loc. cit. n. 7, p. 339. ' Quos vero damnationi addicit, his justo quidem et irreprehensibili, sed incomprehensibili judicio vitæ aditum præcludi.' And how did Calvin treat those who opposed such a doctrine? His work

It is scarcely credible to what truly blasphemous evasions Calvin resorts, in order to impart to his doctrine an air of solidity, and to secure it against objections. As faith was considered by Calvin a gift of the Divine mercy, and yet, as he was unable to deny, that many are represented in the Gospel to be believers, in whom Christ found no earnestness, and no perseverance, and whom consequently he did not recognise to be the elect, Calvin asserts, that God intentionally produced within them an apparent faith; that He insinuated himself into the souls of the reprobate, in order to render them more inexcusable.[1] Instead of acknowledging, in the above-stated facts, the readiness of the Almighty to confer His grace on all, who only wish it, he explains them by the supposition of intentional deceit, which he lays to the charge of the Almighty! Equally strange is the reason assigned for the doctrine of predestination—that God wishes to manifest His mercy towards the elect, and His justice towards the condemned; as if the two divine qualities were severed one from the other, and were mutually ignorant of each other's existence! God will be at once just and merciful to all without exception—not just merely towards these, and merciful only towards those, as the prejudiced judges of this world are wont to be! We must also bear in mind, that the notion of justice, considered in itself, cannot even be upheld, if no fault exists; and no fault can be charged on the reprobate, if, without possessing the use of freedom, they are condemned; nay, have been condemned from all eternity! Equally baseless would be the notion of mercy, as it has necessarily for its subject sinners, who, by the free determination of their own will, and

De æterna Dei prædestinatione, is directed against Albertus Pighius, a very intellectual and learned divine; as also his treatise, *De libero arbitrio*. In the latter work Pighius is treated with sufficient decency, but in the former we read as follows: 'Albertus Pighius Campensis, homo phrenetica plane audacia præditus. . . . Paulo post librum editum, moritur Pighius. Ergo ne cani mortuo insultarem, ad alias lucubrationes me converti. . . . In Pighio nunc et Georgio Siculo, belluarum par non male comparatum,' etc.

[1] Loc. cit. lib. iii, c. 2, n. 11, p. 194. 'Etsi in fidem non illuminantur, nec Evangelii efficacium vere sentiunt, nisi qui præordinati sunt ad salutem; experientia tamen ostendit reprobos interdum simili fere sensu atque electos affici, ut ne suo quidem judicio quicquam ab electis differant. Quare nihil absurdi est, quod cœlestium donorum gustus ab Apostolo, et temporalis fides a Christo illis adscribitur; non quod vim spiritualis gratiæ solide percipiant, ac certum fidei lumen; sed quia Dominus, ut magis convictos et inexcusabiles reddat, se insinuat in eorum mentes, quatenus sine adoptionis spiritu gustari potest ejus bonitas,' p. 195: 'Commune cum illis (filiis Dei), fidei principium habere videntur, sub integumento hypocriseos.'

not by extraneous compulsion, have transgressed the divine moral law, in order then again to receive pardon ; for in this case, the whole process would be a mere absurd farce.

It was, moreover, only by the greatest efforts of Calvin and his disciples, particularly Beza, that this doctrine was enabled to pervert the sound understanding of Christians. Bern especially resisted for a long time, till the *consensus Tigurinorum* was brought about. The Gallic Confession immediately adopted this doctrine,[1] and the Belgic likewise.[2] That the Synod of Dort should sanction Calvin's doctrine of predestination, was to be expected.[3] However, other Reformed communities had, from their very origin, much softened the doctrines of Calvin. Among these we may notice the Articles of the Anglican Church,[4] while the Catechism of the Palatinate maintains silence upon the subject, and the Confession of the Marches positively declares against the decree of absolute predestination.[5]

§ XIII—OF THE CATHOLIC NOTION OF JUSTIFICATION

The want of a deeper acquaintance with the usages of antiquity, particularly of a vivid insight into the spirit of its language, gave the outward occasion at least to a confusion in the notion attached to justification in Christ Jesus, and served strongly to confirm the obstacle which existed in the interior of minds, and prevented the entire appreciation, and comprehensive understanding, of this practical and fundamental doctrine of Christianity.

The ancients are wont to put the form in which the inward essence outwardly manifests and reveals itself, for the inward

[1] Confess. Gallic. c. xii, p. 115.
[2] Confess. Belg. c. xvi, p. 189. 'Credimus, posteaquam tota Adam progenies sic in perditionem et exitium, primi hominis culpa, præcipitata fuit, Deum se talem demonstrasse, qualis est ; nimirum misericordem et justum ; —misericordem quidem, eos ab hac perditione liberando et servando, quos æterno et immutabili suo consilio, pro gratuita sua bonitate in Jesu Christo Domino nostro elegit et selegit, absque ullo operum eorum respectu : justum vero, reliquos in lapsu et perditione, in quam sese præcipitaverant, relinquendo.'
[3] Synod. Dordrac. c. i, art. vi seq., p. 303 seq.
[4] Confess. Anglic. art. xvii, p. 132.
[5] The Scotch Confession (Art. viii, p. 141) speaks a language extremely mild, such as a Catholic might employ. The Declaration of Thorn (Art. xviii, p. 423) is doubtful. Confess. March. Art. xv, p. 383. The Hungarian Confession slurs very well over the matter, p. 252.

spirit itself, because the latter, concealed in its form, is thus brought out. Hence, when in the Old Testament the justification of a man through and before God is represented in the form of a human and judicial act, and consequently of a mere outward acquittal and release, it is the grossest error, and a proof of entire ignorance of the ways of thinking, and modes of speech, among ancient nations, not to connect such impressions with the idea of an inward deliverance and discharge from evil. How much in the Protestant Church the style of the ancient world was misunderstood, we may perhaps most clearly discern from a passage in Gerhard, where he says, the whole act of justification is described only by expressions borrowed from judicial usage. For example: 'judgment,' Psalm cxliii; 'judge,' John v, 27; 'tribunal,' Rom. xiv, 10; 'accused,' Rom. iii, 19; 'accuser,' John v, 45; 'witness,' Rom. ii, 15; 'handwriting,' Col. ii, 14; 'advocate,' 1 John ii, 1; 'acquittal,' Psalm xxxii, 1, etc.[1] Even the multitude of these, and similar expressions, should have inspired a certain caution, and have encouraged the idea, that they must have in part at least a figurative signification. Rarely, even in the Catholic Church was the right view unfolded with perfect scientific exactness, and brought back by means of an accurate philology to its first principles.[2]

---

[1] Gerhard, loci. theolog. Ed. Cotta, tom. iii, p. 6.

[2] Bossuet (Exposition de la doctrine de l'Elise Cathol. c. vi) expresses himself thus briefly, according to the usual interpretation: 'Comme l'Ecriture nous explique la remission de péchés, tantot en disant que Dieu les couvre, et tantôt en disant, qu'il les ôte et qu'il les efface par la grâce du Saint Esprit, qui nous fait nouvelles créatures; nous croyons qu'il faut joindre ensemble ces expressions, pour former l'idée parfaite de la justification du pécheur.' From the want of a deeper knowledge of the Oriental languages, spring so many strange and half explanations of scriptural passages, which were adduced by the Protestants against the Catholics, and vice versa. One example may serve for many. Calvin, in his Instit. iii, 11, appealed to Rom. iv, 8, where from Psalm xxxi the following passages are taken: 'Blessed is he whose transgression is forgiven, whose sin is covered.' 'Blessed is the man, unto whom the Lord imputeth not iniquity.' Now Calvin observes: 'A complete definition of justification is either here given, or it is not: if it be complete, then justification consists merely in the forgiveness of sins, which is sufficiently explained by the words, cover and not impute.' To *justify*, means accordingly, to declare anyone free from punishment, in despite of yet existing sin. But if by the mere covering and remission of guilt and sin, the notion of justification is not completed, how can it be said that he is blessed, whose sins are covered? Bellarmine now answers (De Justificatione, l. 11, c. 9), it is said: 'Beati immaculati in via, qui ambulant in lege Domini;' and in Matthew c. v, 'Blessed are the poor in spirit,

But though the true sense of the ancients might not be explained with the clearest scientific evidence, yet it was adhered to in life. The Church being connected by her origin with the close of the ancient world, the knowledge of the old modes of speech passed to her by a living and immediate contact, although this knowledge did not rise through the medium of reflection to abstract science. If St Augustine says with reason, that the Old is but the New Testament still veiled, and the New the Old Testament unveiled, the true sense of the latter must evidently be better known to the Church than to the synagogue itself. The former imparted to the sense of the Old Testament, in the matter before us, a more appropriate form—and this is the case with all religious ideas, which the Church and the synagogue have in common—in order that the unshackled spirit may show itself purer and more transparent, and that the form may correspond to the matter. It is worthy of remark, that the Protestants conceive justification to be a thing chiefly external, and the Church to be a thing chiefly internal; so that, in either respect, they are unable to bring about a *permeation* of the inward and the outward. The one, however, determines the other; for, as they consider not justification to be internal, the Church, according to their system, could not become external. When justification is not the inmost property of man, it is then too weak to possess the power to produce a complete effect, and to throw out the invisible into the visible, and consequently to make the inward Church simultaneously and indubitably an outward one. Hence that painful oscillation between the invisible and the visible Church, because justification was not conceived to be an internal thing.

The Council of Trent describes justification to be an exaltation from the state of sinfulness to that of grace, and of adoption of the children of God; that is to say, an annihilation of the union of the will with the sinful Adam (a removal of original sin, and of every other sin committed before justification), and the con-

the meek, the merciful, the clean of heart,' etc.; and he asks, 'If the description of the just man be complete, why is no mention made of the covering, and of mere forgiveness? If it be but an incomplete description, how are those called *blessed*, who are only imperfectly just?' Then he adds: 'Potest igitur ad omnes ejusmodi quæstiones responderi, non poni in his locis integram definitionem justificationis, aut beatitudinis; sed explicari solum aliquid, quod pertinet ad justificationem aut beatitudinem acquirendam'—an excellent refutation of Calvin, without, however, being quite satisfactory in a scientific point of view.

traction of fellowship with Christ, the Holy and the Just One—
a state which is, in a negative sense, that of remission of sin,
and in a positive sense, that of sanctification.¹ The Council
further represents justification as a renewal of the inward man,
by means whereof we become really just,² as inherent (*inhærens*)
in the believer, and as a restoration of the primeval state of
humanity. On this account, the same synod observes, that,
by the act of justification, Faith, Hope, and Charity, are infused
into the heart of man; and that it is only in this way he is truly
united with Christ, and becometh a living member of his body.³
In other words, justification is considered to be sanctification
and forgiveness of sins, as the latter is involved in the former,
and the former in the latter : it is considered an infusion of
the love of God into our hearts, through the Holy Spirit; and
the interior state of the justified man is regarded as holy feeling
—as a sanctified inclination of the will—as habitual pleasure
and joy in the Divine law—as a decided and active disposition
to fulfil the same in all the occurrences of life—in short, as a
way of feeling, which is in itself acceptable and well-pleasing
to God. When God declares man to be just and well pleasing
to him, he really is so.⁴

[1] Concil. Trid. Sess. vi, c. 5. 'Quibus verbis justificationis impii descriptio insinuatur, ut sit translatio ab eo statu, in quo homo nascitur filius primi Adæ, in statum gratiæ et adoptionis filiorum Dei per secundum Adam Jesum Christum, salvatorem nostrum.'

[2] Loc. cit. c. vii. 'Quæ (justificatio) non est sola peccatorum remissio, sed et sanctificatio et renovatio interioris hominis per voluntariam susceptionem gratiæ et donorum ; unde homo ex injusto fit justus,' etc.

[3] Loc. cit. c. vii. 'Quamquam nemo possit esse justus, nisi cui merita passionis Domini nostri Jesu Christi communicantur ; id tamen in hac impii justificatione fit, dum ejusdem sanctissimæ passionis merito per Spiritum Sanctum charitas Dei diffunditur in cordibus eorum, qui justificantur, atque ipsis inhæret : unde in ipsa justificatione cum remissione peccatorum hæc omnia simul infusa accipit per Jesum Christum, cui inseritur, per fidem, spem et charitatem. Nam fides, nisi ad eam spes accedat et charitas, neque[unit perfecte cum Christo, neque corporis ejus vivum membrum efficit.'

[4] It may be useful to lay before the reader some descriptions of justification, to enable him, amid the variety of expression, to recognise the unity of idea. Thom. Aq. Prima Sec. q. cxiii. art. i et art. vi : 'Justificatio importat transmutationem de statu injustitiæ ad statum justitiæ prædictæ.' But justice he had described as 'rectitudinem quandam ordinis in ipsa interiori dispositione hominis, prout supremum hominis subditur Deo, et inferiores vires animæ subduntur supremæ, sc. rationi.' Bellarm. de justificatione, lib. ii, c. vi : ' Justificatio sine dubio motus quidam est de peccato ad justitiam, et nomen accipit a termino, ad quem ducit, ut omnes alii similes motus, illuminatio, calefactio, et cæteri : non igitur potest intelligi vera justificatio, nisi aliqua præter remmissionem peccati

The Scriptural word *grace* hath several significations; but not rarely corresponding to it is the German expression, '*gnädige, wohlwollende, huldvolle Gesinnung*'—a gracious, benevolent, condescending feeling, towards anyone: this signification is the basis of all the others; nay, it is, if we will, the only one. But if the question be as to the application of Divine grace towards men, especially sinners, then this feeling is by no means a mere quiescent one, but the condescending will becomes at once an act; is life, and engenders life; so that the grace of God, extended spiritually to the dead, calleth them back to life: the grace of God is sanctifying.

As little can it be disputed, that the words, 'justify,' 'rechtfertigen,' 'dikaioun,' 'justificare,' signify also to acquit. This signification is used when we speak of just or innocent men, who have been acquitted by their judges, of the charges brought against them; who, after inquiry instituted, have been pronounced to be what they are—guiltless. This sense, in the matter under consideration, is inadmissible, because the question is not about just and innocent men, who have been wickedly brought before the judicial tribunal, but about men really and truly guilty, and unrighteous. Here we see the real signification of the Greek word above adduced, and of the corresponding Hebrew and Latin words, namely 'to make just.' The absolving and acquitting word—the word which forgives sin—is a power truly emancipating, dissolving the bonds of evil, and extirpating sin; so that, in the room of darkness, light is admitted: death gives way before life, and despair leads to hope. Hence the forgiveness of sins for Christ's sake, is undoubtedly a remission of the guilt and the punishment, which he hath taken and borne upon himself; but it is *likewise* the transfusion of His spirit to us, so that we enter into a *full* vital communion

justitia acquiratur. Quemadmodum nec vera erit illuminatio, nec vera calefactio, si tenebris fugatis vel frigore depulso, nulla lux, nullusque calor in subjecto corpore subsequatur.' St Augustine says (de Spiritu et lit. c. 17): 'Ibi [among the Jews] lex extrinsecus posita est qua injusti terrerentur, hic [in Christianity] intrinsecus data est, qua justificarentur.' On this observes Bellarmine: 'Quo loco dicit (Augustinus), hominem justificari per legem scriptam in cordibus, quæ, ut ipse ibidem explicat, nihil est aliud, nisi charitas Dei diffusa in cordibus nostris per Spiritum Sanctum, qui datus est nobis,' lib. ii, c. vii. Bellarmine continues: 'Itaque per justitiam, qua justificamur, intelligitur fides et charitas, quæ est ipsa facultas bene operandi.' Pallavicini says (lib. viii, c. 4, p. 259), 'Consenserunt omnes [at Trent] de nominis significatione, justificationem, scilicet, esse transitum a statu inimici ad statum amici filiique Dei adoptivi.'

with the second Adam, in like manner as we had with the first.

There can be no doubt, that the transition from the life of the flesh to the life of the spirit, as above described, cannot ordinarily be sudden; that, on the contrary, the substitution of the latter for the former must be represented as the final term of many preliminary stages in the history of the internal man.[1] The act of justification, indeed, fills up only one portion of time; for the communication of a vital principle cannot be considered other than as consummated in a single moment.[2] However, the development of the same may be subjected to a succession of periods. Susceptibility for the act of Divine justification is dependent on a series of preliminary, mutually qualifying emotions, in the interior of man. From the period wherein our faculties of discernment have clung with undoubting firmness to revealed truths, the struggling soul moves on through fear and hope, through grief and intuitive love, through struggle and victory, up to that happy moment, when all its better energies, hitherto dissipated, unite under the impulse of a higher power, for obtaining a decisive conquest; when, by the full infusion of the Holy Spirit, the union with Christ is consummated, and we belong wholly to Him, and He again joyfully recognises Himself in us. In other words; in order that man may be completely adopted by God in the place of a child, or be justified, He requires on the part of man, a gradually preparatory susceptibility. Hence we may clearly see how singular is the objection urged by Protestants, that the acts preparatory to the great act of justification, indicate a Pelagian tendency in the whole Catholic system.[3] Because, according to our doctrine, so much must be endured, and wrought, so much must be consummated in the spirit, ere the one great divine act can ensue, they think we must needs believe, that, by that prelimi-

---

[1] Bellarmin. de justif. lib. i, c. 13. 'Quos enim diligit (Deus), *primum* vocat ad fidem, *tunc* spem et timorem et dilectionem inchoatam inspirat, postremo justificat, et perfectam charitatem infundit.'

[2] Dun Scotus (l. iv, Sent. dist. i, p. 8) says, justification is momentary: 'Quia non est successio in inductione alicujus formæ, nisi penes partes mobiles, vel penes partes ipsius formæ.' Compare my work, *New Investigations* (in German), second edition, p. 206.

[3] Chemnit. Exam. Concil. Trid. part 1, p. 281; Gerhard loc. tom. vii, p. 221 (loc. xvii, c. 3, sect. v). That to him who has been prepared by faith and fear, by hope and contrition, God doth (through baptism) impart the sanctifying grace, the best schoolmen term, not without reason, a *meritum de congruo*, but not a *meritum de condigno*.

nary spiritual action and suffering, the fulness of God's grace is merited. It is, however, far otherwise. The history of regeneration forms one great whole, most intimately united in all its parts, so that the third and fourth grade cannot be made, till the first and the second have been passed.

As divine grace can alone impart the power for the execution of the first step—and it is so with all the others, as, accordingly, all parts of the great whole are determined by higher aid, and consequently are a work of Divine favour—it follows, that what holds good of the parts, must hold good of the whole. Without human exertion, indeed, the first motion of our spirit cannot be made, precisely because it must move itself. It is so with the second and third motion. In other words, without human agency, God can produce in man no faith, no fear, no germ of love, no hope, no repentance, and, therefore, not the real justification determined by them. But does it follow, that because the Catholic believes this, he must also believe, that God communicates, *on this account*, his further manifestations of grace because man had not refused his co-operation to the earlier ones? The notion of a necessary preliminary condition to a thing, is here confounded with the cause of that thing itself.

In order, however, to complete the Catholic theory of justification, we must, according to the Council of Trent, subjoin two observations. In the first place, the Catholic Church does not dispute, that even in the justified man, notwithstanding that original sin, together with all actual sin, has been forgiven him, and has been obliterated from his soul, there still subsists a perverse sensuality (*concupiscentia*). Yet it is taught that this *in itself* is no sin, and that, if it occurs in Holy Writ under this denomination, it is only because it appears as a consequence of sin, and leads again to real sin, when the will hearkens to its suggestions. The Council saith: 'God hateth nought in the regenerated, because nothing is damnable in those who have been truly buried with Christ in baptism, who walk not according to the flesh, but, putting off the old man, put on the new, created after God, and are become innocent, immaculate, pure, and pleasing unto God, heirs indeed of God, and co-heirs with Christ, so that nothing hindereth their entrance into heaven. That, however, concupiscence, or the stimulus to sin, remains in the baptised, the holy Council avows and acknowledges; but as this stimulus is left for our trial, it is unable to injure those who will not consent, but who resist victoriously by the grace of Christ: for he is not crowned except he strive lawfully.'[1]

As the Catholic Church deduces original sin, and with it all evil in the world, in the last degree, from the abuse of free-will, it cannot find any further traces of sin in man, so soon as his spirit has been averted from the creature, and hath turned to God; so soon as his will hath been again healed, and his inmost feelings been sanctified. By the inborn evil, and by that habit of sin which hath grown out of it, and hath become more or less inveterate, more or less confirmed, a mechanical readiness to incline towards sin hath been engendered in the body and the inferior faculties of the soul. The new bent of the will, therefore, cannot immediately draw into its orbit the movements of the soul and the body. But since, to those regenerated in spirit, such emotions are alien, and even an abomination; since the spirit and the flesh are completely severed one from the other; since they are involved in a decisive, and, for the former, a victorious struggle; so most certainly a carnal emotion in conflict with the will, yet mastered by it, cannot contaminate it, and therefore not convict it of sin. If the will give not in to the desires of the flesh, or the desires of the flesh reach not the will; if, accordingly, there be no consent, then there is no sin.[2] Thus evil, and (in the strict sense of the word) the sinfulness in concupiscence, is removed, as it is driven back from the inward to the outward man, in whom it survives as the consequence and the chastisement of sin, and withal as a temptation, which may conduce either to the more exalted glorification of the soul, or to its relapse into the deepest fall. In the former case, it summons us to struggle and to victory, and to the conformation and expansion of virtue; in the latter, it can easily surprise the inattentive, and draw him into his toils, or penetrate into his inmost soul.

---

[1] Loc. cit. Sess. v, decret. de peccato originali.

[2] Bellarmin. de amiss. grat. et statu peccati, lib. v, c. 5, tom. iv, p. 278. 'Tota controversia est, utrum corruptio naturæ ac præsertim concupiscentia per se et ex natura sua, qualis etiam in baptizatis ac justificatis est, sit proprie peccatum originis. Id enim adversarii contendunt, catholici autem negant; quippe qui sanata voluntate per gratiam justificantem docent reliquos morbos non solum non constituere homines reos, sed neque posse constituere, cum non habeant veram peccati rationem. Addit Thomas Aquinas in sola aversione mentis a Deo consistere proprie et formaliter peccatum originis, in rebellione autem partis inferioris, qui fuit effectus rebellionis mentis a Deo, non consistere peccatum, nisi materialiter.'

But that gap which, in consequence of regeneration, is established between the interior, now sanctified, man, and the outward man, is by no means a fixed, immutable separation. On the contrary, in the believer, faithfully co-operating with sanctifying grace, it is in a state of constant decrease, and gradual declension ; for the continued exercise of virtue, and the ever more and more powerful development of the divine principle of life thereby occasioned, restore the harmony of all the parts of man in his new course, with a constant, though not always perceptible, increase (although, without the extraordinary interposition of a higher power, that harmony in this life is never perfect) ;[1] so that man's inferior faculties learn to move in progressive unison with the sanctified spirit, and have a share in its glorification, as they had before moved in accord with the unholy spirit, and participated in its dissonance. However, the regenerated man looks anxiously for deliverance from the body, not in order to be then only freed from any sinful inclination of the will, but to be delivered from trial, and the fear of trial.

The second observation which we have to make, is, that, according to the doctrine of the Catholic Church, the just man can never hold himself quite free from the so-called venial sins, and transgresses in divers ways, and therefore it is not without reason that he daily, in the Lord's prayer, prays for forgiveness of sins. As the will of the regenerated, however, is not thereby alienated from God, and His holy law which he loves ; and as such transgressions proceed more from the infirmity of the new man, than from any remnant of perverseness in the will, sins of this nature occasion no interruption in the newly established

[1] The Council of Vienna (in the lib. v, Clement, tit. de hæret) has pronounced against the Beguards what Pope Innocent XI repeated against Michael Molinos. He condemned in his bull, the following propositions: ' No. 55. Per hanc viam internam pervenitur ad purgandas et distinguendas omnes animæ passiones, ita quod nihil amplius sentitur, nihil, nihil. No. 56. Duæ leges et duæ cupiditates, anima una, et amoris proprii altera, tamdiu perdurant, quamdiu perdurat amor proprius, unde quando purgatus est et mortuus, ut fit per viam internam, non adsunt amplius duæ illæ leges, nec aliquid sentitur amplius.' A doctrine of this kind is ever connected with the other, that at this grade of the spiritual life a fall is no longer possible. Hence the following propositions of the Quietists are rejected :—' No. 61. Anima, quum ad mortem mysticam pervenit *non potest* amplius velle aliud, quam quod Deus vult, quia non habet amplius voluntatem, et Deus eam illi abstulit.' No 63. ' Per viam internam pervenitur ad statum continuum immobilem in pace imperturbabili.' Compare my work, *New Investigations* (in German), second edition, p. 211.

relations with God; and internal justification, therefore, according to Bossuet's expression, appears not untrue, though it be not perfect. But this infirmity requires us in every instance to observe constant self-watchfulness, and to practise uninterrupted prayer for obtaining Divine grace, and increase of sanctification.[1]

§ XIV—DOCTRINE OF THE PROTESTANTS ON JUSTIFICATION AND SANCTIFICATION

The notion which the Protestants form of justification, is thus briefly defined in the Formulary of Concord: 'The word "justification" signifies, the declaring anyone just, the acquitting him of sins, and the eternal chastisements of sin, on account of the justice of Christ, which is by God imputed to faith;'[2] and it expressly says, our justice is *not of us*.[3] With these declarations Calvin perfectly coincides.[4] Justification, in the Protestant sense, is a judicial act of God, whereby the believing sinner is delivered from the punishments of sin, but not from sin itself; while Catholics teach that, on one hand, the remission of sin, the debt as well as the penalty, and on the other hand, positive sanctification, follows in a like way, through the divine act of justification. The great difference between the confessions consists, accordingly, in this—that, according to the Catholic doctrine the justice of Christ, in the act of justification, is immediately appropriated by the believer, becoming part of his inward self, and changing his whole moral existence; while, according to the Protestant system, justice remains in Christ,

[1] Concil. Trid. Sess. vi, can. 11. 'Si quis hominem semel justificatum dixerit amplius peccare non posse, neque gratiam amittere, atque ideo eum, qui labitur et peccat, nunquam vere fuisse justificatum, *aut contra*, posse in totam vitam peccata omnia, etiam venialia vitare nisi ex speciali Dei privilegio . . . anathema sit.'
[2] Solid, declar. iii, de fid. justif. sect. 11, p. 655. 'Vocabulum justificationis in hoc negotio significat, justum pronuntiare, a peccatis et æternis peccatorum suppliciis absolvere propter justitiam Christi, quæ a Deo fidei imputatur.'
[3] Loc. cit. sect. 48, p. 664. 'Cum igitur in ecclesiis nostris apud theologos Augustanæ Confessionis extra controversiam positum sit, totam justitiam nostram extra nos esse . . . quærendam, eamque in solo Domino nostro Jesu Christo consistere,' etc.
[4] Calvin. Instit. lib. iii, c. 11, sect. 2, fol. 260. 'Ita nos justificationem simpliciter interpretamur acceptionem, qua nos Deus in receptos pro justis habet. Eam in peccatorum remissione ac justitæ Christi imputatione positam esse dicimus.' Sect, 3: 'Ut pro justis in Christo censeamur, qui in nobis non sumus.'

passes not into the inward life of the believer and remains in a purely outward relation to him; covering his injustice, not only past, but still outstanding, since by justification the will is not healed. We therefore may say—according to Catholic principles, Christ, by justification, stamps inwardly and outwardly his living impress on the believer; so that the latter, though a feeble and imperfect, becometh yet a real, copy of the type. On the other hand, according to the Protestant doctrine, Christ casts on the believer his shadow only, under which his continued sinfulness is merely not observed by God. Hence the explicit remark of the Formulary of Concord, that the faithful, on account of the obedience of Christ, are looked upon as just, although by virtue of corrupt nature they be truly sinners, and remain such even unto death.[1]

These avowals prove of themselves, that the Protestants have adopted those notions of grace and justification, which we pointed out above (§ XIII), as one-sided and erroneous. But the opposition between the Confessions, in this matter, derives a stronger illustration from considering the following points, which show the wide practical consequences of this opposition. Concupiscence, which, as Catholics avow, still remains after justification, the mere incitement to sin, is represented by Protestants as sin in itself, and indeed as the yet subsisting original sin; while the distinction between the mere feeling of that incitement to sin and the consent to the same, is rejected by them as unessential, nay, as untrue. It is precisely on this ground they rest the assertion, that justification consists in the mere declaration of the remission of sin, not in the purification from sin itself, because original sin still subsists, and adheres even to the will. In like manner it is asserted, that between venial and mortal sin there is no internal and essential difference; for (so the Protestants teach) all sins, in themselves, whatever be their nature, accuse man in a like degree before the tribunal of God: all merit (eternal) death. Faith in the merits of Christ, according to them, constitutes the only decisive distinction between sinners in the eyes of God. When man believes, and so long as he believes, *all* his sins can be pardoned; for, in reality, unbelief is the only sin.

---

[1] Solid. declar. iii, de fid. justif. sect. 15, p. 657. 'Per fidem propter obedientiam Christi justi pronunciantur et reputantur, etiamsi ratione corruptæ naturæ suæ adhuc sint, maneantque peccatores, dum mortale hoc corpus circumferunt.'

These most astounding maxims involve in themselves the following consequences. If the justified man, *considered in himself*, be as much a sinner and as damnable as the unjust man, then no internal and essential difference, *as to moral being*, is recognised between the converted and the unconverted; the scriptural antitheses of the old and the new man, of the old and the new life, of the new creation of the first birth, and of regeneration, lose not only their point, but in a great degree, their *moral signification* (§ XXIX); the notion of penance whereby the transition from the one state to the other is brought about must be conceived in a one-sided, nay, totally mistaken sense (§ XXXIII); and the impressive language of Holy Writ, respecting the deliverance from sin wrought through Christ, and the mortification (eradication) of sin in believers (Rom. vi, viii, 1-4) is then nothing more than unmeaning bombast, nay, the occasion of the most deplorable and ridiculous self-delusion. But the ulterior consequences of the doctrine, that, in those who believe in the merits of Christ, all distinction between venial and mortal sins is effaced, will in a subsequent part of this work (§ XVI) be made fully manifest. Here we shall cite some passages that will show to what subversion of morality a system leads, that will make no essential distinction between the feeling of the incitement to sin, and the wilful consent to the same. As the former, as long as we live, is unavoidable, so the latter is represented to be simultaneous with it; and from this point of view of moral worthiness, the deed is made to be not more punishable than the most involuntary sensual enticement to the same. Thus Melancthon appeals to the testimony of every Christian conscience, which saith to each one, that even the Christian has nothing less in his power, than his own heart, whose *entire* emotions are unclean.[1] Hence the same Melancthon proposes to Catholics the question: Do not the saints seek their own interest? and he is really of opinion, that the saint, the man truly justified before God, remains *necessarily* enslaved to vain-glory, to avarice, and the like.[2]

---

[1] Melancth. loc. theolog. p. 18. 'Christianus agnoscet, nihil minus in potestate sua esse, quam cor suum,' etc. Melancthon uses the word 'cor,' instead of 'voluntas,' because, according to him, man has really no will, but merely impulses and desires.

[2] Loc. cit. p. 138. 'Annon sua etiam quærunt sancti? Annon in sanctis amor est vitæ, gloriæ, securitatis, tranquillitatis, rerum?' Let the reader observe the singular identification of 'amor gloriæ' and 'securitatis, tranquillitatis,' as if the latter were in itself as much as the

Luther speaks of wicked lust, avarice, anger, immodesty, adding a significant et cetera, which are all to be found in the just man.[1] Calvin, too, makes us acquainted with saints of this sort.[2] A singular saint, forsooth, who seeks his own interest, and not Christ's glory! Equally strange is the combination of ideas, when we are required to conceive an immodest or avaricious saint; for, according to the laws of logic, the predicate destroys the subject. Yet, what is the meaning of the words, when men speak of the covetousness, the avarice, the choler, and immodesty, of saints? Do they mean thereby a stimulus inserted in the flesh, which incites them indeed to works of the flesh, but at last wearies itself out in unsuccessful efforts? Then we cannot understand how such idle, unsuccessful temptations can be denominated covetousness, avarice, choler, and immodesty. But if we imagine this stimulus to be victorious over the will, or its impulse to be consummated into an outward act, how can the conquered be called saints and just ones? (Rom. viii, 1-9, 13.) Such a confusion of language hath its ground in the confusion of essentially different ideas; and we must marvel much, when the identifying of what is most distinct, nay, most opposite in notion and in language, fails to produce in life also a corresponding identification.

Having spoken thus far of the Protestant system of justification, it remains for us to notice their view of sanctification; for it would be in the highest degree unjust, if we did not show, that, according to the Lutheran system, the renovation of sinful man, the moral change—in a word, sanctification—must attach to the confiding reception of the declaration of the forgiveness of sin. Man, conscious of so gracious, so unmerited a remission of sin, must, in thankful return for so great a benefit, earnestly strive to improve, and to observe with ever greater fidelity, the commandments of God. In the justified man, according to the same system, original sin by the communication of the Holy Spirit is weakened, though not extirpated; and, in

---

former, which, a few lines lower, is further explained by the word *kenodoxia*. But when Melancthon says, the Parisienses (the doctors of Sorbonne, as representatives of Catholic theology) did not look to the *affectus internos*, but directed their view to mere outward observances, so for this assertion he may answer at the tribunal of God.

[1] Commentary on the Epistle to the Galatians. Wittenburg, 1556. Part I, p. 202 b.

[2] Calvin. Instit. lib. iii, c. 3, sect. 10, fol. 213. Yet his language is much milder.

proportion as it is weakened, sanctification increases. Calvin, approximating to the Catholic view, goes even so far as to confess, that, as Christ cannot be divided, man in communion with Him must partake at once of justification and sanctification. Thus, whosoever is received by God into His grace, possesses thereby the spirit of the Sonship, through whose power the transformation into the likeness of God ensues.[1] Pleasing as it is to witness this improvement in doctrine, and closely as it is connected with Calvin's representation of original sin, and his description of the process of regeneration; yet an essential difference will ever be found between the two systems, Catholic and Protestant, including, under the latter, the Calvinistic view. For since a mere weakening, not an extirpation, of original sin is admitted, no essential *moral* difference, but a mere *gradual* one, can then be maintained between the old and the new man: but this is as much opposed to the doctrine of the Catholic Church, as it is to the dignity of Christianity, to the notion of a new principle of life communicated by it, which in consequence supersedes the old one, and to the most explicit declarations of Scripture. If the influence of Christ over man were merely confined to this, that the latter was a somewhat morally better, not quite a morally different, man from the heathen, then in a strict sense, it were impossible to speak of sanctification; for both the Heathen and the Christian would, in their inward life, be like, and differ only in their degree of discipline. The Catholic Church, above all things, insists on a radical internal change. Moreover, the difference consists in this, that with the Protestant the external relation to Christ is by far the most important thing; so that at this point of his spiritual life he can calmly sit down, and, without advancing a step further, be assured of eternal felicity; since, by what the Reformers call justification, his sins have been once forgiven, and, at the same time, the gates of heaven opened to him;[2] while the Catholic

[1] Calvin. Instit. lib. iii, c. 11, sect. 6. Compare Calvin. Antidot. in Concil. Trid. opusc. p. 702. ' Neque tamen interea negandum est qua ratione (juxta quorumdam opinionem) per solam quidem fidem coram Deo justificatur; sed tamen ita, ut absque operibus salutem æternam consequi impossibile sit.' Thus, with justification without works, salvation without works is promised.

[2] Calvin (Instit. lib. iii, c. 11, sect. 15) first attacks Peter Lombard, whose doctrine he thus states: ' Primum, inquit, mors Christi nos justificat, dum per eam excitetur charitas in cordibus nostris, qua justi efficimur: deinde quod per eamdem extinctum est peccatum.' He then turns against Augustine: ' Ac ne Augustini quidem sententia recipienda est. Tametsi

can obtain the forgiveness of his sins only when he abandons them, and in this view the justified man—the man acceptable to God—is identical in every respect with the sanctified. Even with Calvin, forgiveness of sins is *quite abstractedly* the only ground for hope of salvation; and if he at length has penetration to perceive, that justification and sanctification cannot be separated in the interior life, he yet divides them in his theory, and deduces from one and the same thing different effects; since he says, that it is only by the declaration of God remitting sins, that righteousness is acquired, and not by any sanctifying power, which, together with the consciousness of such a remission, has been imparted. Hence it follows, that even a minimum of real improvement—without which, according to Calvin, the certainty of being favoured with grace cannot take place—would entirely suffice for salvation.

To this statement of doctrines it will be well to subjoin some remarks, directed towards a deeper scientific appreciation of the Lutheran system. The point to which we would here particularly direct attention, is the fact how well the doctrine of original sin couples with that of justification; how well the one prepares the way for the other! The former was so deeply engraven in the essence of man, that the latter cannot extend beyond his surface. If original sin had been represented as so destructive to man, in order thereby to exalt the power of Christianity, so that it could be said, ' Behold, though original sin had sunk so deep into the inmost core of human existence, yet Christianity sinks still more deeply; it penetrates into the lowest depths of the soul, and works healingly, and creates anew; if the power of the evil principle be great, that of the good principle is still greater;' then this mistaken view of original sin ought to have been entirely excused as a theoretical error. But now it is taught, its ravages are so frightful, that they remain in the will even of the regenerated; the disease under which we labour is so malignant, that we cannot be radically cured of it; and, as we cannot, so we need not be. Hence Christ, our righteousness, is out of us: the unrighteousness in the old Adam is within us; the righteousness in the new Adam out of us.

enim egregie hominem omni justitiæ laude spoliat ... gratiam tamen ad justificationem refert, qua in vitæ novitatem per spiritum regeneramur.' Hereupon he says: ' Scriptura autem, cum de fidei justitia loquitur, longe alio nos ducit.' At last he concludes (sect. 21): ' Ut talis justitia uno verbo appellari queat peccatorum remissio.'

Moreover, the essence of original sin, according to Luther's expression, recurs very evidently here. If Catholics teach that it is only in the case where the solicitation to sin, proceeding from the flesh, is with full consciousness entertained and consented to by the will, that the real character of sin appears; so the Lutherans and Calvinists, with unexampled obstinacy, assert, that that solicitation, even when repelled with decided resistance, is in itself sinful. Let us weigh this doctrine well, and inquire, whether evil be not then considered as something existing apart, independent of the will, and extraneous to it, and be not regarded as an essence? What else can be meant, when it is said, something evil in itself remains in man, and is yet evil, even when the will resists and overcomes it? Here the sinfulness certainly lies no longer in a perverted bent of the will, because the will, in this instance, cannot be perverted; and yet sin, that is to say, original sin, is still in man. This is strikingly corroborated by the assertion, that we can be then only liberated from sin, when we have put off our dear '*corpusculum*'[1] This assuredly is to conceive sin as something very substantial!

And yet it is uncommonly difficult to conceive how Luther should have regarded sin as really something, which, in the strict sense of the word, was an evil essence. Perhaps the following considerations may enable us to understand Luther better than he understood himself. Two facts above all are very remarkable. In the first place, it is asserted of God, that He conceals from His eye the sins of believers, or regards these as just, though they be not so. Now, it is very difficult to imagine, how God can view anything other than it is in itself; or how a really unjust man can be accepted as just by an omniscient Deity. If we would do justice to Divine omniscience, no alternative remains but to suppose, that what is looked upon by man as sin, is really none in the eyes of God, and is a mere consequence of human finiteness; and in this way we can comprehend the security, which is felt in the faith in a mere outward justification. That something of this sort lies concealed in the background of the minds of those who adopt this view of justification, is strongly confirmed by the second fact, to which we must now draw attention. The act of justification,

---

[1] Solid. Declar. de fid. justif. sect. 7, p. 686. 'Dum hoc mortale corpusculum circumferent, vetus Adam in ipsa natura omnibus illius interioribus et exterioribus viribus inhæret.'

and the whole work of regeneration, are represented as the doing of God alone.[1] Now, it must afford ample matter for astonishment, that God, who is here the exclusive agent, should not entirely pervade His own work, and extirpate the very roots of sin, and exert His unshackled might in all its splendour. Man, whose conduct is entirely passive during this process of justification, could yet be entirely transformed. Wherefore does not this change occur ? We are compelled to recur to the same thought which we expressed above, though in a somewhat altered form ; to wit—that sin is an essential condition in the original constitution of man, and, being thus necessary, is therefore not imputed to us by God. For the observation of Calvin—who seems to have felt the revolting nature of the theory, that God is the exclusive agent—the observation of Calvin, that this defective influence was grounded in the motive of God, to be able to summon before His tribunal men at every moment of their lives, cannot seriously satisfy anyone.[2] Calvin should have called to his aid his absolute necessity of all occurrences, as an explanation ready at hand. This necessity of sinning, in the present stage of human existence, is, then, the true ground of this theory, and of the possibility of that profound tranquillity in a state of continued sinfulness—though such never entered into the minds of the Reformers. At least no other speculative notion of the Protestant account of original sin, considered in connection with the doctrine of justification, can be established.

Luther, accordingly, did not express himself well, when he said, *original sin is a part of man's essence;* he should have said, *sin cleaves necessarily to the essence of man.* Thus did the dogmatic decisions of Luther and Calvin against human freedom meet the vengeance due to them : and though they had so much enlarged on the magnitude of sin, yet, in consequence of the relation to man, wherein they placed the Deity, they were at

---

[1] Solid. Declar. ii. de lib. arbit. sect. 44, p. 645. 'Tantum boni, et tamdiu bonum operatur, quantum et quamdiu a Spiritu Dei impellitur.' Far other is the belief of the Catholic, who knows that the divine spirit ever urges man on, but that man will often not let himself be so urged, and, by his own fault, will not correspond to the divine impulse.

[2] Calvin. Instit. lib. iii, c. ii, sect. 11, fol. 169. 'Nam hoc secundum (Reformationem in vitæ novitatem) sic inchoat Deus in electis suis, totoque vitæ curriculo paullatim, et interdum lente in eo progreditur, ut semper obnoxii sint ad ejus tribunal mortis judicio.' Here progress in good is made to depend on God alone, and the cause of retrogression in the path of virtue deliberately referred to the Deity.

last compelled, in despite of themselves, to deny the very existence of sin. What they taught as to the origin of evil, manifests itself again in this matter; and, even in the Lutheran system, the consequences of that doctrine remained, though the doctrine itself the Lutherans rejected. It is far otherwise, as we have above said, in the Catholic Church. Because she clings so firmly, and with such a bleeding heart, to the truth, that it is only in freedom that the ultimate cause of sin is to be sought for—for this very reason, she can, she must, likewise maintain a real redemption from sin.

ON JUSTIFYING FAITH

§ XV—CATHOLIC VIEW OF THIS SUBJECT

The doctrine of justifying faith experienced the same fate as all the other fundamental doctrines of Christianity. For fifteen hundred years, Christians had lived in and by that faith, had formed many intellectual conceptions upon it, and had laid down the same in numerous writings, but had withal felt much deeper things than could be comprehended in notions or defined by words. Yet, in default of an erroneous view of that faith decisively put forth, and asserted by many, men were as far from arriving at a truly sifting point, and at the highest degree of evidence upon the matter, as, before Arius, upon the doctrine of Christ's divinity, and before Pelagius, upon that of Grace. Hence it happened, that, in the same way as in the above-named articles of faith, much that was obscure, much that was self-contradictory, was found among Christian writers before the Nicene Council and the African and Gallic Synods, so it proved in the various expositions of justifying faith, prior to the general Council of Trent; and it became the great and earnest, as well as astonishing task of its assembled Fathers, to define the pure truth, and separate it from the dross of error.[1] As Arius and Pelagius, men widely different in character from Luther, and far his inferiors, did not draw their opinions from their own fancy, but only embraced with warmth, and developed to the fullest extent, obscure conceptions here and there current: so Luther

[1] Pallavic. Hist. Conc. Trid. lib. viii, c. 4, n. 18, p. 262. ' Ingens omnes incesserat cura explicandi effatum apostoli, hominem justificari per fidem.'

merely adhered to some opinions that had previously been started, as we learn from that celebrated Confession delivered by him before the breaking out of the Reformation. In opposition to his teaching, the Church exalted now to the highest degree of certainty, what, from her origin, had been taught perpetually, and universally, established this in the form of a dogma, and separated it from mere individual opinions.

Some of the theologians assembled at Trent applied themselves, especially, to determine the nature of the opposition which St Paul establishes between non-justifying works and justifying faith. The bishops of Agatha and Lanciano showed, at great length, that Paul merely disputes the justifying power of those works, which precede faith, and accordingly, spring not out of it.[1] In conformity with this opinion, the bishop Cornelius Musses observed, that the apostle denies merely the value of the exterior part of the works; for instance, Abraham was not acceptable to God, merely because he offered up his son in sacrifice, or performed other like actions, but he became so by the inward exercise of faith and other virtues, connected with a sanctified course of will proceeding from faith, and manifesting itself actively in good works.[2] Very rightly was it said that Paul had not in view the works of a man sanctified in Christ, and excluded these from consideration, when he denied to works, in opposition to faith, the power of rendering us acceptable to God. In other words—they observed, that Paul opposed to the old, unsatisfactory, legal order of things, the new way of salvation pointed out by God, and attributed only to the living adherence to the same (*pistis*), the power of making us pleasing unto the Deity.

These definitions were, however, of a more negative kind; the following are more positive in their nature. That faith in Christ justifies, observes another theologian, signifies as much, as that faith is the necessary root, from which all spiritual actions, agreeable to God, spring forth; so that consummate righteousness is not conferred by faith, immediately and in itself, but only in its ulterior development. And Claudius Jajus added, with as much brevity as truth—through faith is the grace given to us, not to be absolutely acceptable to God, but to enable us to become so; and this observation Bertonus illustrated, by remarking that Paul did not say, that man is

---

[1] Pallavic. loc. cit. n. 13, p. 261.
[2] Pallavic. loc. cit. n. 14, p. 261.

justified *by* faith, but *through* faith; for our righteousness is not faith itself, but in the latter is the power given to us to acquire the same (John i, 12).[1] An expression of Bernard Diaz is also worthy of mention. This theologian observed, that the justifying power is on this account ascribed to faith—because it raises us from our native lowliness (our earthward views), and consists in certain movements, which transport us to a grade of spiritual life, exalted above natural existence; so that we may be considered by God as having entered on the way to acquire His approval (by attachment to Christ).[2]

All these definitions express only in various ways one and the same thing, which the Council of Trent approves, when it says: 'Faith is the beginning of all salvation—the basis and the root of justification; for, without it, it is impossible to please God, and to attain to His adoption.'[3] Thus is faith *the beginning* of salvation; but yet not a beginning which, during this period of life, can be again abandoned, after important progress hath been made; for it is likewise the permanent *ground-work*, whereon the whole structure of salvation is erected: yet it is not a mere substratum, standing in no immediate organic connection with the superincumbent parts; for it is the *root* of justification. To its power and activity is attributed the justifying grace, the new vital principle, transforming man from an enemy into a friend of God; divine love, in a word (*fides impetrat justificationem*, say the schoolmen), although faith does not merit even this grace. A real definition of faith, however, the Council of Trent has not given: such a one is found in the Roman catechism, when it says: 'The word "faith" signifies not so much the act of thinking, or opining, but it

---

[1] Pallavic. n. 3, p. 260.

[2] Loc. cit. n. 16, p. 262. 'Ideo dici hominem per fidem justificari, quod hæc ex humilitate nativa nos attollit, motusque quosdam super conditionem naturæ nobis imprimit, efficitque ut a Deo respiciamur ceu iter justitiæ jam ingressi.'

[3] Concil. Trid. Sess. vi, c. viii. *Quomodo intelligitur, impium per fidem et gratis justificari.* Cum vero apostolus dicit, justificari hominem per fidem, et gratis; ea verba in eo sensu intelligenda sunt, quem perpetuus ecclesiæ Catholicæ consensus tenuit, et expressit; ut scilicet per fidem ideo justificari dicamur, quia fides est humanæ salutis initium, fundamentum et radix omnis justificationis: sine qua impossibile est placere Deo, et ad filiorum ejus consortium pervenire: gratis autem justificari ideo dicamur, quia nihil eorum, quæ justificationem præcedunt, sive fides, sive opera, ipsam justificationis gratiam promereretur. Si enim gratia est, jam non ex operibus: alioquin, ut idem apostolus inquit, gratia non est gratia.'

has the sense of a firm obligation (contracted in virtue of a free act of submission), whereby the mind decisively and permanently assents to the mysteries revealed by God.'[1] Catholics consider faith as the reunion with God in Christ, especially by means of the faculties of knowledge, illuminated and confirmed by grace, with which the excitement of various feelings is more or less connected. It is in their estimation, a divine light, whereby man discerns, as well as recognises, the decrees of God, and comprehends not only what God is to man, but also what man should be to God.

As justification now, in the Catholic sense, consists in a total change of the whole inward man, we can understand why the Catholic Church should so urgently insist, that faith alone doth not justify before God; that it is rather only the first subjective, indispensable condition to be justified; the root from which God's approval must spring; the first title whereon we can establish our claim of divine filiation. But if faith passes from the understanding, and the feelings, excited through the understanding, to the will; if it pervades, vivifies, and fructifies the will, through the new vital principle imparted to the latter, and engenders, in this way, the new man created after God; or (to make use of the expression of Seripandus at the Council of Trent),[2] if love is enkindled out of faith, as fire out of brimstone, then, only after faith and love doth regeneration or justification ensue.

Hence, the schools of the middle-age recognised, likewise, a faith, whereof they said, that it alone justified; it is known by the designation of the *fides formata*, under which the schoolmen understood a faith, that had love in itself as its vivifying, its plastic principle (*forma*); and on this account it was called *fides charitate formata, animata, fides viva, vivida*. This is that higher faith, which brings man into real, vital communion with Christ, fills him with an infinite devotion to God, with the strongest confidence in Him, with the deepest humility and

---

[1] Catechism. Conc. Trid. p. 17. 'Igitur credendi vox hoc loco putare, existimare, opinari, non significat, sed ut docent sacræ literæ, certissimæ assensionis vim habet, qua mens Deo sua mysteria aperienti firme constanterque assentitur. . . . Deus enim, qui dixit, de tenebris lumen splendescere, ipse illuxit in cordibus nostris, ut non sit nobis opertum Evangelium, sicut iis, qui pereunt.'

[2] Pallav. Hist. Concil. Trid. lib. viii, c. 9, n. 6, p. 270. 'Quemadmodum a sulphure ignis emicat, ita per eam (*fidem*), in nobis charitatem extemplo succendi. Quæ præceptorum observationem et salutem secum trahit.'

inmost love towards Him; liberates him from sin, and causes all creatures to be viewed and loved in God.

We shall take the liberty of quoting some passages, extolling this faith, from writings composed prior, as well as subsequent, to the Reformation. Thomas Aquinas, in answer to the question, whether we were delivered from sin through the sufferings of Christ, says: 'Through faith we appropriate to ourselves the sufferings of Christ, so that we become partakers of the fruits of the same. (Romans iii, 25.) But the faith through which we are cleansed from sin, is not the unliving faith (*fides informis*), which can co-exist with sin, but the faith living through love (*fides formata*); so that the sufferings of Christ, not only by means of the understanding, but by means of feeling, become appropriated by us. In this way are sins forgiven us through the power of Christ's passion.'[1]

Cardinal Nicholas of Cusa, in one of his most intellectual writings—that on religious peace, wherein he lays down principles for the union of all religions in one, observes: 'Faith alone justifies;' but then he adds, 'it must be full-formed faith (*fides formata*), for without works it is dead.'[2] More fully he explains his meaning, in one of his exhortations, to the following effect:[3] 'It is love, the vivifying principle (*amor, qui est forma*),

[1] Thom. Aquin. Summa. tot. theol. p. iii, quæst. xliv, art. i, edit. Thomæ a Vio. Lugd. 1580, vol. iii, p. 233. 'Fides autem, per quam a peccato mundatur, non est fides informis, quæ potest esse etiam cum peccato, sed est fides formata per charitatem, ut sic passio Christi nobis applicetur, non solum quantum ad intellectum, sed etiam quantum ad affectum. Et per hunc etiam modum peccata dimittuntur ex virtute passionis Christi.' Cf. q. cxiii, art. iv. 'Motus fidei non est perfectus, nisi sit charitate informatus, unde simul in justificatione impii cum motu fidei est etiam motus charitatis; movetur autem liberum arbitrium in Deum ad hoc, quod ei se subjiciat, unde et concurrit actus timoris filialis et actus humilitatis,' etc.

[2] Nicol. Cusan. de pace fidei Dial. op. edit. Basil. p. 876. 'Vis igitur, Deum in Christo nobis benedictionem repromisisse vitæ æternæ?—Sic volo. Quapropter oportet credere Deo prout Abraham credidit, ut sic credens justificetur cum fideli Abraham, ad assequendam repromissionem in uno semine Abrahæ Christo Jesu, quæ repromissio est divina benedictio, omne bonum in se complicans.—Vis igitur, quod sola fides illa justificet ad perceptionem æternæ vitæ? . . . . Oportet autem, quod fides sit formata, nam sine operibus est mortua.'

[3] Nicol. Cusan. Excitat. lib. iv, opp. edit. Bas. 1565, p. 461. Confer. Pet. Lombard, lib. iii, dist. 23, c. 1, edit. 1516, p. 136. 'Credere Deum est credendo amare, credendo in eum ire, credendo ei adhærere, et ejus membris incorporari; per hanc fidem justificatur impius, ut deinde ipsa fides incipiat per dilectionem operari; fides ergo, quam da mones et falsi Christiani habent, qualitas mentis est, sed informis; quia sine charitate est.'

which consummates faith and confidence ; which seizes, upholds, and transforms the soul. From Christ the redemption was desired, and he answered. Faith and confidence secure what is loved and wished for. For nothing is anxiously desired, save what we love ; if thus the Redeemer be loved, he then redeems : love consequently redeems, for it is the love of the Redeemer. In love, accordingly, is the beloved object ; hence, too, the beloved Redeemer is in love. For God is love ; and he who abideth in love, abideth in God, and God in him. It is the consummate faith, or the consummate confidence, which we call the faith vivified by love (*fides charitate formata*), whereof the Saviour saith, that it maketh us well-pleasing unto God. Thus he who knoweth Christ, and doth not approach him ; or he who goeth towards him, but doth not enter into fellowship with him ; or he who goeth towards him, and entereth into some fellowship with him, but doth not embrace him, and knit the ties of the closest fellowship with him, hath no part in redemption !'

To the words of this theologian, we shall subjoin a passage from Bellarmine, who flourished nearly about the same length of time after the rise of Luther, as Nicholas of Cusa did before him. On that passage of Galatians v, 6 : ' For in Jesus Christ, neither circumcision availeth anything, nor uncircumcision ; but faith which worketh by charity,' he observes, in order that there may be no occasion for errors, the same apostle (St Paul) declares what sort of faith he calls the justifying one, when he says : in Jesus Christ, neither circumcision availeth anything, nor uncircumcision, that is to say, neither the law given to the Jews, nor the works of the Heathens, can render men acceptable before God, but only faith ; yet not every faith, but solely that ' which worketh by charity,' to wit, the faith which is moved, shaped (*formatur*), and vivified by charity. If love accordingly be the vivifying principle (*forma*) of faith ; then, say the Catholics with reason, faith without love is dead (*informis*) : with love it is living (*formata*).[1]

To this, we may add the explanations which a celebrated Catholic exegetist, at the commencement of the seventeenth century, has given on the 22nd verse of the third chapter of Romans. After the apostle has said, that by the works of the law, no one is justified before God, he adds, a new path of salvation without the law has been now opened by God : to wit,

[1] Bellarm. de justif. lib. ii, c. 4, opp. tom. iv, p. 709.

through faith in Christ; so that all believers may become just. On the word 'believers,' Cornelius à Lapide now observes: 'Those are meant, who are not contented with a mere naked, empty faith, such as the demons possess; but those, who, like friends, have a faith matured by love (*fides charitate formata*), who believe in Christ in such a way, as to fulfil his commandments, who possess an humble, living, and obedient faith; in short, who believe not merely theoretically, but practically (*qui credunt non speculative, sed practice Christo*).'[1] This view presents itself so naturally to the unprejudiced inquirer, that Heinroth, for example, probably without having ever read a Catholic theologian, observed in his *Pisteodicea:* 'Faith is the basis, but love is the principle, of a righteous life.'[2]

§ XVI—LUTHERAN AND CALVINISTIC VIEW OF FAITH

As we now proceed to unfold the Protestant view of faith, it will be desirable in the first place, in order to throw the clearest light on this obscure point, to make our readers acquainted with the position wherein Luther and his followers placed themselves in relation to the Catholic doctrine we have just been stating. Above all, we must observe, that they combated the distinction between the two species of faith, of which we spoke in the preceding section, not to maintain one of the two as alone true, and alone worthy of the name, but to reject both. Had they only represented as inadequate that faith which Catholics denote as insufficient for justification, to wit, the dead faith, their conduct would have been at once intelligible and laudable: but they disputed its very existence, clearly and frequently as it is attested by Holy Writ.[3] The cause of this fact must be

[1] Cornelii a Lap. Comm. in omnes divi Pauli ep. Edit. Antverp. 1705, p. 57.
[2] Heinroth Pisteodicea, Leipzic, 1826, p. 459. We have much pleasure in making mention, on this occasion, of a layman, who has given a very intellectual commentary on the epistle to the Romans (William Beneke, Brief an die Römer, Heidelberg, 1831). Let the reader compare pp. 64, 74, 145, 241. We are at a loss, however, to understand how he could find in the epistle to the Romans, the doctrine of the pre-existence of souls.
[3] Luther, Commentary (in German) on the Epistle to Galatians, loc. cit. p. 70. 'Therefore, faith is not such an *otiosa qualitas*, that is to say, such an useless, lazy, dead thing, that it can lie concealed in the heart, even of a mortal sinner, just like useless chaff, or as a dead fly during wintertime sticks in some chink, till the dear sun comes and rouses it, and warms it into life.'

sought for in the opinion, that faith is the result of exclusive working of the Divinity in man—an opinion which appeared incompatible with the other, that it could show itself dead and ineffectual; whereas the Catholic doctrine explains the want of a progressive movement of faith, not pervading and transforming the whole man by the resistance, which human freedom, everywhere co-operating, or refusing its co-operation, offers. To what surprising interpretations of Scripture the Protestant view leads, in so far as it disputes the distinction between the two aforesaid species of faith, we have already shown in the Twelfth Section, when we had occasion to speak of the Calvinistic theory of predestination.

But even the notion ' of the faith, which worketh by charity,' described by Catholics as the one alone justifying, is rejected by Protestants. When, in the year 1541, deputies of Catholics and Lutherans, assembled at Ratisbon, in order to bring about, if possible, a reconciliation of parties, they agreed on the following exposition of the article on Faith : ' It is a settled and sound doctrine, that sinful man is justified by living and active faith; for by it are we rendered agreeable and well-pleasing unto God for Christ's sake.[1] Luther pronounced condemnation on this article in these words : ' it is a wretched, botched note.' [2]

We will now take the liberty of bringing before our readers the following passages from Luther's Commentary, on the Epistle to the Galatians. ' Our papists, and sophists,' says he, ' have taught the like, to wit, that we should believe in Christ, and that faith was the ground-work of salvation ; but, nevertheless, that this faith could not justify a man, unless it were

[1] ' Firma igitur est et sana doctrina per fidem vivam et efficacem justificari hominem peccatorem ; nam per illam Deo grati et accepti sumus.'

[2] How Plank endeavours to excuse this dissatisfaction on the part of Luther, the reader may see in his *History of the Protestant system of Doctrine*, vol. iii, part ii, p. 91. That very many modern Protestant theologians, even such as are by no means Rationalists—as, for example, the sagacious Menken, should reject Luther's theory, is by no means astonishing. But it is worthy of notice that the untenable nature of this theory is manifest to many Lutheran divines, in proportion as they unconsciously ascribe to Luther and his followers the Catholic doctrine. Thus, Dr Augustus Hahn, professor in Leipsic, in a letter to Bretschneider, entitled *State of Christianity in our Time*, writes as follows : ' Thus Melancthon, in his *Apology* (art. 3), rectifies the Catholic notion of justification through good works, as he shows the Gospel has perfected the Old Testament doctrine respecting the free grace of God in Christ towards all, who with sincere contrition manifest a living faith, working by charity, etc. (p. 64). In fact, the true notion of Lutheran orthodoxy often totally escapes those who, above all things, wish to be orthodox.

the *fides formata* ; that is to say, unless it first received its right form from charity. Now this is not the truth, but an idle, fictitious illusion, and a false, deceitful misrepresentation of the Gospel. On this account, what the senseless sophists have taught respecting the *fides formata*, that is to say, the faith, which should receive its true form and shape from charity, is mere idle talk. For that faith alone justifies, which apprehends Christ by the word of Scripture, and which adorns or decorates itself with Him, and not the faith, which embraces in itself charity. For if faith is to be certain and constant, it should apprehend nought else, save the one Christ. For, in the anguish of the conscience, it hath no other stay, but this precious pearl. Therefore, should the law affright a man, and the weight of sin oppress him, as much as they are able, he can, nevertheless, when he hath apprehended Christ by faith, ever boast that he is yet just and pious. But how cometh this to pass ? And by what is he rendered so just ? By that noble treasure and pearl, which is called Jesus Christ, whom by faith he hath made his own.'[1]

In the same work of the Reformer, we read on the same subject as follows : ' But if a man hears, that he is to believe in Christ, and yet that such faith is of no avail, and profiteth him nothing, unless charity be added thereto, which giveth force to faith, and renders it capable of justifying a man, then it must needs come to pass, that a man will immediately fall away from the faith, despair, and think, if this be so, that faith without charity doth not justify ; then it is undoubtedly useless, and nothing worth, and charity alone can justify : for if faith hath not charity by its side, which imparteth to it the right form, which constitutes it in such a manner, that it can justify, then is it nought ; but if it be nought, how can it then justify ?

' The adversaries, in support of this their pernicious and poisonous doctrine, adduce the text from the thirteenth chapter of the First Epistle to the Corinthians : " If I spake with the tongues of men and of angels, and if I should prophesy, and should know all mysteries, and all knowledge ; and if I should have all faith, so that I could remove mountains, and have not charity, I am nothing." The text the papists regard as their wall of iron. But the dull, stupid asses can neither understand nor perceive anything in the writings of St Paul, and therefore with this their false interpretation they have not only done

[1] Luther's Works, part 1, p. 47, c. 6, ed. Wittenberg.

violence to the words of St Paul, but they have moreover denied Christ, and set all his blessings aside. Therefore we must beware of this doctrine, and regard it as a very diabolical and hellish poison; and conclude with St Paul, that we be justified by faith only, and not *per fidem formatam charitate*.'[1]

What, now, is justifying faith in the Protestant sense? Man believes, when he trusts that he has been received by God into grace, and that, for Christ's sake, who, by his death, has offered up atonement for our sins, he receives forgiveness of the same.[2] Melancthon expresses himself still more clearly, when he says, 'Faith is the unconditional acquiescence in the Divine mercy, without regard to our good or evil works.'[3] By these definitions is the essence of that faith, which the Reformers require, by no means made clear: we must more accurately point out the manner wherein faith exhibits the property of justification. Negatively this is explained by the express observation, that it is not the love connected with faith, or faith, in as far as it manifests its activity in works, which possesses the power of justifying.[4] Positively this is explained by the declaration, that it is the instrument and the mean, which lays hold of the

[1] Loc. cit. p. 70. The Reformers often recur to this *fides formata* in a tone of great indignation. Thus, Luther in a disputation says (Opp. Jen. tom. i, fol. 538, Thes. iv): ' Docent (sophistæ) neque infusam Spiritu Sancto fidem justificare nisi charitate sit formata.' Melancthon, loci theol. p. 85: ' Fingunt (vulgus sophistarum) aliam fidem formatam, id est, charitate conjunctam; aliam informem, id est, quæ sit etiam in impiis carentibus charitate.' Calvin. Instit. lib. iii, c. 4, n. 8, p. 195: ' Primo refutanda est, quæ in scholis volitat nugatoria fidei formatæ et informis distinctio,' etc.

[2] Confess. Aug. art. iv, fol. 13. ' Item docent, quod homines non possint justificari coram Deo, propriis viribus, meritis, aut operibus, sed gratis justificentur propter Christum per fidem, cum credunt se in gratiam recipi, et peccata remitti propter Christum, qui sua morte pro nostris peccatis satisfecit.'

[3] Melancthon loc. theol. p. 93. ' Habes, in quam partem fidei nomen usurpet scriptura, nempe pro eo, quod est fidere gratuita Dei misericordia, sine ullo operum nostrorum, sive bonorum sive malorum, respectu: quia de Christi plenitudine omnes accipimus.' Most complete is the definition which Calvin gives: Instit. lib. iii, c. 2, sect. 7, fol. 195. ' Justa fide definitio nobis constabit, si dicamus esse divinæ erga nos benevolentiæ firmam certamque cognitionem, quæ, gratuitæ in Christo promissionis veritate fundata, per Spiritum Sanctum et revelatur mentibus nostris, et cordibus obsignatur.'

[4] Apol. iv. de justif. sect. 26, p. 76. ' Sola fide in Christum, non propter dilectionem aut opera consequimur remissionem peccatorum, etsi dilectio sequitur fidem.'

grace (the compassion) of God, and the promised merits of Christ.[1]

If this more accurate explanation should not yet place in the fullest light the nature of the Protestant idea of faith, this will be most certainly effected, by considering the comparison, which Calvin, on a certain occasion, employed for this object. Osiander, a preacher in Nuremberg, and afterwards in Königsberg, one of the most celebrated of Luther's followers at the commencement of the Reformation, had taken the liberty to put forth a peculiar theory of justification, which, if we duly elucidate his obscure phraseology, and the want of precision in his ideas, was quite Catholic—a circumstance which was often urged as a matter of reproach against him. He taught, among other things, that the justifying power lies not in faith considered in itself, but only inasmuch as it essentially embraces Christ; that is to say, according to Catholic language, inasmuch as, by the real communication of Christ's righteousness, it places man in a real communion with him. To this Calvin replies: 'Doubtless he is of opinion, that faith by no means justifies through its intrinsic energy; for, as it is always weak and imperfect, it could produce only a defective justification. Faith is only the mean (organ) through which Christ is offered up to God. Thus it blesses man in the same way as an earthen vessel, in which a treasure is found, makes a man happy, although it possess in itself no worth.'[2] Thus is justifying faith regarded,

---

[1] Solid. Declar. iii. de fide just. sect. 36, p. 662. 'Fides enim tantum eam ob causam justificat, et inde vim illam habet, quod gratiam Dei et meritum Christi in promissione evangelii tanquam medium et instrumentum apprehendit et amplectitur.' Sect. 23, p. 659: 'Et quidem neque contritio, neque dilectio, neque ulla alia virtus, sola fides est illud instrumentum, quo gratiam Dei, meritum Christi, et remissionem peccatorum apprehendere et accipere possumus.'

[2] Calvin. Instit. lib. iii, c. 11, sect. 7, fol. 262. 'Quod objicit, vim justificandi non inesse fidei ex se ipsa, sed quatenus Christum recipit, libenter admitto, nam si per se, vel intrinseca, ut loquuntur, virtute justificaret fides, ut est semper debilis et imperfecta, non efficeret hoc, nisi ex parte: sic manca esset justitia, quæ frustulum salutis nobis conferret. . . . Neque tamen interea tortuosas hujus sophistæ figuras admitto, quum dicit fidem esse Christum: quasi vero olla fictilis sit thesaurus, quod in ea reconditum sit aurum. Neque enim diversa ratio est, quia fides etiamsi nullius per se dignitatis sit vel pretii, nos justificat, Christum afferendo, sicut olla pecuniis referta hominem locupletat. . . . Jam expeditus est quoque nodus, quomodo intelligi debeat vocabulum fidei, ubi de justificatione agitur.' Cfr. Apolog. iv, de justif. sect. 18, p. 71. 'Et rursus quoties nos de fide loquimur, intelligi volumus objectum, scilicet misericordiam promissam. Nam fides non ideo justificat aut salvat, quia

not as a morally renovating and vital principle, flowing from the spirit of Christ; but as standing in the same relation to Christ, as the earthen vessel to the treasure. In the same way as the two become not one—the vessel remains earthen, the treasure golden—so the believer is not *inwardly* united with Christ by justifying faith: they stand merely in an outward relation one to the other. Christ is pure; man on the other hand, although he believes in a way agreeable to God, is inwardly impure. Christ is offered up by man to God through faith, the sacrificial vessel, without man himself being a victim acceptable to God through Christ; and as such being just, and, in consequence thereof, obtaining eternal felicity. The belief in an extraneous righteousness, described in the Fourteenth Section required this notion of faith (*justitia extra nos*). A peculiar conception, likewise, of the *appropriation* of the merits and obedience of Christ, must accordingly be formed. Now, this was precisely called appropriation of obedience, whereby it is *not appropriated* by us, not *made our own* in an inward living manner, so that we may become obedient like unto the Redeemer. It is the same with this new mode of appropriation, as if anyone were to purchase a very learned book, and instead of stamping its contents deeply on his mind, and in this way appropriating it, so that he might become a living book, should hold himself very learned, as the learned book was his (outward) property!

Now, the rejection of the above-stated second Catholic view of faith becomes perfectly intelligible. Moreover, Calvin, as it appears, borrowed the simile in question from Luther's writings, in which it frequently occurs, though not so fully carried out.[1]

After these explanations, we can understand the purport of passages, like the following, from Luther's writings: 'Now thou seest how rich is the Christian or the baptised man; for, though he will, he cannot lose his salvation, *however great his sins may be*, unless he refuse to believe. No sin can damn him, but unbelief alone. When faith in the Divine promise given in baptism returns, or is not effaced, then all else will be made to vanish in a moment through faith, or rather the veracity,

ipsa sit opus per se dignum, sed tantum quia accipit misericordiam promissam.' Cf. Chemnit. Exam. Conc. Trid. part 1, p. 294.

[1] Luther's Commentary on the epistle to the Galatians, part 1, p. 70, ed. Wittenberg (in German). 'The reason wherefore faith justifies, is, that it apprehends and brings to itself the costly noble pearl, to wit, Jesus Christ.'

of God; for He cannot belie Himself, if thou confess Him, and acquiese faithfully in His promise. But contrition, and confession of sins, and even satisfaction, and all those efforts invented by man, will quickly leave thee, and make thee unhappier, if thou forgettest this Divine veracity, and busiest thyself about those things. Vanity of Vanities, and vexation of spirit, is all which we strive for, beyond faith in God's fidelity.'[1] In this passage it is asserted, that, by the side of faith, the greatest sins can still be committed; but this certainly is not the faith which St Paul recommends to us, although Luther is ever appealing to the authority of this apostle. But it is that earthen vessel of Calvin, on whose surface, indeed, Christ as the lamb of God is found, but without the spirit of the Redeemer livingly pervading the whole man, destroying sin, and truly engendering a new life within us. Who, that had ever reflected on the Pauline notion of faith, could have ever taken pleasure in defending the thesis, ' that, if in faith an adultery could be com-

---

[1] Luther de captiv. Bab. tom. ii, fol. 264. ' Ita vides, quam dives sit homo Christianus, *etiam volens non potest perdere salutem suam quantiscunque peccatis, nisi nolit credere*. Nulla enim peccata eum possunt damnare, nisi sola incredulitas . . . Cætera omnia, si redeat vel stet fides in promissionem divinam baptizato factam, in momento absorbentur per eandem fidem, etc. Here we may appropriately insert the following celebrated passage from a letter of Luther to Melancthon, although from the evident excitement of mind (so we would willingly believe) under which the author writes, peculiar stress ought not to be laid upon it; but it will still ever remain a characteristic monument in the history of religious opinions. ' Sin lustily,' writes Luther, ' but be yet more lusty in faith, and rejoice in Christ, who is the conqueror of sin, of death, and of the world. Sin we must, so long as we remain here. It suffices, that, through the riches of the glory of God, we know the Lamb which taketh away the sins of the world: from Him no sin will ever sever us, though a million times in a day we should fornicate or commit murder.' Epist. Dr M. Lutheri a Joh. Aurifabro coll. tom. i, Jena, 1556, 4, p. 545, b. Luther says to his friend:—

' Si gratiæ prædicator es, gratiam non fictam sed veram prædica: si vera gratia est, verum non fictum peccatum forto, Deus non facit salvos ficte peccatores.'

' *Esto peccator et pecca fortiter, sed fortius fide et gaude in Christo*, qui victor est peccati, mortis et mundi: peccandum est, quamdiu hic sumus. Vita hæc non est habitatio justitiæ; sed exspectamus, ait Petrus, cœlos novos et terram novam, in quibus justitia habitat.

' Sufficit quod agnovimus, per divitias gloriæ Dei, agnum qui tollit peccata mundi: ab hoc non avellet nos peccatur, *etiamsi millies, millies uno die fornicemur aut occidamus*. Putas tam parvum esse pretium et redemptionem pro peccatis nostris factam in tanto ac tali agno?' The letter was written from the Wartburg, and bears the date of the year 1521.

mitted, it were no sin.'[1] Even in Melancthon, we find similar passages, of which we shall cite only one: 'Whatever thou mayest do, whether thou eatest, drinkest, workest with the hand, teachest, I may add, shouldst thou even sin therewith, look not to thy works; weigh the promise of God; confide in it, and doubt not that thou hast no longer a Judge in heaven, but only a Father, who cherisheth thee in his heart, as a parent doth his child.'[2] In other words, suppose thou shouldst be a drunkard, or a glutton, let not thy hair turn grey; only forget not that God is a kind elder, who learned to forgive much sooner than thou didst learn to sin.

However, we have pointed out only one side of the Lutheran principle of faith, namely, that whereby it works justification. There is another, whereby it becomes the source of love and of good works. Luther, in many places, describes this in nearly the same terms as the Catholics depict the divine love of the regenerated. In this class of the reformer's writings, are included those on Christian freedom and on good works; and who knows not the brilliant description of faith in his preface to St Paul's Epistle to the Romans? 'Faith,' says he, 'is a divine work within us, which changes us, makes us be born again out of God, destroys the old Adam, and transforms us, as it were into other men, in heart, in feeling, and in every faculty, and communicates to us the Holy Spirit. This faith is something living and efficacious; so that it is impossible that it should not always work good. Faith doth not first ask, whether good works are to be done; but, before it inquires about the matter, it hath already wrought many good works, and is ever busied in working.' Here, in the most amiable contradiction with the Lutheran theory of justification, a renovation and entire transformation of the whole inward man is taught. Faith appears as the blossom, springing out of the union of *all* the powers constituting the interior man, as an expression of their combined workings; while a strong testimony is rendered to the power

[1] Luther disput. tom. i, p. 523. '*Si in fide fieri posset adulterium, peccatum non esset.*'

[2] Melancthon loc. p. 92. '*Qualiacunque sint opera, comedere, bibere, laborare manu, docere, addo etiam, ut sint palam peccata,*' etc. I candidly avow, I could as soon imagine the co-existence of day and night, as conceive a man holding the Pauline *pistis* (faith) with the sentiments and conduct described by Melancthon. And what should prevent us from representing to ourselves such a man as unchaste, choleric, etc., if the qualities stated in the text be compatible with faith? In what respect is *gula* morally different from *libido*?

of the Saviour over sin and death. In his commentary, likewise, on the epistle to the Galatians, Luther calls faith ' the righteous heart, the thoroughly good will, and the new-created understanding, or reason.' Here also Luther means to say, that faith is an effect of all the spiritual powers of man, when they are purified and glorified by the Divine Spirit.[1]

APPRECIATION OF THE THEORETIC AND PRACTICAL GROUNDS WHICH THE PROTESTANTS ALLEGE FOR THEIR VIEW OF FAITH

§ XVII—APPRECIATION OF THE THEORETIC GROUNDS

But why, now, do the Reformers so much insist on the distinction of two principles in one and the same faith; to one whereof is reserved the power of working justification, to the other, that of evincing itself in charity and good works, and in unfolding the fulness of all virtues ? Luther and his friends conceived they had very weighty theoretical and practical reasons for this separation. The theoretical reasons will first engage our attention. It is very usual with Luther and his friends to boast of faith, as the instrument of embracing the mercy of God in Christ, as not only the first and original, but also the only pure ordinance of God in man, unmixed, and consequently untroubled, with any human alloy; whereas faith, when it manifests itself in love, and in the whole course of feelings to which it should give rise, on one hand, doth not appear itself, but rather, if we may so speak, as the fruit of itself, and on the other hand, penetrates and pervades the human and the sinful element, and consequently no longer exhibits its pristine purity.[2] Now it is the exclusive act of God, according to them, which maketh men agreeable to Him; it is consequently the instrumental faith only, not the faith working by charity, that justifieth before God, and therefore the distinction in

---

[1] Commentary on the epistle to the Galatians, part 1, p. 143; German edition of Wittenberg. Passages similar to those cited in the text often occur.

[2] Luther de captiv. Babyl. opp. tom. ii, p. 284. ' Opus est enim omnium operum excellentissimum et arduissimum, quo solo, etiamsi cæteris omnibus carere cogeris, servaberis. Est enim opus Dei, non hominis, sicut Paulus docet; cætera nobiscum et per nos operatur, hoc unicum in nobis et sine nobis operatur.'

question must be regarded as well-founded, nay, as absolutely necessary.

The *naïve* simplicity of these theoretic errors, which are entirely based on the doctrine of God's exclusive operation in the work of salvation, is too evident to need any special comment. Luther in one word wished to say: in us God believes—in us God confides in Himself—and as everywhere He can rejoice only in *His own works*, so he rejoiceth solely in *this* His exclusive act. Evident as this is, yet, on account of the importance of the matter, and for the sake of elucidating the notions respecting it, it behoves us not to pass it over with too much haste. The Lutherans describe the *entire* spiritual life of regenerated man as the act of God. Is it not therefore extremely singular and, according to their theoretical doctrines, utterly inconceivable, that they should not likewise say, God in Christ Jesus *loveth* in us, and should not attribute to the Creator as lively a joy in this His work, as that whereby He *believeth* in us ? If the one as well as the other be His work, if both have been obtained for us through the merits of Christ, what imaginable cause is there, why God should look down graciously upon us, inasmuch as he excites within us faith in the Redeemer; but cannot love us, inasmuch as he produces within us love for Christ ? The doubt that in love something human, and therefore, as they say, something meagre and insufficient, exists, the peculiar theory of Protestants cannot allege ; for what is weak and sinful in love, that is to say, what is not love itself they will not denominate God's work, but only love itself. The exotic and impure elements in this love God could always separate, and, as to that which should be proved to be his own work, graciously accept, and even as graciously as anything else, which He hath ordained. A very peculiar reason must have induced the Lutherans to adopt this view; for although, as they conceive, faith is the exclusive work of God, yet it still frequently trembles, becomes now and then even according to the symbolical books (for example, the *Apology*), extremely weak, is scarcely able at times to cling to the staff of Divine Providence, and forgets itself even so far as to doubt the existence of God. And as regards Luther himself, he was often unable to put off the doubt, whether he had conceived justifying faith in a very believing spirit, and dispelled awakening scruples, not by the power of faith, but after a very human fashion, to wit, by resolving in such moments to inveigh instantaneously and energetically against the papacy, and in this way to set aside disgust by pleasure.[1] Now this dismay, and this doubting in divine truths and divine promises, are most assuredly no gracious work of God; but in both we recognise the human alloy, and (in the sense of the Reformers), we must say: ' In us God believes; it is man, on the contrary who trembles and who doubts. In despite of this perturbation of the divine element within us, God doth not yet cease to look down graciously upon the seed he hath sown in man.' Why should the Deity, then, on account of the human alloy intermingled with charity, be induced to cast no friendly eye upon it, and not graciously to recognise that portion of it, which is His own work?

Love, then, is an effect of faith, and consequently not the first of the divine workings within us; for as it is only faith which with God's aid brings forth charity, and certainly not any unbelief ingrafted on faith, love must in consequence be as divine as faith; because it is the pure, though (as the Lutherans assert) the later, production of a divine principle. For whatever would be defective in charity, would be, as we remarked above, not charity itself, but only the effect of a deficiency in faith; or, to express ourselves more accurately (for a deficiency, that is to say, the absence of being can do nothing) a smaller degree of charity presupposes a small degree of faith; though the former, be it even subsequent in its origin, is as divine as the

[1] Some passages of this kind we must here lay before the reader. Luther, in his *Table-talk* (p. 166, ed. Jena, 1603), says: ' I once believed all that the Pope and the monks told me. But now what Christ saith, who cannot lie, this I cannot put too strong a faith in. But this is a wearisome subject; we must defer it to another day.' P. 167: ' The spirit is indeed willing, but the flesh is weak, saith Christ, when he speaks of himself. St Paul also saith: The spirit will give itself up to God, and trust in him and obey; but reason, flesh, and blood resist, and will not and cannot upward rise. Therefore must our Lord God bear with us; the glimmering wick he will not put out; the faithful have only the first fruits of the spirit, not the full perfection, and the ten commandments.' One person asked, Wherefore doth not God impart to us full knowledge? Dr Martin replied: If anyone could indeed believe, then for very joy he would be able neither to eat, nor to drink, nor do aught else. As at Dr Martin's table the text from the prophet Hosea, *Hæc dicit Dominus*, was sung, he said to Dr Jonas, ' As little as you believe that this singing is good, so little do I firmly believe that theology is true. I love my wife, I love her more dearly than myself—that is most sure—I mean to say, I would rather die than that she or the little ones should die. I love Christ very dearly, who with His blood hath redeemed me from the power and tyranny of the devil: but by faith ought in justice to be greater and more ardent than it is; ah! Lord! enter not into judgment with thy servant,' etc.

latter. A flame is not less fire than a spark, though the spark precedes the flame; it is the same with a little flame, though it were only the effect of a little spark, and both in the same way would be comprised in the notion of a little fire.

Whithersoever we turn our inquiring glance, we can discover nothing which should have brought charity into such discredit, that it were only by faith, and not by love, we can be acceptable to God. Holy writ is not in the slightest degree chargeable with the evil repute into which love is fallen. Let us compare only John xiv, 21, 23, and 1 Cor. viii, 3. If the Saviour saith in the former place, 'He who loveth me shall be loved of my Father, and I will love him, and will manifest myself to him;' so we may be allowed to put the question, what distinction can exist ' between receiving anyone into his grace,' ' assuring anyone of his good-will,' (declaring him just) and ' loving anyone ?' It is also useful attentively to consider, who it is, according to this passage, whom the Father and the Son love ;—him, it saith, 'who loveth Christ.' Thus, it would be Faith, in so far as it loves, and is active in love, wherein consists the righteousness that availeth before God, and whereby we become well-pleasing unto Him.

To speak out plainly our own opinion, it appears to us, that in the Protestant mode of distinguishing between the instrumental faith, and the faith working by charity, there has been always wanting a clearness of conception. This will be proved most evidently, if we take the pains of inquiring, what is this faith considered *in itself*, and what, on the other hand, it ought to be, *according to Protestants ;* this faith, as we should premise, being always understood, in the Protestant sense, of confidence in the Saviour, as the Forgiver of sins. The discussion, which we have just concluded, leads us to a certain result. Let us once more place ourselves in the Protestant point of view, which looks on charity as an effect, or a fruit of faith. If charity stands really in this relation to faith, it is necessarily comprised in it, for, otherwise, it could not proceed from it; it would be, therefore, most certainly only another form of Faith's existence, or faith in another shape, and would determine its essence in such a degree, that it could not be conceived without it, and could only be, through it, what it is. It would, therefore, be no error to assert, that love were the essence of faith, and so in a higher, more developed, and more distinct manner; it would be the essence of the latter, because it is the latter which is manifested in it, as the cause in its effect, the reason in its consequence, the root in the tree. Love would be faith, even in a more consummate form, because faith only, after a gradual growth, hath become love. Faith, in so far as it embraces Christ, and the forgiveness of sins in him, is, consequently, love itself, although (as, until more accurate definitions be given, we are willing, for argument's sake, to concede) it be at first only love in its infancy. Love is thus, without doubt, the organ, which rests with confidence in Christ, and the efficacious faith is the instrumental one, only, as we said, in a more mature and a more confirmed shape.

The truth of what has been stated, and, consequently, the due relation in which faith stands to charity, may, in various ways, be made evident. The first is as follows :—To the abstract idea of God, as a Being infinitely just, corresponds the sentiment of fear. If, on the other hand, God be conceived as the all-loving, merciful, and forgiving Father, this is most assuredly possible only by a kindred sentiment in our souls, corresponding to the Divine love, that is to say, by a love germinating within us. It is awakening *love* only that can embrace the loving, pardoning, compassionate God, and surrender itself up entirely to Him, as even the Redeemer saith, ' He who loveth me, shall be loved of my Father, and I will love him, and will *manifest myself to Him*.' Thus it would not be faith (confidence) which would be first in the order of time, and love in the next place, but faith would be an effect of love, which, after she had engendered faith as confidence, supported by this her own self-begotten help-mate, would come forward more vigorously and efficaciously. This, at least, Holy Writ teaches very clearly. Compare Romans v, 5, with viii, 15, 16. The second mode, wherein what we have said may be made evident, is as follows : Confidence in the Redeemer (for this, we repeat it again, the Reformers denominate faith), necessarily presupposes a secret, hidden desire—a longing after Him. For our whole being, having received the impulse from God, forces and urges us to apply to ourselves what is offered through the mediation of Christ; and our deepest necessities, whereof we have attained the consciousness through His Holy Spirit, are satisfied only in Him. But what is now this longing, this desire, other than love ? Assuredly, this aspiring of our whole being towards Christ, this effort to repose in Him, to be united with Him, to find in Him only our salvation, is nought else than love. It follows, then, that love, even according to this view of things, constitutes the foundation and internal condition of confidence—nay, its very essence ; for, in every internal consequence, the essence is again manifested.[1]

It was only a very singular confusion of the manner wherein the Gospel is announced to us, with the interior, living acceptance of the same in our souls, that could ever have given rise to a different opinion. The Redeemer, doubtless, announces himself to us from without (*Justitia nostra extra nos*) as Him, for the sake of whose merits, the forgiveness of sins is offered to us, with the view of restoring us to communion with God. But when we have once clearly apprehended and recognised this righteousness, which is without, then first awakes within us the feeling kindred to divinity : we find ourselves to be beings designed and created for God ; we feel ourselves attracted towards Him (this is the first germ of love) ; we find, even in our sins, no further obstacle ; we pass them by, and move consoled onward towards God and Christ (this is confidence in the latter) ; and, by the progressive development of such feelings, we at last disengage ourselves from the world, and live entirely in God (*Justitia intra nos, inhærens, infusa*). Thus the recognition of the truths revealed in Christ, and especially of the forgiveness of sins in Him (this is faith, in the ordinary Catholic sense) is, undoubtedly, the primary thing preceding all others—

[1] Cardinal Sadolet (ad Principes Germ. oratio. Opp. ed. Ver. MDCCXXXVIII, tom. ii, pp. 359, 360) observes with great truth : ' Illud præterea docto homine indignum, quod, cum istam ipsam fidem, in qua una hæretis, a Spiritu Sancto nobis conceditis dari, non videtis eam in amore et charitate esse datam. Quid enim aliud Spiritus Sanctus est, quam amor ? Quod etiam ut prætereatur, cum fidem esse fiduciam affirmatis, qua certo confidimus nostra nobis peccata a Deo per Christum fuisse ignota, spem, quamvis imprudens, in hac fiducia inseritis : non enim sine spe potest esse fiducia. Quod si spem, profecto etiam, amorem ; sic enim confidimus nostra peccata nobis condonari, ut non modo id speremus, sed etiam amando optandoque expectemus, ut ita sit : quoniam omnis ratio spei et fiduciæ, quacunque versetur in re, amore rei illius innixa est, quam nos esse adeptos aut adepturos confidimus. Ita in fide vera spes et charitas sic implicita est, ut nullum eorum ab aliis possit divelli.' S. Ambrose admirably observes (Exposit. Evang. Luc. viii) : ' Ex fide charitas, ex charitate spes et rursus in se sancto quodam circuitu refunduntur.' *Fiducia* is the *corroborata spes*, as defined by the schoolmen. Bellarmin. de justif. lib. i, c. 13 : ' Quarta dispositio (ad justificationem) dilectio est. Statim enim ac incipit aliquis sperare ab alio beneficium, incipit etiam eundem diligere ut benefactorem, atque auctorem omnis boni, quod sperat. . . . Porro dilectionem aliquam priorem esse remissione peccatorum, vel tempore, si sit dilectio imperfecta, vel certe natura, si sit perfecta et ex toto corde, atque ad eam disponere,' etc.

the groundwork and the root of justification (*radix et funda-mentum justificationis*); so that, *from this sort of faith*, love emanates. But, if faith be taken in the sense of *confidence* (*fiducia*), then it is far from the truth to assert, that it is only followed by love, and, still more, that, separated from love, or conceived without it, it is capable of justifying. This confidence is itself only one phase in the history of love. Accordingly, our sins are not, in the first place, forgiven us, so that, in consequence of this consciousness, we love, but because we confidingly love, and lovingly confide, they are forgiven. *In our interior life*, forgiveness of sins and sanctification are simultaneous; or, as St Thomas Aquinas excellently expresses it,[1] 'the infusion of grace, and the remission of sin, like the illumination of any space, and the dispersion of darkness, are one and the same thing.' But, according to the Apology, and the Formulary of Concord it is *Faith exclusively alone*, wherein the appropriation of the merits of Christ and justification consist; and, consequently neither charity nor any other virtue,[2] that is to say, no holy feelings on the part of men, have any share in this work. Accordingly, faith or confidence in Christ, in so far as it justifies, is something quite distinct from every holy sentiment, especially charity, which is the one expressly named. Whether this doctrine can be in any way justified—whether it offer any sense whatever—the discussion in which we have just been engaged may suffice to show.

§ XVIII—APPRECIATION OF THE PRACTICAL GROUNDS

Let us now endeavour to comprehend the meaning of those practical reasons, which the Protestants allege in their cause. These reasons are the following:—

1. The first is, that in this way only 'troubled consciences' can receive a powerful and adequate solace. For, so say the Protestants, if instrumental faith, which clings to Christ alone who hath offered up satisfaction for us, possess the power of justifying, hearts, sorely grieved on account of their sins, will

[1] Prim. sec. 9, cxii, art. vi. 'Idem est gratiæ infusio et culpæ remissio, sicut idem est illuminatio et tenebrarum expulsio.'

[2] Solid. declar. iii. de fide justif. sect. 23, p. 659. 'Neque contritio, neque dilectio, neque ulla alia virtus est illud instrumentum, quo gratiam Dei meritum Christi, et remissionem peccatorum apprehendere et accipere possumus.'

then enjoy a steady interior peace. But this they never can attain to, if only the faith, which is manifested in love—faith evidenced in holiness of sentiment—be considered as the test of the children of God; for who is conscious of possessing the true love of God, and holiness of feeling?

2. In the second place, the Protestants contend, that, if the instrumental faith be regarded as the one conferring justification, everything is then referred to the divine mercy in Christ, and all glory rendered to the Redeemer. But so soon as faith inasmuch as it comprises a circle of holy feelings, is to earn for us the approbation of heaven, then the glory, due to the Saviour alone, is divided between him and us, or rather withdrawn from him. In a word, by this way only can the merits of Christ, in their entire magnitude, be gratefully acknowledged.[1]

3. The reason, first assigned, offers us, in fact, a very beautiful, and very pleasing motive, and we see at once the sentiment which it is intended to cherish in the breast of men. This sentiment is *humility*, which, with an honest self-denial, refers all good to God, as its primary source, and ascribes nothing good to man, as such: and humility, therefore, must be regarded in fact as the motive of the third ground for this distinction between the two kinds of faith.[2]

[1] Apolog. iv de dilect. et implet. leg. sect. 48, p. 90. 'De magna re disputamus, de honore Christi, et unde petant bonæ mentes certam et firmam consolationem.' Calvin. Instit. lib. iii, c. 1, sect. 13, p. 273: 'Atque omnino quidem duo hic spectanda sunt, nempe ut Domino illibata constet et veluti sarta tecta sua gloria, conscientiis vero nostris coram ipsius judicio placida quies ac serena tranquillitas.' De necessitate reformandæ ecclesiæ opusc. p. 429: 'Neque inter opera et Christum dimidiat, sed in solidum Christo adscribit (Paulus), quod coram Deo justi censemur. Duo hic in quæstionem veniunt: utrum inter nos et Deum dividenda sit salutis nostræ gloria,' etc. Compare Chemnit. Exam. Concil. Trid. part 1, p. 296, and in other passages.

[2] Luther adv. Erasmus. Roterod. Opp. tom. iii, p. 176, b. 'Duæ res exigunt talia prædicari. Prima est humiliatio nostræ superbiæ et cognitio gratiæ Dei, altera ipsa fides Christiana. Primum, Deus certo promisit humiliatis, id est deploratis et desperatis, gratiam suam. Humiliari vero penitus non potest homo, donec sciat, prorsus extra suas vires, consilia, studia, voluntatem, opera, omnino ex alterius arbitrio, consilio, voluntate, opere suam pendere salutem, nempe Dei solius. Siquidem, quamdiu persuasus fuerit, sese vel tantulum posse, pro salute sua, manet in fiducia sui, nec de se penitus desperat, ideo non humiliatur coram Deo, sed locum, tempus, opus aliquod sibi præsumit, vel sperat, vel optat saltem, quo tandem perveniat ad salutem. Qui vero nihil dubitat, totum in voluntate Dei pendere, is prorsus de se desperat, nihil eligit, sed exspectat operantem Deum, is proximus est gratiæ, ut salvus fiat. Itaque propter electos ista

Let us now examine the intrinsic worth of the first reason. It is certainly a great task for the true Church to administer solid consolation to consciences sorely troubled and deeply agitated on account of their sins. But the solace so extended should be no false one ; and that such an epithet must attach to the Protestant consolation, we have already, on account of the distinction between the instrumental and the efficacious faith, full and just cause to apprehend. And why so ? Let us hear the following dialogue betwixt Luther and a heart seeking consolation :—' Thou sayest, I have done no good work : I am for this too weak and frail. Such a treasure thou wilt not acquire by thy works ; but thou shouldst hear the joyous message, which the Holy Ghost proclaims to thee, through the mouth of the prophet, for he saith to thee—Be joyous, thou barren, that bearest not ; that is to say, that art not active in charity. As if he would say, why art thou anxious and art so troubled ? for thou hast no cause to be anxious and to be troubled. But I am barren, and lonely, and bear no children. Although thou buildest not on the righteousness of the law, nor bearest children like Hagar, it matters not ; thy righteousness is far higher and better, to wit, Christ, who is able to defend thee against the terrors and the curses of the law ; for he became an anathema for thee, that he might redeem thee from the anathema of the law.' [1]

What an utterly false and dangerous application of the twenty-seventh verse of Galatians, chapter iv ! Is not this replacing one part of faith by the other ? And distinguishing the efficaci-

---

vulgantur, ut isto modo humiliati et in nihilum redacti, salvi fiant : cæteri resistunt humiliationi huic, imo damnant doceri hanc desperationem sui ; aliquid vel modiculum sibi relinqui volunt, quod possint : hi occulte manent superbi et gratiæ Dei adversarii. Hæc est, inquam, una ratio, ut pii promissionem gratiæ humilitati cognoscant, invocent, et accipiant.' Calvin. Instit. lib. iii, c. 12, sect. 6, p. 272 : ' Hactenus perniciosam hypocrisin docuerunt, qui hæc duo simul junxere, humiliter sentiendum, et justitiam nostram aliquo loco habendam.'

[1] Luther's Commentary on the epistle to the Galatians, p. 258. It is self-evident that the soul in question is not one which is in a state of anxiety, because, on account of the relations wherein it is placed, it cannot perform the works it would desire, nor confer happiness on its fellow-creatures. In this case the solace administered would have been of a very different kind, and could not have been brought in connection with the passage relative to Hagar. It should then only have been said, the charity, wherewith this soul is animated, sufficeth ; for love is the fulfilment of the law. But this it was precisely, which Luther did not wish to assert.

ous from the instrumental faith, in order that not merely in the defective condition, but in the utter absence, of the former, the latter might be made to represent it? Here we find no solace, but the encouragement of a false security; and the doctrine, that it is only the faith working by charity which justifies, is reproached with being unable to rise above the low level of a mere legal justice! And what contradictions, too, we find here! Above, as we have seen, Luther termed faith the thoroughly good-will, and here we find faith destitute of all will. Above, faith was described as an eternal, active principle, and here it appears before us as indolence itself? Above, it was a fresh living power, which doth not first ask, whether and what it should do; but, before the question is put, is already prepared: here it appears a thing that can only sigh and lament, and can never make progress, and which still, however, remains the true faith! Should the distinction accordingly between the active and the instrumental faith be meant undoubtedly to express the idea, that faith justifies, yet not in so much as it is active, still it would convey the sense, that it justifies, even when it is not active! Let us attentively consider once more some passages previously cited from Luther's writings (see § XVI) passages which only now perhaps will be completely understood. Let us especially weigh the words: ' But if a man heareth, that he should believe in Christ, and yet that this belief availeth him nothing, nor is of use, *unless love be added thereto*, which imparts vigour to faith, and renders it capable of justifying man; then without doubt he will fall away from faith, despair, and think that if it be really so, that *faith without love* doth not justify, then it is undoubtedly profitless and nothing worth.' Luther's already cited description of the riches, which flow to us from baptism, is well worthy of our repeated attention. All these passages furnish so many evidences of the opinion which we have advanced, respecting the real practical importance of the here alleged distinction between the two forms of one and the same faith. It is not to be denied, that, according to Luther, the form of faith efficacious to holiness cannot appear without the other, which consists in the solacing apprehension of Christ's merits. But the latter can exist without the former, and indeed, in such a way, that, according to Luther's opinion, the faith in the forgiveness of sins through Christ would lose all value and all importance, if such were not the case.

This now is not the doctrine of St Paul, who consoles us in a very different manner. Compare Romans v, 1-6, viii, 1-16; Galatians, v, 6-22. In the Holy Spirit let us cry out, ' Abba, dear Father! But the fruits of the Spirit are charity, joy, peace, patience, benignity, goodness, longanimity, mildness, faith, modesty, continency, chastity.' Peace and joy in the Holy Spirit are accordingly not to be gained without love, and all other holy sentiments. And this the soul, whose scruples are silenced by Luther, clearly proves. Because it possessed no loving, gentle, and meek faith, therefore joy and peace were not its portion, and never would it obtain these *alone*, unless it were seduced into a culpable levity, or sought its satisfaction in carnal pleasures. The nature of that consolation, which the Catholic Church administers, we shall later have occasion more accurately to define.

2. Let us now proceed to the appreciation of the second of the practical grounds, which, in the opinion of the Reformers, so strongly enforce their view of faith, as to render it not only laudable, but even commanded by the spirit of Christianity to such an extent, that they characterise the opposite opinion as absolutely wicked. It would have been, in truth, a noble struggle between the different confessions, if they had striven in an *enlightened manner* to surpass each other in the glorification of Him, whom they mutually revere as the source of all salvation. But the sovereign rule, according to which judgment should be given in this strife, is this; when we praise the holiest, let there be nothing unholy! Let us first endeavour clearly to apprehend the meaning of the Reformers' assertion! They think the doctrine of Catholics, that only the sanctified is the justified man, only the lover of God is the beloved of God, has nothing above the level of vulgar and every-day maxims; for to love him, who loves us, is not rare even among men. Thus if we would be agreeable to God, only in so far as the power of Christ really transforms us, puts aside sin, and makes us in fact worthy of becoming children of God, this is not a sufficient honour of the Redeemer; the conception of Christ and the value of his sufferings before God are not estimated sufficiently high. But if the merit of the sufferings of the son of God be so exalted, that its power can introduce us into heaven, without its costing him, or ourselves, any effort for our preparatory purification, then what he hath achieved for us, and what he is able to achieve with his Father, appears in all its

lustre.[1] The Reformers conceived that the case was nearly the same, as if a gentleman were to testify his favour to a friend, by letting him introduce guests in their soiled travelling clothes, without giving them on that account a less gracious welcome. But here the question is not about forms of decorum and ceremonial frivolity:—it is about that inward adornment, that nuptial garment, which, under pain of removal from the banquet, according to the sentence of the Lord of grace, who is also the Holy One, ought not to be wanting. Even the gentleman, in the case referred to, would suppose that *the guests* introduced to him in the manner described, would entertain the same kindly feelings towards himself, *as the friend* under whose auspices they were admitted. Having thus formed clear notions of the mode, which the confessions deem most fitting for showing forth the glory of the Redeemer, it can no longer be a matter of doubt, which of them renders the tribute most worthy of that Redeemer. And now let us inquire into the misunderstandings, that have led to a condemnation of the Catholic doctrine.

It is scarcely possible, perhaps, to conceive any objection less cogent against the peculiar doctrines of the Catholic Church, than the assertion that it considers the reconciliation of man with God, *partly* as the work of Christ, *partly* as the work of man, or what is the same, that it divides between the Saviour and the believer the glory of bringing the latter back to God; and this forsooth, because Catholics represent the faith animated by love as agreeable to God! If the doctrine of Catholics were this, that the holy sentiments required of the Christian were obtained independently of Christ, and, in this independence, were acceptable to God; or even that Christ supplied only those virtues, wherein we were deficient; then the above objection would doubtless be well founded. But as the Church expressly teaches, that the entire spiritual life of the faithful, in so far as it is agreeable to God, flows absolutely from the source which is called Christ, how can there be here any question of a division of glory, or of a thankless conduct towards the Redeemer, and of a want of pious feeling! Undoubtedly, the Church urgently demands of everyone, to appropriate in a com-

[1] Chemnit. Exam. Conc. Trid, part 1, p. 265. 'Videt enim pius lector, remissionem peccatorum, adoptionem, ipsam denique salutem et vitam æternam adimi et detrahi satisfactioni et obedientiæ Christi, et transferri in nostras virtutes, Christo vero mediatori *hoc tantum* relinquitur, quod propter ipsius meritum accipiamus charitatem. . . . Exinanita est fides, et abolita promissio, si hæreditas ex lege, cujus summa est charitas.'

plete and vivid manner the power proffered in the Redeemer; undoubtedly, she teaches, that it is only by this living appropriation, by stamping Christ on our souls, we can become pleasing unto God; namely, when all our feelings, all our thoughts, and will, are filled with His vital breath. But to call this a dividing of glory with Christ, is tantamount to asserting, that a man, exposed to danger of death from hunger, divides the honour of his deliverance with him who benevolently offers him food and drink; because the unhappy man makes use of the strengthening nurture, and by that participation appropriates it to his own substance, and does not merely content himself with turning up a look of hope and confidence towards his benefactor. With this case, in fact, may be aptly compared the theory of Protestants in respect to the relation of the believer to Christ. But whoever is entangled in this error, will perish in his sins, like the starving man whom he would take for his model, while he fancies he is rendering glory to the Saviour alone. He will be comprised in the number of those, who exclaim, ' Lord, Lord ' (be thou alone praised !), but who ' do not the will of the heavenly father.'

But this whole error is here based on a confusion of the objective consummation of the atonement with its subjective appropriation (see § XI);[1] and the love which must first ger-

[1] The Council of Trent distinguishes five causes of justification, the sense whereof Sarpi should have fathomed before he presumed to express a censure. 'Hujus justificationis causæ sunt *finalis* quidem gloria Dei et Christi, ac vita æterna : *efficiens* vero misericors Deus, qui gratuito abluit : *meritoria* autem dilectissimus unigenitus suus, Dominus noster Jesus Christus, qui, cum essemus inimici, propter nimiam caritatem, qua dilexit nos, sua sanctissima passione in ligno crucis nobis justificationem meruit et pro nobis Deo patri satisfecit : *instrumentalis* item, sacramentum baptismi: . . . demum unica *formalis* causa est justitia Dei ; non qua ipse justus est, sed qua nos justos facit : qua videlicet ab eo donati, renovamur spiritu mentis nostræ, et non modo reputamur, sed vere justi nominamur et sumus, justitiam in nobis recipientes.' (Sess. vi, c. viii.) It is the *justificationis causa formalis*, which gives so much offence to the Protestants. The *causa formalis* is, in the technical language of the mediæval schools, the *dans esse in aliquo, dans actualitatem ;* and accordingly, here it is that whereby the righteousness, which God desireth of us, becomes real within us forming (*forma*) the vivifying principle within us. The Council says, the righteousness becomes living and is formed within us, through the impression of God's holy will (*justitia Dei*) upon our souls. This doctrine the Protestants take quite abstractedly, just as if it signified : ' the sanctified will is what is acceptable to God in us,' without attending to what immediately before was said respecting the *causa finalis, efficiens,* and *meritoria*, to wit that it is only the mercy of God and the merits of Christ which are the source, whence flow the release of the human will

minate from faith in the grace and the love of God in Christ, though in a living faith it has already ripened into blossom and fruit, is so understood, as if God remitted us our sins on account of our love, whereas it is His voluntary gift. A misunderstanding of Scripture has had great share in producing this error. In the Bible, God is represented as loving men *before* they love Him (see 1 John iv, 10); that is to say, as loving them *without* their love; whereas, the Catholic Church teaches that he only, who loves God, is beloved of God. Hereby the free, unmerited, grace of God in Christ seems totally rejected, as if only through our love, the love of God deserved to be acquired. What is to be said in reply to this? In answering this question, we connect with the first epistle of John iv, 10, numerous other passages which appear to contradict it—passages wherein it is expressly said, that God loves only those who love Him. In the verse referred to, the love of God embracing the human race (τὸν κοσμόν) in the Redeemer, is announced, and at the same time the eternal mystery is unveiled, that God, through his Son, proffers forgiveness to all. But this universal, eternal love of God is *realised in the individual*, only

from sin and its sanctification, and on this account it is said, God stamps His will upon us, *nos justos facit Deus.* Luther says, the *causa formalis justificationis* is the instrumental faith (Commentary on the epistle to the Galatians, loc. cit. p. 70); and in his system he is right, for, according to it, man is already completely righteous and regenerated, so soon as he possesses that faith—so soon as he apprehends Christ—the extraneous righteousness. But the Catholic denies that by this theory the scriptural, or even scientific, notion of a living appropriation is realised; and he is equally far from conceding, that by upholding this notion the Catholic Church withholds the glory due to Christ, the Lord, or in other words, fails to recognise in its full extent the power of the atonement. Calvin (in Antidot. in Concil. Trid. opusc. p. 704) expresses himself with great naïveté: 'Porro quam frivola sit et nugatoria causarum partitio . . . supersedeo dicere.' He is also perfectly right in avoiding all clear scientific definitions on this matter: for the very existence and maintenance of the whole Protestant system of doctrine is connected with this point. Chemnit. Exam. Concil. part 1, p. 266, ' Sed Andradius hanc Christi mediatoris justitiam fide nobis imputatam blasphemat esse commentitiam, adumbratam et fictitiam. Nullum autem habent aliud argumentum, nisi (!) quod opponunt absurditatem ex physica et ethica: absurdum scilicet esse (sicut Osius inquit) dicere alicujus rei formam esse, quæ ipsi rei non insit, ut si dicam, parietem esse album albedine, quæ vesti meæ inhæreat, non parieti: vel Ciceronem esse fortem fortitudine, quæ non ipsi, sed Achillis animo inhæreat. Quid vero hæc argumenta aliud ostendunt quam Pontificios in doctrina justificationis, relicta evangelii luce, quærere sententiam, quæ conformis et consentanea sit philosophicis opinionibus, aut certe legalibus sententiis de justitia? Evangelium vero pronuntiat esse sapientiam in mysterio absconditam, quam nemo princi-

K

at the moment wherein he co-operates with the love of God revealed in the Redeemer, and, full of faith, stamps it on his heart and his will; so that, as this specific individual, he is, in effect, beloved of God at the moment only when the love hath become mutual. (John xiv, 21-23.) Hence both forms of speech in Holy Writ are equally true; hence the truth of the Catholic doctrine, which, in the article of justification, *wherein this personal appropriation of God's unmerited grace is the question at issue*, necessarily adheres to the words of the Scriptural text last referred to.

3. Let us now turn to the relation which the distinction in question bears to humility. The principal virtue of the Pauline faith is, doubtless, humility—the unconditional resignation to God in Christ, self-renunciation on the part of man, and his deep conviction of possessing no sentiment agreeable to God, without Christ—and it is not to be denied, that a perception of this truth mainly influenced the Reformers in their definition. But as they asserted that it was not the intrinsic worth of faith —that is to say, it was not a circle of closely-connected virtues involved in faith, such as humility, love, self-denial, and the rest, which stamped on it the character of justification; a

pum hujus sæculi cognovit. Ideo cum habeamus sententiæ nostræ in scriptura certa et firma fundamenta (?), non est curandum, *etiamsi incurrat in absurditatem philosophicam.*' Here it is openly avowed, that the Protestant theory of appropriation of the merits of Christ, cannot stand the test of scientific investigation. And such is the fact; for, as was said above, we are to appropriate to ourselves the obedience of Christ without his becoming our own true and inmost property; He is to become subjective, without becoming so; and this is, in truth, a philosophic absurdity. In the same way, no philosophic notion of Protestant faith can be formed, because it is to be an organ of appropriation *without appropriating.* To the same confusion of ideas we may ascribe charges like the following: 'Sed hoc dicunt esse totum meritum Christi, quod propter illud misericordia Dei infundat nobis novam qualitatem justitiæ inhærentis, quæ est caritas, ut illa justificemur: hoc est, ut non propter Christi obedientiam, sed propter nostram charitatem, absolvamur coram judicio Dei adoptemur in filios.' (Chemnit. lib. i, p. 263.) Here again we find the divine and the human, the objective atonement and the subjective appropriation confounded with each other. When Chemnitius, in a tone of lament, proceeds to observe, 'Ut ita misericordia Dei *tantum* sit causa efficiens, et obedientia Christi *tantum* sit meritoria causa,' we can only express our astonishment; for what more can they be *in themselves?* Chemnitius desires the obedience of Christ should be also the *causa formalis*, that is to say, should become our own, without ourselves being obliged to be obedient: it is to become subjective without becoming subjective! In a word, the theory of Chemnitius is what we have already commented on in the text; to wit, that the merits of Christ stand forth in a far more glorious light, when we not merely believe they work out our forgiveness,

method was found of dispensing with humility even in humility itself, and, in order to evince a true humility, it was taught, that it was not humility in faith which rendered us acceptable to God! It is indeed a sign of true humility, to be ignorant of itself, and to conceal itself from its own view; but never hath a truly humble man taught, that humility doth not render us agreeable to the Deity. Were there any other means of awakening in our souls a heartfelt, vivid, persevering sense of the virtue of humility, than faith in the merits of the Redeemer, by the acknowledgment of which alone man is compelled to go out of himself, to renounce, without reserve, his own self-produced virtue, in order to live entirely in and by God; we should not then even stand in need of the merits of the Redeemer. So much is humility the cardinal point, on which everything hinges, which must be called forth before everything else, because in this negative, all positive is comprised. And this is not to make us acceptable to God, because, forsooth, no virtue can make us so! And it is precisely in the avowal, that it is not humility, but faith only which possesses this property, that true humility is to consist! Here the Reformers were evidently misled by the most vague, the most confused, yet withal honourable, feelings. Of the

in so far as they work out at the same time our improvement, but when we also assume, that for the sake of these merits sin is forgiven us, even when we reform not our conduct, but merely believe. Chemnitius (p. 263-4) censures Catholics for denying forgiveness of sins on account of Christ's satisfaction, because they make the same tantamount to a real extirpation of sin, and the implanting of charity in the room of the old debt of sin. But Catholics teach that through faith in the divine mercy in Jesus Christ, and all connected therewith, love for God is awakened in our souls, and thereby the affection for sin effaced. But is this to deny the objective forgiveness of sins, or is it not rather to appropriate the same to ourselves? Is it not to protest against a notion of appropriation, which is none at all? Calvin, especially, entertained the singular opinion, that Catholics believed justification to consist, *partly* in the forgiveness of sins, *partly* in the spiritual regeneration. Antidot. in Condc. Trid. opusc. p. 704: ' Sed quid facis istis bestiis (the Catholics) . . . Nam justitiæ partem operibus hinc constare colligunt, quod nemo absque spiritu regenerationis per Christum Deo concilietur,' and so on : ' Ac si *partim* remissione, *partim* spirituali regeneratione justi essemus.' Calvin having already taught, that by instrumental faith, and apart from all newness of life, man becomes righteous, must needs further teach, that by forgiveness of sins alone is man justified. But although under righteousness Catholics include newness of life, it by no means follows that they hold justification to consist, *partly* in this newness of life, and *partly* in the forgiveness of sins, for out of faith is unfolded the entire new life, and the latter is ever determined by the former. Thus, in the righteous man, faith and the inner new-born life form an inseparable unity (*fides formata*), as in God do forgiveness of sins and sanctification.

truly positive principle in the negative character of humility, they had no clear conception. Still less did they pause to reflect, that it is one thing to lay down the doctrine, that a man can be thoroughly good, and another to hold oneself as personally good. The latter would be the destruction of all religious life, while the former is its essential condition.

The inextricable contradiction, in which this doctrine involved the Protestants, is well worthy of notice. According to their teaching, humility, like every other virtue, can be *rightly* found, only where it is most urgently inculcated, that the believer needs it not to render himself acceptable to God. And yet it is taught at the same time, that *on that account* the Christian needs it not, as a holy sentiment, to obtain the favour of the Deity, because, like every other virtue, it appears *always impure* in man, that is to say, always marred by self-complacency and arrogance. Hence, if it were exacted as necessary to justification, man would never become just in the eyes of God. Thus, forsooth, true humility is to be engendered by a system of faith which establishes, that there is no true humility even in the new-born; and true humility can acquire a solid foundation only by the doctrine of its impossibility, or at least its non-existence in this system. Either the doctrine, that there is no true humility, is right—and then such a doctrine can never produce true humility, because otherwise the doctrine itself would be false—or, there is such a thing as true humility, and then the doctrine is false.

Akin to this contradiction, or, rather, identical with it, though only in another form, is the following: in studying the writings of the Reformers, the thought has often involuntarily occurred to us, that they entertained the opinion that it was something extremely dangerous to be really good; nay, that the principle of sanctity, so soon as it was on the point of acquiring complete dominion over a man, contained the germ of its own destruction, as such a man must needs become arrogant, fall into vain-glory, liken himself to the Eternal, and contend with him for divine sovereignty. Hence the securing of believers seemed to require, that they should ever keep within themselves a good germ of evil, because in this state we are better off! Accordingly the matter was so handled, as if real goodness were incompatible with humility, and as if it were in evil only, that this virtue flourished; whereas it was not considered, that wickedness was in itself the contrary of true humility, and utterly excluded it.

In the following passage, replete with wonderful *naïveté* the impression which, as we just said, the reading of the Reformers' writings has produced on our mind, has been recorded in felicitous language by Luther himself. 'Doctor Jonas said to Dr Martin Luther at supper-time: he had that day in his lecture been commenting on that sentence of Paul in 2 Timothy iv, "*Reposita est mihi corona justitiæ*," "there is laid up for me a crown of justice," "Oh! how gloriously doth St Paul speak of his death! I cannot believe it!" Whereupon Dr Martin replied, "I do not believe St Paul was able to have so strong a faith on this matter as he asserts. In truth, I cannot, alas! believe so firmly as I preach, talk, and write, and as other people think I believe. AND IT WOULD NOT BE QUITE GOOD FOR US TO DO ALL THAT GOD COMMANDS, FOR HE WOULD THEREBY BE DEPRIVED OF HIS DIVINITY, AND WOULD BECOME A LIAR, AND COULD NOT REMAIN TRUE. The authority of St Paul, too would be overturned, for he says in Romans: "God hath concluded all things under sin, in order that He might have mercy on all men."'[1]

§ XIX—SURVEY OF THE DIFFERENCES IN THE DOCTRINE OF FAITH

We will now endeavour, briefly, to state the points of agreement and of divergence in the article of faith. They are as follows:—

1. If 'Faith' be taken in an objective sense, that is to say, as an establishment instituted by God, in Jesus Christ, in opposition to Mosaism, or any human and arbitrary system of religion, and the modes of thinking, feeling, and acting, which such prescribe, then the Catholic can without restriction assert: it is by faith alone man is able to acquire God's favour: there is no other name given to men whereby they may be saved, save Christ Jesus alone. And it is *only* through the mercy of God, we say this name is given; consequently without any merit on the part of mankind in general, or of individual man in particular.

2. The divergence commences only when the objective must become subjective—when the question regards the conditions under which that institution of salvation is to conduce towards

[1] See Luther's Table-talk, p. 166 (in German): Jena, 1603.

our personal salvation. But here, also, each confession teaches, that man should adhere to Christ, and enter into a spiritual connection with him, in order to partake of the blessings proffered through and in Him. But the Catholic says, if this adherence be a mere connection of ideas—an empty union of feeling or phantasy with Christ—a mere theoretic faith in him—a mere recognition of Christian truths, in opposition to *works wrought in the vital communion of the will* with Christ, as well as to the love engendered by faith, and to all other virtues ; then this faith is in itself by no means sufficient to render men acceptable to God, or to justify. But if faith, on the other hand, be understood as a new divine sentiment, regulating the whole man— as the new living spirit (*fides formata*) ; then to this *alone*, even according to the Catholic system, is the power given to make us the children and heirs of eternal happiness; for, in this sense, faith alone embraces everything.[1] But let it be observed, that, by the Catholic Church, sacred charity is regarded as the substantial form of the faith, which alone justifies, not as a consequence, as a fruit *in expectancy*, but which, perhaps, may never come forth. *Love must already vivify faith*, before the Catholic Church will say, that through it man is really pleasing unto God. Faith in love and love in faith, justify ; they form *here* an inseparable unity.[2] This justifying faith is not merely

[1] We should here observe, that, at the commencement of the Reformation, the proposition, ' that faith alone justifies,' often bore the sense, ' that even the sacraments are unnecessary.' On which account, at several religious conferences, the Catholics, under the article of faith, insisted on the necessity of the sacraments as means of justification. Of these external means of grace we are not here speaking, where we have to treat merely of the internal acts agreeable to God, the spiritual state of the soul, and its outward manifestations in moral conduct.

[2] A very comprehensive view of this subject has been taken by Cardinal Sadoletus, Bishop of Carpentras, in his letters to the Genevans. (Epp. c. xvii, n. 25, Opp. ed. Veron. 1738, tom. ii, p. 176.) ' Assequimur bonum hoc nostræ perpetuæ universæque salutis, fide in deum sola et in Jesum Christum. Cum dico fide sola, non ita intelligo, quemadmodum isti novarum rerum repertores intelligunt, *ut seclusa charitate et cæteris Christianæ mentis officiis*, solam in Deum credulitatem et fiduciam illam, qua persuasus sum in Christi cruce et sanguine mea mihi delicta omnia esse ignota : est hoc quidem etiam nobis necessarium, primus hic nobis patet ad Deum introitus : sed is tamen non est satis. Mentem enim præterea afferamus oportet pietatis plenam erga summum Deum, cupidamque efficiendi quæcunque illi grata sint : in quo præcipue virtus Spiritus Sancti inest. Quæ mens etiamsi interdum ad exteriora opera non progreditur, ipsa tamen ex sese ad bene operandum jam intus parata est, promptumque gerit studium, ut Deo in cunctis rebus obsequatur : qui verus divinæ justitiæ in nobis est habitus.' After citing several scriptural texts, Sadoletus continues :

negative, but positive, withal; not merely a confidence, that, for Christ's sake, the forgiveness of sins will be obtained, but, a sanctified feeling, in itself agreeable to God. Charity is, undoubtedly, according to Catholic doctrine, a fruit of faith. But faith justifies, *only when it has already brought forth this fruit.* Faith is also, in our view, a vivifying principle; but it obtains for us the favour of God, *only when it has already unfolded its vivifying power.*[1]

3. The justifying subjective faith, in the Protestant sense, is described, not merely as a recognition of the New Testament Revelation,[2] but as an assurance of the Divine Grace in Christ

' Certe fides, quæ in Deum nostra per Jesum Christum est, non solum ut confidamus in Christo, sed bene in illo operantes, operarive instituentes, ut confidamus, imperat nobis ac præscribit. Est enim amplum ac plenum vocabulum fides, nec solum in se credulitatem et fiduciam continet : sed spem etiam et studium obediendi Deo, et illam, quæ in Christo maxime perspicua nobis facta est, principem et dominam Christianarum omnium virtutum, charitatem.'

[1] Sadoleti Epp. lib. xiii, n. 2 ; Gaspari Contareno Card. opp. ed. Veron. tom. ii, p. 45. ' De justificatione et justitia placet mihi vehementer tuarum rationum contextus et distinctio ex Aristotele sumpta. Sequitur enim certe charitas cursum illum antecedentem, quo ad justitiam pervenitur : non tamen sequitur eadem charitas (meo quidem animo opinioneque) justitiam, *sed eam ipsa constituit :* vel potius charitas ipsa est justitia. Habet enim formæ vim charitas : forma autem est id, quod ipsa res. Cum ergo acceditur, præeunte illa præparatione ad justitiam, acceditur una et ad charitatem : ad quam cum est perventum, tum justitia per ipsam charitatem constituitur. Justitiam voco, non vulgari, neque Aristotelico nomine, sed Christiano more ac modo, eam quæ omnes virtutes complexa continet : neque id humanis viribus, sed instinctu influxuque divino,' etc.

[2] On this matter as in other articles, we find in Luther little permanent uniformity; and this may be accounted for by the obscurity and confusion in the notion which he *commonly* attached to justifying faith. Very often with him, ' faith' is belief in the truth of anything. Thus, in his commentary on the epistle to the Galatians (loc. cit. p. 70), he calls faith ' a hidden, lofty, secret, incomprehensible *knowledge ;*' but immediately thereupon, ' a true confidence and assurance of the heart.' Elsewhere, in the same work, he compares faith to dialectics, and hope to rhetoric; that is to say, faith floated before his mind as something theoretical, and not as anything practical. In his work, *De servo arbitrio* (lib. i, p. 177, b), faith is again described, in a long passage, as a firm persuasion ; and so also in the numerous passages where he opposes it to the future intuition. In his book *De captivitate Babylonica* (opp. tom. ii, p. 279, b), he says : ' Verbum Dei omnium primum est quod sequitur fides, fidem charitas, charitas deinde facit omne bonum opus.' Here one act on the part of men is overlooked : the preaching of the truth is followed, first, by *knowledge and recognition of the truth,* next, by confidence, and so on ; but which of these acts is here denoted by *fides ?* Probably it includes at once knowledge and confidence. Such indefiniteness in language is attended with very pernicious consequences, and, in later

Jesus, as confidence in the merits of the Redeemer, by the power whereof sins are forgiven. And this confidence is held up as being able, abstractedly and entirely of itself, to win for its possessor the favour and friendship of the Almighty. This consciousness of the Divine favour must see charity and good works in its train ; but as by their presence the latter contribute nought towards justification, so by their absence they take nothing from the state of the justified. Here, accordingly, charity is not regarded as the substantial form of the alone-justifying faith : man is already justified, so soon as he confides in Christ ; the seed is sown for heaven, and brings us thither, even when, under unfavourable circumstances, as, for instance, the sluggishness of the will, and the like, it bears absolutely no fruit. Thus the Protestant doctrine excludes works wrought before, as well as after, conversion to Christ, and, moreover, all holy sentiments, when it attributes to faith alone the power of saving—a doctrine which we may say, in passing, has not even the *very slightest* foundation in Scripture. Of *such* an opposition between faith, charity and works, *Paul did not even once think*, and James is absolutely opposed to it. (See section XXII.)[1]

§ XX—ON THE ASSURANCE OF JUSTIFICATION AND ETERNAL FELICITY

The opinion, that the believer must be perfectly convinced of his justification before God, and of his future felicity, is so closely connected with the doctrine of faith, in the Protestant

times, was productive of an utter indifference to *the truth*, just as if the having confidence were alone sufficient, or as if 'confidence' were intelligible without the firm conviction of the truth.

[1] After this investigation we shall be enabled to appreciate Gerhard's *Loci Theologici* (tom. vii, p. 206, loc. xvii, c. iii, sect. v), where he endeavours to base on tradition the Protestant doctrine of faith. It is a compilation totally unworthy of a man like Gerhard. Every passage wherein any doctor of the Church asserts that faith in Christ alone conducts to salvation, he alleges in favour of the Protestant theory, without at all inquiring what sense the author attached to these words. He was even so foolish as to make use of those passages wherein fathers of the Church (for example, St Irenæus), assert of the Catholic faith, in opposition to heretical systems of doctrine, that it can alone insure salvation ! The perception that a father of the Church, like Chrysostom, who held anything but the Protestant doctrine respecting original sin, free-will, and its relation to grace, could not possibly have entertained the Lutheran view of faith, it would be perhaps too much to expect from Gerhard ; for any desire to investigate the internal connection between different doctrines as he did not even feel.

system,[1] that Melancthon says of the schoolmen, who deny it, '"We see clearly, from this alone, how utterly devoid of intellect this species of men are.'[2] The close connection of this position with the whole Protestant system is undeniably clear. We have before observed, that, from the doctrine of the total extirpation of all seeds of good out of the human breast, one advantage in regard to Christian life might be gained—that man, so soon as he perceived any little sparks of a higher life within him, might be well assured that God had begun His work of redemption, which would be as certainly consummated (chap. xi, § vi). Secondly, that theory of faith according to which men are to direct their view towards God's mercy, and to turn it away from their own moral state,[3] necessarily involves the opinion we have advanced. Moreover this assurance of salvation presupposes absolute predestination, and the doctrine, that God's grace works only in the elect; for if a man can at any time repel the grace once felt, then, by the very idea of this possibility, the sense of certitude is at once shaken. Hence, it is only by the Calvinists this doctrine hath been carried out to its full extent; while on the part of the Lutherans it betrays that original adherence to the principles of predestination, which in other matters also have left traces of their influence, and the later rejection whereof has so materially impaired the internal harmony of their system.

[1] Apolog. iv, sect. 40, p. 83. 'Non diligimus, nisi *certo* statuant corda, quod donata sit nobis remissio peccatorum.' XII. De pœnitent. sect. 20, p. 157: 'Hanc certitudinem fidei nos docemus requiri in evangelio.' Calvin. Instit. lib. iii, c. 2, sect. 16, fol. 197: 'In summa, vere fidelis non est, nisi qui solida persuasione Deum sibi propitium benevolumque patrem esse persuasus, deque ejus benignitate omnia sibi pollicetur: nisi qui divinæ erga se benevolentiæ promissionibus fretus, indubitatem salutis expectationem præsumit.'

[2] Melancth. loc. theolog. p. 116. 'Ut vel hoc solo loco satis appareat, nihil nisse spiritus in toto genere.'

[3] Melancth. loc. theolog. p. 92, says, in this respect: 'Debebant enim non opera sua, sed promissionem misericordiæ Dei contemplari. *Quid est enim iniquius, quam æstimare voluntatem Dei ex operibus nostris, quam ille suo verbo nobis declaravit?*' True, if man hath no freedom; and hence it is by no means surprising, that Melancthon requires us to be certain of our salvation (for the certitude of the forgiveness of sins is, with the Reformers, tantamount to the certitude of salvation), although, the believer be not assured of his perseverance in good. 'Certissima sententia est, oportere nos certissimos semper esse de remissione peccati, de benevolentia Dei erga nos, qui justificati sumus. Et norunt quidem fide sancti, certissime se esse in gratia, sibi condonata esse peccata. Non enim fallit Deus, qui pollicitus est, se condonaturum peccata credentibus, *tametsi incerti sint, an perseveraturi sint.*'

Catholics, from opposite reasons, believe not that a quite unerring certitude of salvation can be acquired.[1] As they consider not fallen man to be devoid of all moral and religious qualities and signs of life, they are unable to discover a criterion, absolutely beyond the reach of illusion, whereby they can distinguish between the operations of grace, and the effects of those feelings in man akin to the Deity, and uneradicated by His fall.[2] But even if they were fortunate enough to possess

[1] Concil. Trident. sess. vi, cap. ix. 'Sicut nemo pius de Dei misericordia, de Christi merito, de sacramentorum virtute et efficacia dubitare debet, sic quilibet, dum se ipsum suamque propriam infirmitatem et indispositionem respicit, de sua gratia formidare et timere potest, *cum nullus seire valeat certitudine fidei*, cui non potest subesse falsum, se gratiam Dei esse consecutum.' Cap. xii. 'Nemo quoque, quamdiu in hac mortalitate vivitur, de arcano divinæ prædestinationis mysterio usque adeo præsumere debet, ut certo statuat se omnino esse in numero prædestinatorum : quasi verum esset, quod justificatus amplius peccare non possit, aut, si peccaverit, certam sibi resipiscentiam promittere debeat. Nam, nisi ex speciali revelatione, sciri non potest, quos Deus sibi elegerit.' C. xiii. 'Similitere de perseverantiæ munere, de quo scriptum est,—Qui perseveravit usque in finem, hic salvos erit : quod quidem aliunde haberi non potest, nisi ab eo, qui potens est eum, qui stat statuere, ut perseveranter stet, et eum, qui cadit, restituere. Nemo sibi certi aliquid absoluta certitudine polliceatur : tametsi in Dei auxilio firmissimam spem collocare, et reponere omnes debent. Deus enim, nisi ipsi illius gratiæ defuerint, sicut coepit opus bonum, ita perficiet, operans velle et perficere. Verumtamen qui se existimant stare, videant, ne cadant, et cum timore ac tremore salutem suam operentur. (Phil. ii. 12) . . . Formidare enim debent, scientes quod in spem gloriæ, et nondum in gloriam renati sunt, de pugna quæ superest cum carne, cum mundo, cum diabolo : in qua victores esse non possunt, nisi cum Dei gratia apostolo obtemperent, dicenti : Debitores sumus, non carni, ut secundum carnem vivamus ; si enim secundum carnem vixeritis, moriemini : si autem spiritu facta carnis mortificaveritis, vivetis.'

[2] Melancthon (loc. theol. p. 121) says, 'The fruits of the Holy Spirit testify that he worketh in our breast (*quod in pectore nostro versetur*); everyone, to wit, knoweth from his own experience whether he hateth sin from the bottom of his heart.' This criterion sounds the more strange from the lips of Melancthon, because he at the same time teaches, that even in the will of the regenerated sin remains ; that is to say, it is not detested from the heart. Hereby, accordingly, confidence would be placed in our own worthiness, whereas the Protestant doctrine of the solace of faith is to be zealously upheld, precisely because, if man look to himself, despair must take possession of his soul. The principles, which Melancthon here lays down for discerning the state of grace, are those of the Catholic theologians of the Middle Ages, and suit only the Catholic point of view.

So speaks St Thomas Aquinas, loc. cit. quæst. cxii. art. v. 'Hoc modo aliquis cognoscere optest, se habere gratiam, in quantum scilicet percipit se delectari in Deo, et contemnere res mundanas, et in quantum homo non est conscius peccati mortalis. Secundum quem modum potest nitelligi, quod habetur Apoc. i : "Vincenti dabo manna absconditum,

such a criterion, the confidence built thereon would be again damped, by the remembrance of the doctrine of human and divine co-operation in the second birth and its consummation, and be reduced to a more modest tone. For, together with the deepest confidence in God's mercy, Catholics are taught, by reason of those humiliating experiences, which we all make in the course of our lives, to entertain a great distrust of human fidelity ; and an absolute predestination, that would bid them overlook such scruples, is rejected by their Church. Thus the Catholic Christian, without a false security, yet full of consolation, calm, and entirely resigned to the divine mercy, awaits the day on which God shall pronounce his final award.

The avowals of Calvin in this matter are very remarkable, as well as the strenuous exertions he must have recourse to, in order to awaken in the souls of his disciples the desired assurance. He observes, that no temptation of Satan is more dangerous, than when he seduces believers to doubt of the certainty of their salvation, *and tempts them to seek the same in evil ways.* To this he subjoins the remark, that such temptations are the more dangerous, *because to none are the generality of men more inclined than to these.* Rarely do we find a man, whose soul is not at times disturbed by the thought—' Nowhere is the source of thy salvation to be found, but in the Divine election ; but in what manner hath this election been revealed to thee ? ' This train of thought Calvin concludes with a proposition drawn from his own experience : ' When once such doubts have become habitual in anyone, then the unhappy man is either constantly tortured with dreadful anxiety, or entirely deprived of all consciousness.'[1]

By this rash endeavour to obtain the assurance of our future salvation, various kinds of superstition, as well as a distracting uncertainty, were occasioned: so that the very reverse of Calvin's wishes occurred ; and it soon became manifest, that the effects of an unnatural desire were ever pernicious. With sin, and the combat against sin, came the restlessness of the

quod nemo novit, nisi qui accipit," quia sc. ille, qui accipit, per quandam experientiam dulcedinis novit, quam non experitur ille qui non accipit. Ista tamen cognitio imperfecta est. Unde apostolus dicit. 1, ad Cor. iv : " Nihil mihi conscius sum, sed non in hoc justificatus sum," ' etc.

[1] Lib. iii, c. 24, sect. 3, fol. 353, ' Eoque exitialior est hæc tentatio, quod ad nullam aliam propensiores simus fere omnes. . . . Quæ si apud quempiam semel invaluit, aut diris tormentis miserum perpetuo excruciat, aut reddit penitus attonitum.'

spirit; the latter never capable of being stilled, till the former had ceased to exist.[1] Undoubtedly, according to the sentence of the apostle, the spirit testifies to the spirit, that we are the children of God;[2] but this testimony is of so delicate a nature, and must be handled with such tender care, that the Christian in the feeling of his unworthiness and frailty, approaches the subject only with timidity, and scarcely ventures to take cognisance of it. It is a holy joy, which would fain conceal itself from its own view, and remain a mystery to itself; and the more exalted the Christian stands, the more humble is he, and the less is he disposed, without an extraordinary revelation, to vaunt a certainty, which so little accords with the uncertainty and mutability of all earthly things. The higher the duties which the Catholic Church imposes on man, the more obvious the reason wherefore she will acknowledge no absolute certainty of salvation. And herein precisely we must look for the motive of her teaching, that the believer can and must become worthy of salvation while yet she denies the certainty thereof; whereas the Protestants, who assert that man can in no wise become worthy of heaven, exert their utmost endeavours to call forth such a sense of security.

Moreover, in many other cases of spiritual life, it is the same as with the point in question. The innocence that would become conscious of itself, is usually lost by that very act; and the reflexion, whether the act we are about to perform be really

---

[1] Calvin. loc. cit. c. 2, sect. 17, fol. 198. 'Nos certe dum fidem docemu esse certam ac securam, non certitudinem aliquam imaginamur, quæ nullas tangatur dubitatione, nec securitatem, quæ nulla sollicitudine impetatur; quin potius dicimus, perpetuum esse fidelibus certamen cum sua ipsorum diffidentia.' But by this sentence the whole doctrine of assurance is given up. These striking contradictions are inherent in the very effort to force artificially on the human consciousness something in contradiction to that consciousness itself.

[2] Sarpi histoire du concile de Trent traduite per Amelot de la Houssaie, Amst. 1699, p. 198. 'Au commencement du ix chapitre, oǹ l'on disait, *que les péchés ne sont pas remis par la certitude qu'on a de la remission*, le legat changea le mot de *certitude* en ceux de jectance et de confiance présomptueuse en vertu de cette certitude de la grâce. Et à la fin du meme chapitre, au lieu de dire, *parceque personne ne peut savoir certainement, qu'il ait reçu la grâce de Dieu*, le mot *certainement* fut changé en ceux-ci, de certitude de foi.' This is further below explained, that faith is eternally true and unchangeable itself, however believing man may change; whereas, he who by an inward feeling is convinced of his state of grace, cannot yet be sure whether through sin he may not fall from that state: and therefore man in general cannot be assured of his salvation, *cum certitudine fidei*, although he may with confiding hope look forward to it.

pure, makes it not unfrequently impure. Hence the Saviour saith, ' let not thy right hand know what thy left doeth.' Joyful, yet full of sorrow, calm, and without precipitancy, the true saints pursue their way—they boast not on that account of being in the number of the elect, but resign their fate to God. According to the Protestant theory, everyone should be asked what he thought of himself, and he must in his own life be regarded as a saint. The doubt of others as to the truth of his own declaration would invalidate the doctrine of the symbolical books. As if in irony of their own doctrine, the Protestants would recognise no saints! I think that, in the neighbourhood of any man, who would declare himself under all circumstances assured of his salvation, I should feel very uncomfortable, and should probably have some difficulty to put away the thought, that something like diabolical influence was here at play.

But the truth, which even this Protestant doctrine darkly divined, must not be overlooked. It consists in the individualising of evangelical truths—in pointing to the necessity of the personal application of them, and of the relation of the Divine promises to ourselves, so that we should not regard them as undefined, and as merely relative to others.

OF GOOD WORKS

§ XXI—DOCTRINE OF CATHOLICS RESPECTING GOOD WORKS

By good works the Catholic Church understands all the moral actions and sufferings of the man justified in Christ, or the fruits of holy feeling and believing love. Of the observance of certain ecclesiastical ceremonies, external rites, and the like, we have not *here* occasion to speak, as the following exposition will very clearly show. As in the man truly born again from the Spirit the Catholic Church recognises a real liberation from sin, a direction of the spirit and the will truly sanctified and acceptable to God, it necessarily follows that she asserts the possibility and reality of truly good works, and their consequent meritoriousness. It is evident, too, that in consequence of this doctrine, she can and must exact the fulfilment of the moral law, as laid down by the Apostle Paul, in Rom. viii, 3, 4.

Thus, we must especially observe, that it is only on works

consummated in a real vital communion with Christ, the Church bestows the predicate 'good'; and of a fulfilment of the law, she speaks only in so far as the power to this effect hath been given in fellowship with Christ. The Fathers of Trent express themselves in the following manner:—' As a constant power flows from Christ, the Head, on the justified, who are his members, as from the vine to its branches, a power, which precedes their good works, accompanies the same, and follows them—a power without which they can be in nowise agreeable to God, and meritorious; so we are bound to believe, that the justified are enabled through works performed in God, to satisfy the divine law, according to the condition of this present life, and to merit eternal life, when they depart in a state of grace.[1]

From this we may, at the same time, clearly see, how far works are called meritorious. When we presuppose, what must be here of course taken for granted, the fundamental doctrine of all true religion, to wit, that it was out of *pure love itself* that God conferred on us life, all our faculties, and the destination for eternal happiness; and that the agent expressly acknowledges these truths; then we may briefly describe those works as meritorious, which our freedom (and without freedom it were idle to talk of man's moral relations) hath wrought in *the power of Christ*. Hence the holy fathers of Trent observe at the same time: ' So great is the goodness of the Lord towards all men, that He considers His own gifts as their merits.' [2] This is the idea which the ancient Church attached to merit, and which is founded on Holy Writ. Can heaven then be merited by believers? Undoubtedly; they must merit it, that is to say, become worthy of it, through Christ. Between them and heaven there must be a homogeneity—an internal relation; that relation, which, by God's eternal ordinance and His express promises, exists between sanctity and beatitude; terms which

---

[1] Concil. Trident. sess. vi, c. 16.
[2] Even Calvin allows this to be the doctrine of Catholics. He says as follows (Instit. lib. iii, c. 11, sect. 14, p. 266): 'Subtile effugim se habere putant sophistæ, qui sibi ex scripturæ depravatione et inanibus cavillis ludos et delicias faciunt: nam opera (of these St Paul saith that they do not justify) exponunt, quæ literaliter tantum et liberi arbitrii conatu extra Christi gratiam faciunt homines necdum regeniti, id vero ad opera spiritualia spectare negant. (This is right.) Ita, secundum eos, tam fide, quam operibus justificatur homo, modo ne sint propria ipsius opera, sed dona Christi et regenerationis fructus.' However, the Catholic doth not say, man is justified, *tam fide quam operibus*, as if both existed independently of each other.

are not only inseparable, but which stand also in the same relation to one another, as cause and effect.¹ The Catholic Church, as she maintains that the genuine Christian possesses in Christ an inward righteousness proper to himself, and deeply rooted in his being, cannot do other than teach that salvation is to be derived from this source. A heavenly seed having been sown in the soul of the just, it must bear its fruits for heaven.²

¹ St Thomas Aquinas has expressed himself admirably on this matter. He says (loc. cit. quæst. cxiv, art. 1) that the notion of merit is founded on the notion of justice, in the Hellenic and Roman sense of the word. But absolute justice, strictly speaking, exists only between absolute equals. To give back *of our own* as much as we have received, or will receive, is to give according to merit, and to act justly, which absolutely presupposes the equality of both parties. In this sense there can be no question of merit before God; for we should be obliged to offer to God what is our own, not what we have received from him, whereupon he would repay us with as much of his own. Hence, when in Holy Writ so much is said of a reward, which the good receive in the next life; or when it is said there will be a remuneration, according to works, it is only a conditional merit and a conditional justice which is meant. He says: 'Manifestum est autem, quod inter Deum et hominem est maxima inæqualitas, in infinitum enim distant; totum, quod est hominis bonum, est a Deo, unde non potest hominis a Deo esse justitia secundum absolutam æqualitatem, sed secundum proportionem quandam, in quantum scilicet uterque operatur secundum modum suum. Modus autem et mensura humanæ virtutis homini est a Deo, et ideo meritum hominsi apud Deum esse non potest, nisi secundum præsuppositionem divinæ ordinationis: ita scilicet ut id homo consequatur a Deo, per suam operationem, quasi mercedem, ad quod Deus ei virtutem operandi deputavit. Sicut etiam res naturales hoc consequuntur per proprios motus et operationes, ad quod a Deo sunt ordinatæ, differenter tamen, quia creatura rationalis se ipsam movet ad agendum per liberum arbitrium. Unde sua actio habet rationem meriti; quod non est in aliis creaturis.'

² St Thomas in answer to the questions, whether eternal life can be obtained without grace? and whether with grace, we become *worthy* of the same? says as follows: (Q. cxiv, art. ii) 'Non potest homo mereri absque gratia vitam æternam per *pura* naturalia, quia scilicet meritum hominis dependet ex præordinatione divina. Actus autem, cujuscunque rei non ordinatur divinitus ad aliquid excedens proportionem virtutis, quæ est principium actus: hoc enim est ex institutione divinæ providentiæ, ut nihil agat ultra suam virtutem. Vita autem æterna est quoddam bonum excedens proportionem naturæ creatæ: quia etiam excedit cognitionem et desiderium ejus, secundum illud 1, ad Cor. 2: nec oculus vidit, etc. Et inde est, quod nulla natura creata est sufficiens principium actus meritorii, vitæ æternæ, nisi superaddatur aliquid supernaturale donum, quod gratia dicitur. Si vero loquamur de homine sub peccato existente, additur cum hoc secunda ratio propter impedimentum peccati,' etc. Art. iii: 'Si loquamur de opere meritorio, secundum quod procedit ex gratia Spiritus Sancti, sic est meritorium vitæ æternæ ex condigno. Sic enim valor meriti attenditur secundum virtutem Spiritus Sancti, moventis nos in vitiam æternam, secundum illud Joann. iv. fiet in eo fons aquæ salientis in vitam æternam, etc. . . . Gratia Spiritus Sancti, quam in præsenti habe-

If Catholics teach, that the divine grace which precedes the first beginnings of regeneration, cannot be merited, this is a far different case; and this remark should serve to place in the strongest light our doctrine respecting good works. In the former instance, nature, yea, fallen nature and grace stand opposed to one another—humanity, thoroughly polluted with sin, on one side, and the Deity on the other: but in the latter instance, this is by no means the case. Although the greatest effort of nature cannot draw down to itself the supernatural power (for this must condescend), in the regenerated, however, exist qualities truly divine and supernatural—a holy energy, which stamps its impress on the whole inward life of the believer, and contains, as in a germ, the beatitude which still, however, retains a supernatural and divine character. Thereby, however, the grace of beatitude doth not cease to be a grace; but it is already comprised in the grace of sanctification. If God gave the latter, then was the former, too, communicated. Hence also, the Council observes, this doctrine can give no occasion to self-confidence or to self-glory; but 'he who glorieth, must glory only in the Lord.'

It is, moreover, scarcely necessary to observe, that it is not to works considered abstractedly, but to works in connection with the feelings in which they have their source, that salvation is awarded: it is promised to works only in so far as they are the expression and the blossom, the consummation and the proof, of feeling, or love in its outward and active manifestation. By a metonymy, the outward is put for the inward thing, which constitutes with the former an indivisible whole—a one act, and this, too, *in consequence of a biblical usage of speech*. It is, also, self-evident, that sanctified feelings which remain unmanifested in deeds, because they fail of an outward occasion, or even of the physical means, possess as much worth, as if they had been revealed in works.[1] Lastly, it is taught that the

mus, etsi non sit æqualis gloriæ in actu, est tamen æqualis in virtute: sicut et semen arbori, in quo est virtus ad totam arborem.'

[1] Jacob Sadolet. card. ad. princip. Germaniæ oratio, loc. cit. p. 360. ' Quomodo igitur opera cum fide simul justificant, cum sæpe absque operibus faciat sola fides justitiam, uti in latrone fecit, ut in aliis multis, quos ex historiis ecclesiasticis possumus colligere? Nempe, quia habitus justitiæ, quo ad bene operandum propensi efficimur, fidei ipsi ab initio statim propter amorem et charitatem est annexus; ubi enim amor Dei inest, qui in vera illa fide protinus elucet, simul illa subito ades propensio animi et cogitatio, esse in actionibus rectis amori nostro in Deum, et Deo ipsi satisfaciendum admonenti nos illi et docenti, si diligamus eum, et

performance of good works augments grace. Exercise in good, the faithful co-operation with grace, renders the soul ever more susceptible to its influence. The general maxim, that the exercise of any faculty serves to strengthen it, holds good in this case also ; and that he who doth not bury the talent he hath received, but puts it out to interest, will receive still more, is the promise of our Lord.

But doth not this doctrine promote mere outward holiness ? Its object is precisely to encourage *holiness in deeds*. Doth it not produce self-righteousness ? This should it do—namely, cause that we *ourselves* become righteous. Yes, indeed, the Church requires works emanating from the sanctified soul, and knows well how to appreciate the mere exterior works. Nay, she urges us to become righteous *in our own persons*, distinguishing this very accurately from the conceit that we can become righteous *through ourselves;* but she calls on the Protestants to learn this distinction, not to hold the one as synonymous with the other, and, in consequence, to reject both alike.

§ XXII—DOCTRINE OF THE PROTESTANTS RESPECTING GOOD WORKS

Let us now turn to the exposition of the Protestant doctrine on good works. Above all, we must describe what they are in themselves, according to the Lutheran and Calvinistic writings ; next, what is their merit, and whether and how far they be deemed necessary. That this whole article of doctrine must,

mandata ejus servemus. Hinc intestinus justitiæ habitus, non conflatus ex actionibus et operibus nostris, sed cum ipsa fide charitateque conjunctim divinitus nobis impressus, is ille ipse est, qui justos nos facit. Et sane convenientius est, ut a justitia justi, quam a fide nominemur. Tametsi (ut dixi) omnia hæc in unum connexa sunt et cohærent. Hunc habitum præclare exprimit Paulus divinis illis verbis, quibus ad Ephesios utitur, sic scribens : gratia servati estis per fidem, idque non ex vobis, Dei donum est ; non ex operibus, ne quis glorietur, Dei enim ipsius sumus effectio, ædificati in Christo Jesu ad opera bona, quibus præparavit Deus in illis ut ambularemus. Ad Deum itaque per Christum accedenti, statim ad recte faciendum prompta facilitas quædam et voluntas bona agnoscitur. Porro iste ipse habitus justitiæ tunc absolute in nobis perfectus est, cum explicat sese, et exerit in sanctas actiones : exercitationemque continet justitiæ cum ipsa exercendi voluntate conjunctam. Ipso autem fidei initio, aut si spatium non est recti faciendi, licet totam perfectionem justitiæ non teneat, idem tamen nobis potest ad salutem, quod absoluta plenaque justitia.'

L

in every respect, be only a further development of the Protestant principles on justification and justifying faith, is evident of itself; for the view which the Protestants have formed of the latter, that it possesses no power of moral renovation, no power for the expiation of sin, pervades their whole conception of Christian works. In a word, the same relation which they, as we have before shown, establish betwixt justifying faith and charity, recurs here, applied to good works.

Luther, asserting the continuance and operation of original sin, even in the will, of the justified, maintained, immediately after the commencement of his Reforming career, that no works could possibly be *pure and acceptable to the Deity;* and used the expression, that even the best work is a venial sin. This proposition was, as may be supposed, condemned in the papal censure of his opinions. But the Reformer went a step further, and laid down the doctrine, that every so-called good work— that is to say, every act of a believer—is, when considered in itself, a mortal sin, though, by reason of faith, it is remitted to him.[1] Melancthon not only expressed full concurrence in the doctrine of his master, but carried it out to an extreme, by asserting that all our works, all our endeavours, are *nothing but sin*;[2] and Calvin, though in more measured language, corroborated the assertions of both.[3]

[1] Luther. assert. omn. art. op. tom. ii, fol. 325, b. 'Opus bonum optime factum est veniale peccatum. Hic (articulus) manifeste sequitur ex priori, nisi quod addendum sit, quod alibi copiosius dixi—hoc veniale peccatum non natura sua, sed misericordia Dei, tale esse. . . . Omne opus justi damnabile est et peccatum mortale, si judicio Dei judicetur.' Cfr. Antilatom. (confut. Luth. rat. latom.) l. c. fol. 406, b, 407, seq.

[2] Melancth. loc. theolog. p. 108. 'Quæ vero opera justificationem conequuntur, ea, tametsi a spiritu Dei, occupavit corda justificatorum, proficiscuntur, tamen quia fiunt in carne adhuc impura, sunt et ipsa immunda.' P. 158: 'Nos docuimus, justificari sola fide, . . . opera nostra, conatus nostros nihil nisi peccatum esse.'

[3] Calvin. Instit. lib. ii, c. 8, sect. 59; lib. iii, c. 4, sect. 28. He says the same also in his work, *De necessit. Reformandæ eccl. opuscul.* p. 430; yet his expressions are much milder than Luther's. He says here: 'Nos ergo sic docemus; semper deesse bonis fidelium operibus *summam* puritatem, quæ conspectum Dei ferre possit, imo etiam *quodammodo* inquinata esse,' etc. Quite falsely doth Zwingle state the Protestant doctrine. He says (in fidei Christianæ exposit. ad regem christianiss. Gall. opp. tom. ii, p. 558): 'Fidem oportet esse fontem operis. Si fides adsit, jam opus gratum est Deo: si desit, perfidiosum est, quicquid fit, et subinde non tantum ingratum, sed et abominabile Deo. . . . Et ex nostris quidem παραδόξως adseruerunt (?), omne opus nostrum esse abominationem. Qua sententia nihil aliud voluerunt, quam quod jam diximus!' This Luther did not mean to say, for otherwise there would be no difference.

It may not be unworthy of our attention, and at any rate it will conduce to the elucidation of the subject before us, to examine, in a few words, the course of argument pursued by Luther. He says: in the saint two men are to be distinguished —a slave of sin, and a servant of God; the former is holy according to the flesh, the latter according to the spirit. Accordingly, the person of the just man is in part holy, in part sinful; and the entire personality being thus divided between sin and holiness, every good work partakes of the character of both—for a holy and an unholy sentiment co-exist in the breast of the believer.[1] Even Melancthon expressly affirms, that the believer, in despite of the spirit of Christ working within him, is unable to exalt himself above this dualism; that *two natures* ever survive in him, the spirit and the flesh.[2] If we only recollect that by the word 'flesh' is understood, not the body merely, but the entire man, independent of the new powers imparted to him through the Holy Ghost, there can no longer remain, it appears to us, any obscurity in this article.[3]

The spirit of Christ is too powerless to be able, like a purifying fire, totally to cleanse the nature of man, and to produce in him pure charity and pure works. Hence the assertion so often and so energetically repeated by the leaders of the Reformation, at the outset of their career, that even the regenerated cannot fulfil the law.[4] On this subject Luther expresses himself with great *naïveté*. In reply to the observation of the Catholics— that God commands not impossibilities, and that, if we have only the will, we have the power of loving Him with our whole hearts, and thereby of fulfilling the law, he observes: 'Commanding and doing are two things. Commandment is soon given, but it is not so easily executed. It is, therefore, a wrong conclusion to say, God has commanded me to love Him; therefore I can do so.'[5]

The intrinsic inanity of this doctrine, its evident repugnance to Scripture—which only the most forced interpretation could

[1] Luther. Assert. omn. art. n. 31, opp. tom. ii, fol. 319.
[2] Melancth. loc. theolog. 'Ita fit, ut duplex sit sanctorum natura spiritus et caro.'
[3] Melancth. loc. theolog. p. 138.
[4] Melancth. loc. theolog. p. 127. 'Maledixit lex eos, qui non universam legem semel absolverint. At universa lex nonne summum amorem erga Deum, vehementissimum metum Dei exigit? a quibus cum tota natura sit alienissima, utut maxime pulcherrimum pharisæismum, præstes maledictionis tamen rei sumus.'
[5] Luther, Commentary on Epistle to Galatians, loc. cit. p. 233.

conceal—and the very pernicious influence which it too evidently exercised over the morals of those professing it, as well as the cogent objections of Catholics, gradually brought about some ameliorations, which passed into the later writings of Melancthon, and even into the public formularies, but still fell very far short of that standard, which the Catholic Church deems herself authorised, both by the spirit and the letter of the Gospel, to propose to her children.[1]

If, now, the question be asked, what do good works, or rather the sentiments pervading them—the inward kernel of the regenerated—the fulfilment of the law through charity—what do good works merit ? it is clear that this question must be answered in a sense very different from that of Catholics. Already the rejection of the co-operation of free-will necessarily involved the denial of every species of merit, and rendered the very notion of such a thing utterly unintelligible. As, moreover, no true sanctity was believed to exist in the justified, so no felicity could be derived from it. Accordingly, it was most zealously contended, that, when the question was about good works, and the observance of the moral precepts, the former should not be represented as having reference to the acquisition of eternal happiness, nor the latter as having any internal connection with works and the fulfilment of the law ; and both should be stated as utterly independent one of the other, in the same way as justification is something very different from sanctification.[2] To estimate the whole extent of that separation, which in this article of doctrine divides the Christian Confessions, we need only be reminded of George Major, a very esteemed Protestant, who ventured to teach, that good works are necessary to salvation. His motive in the introduction of this innovation was very laudable. He believed that a true Christian bearing and deportment was most painfully neglected among the members of his Church, and that the preaching of what was then called ' the

[1] Apolog. iv, de dilect. et implet. legis. sect. 50, p. 91. ' Hæc ipsa legis impletio, quæ sequitur renovationem, est *exigua* et *immunda*.' Sect. 46, p. 88 : ' In hac vita *non possumus* legi satisfacere.

[2] Solid. Declare. iv, sect. 15, p. 672. ' Interim tamen diligenter in hoc negotio cavendum est, ne bona opera articulo justificationis et salutis nostræ immisceantur. Propterea hæ propositiones rejiciuntur : '' Bona opera piorum necessaria esse ad salutem,'' ' etc. III De fidei justitia, sect. 20, p. 658 : ' Similiter et renovatio seu sanctificatio, quamvis et ipsa sit beneficium mediatoris Christi et opus Spiritus Sancti, non tamen ea ad articulum aut negotium justificationis coram Deo pertinet : sed eam sequitur.'

new obedience,' was not adequately discharged; and, under this impression, he conceived, that, if the necessity of good works for ensuring salvation was generally recognised, a salutary change in this respect would take place. By this step he advanced scarcely a whit nearer to the Catholic doctrine than the other Lutherans; for, like them, he did not uphold an internal connection between holiness and salvation. He only conceived that good works must be there (outwardly present), if eternal happiness was to be the reward of faith.[1] Nevertheless, his doctrine excited general opposition; and Von Amsdorf, the old friend of Luther, composed, under these circumstances, a work, wherein he professed to show that good works were even hurtful to salvation.[2] The Formulary of Concord, which, among other things, undertook to adjust the controversies pending on this subject, disapproves, indeed, of Amsdorf's doctrine, yet expresses that disapprobation in very mild terms; while it rejects

[1] Marheineke thinks the distinction between the Catholic and the Protestant doctrine, respecting works, consists herein: that these are considered by Catholics as a *conditio sine qua non* to salvation, but not so by Protestants. This is by no means the case. Such, indeed, was the opinion of Major; but it is not the Catholic doctrine. Melancthon in his *Erotemat. Dialectices*, p. 276 (ed. Wittenberg, 1550), defines the notion of the *conditio sine qua non*, to be, not the internal condition to, or primary cause of, an effect, but something by the absence whereof the effect doth not take place: as, for instance, if a king should offer his daughter in marriage to anyone, who should with great elegance ride up and down a public place, the *conditio sine qua non* would have no manner of internal relation to the effect, which is to follow. On the other hand, the doctrine of the Catholic Church may be represented under the image of a father promising the hand of his daughter to a youth who sincerely loved her, and was favoured with her affection. This mutual inclination of hearts is an internal condition to the solemnisation of marriage—something required by the essence of the latter.

[2] The work is entitled, 'The Proposition of Nicholas von Amsdorf, that good works are hurtful to salvation, shown to be a right, true, Christian proposition, preached by St Paul, and St Luther,' 1559. He defended the proposition in the same sense, as Luther might have defended the thesis of a disputation: 'fides nisi sit sine ullis, etiam minimis operibus, non justificat, imo non est fides' (Op. tom. i, p. 523). The sense of this thesis must be clear from the preceding statements in the text. Doubtless it was immediately followed by the other thesis, '*impossibile esse fidem esse sine assiduis multis et magnis operibus*. Both theses comprise *exaggerated opinions*, whose limitation must be drawn from the whole argument in our text. The editor of Luther's works, in the introduction prefixed to the general collection of that Reformer's public Disputations, which are found in great numbers at the end of the first volume, observes, that from these disputations we may learn, in the surest as well as the shortest way, Luther's true doctrine; and this observation we have found very true.

Major's view as incompatible with the exclusive particles—
'Faith *alone* saves, by faith alone we are justified *without* works.'[1]

If good works, according to the doctrine of the Lutherans, be not necessary to salvation, are they in any respect necessary? This question was agitated among the Lutherans, and resolved in various senses. But the very possibility of such a question, in a doctrinal system, presupposes a strange obliquity of all ideas. The Augsburg Confession and the Apology frequently employed the expression, 'they are necessary;' and the Formulary of Concord appeals to their authority.[2] But what notion, after all we have set forth, is to be connected with the word 'necessary,' it were no easy matter to discover. Perhaps it was meant to be said: 'We may take it as certain, that faith will ever achieve something.' Moreover, works go not entirely unrewarded. The Formulary of Concord assures to them *temporal* advantages, and, to those who perform the most, a greater recompense in heaven.[3] Accordingly, faith without works would absolutely merit heaven; but works would only contribute something thereto!

In how much more enlightened a way have the schoolmen explained the relation of faith to works, as conducive to Divine favour and eternal happiness![4] What is the (living) faith, other than the good work, still silently shut up in the soul; and what is the good Christian work other than faith brought to light? They are one and the same, only in a different form; and hence, Catholic theologians explain the fact, why in Scripture salvation is promised sometimes to works, sometimes to faith. From this conception of the relation between faith and good works, Luther in one place attempted to meet the objection against his doctrine, founded on the very numerous passages in Holy Writ, that promise to a virtuous conduct eternal felicity. He replies, namely, that faith and works are 'one cake,' and therefore, on account of that inseparable unity, exchange their predicates; so that to works is ascribed what really belongs

---

[1] Solid. Declar. iv, sect. 15, p. 672. 'Simpliciter pugnant cum particulis exclusivis in articulo justificationis et salvationis.' Sect. 25, p. 676: 'Interim haudquaquam consequitur, quod simpliciter et nude asserere liceat, opera bona credentibus ad salutem esse perniciosa.'

[2] Solid. Declar. iv, sect. 10, p. 670: 'Negari non potest, quod in Augustana Confessione ejusdemque Apologia hæc verba sæpe usurpentur atque repetantur: "bona opera esse necessaria,"' etc.

[3] Loc. cit. iv, sect. 25, p. 676.

[4] See for instance, H. Smid's *Mysticism of the Middle Age*, p. 245, Jena, 1824. (In German.)

to faith, in the same way as the Scripture refers to the Divine nature in Christ the attributes of his humanity, and *vice versa*.[1] But Luther did not perceive, that by such a mode of explanation he placed himself on Catholic ground and utterly annihilated his doctrine, that faith without works could justify. For if works together with faith constitute an unity—that is to say, if works be absolutely implied by faith, in the same way as, when no outward, accidental hindrance occurs, the inference is implied in the reason, the effect in the cause, how can it be asserted that faith without works justifies ? Does it not, then, follow that faith is of value, only in so far ' as it worketh by charity ' ? and thereby alone, would not the whole Lutheran theory of justification be given up ? Luther became entangled in his own distinctions, for he here ascribes to faith *as the moral vivifying sentiment*, the power of justification ; whereas, according to the whole tenor of his system, it is to faith as *the organ* which clings to the merits of Christ, that he must impute this power.[2] It was precisely from this point of view, that Luther might have discovered how utterly erroneous was his whole system; for never certainly would the Scripture have promised eternal life to works, nor that *communicatio idiomatum* have been possible, if faith could justify, merely as *the instrument* so often boasted of, and not as involving an abundance of moral and religious virtues. Thus, that in Holy Writ eternal felicity should be promised to works, in so far as they emanate from faith unquestionably supposes that this faith is, absolutely and without restriction, the one which Catholic theologians are wont to designate as the *fides formata*. Hence, Luther elsewhere

[1] Luther, Comment. on Ep. to Galat. loc. cit. p. 145.
[2] It was a very favourite saying of Luther's, that, as good works are the fruits of the spiritual birth and the new inward life, we cannot be justified through the same : on the contrary, works are then only good, when man is already righteous. ' That good works,' says he, ' merit not grace, life, and salvation, is evident from the fact, that good works are not the spiritual birth, but only fruits of it : by works we become not Christians, righteous, holy, children and heirs of God ; but when we have become righteous through faith, from God's pure mercy, for Christ's sake, and when we have been created anew and born again, then only we perform good works. If we only insist upon regeneration and *substantialia*, on the essence of a Christian, we have at once overturned the merit of good works towards salvation, and reduced them to nothing.' (Luther's *Table-talk*, p. 171 : Jena, 1603.) This view of works affects not the Catholic doctrine, for this likewise teaches, that it is not by works that grace and regeneration are merited, but that works are the fruits of the new spirit. But since Catholics represent the fruits as forming one with the tree, they cannot say that the new spirit without its fruits insures salvation.

abandons this mode of enfeebling the objection adverted to ; and, in all the plenitude of his power, he commands his followers, not once, but a thousand times, to observe silence on the subject of works, when justifying faith was spoken of, and, consequently, to consider both, not as one, but as two cakes of very different substances.[1] Hence, in defining the relation of faith to works as conducive to salvation, the Formulary of Concord very wisely shuns the allusion to a one cake, but proposes to works temporal rewards and a sort of decoration in heaven. We cannot, however, refrain from expressing our astonishment, that men, like Reinhardt and Knapp, as we see from their *Manuals of Dogmatic Theology*, could believe that by such definitions as those respecting the recompenses in question, a faith active in good works could be promoted; and still more, that, in their capacity of exegetists, they could find such a doctrine reconcilable with Scripture, which, in the most unqualified manner, promises *salvation* to good works : see, for example, Matthew v, 1 ; xxv, 31 ; Romans viii, 17.[2]

[1] Comment. on Ep. to Galat. p. 74. Solid. declar. iii. de fide justif. sect. 26, p. 660 : ' Etsi conversi et in Christum credentes habent inchoatam in se renovationem, sanctificationem, dilectionem, virtutes et bona opera : tamen hæc omnia nequaquam immiscenda sunt articulo justificationis coram Deo : ut Redemptori Christo honor illibatus maneat, et cum nostra nova obedientia imperfecta et impura sit, perturbatæ conscientiæ certa et firma consolatione sese sustentare valeant.'

[2] A most superficial view of the relation between good works and eternal felicity, as stated in Holy Writ, as well as a remarkable specimen of fanciful and shallow interpretation of Scripture, we find in Luther's *Table-talk* (p. 176, Jena, 1603), where the recompenses promised to holiness of conduct are represented only as a tutorial stimulus, without any reference to the inward life of the soul. It is as follows :—' In the year 1542 (accordingly in his ripest years, shortly before his death), Dr Martin Luther said, touching the article of our justification before God, that it was in this case precisely the same as with a son, who is born, and not made by his own merit, heir to all the paternal estates ; he succeeds, without any act or merit of his own, to all his father's properties. But nevertheless the father exhorts him to do this or that diligently ; promises him a present, to engage him to perform his task with greater readiness, love, and pleasure. As if he should say to the son : if thou be pious, obedient to my commands, and diligent in thy studies I will buy for thee a fine coat. So also : come to me and I will give thee a pretty apple. Thus he teaches his son to obey him and although the inheritance will naturally fall to the son, yet by such promises the father will engage his son to do with cheerfulness what he bids him ; and thus he trains up his son in wholesome discipline. Therefore we must consider all such promises and recompenses, as only a pedagogical discipline, wherewith God incites and stimulates us, and like a kind pious father, makes us willing and joyous to do good, and to serve our neighbour, and not thereby to gain eternal life, for this he bestows on us entirely from his pure grace.' From these so very different

What especially confirmed the Reformers in their errors, was the explanation (derived, indeed, from their own system) of several passages of St Paul—for instance, of Romans iii, 28—where it is said, that it is not through the works of the law, but through faith, that man is justified: a passage, in writing which the apostle did not dream of the opposition existing between Catholics and Protestants. St Paul here contends against the Jews of his own time, who obstinately defended the eternal duration of the Mosaic law, and asserted, that, not needing a Redeemer from sin, they became righteous and acceptable before God by that law alone. In opposition to this opinion, St Paul lays down the maxim, that it is not by the works of the law, that is to say, not by a life regulated merely by the Mosaic precepts, man is enabled to obtain the favour of Heaven, but only through faith in Christ, which has been imparted to us by God for wisdom, for sanctification, for righteousness, and for redemption. Unbelief in the Redeemer, and confidence in the fulfilment of the law performed, through natural power alone, on the one hand, and faith in the Redeemer and the justice to be conferred by God, on the other (Romans i, 17, x, 3; Philippians iii, 9)—these, and not faith in the Redeemer and the good works emanating from its power, constitute the two points of opposition, here contemplated by the apostle. *The works of the law*, ἔργα τοῦ νόμου, St Paul accurately distinguishes everywhere from *good works*, ἔργα ἀγαθὰ, καλὰ ; as indeed in their inmost essence they are to be distinguished from one another: for the former are wrought without faith in Christ, and without his grace; the latter with the grace and in the spirit of Christ. Hence St Paul never says, that man is saved not through *good* works, but through faith in Christ! This marvellous opposition is a pure invention of the sixteenth century. Nay, the doctrine that to good works eternal felicity will be allotted, has been positively announced by this apostle, Romans ii, 7-10.

and opposite views of the same subject, it is again evident that upon this important article of belief Luther had never formed clear and settled notions, and that this inward unsteadiness and obscurity made him ever vacillate from one extreme to another.

§ XXIII—THE DOCTRINE OF PURGATORY IN ITS CONNECTION WITH THE CATHOLIC DOCTRINE OF JUSTIFICATION

The doctrine of the possibility of the fulfilment of the law, touched on in the last section, must now be treated more fully and minutely. The conflicting doctrines are of such importance, as to deserve a more precise statement of the arguments on either side. Calvin says: 'Never hath a man, not even one regenerated in the faith in Christ, wrought a morally good work—a work which, if it were strictly judged, would not be damnable.' Admitting even this impossibility to be possible, yet the author of such an action would still appear impure and polluted, by reason of his other sins. It is not the outward show of works, which perhaps in their external character may satisfy the moral law, but it is the purity of the will, which is regarded by God. Now, if we but raise our eyes to the judgment-seat of the Almighty, who will venture to stand before it? It is, therefore, evident, that the doctrine of an internal justification, involving the necessity of the fulfilment of the law, is reprehensible, because it must precipitate troubled consciences into despair.[1]

In reply to this, the Catholic observes: Either it is possible for man, strengthened and exalted by the Divine aid, to observe the moral law, in its spirit, its true inward essence, or it is impossible to do so. If the former be the case, then, undoubtedly, such observance cannot be too strongly urged; and everyone may find a proof for its possibility in the fact, that, on every transgression of the law, he accuses himself as a sinner: for every accusation of such a kind, involves the supposition, that its fulfilment is possible, and even, with assistance from above, not difficult. But if the latter be the case, then the cause must be sought for only in God, and in such a way, that either the

[1] Calvin. Instit. lib. iii, c. 14, sect. 11, fol. 279. 'Duobus his fortiter insistendum, nullum unquam extitisse pii hominis opus, quod, si severo Dei judicio examinaretur, non esset damnabile. Ad hæc, si tale aliquod detur, quod homini possibile non est, peccatis tamen, quibus laborare autorem ipsum certum est, vitiatum ac inquinatum, gratiam perdere; atque hic est præcipuus disputationis cardo.' C. 14, sect. 1, fol. 270: ' Huc, huc referenda mens est, si volumus de vera justitia inquirere: quomodo cœlesti judici respondeamus, cum nos ad rationem vocaverit.' Sect. 4: 'Illic nihil proderunt externæ bonorum operum pompæ. . . . Sola postulabitur voluntatis sinceritas.' Cf. Chemn. Exam. Conc. Trid. part I, p. 294.

Almighty hath not framed human nature for the attainment of that moral standard which He proposes to it, or He doth not impart those higher powers, which are necessary to the pure and not merely outward, but internal, compliance with His laws. In both cases, the cause of the non-fulfilment lies in the Divine will; that is to say, God is represented as not willing that His will should be complied with, which is self-contradictory. But in any case, there could be no conconceivable guilt in respect to this non-obedience to the law, and, accordingly, there could be, notwithstanding the non-observance of the Divine precepts, no obstacle to the attainment of eternal felicity.[1]

If it be urged, that reference is had exclusively to man's fallen nature, which is in a state of incapacity for the fulfilment of the law, we may reply, that God in Christ Jesus hath raised us from this fall; and it was justly observed by the Council of Trent, that, in virtue of the power of Christ's spirit, no precept was impracticable to man. For to the heritage of corruption, a heritage of spiritual power in Christ hath been opposed, and the latter can in every way be victorious over the former. Or do we believe the moral law to have been framed merely for the nature of Adam, for his brief abode in paradise, and not for the thousands of years that humanity was to endure?[2]

In modern times, some men have endeavoured to come to the aid of the old orthodox Lutheran doctrine, by assuring us

[1] It many times really occurred to Luther, as if his doctrine led to the conclusion, that the eternal order of things prevented our observance of the law. So he says (*Table-talk*, p. 162, b. Jena, 1603), 'God hath indeed known that we would not, *and could not*, do everything; *therefore* hath he granted to us *remissionem peccatorum*.' Indeed!

[2] Concil. Trid. sess. vi, c. xi. '*De observatione mandatorum, deque illius necessitate et possibilitate.* Nemo autem, quantumvis justificatus, liberum se esse ab observatione mandatorum putare debet: nemo temeraria illa et a patribus sub anathemate prohibita voce uti, Dei præcepta homini justificato ad observandum esse impossibilia. Nam Deus impossibilia non jubet, *sed jubendo monet et facere quod possis, et petere quod non possis, et adjuvat, ut possis.* Cujus mandata gravia non sunt, cujus jugum suave est et onus leve. Qui enim sunt filii Dei, Christum diligunt; qui autem diligunt eum, ut ipsemet testatur, servant sermones ejus. Quod utique cum divino auxilio præstare possunt,' etc. Hence Innocent X, in his constitution against the five propositions of Jansenius, has rightly condemned the following proposition (Hard. Concil. tom. xi, p. 143, n. 1): 'Aliqua Dei præcepta justis volentibus et conantibus, secundum præsentes quas habent vires, sunt impossibilia: deest quoque illis gratia, qua possibilia fiant.'

that the moral law proposes to men an ideal standard, which, like everything ideal, necessarily remains unattained. If such really be the case with the moral law, then he who comes not up to it, can as little incur responsibility, as an epic poet for not equalling Homer's Iliad. More intellectual, at least, is the theory, that the higher a man stands on the scale of morality, the more exalted are the claims which the moral law exacts of him; so that they increase, as it were, to infinity with the internal growth of man, and leave him ever behind them. When we contemplate the lives of the saints the contrary phenomenon will arise to view. The consciousness of being in the possession of an all-sufficing, infinite power, ever discloses the tenderer and nobler relations of man to God and to his fellow-creatures so that the man sanctified in Christ, and filled with his Spirit, ever feels himself superior to the law. It is the nature of heaven-born love—which stands so far, so infinitely far, above the claims of the mere law, never to be content with its own doings, and ever to be more ingenious in its devices; so that Christians of this stamp not unfrequently appear to men of a lower grade of perfection, as enthusiasts, men of heated fancy and distempered mind. It is only in this way that remarkable doctrine can be satisfactorily explained, which certainly, like every other that hath for centuries existed in the world, and seriously engaged the human mind, is sure to rest on some deep foundation—the doctrine, namely, that there can be works which are more than sufficient (*opera supererogationis*)—a doctrine, the tenderness and delicacy whereof eluded, indeed, the perception of the Reformers; for they could not even once rise above the idea, that man could ever become free from immodesty, unjust wrath, avarice, and the rest. The doctrine in question, indeed, on which the Council of Trent does not enter into detail, in proportion as the principle, whereon it is based, is more exalted, is on that account the more open to gross misrepresentation; especially if, as the Reformers were imprudent enough to do, we look to mere outward, arbitrary actions. Quite untenable is the appeal to experience, that no one can boast of having himself fulfilled the law; or the assertion, that the question is not as to the possibility but the reality of such a fulfilment. In the first place, no argument can be deduced from reality, because we are not even capable of looking into it, and we must not, and cannot, judge of the hearts of men. We are not even capable of judging ourselves; and therefore St Paul saith '*he is conscious to himself of nothing*, but he leaveth judgment to the Lord.'[1] Accordingly, the desire to determine the limits of our power in Christ, by the reality of every-day life, would lead to the worst conceivable system of ethics. Once regulate the practicable by the measure of ordinary experience, and you will at once see the low reality sink down to a grade still lower. Lastly, this view alleges no deeper reason for what it calls reality, and we learn not why this hath been so, and not otherwise; so that we must either recur to the first or the second mode of defending the orthodox Protestant view, or seek out a new one.

Calvin commands us to raise our eyes to the judgment-seat of God. In truth, nothing is more fit to avert the sinner from himself, and to turn him to Christ, than calling to mind the general judgment—not merely that which the history of the world pronounces, but that which the all-wise, holy, and righteous God doth hold.[2] Woe to him who hath not turned to Christ; but woe likewise to him whom the blood of Christ hath not really cleansed, whom the living communion with the God-man Himself hath not rendered godly. Can our adversaries even imagine, that the elect are still stained with sin before the judgment-seat of God, and that Christ covers them over, and under this covering conducts them into heaven? It is the most consummate contradiction to talk of entering into heaven, while stained with sin, be it covered or uncovered. Hence, the question recurs: how shall man be finally delivered from sin, and how shall holiness in him be restored to thorough life? Or, in case we leave this earthly world, still bearing about us some stains of sin, how shall we be purified from them? Shall it be by the mechanical deliverance from the body, whereof the Protestant Formularies speak so much? But it is not easy to discover how, when *the body* is laid aside, sin is therefore purged out from *the sinful spirit*. It is only one who rejects the principle of moral freedom in sin, or who hath been led astray by Gnostic or Manichean errors, that could look with favour upon a doctrine

---

[1] Concil. Trident. sess. vi. 'Quia in multis offendimus omnes unusquisque sicut misericordiam et bonitatem, ita et severitatem et judicium ante oculos habere debet, neque se ipsum aliquis, etiamsi nihil sibi conscius fuerit, judicare: quoniam omnis hominum vita non humano judicio examinanda et judicanda est, sed Dei: qui illuminabit abscondita tenebrarum, et manifestabit consilia cordium: et tunc laus erit unicuique a Deo, qui, ut scriptum est, reddet unicuique secundum opera.'

[2] Dr Moehler here alludes to a celebrated saying of the German poet, 'that the history of the world is the judgment of the world.'—*Trans.*

of this kind. Or are we to imagine it to be some potent word of the Divinity, or some violent mechanical process, whereby purification ensues? Some sudden, magical change the Protestant doctrine unconsciously presupposes; and this phenomenon is not astonishing, since it teaches, that by original sin the mind had been deprived of a certain portion, and that in regeneration man is completely passive. But the Catholic, who cannot regard man other than as a free independent agent, must also recognise this free agency in his final purification, and repudiate such a sort of mechanical process, as incompatible with the whole moral government of the world. If God were to employ an economy of this nature, then Christ came in vain. Therefore is our Church forced to maintain such a doctrine of justification in Christ, and of a moral conduct in this life regulated by it, that Christ will, at the day of judgment, have fulfilled the claims of the law outwardly *for* us, but on that account inwardly *in* us. The solace, accordingly, is to be found in the power of Christ, which effaces as well as forgives sin—yet in a two-fold way. Among some, it consummates purification in this life: among others, it perfects it only in the life to come. The latter are they, who by faith, love, and a sincere penitential feeling, have knit the bond of communion with Christ, but only in a partial degree, and at the moment they quitted the regions of the living, were not entirely pervaded by His spirit: to them will be communicated this saving power, that at the day of judgment they also may be found pure in Christ. Thus the doctrine of a place of purification is closely connected with the Catholic theory of justification, which, without the former, would doubtless be, to many, a disconsolate tenet. But this inward justification none can be dispensed from;—the fulfilment of the law, painful as it undoubtedly is, can be remitted to none. On each one must that holy law be inwardly and outwardly stamped. The Protestants, on the other hand, who, with their wonted arrogance, have rejected the dogma of purgatory, so well founded as it is in tradition, saw themselves thereby compelled, in order to afford solace to man, to speak of an impossibility of fulfilling the law—a thought which is confuted in every page of scripture, and involves the Almighty in contradiction with Himself. They saw themselves compelled to put forth a theory of justifying faith, which cannot even be clearly conceived. Lastly, they saw themselves compelled to adopt tacitly at least, the idea of a mechanical course of operations practised on man after death—new authoritative decrees of the Deity, and left unexplained how a deep-rooted sinfulness, even when forgiven, could be at last totally eradicated from the spirit. Thus do both communions offer a solace to man, but in ways totally opposite; the one in harmony with Holy Writ, which everywhere presupposes the possibility of the observance of the law; the other in most striking contradiction to it: one in maintaining the whole rigour of the ethical code; the other by a grievous violation of it: one in accordance with the free and gradual development of the human mind, which only with a holy earnestness, and by great exertions, can bring forth and cultivate to maturity the divine seed once received; the other without regard to the eternal laws of the human spirit, and by a very guilty encouragement to moral levity.

§ XXIV—OPPOSITION BETWEEN THE COMMUNIONS IN THEIR GENERAL CONCEPTION OF CHRISTIANITY

In many an attentive reader the statements we have made may have already awakened the thought, that the Catholic Church views the whole system of Christianity, and the immediate objects of the Saviour's advent, in a manner essentially different from the Protestant communities. That such a thought is not entirely unfounded, the following investigations will show, in proportion as they will at the same time shed the clearest light on all that has been hitherto advanced, dissipate many doubts, and confirm, with more accuracy and vividness, the views we have put forth as to the nature of the Protestant doctrines.

According to the old Christian view, the Gospel is to be regarded as an institution of an all-merciful God, whereby through His Son He raises fallen man to the highest degree of religious and moral knowledge which he is capable of attaining in this life, proffers to each one forgiveness of sins, and withal an internal sanatory and sanctifying power. But, how now does Luther look upon the Gospel?

1. He asserts, that Christ hath only in an *accidental way* discharged the office of teacher; and that his real and sole object was, to fulfil the law in our stead, to satisfy its demands, and to die for us. Hence he reproaches the Papists with teaching, that the Gospel is a law of love, and comprises a less easy, that

is to say, a purer and more exalted morality than the Mosaic dispensation. In his Commentary on the Epistle to the Galatians, he says, 'On this account principally hath Christ come upon the earth, not to teach the law, but only to fulfil it. That he occasionally teaches, is merely accidental, and foreign to his office; in the same way, as, beside his real and proper duty, which was to save sinners, he accidentally restored the sick to health.'[1] In another place he makes a similar remark: 'Although this is as clear as the dear sun at noon-day, yet the Papists are so senseless and blind, that out of the Gospel they have fashioned a law of love, and out of Christ a law-giver, who hath imposed far more burthensome laws than Moses himself. But let the fools go on in their blindness, and learn ye from St Paul, that the Gospel teacheth, Christ hath come not to give a new law, whereby we should walk, but to offer himself up as a victim for the sins of the whole world.'

What a one-sided view did Luther here take of the mission of Christ! His teaching office he calls something accidental, and entirely forgets, that, in formal opposition to the Mosaic dispensation, Christ proclaimed a new, purer, more exalted, and therefore severer, law of morality (Matthew v, 31-48), and uttered himself those words: 'A new commandment I give ye, that ye love one another.' (John xiii, 34.) The misconception, moreover, whereon Luther's complaint is founded, that the Papists degrade Christ into a mere law-giver and ethical teacher, will shortly be more closely examined.

2. Yet Luther not only taught, that Christ had not come to impart to men a purer ethical code, but even maintained, that he had come to *abolish* the moral law, to liberate true believers from its curse, both for the past and for the future, and in this way to make them free. The theory of evangelical liberty, which Luther propounded, announces, that even the Decalogue shall not be brought into account against the believer, nor its violation be allowed to disturb the conscience of the Christian; for he is exalted above it and its contents. Luther called attention to a two-fold use of the moral law, the Mosaic as well as the Evangelical, to which somewhat later a third was added. The first consists herein, that it convinces the unconverted of their sinfulness, and, by menacing its transgressors with the divine judgments, throws them into a state of terror: the second, that it conducts those, sufficiently shaken and

---

[1] Comment. on Ep. to Galat. loc. cit. p. 219.

intimidated, unto Christ, in order to obtain through him forgiveness of sins. Moreover, the Saxon Reformer maintained, that the believer, *as such*, was to make no use of the moral law.[1] When the sinner hath come unto Christ, the law ceases for him, and the Gospel begins ; he is free from the terrors which the *continued* transgressions of the former produce, and Christ unconditionally makes good all deficiencies. Hence, Luther so often insists on the necessity of separating most pointedly the law and the Gospel, of no longer molesting and tormenting the faithful with the former, but only of cheering and solacing them with the latter. He says, ' It is of very great importance, that we should rightly know and understand, how the law hath been abolished. For such a knowledge, that the law is abolished, and its office totally set aside, that it can no longer be a ground of accusation and condemnation against the believers in Christ, confirms our doctrine on faith. From this our consciences may derive solace, especially in their moments of great fearful struggle and mental anguish. I have before earnestly and frequently said, and repeat it now again (for this is a matter which can never be too often and too strongly urged), that a Christian, who grasps and lays hold on Christ, is subject to no manner of law, but is free from the law, so that it can neither terrify nor condemn him. This Isaiah teacheth in the text cited by St Paul : " Give glory, thou barren one, that bearest not."

'When Thomas of Aquino, and other schoolmen assert, that the law hath been abolished, they pretend that the Mosaic ordinances respecting judicial affairs and other secular matters (which they call *judicialia*), and in like manner the laws respecting ceremonies and the services of the Temple (*kirchwerken*), were after the death of Christ pernicious, and on that account were set aside and abolished. But when they say the Ten Commandments (which they call *moralia*) are not to be abrogated, they themselves understand not what they assert and lay down.

'But thou, when thou speakest of the abolition of the law, be mindful that thou speakest of the law, as it really is, and is rightly called, to wit, the spiritual law, and understand thereby the whole law, making no distinction between civil laws, ceremonies, and Ten Commandments. For when St Paul saith, that through Christ we are redeemed from the anathema of the

---

[1] The Formulary of Concord hath also a special article upon a third use of the law (*tertius usus legis*) ; its use, namely, as a standard of Christian life.

M

law, he speaketh certainly and properly of the whole law, and especially of the Ten Commandments; since these alone accuse the conscience before God and terrify it; whereas the other two species of law, that treat, so to speak, of civil affairs and ceremonies, do not so. Therefore, we say, that even the Ten Commandments have no right to accuse nor to alarm the conscience, wherein Christ reigns by his grace; since Christ hath abolished this right of the law, when he became an anathema for us.' [1]

In the writings of Melancthon reigns, in a no less striking degree, the same one-sided view, which can neither satisfy human reason—desirous in everthing of unity of principle—nor meet in all respects the practical wants of man. Melancthon, at times, defines very well the true notions of Christian freedom. For instance, when he says (what undoubtedly is acknowledged on all sides), that we are released from the obligation of observing the ritual law of Moses, and when he adds, that the believer, being inwardly and freely moved by the Divine Spirit practises the moral law, and would fulfil it, when even it did not make any outward claims; the Reformer here excellently describes Christian freedom as a voluntary obedience to God, and consequently as a release from the fetters, wherein evil held men enchained. But immediately, again, he falls back into pure Lutheran definitions, by distinguishing, in the Christian liberty just described, two things. The first is, that, by reason of this freedom, the Decalogue condemns not believers, even though they be sinners; the second is, that they fulfil the moral law of themselves. Lastly, he expresses himself briefly and clearly to this effect—' The law is abrogated, not that it should not be fulfilled, but that it may be fulfilled, and may not condemn, even when it is not fulfilled.' [2] Here a multitude of

---

[1] Luther, Comment. on Ep. to Galat. loc. cit. p. 257, b; 258, b. Compare his instruction how the books of Moses are to be read. Part v, ed. Wittenberg, p. 1, b. ' The law signifies and demands of us, what we are to do, what we are not to do, and how we are to be in respect to God; it is exclusively directed to our conduct, and consists in demands; for God speaks through the law—do this, do not this, this I will require of thee. But the gospel preacheth not what we are to do, and not do; requires nothing of us, but turns round, doth the reverse, and saith not, do this, do that, but bids us only hold out our laps, and saith, dear man, this hath God done, for thee—He hath sent His Son into the flesh for thee, He hath let Him be slain for thy sake, and hath redeemed thee from sin, death, the devil, and hell: this believe and hold, and then thou art saved.'

[2] Melancthon (in his Loci Theolog. p. 127) says very well of Christian freedom: ' Postremo libertas est Christianismus, quia qui spiritum Dei

questions press themselves on our consideration. For instance, if *the essence* of freedom consists in the fact, that it can fulfil, and really doth fulfil, the law, how can those, who fulfil it not, be numbered among the free ? How can one and the same freedom love inconstancy to such a degree, that here it proves itself obedient, there disobedient, and is only uniform in one thing, that in either case it doth not condemn. We may ask further, whether the strange freedom of those, who are free with respect to condemnation, but are not free from evil and disobedience, extends to every point of the Decalogue ? Whether, in general, a limit can be traced, down to which freedom from condemnation can render innoxious the servitude to evil co-existing with it ? We content ourselves with proposing these questions, and shall now proceed in our inquiry.

Strobel announced to the learned world, as a great novelty, that already, in the year 1524 (thus seven years after the commencement of the great revolution in the Church), Melancthon *called the Gospel a preaching of penance ;* [1] for, before that literary discovery, it was believed, that he had only much later risen to this idea. What astonishment do we feel, when we reflect on the notion which he attaches *to the new vivification* of the Christian by the gospel ! He constantly takes *vivificatio* as the opposite to *mortificatio ;* and as by the latter he understands only the mortal terrors at the vengeance which the law announces to all its transgressors ; so to his mind the former signifies merely the resuscitation, the recovery from these terrors, brought about by the tidings, that in Christ sins are remitted.[2]

---

non habent, legem facere neutiquam possunt, suntque maledictionum legis rei. Qui spiritu Christi renovati sunt, ii jam sua sponte, etiam non præeunte lege, feruntur ad ea, quæ lex jubebat. Voluntas Dei lex est. Nec aliud Spiritus Sanctus est, nisi veri Dei voluntas et agitatio. Quare ubi Spiritu Dei, qui viva voluntas Dei est, regenerati sumus, jam id ipsum volumus sponte, quod exigebat lex.' P. 130, we read as follows : ' Habes quatenus a Decalogo liberi sumus, primum, *quod tametsi peccatores*, damnare non possit eos, qui in Christo sunt. Deinde, quod, qui sunt in Christo, spiritu trahuntur *ad legem faciendam*, et spiritu faciunt, amant, timent Deum,' etc. P. 131: ' Ergo abrogata lex est, non ut ne fiat, sed ut, et non facta, non damnet et fieri possit.' Here one assertion evidently destroys the other. Hence, as stated above in the text, it is taught by Melancthon in his Apology, that we *cannot* fulfil the law.

[1] Strobel, Literary History of Melancthon, loc. theol. p. 240.
[2] Luther also, De Captiv. Babyl. eccles. Opp. tom. ii, fol. 287, and in several other places attaches to the same idea to *novitas vitæ*. But Melancthon is clearer, in loc. theol. p. 147, ' Qui rectissimi senserunt, ita judicarunt : Joannis Baptismum esse vivificationis, quod ei addita sit gratiæ promissio seu condonatio peccatorum.' When Melancthon attempts

The *inward* resuscitation from the death of sin, the immediate communication of a new, higher, vital energy, which annihilates the earlier weakness, transforming it into a victorious, all-conquering power over flesh, Melancthon was unable to understand (as the Church had always done) by the word *vivificatio*. Even Calvin took scandal at this opinion of Melancthon's; at least, I am at a loss to know to whom his counter-statements can be applicable, except to his Wittenberg friend.[1] Even in the Apology composed by Melancthon for the Confession of Augsburg, the new resuscitation, nay, even the expression, 'regeneration,' are referred to this solace alone,[2] as is remarked by the Formulary of Concord.[3]

No one can call to mind, that, in the symbolical books of the Lutherans, the believing sinner, when disquieted on account of his moral conduct, is ever consoled by the encouraging words: 'thou canst do all in Him, who strengthened thee: not thou, but Christ with thee.' Not to Christ, the strengthener and the sanctifier, do they refer him, but exclusively to Christ, the forgiver of sins. This solace they really impart in almost countless passages—on this they constantly insist. To make moral indolence attentive to itself, would have appeared to them a reprehensible transmutation of the gospel into the law.[4] It

to give any definition of the Gospel, he is usually as one-sided as Luther. 'Novum Testamentum non aliud est, nisi bonorum omnium promissio citra legem, nullo justitiarum nostrarum respectu. Vetere Testamento promittebantur bona, sed simul exigebatur a populo legis impletio: novo promittuntur bona citra legis conditionem, cum nihil a nobis vicissim exigatur. Atque hic vides, quæ sit amplitudo gratiæ, quæ sit misericordiæ divinæ prodigalitas' (Loc. theolog. p. 126). Passages, such as at p. 140, are true rarities, and do not agree with the rest.

[1] Calvin. Instit. 1. iii, c. 3, sect. 4, fol. 210. 'Vivificationem interpretantur consolationem, quæ ex fide nascitur: ubi scilicet homo, peccati conscientia prostratus, ac Dei timore pulsus, postea in Dei bonitatem, in misericordiam, gratiam, salutem, quæ est per Christum, respiciens, sese erigit, respirat, animum colligit, et velut e morte in vitam redit . . . *non assentior, quum potius sancte pieque vivendi studium significet, quod oritur ex renascentia: quasi diceretur hominem sibi mori, ut Deo vivere incipiat.*'

[2] Apolog. iv, sect. 21, p. 73. 'Corda rursus debent concipere consolationem. Id fit, si credent promissioni Christi, quod propter eum habeamus remissionem peccatorum. Hæc fides, in illis pavoribus erigens et consolans, accipit remissionem peccatorum, justificat et vivificat. Nam illa consolatio est nova et spiritualis.' On regeneration, see sect. 26, p. 76.

[3] Solid Declar. iii, de fidei justif. sect. 13, p. 656.

[4] On this ever-recurring consolation, see Apology iv, sect. 11, p. 68; sect. 13, p. 69; sect. 14, p. 70; sect. 19, p. 72 and 73; sect. 20, p. 73; sect. 21, p. 73; sect. 26, p. 76; sect. 27, p. 77; sect. 30, p. 78; sect. 38,

must be obvious to every man, that they could not urge to moral exertion, because such an act would have overthrown their leading doctrine, that, in the production of all good, man is utterly passive. Most striking in this respect is the decision, which the Formulary of Concord pronounced in the Antinomian controversies, which in themselves presuppose a most strange aberration of the human mind. It is there especially enjoined, *that the gospel should not be mixed up with the law ;* for otherwise the merits of Christ would be abridged, and troubled consciences be robbed of their sweetest solace.[1] Accordingly, it is there said, that in a wider sense, undoubtedly, the gospel is the preaching of penance, as well as of the forgiveness of sins ; but in its most proper sense, it is *only* the latter—*only* the announcement of the pardoning mercy of God.[2] If to one, who recalls to mind the epistle to the Romans, i, 15-18, this opposition must appear singular enough, so the fact is still more remarkable, that, under the grace to be announced, absolution from sin is alone understood ; and the truly sanctifying grace is passed over in utter silence. In one passage, indeed, the communication of the Holy Spirit is vaguely mentioned ;[3] but should anyone wish to refer this to the truly purifying, and effectually sanctifying Spirit, he would most certainly err ; for the activity of the Spirit is, in this formulary, expressly confined to *consolation ;* on which account, He is termed the Paraclete ; and his office

p. 81 ; sect. 40, p. 83 ; sect. 45, p. 87 ; sect. 48, p. 90, and so on. In the Formulary of Concord there occurs as repeated mention of this solace, as in the Apology.

[1] Solid. Declar. v, de lege et Evang. sect. 1, p. 676. 'Cavendum est ne hæc duo doctrinarum genera inter se commisceantur, aut Evangelion in legem transformetur. Ea quippe ratione meritum Christi obscuraretur, et conscientiis perturbatis dulcissima consolatio (quam in Evanlio Christi, sincere prædicato, habent, qua etiam sese in gravissimus tentationibus adversus legis terrores sustenant) prorsus eriperetur.'

[2] Loc. cit. sect. 4, p. 678. It is said of the Gospel in a wider sense : 'Est concio de pœnitentia et remissione peccatorum.' Sect. 5, p. 678 : 'Deinde vocabulum Evangelii in alia et quidem propriisima sua significatione usurpatur : et tum non concionem de pœnitentia, sed tantum prædicationem de clementia Dei complectitur.' Compare sect. 15, p. 681 and 682 ; sect. 16, p. 682 : 'Quidquid enim pavidas mentes consolatur, quidquid favorem et gratiam Dei transgressoribus legis offert, hoc proprie est, et recte dicitur Evangelion, hoc est lætissimum nuntium. Gratia (is only) remissio peccatorum.' Apolog. iv, sect. 13, p. 69 : 'Evangelium, quod est proprie promissio remissionis peccatorum.'

[3] Loc. cit. sect. 17, p. 682. 'Lex ministerium est, quod per literam occidit et damnationem denuntiat : Evangelium autem est potentia Dei ad salutem omni credenti, et hoc ministerium justitiam nobis offert et Spiritum Sanctum donat.'

to convince the world of sin (*arguere de peccato*) is represented as one, not peculiar but foreign to Him, under the new covenant.[1] If it be said, however, by way of excuse, that in other parts the sanctifying spirit of Christ is spoken of, let no one rest satisfied therewith: for the article which undertakes to treat of the signification of the gospel, is certainly the place where such a subject must be handled in all its bearings.

What gross misconceptions, what profound errors, do we encounter here! A feeling of infinite pain seizes on the Christian observer, at witnessing such doctrines—at witnessing such fierce divisions in one and the same revelation! And most painful is the experience he makes, that not even one man felt the necessity of seeing those divisions composed! The controversies, indeed, which upon this matter, were carried on in the Lutheran Church, indicate a sense of uneasiness, prevailing among many of its members—an obscure perception, that some prodigious mistakes had been committed; but to reconcile effectually those feuds, was a thing which occurred to no man. This inward disquiet it was which drove Agricola of Eisleben into thorough Antinomianism: a hidden impulse, unknown to himself, urged him to escape from this turmoil of contradictions, to pour out his insane blasphemies against Moses, to demand that *no further use* should be made of the law, to require that for the future grace only should be preached up in the Christian churches, and in this way to cut the Gordian knot, and to rush into the wildest extremes. In this, as in other matters, the Formulary of Concord has restored no inward and essential harmony; and without entirely giving up the Lutheran point of view, it was out of its power so to do.

The life of the Saviour constitutes, in every relation, an organic unity; and everything in him, his sufferings and his works, his doctrines, his conduct, his death on the cross, were in a like degree calculated for our redemption. It is the merits of the entire, undivided God-man, the Son of God whereby we are won again to God. His three offices, the prophetic, the high-priestly, the royal, are alike necessary; take one away, and

---

[1] Loc. cit. sect. 8, p. 679. 'Manifestum est, Spiritus Sancti officium esse, non tantum consolari, verum etiam (ministerio legis) arguere mundum de peccato (Joh. xvi, 8) et ita etiam in Nova Testamento facere *opus alienum*, quod est arguere: ut postea faciat opus proprium, quod est consolari et gratiam Dei prædicare. Hanc enim ob causam nobis Christus precibus suis et sanctissimo merito eundem nobis a Patre impetravit et misit; unde et Paracletus seu consolator dicitur.'

the remaining immediately appear as unintelligible, as devoid of consistency. Thus, by the advent of the Son of God into the world, there were proffered to men, not by accident, but by *necessity*, at once, the highest degree of religious and ethical knowledge; the ideal of a life agreeable to God; forgiveness of sins, and a sanctifying power: and, as in the one life of the Saviour we find all these united, so they must, in like manner, be adopted by us.

It is undeniable, and no arts can long conceal the fact, that Christ proposed, in the most emphatic manner, to his followers, the highest ethical ideal, corresponding to the new theoretical religious knowledge, and further developing the Old Testament precepts. It is likewise equally certain, that in his name are announced to all, who believe in him, grace and forgiveness of sins; that is to say, pardon for every moral transgression. These are two phenomena, which, as they stand in direct opposition one to the other, require, in consequence, some third principle which may mediate their union. This third conciliating principle, as it is to unite the two, must be akin alike to law and to grace, to the rigid exaction and to the merciful remission. This is the sanctifying power which emanates from the living union with Christ; the *gratuitous grace* of holy love, which, in justification, he pours out upon his followers. In this grace all law is abolished, because no outward claim is enforced; and, at the same time, the law is confirmed, because love is the fulfilment of the law: in love, law and grace are become one. This is the deep sense of the Catholic dogma of justification, according to which, forgiveness of sins and sanctification are one and the same; according to which, justification consists in the reign of love in the soul. Hence the maxim which the ancient Church, after St Paul (Rom. iii, 25), so frequently repeated, that, on entering into communion with Christ, the sins committed *before* that event, were forgiven, but not future sins; implying that now Christ would fulfil the law in us, and we in him. In the Catholic Church, therefore controversies could never be prolonged as to the relation between law and grace, because, by its doctrine of justification, such an opposition was essentially and eternally precluded: while on the other hand, the Reformers misapprehended the essence of love to such a degree, that, instead of recognising in it whatever was most spiritual, most vital, most resuscitating, and thereby, in consequence, the fulfilment of the law, they looked on it as merely the law itself.

Instead of raising themselves to the heights of Catholicism, and thence beholding how in love the entire undivided Christ becometh living within us, and the moral teacher and forgiver of sins is alike glorified, they urged it as a matter of reproach against the Catholic Church, that *it buried Christ* because, in their one-sided view, they regarded the Mediator only in his capacity of Pardoner.[1]

§ XXV—THE CULMINATING POINT OF INQUIRY—LUTHER MAINTAINS AN INWARD AND ESSENTIAL OPPOSITION BETWEEN RELIGION AND MORALITY, AND ASSIGNS TO THE FORMER AN ETERNAL, TO THE LATTER A MERE TEMPORAL, VALUE

This so decided and unreconciled opposition between gospel and law leads to a total degradation of the latter; so that all differences between Catholicism and Protestantism, in the article of justification, may shortly be reduced to this; namely, that the Catholic Church considers religion and morality as inwardly one and the same, and both equally eternal; while the Protestant Church represents the two as essentially distinct —the former having an eternal, the latter a temporal, value. Luther, in numberless passages of his writings, insists on keeping both principles, the religious and the ethical, as far apart, nay, further apart, than heaven and earth; on separating them, like day and night, like sunshine and darkness. He teaches, that we are not to let the moral law by any means intrude on the conscience; that, in considering our relations to God, we are not to look to our personal bearing to that law, and that, in general, we are to attend to it only in the conduct of our everyday earthly existence. When the question recurred to him, wherefore then, was the moral law given, he could make no other reply, than ' that it was given for the sake of civil order '; or, that it had so pleased God to establish such an ordinance, the observance whereof, as might be said of any mere legal institution, afforded him pleasure. The maintenance of the moral law, accordingly, he would leave to the jurisdiction of the State

---

[1] Apolog. iv, de justific. sect. 23, p. 75. ' Itaque, qui negant fidem (solam) justificare, nihil nisi legem, abolito Christo, docent.' Sect. 26, p. 77 : ' Adversarii Christum ita intelligunt mediatorem et propitiatorem, quia meruerit habitum dilectionis . . . Annon est hoc prorsus sepelire Christum, et totam fidei doctrinam tollere.'

and not by any means include among real religious concerns. It will be well, however, to hear Luther's own words, who, if anywhere, is in this matter his own best interpreter. He says, 'We must thus carefully distinguish between both, placing the gospel in the kingdom of heaven above, and the law on the earth below, calling and holding the righteousness of the gospel a heavenly and godly righteousness, and that of the law a human and earthly one. And thou must separate and distinguish the righteousness of the gospel as peculiarly and carefully from the righteousness of the law, as our Lord God hath separated and divided the heavens from the earth, light from darkness, and day from night. So is the righteousness of the gospel light and day; the righteousness of the law darkness and night; and would to God we could divide them still further one from the other.

'Therefore, as often as we have to treat of, and to deal with, faith, with heavenly righteousness, with conscience, etc. etc., let us cut off the law, and let it be confined to this lower world. But if the question be about works, then let us enkindle the light which belongeth to works of legal justice, and to the night. Thus will the dear sun, and the clear light of the Gospel and of grace, shine and illumine by day, the light of the law shine and illumine by night. And so these two things must ever be separated one from the other, in our minds and our hearts, that the conscience, when it feels its sins and is terrified, may say to itself, now thou art on the earth; therefore let the lazy ass there work, and serve, and ever carry the burden imposed upon it. That is to say, let the body, with its members, be ever subjected to the law. But when thou mountest up to heaven, leave the ass with its burden upon the earth. For the conscience must have nothing to do with the law, works, and earthly righteousness. So the ass remains in the valley, but the conscience ascends with Isaac up the mountain, and knows nothing either of the law, or of works, but seeks and looks only for the forgiveness of sins, and the pure righteousness which is proffered and imparted to us in Christ.

'On the other hand, in civil government we must most rigidly exact, and observe, obedience to the law; and, in that department, we must know nothing, either of gospel, or conscience, or grace, of forgiveness of sins, of heavenly righteousness, or even of Christ himself; but we must know only how to speak of Moses, the law and works. Thus both things, to wit, the law, and the Gospel, are to be severed as far as possible one from the other, and each is to remain in the separate place to which it appertains. The law is to remain out of heaven, that is to say, out of the heart and the conscience. On the other hand, the freedom of the Gospel is to remain out of the world, that is to say, out of the body and its members. On this account, when law and sin shall come into heaven—that is to say, into the conscience—we must immediately drive them out; for the conscience must at no time know of law or sin, but of Christ only. And again, when grace and freedom come into the world—that is to say, into the body—we must say to them: "hearken, it becometh not ye to walk and dwell in the hog-sty and on the dung-heaps of this earthly life, but upwards to heaven ye shall ascend." '[1]

Luther cannot often enough recur to the idea of the internal and essential difference of the religious from the ethical principle, as in the case of such an excellent discovery was to be expected. Elsewhere he says, 'Because it is so hazardous and dangerous to have anything to do with the law, and it may easily occur that herein we sustain a perilous and grievous fall, as if we were to be precipitated from heaven into the very abyss of hell; it is very necessary that every Christian should learn to separate the two things most carefully, one from the other. Thus, he can let the law rule and govern his body and its members, but not his conscience. For the same bride and queen must remain unspotted and unpolluted by the law, and be preserved in all her integrity and purity for her only one and proper bridegroom—Christ. As St Paul saith, in another place, I have entrusted ye to a man, that I may bring a pure virgin to Christ.

'Therefore must conscience have its bridal bed, not in a deep valley, but on a high mountain, where Christ holds sway and jurisdiction; who neither terrifies nor tortures poor sinners, but, on the contrary, consoles them, forgives sins, and saves them.'[2]

Luther's reply to the question, 'What need is there then of the moral law?' is recorded in the following passage:—
'Why do men keep the law, if it do not justify? They who are just observe it, not because they are thereby justified before God (for through faith only doth this occur), *but for the sake of civil order*, and because they know that such obedience

---

[1] Comment. on Ep. to Galat. loc. cit. p. 62.
[2] Loc. cit. p. 64. Compare pp. 79, 168, 172.

is well-pleasing and agreeable to God, and a good example and pattern for improvement to others, in order that they may believe in the gospel.' (Let the reader remember Zwingle's views on the same subject, c. 1, § iv.)

Had Luther felt, in a higher degree than we can discover in him, the want of a more general completion and more consistent development of his views, he would most certainly have embraced the opinion of a merely righteous Demiurgos, as asserted by the Gnostics; laid claim to their heretical antinomianism in behalf of the Pneumatici; and, like Marcion, have separated the Old from the New Testament. Marcion, too, was unable to reconcile law and grace, the all-good, merciful God, with the God who imposes moral precepts, and who chastises; and proceeded so far as to hold the legislative God of the old covenant to be essentially distinct from the God of the new. This opinion, absurd as it is in itself, possessed, however, a certain consistency, as did also the assertion of the Valentinians that they were exempt from the law, but that Catholics, on the other hand, could be saved only by its observance; for they entertained the opinion that they were substantially different from the latter; that they were Pneumatici, and the Catholics Psychici—beings belonging to an inferior grade of existence. But in Luther we discover no cohesion nor connection of ideas; and his point of view is in itself utterly untenable. To the moral law he assigned the destination of terrifying the conscience; and yet the law and the conscience are to stand in no inward relation, one to the other; an association of ideas, which is utterly inconceivable! By holding up the moral law, the sinner is to be terrified into the conviction, that for having violated it he has deserved the *eternal* torments of hell; and yet it is to possess a mere *temporal* worth, and be destined for merely *transitory* relations! How then are we to understand the mission of Christ, and especially His atonement? Did not the latter take place, in order to deliver us from the *eternal* punishment that had been affixed to the transgression of the moral law? But how, we must repeat it, can the violation of a finite law, merely adapted for this period of earthly existence, entail an eternal chastisement? Was it for the fulfilment of so miserable an end that the Son of God was to become incarnate? It might, at least, have occurred to Luther's mind, that, if in the unconverted the consciousness of violating the law were accompanied with such deep sorrow, and produced such terrors of conscience, he ought not to expel it from the conscience of the converted. It might have been expected that he would, at least, be sensible that the law would lose all its efficacy on the unbelieving, if, in relation to the regenerated, he represented it as so paltry ! The law, then, is to lead to Christ ! Strange conceit ! If the law stand in no essential, intimate relation to Christ, how can it conduct to him ? How can that, which abideth not in him, and hath not root in him, smooth the way to him ? For so Luther teaches, when the law hath brought the sinner to Christ, it must be again banished from the interior of man—his conscience and his heart—and be confined to his body ! What doth not belong essentially and eternally to the spiritual part of man, can at no period of time, and in no state of existence, very strongly affect it. If thus the conscience of the *sinner* is to be moved by the law, and in order to rid himself of his own anguish he is to embrace the forgiver of sins, then, surely, in the man *justified* in Christ, the law is not to be limited to this earthly and transitory existence. Therefore hath Christ not abolished, but fulfilled, the law, which was to conduct to him ! Rightly hath it been represented as Israel's distracting grief, that her God abode without her, far removed from her, and thundering forth terror and despair. *But, at the same time, and in most intimate connection with this state of things*, the law of Israel was likewise only extraneous, and widely remote from her, and therefore menacing on stony tablets, and not inscribed on the living heart ; for the law is God's declared will ; and thus alienation from God involved also alienation from his law. By the coming of the Son of God into the world, and his reception into our souls, this disunion between God and man terminated :— in Christ both are reconciled, and are become one. Shall then the law, which had been extraneous, not penetrate also into the interior of man, and there become living, and, consequently, be fulfilled ? Yea, by reconciliation with God we are reconciled and become one with His law also. By the living reception of God into our hearts, through the means of faith we likewise, and necessarily, receive His law ; for the latter is God's eternal will, and one with Him ; so that, where God is, there also is His law.

Religiousness and virtue ! how intimately, how vitally, are they united ! And in the same degree, therefore, religion and morality—faith and the law ! Contemplate the immoral man —see how fading, how drooping, too, is all religious life within him, how utterly incapable it is of putting forth blossoms! How the clear, pure knowledge of divine things is obscured within him! Contemplate the history of nations, and ye will learn how ever immorality and unbelief, of misbelief, have gone hand in hand! This truth the progress of heathenism has inscribed in frightful characters in the book of history. On the other hand, when the Saviour would lay the foundation for Christian piety—for faith in himself, he commands us to observe in life what he hath taught! And this was the experience of all the saints, that the more moral they became the more their piety increased; that, in proportion to the fidelity and purity wherewith the Divine law was realised within them, the deeper their religious knowledge became! Whence comes the fact, that a genuine piety evaporates, when a violation of the moral law occurs; and, again, that to the observance of the latter the former is so easily annexed? Doth not this point incontrovertibly to an essential unity of the two? Oh, believe me, whoso sees himself forced, in order to preserve in his heart and conscience a confiding faith, to banish thence the moral law, hath in his heart and conscience an erroneous faith; for the true living faith not merely agrees with the moral law—it is one with it. Again, too, whence the fact, that the religious and moral elements cannot really exist asunder; that the one perpetually seeks the other, nay, bears it in its own bosom? From the living sense and the clear acknowledgment of our dependence on the all-gracious and merciful God, humility and confidence first spring, next the fulness of love, which already includes obedience and resignation to the will of heaven, whereby we tread immediately on ethical ground. If the first virtues be more religious, the last are more ethical; but the distinction between them is absorbed in love—their living centre—the point wherein religiousness and morality unite.[1]

Now only have we obtained a complete solution to the Protestant doctrine, that faith, in its abstract sense, alone saves. Salvation the Catholic attaches only to the undivided interior life of the regenerated—to faith and love—to the fulfilment of the law, or to the concurrence of the religious and ethical principles: he places both in an equal relation to a future life, for

[1] In modern times Schleiermacher, Twesten, and Sack, have shown themselves to be genuine Protestants, in severing, quite immoderately, the ethical and the religious principle one from the other; this, however, has been done more by the two former than by the latter.

both alike possess an eternal value. Luther, on the other hand, recognises faith alone as the principle of eternal felicity, because he ascribes to morality only an earthly, perishable worth. The above alleged argument of the Protestants, that works, on account of the partly sinful faculty whence they emanate, have not a saving efficacy, is in itself inadequate; for from the same motive they should represent faith as weak and defective; and, consequently, deny it the power of insuring salvation. But from the point of view which we have now reached, we can survey the whole, and all becomes perfectly clear and luminous. Hence it was quite in the spirit of Luther, and even better than he understood himself, that Andrew Poach—a writer who took part in the controversies raised by Major—advanced the proposition, that even the perfect fulfilment of the law, that is to say, the purest morality, had no claim to eternal happiness.[1]

Now have we at last succeeded in completely unfolding the speculative idea, which lies at the bottom of the Protestant doctrine of justification. We have before observed, that the relation towards evil, wherein the Reformers placed the Almighty, and their ulterior doctrine, that it cannot even by Divine power be rooted out from the regenerated, are based upon the idea that evil necessarily adheres to everything finite. The same thought may also be expressed in the following manner. The sense of sin cannot be effaced from all finite consciousness—from the consciousness of man—it constantly accompanies and tortures man, because evil is inseparable from him, as a limited being; to this he is predestined. But how doth he obtain quiet ? By the lifting up of the mind to a higher point of view —to the inward essence of things—to the Infinite: in the consciousness of God, in faith, evil vanishes. Hence, moral freedom annihilated was converted into freedom from the moral law, which has relation merely to the temporal, limited, external world, but has no kind of reference to that which is eternal and exalted above space and time. But, however, we by no means intend to assert, that the Reformers were conscious of this fundamental principle of their system; on the contrary, had they understood themselves—had they conceived whither their doctrines led—they would have rejected them as un-Christian.

[1] 'Propositio " bona opera sunt necessaria ad salutem " non potest consistere in doctrina legis, neque lex ullas habet de æterna vita promissiones, etiam perfectissime impleta.' Auctore Andrea Poach, 1535. The orthodox Lutherans, indeed, would not admit this view.

Yet we may also understand wherefore the Catholics, if they wished to uphold the idea of the holiness and justice of God; if they wished to maintain human freedom, insure the dignity of the moral law, confirm the true notion of sin, and the debt of sin, and not suffer the doctrine of redemption in Christ to be converted into a very folly, should with all their energy, have opposed the Protestant theory of faith and justification.

XXVI—ANALYSIS OF THE ELEMENTS OF TRUTH AND OF ERROR IN THE PROTESTANT DOCTRINE OF FAITH, AS HITHERTO STATED

If we now take a retrospective view of all that has been advanced, and reduce all to a short summary, it will follow that in Protestantism the religious element formed the more luminous side, and the ethical the darker; and this, of course, was attended with the consequence, that ultimately the religious element was regarded only with a very oblique and distorted view.

The religious element no one will fail to notice in Protestantism, who only recalls to mind that notion of Divine Providence, which Luther and Melancthon put forth at the commencement of the Reformation, but which Calvin defended to the end of his days. The action of Providence the Reformers by no means made to consist merely in the guidance of all things little and great, in the wise and tender conduct of individuals, as of the whole human race. No; according to them, all the phenomena in the world of man are God's own work, and man is the mere instrument of God: everything in the world's history is God's invisible act, visibly realised by the agency of man. Who can here fail to recognise a religious contemplation of all things? All is referred to God—God is all in all.

The same pious view of the world, and the world's history, extends to the more special circle of Christian doctrines. The fundamental principles of Christian piety are, doubtless, rigidly maintained; but only a perverse application of them is made; for the same relation, wherein, as we have seen, the Deity is represented to be in respect to man, is established between Christ and the believer. The Redeemer is, in such a way, all in all, that he and his spirit are alone efficacious, and faith and regeneration are exclusively his act; so that, as, according to

Luther's doctrine, man disappears before God, so the Christian likewise disappears before Christ. The following passage will furnish us with the clearest insight into Luther's feelings on this subject:—'I can well remember,' he remarks, 'that Dr Staupitz, who was provincial vicar of the Augustinians, when the gospel first began to be preached, said to me, "it affords me the greatest consolation, that this doctrine of the gospel, which is now coming to light, gives all honour and praise to God alone, and nothing to men. Now it is clear and evident that we can never ascribe too much honour, goodness, etc., to our Lord God." So he then consoled me: and it is the truth, that the doctrine of the gospel takes from men all honour, wisdom, and justice, and ascribes them to the one just Creator, who creates all things out of nothing. Now it is much safer to ascribe too much to our Lord God; albeit, however, we can never too much ascribe to Him. Herein do I not err and sin, for I give to both—to wit, God and man—what appertaineth to each.'[1]

The feelings whereby Luther was guided, are, to judge from such appearances, sound to their inmost core; but as, in feeling truth and error can lie enclosed, and only in a higher grade of intellectual life are separated one from the other, so this is here the case. In Luther we imagine ourselves to be transported to the primitive times of our race, when, before the mind of man yet giddy from his fall, all forms pass in motley confusion; God and man are no longer kept distinct, and the acts of both are blended together.

The principle of freedom Luther did not apprehend; since in it he abhorred the destruction of all deeper religious feeling and true humility; viewing in it an encroachment on the rights of the Divine Majesty, nay, the self-deification of man. To be free and to be God was, in his opinion, synonymous.[2] But what was the consequence? While he desired to oppose the self-will, he annihilated the free-will, of man; and, in combating his self-

---

[1] Luther, Comment. on Ep. to Galat. loc. cit. p. 35.
[2] Luther de servo arbitrio ad Erasm. Roterod. l. l. fol. 117, b. 'Sequitur nunc, liberum arbitrium esse plane divinum nomen, nec ulli posse competere, quam soli divinæ majestati; ea enim potestate facit omnia, quæ vult in cœlo et in terra. Quod si hominibus tribuitur, nihil rectius tribuitur, quam si Divinitas quoque ipsa eis tribueretur, quo sacrilegio nullum esse majus possit. Proinde theologorum erat, ab isto vocabulo abstinere, cum de humana virtute loqui vellent, et soli Deo relinquere; deinde ex hominum ore et sermone id ipsum tollere, tanquam sacrum ac venerabile nomen Deo suo asserere.'

seeking, he assailed, withal, his self-existence and individuality. It is a circumstance worthy of special consideration, that Luther so often as he will prove man to be no longer in possession of the higher freedom—that freedom which truth, piety, and virtue insure, shows also involuntarily, that he no longer possesses the freedom of election, and confounds both species of freedom, which are yet so very distinct one from the other ! The freedom of election is for man the necessary condition to a higher freedom, but not the same. Thus the Reformer worked himself up to an incapacity to discover in the Catholic notion of humility any humility at all ; for humility, according to him, consists in the renunciation of an independent personality, and of personal dignity, and is of an essentially physical nature ; whereas, according to the genuine and old Christian view, humility is of a moral essence, and must depend on a free homage, a free oblation of oneself. The Reformers said : ' See, thou art not thyself free, and yet thou wouldst fain be free ; in this consists all thy perverseness.' The Catholic, on the other hand, said : ' O man, thou art created free ; but if by thy freedom thou becomest a bond-slave to God, thou wilt receive thy freedom glorified back.' Hereby it was possible for the Catholic to explain how a false freedom could be sought after ; and his whole system became at once a Theodicea—a justification of God on account of evil in the world, which Protestantism must absolutely renounce, as it can never explain how man, whom it believes to be absolutely devoid of free-will, could ever come to believe himself a free agent, and thereby become evil ; unless, with the want of freedom, he be destined to this longing after freedom, and in this way be he doomed to an annihilating contradiction of his own nature with itself, and thereby all evil be referred to God.

In fact, this course of reasoning the Reformers fearlessly pursued ; misapprehended, together with free will, the essence of the moral law and morality, which, without free will, is inconceivable ; and yet ventured withal to accuse Catholics of want of humility—Catholics, according to whose doctrine that word can alone possess a rational sense ; and who, when they say of a man that he confesses himself a sinner before God (and this is the principle of all humility in fallen creatures), are alone consistent.

These grievous perplexities necessarily required a theory of justifying faith, such as the new Church gave. Reduced to a rational expression, this faith accordingly signifies the giving ourselves back full of confidence to God, as at our birth, and through the course of our lives, He hath constituted us;—a well-grounded expectation that He will grant us a favourable issue out of the enigmatic labyrinth of evil, which He hath himself prepared and into which He hath conducted us. By such a method, undoubtedly, no glory accrues to man; but whether any glory be thereby rendered to God, the enlightened observer will be able to judge.[1]

§ XXVII—AFFINITY OF PROTESTANTISM WITH GNOSTICISM, AND SOME PANTHEISTIC SYSTEMS OF THE MIDDLE AGE—MORE ACCURATE DETERMINATION OF THE DIFFERENCE BETWEEN ZWINGLE'S AND LUTHER'S PRINCIPLES

There is no religious phenomenon, to which the system of the Reformers offers more resemblance, than Gnosticism, to which we have already had, now and then, occasion to advert. In the first place, the latter sprang out of a glowing desire after eternal life, and the deepest sense of human misery in general, and of the misery of sin in particular. So deep a horror for

[1] Luther (de servo arbitrio ad Erasm. Roterod. l. l. fol. 236), expresses this thought in the following way: ' Ego sane de me confiteor, si qua fieri possit, nollem mihi dari liberum arbitrium aut quippiam in manu mea relinqui, quo ad salutem conari possem; non solum ideo, quod in tot adversitatibus et periculis, deinde tot impugnantibus, dæmonibus, subsistere et retinere illud non valerem, cum unus dæmon potentior sit omnibus hominibus, neque ullus hominum salvaretur; sed quod etiam, si nulla pericula, nullæ adversitates, nulli dæmones essent, cogerer tamen perpetuo in incertum laborare et aerem pugnis verberare. Neque enim conscientia mea, si in æternum viverem et operarer, unquam certa et secura fieret, quantam facere deberet, quo satis Deo fieret. Quocumque enim opere perfecto reliquus esset scrupulus, an id Deo placeret, vel an aliquid requireret, sicut probat experientia omnium justiciariorum, et ego meo magno malo tot annis satis didici. '*At nunc cum Deus salutem meam, extra meum arbitrium tollens, in suum receperit, et non meo opere aut cursu, sed sua gratia et misericordia, promiserit me servare, securus et certus sum, quod ille fidelis sit, et mihi non mentietur, tam potens et magnus, ut nulli dæmones, nullæ adversitates eum, frangere, aut me illi rapere, potuerunt. Nemo (inquit) rapiet eos de manu mea, quia pater, qui dedit, major omnibus est. Ita fit, ut si non omnes, tamen aliqui et multi salventur, cum per vim liberi arbitrii nullus prorsus servaretur, sed in unum omnes perderemur. Tum etiam certi sumus et securi, nos Deo placere, non merito operis nostri, sed favore misericordiæ suæ nobis promissæ, atque si minus aut male egerimus, quod nobis non imputet, sed paterne ignoscat et emendet. Hæc est gloriatio omnium sanctorum in Deo suo.*'

evil filled its disciples, that they deemed it absolutely incompatible with the creation of the good God, and thence proceeded even to uphold a dualism of principles. From the present form of human existence, which arose out of the mysterious concurrence of these principles, evil, according to them, was quite inseparable; it could, though combated, never be overcome.

Down to the fourteenth and fifteenth centuries, we find Gnosticism continuing in broken and detached systems. The Reformers in the sixteenth century embraced it under a milder form. It is not to be doubted, but that they were moved by the like feelings; that they were deeply impressed with the sinfulness of the world, and on that account represented human nature as so thoroughly corrupted, that the disease was in this life absolutely incurable.

Secondly, this sense of sin, pious, doubtless, but confused and distempered in itself, tended, among the Protestants as well as the Gnostics, towards its own destruction; and, as it did not comprehend, and thereby maintain itself, it became utterly extinct.

The higher the degree of objective sinfulness is considered, wherein the subject sees himself involved without personal guilt, the more the magnitude of subjective self-committed evil disappears; and human nature is then charged with the debt, which the individual had contracted. How much the Gnostics sought to excuse themselves, by means of their theory of evil, is well known. In like manner, the Protestants represent Adam, who is accounted the only sinner, as succeeded by Christ, who alone worketh good; and if, by the former, all personal guilt is made impossible, so, through the latter, all personal merit is rendered unnecessary. If the former hath bereaved man of all moral freedom, and, consequently, of all capacity for good, the latter is so constituted, that all liberty, all independent working of good on the part of man, becomes unnecessary; and the more unavoidable the necessity of sinning is represented to have been in the first Adam, the more easily obtainable is forgiveness through the second Adam described to be. The error here is precisely the same as if one were to believe, that a deep sense of guilt was possible only under the condition of a prodigious magnitude of evil deeds committed by us; for, on the contrary, experience shows, that when the amount of evil, objectively considered, is small, it is always *most deeply felt*, and most strongly detested. In fact, no blood-guiltiness, no perjury, no adultery is necessary, in order to make one weep out his whole life in penitential tears. In like manner, it is quite unnecessary, that, through Adam, men should have been bereaved of all reason, and their every fibre infected, in order to inspire them with a deep sense of the misery under which they languish, and to make them hail a Redeemer with joy. In Adam we were wounded, but not killed: the wound causes a pain to be felt, and the physician to be welcomed, and admits of a perfect cure; but in death all pain is extinguished, and no life returns.

Thirdly, Gnosticism desired of its followers the consciousness, the knowledge (γνῶσις), that they were the sons of the good God; that they could not be lost; that they were quite certain of salvation; and with this claim was associated the doctrine, that some men are by birth οἱ Πνευματικοί (men of the spirit), others οἱ Ψῡχικοί (men of the soul), and others, again οἱ χοϊκοί (men of clay). In Protestantism, we find, as parallels, *Faith*, which comprises the absolute assurance of eternal life, and the doctrine, that some are, from eternity, predestined to happiness, others to damnation; and this is merely another mode of expressing the Gnostic classification of men. Even the Gnostic doctrine of the Pneumatici contains a principle, that incited to the highest moral enthusiasm, to the most perseverant struggle against all evil; but it is well known how horribly this doctrine was abused in life. It is the same with the Protestant certitude of eternal life, and of absolute predestination. The conviction, that, through God's mercy, and without any moral obligation on my part, I shall infallibly have a share in eternal happiness, can inspire me with gratitude the warmest, and the most capable of producing the fairest fruits in life; and this it was which Luther expected to be the result of his doctrine. But the notion, that heaven will not be lost to the believer, or to him who firmly confides; and that no merit, that is to say, no personal worth bears any inward relation to salvation, could as easily produce the opposite effects in practice; and that these did not fail to ensue, Luther himself often enough complains, and the course of our investigations will furnish us with numerous proofs. We do not contend, that such an assurance, in noble, tender, and sensitive souls, if such can vaunt of this assurance, is not capable of bearing the most abundant fruits; but how doth the view, which the Reformers entertain of human sinfulness, entitle them to reckon upon souls of such a stamp? If to this it be objected, that every doctrine can be abused, we admit the fact, but maintain, that truth of itself never gives occasion to abuse ; that, on the contrary, abuse springs only from the false position, wherein anyone sets himself in relation to the truth : whereas with an erroneous doctrine, abuse is necessarily intertwined, and it is a mere matter of chance whether it conduce to anyone's spiritual welfare. This is the case with the doctrine, that, without fulfilling any moral obligations, we become, by faith alone, partakers of Divine grace ; this is the case with the Gnostic and Protestant feeling of assurance, and with the doctrine of predestination, which it presupposes.

Fourthly, Marcion was so impressed with the loftiness of the New Testament revelation, with the revelation of God as a gracious, loving, and merciful Father, that, on that account, he held the divinity in Christ to be essentially different from the one that created the world filled with evils of every kind, gave in the old covenant such severe laws, and so strictly, according to them, meted out rewards and punishments. Into what contradictions Luther brought Nature and Grace, Law and Gospel, we have already seen, and not less so, how, in the Redeemer, he saw exclusively the merciful Forgiver of sins.[1] Marcion, the most pious of Gnostics, but who evinced scarcely any trace of a scientific spirit, supposed, that the good God in Christ took compassion on men, without incurring any obligation to concern Himself as to their destiny ; since they belonged to a creation to which He was a stranger : but he forgot, that it was inconceivable how men could even understand Him, and enter into communion with Him, because, as beings created by the Demiurgos (a spirit independent of God), they possessed nothing akin to God, no manner of likeness unto God. In his folly, he thought he more highly exalted the mercy of God, by representing Him as redeeming creatures, not only estranged from Him by sin, but, in their very essence, aliens to Him. In like manner Luther. Fallen man, according to him, was nothing but sin, entirely bereft of the Divine image ; a doctrine by which he thought to exalt the glory of the Saviour ; without considering, that he, who has no longer anything to be redeemed, cannot possibly be susceptible of redemption. Yet these

[1] Tertull. adv. Marc. l. i, c. 2. 'Et ita in Christo quasi aliam inveniens dispositionem solius et puræ benignitatis et diversæ a Creatore, facile novam et hospitam argumentatus est divinitatem in Christo suo revelatam.'

parallels must now be closed, especially as we should be thrown into no small embarrassment, were we to compare Luther's ascetic exercises with those of Marcion. Such very opposite practical results flowed from theories which have the closest affinity with each other. But even Prodicus, the most libertine enemy to the law, and the Cainites professed theoretical maxims similar to those of Marcion!

Another doctrine to which Protestantism bears undeniable relationship, is the ideal Pantheism, whose adherents, through the whole course of the middle age, were arrayed against the Church, in no less violent opposition than that which she encountered from the Gnostico-Manichean Dualists. To the former class belong Amalrich of Chartres, and his disciple, David of Dinant, with their followers, various classes of the Fraticelli, Lollards, and Beghards, the brothers and sisters of 'the Free Spirit,' together with several others. They held the doctrine of the One and All of things—of the absolute necessity of everything which occurs—and, consequently, of evil in the creation, of the want of free-will in man, and yet of the utmost latitude of freedom, which he can enforce against the dictates of the moral law—of the certainty of salvation—that is to say, the return to the deity, or absorption in His bosom, which indeed, forms a necessary part of Pantheism, and of every doctrine that ascribes a divine essence to man. To this class Wycliff belongs, who only further expanded the fatalistic doctrines more hesitatingly taught by Thomas Bradwardine; ascribed, in his Trialogus, evil to God; and, with the denial of freedom of election in man, admitted in his system an absolute predestination, and on this account was censured by an English synod.

Luther and Zwingle, to a certain extent, diverged into these opposite courses; and herein consists, if we judge rightly, the real difference between them. Luther approximates more to the Gnostico-Manichean view of the world;—Zwingle to the Pantheistic. In the first period of his opposition against the Church, Luther, in his peculiar humility, wished to refuse, *to fallen man only*, every species of freedom in what concerned holiness. But, in the course of his hostility, he thought to give a further support to his notion of humility, by representing man, *as in himself*, devoid of freedom—a proof of his unscientific spirit—for by this second doctrine, he entirely took away all weight from the first. It is, however, evident, from numerous passages in his writings, that his principal object was to inspire men with humility and piety, by consideration of their deep guilt in Adam ; and that, in the course of the struggle, he evinced a disposition to cling only to this groundwork of his system— which we may call the would-be Christian—and to give up the other, which we may characterise as the speculative one.[1] Zwingle, on the other hand, leant almost exclusively on the latter (for what he alleged respecting original sin, and evil in general, is scarce worthy of attention), he pretty openly declared for Pantheism, and thereby attached himself to the principles of that second party described above, which, in the middle age, unfurled the banner of opposition against the Church. The following statement will furnish the reader with more detailed explanations.

The leading principles in his writing on providence are as follows: All power is either created or uncreated. If it be uncreated, it is God himself ; if it be created, it must needs be created by God. But to be created by God, signifies nought else than to be an emanation of His power ; for whatever is, is from Him, and in Him, *nay, is Himself.* Thus, created power is ever but a phenomenon of universal power, in a new subject, and a new individual.[2] The notion of a power, peculiar to a created being, is as incompatible with the notion of the Deity, as with the notion of a created being, since this would thereby be conceived as uncreated. To wish to be free, is accordingly identical with wishing to be one's own God ; and the doctrine

---

[1] Luther de servo arbitr. adv. Erasm. loc. cit. p. 177, b. ' Nonne agnoscis ? Jam quæro et peto, si gratia Dei desit, aut separetur ab illa vi modicula, quid ipsa faciet ? Inefficax (inquis) est, et nihil facit boni. Ergo non faciet, quod Deus aut gratia ejus volet ; siquidem gratiam Dei separatam ab ea jam posuimus, quod vero gratia Dei non facit, bonum non est. Quare sequitur, liberum arbitrium sine gratia Dei prorsus non liberum, sed immutabiliter captivum et servum esse mali, cum non possit vertere se solo ad bonum. *Hoc stante, dono tibi, ut vim liberi arbitrii non modo facias modiculam, fac eam angelicam, fac, si potes, plane divinam, si adjeceris tamen hanc illætabilem appendicem, et citra gratiam Dei inefficacem dicas ;* mox ademeris illi omnem vim : quid est vis inefficax, nisi plane nulla vis ? ' But as might be expected from this conclusion, we find immediately a recurrence to the old doctrine : ' Fixum ergo stet . . . nos omnia necessitate, nihil libero arbitrio facere, dum vis liberi arbitrii nihil est, neque facit, neque potest bonum, absente gratia.'

[2] Zwingli de providentia, tom. i, fol. 354, a. ' Quæ tamen creata dicitur, cum omnis virtus numinis virtus sit, nec enim quidquam est, quod non ex illo, in illo, et per illud, imo illud sit, creata, inquam, virtus dicitur, eo quod in novo subjecto, et nova specie, universalis aut generalis atis virtus exhibetur. Testes sunt Moses, Paulus, Plato, Seneca.' (!!)

of freedom leads at once to self-deification, and to polytheism. The predicate ' freedom,' and the subject ' creature,' are mutually incompatible ; and the expression ' a free creature,' involves a contradiction.

He continues : Freedom as a self power, being inconsistent with the omnipotence of God, the notion of a creature living according to its own design is evidently subversive of the wisdom of God. For this is as much as to suppose, that God would alter his decree, which can only be eternal, and consequently immutable, according to human caprices and actions, the result of human prudence. The notion of Divine Providence is, therefore, according to Zwingle, in every respect, one and the same with that of the inevitable necessity of all occurrences ; and quite consistently, therefore, he rejects, with the idea of free-will, all freedom of thinking also.[1]

His thoughts on the essence of created energies Zwingle discloses further, when he says, the being of all things is the being of God, and God Himself ; for, should we assert the contrary, then the notion of the infinite, which appertains to God, is destroyed ; since anything, which *is not Himself*, is placed *beside Him*, and *out of Him*.[2] To render his ideas more intelligible to the Landgrave of Hesse, he makes use of the following comparison. As plants and animals grow out of the earth, and, when their individual life is extinct, dissolve again into its bosom, so it is with the universe in respect to God :—and he adds, in passing, the consoling observation, that from thence the immortality of man is very apparent, since we see, that nought which has ever been, can quite cease to be, as it only

[1] Loc. cit. ' Jam si quicquam sua virtute ferretur aut consilio, jam isthinc cessarent sapientia et virtus nostri numinis. Quod si fieret, non esset numinis sapientia summa, qui non comprehenderet ac caperet universa ; non esset ejus virtus omnipotens, quia esset virtus libera ab ejus potentia, et idcirco alia. Ut jam esset vis, quæ non esset vis numinis, esset lux et intelligentia, quæ non esset numinis istius sapientia.'
What conclusions for a Reformer ! Above all, Zwingle should have been advised to reform his logic. More plausible, yet still devoid of all true solidity, is the following : ' Immutabilem autem diximus administrationem ac dispositionem, hanc ob causam, ut et eorum sententiam, qui hominis arbitrium liberum esse adseverant, non undique firmam, et summi numinis sapientiam certiorem ostenderem, quam ut eam eventus ullus latere possit, qui deinde imprudentem cogeret aut retractare aut mutare consilium.'

[2] Loc. cit. fol. 355, b. ' Cum autem infinitum, quod res est, ideo dicatur, quod essentia et existentia infinitum sit, jam constat extra infinitum hoc " Esse nullum esse posse." ' Fol. 356 : ' Cum igitur unum ac solum infinitum sit, necesse est præter hoc nihil esse.'

returns to the Universal Being. He even cannot refrain from a digression, to the effect that the Pythagorean doctrine of the transmigration of souls is not quite groundless, and presents one very favourable side.[1]

From all this Zwingle infers, that there can be but one cause, and that the so-called secondary causes should not be regarded as causes, but only as means and instruments of the first, which is at once the only cause.[2] By this he utterly denies, that man can be the free principle of causation in a series of actions, and represents him as a completely passive instrument—a living machine, which never acts from itself, which is only set in motion, and is alike incapable either of good or of evil. So far Zwingle, who only reduces to its first principles Luther's doctrine of the servitude of the human will. We have often wondered at the so-called orthodox Protestant theologians of our days, when they opposed modern theological, and philosophical systems, which more consistently carried out the principles of the Reformers, so little did Protestant orthodoxy understand itself ! With all his deviations on particular points, Schleiermacher is, in my opinion, the only genuine disciple of the Reformers.

[1] Loc. cit. ' Sed hanc sententiam paulo φιλοσοφικώτερον tractatam . . . exemplo . . . confirmabimus,' etc.
[2] Loc. cit. fol. 358, b.

CHAPTER IV

DIFFERENCES IN THE DOCTRINE OF THE SACRAMENTS

§ XXVIII—DOCTRINE OF CATHOLICS ON THE SACRAMENTS IN GENERAL

THE doctrine of the sacraments we shall now treat immediately after the exposition of the doctrine of justification; since, according to the expression of the Council of Trent, justification is, by means of the sacraments either originally infused into us, or subsequently increased, or, when lost, is again restored.[1] We shall begin with stating the Catholic doctrine. The nature of the sacraments in general will first be defined; next the object of their institution; then the manner in which they communicate grace will be explained; and, lastly, their number will be stated.

A sacrament is defined, by the catechism of the Council of Trent, to be an outward sign, which, in virtue of the divine ordinance, not only typifies, but works, the supersensual; to wit, holiness and justice.[2] Here the same manual notices the distinction which, according to the definition we have cited, exists between a sacrament and an image, or the sign of the cross and the like.

On the object of their institution, the same catechism enlarges in the following manner. In the first place, man, as a being belonging to the world of sense, stands in need of a sensible type, to obtain and to preserve the consciousness of what passes in his supersensual part. It adds, if a man were a pure spirit, then would the divine powers, which produce justice and holiness, require no sensible medium. In the second place, the catechism represents the sacraments as pledges of the Divine will in regard to man, as sureties of the truth of God's promises. It is only with difficulty, it continues, that men can be brought into belief; hence it was, that God, in the Old Testament, in corro-

---

[1] Concil. Trident. sess. vii, decret. de Sacram.

[2] 'Quare ut explicatius, quid sacramentum sit, declaretur, docendum erit, rem esse sensibus subjectam, quæ ex Dei institutione sanctitatis et justitiæ tum significandæ, tum efficiendæ, vim habet.'

boration of His word, made use of outward signs to strengthen the confidence of man in the Divine assurances. In like manner, such signs have been instituted by Christ, to serve to men as pledges of the forgiveness of sin, of heavenly grace, and of the communion of the Holy Spirit. Thirdly, the sacraments are represented as the channels (*quasi alvei*), whereby the power which flows from the sufferings of Christ, the grace which the Saviour hath merited for us, is individualised, and applied to each one; in order that by aid thereof, the health of the soul may be re-established, or confirmed. Fourthly, remarks the catechism, they are to be considered as outward marks and tokens of confession among the faithful. Lastly, the idea, with which this exposition of the cited manual concludes, is far more ingenious and more profound than it may at first sight appear— the idea, namely, that the sacraments contribute the more to cherish Christian piety as they are well calculated to humble arrogance by the reflection, that, as man had ignominiously delivered himself over to the dominion of the lower world, so he needs its mediation to enable him to rise above it. That false spiritualism, which, during a considerable part of the Middle Age, as well as at the period of the Reformation, everywhere burst forth, and sought to obtain ascendancy, might, by an earnest consideration alone of the great humiliating truth which this idea involves, have attained to a consciousness of its fearful aberrations.[1]

As regards the mode in which the sacraments confer on us sanctifying grace, the Catholic Church teaches, that they work in us, by means of their character, as an institution prepared by Christ for our salvation (*ex opere operato, scilicet a Christo*, in place of *quod operatus est Christus*),[2] that is to say, the sacraments convey a divine power, merited for us by Christ, which cannot be produced by any human disposition, by any spiritual effort or condition; but is absolutely, for Christ's sake, conferred by God through their means. Doubtless, man must *receive* this grace, and therefore be *susceptible* of it; and this suscepti-

---

[1] Loc. cit. p. 167. The whole exposition of the catechism is taken from the manuals of the theologians of the Middle Age; for example, from Hugh St Victor, Alexander Hales, Bonaventura, and Thomas Aquinas. See the last-named schoolman's Summ. tot. theolog. Par. 3, Q. lxi, Art. I. p. 276.

[2] Concil. Trid. sess. vii, can. viii. 'Si quis dixerit, per ipsa novæ legis sacramenta ex opere operato non conferri gratiam, sed solam fidem divinæ promissionis ad gratiam consequendam sufficere, anathema sit.'

bility is evinced in repentance and sorrow for sin, in the desire after divine aid, and in confiding faith. But he can *only* receive it, and therefore be *only* susceptible of it. By this doctrine, accordingly the objectivity of Divine grace is upheld; and we are prevented from drawing down the effects of the sacrament into the region of the subjective; and, from entertaining the opinion, that these consisted in mere moral and dialectic results, in human feelings, considerations, and resolves, which, as at the view of a picture representing Christ crucified, are excited within us at the moment of receiving, or even may precede the reception. This human activity, except in the case of infants to be baptised, is indeed necessary; but it is not the divine grace promised in the sacrament, nor doth it even merit it. Nay, the religious energies of the human soul are set in new motion by the sacrament, since its divine matter impregnates the soul of man, vivifies her anew, establishes her in the most intimate communion with God, and continues to work within all men, who do not show themselves incapable of its graces, or, as the council expresses it, do not place an obstacle in the way.[1]

[1] Concil. Trid. loc. cit. can. vi. 'Si quis dixerit, Sacramenta novæ legis non continere gratiam, quam significant, aut gratiam ipsam non ponentibus obicem non conferre, quasi signa tantum, etc., anathema sit.' Bellarmine has treated this subject of the sacraments with the felicity which he always evinces in doctrinal investigations: 'Igitur ut intelligamus,' says he, 'quid sit opus operatum, notandum est in justificatione quam recipit aliquis, dum percipit sacramenta, multa concurrere, nimirum, ex parte Dei, voluntatem utendi illa re sensibili; ex parte Christi, passionem ejus: ex parte ministri, voluntatem, potestatem, probitatem; *ex parte suscipientis, voluntatem fidem, et pænitentiam;* denique ex parte sacramenti, ipsam actionem externam quæ consurgit ex debita applicatione materiæ et formæ. Cæterum ex his omnibus id, quod active et proxime et instrumentaliter efficit gratiam justificationis, est sola actio illa externa, quæ sacramentum dicitur, et hæc vocatur opus operatum, accipiendo passive (operatum), ita ut idem sit sacramentum conferre gratiam ex opere operato, quod conferre gratiam ex vi ipsius actionis sacramentalis a Deo ad hoc institutæ, non ex merito agentis vel suscipientis.' After proving all that has been here stated, and in reference to what has been said of the minister, after showing that his will only *is necessary*, Bellarmine continues: 'Voluntas, fides, et pœnitentia in suscipiente adulto necessario requiruntur, ut dispositiones ex parte subjecti, non ut causæ activæ; non enim fides et pœnitentia efficiunt gratiam sacramentalem, neque dant efficaciam sacramenti, sed solum tollunt obstacula, quæ impedirent, ne sacramenta suam efficaciam exercere possent, unde in pueris ubi non requiritur dispositio, sine his rebus fit justificatio. Exemplum esse potest in re naturali. Si ad ligna comburenda primum exsiccarentur ligna, deinde excuteretur ignis ex silice, tum applicaretur ignis ligno, et sic tandem fieret combustio, nemo diceret

The doctrine of justification—according to which the divine activity precedes the human, and then both, in case the latter doth not obstinately resist, constitute one and the same divine and human work—recurs in the theory of the sacraments. And from the universal relation which, according to Catholic doctrine, exists between grace and free-will, we might infer that, the *opus operatum* doth not establish a divine activity only, nor imply a mere inertness on the part of man.[1]

That Catholics reckon seven sacraments, needs no further evidence; but Catholics, we may notice in passing, assert of no sacrament, that its reception is entirely and absolutely necessary to salvation. So, for instance, the ardent desire of a catechumen for baptism, when invincible outward obstacles prevent its accomplishment, is sufficient. God, who freely chooses one mode of communicating to us His grace, can make use of another; but it is not for man to reject, according to his caprice, the means of salvation offered to him by Christ, and to prefer another path of grace. This would argue a very gross presumption, and be a most culpable contempt of the divine ordinances. A spirituality of this kind is, with all its pretensions to refinement nought else than a coarse, carnal arrogance.

§ XXIX—LUTHERAN DOCTRINE OF THE SACRAMENTS IN GENERAL—CONSEQUENCES OF THIS DOCTRINE

At the commencement of the Reformation, Luther and Melancthon evinced on this matter the most decided opposition to the Catholic Church; and the internal ground of this opposition lay entirely in their one-sided conception of the justification of man before God. Hereby especially the communication of *really sanctifying* graces, by means of the sacraments, was thrown into the background, nay, even totally called in question; just as if the Reformers dreaded being sanctified. The highest

causam immediatam combustionis esse siccitatem, aut excussionem ignis ex silice, aut applicationem ignis ad ligna, sed solum ignem, ut causam primariam, et solis calorem, seu calefactionem, ut causam instrumentalem' (Bellarm. de Sacram. l. ii, c. 1, t. iii, p. 108, 109).

[1] Let the reader compare sess. vi, c. vi, of the Council of Trent with what will be said below respecting penance. Many divines, moreover, along with Bellarmine in the passage just cited, bring, in connection with the doctrine of the *opus operatum*, the fact, that the efficacy of the sacraments is not determined by the virtue and piety of those who dispense them.

point to which they could rise, was the one-sided view of the sacraments, considered as pledges of the truth of the Divine promises for the forgiveness of sins. The sacraments, accordingly, were to have no other destination, than to make the faithful receiver assured that his debt of sins was remitted, and to console and to quiet him.

The sacraments being now no longer used as channels of grace, which *convey* an internal sanctifying power, and *proffer* it to man, their effects were necessarily confined to the subjective acts of the individual at the moment of reception; and it was asserted, that the participation of them was only in so far attended with fruit, *as faith in the forgiveness of sins existed*.

Hereby, therefore, in the first place, the *opus operatum*—the objective character of these means of grace—was of necessity rejected; and everything drawn down into the sphere of the subjective. A second point of opposition was formed by the Lutheran notion of a sacrament, as above described; inasmuch as Catholics, with whom forgiveness of sins and sanctification are one and the same divine act, understand both, by the justification produced or augmented by the medium of the sacraments.

As it is by the right use of the sacraments that man is sanctified, so it is by the same means that his sins are forgiven him, or, when these are already forgiven, that sanctifying grace is increased. On the other hand, the Reformers, whose system everywhere lays too exclusive a stress on the pardon of sins, teach that even the sacraments serve only as instruments for confirming faith in this remission of sins. In the first edition of his 'Loci Theologici,'[1] Melancthon betrays not even a perception of any deeper or more comprehensive notion of the sacraments, than the one here stated; and Luther, in his work

[1] P. 46: 'Apparet quam nihil sacramenta sint, nisi fidei exercendæ μνημόσυνα.' P. 141, et seq: 'Nostra imbecillitas signis erigitur, ne de misericordia Dei inter tot insultus peccati desperet. Non aliter atque pro signo favoris divini haberes, si ipse tecum coram colloqueretur, si peculiare aliquod pignus misericordiæ, qualecunque miraculum tibi exhiberet : decet de his te signis sentire, ut tam certo credas, tui misertum esse Deum, cum beneficium accipis, cum participas mensæ Domini, quam crediturus tibi videris, si ipse tecum colloqueretur Deus, aut aliud quidquam ederet miraculi, quod ad te peculiariter pertineret. Fidei excitandæ gratia signa sunt proposita—Probabilis et illi voluntatis sunt, qui symbolis seu tesseris militaribus hæc signa comparaverunt, quod essent notæ *tantum*, quibus cognosceretur, ad quos pertinerent promissiones divinæ.'

on the Babylonish captivity of the Church, unfolds no other view.[1]

In regard to the distinction between the symbols of the Old Testament and the sacraments of the New, Catholic theologians were wont to teach, that the former imparted no justifying grace, that placed us in a real, vital communion with God, but that the latter did so. This distinction the Protestants evidently could not approve, since they held justification and sanctification as separate things, and asserted that the former was determined only by faith. What prevented them, however, from maintaining that our means of salvation were the channels of truly *sanctifying* graces, as cannot be asserted of the Jewish symbols? But Melancthon writes:—'Circumcision is nothing; so is baptism nothing; the communion of the Lord's Supper is nothing; they are rather testimonies and σφραγίδες (seals) of the Divine will toward thee; through them is thy conscience assured, if it ever doubted of the graciousness and the good-will of God in thy regard.' Here baptism and the holy communion are ranked indiscriminately with circumcision; and, like it, are represented as mere signs of covenant. Melancthon, however, expresses himself still more distinctly on this point: he likens the sacraments of the New Law to the signs, which were given to Gideon to assure him of the victory he would gain. Herein, however, we must beware not to alter the point of comparison, which Melancthon wishes to institute. He does not mean to say, that in the same manner as the pledge, given to Gideon, afforded him the certainty that he would overcome the adversaries of God's people, so the sacraments are to us a sign of victory that we shall conquer our enemy, namely, evil. No, in the opinion of Melancthon, the resemblance consists only in the abstract assurance. In the one case, the assurance refers to the fact, that Israel would come victorious out of the impending contest; in the other, it implies only that we should derive consolation, even were we to succumb in the struggle. So mean a conception of the sacraments necessarily led to the

---

[1] Op. Jen. tom. iii, fol. 266, b. 'Omnia sacramenta ad fidem alendam sunt instituta.' 289, b: 'Error enim est sacramenta novæ legis differre a sacramentis veteris legis penes efficaciam significationis.' 287: 'Ita nec verum esse potest, sacramentis inesse vim efficacem justificationis, seu esse signa efficacia gratiæ. Hæc enim omnia dicuntur in jacturam fidei, ex ignorantia promissionis divinæ. Nisi hoc modo efficacia dixeris, quod si adsit fides indubitata, certissime et efficacissime gratiam conferunt.'

view, that they operate only through faith in the Divine promise of the forgiveness of sins.

It was only in course of the disputes with the fanatics, as Luther called them, or with the Sacramentarians, that the Reformers of Wittenberg approximated again to the doctrine of the Church. Already the Confession of Augsburg expresses itself, though indefinitely enough, yet still in a manner to enable Catholics to declare themselves tolerably satisfied with it.

The 'Apology' is still more explicit, for, in a few brief words, it says, that a sacrament is a ceremony, or a work instituted by God, wherein that is represented to us, which the grace annexed to the ceremony proffers.[1]

But, by degrees, the Lutherans again adopted the entire notion of the *opus operatum*, although they continue, even down to the present day, to protest against it—a protest which can be accounted for only by their apparent ignorance of the origin of the Lutheran opposition to the same, and by the arbitrary signification they have attached to the Catholic doctrine.[2] Thus, in course of time, no important difference inherent in the nature of things could be pointed out: but, as a dispute had once existed between Catholics and Protestants, and the later Protestants would not acknowledge the mistakes of the elder ones, they saw themselves forced to invent differences. Even Chemnitius gave Luther's original doctrine in a very disfigured form, and would not avow that he indulged in any such one-sided view of the sacraments, and even took the trouble to misrepresent the schoolmen, particularly Gabriel Biel, in order to

[1] Confess. August. Art. xiii. 'De usu sacramentorum docent, quod sacramenta instituta sint, non modo ut sint notæ professionis inter homines, sed magis ut sint signa et testimonia voluntatis Dei erga nos, ad excitandam et confirmandam fidem in his, qui utuntur, proposita. Itaque utendum est sacramentis, ita ut fides accedat, quæ credat promissionibus, quæ per sacramenta exhibentur et ostenduntur.' Apolog. p. 178: 'Sacramenta vocamus ritus, qui habent mandatum Dei, et quibus addita est promissio gratiæ.' P. 206: 'Sacramentum est ceremonia vel opus, in quo Deus nobis exhibet hoc, quod offert annexa ceremoniæ gratia.'

[2] Marheinke admits this at least, and says the difference between the two confessions consists simply in this, that Catholics teach 'sacramenta *continere* gratiam,' Protestants, on the other hand, inculcate 'sacramenta *conferre* gratiam.' Catholics make use of both expressions, as may be seen from what has been already stated. But how far the *continere* is unsuited to the Protestant theory, the *in, sub,* et *cum* pane clearly point out.

conceal from the eye of uninformed readers Luther's own variations.[1]

Meanwhile the original view of Luther on the sacraments (though, as the correction, which shortly after was made in it, showed, it had arisen out of a heedless spirit of opposition, and from want of serious reflection), produced very important consequences. As the aforesaid means of salvation, according to this theory, were, by their symbolical character, destined only to confirm and consolidate faith in the forgiveness of sins; so the number of the old ecclesiastical sacraments must of necessity be diminished. Everyone at the first glance must perceive, that matrimony could no longer be numbered among these, for it was assuredly not instituted to serve as a pledge for the forgiveness of sins. Even the signification of holy orders could no more be appreciated, since this sacrament was as little destined to nourish and foster the faith of the person ordained, that his sins were remitted.[2] In short, the number of seven sacraments (in direct contradiction to Scripture, and the well-founded tradition of the Catholic, as well as of the orthodox Greek Church, nay, even of the Nestorians and Monophysites, who, fourteen hundred years ago, separated from the communion of these Churches) was reduced to two; and merely the sacraments of baptism and the Lord's supper retained, although the two so retained could not even be understood. Confirmation was only to be a renewal of baptism; and the Lord's supper, which was considered merely as a pledge for the forgiveness of sins, was to supply the place of extreme unction; for, in danger of death, man needed most the assurance of the pardoning mercy of God. Of penance we shall have to speak more in detail.[3]

---

[1] Chemnit. Exam. sect. 11, p. 39. His misrepresentations are well pointed out by Bellarmine in his work 'De Sacramentis,' l. ii, p. 110.

[2] Melancth. loc. theolog. p. 157. 'Matrimonium non esse institutum ad significandam gratiam' (*gratia* is here only the divine forgiveness of sins) 'non est quod dubitemus. Quid autem in mentem venit iis, qui inter signa gratiæ ordinem numerarunt? Cum non aliud sit ordo, quam deligi ex *ecclesia* eos, qui docent,' etc.

[3] Melancth. loc. cit. p. 156. 'Signum gratiæ certum est participatio mensæ, hoc est, manducare corpus Christi et bibere sanguinem. Sic enim ait . . . quoties feceritis, facite in memoriam mei. Id est: cum facitis, admoneamini Evangelii, seu remissionis peccatorum . . . Est autem significatio hujus sacramenti, confirmare nos toties, quoties labescunt conscientiæ, quoties de voluntate Dei erga nos dubitamus.' (That is to say, as often as we doubt, whether God be earnest in forgiving us our sins). 'Id cum alias sæpe, tum maxime, cum moriendum est, accidit.

On the other hand, it is evident that the Catholic, who does not conceive the believer under the one-sided view of a man that, for Christ's sake, has obtained merely the remission of his sins; but, under the living believer, understands a man redeemed from sin, and consecrated to God in mind and sense, needs a circle of sacraments, embracing all the important events of life, and reflecting the ever-recurring view of his earthly pilgrimage—a circle of sacraments which symbolically express the high relation of each passage of his life to the atonement of Christ, and guarantee and really impart the divine energy, which is requisite to its beginning and its consummation.

The entanglement of man with the lower world, which, since Adam's disobedience, hath been subjected to a curse, is revealed in the most diverse ways. Even so diverse are the ways whereby we are raised up to a world of a higher order, in and by the fellowship with Christ.[1] If, by earthly generation and birth,

Unctionem arbitror esse eam, de qua Marci vi' (the fourteenth verse of the fifth chapter of James did not then occur to his mind!). 'Sed ea signa esse tradita ut certo significent gratiam, non video.' (As if it were not expressly stated in James: κἂν ἁμαρτίας ᾖ πεποιηκώς, ἀφεθήσεται αὐτῷ.

[1] Thom, Aquinas (Summ. p. iii, q. lxv, art. i, p. 296) objects: 'Videtur, quod non debeant esse septem sacramenta. Sacramenta enim efficaciam habent ex virtute divina et ex virtute passionis Christi. Sed una est virtus divina et una Christi passio: una enim oblatione consummavit in sempiternum sanctificatos.' Among other things, he replies: 'Dicendum quod sacramenta ecclesiæ ordinantur ad duo, scilicet ad perficiendum hominem in his, quæ pertinent ad cultum Dei secundum religionem Christianæ vitæ, et etiam in remedium contra defectum peccati. Utroque autem modo convenienter ponuntur septem sacramenta. Vita enim spiritualis conformitatem aliquam habet ad vitam corporalem, sicut et cætera corporalia conformitatem quandam spiritualium habent. In vita autem corporali dupliciter aliquis perficitur. Uno modo quantum ad personam propriam, alio modo per respectum ad totam communitatem societatis, in qua vivit: quia homo naturaliter est animal sociale. Respectu autem sui ipsius perficitur homo in vita corporali dupliciter. Uno modo per se, acquirendo scilicet aliquam vitæ perfectionem: alio modo per accidens, scilicet removendo impedimenta vitæ puta ægritudines vel aliquid hujusmodi. Per se autem perficitur corporalis vita tripliciter. Primo quidem per generationem, per quam homo incipit esse et vivere. Et loco hujus in spirituali vita est baptismus, qui est spiritualis regeneratio: secundum illud ad Titum iii. Secundo, per augmentum quo aliquis perducitur ad perfectam quantitatem et virtutem. Et loco hujus in spirituali vita est confirmatio, in qua datur sanctitas et robur. Unde dicitur discipulis, jam baptizatis, Luc. ult: "Sedete in civitate, quoadusque induamini virtute ex alto." Tertio per nutritionem, qua conservatur in homine vita et virtus. Et loco hujus in spirituali vita est Eucharistia, unde dicitur, Joann. vi, "Nisi manducaveritis carnem filii hominis et biberitis ejus sanguinem, non habebitis vitam in vobis." Et hoc quidem sufficeret homini, si haberet et corporaliter et spiritualiter impassibilem vitam.

we have been brought into a general connection with this distracted world; so, in our maturer years, this connection ever meets us in more special relations, and in more definite forms: and what, by our birth, was deposited as a germ, is now expanded, and thereby realised and strengthened. But man feels himself ever more and more strongly straitened by the laws of this world—they encompass him with ever-growing force; and of his own free choice, as well as under a sort of mysterious necessity, he contracts, with a being of his own kind, the closest alliance in the bonds of earthly and sexual love, in order to provide for the perpetuity of his species, and thereby for the whole economy of this lower world. Hereby he becomes at once an active and efficient member of the state, which is itself a larger, but ever limited circle of families, who, usually having all sprung from one and the same progenitor, have, through their opposition to other associations of families, been drawn into peculiar destinies, and thereby received the impress of a special character; while, in a common order, and for mutual protection against such an opposition, they maintain themselves with all the individual interests determined by such a state of things. If, when once man hath come into the world, all the relations we have adverted to take place only at particular periods of his life, there are others again which pervade every stage of his existence. Self-preservation forms the centre point of all earthly exertion, which is concentrated in the care for one's livelihood. Much as thou mayst strive, O man! by a new

Sed quia homo incurrit interdum et corporalem infirmitatem et spiritualem, scilicet peccatum, ideo necessaria est homini curatio ab infirmitate. Quæ quidem est duplex, una quidem est sanatio, quæ sanitatem restituit. Et loco hujus in spirituali vita est pœnitentia, secundum illud Psalmi: "sana animam, meam quia peccavi tibi." Alia autem est restitutio valetudinis pristinæ per convenientem diætem et exercitium. Et loco hujus in spirituali vita est extrema unctio, quæ removet peccatorum reliquias, et hominem paratum reddit ad finalem gloriam, unde dicitur, Jac. v. . . . Perficitur autem homo in ordine ad totam communitatem dupliciter. Uno modo per hoc, quod accipit potestatem regendi multitudinem seu exercendi actus publicos. Et loco hujus in spirituali vita est sacramentum ordinis, secundum illud, Hebr. vii, " quod sacerdotes hostias offerunt non tantum pro se, sed etiam pro populo." Secundo, quantum ad naturalem propagationem: quod fit per matrimonium tam in corporali quam in spirituali vita, ex eo quod non solum est sacramentum, sed naturæ officium. Ex his etiam patet sacramentorum numerus, secundum quod ordinantur contra defectum peccati. Nam baptismus ordinatur contra carentiam vitæ spiritualis: confirmatio contra infirmitatem animi, quæ in nuper natis invenitur: Eucharistia contra labilitatem animi ad peccandum: pœnitentia contra actuale peccatum, post baptismum commissum,' etc.

recruiting of thy bodily strength, to renovate thy earthly existence, the seed of death was laid in the first moment of thy life—it announces its being amid the fairest bloom of personal charms—it waxes more and more in strength, and at last overmasters life itself. Thus, in various alternations of earthly action and suffering, of joy and of sorrow, doth the end of life unavoidably grow out of the beginning; it is betokened by sicknesses of various kinds, until the creature, that had sprung out of dust and ashes, again resolves into the same.

To this inferior order of things, the Church, in virtue of the commission given to her by Christ, opposes a higher order, not to annihilate the former, but to bestow on it the blessings of redemption, to explain its significance, and to purify, by heavenly influences, all the stages of earthly and sinful existence; to raise humanity again up to God, as through Adam it had fallen, and to exalt time into eternity. Symbolical signs bring the higher world more immediately within the perception of sense, and withal convey from that world the capacity for its influence. To the earthly birth, stained with sin, the spiritual second birth for heaven is annexed. At the moment when the growing perils of the world threaten to encompass the individual, and lay fast hold upon him, cometh the *confirmation* of his spirit, by the Spirit from above, to enable him to encounter the arduous impending struggle. The earthly sexual intercourse, calculated as it is to draw down man to destruction, into the lowest depths of terrestrial existence, is transformed into a heavenly alliance; and sensuality, which is opposed to all permanent connection, is subdued in Christ the Lord, and made instrumental to the indissoluble union of spirits. If by marriage man contracts a more intimate alliance with the earthly and limited existence of the state; so marriage is sanctified by a symbolical action, which, while it consecrates it to be the central organ for the union of all believers, makes them consider themselves members of an all-embracing divine kingdom on earth, which, totally distinct from circumscribed terrestrial kingdoms is destined to permeate all these, and to vivify them with its spirit; in the same way as the individual's ecclesiastical life should pervade his civil existence. If Matrimony be the vital condition not only of states, but of all earthly existence, and of its regular progress; so Holy Orders are the condition to all ecclesiastical life, and all the other sacraments. In opposition to the earthly nurture, and the perishable food, the celestial Bread is offered us for our lasting spiritual sustenance through life; so that the Table of the Lord forms the centre-point of divine service and religious existence, as the table of the father of the family constitutes the centre of domestic service and civil life. If in the violent obstructions of bodily organism the foe of earthly life manifests himself, so Extreme Unction imparts strength and consolation—warning us, that, in every case, the real man is redeemed by a higher power; and this, especially in the approaching dissolution of the bond between body and soul, never fails of its effect. The holy action devoted to the cure of the penitent sinner, who, after being incorporated into the Church, hath grievously fallen, cannot be conceived as a normal principle in the history of the spiritual life; for, otherwise, the fall after regeneration would come to be regarded as unavoidable and necessary—that is to say, as no sin. But yet it hath been ordained by God's mercy as an extraordinary dispensation of grace; and so the septenary number of sacraments is now filled up.

Protestantism despaired of the possibility of the earthly being quite pervaded by the heavenly element, and of the former being viewed through the medium of the latter; and hence it was forced, not only to reject the doctrine of seven sacraments as the effect of human presumption, struggling against an unavoidable necessity; but, in the two sacraments it retained, it saw only the principle of the forgiveness of sins, rendered necessary in consequence of the indomitable carnal spirit of man.

§ XXX—FURTHER CONSEQUENCES OF THE ORIGINAL LUTHERAN VIEW OF THE ESSENCE OF A SACRAMENT

That infant baptism, according to the Protestant view of the sacraments, is an act utterly incomprehensible, cannot be doubted; for if it be through faith *only* that the sacrament takes effect, of what value can it be to the unconscious child? The Anabaptists, against whom Luther was so incensed, drew but the natural inferences from the premises which he had laid down, and could not be refuted by him without his proving unfaithful to his own principle.

In the same way, it was not difficult to come to the conclusion, that, with such views, there was not the slightest reason for adopting a real presence of Christ in the Eucharist. For if the

Lord's Supper, as Luther said, be only a pledge of the forgiveness of sins no reason can be assigned why Christ should be present. The bare bread, and the bare wine, would achieve all which was expected of the sacrament. As little as God need be personally present in the rainbow, to make that natural phenomenon—selected as a token of promise to the infant world, that the inhabitants of the earth should never more be destroyed by deluge—attain its pacifying end; so little is the real presence of the Saviour necessary in the sacrament of the altar, if it be to serve only as a pledge of the remission of sins. This Andrew Carlstadt perceived; and, from the very principle laid down by Luther, as to the mode of viewing a sacrament, he drew conclusions against the real presence of Christ in the Lord's Supper; and, in our opinion, Plank should not have doubted whether Carlstadt had not really been conducted in this way to the denial of the real Presence, as in one of his writings he himself stated it.[1] We recognise the internal consistency and necessity of Carlstadt's view, so soon as he had fallen into Luther's one-sided conception of the sacraments. Here, it appears to us, we have found the clue for explaining the fact, that, shortly after the breaking out of the dispute adverted to, Luther wrote, in the following manner, to Bucer and Capito, who had requested of him an elucidation of the difficulties which Carlstadt had raised against the real presence of Christ in the sacrament of the altar. He says, that five years previously he had come to the same opinion as Carlstadt had arrived at, and would willingly have enforced it, 'in order to be able to give a blow to the Papacy,' had he not been deterred by the clear words of Scripture.[2] His whole theory of the sacraments led him to the adoption of Carlstadt's view; and what with repugnance he saw himself forced to revere as Scriptural, possessed in his system no internal consistency. With the same urgency should Luther's opinion, that the foundations of the Church had been

[1] Plank, History of the rise, etc., of the Protestant system of doctrine, 2nd book, p. 215.

[2] E. Münch, in *Bilibald Pirkheimer's Schweizer-Krieg*, p. 54, communicates a letter of this scholar to Melancthon, wherein the same view appears to be stated. It is said: 'So Œcolampadius, Zwingle, and others, are highly opposed to Luther; and if Luther had not investigated the matter so deeply, and had not engaged in so strenuous an opposition against Dr Carlstadt, he would have been the leader in this cursed error.' Pirkheimer means to say, that it was only out of opposition to Carlstadt, that Luther had been brought back to the doctrine of a real presence of Christ in the Lord's supper.

shaken, since it had fallen into essential errors, have led him to dispute the true presence of the Lord in the Sacrament. For it was, doubtless, inconsistent to admit on the one hand, a real, and therefore *efficacious*, presence, of Christ in the Church; and, on the other hand, to assert, that she had fallen away from him, or rather, he had withdrawn from her, and, in matters of such vast moment, had suffered her to walk her own way.

If we be justified, perhaps, in assuming, that Luther's, and, more especially, Melancthon's, general exposition of the sacraments, had prepared the way for the original Helvetic view of the Lord's supper (for the conclusions, which Luther himself was so disposed to draw, pressed not less urgently on the minds of others); so, on a nearer consideration, we may discover, in this exposition, the source whence emanated the rejection of all the sacraments, or, at least, that indifference for them, to which, in the first period of the Reformation, we discern so strong a propensity, as for instance, in Carlstadt and Schwenkfeld. Luther, and especially Melancthon, had more than once asserted, that he, who held fast in faith to the Divine promise, did not even need the sacraments.[1] Hence, against the doctrine, that sacraments are the pledges of the forgiveness of sins Carlstadt observes: 'he who hath the right remembrance of Christ, is sure of his redemption, and hath peace in God through Christ—not through the sacrament. If Christ be our peace and our assurance, then creatures without soul cannot tranquillise us and make us secure.'[2] It was only when Luther heard his own thoughts uttered from the lips of others, that he found them dangerous and untrue. Hence, in his larger catechism, he suffers not a word to escape him, whereby the sacraments could be represented as anywise superfluous; nay, with all earnestness, and the greatest urgency, he exalts their power and efficacy.[3]

---

[1] Melancthon, loc. theol. p. 142. 'Sine signo restitui Ezechias potuit, si nudæ promissioni credere voluisset: vel sine signo Gideon victurus erat, si credidisset. Ita sine signo justificari potes, modo credas.' Luther de captivit. Babylon. l. c. fol. 280: ' Neque enim Deus aliter cum hominibus egit aut agit quam verbo promissionis. Rursus nec nos cum Deo unquam aliter agere possumus, quam fide in verbum promissionis ejus. Opera ille nihil curat, nec eis indiget, quibus potius erga homines et cum hominibus et nobis ipsis agimus.' Fol. 286, b: ' Qui eis credit, is implet ea, etiamsi nihil operetur.'

[2] See the extracts from Carlstadt's writing, in the above-cited work of Plank, p. 218.

[3] Catech. maj. p. 510.

§ XXXI—ZUINGLIUS AND CALVIN ON THE SACRAMENTS

Zuinglius formed the worst and most miserable conception of the sacraments, that it is possible to imagine; yet, in doing so, as we have said, he merely followed out the hints given him by Luther and Melancthon.

He considers the sacraments only as ceremonies whereby a man professes himself a member of the Church, and follower of Christ. He accordingly very much approves of the Lutherans throwing aside the belief that the sacraments contribute aught towards justification; but he laments the more that they should still regard them as pledges of the Divine mercy and favour; since he, whose faith needs such a confirmation, actually possesses none. In this respect, he says, the reception of the sacraments rather affords the Church an assurance that her followers believe, than that they themselves become thereby more sure and steadfast in their faith.[1]

If contrary to the clearest teaching of Holy Writ, and the testimony of all Christian ages, Luther and Melancthon had degraded the sacraments into mere tokens of covenant between God and men; so Zuinglius advanced a step further and re-

[1] De vera et falsa religione Commentar. Op. tom. xi, fol. 197-9. He thus concludes: 'Sunt ergo sacramenta, signa vel ceremoniæ, pace tamen omnium dicam, sive neotericorum sive veterum, quibus se homo ecclesiæ probat aut candidatum aut militem, esse Christi, redduntque ecclesiam totam potius certiorem de tua fide, quam te. Si enim fides tua non aliter fuerit absoluta, quam ut signo ceremoniali ad confirmationem egeat, fides non est.' De peccato originali declarat. 1. c. fol. 122 : ' Signa igitur nihil quam externæ res sunt, quibus nihil in conscientia efficitur. Fides autem sola est qua beamur. . . . Symbola igitur sunt externa ista rerum spiritualium, et ipsa minime sunt spiritualia, nec quidquam spirituale in nobis perficiunt : sed sunt eorum, qui spirituales sunt, quasi tesseræ.' Elsewhere he expresses himself, however, in a somewhat milder strain; for instance, in his *Fidei Ecclesiasticæ Expositio*, 1. c. p. 551 : ' Docemus ergo, sacramenta coli debere, velut res sacras, ut quæ res sacratissimas significent, tam eas, quæ gestæ sunt, tam eas quæ nos agere et exprimere debemus. Ut baptismus significat et Christum nos sanguine suo abluisse, et quod nos illum, ut Paulus docet, induere debemus, hoc est ad ejus formulam vivere; sic Eucharistia quoque significat cum omnia, quæ nobis divina liberalitate per Christum donata sunt, tum quod grati debemus ea charitate fratris amplecti, qua Christus nos suscepit, curavit, ac beatos reddidit.' Here accordingly, the sacrament signifies something for the receiver, not for the Church only. But this writing of Zuinglius was his swan-like song, as Bullinger in the preface to it asserts, p. 550 : ' Nescio quid cygneum vicina morte cantavit.' A very high strain of song truly ! Yet in his work, *De vera et falsa religione*, p. 108, he had already expressed himself in a similar way.

presented them as signs of covenant between man and man. Who could now connect any sense with the words of Christ: ' He who believeth, and is baptised, shall be saved ? ' And how powerless and unmeaning must the passage of Paul appear, wherein he calls baptism ' the laver of regeneration, and of the newness of the Holy Spirit ? ' But the uncertainty of belief, which Zuinglius exhibits at the beginning of his treatise on the sacraments, is worthy of notice. He begs pardon, if he offend the opinions of others, and he declares that, with the exception of Eck and Emser, he is at peace with everyone, and in return claims the indulgence of others for himself.[1] He speaks as if the question turned on mere human opinions—on things of a doubtful nature ; just as if the Christian Church were such a wretched, mismanaged body, that she did not even know, and could not know, with certainty, what it was which she daily practised, and practised at the command of Christ and must through all centuries continue to practise. When once the firm ground, and sure and eternal footing is abandoned then all must indeed vacillate, and all doctrines be abandoned to mere conjecture.

It was quite in the opposite sense that Calvin taught. His doctrine, with the exception of one point, differs not at all from that of the Lutheran formularies. Calvin carefully points out all the parts of what is understood by a sacrament, and recommends, with much urgency, its use.[2] The point in which he deviates from the Catholics and the Lutheran doctrine, consists especially herein, that he will have the sanctifying grace distinct

[1] De vera et falsa relig. lib. i, p. 197.
[2] Calvin. Institut. lib. iv, sect. 3, fol. 471. ' Ut exigua est et imbecillis nostra fides, nisi undique fulciatur, ac modis omnibus sustentetur, statim concutitur, fluctuatur, vacillat adeoque labescit. Atque ita quidem hic se captui nostro pro immensa sua indulgentia attemperat misericors Dominus, ut quando animales sumus, qui humi semper adrepentes et in carne hærentes nihil spirituale cogitamus, ac ne concipimus quidem, elementis etiam istis terrenis nos ad se deducere non gravetur, atque in carne proponere spiritualium bonorum speculum,' etc. Helvet 1, cap. xix, p. 65: ' Prædicationi verbi sui adjunxit Deus mox ab initio in ecclesia sua sacramenta vel signa sacramentalia. Sunt autem sacramenta symbola mystica, vel ritus sancti aut sacræ actiones, a Deo ipso institutæ, constantes verbo suo, signis, et rebus significatis, quibus in ecclesia summa sua beneficia homini exhibita retinet in memoria, et subinde renovat, quibus item promissiones suas obsignat, et quæ ipse nobis interius præstat, exterius representat, ac veluti oculis contemplanda subjicit, adeoque fidem nostram, spiritu Dei in cordibus nostris operante, roborat et auget, quibus denique nos ab omnibus aliis populis et religionibus separat, sibique soli consecrat et obligat, et quid a nobis requirat significat.'

and separate from the sacrament, as the sensible sign. The
former, according to him, is not conjoined with the material
element : and hence to every Christian is this element tendered,
but not so the divine nourishment.[1] The necessity of this
doctrine, in the system of Calvin, is evident; for as it is only
to the elect the Divine grace is imparted, and the rest are passed
over by God, so grace must by no means be connected with
the visible sign.[2] Nay, the Divine grace worketh irresistibly :
It might, therefore, easily happen, that some, not among the
chosen, should, without the Divine will, be classed among the
elect, if the heavenly nurture and power united with the sensible
sign itself were offered to everyone ! Hence in baptism the non-
elect are only outwardly washed ; and the same receive in the
Lord's Supper but mere bread and wine ; a view which Gotts-
chalk, a predestinarian of the ninth century, likewise entertained ; at least such an opinion is imputed to him. Moreover,
Calvin also admits but two sacraments.[3]

§ XXXII—BAPTISM AND PENANCE

After having pointed out the divergences of opinion as to
the nature of a sacrament in general, we must now proceed

[1] Loc. cit. sect. 9, fol. 474. ' Cæterum munere suo tunc rite demum per
funguntur (sacramenta) ubi interior illi magister spiritus accesserit : cujus
unius virtute et corda penetrantur, et affectus permoventur, et sacramentis
in animas nostras aditus patet. Si desit ille, nihil sacramenta plus præstare
mentibus nostris possunt, quam si vel solis splendor cœcis oculis affulgeat,
vel surdis auribus vox insonet. Itaque sic inter spiritum sacramentaque
partior, ut penes illum agendi virtus resideat, his ministerium duntaxat
relinquatur ; idque sine spiritus actione manet frivolum, illo vero intus
agente, vimque suam exercente multæ energiæ refertum.'

[2] Loc. cit. sect. 17, fol. 477. ' Spiritus Sanctus (*quem non omnibus pro-
miscue sacramenta advehunt, sed quem peculiariter suis confert*) is est, qui
Dei gratias secum affert, qui dat sacramentis in nobis locum, qui efficit, ut
fructificent.' Here lies the real point of difference. Now Calvin makes
the matter appear, as if the Catholics separated the power working in the
sacraments from their primary fountain, and looked upon them as working
of themselves. ' Tantum hic quæritur, propriane et intrinseca (ut loquuntur) virtute operetur Deus, an externis symbolis suas resignat vices. Nos
vero contendimus, quæcunque adhibeat organa primariæ ejus operationi
nihil decedere.' And now, ' Interim illud tollitur figmentum, quo justificationis causa virtusque Spiritus Sancti elementis, ceu vasculis ac
plaustris, includitur.'

[3] Loc. cit. sect. 19, fol. 478. ' Sacramenta duo instituta, quibus nunc
Christiana ecclesia utitur, baptismus et cœna Domini.' Quite in the same
sense are the first Helvetic Confession, c. xix : the Augsburg, art. xxv ;
the Gallic, art. xxxv, p. 123 ; the Belgic, art. xxxix-v, p. 192.

with details, and begin with baptism.[1] It is principally in describing the effects of this means of salvation, that the Christian Communities differ from one another; and indeed, the different notion which each entertains of justification, determines, as we may suppose, this diversity of opinion. If, according to Catholic doctrine, original sin in children, in adults original sin together with actual sins, is by the due reception of baptism removed, according to that process of regeneration above described :—so that the believer, having become a member of Christ, walketh no more according to the flesh, but interiorly quickened by the Divine Spirit, showeth himself a new man : so among the Protestants, their well known theory of the mere forgiveness of sins is here again predominant. Through the faith received before baptism, is the adult justified; but through baptism, in which all that Christ hath done for us is applied, and the Holy Ghost with all his gifts is imparted, this faith is sealed. This certainly is a far more elevated theory of baptism; one, unquestionably, more consonant to Holy Writ, than that adopted by Luther, at the commencement of the Reformation. However, according to the Lutherans, original sin still remains in the baptised—an opinion, which cannot in this place be matter of any further investigation. The Calvinistic formularies point out very beautifully the new life, commencing with baptism, and they do so still better than the Lutheran.[2]

The Catholic Church, moreover, from the second century, hath invested the original simple act of baptism with a rich

---

[1] In its sixth session, the Council of Trent supposes the case of an adult, who by baptism is received into the Christian Church; and, in fact, in this way the holy act can best be understood.

[2] Catechism. maj. part iv, sect. 9, p. 12. 'Sola fides personam dignam facit, ut hanc salutarem et divinam aquam utiliter suscipiat.' Sect. 14, p. 54 : 'Quapropter quivis Christianus per omnem vitam suam abunde satis habet, ut baptismum recte perdiscat atque exerceat. Sat enim habet negotii, ut credat firmiter, quæcunque baptismo promittuntur et offeruntur, victoriam nempe mortis ac diaboli, remissionem peccatorum, gratiam Dei, Christum cum omnibus suis operibus [his sufferings and death and the like] et Spiritum Sanctum cum omnibus suis dotibus.' (This is not true, see 1 Cor. xii.) The *Smalcald Article*, part iii, c. 5, sect. 1, in order to be able to say something against Catholics, confounds scholastic opinions with the doctrine of the Church. Helvetica i, cap. xx, p. 71 : 'Nascimur enim omnes in peccatorum sordibus, et sumus filii iræ. Deus autem, qui dives est misericordia, purgat nos a peccatis gratuite, per sanguinem filii sui, et in hoc adoptat nos in filios, adeoque fœdere sancto nos sibi connectit, et variis donis didat, ut possimus novam vivere vitam. Obsignantur hæc omnia baptismo. Nam intus regeneramur, purificamur, et renovamur a Deo per Spiritum Sanctum,' etc.

abundance of symbolical ceremonies, in order to stamp more deeply on the minds of her children the idea of this sacrament, and to symbolise, by various emblems, the exalted nature of the newness of life in Christ. Although, doubtless, the symbolisation of this sacrament, unessential in itself, belongs not to this place, but only the doctrine itself; yet we may be permitted to draw, in a few words, the attention of the reader to this ceremonial, and thereby render him more familiar with the Catholic view of baptism, whereby it will become more evident what a decided influence this view hath on the conception of the other sacraments. As the Lord once, by a mixture of spittle and dust, cured the corporeal deafness of a man; so the same mixture, applied in baptism, denoteth the fact, that the spiritual organs are henceforth opened for the mysteries of God's kingdom. The burning candle signifieth that now truly the divine light from above hath fallen upon the mind, and the darkness of sin been changed into a celestial splendour. The salt denoteth the wise man, freed from the folly of this world: the anointing with oil, the new priest; for every Christian is, in the spiritual sense of the word, a priest who hath penetrated into the inmost sanctuary, and hath renewed the most living communion with God in Christ Jesus; and the white garment imports that the believer, washed clean in the blood of the Lamb, must henceforth preserve, unto the second coming of the Lord, the innocence which he had lost in the first Adam, and won again in the second. Symbol is crowded upon symbol, in order to express, in the most manifest way, the one idea; that a total, permanent change is to occur in man, and a new, higher, and lasting existence is henceforward to commence; and hence, among other reasons, baptism is not repeated.

Hereby, on the part of the Church, the confident expectation —on the part of the believer, the solemn vow, is declared, never more to fall into any grievous (mortal) sin; but rather to wax, more and more in holiness of life. If such a sin be committed, then the darkness, the folly of the world, and the unpriestly life, take again possession of the soul; and thereby is communion with God broken off, and the baptismal grace forfeited. Hence, if the sinner wish to be converted from his evil ways, he needs a *new* reconciliation with God, and therefore another sacrament; and such a sacrament is penance conceived to be. Yet it ought not to be hence inferred, that penance, as a sacrament, is instituted *only* for such as return from a course of conduct, and a state of feeling, absolutely incompatible with the abode of Christ in their souls. It is for all believers an institution of fatherly instruction, exhortation, correction, quieting, and solace.

But it is quite otherwise in the Lutheran, and even in the Calvinistic creed. Since, according to this creed, the power of the Divine Spirit in regeneration is able to work no extirpation of sin; since, on the contrary, original sin as such, the carnal sin as such, though weakened, is still considered to endure in the man, ' born again of water and the spirit '; a totally different view of the relation of the baptised to Christ is necessarily entertained. And the sins—even the more grievous sins—of the former, appear not as anything which hath dissolved that state of grace obtained in baptism, and therefore not as anything whereby the fellowship with Christ would be again broken off. All sins, moreover, being but the particular forms of original sin, not extirpated, but *only forgiven in baptism*, and in all this God only working salvation, but man, on the other hand, not acting independently, baptism not only imparts the assurance, that all our sins committed before baptism are forgiven, but gives the pledge of the remission of all the sins to be afterwards committed.[1] Baptism is a letter of indulgence sealed by God for one's own life, and therefore, in every transgression, we need only recall and resuscitate in our minds the promises recorded in that letter; and this is what the Reformers call a *regressus ad baptismum*. Hence, baptism is characterised also as the sacrament of penance, that is to say, as the moral pledge given by God, that sins at every moment of his life, are remitted to the believer, and that he is admitted to grace; or in other words, penance is no peculiar sacrament.[2] Hence, Luther

---

[1] See Luther's Commentary on the epistle to the Galatians. ' Therefore we say that man is a true Christian; not one who hath and feeleth no sin, but one to whom the sins which he hath and feeleth are not imputed by our Lord God, and on account of the faith which he has in Chiist. And this doctrine ministers to the poor conscience a mighty and steady solace, when it would be like to quake before God's wrath and judgment. Wherefore is a Christian, when he is what he ought to be, perfectly and entirely free from all laws, and subject to no law whatever, whether internal or external.'—p. 68. (Nothing conduces to his condemnation provided he only believe.)

[2] Melancthon, however, occasionally makes an exception, the cause whereof we shall hereafter have occasion to show. Apolog. art. iv: ' In ecclesiis nostris plurimi sæpe in anno utuntur sacramentis, *absolutione* et cœna Domini.' Art. v: ' Absolutio *proprie* dici potest sacramentum pœnitentiæ, ut etiam scholastici theologi eruditiores (?) loquuntur.' Art vii: ' Vere igitur sunt sacramenta, baptismus, cœna Domini, absolutio,

could not pardon St Jerome for having called penance the second plank redeeming from shipwreck; since, as he says, the first, namely, baptism, could never be lost, provided only man, so often as he was seized with terror for his sins, renewed the promises made in baptism. He is even of opinion, that this view is borne out by the principle of the Church, forbidding the repetition of baptism. Accordingly, while Catholics conceive the effects of baptism to extend to our whole lives, in such a way, that, from the moment of baptism to the close of our earthly career, life ought to flow on pure, stainless, and ever consecrated to God; Luther looks on these effects of baptism as administering consolation to man, even amid all his transgressions. Thus, had the Reformers considered the real internal renovation and sanctification of man to be possible through baptism, and regarded this renovation as one with justification, they would have seen clearly, that by any grievous sin, the grace of baptism could be lost, and penance would then have been acknowledged as a second sacrament. But, since they look on justification as merely the forgiveness of sins, and the sacrament of baptism as its seal or letter the operation of baptism according to them, continues uninterrupted.[1]

The particular parts of penance are accordingly very differently

quæ est sacramentum pœnitentiæ.' In the third revisal of his *Loci*, after 1545, he says: 'Cum autem vocabulum sacramenti de ceremoniis intelligitur in stitutis in prædicatione Christi, numerantur hæc sacramenta, baptismus, cœna Domini, absolutio.' Compare Augusti's *Christian Archæology*, vol. ix, p. 28.

[1] Melancthon loc. theol. p. 145. 'Usus vero signi (baptismi) hic est, testari quod per mortem transeas ad vitam, testari quod mortificatio carnis tuæ salutaris est.' [The notion of *mortificato* and of the *transitus ad vitam* or of the *vivificatio*, has been explained above, and is evident from what follows.] 'Terrent peccata, terret mors, terrent alia mundi mala; confide quia σφραγῖδα accepisti misericordiæ erga te, futurum ut salveris, quomodocumque oppugneris a portis inferorum. Sic vides, et significatum baptismi et signi usum durare in sanctis per omnem vitam.' P. 146: 'Idem baptismi usus est in mortificatione. Monet conscientiam remissionis peccatorum, et certam reddit de gratia Dei, adeoque efficit ut ne desperemus in mortificatione. *Proinde quantisper durat mortificatio tantisper signi usus est.* Non absolvitur autem mortificatio, dum vetus Adam prorsus extinctus fuerit.' P. 149: 'Est enim pœnitentia vetustatis nostræ mortificatio, et renovatio spiritus: sacramentum ejus, vel signum, non aliud, nisi baptismus est.' P. 150: 'Sicut evangelium non amisimus alicubi lapsi, ita nec evangelii σφραγῖδα baptismum. Certum est autem, evangelium non semel tantum, sed iterum ac iterum remittere peccatum. Quare non minus ad *secundam* condonationem, quam ad primam, baptismus pertinet.' All these passages are but extracts from Luther's work, *De captivitate Babylonica*. Op. tom. ii, fol. 287, b.

described by the two confessions. The Protestants regard contrition and faith, as the stages through which a particular penitential act takes its course. Contrition they explain by 'terrors of conscience' (*conscientiæ terrores*), which consist in that dread of the Divine judgment, that attends the consciousness of the non-fulfilment of the Law. This fear is next banished by instrumental faith: and the conscience hereby obtaining the solace and the quiet which the Lutherans so exclusively look to, the whole penitential act is terminated. Hence, absolution is nothing more than a *declaration* that sin is forgiven.[1] Even the Calvinists have not refused their approbation to this decision; yet they have received it with the modification which their, in some degree profounder, doctrine of justification demanded.[2]

§ XXXIII—CONTINUATION OF THE DOCTRINE OF PENANCE

The Catholics raise the same objections to the Lutheran view of penance, as to Luther's doctrine of justification. They accuse it of poverty, and they charge it with holding down the believer to an extremely low grade of the spiritual life, allowing him scarcely a perception of the fulness of the riches of evangelical grace, while it is very far from expressing the biblical idea of μετάνοια. The doctrine of the Catholic Church is, that the sacramental penance should pass through three stages; whereof the first is contrition, with the firm purpose of change of life; the second, confession; the third, satisfaction: and hereby the sacerdotal absolution also receives a signification, wholly different from that which is attached to it by the Protestants. As regards, in the first place, contrition, it is of an essence far more exalted than what the Lutherans term *conscientiæ terrores*, above which

[1] Confessio Augustana, art. xxii. 'Constat autem pœnitentia proprie his duabus partibus; altera est contritio, seu terrores incussi conscientiæ, agnito peccato; altera est fides, quæ concipitur ex evangelio seu absolutione, et credit propter Christum remitti peccata, et consolatur conscientiam, et ex terroribus liberat.'

[2] Calvin. Instit. lib. iii, c. 34, sect. 8. The Lutheran denomination of the two parts here occurs under the name of *mortificatio* and *vivificatio*. But, as we remarked above, by the former expression, the putting off of the old man, and by the latter the putting on of the new man, are to be understood: so signifying something other than the Lutheran *contritio et fides*. When Augusti, in his *Archæology* (vol. ix, p. 25) says, the terminology of the Calvinists is either borrowed from Melancthon or made to harmonise with his, the first assertion is decidedly true, but the second is not at all so.

only the rudest natures are incapable of rising; for these terrors involve no detestation of sin, as such, and contain no trace of the tenderer emotions: they are but the dread of sensible evil. It is contrary to all experience, that, within the circle of Christian life, sorrow for moral transgressions, and for the falling short of evangelical perfection, can or ought to be called forth only by the representation of hell-torments: and he who would obstinately insist thereon, would merely deduce a general rule from the experience of his own individual feelings, and, in the same measure, furnish a remarkable example of his own narrow-mindedness, as well as of his ignorance of the plastic power of Christianity. It would be even contrary to the most clearly attested facts, to represent the dread of Divine chastisements as the only path which first leads men into the bosom of the Christian Church. Christ is the divine teacher of truth; and we need only peruse the Clementines, and the account which Justin hath given of his conversion to Christianity, at the commencement of his dialogue with the Jew Trypho, as well as the narrative which Tatian, in his apology for the Christian religion, and Hilarius of Poictiers, in his work on the Trinity, have furnished of their respective conversions,[1] to convince ourselves that the transition from heathenism to Christianity was especially brought about by the following means, to wit—the recognition of reason, that Christ had communicated most credible revelations respecting divine things, and freed the frail heart of man from uncertainty and distracting doubt. We should not look on the teaching office of Christ as merely accidental as Luther did, and thereby fell into such a narrow conception of things. He who, from a desire of truth, first embraces the Son of God manifested in the flesh, stands on much higher ground than one who has been induced to do so from the fear of hell; and other motives at least will concur to produce the sorrow for sin.

---

[1] Lactantius divin. Instit. lib. i, c. 1, is brief enough to permit our citing a passage in reference to this subject. After having described the assiduity with which the ancient philosophers sought for the truth, he says: 'Selneque adepti sunt id, quod volebant, et operam simul atque industriam perdiderunt: quia veritas, id est arcanum summi Dei, qui facit omnia, ingenio ac propriis non potest sensibus comprehendi: alioquin nihil inter Deum hominemque distaret, si consilia et dispositiones illius majestatis æternæ cogitatio assequeretur humana. Quod quia fieri non potuit, ut homini per seipsum ratio divina innotesceret, non est passus hominem Deus, lumen sapientiæ requirentem, diutius oberrare, ac sine ullo laboris effectu vagari per tenebras inextricabiles. Aperuit oculos ejus aliquando et notionem veritatis munus suum fecit,' etc.

How, then, within the pale of Christianity, should this sorrow consist only in that fear ? But even where it exists, it is very far, according to Catholic principles, from completing the notion of repentance. The dread of the divine judgments is deemed by Catholics to be only an incitement to repentance—a germ from which, after it hath been further expanded, something far nobler must grow out, if a true or perfect contrition is to be manifested. Out of faith and confidence, which, according to Catholics, *must precede, and not follow repentance*, the hatred to sin, and the germs of Divine love are to be unfolded ; so that these must concur to make up the penitential feeling. Contrition (*contritio charitate formata*) is with them a profound detestation of sin, springing out of the awakened love for God, with the conscious, deliberate determination *never more to sin*, but rather to fulfil the Divine law from and in a love for Him. In every case, they hold no emotion of the soul worthy the name of repentance, unless with this emotion be connected at least a firm determination of the will to abstain from all sin, though even this resolution may not be determined by clearly defined motives of a higher kind.[1]

Moreover, it is scarcely necessary to call attention to the frequency with which the differences between the Christian communions in the doctrine of justification recur in the matter before us. The Protestants suppose the terrors of conscience to be the only condition necessary to render us susceptible of the blessings manifested to us in Christ Jesus. Instrumental faith delivers from these terrors, and man is justified by it

---

[1] Bellarm. de pœnitent. lib. 1, c. xix, tom. iii, p. 948 : ' Cum partes pœnitentiæ quærimus, non quosvis motus, qui quocunque modo ad pœnitentiam pertinent, quærimus, sed eos duntaxat, qui ex ipsa virtute pœnitentiæ prodeunt. Porro terreri, cum intentantur minæ, non est ullius virtutis actus, sed naturalis affectus, quem etiam in pueris et in ipsis bestiis cernimus. Ad hæc sæpe terrores in iis inveniuntur, qui pœnitentiam nullam agunt, ac ne inchoant quidem, ut in dæmonibus, qui credunt et contremiscunt. Jac. 11.' [There is, however, a distinction between believe and tremble, and tremble and believe, which Bellarmine has here overlooked.] 'Sæpe etiam nonnulli veram pœnitentiam agunt, nullo pœnæ terrore, sed solo Dei et justitiæ amore impulsi, qualem credibile est fuisse beatam illam fæminam, de qua Dominus ait Luc. vii : " dimittuntur ei peccata multa, quoniam dilexit multum." Quod si terrores sine pœnitentia, et pœnitentia sine terroribus aliquando esse potest, certo non debent terrores illi inter partes pœnitentiæ numerari. Denique fides, ut mox probabimus, non est pars pœnitentiæ, sed eam præcedit.' See the work ' Hugo of St Victor, and the theological tendencies of his age,' by Albert Liebner, Leipzig, 1832, p. 465, where we may see how much more deeply the schoolmen have treated this subject than the Reformers.

alone. But, from faith, the resolution to begin a new life, and the germs of love, are *expected*, indeed, as the fruit, but of themselves contribute nought towards making us acceptable to God, and are, therefore, no sign of the Protestant notion of contrition, in so far as it is the condition of faith. With Catholics, on the other hand, sanctification and forgiveness of sins are one act : accordingly should the latter ensue, the spirit of man must be moved by far other motives than mere fear.

The Lutheran doctrine of contrition has exerted a determining influence on that of confession. Everything which is truly interior must according to Catholic doctrine, be outwardly expressed : the love for Christ in our interior must manifest itself externally in works of charity to the brethren, and what we do unto these, we do to him also. It is the same with contrition and the confession of sins before God—an act itself purely internal ; if it be deep, strong, and energetic, it seeks an outward manifestation, and becomes the sacramental confession before the priest ; and what we do to him, we do again unto Christ likewise, whose place he represents. Origen rightly compares sin to an indigestible food, which occasions sickness at the stomach, till it has been thrown off by a motion in the bowels. Even so is the sinner tormented with internal pain, and then only enjoys quiet and full health, when, by means of confession, he hath, as it were, eased himself of the noxious internal stuff. Two enemies, who wish for a sincere reconciliation, and, in their hearts, despise their hatred, will certainly feel themselves forced to avow to each other their mutual injustice ; and it is only by means of this confession that their reconciliation becomes sincere, and peace is restored to their souls. For man is so constituted, that he doth not believe in his interior feelings, unless he see them in an outward manifestation ; and, in fact, an internal sentiment is then only ripened to consummation, when it has acquired an outward shape. Moreover, a true confession to God cannot be indefinite ; for, our sins are not merely abstract ; we are guilty of specific, definite transgressions : and so a true confession of sins to God is one necessarily entering into minute details ; consequently, a confession to the priest is necessary.

But now the internal confession of sins—the interior pain, which is required by the Lutherans for penance—is merely a dread of the Divine judgments : it is no detestation of sin ; no hearty, inward hatred of sin, which can only spring up by degrees *after* absolution—*after* the assurance of the forgiveness of sins hath been already obtained. Hence, an outward unbosoming of the conscience is absolutely impossible because the sinner is really not yet in that spiritual disposition to induce him to confess. Sin is not internally rejected; how then should the rejection of it be outwardly manifested? Humility is still wanting: shame still confounds the sense of the sinner; because sin is too much his own, and is not yet estranged from his will. On the other hand, he who truly and heartily hates sin, confesses it with an involuntary joyful pain; with pain, because it is *his own;* but with a joyful pain because it now *ceases* to belong to him and to be his own. Hence, too, we can understand why Protestants look on Catholic confession as a *carnificina conscientiarum, a racking of the conscience.* However much, accordingly, the Reformers did homage to the principle of ecclesiastical, and particularly of auricular, confession, this institution could not long endure.[1] The faithful were taught to do something, which according to the general views of their teachers respecting penance, they could not do: they were to confess, and yet the sin surviving in their soul closed their lips; they were, by confession, to free their breast from sin, and yet they could never properly extricate themselves from its entanglements.

Private absolution, however, the Reformers, from a particular motive, wished, in every case, to retain; for as the individual was to refer *to himself* the general forgiveness of sins, they deemed it right to give them a special absolution.[2]

[1] Luther de captiv. Babyl. Opp. t. ii, fol. 292. ' Occulta autem confessio quæ modo celebratur, etsi probari ex scriptura non possit, miro modo tamen placet, et utilis, imo necessaria est, nec vellem eam non esse, imo gaudeo eam esse in Ecclesia Christi.' Art. Smalcald. P. iii, c. viii, p. 303 : ' Nequaquam in Ecclesia confessio et absolutio abolenda est : præsertim propter tenaras et pavidas conscientias, et propter juventutem indomitam et petulantem, ut audiatur, examinetur et instituatur in doctrina Christiana.' And we often find the same doctrine elsewhere laid down.

[2] The twenty-first canon of the fourth council of Lateran (Hard. Conc. tom. vii, p. 35) says : ' Omnis utriusque sexus fidelis, postquam ad annos discretionis pervenerit, omnia sua solus peccata confiteatur fideliter, saltem semel in anno, proprio sacerdoti, et injunctam sibi pœnitentiam studeat pro viribus adimplere, suscipiens reverenter ad minus in pascha Eucharistiæ sacramentum.' This canon is to be ranked merely among disciplinary observances, for the determining of the time when anyone should confess doth not belong to the essence of the sacrament. Even the present very laudable practice of always going to confession before communion, doth not rest on any general law of the Church. He who doth not feel himself guilty of any grievous transgression, can, without confessing to the priest, approach of his own accord to the table of the

If in confession internal repentance is outwardly manifested, and the sinner thereby reveals his hidden spiritual condition to the priest of the Church, the Church, in her turn, acts on him again by the claim of satisfaction; so that, if contrition forms the essence of penitential feeling, and the confession of sins its form and its completion, its confirmation is secured by satisfaction. These three acts of the sinner—for satisfaction, as far as regards his will, is already performed, though its execution be delayed—are the conditions to the priestly absolution, wherewith the sacramental penance is concluded. We may easily perceive, that absolution, according to Catholic principles, can by no means be a mere declaration that sins are forgiven, because the contrition required does not consist in mere terrors of conscience; and something, far other than a mere instrumental faith in the merits of Christ, is demanded of the penitent. The above-described succession of acts on the part of the sinner, united with the sacerdotal function (or, in other words, the full sacrament) is the organ of God's justifying grace, whereby man

Lord; and so, doubtless, what was formerly the practice might again be renewed, and each one resort to confession, only when he found his conscience particularly burdened. But every well-thinking man, acquainted with the human heart and its wants, must deeply lament, if ever the present practice should be changed; and it is only the indolent priest, who reluctantly discharges his undoubtedly painful office, that could desire such a change. The intellectual Pascal, who, perhaps, of all theologians and philosophers of modern times, has, in his *Pensées*, cast the deepest glance into the misery of man, unfolds in one passage his arrogance and his inclination to deceive himself, and never to trace a faithful image of his own interior. He then, with reference to the differences between the Christian communions, proceeds to say: ' En voici une preuve qui me fait horreur : La religion Catholique n'oblige pas à découvrir ses péchés indifféremment à tout le monde : elle souffre qu'on demeure caché à tous les autres hommes, mais elle en excepte un seul, à qui elle commande à découvrir le fond de son cœur, et de se faire voir tel qu'on est. Il n'y a que ce seul homme au monde qu'elle nous ordonne dédesabuser, et elle l'oblige à un secret inviolable, qui fait que cette connaissance est dans lui, comme si elle n'y était pas. Peut-on s'imaginer rien de plus charitable et de plus doux ? Et néanmoins la corruption de l'homme est telle, qu'il trouve encore de la dureté dans cette loi , et c'est une des principales raisons qui a fait revolter contre l'Eglise une grande partie de l'Europe. Que le cœur de l'homme est injuste et déraisonnable, pour trouver mauvais qu'on l'oblige de faire, à l'égard d'un homme, ce qu'il serait juste en quelque sort, qu'il fît à l'égard de tous les hommes ! Car est-il juste que nous les trompions ? Il y a différens dégrés dans cette aversion pour la vérité : mais on peut dire qu'elle est dans tous en quelque dégré, parcequ'elle est inséperable de l'amour propre. C'est cette mauvaise délicatesse qui oblige ceux qui sont dans la nécessité de reprendre les autres, de choisir tant de détours et de tempéramens pour éviter de

obtains the forgiveness of sins in sanctification, and sanctification in the forgiveness of sins.

Those theologians who pretend that the differences between the Christian communions, in the article of absolution, consist only herein—that, according to Catholic principles, the priest acts merely from the fulness of his power, while the Protestant minister declares only the will of God, and announces the same to the sinner; those theologians, we say, understand not a single syllable of the doctrinal peculiarities of the two communions. For never did any man entertain the opinion, that he could of himself forgive sins; and the Protestant declaration, that sins are remitted, bears quite another sense, than scholars of this sort suppose.

Respecting satisfaction, which, before absolution, we considered consummated, at least as regards the will, it is now necessary to enter into a few details. It is of a two-fold kind; the one referring to the past, the other both to the future and the past. For example, if anyone accuses himself of possessing

les choquer. Il faut qu'ils diminuent nos défauts, qu'ils fassent semblant de les excuser, qu'ils y mêlent des louanges et des temoignages d'affection et d'estime. Avec tout cela, cette médicine ne laisse pas d'etre amère à l'amour propre. Il en prends le moins qu'il peut, et toujours avec dégout, et souvent même avec un secret dépit contre ceux qui la lui présentent. Il arrive de là que, si on a quelque intérêt d'être aimé de nous, on s'éloigne de nous rendre un office qu'on sait nous être désagréable : on nous traite comme nous voulons être traité : nous haissons la vérité, on nous la cache ; nous voulons être flattés, on nous flatte ; nous aimons à être trompés, on nous trompe. C'est qui fait, que chaque dégré de bonne fortune, qui nous élève dans le monde, nous éloigne davantage de la vérité, parcequ'on apprehende plus de blesser ceux dont l'affection est plus utile et l'aversion plus dangereuse. Un prince sera la fable de toute l'Europe, et lui seul n'en saura rien. Je ne m'étonne pas ; dire la vérité est utile à celui à qui on la dit, mais désavantageux à ceux qui la disent, parcequ'ils se font haïr. Or ceux qui vivent avec les princes aiment mieux leur intérêts que celui du prince qu'ils servent, et ainsi ils n'ont garde de lui procurer un avantage, en se nuisant à eux-mêmes. Ce malheur est sans doute plus grand et plus ordinaire dans les plus grandes fortunes ; mais les moindres n'en sont pas exemptes, parcequ'il y a toujours quelque intérêt à se faire aimer des hommes. Ainsi, la vie humaine n'est qu'une illusion perpetuelle ; on ne fait que s'entre-tromper et s'entreflatter. Personne ne parle de nous en notre présence, comme il en parle en notre absence. L'union qui est entre les hommes n'est fondée que sur cette mutuelle tromperie ; et peu d'amitiés subsisteraient, si chacun savait ce que son ami dit de lui, lorsqu'il n'y est pas quoiqu'il parle alors sincèrement et sans passion. L'homme n'est donc que déguisement, que mensonge, et hypocrisie, et en soi-même et à l'égard des autres. Il ne veut pas qu'on lui dise la vérité il évite de la dire aux autres ; et toutes ces dispositions, si éloignées de la justice et de la raison, ont une racine naturelle en nous.'—
Pensées de Pascal, p. 1, art. v, n. 8, t. i, p. 194, etc. Paris, 1812.

unlawful goods, by theft, usury, robbery, cheating, or any other way, it is required, that the penitent should make restitution of the same, *if he wish to obtain the forgiveness of his sins*. But, as, in many cases, those robbed or defrauded cannot obtain possession of their lost property, so a corresponding renunciation of the unlawful goods, in some other appropriate way, is *enjoined;* for it is evidently in the very nature of things, that no one, while retaining the purloined goods, can truly repent of his theft. Hence the forgiveness of sins, which, according to Catholic doctrine, is identical with the internal extirpation of sin, appears determined by satisfaction ; for the willing, joyous, restitution of property unrighteously acquired, is, in itself, satisfaction. According to the different transgressions, satisfaction, as is obvious, must take a different form. This is the first species of satisfaction, consisting in the performance of what true contrition absolutely requires. The cure that follows needs the most careful attention, and the still debilitated moral powers require the application of strengthening remedies. The priest, who has learned to know the spiritual state of the sinner, ordains, accordingly, the fitting remedies—pious exercises, calculated to keep up his self-vigilance, and to impart to the will a safe, lively, and vigorous impulse, in the direction it most needs. The enjoining of such remedies belongs to the active superintendence of the Church ; and he who knows the nature of man, his effeminate tenderness towards himself, his timorous unsteadiness in the choice of vigorous means conducive to his salvation, will easily understand why the Church should have come in aid of his weakness, and been directed by Christ to support and to determine, by the declaration of her own firm and manifest will, the will of her children. The declared will of the parent is the stay to the will of the child ; it comes in to its aid, doubling it, as it were, till it has attained sufficient strength.[1]

[1] Catechismus ex decreto Concil. Trident. 343. ' Satisfacere est causas peccatorum excidere, et eorum suggestioni aditum non indulgere. In quam sententiam alii assenserunt, satisfactionem esse purgationem, qua eluitur quidquid sordium propter peccati maculam in anima resedit, atque a pœnis tempore definitis, quibus tenebamur, absolvimur. Quæ cum ita sint, facile erit fidelibus persuadere, quam necessarium sit, ut pœnitentes in hoc satisfactionis studio se exerceant. Docendi enim sunt, duo esse quæ peccatum consequuntur, maculam et pœnam : ac quamvis semper, culpa dimissa, simul etiam mortis æternæ supplicium, apud inferos constitutum, condonetur, tamen non semper contingit, quamadmodum a Tridentina Synodo declaratum est, ut Dominus peccatorum reliquias et pœnam,

Considered from one point of view, however, these penitential exercises, imposed by the Church, bear the character of real punishments, and, from the foundation of the Church, were ever regarded in this light : and this again drew down upon her the charge of Pelagianism. The matter accordingly stands thus : By the transgression of the eternal moral law, man contracted an infinite debt, which he was totally incapable of discharging. Christ took it upon himself : and to all, who will enter into a true, interior, living communion with him, the Righteous one, that debt is remitted. But, as in the fulness of His mercy the Almighty instituted this ordinance, it was not His will to release all who should return to Him, after personal guilt, from the temporal punishments which man is capable of enduring. And justice, which is not superseded by love, requires the imposition of such penalties, the more especially as those who believe in Christ and by baptism are become members of His body, have received full strength to observe the Divine law; for it is of such only there is question in the article of penance.

The contempt of God's commandments, on the part of these, and, still more, the grievous violation of them by a believer, is, even in case of amendment, deservedly punishable, and must be atoned for. Holy writ abounds in examples of men who, after having obtained the remission of their sins, still received temporal chastisements at the hand of God;—a fact utterly inexplicable, if a man, being once justified, could escape entirely without punishment. The Reformers, indeed, explained these chastisements, as having a mere correctional tendency, yet in such glaring contradiction to many passages of the Bible, that,

certo tempore definitam, quæ peccatis debetur, remittat,' etc. P. 347 : ' Divus etiam Bernardus duo affirmat in peccato reperiri, maculam animæ et plagam : ac turpitudinem quidem ipsam Dei misericordia tolli : verum sanandis peccatorum plagis valde necessarium esse eam curam, quæ in remedio pœnitentiæ adhibetur, quemadmodum enim sanato vulnere, cicatrices quædam remanent, quæ et ipsæ curandæ sunt : ita, inanima culpa condonata, supersunt reliquiæ peccatorum purgandæ,' etc. P. 352 : ' Sed illud imprimis a sacerdotibus observari oportet, ut, audita peccatorum confessione, antequam pœnitentem a peccatis absolvant, dilligenter curent, ut, si quid ille forte de re aut de existimatione proximi detraxerit, cujus peccati merito damnandus esse videatur, cumulata satistactione compenset : nemo enim absolvendus est, nisi prius, quæ cujuscunque fuerint, restituere polliceatur. At quoniam multi sunt, quibus etsi prolixe pollicentur, se officio satis esse facturos, tamen certum est ac deliberatum nunquam promissa exsolvere, omnino ii cogendi sunt, ut restituant,' etc.

so interpreted, they offer no sense.[1] From this emasculated opinion the Reformers might well have turned away, had they but calmly interpreted the language of the uneducated man, on meeting with misfortunes : ' I have *deserved* them,' is his ordinary exclamation. They would then have perceived, that undebauched feeling regards suffering as something far different from mere *means of correction;* and humility would not have failed to suggest a view more consonant with its own spirit.

Moreover, if there be no temporal punishments for the righteous, there are then no eternal ones for the unrighteous. On the other hand, if there are eternal punishments for the latter, so there must be temporal punishments for the former, when after baptism they relapse into sin ; for the question here is as to the notion and essence of punishments, and not as to any of their accidental qualities. If they be in their nature purely remedial, they cannot, in the one case, be destined solely for cure, and, in the other, only for chastisement, in the strict sense of the word ; and *vice versa*, if they be in their essence solely vindicative, they must everywhere retain this character. Both exclusive views, however, are erroneous. Nay, as in God goodness and justice are one, so each of those attributes concurs in determining the object of punishments ; and it is only when man has wilfully repelled the pardoning and reconciling goodness of God, that he feels the arm of His justice alone. It was therefore an inconsistency, on the part of the Reformers, to leave intact the Scriptural doctrine of hell-torments, and yet to look on punishments *solely* as the means of amelioration.

The Church, which, in the tribunal of Penance, recognises a divine institution, must contemplate all the relations wherein the sinner stands to God, and foster in him the feeling that he is deserving of chastisement for his transgressions. She must attentively consider punishment in all its bearings, and impose satisfaction in the strict sense of the word, so as withal to prevent the relapse of the penitent, to confirm him in virtue, and to cherish the feeling of repentance. The primitive Church took precisely this view of penitential exercises ; and it is contrary to history to assert that the satisfactions it required, were directed solely to the conciliation of the Church. The old visible Church did not separate itself from Christ, as in modern times has been done, out of the pale of Catholicism ; and men therefore transferred to primitive Christianity their own modern

[1] See Note A in Appendix.

conceptions, arising out of very opposite principles, when they endeavoured to enforce this unfounded theory touching the ancient satisfactions.

The Church, moreover, has repeatedly, in language as unequivocal as it was affecting, declared, that through the satisfactions she exacted, the merits of Christ could be in no wise impaired; that this species of satisfaction ought not to be confounded with that achieved by Christ; and lastly, that the works of satisfaction which she required, must emanate from the penitential spirit that Christ himself inspires, and from thence solely derived their value. Those works on the other hand, she declared, which are not offered up by a sinner justified and regenerated, being perverse in themselves, must not be included in the above denomination.[1] Nevertheless, down to the present day, the Church has never been able to convince her adversaries, that, by these ordinances, the glory of Christ is not obscured, nor human self-righteousness promoted. But who does not perceive the necessity of such an opinion on the part of the Protestants, when he maturely weighs the Protestant doctrine of justification, which we have above described? If satisfaction in the form of restitution were made a condition to the forgiveness of sins, what was this but to declare works as necessary to *salvation?* If the Protestants exacted satisfactions as spiritual remedies, they would give countenance to the principle that man must co-operate with God, and that the forgiveness of sins depended on sanctification. If they declared satisfaction, in the proper sense of the word, to form an integral part of Penance; then this were tatamount to the opinion, that the just man could fulfil the law; for punishment is inflicted on the sinner baptised, in order precisely to impress him with the conviction that he was enabled to observe the precepts of the law. Whichever way, accordingly, we look at satisfactions, the fundamental doctrines of Protestantism forbid their forming part of their penitential system.[2]

[1] Concil. Trid. sess. xiv, c. viii. ' Neque vero ita nostra est satisfactio hæc, quam pro peccatis nostris exsolvimus, ut non sit per Christum Jesum. Nam qui ex nobis, tanquam ex nobis, nihil possumus, eo co-operante, qui nos confortat, omnia possumus. Ita non habet homo unde glorietur, sed omnis gloriatio nostra in Christo est, in quo vivimus, in quo meremur, in quo satisfacimus, facientes fructus dignos pœnitentiæ; qui ex illo vim habent, ab illo offeruntur Patri, et per illum acceptantur a Patre.'

[2] Melancth. loc. theol. p. 65. ' Quid enim videtur magis convenire, quam ut sint in ecclesia publicorum scelerum satisfactiones? At illæ obscurarunt gratiam.' Calvin. Instit. lib. iv, c. 4, sect. 25: ' Talibus

With the ecclesiastical punishments we have described as remedies and satisfactions, the doctrine of Indulgences is connected, the abuse whereof, real and undeniable, led the Reformers into so many false steps, and would have been calculated to furnish them with some excuse, were it not expected of great men, for which they wished to pass, and, especially, of a Divine envoy (and such Luther was inclined to regard himself) that they should not take occasion, from the abuse of truths, to reject those truths themselves. From the earliest ages of Christianity, indulgences were understood to be, the shortening, under certain conditions, of the period of penance, imposed by the Church, and, withal, the remission of the temporal punishment.[1] The most important condition was fulfilled, when the sinner furnished such proofs of contrition, and of newness and holiness of heart, that he seemed no longer to need the special ecclesiastical remedies we have described, and appeared worthy to be released from the temporal penalty.[2]

At a later period, many theologians gave greater extension to the doctrine of indulgences; but their opinions, though very well grounded, have not been declared articles of faith in any formulary of the Church, and, therefore, enter not into the plan of this work. The Council of Trent, with wise precaution, decreed no more, than that the Church has the right

mendaciis oppono gratuitam peccatorum remissionem: qua nihil in scripturis clarius prædicatur.'

[1] Concil. Ancyran. (an. 314) c. v; Hard. Concil. tom. i, p. 273 : τοὺς δὲ ἐπισκόπους ἐξουσίαν ἔχειν τὸν τρόπον τῆς ἐπιστροφῆς δοκιμάσαντας φιλανθρωπεύεσθαι, ἢ πλείονα προστιθέναι χρόνον· πρὸ πάντων δὲ καὶ ὁ προάγων βίος, καὶ ὁ μετὰ ταῦτα ἐξεταζέσθω· καὶ οὕτως ἡ φιλανθρωπία ἐπιμετρείσθω. Concil. Nicen. an. 325, c. xii, lib. i, p. 327 : ἐφ' ἅπασι δὲ τούτοις προσήκει ἐξετάζειν τὴν προαίρεσιν, καὶ τὸ εἶκος τῆς μετανοίας. ὅσοι μὲν γὰρ καὶ φόβῳ καὶ δάκρυσι καὶ ὑπομονῇ καὶ ἀγαθοεργίαις τὴν ἐπιστροφὴν ἔργῳ καὶ οὐ σχήματι ἐπιδείκνυνται, etc. Compare Concil. Carth. iv, c. 75.

TRANSLATION

Concil. Ancyr. (anno 314) c. v; Hard. Concil. tom. i, p. 273. 'But bishops have the power, when they have examined into the character of the conversion, to exercise clemency, or to prolong the time: above all, let the anterior and the subsequent course of life be thoroughly sifted, and so let mercy be exercised.' Concil. Nicæn. anno 325, c. xii, lib. i, p. 327 : 'But in all these things it is proper to investigate the object and the nature of the repentance. But such as, by dread, and tears, and patience, and good works, manifest their conversion in deed, and not in appearance,' etc.

[2] In the ancient Church, the absolution was given only after the satisfaction had been performed.

to grant indulgences, and that these, dispensed with wisdom, are useful.¹

Of the relation which the doctrine of purgatory bears to these satisfactions, we shall elsewhere have occasion to speak.

§ XXXIV—DOCTRINE OF THE CATHOLICS ON THE MOST HOLY SACRAMENT OF THE ALTAR, AND ON THE MASS

The mighty subject, which is now about to engage our attention, gave birth to the most important controversies between the Christian communions. All the other distinctive doctrines are here combined, though in a more eminent degree; for although, as has been clearly shown, in every point of difference the whole system of doctrine is mirrored forth, yet here this is more especially the case. On the view, too, which we take of this subject, depends the fact, whether the Church be destined to possess a true and vital worship, or ought to be devoid of one.

According to the clear declarations of Christ and his apostles, and the unanimous teaching of the Church, attested by the immediate followers of our Lord's disciples, Catholics firmly hold that in the sacrament of the altar Christ is truly present, and indeed in such a way, that Almighty God, who was pleased at Cana, in Galilee, to convert water into wine changes the inward substance of the consecrated bread and wine into the body and blood of Christ.²

---

[1] Concil. Trident. sess. xxv, decret. de indulg. At the same time the abuses in the dispensation of indulgences are openly and sharply rebuked and forbidden. ' In his tamen concedendis moderationem, juxta veterem et probatam in ecclesia consuetudinem, adhiberi cupit : ne nimia facilitate ecclesiastica disciplina enervetur. Abusus vero, qui in his irrepserunt, et quorum occasione insigne hoc indulgentiarum nomen ab hæreticis blasphematur, emendatos et correctos cupiens, præsenti decreto generaliter statuit, pravos questus omnes pro his consequendis, unde plurima in Christiano populo abusuum causa fluxit, omnino abolendos esse. Cæteros vero, qui ex superstitione, ignorantia, irreverentia, aliunde quomodocunque provenerunt . . . mandat omnibus episcopis, ut diligenter quisque hujusmodi abusus ecclesiæ suæ colligat, eosque in prima synodo provinciali referat,' etc.

[2] Concil. Trid. sess. xiii, c. iv. ' Quoniam autem Christus, redemptor noster, corpus suum id, quod sub specie panis offerebat, vere esse dixit ; ideo persuasum semper in ecclesia Dei fuit, idque nunc denuo sancta hæc synodus declarat, per consecrationem panis et vini, conversionem fieri totius substantiæ panis in substantiam corporis Christi Domini nostri, et totius substantiæ vini in substantiam sanguinis ejus. Quæ conversio convenienter et proprie a sancta Catholica ecclesia transubstantiatio est appellata.'

We therefore adore the Saviour mysteriously present in the sacrament;[1] rejoice in his exceeding condescending compassion; and express, in canticles of praise and thanksgiving, our pious emotions, as far as the divinely enraptured soul of man can express them.[2]

Out of this faith sprung the Mass, which, in its essential purport, is as old as the Church, and even in its more important forms can be *proved to have been already in existence* in the second and third centuries. But to unfold more clearly the Catholic doctrine on this point, it is necessary to anticipate somewhat of our reflections on the Church. The Church, considered in one point of view, is the living figure of Christ, manifesting himself and working through all ages, whose atoning and redeeming acts, it, in consequence, eternally repeats, and uninterruptedly continues. The Redeemer not merely lived eighteen hundred years ago, so that he hath since disappeared, and we retain but an historical remembrance of him, as of a deceased man: but he is, on the contrary, eternally living in his Church; and in the sacrament of the altar he hath manifested this in a sensible manner to creatures endowed with sense. He is, in the announcement of his word, the abiding teacher; in baptism he

---

[1] Loc. cit. c. v. ' Nullus itaque dubitandi locus relinquitur, quin omnes Christi fideles, pro more in catholica ecclesia semper recepto, latriæ cultum, qui vero Deo debetur, huic sanctissimo sacramento in veneratione exhibeant. Neque enim ideo minus est adorandum, quod futeri a Christo Domino, ut sumatur, institutum. Nam illum eundem Deum præsentem in eo adesse credimus, quem Pater æternus introducens in orbem terrarum dicit : " et adorent eum omnes Angeli Dei," quem magi procidentes adoraverunt, quem denique in Galilæa ab apostolis adoratum fuisse, scriptura testatur.'

[2] The well-known Christian hymn saith :—

' Lauda Sion salvatorem,
Lauda ducem et pastorem,
In hymnis et canticis.
Quantum potes, tantum aude,
Quia major omni laude ;
Nec luddare sufficis.
Laudis thema specialis
Panis vivus et vitalis
Hodie proponitur,' etc.

In another we find the following :—

' Pange lingua gloriosi
Corporis mysterium,
Sanguinisque pretiosi,
Quem in mundi pretium,
Fructus ventris generosi
Rex effudit gentium,' etc.

perpetually receives the children of men into his communion; in the tribunal of penance he pardons the contrite sinner; strengthens rising youth with the power of his spirit in confirmation; breathes into the bridegroom and the bride a higher conception of the nuptial relations; unites himself most intimately with all who sigh for eternal life, under the forms of bread and wine; consoles the dying in extreme unction; and in holy orders institutes the organs whereby he worketh all this with never-tiring activity. If Christ, concealed under an earthly veil, unfolds, to the end of time, his whole course of actions begun on earth, he of necessity, eternally offers himself to the Father as a victim for men; and the real permanent exposition hereof can never fail in the Church, if the historical Christ is to celebrate in her his entire imperishable existence.[1]

The following may perhaps serve to explain the Catholic view on this subject, since it is a matter of so much difficulty to Protestants to form a clear conception of this dogma.[2]

Christ, on the cross, has offered the sacrifice for our sins. But the incarnate son of God, who hath suffered, died, and risen again from the dead for our sins, being according to his own teaching, present in the Eucharist, the Church from the beginning hath, at His command (Luke xxii. 20), substituted the Christ mysteriously present, and visible only to the spiritual eye of faith, for the historical Christ, now inaccessible to the corporeal senses. The former is taken for the latter, because the latter is likewise the former—both are considered as one and the same; and the eucharistic Saviour, therefore, as the victim also for the sins of the world. And the more so, as, when we wish to express ourselves accurately, the sacrifice of Christ on the cross is put only as a part for an organic whole. For his

---

[1] Conc. Trid. sess. xxii, c. 1. ' Is igitur Deus et Dominus noster, etsi semel seipsum in ara crucis, morte intercedente, Deo patri oblaturus erat, ut æternam illic redemptionem operaretur; quia tamen per mortem sacerdotium ejus extinguendum non erat, in cœna novissima, qua nocte tradebatur, ut dilectæ sponsæ suæ ecclesiæ visibile, sicut hominum natura exigit, relinqueret sacrificium, quo cruentum illud, semel in cruce peragendum, repræsentaretur, ejusque memoria in finem usque sæculi permaneret, atque illius salutaris virtus in remissionem eorum, quæ a nobis quotidie committuntur, peccatorum applicaretur,' etc. C. ii: ' Et quoniam in divino hoc sacrificio, quod in missa peragitur, idem ille Christus continetur, et incruente immolatur, qui in ara crucis semel se ipsum cruente obtulit, docet sancta synodus, sacrificium istud vere propitiatorium esse, per ipsumque fieri, si cum vero corde et recta fide, cum metu et reverentia, contriti ac pœnitentes ad Deum accedamus,' etc.

[2] See Note B in Appendix.

whole life on earth—his ministry and his sufferings, as well as his perpetual condescension to our infirmity in the Eucharist—constitute one great sacrificial act, one mighty action undertaken out of love for us, and expiatory of our sins, consisting, indeed, of various individual parts, yet so that none by itself, is strictly speaking the sacrifice. In each particular part the whole recurs, yet without these parts the whole cannot be conceived. The will of Christ, to manifest his gracious condescension to us in the Eucharist, forms no less an integral part of his great work, than all besides, and in a way so necessary, indeed, that, whilst we here find the whole scheme of Redemption reflected, without it the other parts would not have sufficed for our complete atonement. Who, in fact, would venture the assertion that the descent of the Son of God in the Eucharist belongs not to his general merits, which are imputed to us? Hence the sacramental sacrifice is a true sacrifice—a sacrifice in the strict sense, yet so that it must in no wise be separated from the other things which Christ hath achieved for us, as the very consideration of the end of its institution will clearly show.[1] In this last portion (if we may so call it) of the great sacrifice for us, all the other parts are to be present, and applied to us: in this last part of

[1] In Theophilus L. S. register. Annæ Comnenæ Supplementa (Tub. 1832, c. iv, pp. 18-23) a fragment from the still unprinted panoply of Nicetas is communicated in reference to Soterichus Panteugonus—the oldest document, to our knowledge, informing us of any doubt being entertained, whether the mass be really a sacrifice. Soterich lived in the twelfth century, under Manuel Comnenus, and maintained the opinion that it was only in an improper sense that Christ in the Eucharist was said to be offered up as a victim to God. But the Greek bishops assembled together rejected this view, and Soterich presented a recantation, which is not contained in the above-named writing, but which I printed in the *Theological Quarterly Review* of Tübingen. (See the *Tubinger Quartalschrift*, 1833, No. ι, p. 373.) The recantation runs thus: ὁμοφρονῶ τῇ ἁγίᾳ καὶ ἱερᾷ συνόδῳ ἐπὶ τῷ τὴν θυσίαν καὶ τὴν νῦν προσαγομένην καὶ τὴν τότε προσαχθεῖσαν παρὰ τοῦ μονογενοῦς καὶ ἐνανθρωπήσαντος λόγου, καὶ τότε προσοχθεῖσαν [it stands so written in the Paris codex, but it ought evidently to be προσαχθῆναι] καὶ νῦν πάλιν προσάγεσθαι, ὡς τὴν αὐτὴν οὖσαν καὶ μίαν, καὶ τῷ μὴ οὕτω φωνοῦντι ἀνάθεμα. Κἄν τι πρὸς ἀνατροπὴν εὑρίσκηται λεγραμμένον, ἀναθέματι καθυποβάλλω. Ἡ ὑπογραφή Σωτηρίχος ὁ Παντεύγονος.

TRANSLATION

'I agree with the holy synod herein, that the sacrifice now to be offered up, and once offered up by the only-begotten and incarnate Word, was once offered up, and is now offered up, because it is one and the same. To him who doth not so believe, anathema: and if anything hath been found written in refutation hereof I subject it to the anathema.

'(Signed)   SOTERICHUS PANTEUGONUS.'

the objective sacrifice, the latter becomes subjective and appropriated to us. Christ on the cross is still an object strange to us : Christ, in the Christian worship, is our property, our victim. There he is the universal victim—here he is the victim for us in particular, and for every individual amongst us ; there he was only the victim ;—here he is the victim acknowledged and revered : there the objective atonement was consummated ; —here the subjective atonement is partly fostered and promoted, partly expressed.

The Eucharistic sacrifice, in conformity to its declared ends, may be considered under a two-fold point of view. The Church, in general, and every particular community within her, being founded by the sacrifice of the son of God, and by faith in the same, and thus owing their existence to him, the Eucharistic sacrifice must, in the first place, be regarded as one of praise and thanksgiving. In other words, the Church declares that she is incapable of offering up her thanks to God in any other way, than by giving him back who became the victim of the world ; as if she were to say : ' Thou didst, O Lord, for Christ's sake, look down, with graciousness and compassion, upon us as *Thy children;* so vouchsafe that we, with grateful hearts, may revere Thee as *our Father* in Christ, thy Son, here present. We possess nought else that we can offer Thee, save Christ ; be graciously pleased to receive our sacrifice.' While the community, in the person of the priest, performeth this, it confesses perpetually what Christ became, and still continues to be, for its sake. It is not however the interior acts of thanksgiving, adoration, and gratitude, which it offers up to God, but it is Christ himself present in the sacrament. These emotions of the soul are indeed excited, unfolded, kept up, and fostered by the presence and the self-sacrifice of the Saviour ; but of themselves they are deemed unworthy to be presented to God. Christ, the victim in our worship, is the copious inexhaustible source of the deepest devotion ; but, in order to be this, the presence of the Saviour, sacrificing himself for the sins of the world, is necessarily required—a presence to which, as to an outward object, the interior soul of man must attach itself, and must unbosom all its feelings.

The community, however, continually professes itself a sinner, needing forgiveness, and striving, ever more and more, to appropriate to itself the merits of Christ. Now the sacrifice appears propitiatory, and the Redeemer present enables us to be entirely his own children, or to become so in an ever-increasing degree. The present Saviour, in a voice audible to the spiritual-minded, incessantly addresses His Father above : ' Be graciously pleased to behold in me the believing and repentant people : ' and then he crieth to his brethren below : ' Come to me, all you that labour and are heavy laden, and I will refresh you : each one, who returneth to me with all his heart, shall find mercy, forgiveness of sins, and every grace.' Hence, in the liturgy of the Latin, as well as of the Greek Church, it is rightly said, that it is Christ, who, in the holy action, offers himself up to God as a sacrifice ; he is at once the victim and the high-priest. But we, recognising, in the Eucharistic Christ, that same Christ, who, out of love for us, delivered himself unto death, even the death of the cross, exclaim, at the elevation of the Host, wherever the Catholic Church extends, with that lively faith in his manifest mercy, from which humility, confidence, love, and repentance spring ' O Jesus ! for Thee I live ; for Thee I die ! O Jesus ! Thine I am, living or dead.'

It is now evident to all, that the belief in the real presence of Christ in the Eucharist, forms the basis of our whole conception of the mass. Without that presence, the solemnity of the Lord's supper is a mere reminiscence of the sacrifice of Christ, exactly in the same way as the celebration by any society of the anniversary of some esteemed individual, whose image it exhibits to view, or some other symbol, recalls to mind his beneficent actions. On the other hand, with faith in the real existence of Christ in the Eucharist, the past becomes the present—all that Christ hath merited for us, and whereby he hath so merited it, is henceforth never separated from his person : He is present as that which he absolutely is, and in the whole extent of his actions, to wit, as the real victim. Hence the effects of this faith on the mind, the heart, and the will of man, are quite other than if, by the mere stretch of the human faculty of memory, Christ be called back from the distance of eighteen hundred years. He himself manifests his love, his benevolence, his devotedness to us : He is ever in the midst of us, full of grace and truth.

Accordingly, the Catholic mass, considered as a sacrifice, is a solemnisation of the blessings imparted to humanity by God in Christ Jesus, and is destined, by the offering up of Christ, partly to express in praise, thanksgiving, and adoration, the joyous feelings of redemption on the part of the faithful ; partly to make the merits of Christ the subject of their perpetual appropriation. It is also clear, why this sacrifice is of personal utility to the believer; namely, because, thereby pious sentiments, such as faith, hope, love, humility, contrition, obedience, and devotion to Christ, are excited, promoted, and cherished. The sacrifice presented to God, which, as we have often said, is not separated from the work of Christ, merits internal grace for the culture of these sentiments, which are psychologically excited from without, by faith in the present Saviour, whose entire actions and sufferings are brought before the mind. As, according to Catholic doctrine, forgiveness of sins cannot take place without sanctification, and a fitting state of the human soul is required for the reception of grace as well as an active concurrence towards the fructification of grace, the reflecting observer may already infer, that it is not by a mere outward or bodily participation, on the part of the community, that the mass produces any vague indeterminate effects.

The sacrifice of the mass is likewise offered up for the living and the dead; that is to say, God is implored, for the sake of Christ's oblation, to grant to all those who are dear to us, whatever may conduce to their salvation. With the mass, accordingly, the faithful join the prayer, that the merits of Christ, which are considered as concentrated in the Eucharistic sacrifices, should be applied to all needing them and susceptible of them. To consider merely himself is a matter of impossibility to the Christian, how much less in so sacred a solemnity can he think only of himself, and omit his supplication, that the merits of Christ, which outweigh the sins of the whole world may likewise be appropriated by all ? The communion with the happy and perfect spirits in Christ is also renewed; for they are one with Christ, and his work cannot be contemplated without its effects. Lastly, all the concerns of inward and outward life—sad and joyful events, good and ill fortune—are brought in connection with this sacrifice; and at this commemoration in Christ, to whom we are indebted for the highest gifts, we pour out to God our thanksgivings and lamentations, and in Him, and before Him, we implore consolation, and courage, and strength, under sufferings; self-denial, clemency, and meekness, in prosperity.

Hitherto, however, we have considered the mass merely as a sacrificial oblation; but this view by no means embraces its whole purport. The assembled congregation declares, from what we have stated, that *in itself without Christ*, it discovers nothing—absolutely nothing—which can be agreeable to God: nay, nothing, but what is inadequate, earthly, and sinful. Renouncing itself, it gives itself up to Christ, full of confidence, hoping for his sake forgiveness of sins and eternal life, and every grace. In this act of self-renunciation and of entire self-abandonment to God in Christ, the believer has, as it were, thrown off himself, excommunicated himself, if I may so speak, in his existence, as separated from Christ, in order to live only by him, and in him. Hence he is in a state to enter into the most intimate fellowship with Christ, to commune with him, and with his whole being to be entirely absorbed in him. For the unseemliness of the congregation no longer communicating every Sunday (as was the case in the primitive Church), and of the priest in the mass usually receiving alone the body of the Lord, is not to be laid to the blame of the Church (for all the prayers in the holy sacrifice presuppose the sacramental communion of the entire congregation), but it is to be ascribed solely to the tepidity of the greater part of the faithful. Yet are the latter earnestly exhorted to participate, at least spiritually, in the communion of the priest, and in this way to enter into the fellowship of Christ.[1]

Who will not call such a worship most Christian, most pious, and real:—a worship wherein God is adored in spirit and in truth? Indeed, how can a carnal-minded man, who will not believe in the incarnation of the Son of God—for the most powerful obstacle to this belief is in the fact that man clearly perceives, he must be of a godly way of thinking, so soon as he avows that God has become man—how can such a man look upon the mass as other than mere foolishness? The mass comprises an ever-recurring invitation to the confession of our sins, of our own weakness and helplessness. It is a living representation of the infinite love and compassion of God towards us, which He hath revealed, and daily still reveals, in the delivering up of His only-begotten Son: and therefore it contains the most

---

[1] Loc. cit. sess. xiii, c. viii. 'Quoad usum autem, recte et sapienter patres nostri tres rationes hoc sanctum sacramentum accipiendi distinxerunt. Quosdam enim docuerunt sacramentaliter duntaxat id sumere, ut peccatores, alios autem spiritualiter, illos nimirum, qui voto propositum illum coelestem panem edentes, fide viva, quæ per dilectionem operatur, fructum ejus et utilitatem sentiunt; tertios porro sacramentaliter simul et spiritualiter: hi autem sunt, qui se prius probant et instruunt, ut vestem nuptialem induti,' etc.

urgent exhortation to endless thanksgiving, to effective mutual love, and to our heavenly glorification. Hence an adversary to such a worship must be one whose thoughts creep exclusively on the earth, or who of the whole act understands nought else, but that the priest turns sometimes to the right, sometimes to the left, and is clothed in a motley-coloured garment. On the other hand, he who misapprehends the wants of man, and the high objects of our Divine Redeemer, in the establishment of the sacraments; he who, like the Manicheans, rejects the sacraments as coarse, sensual institutions, and follows the track of a false spirituality, will regard the Catholic dogma as incomprehensible. In the opinion of such a man, a worship is in the same degree spiritual, as it is untrue. He lays before his God the lofty conceptions that have sprung out of the fulness of his intellectual powers, his holy feelings, and inflexible resolves; these have no reference to the outward historical Christ, but only to the ideal one, which is merged in the subjectivity of these feelings and ideas; while yet, by the fact of the external revelation of the Logos, internal worship must needs obtain a perpetual outward basis, and, in truth, one representing the Word as delivered up to suffering, because it was under the form of a self-sacrifice for the sins of the world that this manifestation occurred. How, on the other hand, anyone who has once apprehended the full meaning of the incarnation of the Deity, and who with joy confesses that his duty is the reverse —namely, to pass from seeming to real and divine existence, and has accordingly attained to the perception that the doctrine of a forgiveness of sins in Christ Jesus, of an exaltation of man unto God, and of a communication of divine life to him, through our Lord, must remain unprofitable until it be brought before us in concrete forms, and be made to bear on our most individual relations—how anyone, I say, who clearly perceives all this, can refuse to revere in the Catholic mass a divine institution, I am utterly at a loss to conceive.

After this exposition, we are probably now enabled to give a satisfactory solution to the chief objection which the Protestant communities have urged against the Catholic sacrifice of the mass. It is argued, that by the mass the sacrifice of Christ on the cross is abolished, or that, at any rate, it receives a detriment, since the latter is considered as incomplete, and needing a supplement. Now, it is self-evident, that the sacrifice of the mass, by keeping the oblation of Christ on the cross, or rather his whole ministry and sufferings, eternally present, presupposes the same, and in its whole purport maintains the same; and so far from obliterating, it stamps them more vividly on the minds of men; and, instead of supplying the bloody sacrifice of the cross with some heterogeneous element, it brings that sacrifice in its true integrity and original vitality to bear the most individual application and appropriation throughout all ages. It is one and the same undivided victim, one and the same High Priest, who on the mount of Calvary and on our altars hath offered himself up as an atonement for the sins of the world. But, as this view is so obvious, and as the Reformers nevertheless constantly repeated their objections, and impressed them so strongly on the minds of their followers, that, down to the present day, they are repeated; something deeply rooted in the constitution of Protestantism itself seems to lurk under these objections, and requires to be dragged to light. The decisive, conscious, undoubting faith that Christ before our eyes offers himself up for us to his eternal Father, is quite calculated to produce an effect piercing into the inmost heart of man—far below the deepest roots of evil, so that sin in its inmost germ should be plucked from the will, and the believer be unable to refuse to consecrate his life to God.[1] This ordi-

[1] Luther (de captivit. Bab. opp. ed. Jen. tom. ii, p. 279, b, and 280) still expresses the glorious reminiscences of his Catholic education, which, however, became always feebler, till at last they were totally extinguished, 'Est itaque missa, sed secundum substantiam suam, proprie nihil aliud, quam verba Christi prædicta : " accipite et manducate," etc. Ac si dicat : ecce o homo peccator et damnatus, ex mera gratuitaque charitate, qua diligo te, sic volente misericordiarum patre, his verbis promitto tibi, ante omne meritum et votum tuum, remissionem omnium peccatorum tuorum et vitam æternam. Et ut certissimus de hac mea promissione irrevocabili sis, corpus meum tradam et sanguinem fundam, morte ipsa hac hanc promissionem confirmaturus, et utrumque tibi in signum et memoriale ejusdem promissionis relicturus. Quod cum frequentaveris, mei memor sis, hanc meam in te charitatem et largitatem prædices et laudes et gratias agas.' (Here, however, it is merely the subjective, and not the objective part which is brought forward.) ' Ex quibus vides ad missam digne habendam aliud non requiri quam fidem, qua huic promissioni fideliter nitatur, Christum in suis verbis veracem credat, et sibi hæc immensa bona esse donata non dubitet. Ad hanc fidem mox sequetur sua sponte dulcissimus affectus cordis, qua dilatatur et impinguatur spiritus hominis (hæc est charitas, per Spiritum Sanctum in fide Christi donata), ut in Christum, tam largum et benignum testatorem, rapiatur, fiatque penitus alius et novus homo. Quis enim non dulciter lacrymetur, imo præ gaudio in Christum pene exanimetur, si credat fide indubitata, hanc Christi promissionem inæstimabilem ad se pertinere? Quomodo non diliget tantum benefactorem, qui indigno et longe alia merito tantas divitias et

nance of divine compassion necessarily leads, along with others to the doctrine of internal justification; as, on the other hand, the mass must be rejected with a sort of instinct, wherever that doctrine is repudiated. If such great and living manifestations of the Redeemer's grace be unable thoroughly to purify the heart of man; if they be incapable of moving us to heartfelt gratitude and mutual love, to the most unreserved self-sacrifice and to the supplication, that God would accept the oblation of ourselves; then we may with reason despair of our sanctification, and abandon ourselves to a mere *theory of imputation*. Now, perhaps, we may understand the full sense of the prayer, which the Catholic at the elevation of the host utters to his Saviour: ' To thee let my whole life be consecrated!'

Yet it ought not to be overlooked, that the Reformers might be led into error through various, and some extremely scandalous, abuses, especially an unspiritual, dry, mechanical performance and participation in this most mysterious function. Moreover, in default of historical learning, the high antiquity and apostolic origin of the holy sacrifice was unknown to them. If it cannot even be denied, that their whole system, when regarded from one point of view, should have led them rather zealously to uphold, than to disapprove of the sacrificial worship; yet they instinctively felt that, in that worship, there lay something infinitely more profound than all the doctrinal foundations of their own theological system; and, accordingly, they were driven by an unconscious impulse into a negative course.

There are now some particulars which remain to be considered. The doctrine of the change of bread and wine into the body and blood of Christ occupies an important place in the Catholic system of theology. Who doth not immediately think of that true, moral change which must take place in man, so soon as he enters into communion with Christ, when the earthly man ceases, and the heavenly one begins, so that not we, but Christ liveth in us? In the Lord's supper Luther could not

hereditatem hanc æternam præveniens offert, promittit et donat.' Compare Sancti Anselmi orationes n. xxv-xxxv, opp. edit. Gerberon, Par. 1721, p. 264, seq. But at page 281 of this work Luther says: ' Ita possum quotidie, imo omni hora, missam habere, dum quoties voluero, possum mihi verba Christi proponere et fidem meam in illis alere,' etc. This is indeed true, but to overlook every other consideration, such an idealism would render the sacraments utterly unnecessary, and *public* worship useless, since something external *must* always form the foundation of the latter.

find Christ alone—bread and wine ever recurred to his mind, because, in the will of those regenerated in Christ, he saw a permanent dualism, a perpetual co-existence of a spiritual and a carnal inclination, so that the latter—evil principle in man— could never be truly converted into the former. Moreover, the doctrine of transubstantiation is the clearest representation of the objectivity of the food of the soul offered to us in the sacraments ; and, if we may dare to speak of the internal motives of the Divine economy, we should affirm that, by this transubstantiation, wrought through a miracle of God's omnipotence, the strongest barrier is raised against any false subjective opinion. This doctrine, which most undoubtedly was at all times prevalent in the Church,[1] though at one time more clearly, at another less clearly, expressed, according as occasion seemed to require, was, in the Middle Age, laid down as a formal dogma, at a period, when a false pantheistic mysticism, which we have elsewhere described, confounded the distinctions between the human and

[1] In the Liturgy of St Chrysostom (Goar, Eucholog. p. 77) we meet with the following forms of prayer ; Εὐλόγησον δέσποτα τὸν ἅγιον ἄρτον: ' Bless, O Lord, the holy bread,' saith the deacon ; hereupon the priest saith : ποίησον τὸν μὲν ἄρτον τοῦτον τίμιον σῶμα τοῦ Χριστοῦ σοῦ : ' Make this bread the venerable body of thy Christ.' Then the deacon calls upon the priest to bless the wine ; whereupon the latter saith : Τὸ δὲ ἐν ποτηρίῳ τούτῳ τίμιον αἷμα τοῦ Χριστοῦ : ' Make what is contained in this chalice the venerable blood of thy Christ.' Then over both the priest saith : ' Converting them through thy Holy Spirit,' μεταβαλὼν τῷ πνεύματί σου τῷ ἁγίῳ. The Liturgy of St Basil has the same forms, with even a verbal coincidence (p. 166).

In Renaudot's *Collectio Liturgiarum Orientialium* (tom. i, p. 157), we read as follows in the Liturgy of the Alexandrine Church : "Ἔτι δὲ ἐθ' ἡμᾶς καὶ ἐπὶ τοὺς ἄρτους τούτους, καὶ ἐπὶ τὰ ποτήρια ταῦτα τὸ πνεῦμά σου τὸ ἅγιον, ἵνα ταῦτα ἁγιάσῃ καὶ τελειώσῃ, ὡς παντοδύναμος θεός. Καὶ ποιήσῃ, τὸν μὲν ἄρτον σῶμα . . . τὸ δὲ ποτήριον αἷμα τῆς καινῆς διαθήκης αὐτοῦ τοῦ κυρίου καὶ θεοῦ καὶ σωτῆρος, καὶ παμβασιλέως ἡμῶν Ἰησοῦ Χριστοῦ : ' Send down upon us, and upon these breads, and upon these chalices, thy Holy Spirit that he may consecrate and consummate these as the omnipotent God ; and that he may make the bread the body, and the chalice the blood of the New Testament of him our Lord, and God, and Saviour, and universal King, Jesus Christ.'

The so-called universal canon of the Ethiopians says, loc. cit. p. 504 : ' Ostende faciem tuam super hunc panem et super hunc calicem, quos proposuimus super hoc altare spirituale tuum : benedic, sanctifica, et purifica illos ; et transmuta hunc panem, ut fiat corpus tuum purum, et quod mistum est in hoc calice, sanguis tuus pretiosus.' Hereupon Renaudot observes (p. 527) : ' Veram mutationem significat vox Æthiopica, rei scilicet unius in aliam, ut agnoscit ipse Ludolfus in lexicis suis, multique scripturæ loci in quibus usurpatur, palam faciunt. Si vel levissima de ejus significatione esset dubitatio, vox Coptica, cui respondet, et versiones Arabicæ illam plene discuterent.'

the divine, and identified the Father with the world, the Son of God with the eternal idea of man, and the Holy Ghost with religious feelings. Several Gnostic sects, and afterwards Amalrich of Chartres, and David of Dinant, inculcated these errors. They regarded the historical revelation of God in Christ Jesus as a self-revelation of man, and the sacraments were, therefore, in the eyes of these people nought else than what man chose of himself to attribute to them. Hence, they rejected them as useless; and, identifying with God the energies of the world, they conceived it singular that those powers, which in themselves were thoroughly divine, should receive, from any external cause, a divine nature or property. In this juncture of time, it appeared necessary to point out more clearly than had been done at any previous period, the primitive doctrine that had been handed down, and to set it in the strongest light with all the consequences deducible from it. The doctrine of a change of *substance* in created powers, to be applied as a divine and sanctifying nourishment of the spirit, most clearly established the opposition of Christianity to the fundamental tenet of these sects, which took so much pleasure in the world as to confound it with the divinity; failing to observe that, through the creative energy of the Redeemer, only could a new world be called into existence, and that, consequently, it was impossible for him to be engendered by the world. Moreover, out of the general movement of the age sprang a peculiar form of the most solemn adoration of the Eucharist (*festum corporis Christi*) so that it should be no longer possible to confound the internal acts of the human mind with the historical Christ; for, by the very nature of the festival, Christ was represented as *extraneous* to man, and neither as one in himself with us, nor as evolved out of us, but as coming to us only from without.[1] In the doctrine of tran-

[1] That it was not in the Middle Age, as a frivolous ignorance has often asserted, that the adoration of the Eucharist first arose, numberless authorities can prove. For example, to pass over the testimonies of the much more ancient Origen, we read in the Liturgy of St Chrysostom (Goar's Eucholog. p. 81), at the elevation of the Host, the following words: εἶτα προσκυνεῖ ὁ ἱερεὺς, καὶ ὁ διάκανος, ἐν ᾧ ἐστιν τόπῳ· λέγοντες μυστικῶς τρίς· ὁ θεὸς ἱλάσθητί μοι τῷ ἁμαρτωλῷ. Καὶ ὁ λάος ὁμοίως πάντες μετ' εὐλαβείας προσκυνοῦσιν.

TRANSLATION

'Then the priest and the deacon worship, each in the place where he stands, saying in secret three times: "O God! be propitious to me a sinner." And the people in like manner all worship with reverence.'

substantiation, Christianity with its entire essence exhibits itself as an external, immediate divine revelation. At the period of the Reformation, therefore, it was the more necessary to bring out this doctrine, and the ecclesiastical rites connected with it, in the most prominent form, as an empty, erroneous spiritualism was everywhere manifesting itself.

Lastly, in the Catholic Church the custom prevails of receiving communion only under one kind :—a matter, as is evident, belonging to discipline, and not to doctrine.[1] It is well-known that this custom was not first established by any ecclesiastical law : but, on the contrary, it was in consequence of the general prevalence of the usage, that this law was passed in approval of it. It is a matter of no less notoriety, that the monasteries in whose centre this rite had its rise, and thence spread in ever wider circles, were led by a very nice sense of delicacy to impose on themselves this privation. A pious dread of desecrating, by spilling and the like, even in the most conscientious ministration, the form of the sublimest and the holiest, whereof the participattion can be vouchsafed to man, was the feeling which swayed their minds. Some may hold this opinion for superstitious ; and, according as they see in the consecrated elements but mere material species, the more easily will such an opinion occur to their minds. But the Catholic who, even in this formality, proves that it is not with him a mere matter of form when he abstains from the consecrated chalice, and who, taught by examples in Scripture, or, at any rate, by the authority of the primitive Church, thinks himself justified in so abstaining, without becoming alienated from the spirit of Jesus Christ, or losing any portion of his Eucharistic blessings :—the Catholic, we say, rejoices that though in his Church there may be men of a perhaps exaggerated scrupulosity, yet none are found so carnal-minded as to desire to drink in the communion not the holy blood but the mere wine, and often, on that account, protest, among other things, against what they call a mutilation of the ordinance of Christ. We regret the more to be obliged to call the attention of our separated brethren to this abuse in their Church, as we must add, that the number of those in their communion is not less considerable, who forego the partaking of the sacred blood, not from any spiritual dread of desecrating it by spilling, but from a mere sensual feeling of disgust at the

[1] Concil. Trident. sess. xxi. can. i-iv, sess. xxii, Decret. sup. concess. calicis.

uncleanliness of those with whom they are to drink out of the same cup. When even the Zwinglians complain of this mutilation—they who have taken away the body with the blood of Christ, and left in the room of them mere bread and mere wine —it is difficult not to think of that passage in Holy Writ, wherein the Redeemer reproaches the Pharisees, that they strain at gnats, but swallow camels. However, we should rejoice, if it were left free to each one to drink or not of the consecrated chalice: and this permission would be granted, if with the same love and concord an universal desire were expressed for the use of the cup as, from the twelfth century, the contrary wish has been enounced.

§ XXXV—DOCTRINE OF THE LUTHERANS, ZWINGLIANS, AND CALVINISTS, ON THE EUCHARIST

The Reformation had run its course but for a few years, when there arose among its partisans, in relation to the holy Eucharist, very important points of difference. Luther taught a real and substantial presence of the body and blood of Christ in the holy communion, without, however, adhering to the doctrine of transubstantiation, which he rejected, not on exegetical grounds, but on account of an expression accidentally thrown out by Pierre d'Ailly.[1] But we have already observed that Carlstadt, a colleague of Luther's in Wittenberg, drew from those very opinions which Luther and Melancthon had put forth, upon the nature of the sacraments, conclusions which, according to the principles of those Reformers, could not be easily invalidated. The exegetic proofs, on the other hand, which Carlstadt adduced in support of his views, were most feeble, nay, perfectly contemptible: but what he was unable to accomplish, Zwingle and Œcolompadius, who hastened to his assistance attempted with

[1] Even the tenth article of the Augsburg Confession teaches: 'De cœna Domini docent, quod corpus et sanguis Christi vere adsint et distribuantur vescentibus in cœna Domini, et improbant secus docentes.' The words 'sub specie panis et vini,' were originally inserted, but, as early as the year 1531, Melancthon suppressed them. See Salig's complete history of the Augsburg Confession (in German), vol. iii, c. l, p. 171. In the copy of the Confession presented to the Emperor Charles V, in the year 1530, the tenth article ran thus: 'Touching the Lord's Supper, it is taught, that the true body and blood of Christ are, under the form of bread and wine, truly present, given, distributed, and taken in the Eucharist. On which account the contrary doctrine is rejected.'

much dexterity to effect. If the first Swiss Reformers in more than one respect evinced a shallowness without example, this was here more pre-eminently the case. They saw in the holy Eucharist a mere remembrance of Christ, of his sufferings and his death; at least, whatever traces of a deeper signification they might yet find in this mystery, were so feeble as to be rarely discerned by anyone.[1] Moreover, Zwingle and Œcolompadius variously interpreted the well-known classical passage in Matthew, though they agreed in the result. The former maintained that ἐστί (is) was the same as 'signifies': the latter took ἐστί in its proper sense, but, asserted that σῶμα (body) was put metaphorically for 'sign of my body.' Luther had then indeed already rejected the doctrine of transubstantiation; but he still continued, with his accustomed coarseness and violence, yet with great acuteness and most brilliant success, to defend against Zuinglius the real presence of Christ in the Eucharist. For, whenever the doctrinal truth is in any degree on his side, he is always an incomparable disputant: and what he put forth on this subject in his controversial writings is still well deserving of attention.

Between the Saxon and the Helvetic opinions, Capito and the pliant Bucer attempted to steer an untenable middle course, without being able to reduce their ideas to clear, simple forms of expression.[2] More successful was Calvin in holding such a middle course; and his acuteness would not have failed finding

---

[1] Huldrichi Zuinglii Op. t. ii. In the essay (Illustrissimis Germaniæ Princip. in Conciliis Aug. Congreg. p. 546, b), he gives an explanation not unworthy a Rationalist of our time, how it came to pass that Christians said, Christ is present in the Eucharist: 'Quo factum est, ut veteres dixerint corpus Christi vere esse in cœna; id autem duplici nomine, cum propter istam, quæ jam dicta est, certam fidei contemplationem, quæ Christum ipsum in cruce propter nos deficientem nihil minus præsentem videt, quam Stephanus carnalibus oculis ad dexteram Patris regnantem videret. Et adseverare audeo, hanc Stephano revelationem et exhibitionem sensibiliter esse factam, ut nobis exemplo esset, fidelibus, cum pro se paterentur eo semper modo fore, non sensibiliter, sed contemplatione et solatio fidei.' P. 549: Cum paterfamilias peregre profecturus nobilissimum annulum suum, in quo imago sua expressa est, conjugi matrifamiliæ his verbis tradit: En me tibi maritum, quem absentem teneas, et quo te oblectes. Jam ille paterfamilias Domini nostri Jesu Christi typum gerit. Is enim abiens ecclesiæ conjugi suæ imaginem suam in cœnæ sacramento reliquit.'

[2] Confess. Tetrapolitan. c. xviii. p. 352. 'Singulari studio hanc Christi in suos bonitatem semper deprædicant, qua is non minus hodie, quam in novissima illa cœna, omnibus qui inter illius discipulos ex animo nomen dederunt, cum hanc cœnam, ut ipse instituit, repetunt, verum suum corpus verumque suum sanguinem vere edendum et bibendum, in cibum potumque animarum, quo illæ in æternam vitam alantur, dare per sacramenta

the most fitting expression for his ideas, had he not purposely preferred a certain obscurity. He taught that the body of Christ is truly present in the Lord's Supper, and that the believer partook of it. But he only meant that, simultaneously with the bodily participation of the material elements, which in every respect remained what they were, and merely signified the body and blood of Christ, a power, emanating from the body of Christ, which is now in heaven only, is communicated to the spirit.[1] He had the pleasure of seeing his opinion adopted in the 'Agreement of Zurich' by the Swiss Reformed; and the later Calvinistic formularies of faith in like manner all adhere to it.[2]

We must, however, examine this subject more nearly. The dignatur, ut jam ipse in illis, et illi in ipso vivant et permaneant, in die novissima in novam et immortalem vitam per ipsum resuscitandi,' etc. But as even Zuinglius made use of the expression, ' Christ is truly present in the Lord's supper,' and the cities of Upper Germany were in close connection with him, no one confided in this declaration of the formulary. Compare Salig's complete history of the Augsburg Confession (in German), vol. ii, c. 12, p. 400 : ' The praise,' says he, ' cannot be refused to the Confession of the four cities, that on many points it has a good and Christian bearing ; but in the article of the Lord's supper, it was very ambiguously worded, so that it might be interpreted in favour of Zwingle's, as well as of Luther's doctrine. . . . Hence must the aforesaid article of this Confession be understood and explained from the previously cited correspondence between Bucer and Melancthon.'

[1] Calvin. Instit. lib. iv, c. 17, fol. 502; Consens. Tig. Calvin. opp. tom. viii, p. 648.

[2] Confess. Helvet. II, art. xx, xxii, p. 99, et seq. ' Cœnam vero mysticam,' it is said (art. xxii), ' suis vere ad hoc offert, ut magis magisque in illis vivat, et illi in ipso : non quod pani et vino corpus Domini et sanguis vel naturaliter uniantur, sed quod panis et vinum ex institutione Domini symbola sunt, quibus ab ipso Domino, per ecclesiæ ministerium, vera corporis et sauguinis ejus communicatio, non in periturum ventris cibum, sed in æternæ vitæ alimoniam, enhibeatur. Hoc sacro cibo ideo sæpe utimur, quoniam hujus monitu in crucifixi mortem sanguinemque fidei oculis intuentes ac, salutem nostram non sine cœlestis vitæ gustu et vero vitæ æternæ sensu meditantes, hoc spirituali, vivifico intimoque pabulo ineffabili cum suavitate reficimur, ac inenarrabili verbi lætitia propter inventam vitam exultamus, totique ac viribus omnino nostris omnibus in gratiarum actionem, tam pro admirando Christi erga nos beneficio effundimur,' etc. This form belongs properly to the category of the Tetrapolitana. Confess. Gall. art. xxxvi, p. 123 : ' Affirmamus sanctam cœnam Domini, alterum videlicet sacramentum, esse nobis testimonium nostræ cum Domino nostro Jesu Christo unitionis, quóniam non est duntaxat mortuus semel et excitatus a mortuis pro nobis, sed etiam vere nos pascit et nutrit carne sua et sanguine, ut, unum cum ipso facti, vitam cum ipso communem habeamus. Quamvis enim nunc sit in cœlis, ibidem etiam mansurus, donec veniat mundum judicaturus ; credimus tamen eumarcan a et incomprehensibili spiritus sui virtute nos nutrire et vivificare sui corporis et sanguinis substantia per fidem apprehensa. Dicimus autem hoc spiritualiter fieri, non ut efficaciæ et vertitatis loco imaginationem aut

disputes prevailing between the Wittenberg and Helvetic Reformers could, for many reasons, be viewed only with the greatest pain by the advocates and friends of the ecclesiastical revolution. Independently of the fact, that, from the existence of such disputes, the Catholics did not unsuccessfully draw conclusions against important principles of the Reformers, these controversies prevented the union of all the Protestant Churches in one common struggle against their adversaries—a struggle which threatened ever more and more to terminate in a bloody civil war; and of what importance in the latter case must not concord prove! Most critical was the situation of the Sacramentarians—such was the name given by Luther to the disciples of Zwingle, Carlstadt and others; for their party was confined to only four cities within the whole compass of the German empire; and therefore, abandoned to themselves alone, they could make no vigorous resistance. Hence, at the celebrated diet of Augsburg, in the year 1530, they exerted every imaginable effort, and, under the guidance of Bucer, employed every subterfuge of equivocation, in order to be received into the association of the German Protestants. But all their endeavours failed, especially through the German honesty of Luther, who expressed himself in the harshest strain against their evasions. Even in the religious peace of Nuremberg, it was only to the adherents of the Augsburg Confession that final quiet was granted.

If the middle opinion respecting the Eucharist, framed under these circumstances, was originally far more the result of political embarrassment, than the fruit of a sincere conviction obtained by earnest investigation; it now began to make its way, and include an ever greater number of Lutherans among its supporters. Even Melancthon, who was not entirely a stranger to it, had the complaisance to make in the later editions of the Augsburg Confession (that appeared subsequent to the year 1540), some important changes in its favour; just as if his having composed this public formulary of faith gave him the

cogitationem supponamus, sed potius, quoniam hoc mysterium nostræ cum Christo coalitionis tam sublime est, ut omnes nostros sensus totumque adeo ordinem naturæ superet: denique quoniam cum sit divinum ac cœleste, non nisi fide percipi et apprehendi potest.' Confess. Anglic. art. xxxviii, p. 137: 'Cœna domini non est tantum signum mutuæ benevolentiæ Christianorum inter sese, verum potius est sacramentum nostræ per mortem Christi redemptionis. Atque adeo rite, digne, et cum fide sumentibus panis, quem frangimus, est communicatio corporis Christi: similiter poculum benedictionis est communicatio sanguinis Christi.'

right to dispose of it according to his good pleasure![1] As the advocates of this new opinion employed without hestitation the expression, that Christ is really present in the Eucharist, and his body and blood given to believers for participation, and as the altered edition of the Augsburg Confession favoured a certain indefiniteness of meaning, it was unhesitatingly asserted, after Luther's death, that the opinion of the innovators was, even according to the principles of the Saxon Reformation, perfectly orthodox. If John à Lasko, who was so ill treated by the English, Danish, and German Protestants, deserves to be forgiven for having, contrary to all the laws of historical interpretation, affixed his own meaning to the original formulary delivered to the emperor, because, by this expedient, he thought to ensure his temporal safety; the two-faced conduct of Melancthon, on the other hand, will remain an eternal stigma on his memory; and all the apologies attempted in his behalf can proceed on no other principle, than that his pretended good intention sanctified the means employed. With the most touching confidence did the remotest communities apply to him, to learn with certainty from his own lips the true Lutheran doctrine; and yet he could bring himself to meet that confidence with crafty and evasive replies, that were perfectly inconsistent one with the other. A few months only before his death, when he had nothing more to fear for his own personal safety, he declared himself decidedly for Calvin's view. This hypocrisy of Melancthon was imitated by his disciples, the professors of theology in Wittenberg, as well as by many others; and we might call the fate which, on discovery of their undoubtedly shameful deception they met with at the hands of the elector of Saxony, a merited chastisement, had it not been in some respects too severe.

It was now the object of the Lutherans not only to assert against the Crypto-Calvinists the original doctrine of their Church, but to express it in the most definite forms. This occurred in the following manner: Calvin having spoken indeed

[1] The following is the difference between the unchanged and the changed Augsburg Confession; but what we shall have occasion to relate subsequently will best illustrate this difference. The unchanged edition: 'De cœna Domini docent, quod corpus et sanguis Christi *vere adsint et distribuantur* vescentibus in cœna Domini, *et improbant secus docentes.*' It is to be observed, that even here the ' sub specie panis et vini ' is already wanting, but which, as Salig says, was no change in *realibus*. (Vol. iii, c. i, p. 477.) The changed edition: ' De cœna Domini docent, quod *cum* pane et vino vere *exhibeantur* corpus et sanguis Christi, vescentibus in cœna Domini.'

of a true partaking of the body of Christ, but acknowledging only a certain spiritual reception of it, which, at the same moment when the bread is taken in by the mouth, is by means of faith enjoyed by the soul, and having accordingly, connected only by time the spiritual food with the participation of the material elements, the orthodox Lutherans decreed in the 'Formulary of Concord,' that the body of Christ is administered *in*, *with*, and *under* the bread. Further, it is well known that, according to Calvin's theory, it is only the justified who are in communion of life and faith with Christ—in other words, the elect only that can receive the body of the Lord, while the unbeliever receives only bread and wine. Against this theory the 'Formulary of Concord' teaches, that the unworthy communicant also receives the body of the Lord, yet to his own judgment. Lastly, an argument was answered which the Calvinists had constantly alleged as one in itself of great weight. Against the bodily presence of Christ in the sacrament of the altar, they observed that the doctrine which inculcated that, from the moment of his ascension up to heaven, Christ sat at right hand of God, was incompatible with the one, according to which he was at the same time present on earth in the Eucharist. In conformity with this Beza, at the religious colloquy of Poissy, which the Lutheran theologians, in the course of their disputes on the sacrament, often adverted to, had declared that Christ was as far removed from the Eucharist as heaven from earth. In answer to this objection, Luther and his disciples had long asserted that Christ, even according to his humanity, was everywhere present (*ubiquitas corporis Christi*). This strange opinion, which the inhabitants of Wurtemberg in defiance of those of the Palatinate, had, at the instigation of the Reformer Brentius, already admitted into their confession of faith, was now consecrated by the 'Formulary of Concord' and raised to a formal article of faith. The objection of the Calvinists was met by observing that, in reverence to God, there could be no question of a right or left side, since He was everywhere present: and that, in the same way, Christ, even according to his humanity, was in every place. With this was closely connected the much-handled doctrine of the *communicatio idiomatum*, which had long been a subject of strife: for the Calvinists brought the charge of Monophysitism against the Lutherans, and were by the latter in turn accused by the heresy of Nestorius.[1]

[1] Solid. Declar. pp. 659, 691, 724.

CHAPTER V

DIFFERENCES IN RESPECT TO THE DOCTRINE ON THE CHURCH

§ XXXVI—NOTION OF THE CHURCH—COMBINATION OF DIVINE AND HUMAN ELEMENTS IN HER—INFALLIBILITY OF THE CHURCH

It has, undoubtedly, excited surprise, and it has even been made a matter of reproach against us by well-meaning readers, that we have not, prior to all the subjects here discussed, treated of the article of Church authority. For it appears a matter of self-evidence, that any discussion respecting the doctrines of a confession, should be postponed to the inquiry into the authority which that confession follows, and into the sources from which it derives its tenets. In fact, this *appears* indeed to be self-evident, if we merely look at the matter from without; and such an appearance has misled many. But, as we have made it our duty everywhere to trace the inward bond of connection pervading all the details of the subject treated by us, and forming them into one living connected whole, we saw ourselves compelled to accord the precedence to the matter giving light before that which receives it, and to the inwardly determining principle before that which is determined; and precisely for this reason we here insert the article on the Church, and the authoritative sources of the different confessions. History teaches us, that out of the pale of the Church, from the earliest Egyptian Gnostic, down to the two general superintendents of Weimar and Gotha,[1] Messrs Röhr and Bret-

---

[1] See Röhr, Letters on Rationalism, p. 15. The writer, after asserting that in matters of faith and in the adoption of religious doctrines, reason alone decides, goes on to say, ' The Bible is, in his estimation, nothing more than any other book. He holds its declarations to be valid only when they are in accordance with his own convictions; and these declarations do not constitute the ground of determination (for these depend on their own rational proofs), but serve merely as an illustration, that others also, wise men of antiquity, have so thought and believed.'

schneider,[1] Holy Writ never enjoyed the anthority, which it must lay claim to among Christians, of determining by its purport their mode of thinking. On the contrary, it was always preconceived opinions—opinions derived from sources extraneous to Christianity—that were made the standard for estimating the authority of Scripture, the extent of that authority, and the mode of its use, although this might not always be so openly and candidly confessed, as in the case of the two above-mentioned rationalists. Several of the smaller religious sects—the Anabaptists, the Quakers, the Swedenborgians, and others—are in modern times irrefragable vouchers for the truth of what is here asserted. As regards Luther, he by no means first abandoned the faith in the Catholic doctrine of the Church, and of the relation of the same to Holy Writ, and then changed what he found reprehensible in the dogmas of the Church. Still less did he make use of the principles, according to which he formed his theory of the Church, to deduce from them his other doctrines. On the contrary, the very reverse took place *in both respects*. In regard to the first assertion, it is well known that the earliest attacks of Luther were by no means directed against the principle of the Catholic Church and her authority; nay, he declared himself at the outset ready to submit his peculiar doctrines to the judgment of the Church, and he had to endure a grievous struggle with his conscience, whereof he himself has given us a most interesting description, until he at length obtained a melancholy victory, and until the troubled spirit departed from him. Had the Catholic Church agreed to recognise his doctrine, he in his turn would ever have acknowledged her authority. And assuredly, as far as he was concerned, he would have found no difficulty in uniting two things so contradictory, as *his dogma* and *the Catholic Church*; and, as he had

---

[1] See Bretschneider's 'St Simonianism and Christianity, or Critical Exposition of the St Simonian religion, its relation to the Christian Church, and of the state of Christianity in our times.' Leipzig, 1832. As the result of the progress of intelligence in theological matters, in modern times, we are told by this author, ' Not only is the interpretation of Scripture to be abandoned to science, but even the contents of Scripture discovered by such interpretation are to be estimated according to the sciences.' This assertion, more closely analysed, would signify that the sum total of all the truths, which the sciences in general, metaphysical as well as empirical, had brought forth, or might yet bring forth, as common property, are the standard for estimating the contents of the Bible. What then is the Deity in the opinion of Mr Bretschneider? And what will he be yet?

often succeeded in coupling, as a peaceful pair, two things inwardly opposed to each other, so he would have made the attempt here. But, with sound perception, the organs of the Church observed, that deleterious matter was infused by him into ecclesiastical life. Summoned now, either to renounce as erroneous his peculiar doctrine of Justification, together with the propositions determining the same or determined by it, or no longer to flatter himself with the title of a son of the Church, he felt necessitated, as he was the parent of a new doctrine, to become the father of a new Church. Hence, it appeared to him more honourable to execute what *his own* spirit had suggested rather to command as a father, than to obey as a son. He now laid the foundations for another Church, to be erected *by himself;*—whether on a rock, or in the sand, the sequel will show.

Yet that Luther had formed a peculiar theory of Justification, before he entertained the clear idea of founding a new Church, is only a subordinate motive for our setting forth the exposition of doctrine, before the explanation of the article on the Church. For it not rarely happens, that what is merely an effect, is already clearly recognised, while its cause, though long busy in the background of human consciousness, exhibits itself only later in its full light, and with entire clearness. Accordingly, it is perhaps possible, that Luther's other tenets may stand in a relation of internal independence on his view of the Church, although he may have been clearly conscious of his doctrine of Justification by faith alone, prior to his doctrine on the Church, and consequently may have given utterance to the former tenet, previously to the latter. The principal point is, consequently, which of the two furnishes a scientific explanation of the other? We must thus adhere to the latter of the two above-stated propositions. In the course of our inquiries it will be made manifest, that Luther's as well as Calvin's and Zwingle's general moral views, especially their conception of the relation of the believer to Christ, entirely pervade their theory of the Church and of Scripture, and constitute the foundation of the same. As, moreover, we consider the Catholic doctrines only in their opposition to the peculiar tenets of Protestantism, and the latter must accordingly determine what Catholic doctrines are to be here discussed, so they must also regulate the *mode* of the discussion. As thus the Catholic doctrines are in a purely passive relation, and the Protestant, if we are to pursue a scientific course, assign *the present place* to the article on the Church; so our method, quite independently of the reasons assigned in the first section, is in every way justified.

By the Church on earth, Catholics understand the visible community of believers, founded by Christ, in which, by means of an enduring apostleship, established by him, and appointed to conduct all nations, in the course of ages, back to God, the works wrought by him during his earthly life, for the redemption and sanctification of mankind, are, under the guidance of his spirit, continued to the end of the world.

Thus, to *a visible society of men*, is this great, important, and mysterious work entrusted. The ultimate reason of the visibility of the Church is to be found in the *incarnation* of the Divine Word. Had that Word descended into the hearts of men, without taking the form of a servant, and accordingly without appearing in a corporeal shape, then only an internal, invisible Church would have been established. But since the Word became *flesh*, it expressed itself in an outward, perceptible, and human manner; it spoke as man to man, and suffered, and worked after the fashion of men, in order to win them to the kingdom of God; so that the means selected for the attainment of this object, fully corresponded to the general method of instruction and education determined by the nature and the wants of man. This decided the nature of those means, whereby the Son of God, even after He had withdrawn himself from the eyes of the world, wished still to work in the world, and for the world. The Deity having manifested its action in Christ according to an *ordinary human fashion*, the form also in which His work was to be continued, was thereby traced out. The preaching of his doctrine needed now a *visible, human* medium, and must be entrusted to visible envoys, teaching and instructing after the wonted method; men must speak to men, and hold intercourse with them, in order to convey to them the word of God. And as in the world nothing can attain to greatness but in society; so Christ established a community; and his divine word, his living will, and the love emanating from him exerted an internal, binding power upon his followers; so that an inclination implanted by him in the hearts of believers, corresponded to his outward institution. And thus a living, well-connected, visible association of the faithful sprang up, whereof it might be said—there they are, there is his Church, his institution wherein he continueth to live, his spirit continueth to work, and the word uttered by him eternally resounds. Thus, the visible Church, from the point of view here taken, is the Son of God himself, everlastingly manifesting himself among men in a human form, perpetually renovated, and eternally young—the permanent incarnation of the same, as in Holy Writ, even the faithful are called 'the body of Christ.' Hence it is evident that the Church, though composed of men, is yet not purely human. Nay, as in Christ the divinity and the humanity are to be clearly distinguished, though both are bound in unity; so is he in undivided entireness perpetuated in the Church. The Church, his permanent manifestation, is at once divine and human— she is the union of both. He it is who, concealed under earthly and human forms, works in the Church; and this is wherefore she has a divine and a human part in an undivided mode, so that the divine cannot be separated from the human, nor the human from the divine. Hence these two parts change their predicates. If the divine—the living Christ and his spirit— constitute undoubtedly that which is infallible, and eternally inerrable in the Church; so also the human is infallible and inerrable in the same way, because, the divine without the human has no existence for us; yet the human is not inerrable in itself, but only as the organ and as the manifestation of the divine. Hence, we are enabled to conceive, *how* so great, important and mysterious a charge *could* have been entrusted to men.

In and through the Church the redemption, announced by Christ, hath obtained, through the medium of his spirit, a reality; for in her his truths are believed and his institutions are observed, and thereby have become living. Accordingly, we can say of the Church, that she is the Christian religion in its objective form—its living exposition. Since the word of Christ (taken in its widest signification) found, together with his spirit, its way into a circle of men, and was received by them, it has taken shape, put on flesh and blood; and this shape is the Church, which accordingly is regarded by Catholics as the essential form of the Christian Religion itself. As the Redeemer by his word and his spirit founded a community, wherein his word should ever be living, he entrusted the same to this society, that it might be preserved and propagated. He deposited it in the Church, that it might spring out of her ever the same, and yet eternally new, and young in energy; that it might grow up and spread on all sides. His word can never more be separated from the Church, nor the Church from his word. The more minute explanation, how in the community established by Christ this word is maintained and propagated, and each individual Christian can attain to the undoubted true possession of Christian doctrine, is accordingly the first and most important matter, to which we must direct attention. But as the Church is connected with the apostleship established by Christ, and can by this only maintain itself; so this, in the second place, must come under consideration. But it is necessary to premise a closer examination of the leading propositions, on which all others turn—a more detailed exposition of the ultimate reasons for that high reverence which Catholics pay to this Church.

§ XXXVII—MORE DETAILED EXPOSITION OF THE CATHOLIC VIEW OF THE CHURCH

When the time appointed by Christ for the sending down of the spirit was come, he communicated himself to the apostles and the other disciples, when gathered together in one place, and all of 'one accord' (ὁμοθυμαδόν), they were longing for his coming. It was not while one here, the other there, abode in some hidden place: nay, they were expressly commanded (Acts i. 4) to wait for him, while assembled in Jerusalem. At last the Holy Spirit, that had been promised, *appeared:* he took an outward shape—the form of fiery tongues—an image of his power that cleansed hearts from all wickedness, and thereby united them in love. He wished not to come inwardly, as if he designed to uphold an invisible community; but in the same way as the Word was become *flesh,* so he came in a manner obvious to the senses, and amid violent sensible commotions, like to 'a rushing mighty wind.' If individuals were filled with power from above in such a way, that, only in as far as they constituted an *unity,* could they become participators of the same; and if the hallowing of the spirit took place under sensible forms; so, according to the ordinance of the Lord for all times, the union of the interior man with Christ could take effect only under outward conditions, and in communion with his disciples. *Under outward conditions:* for independently of outward instruction, what are the sacraments but visible signs and testimonies of the invisible gifts connected with them? *In communion:* for no one by the act of baptism sanctifies himself; each one is, on the contrary, referred to those who already belong to the community. Nor is anyone but momentarily introduced into fellowship with the members of the Church—to remain only until, as one might imagine, the holy action should be consummated ; for the fellowship is formed in order to be permanent, and the communion begun, in order to be continued to the end of life. Baptism is the *introduction* into the Church—the reception into the community of the faithful, and involves the duty, as well as the right, of sharing for ever in her joys and her sorrows. Moreover, the administration of the sacraments, as well as the preaching of the word, was intrusted by the Lord to the apostolic college and to those commissioned by it ; so that all believers, by means of this Apostolic College are linked to the community, and in a living manner connected with it. The fellowship with Christ is accordingly the fellowship with his community—the internal union with him a communion with his Church. Both are inseparable, and Christ is in the Church, and the Church in him. (Eph. v, 29-33.)

On this account, the Church, in the Catholic point of view, can as little fail in the pure preservation of the word, as in any other part of her task :—she is infallible. As the individual worshipper of Christ is incorporated into the Church by indissoluble bonds, and is by the same conducted unto the Saviour, and abideth in him only in so far as he abideth in the Church, his faith and his conduct are determined by the latter. He must bestow his whole confidence upon her ; and she must therefore merit the same. Giving himself up to her guidance, he ought in consequence to be secured against delusion : she *must* be inerrable. To no individual, considered as such, doth infallibility belong ; for the Catholic, as is clear from the preceding observations, regards the individual only as a member of the whole ; as living and breathing in the Church. When his feelings, thoughts, and will are conformable to her spirit, then only can the individual attain to inerrability. Were the Church to conceive the relation of the individual to the whole in an opposite sense, and consider him as personally infallible, then she would destroy the very notion of community ; for communion can only be conceived as necessary, when the true faith and pure and solid Christian life cannot be conceived in individualisation.

Hence, it is with the profoundest love, reverence, and devotion, the Catholic embraces the Church. The very thought of resisting her, of setting himself up in opposition to her will, is one against which his inmost feelings revolt, to which his whole nature is abhorrent : and to bring about a schism—to destroy unity—is a crime, before whose heinousness his bosom trembles, and from which his soul recoils. On the other hand, the idea of community, in the first place, satisfies his feelings and his imagination, and in the second place, is equally agreeable to his reason ; while, in the third place, the living appropriation of this idea by his will appears to him to concur with the highest religious and ethical duty of humanity. Let us now consider the first of these reasons. No more beautiful object presents itself to the imagination of the Catholic—none more agreeably captivates his feelings, than the image of the harmonious inter-workings of countless spirits, who, though scattered over the whole globe endowed with freedom and possessing the power to strike off into every deviation to the right or to the left ; yet, preserving still their various peculiarities, constitute one great brotherhood for the advancement of each other's spiritual existence—representing one idea, that of the reconciliation of men with God, who on that account have been reconciled with one another, and are become one body. (Eph. iv, 11-166.) If the state be such a wonderful work of art, that we account it, if not a pardonable, yet a conceivable act, for the ancients to have made it an object of divine worship, and almost everywhere considered the duties of the citizen as the most important—if the state be something so sacred and venerable, that the thought of the criminal, who lays on it a destroying and desecrating hand, fills us with detestation —what an object of admiration must the Church be, which, with the tenderest bonds, unites such an infinite variety of subjects ; and this unimpeded by every obstacle, by rivers and mountains, deserts and seas, by languages, national manners, customs, and peculiarities of every kind, whose stubborn, unyielding nature defies the power of the mightiest conquerors ? Her peace, which cometh down from Heaven, strikes deeper roots, into the human breast, than the spirit of earthly contention. Out of all nations, often so deeply divided by political interests and temporal considerations, the Church builds up the house of God, in which all join in one hymn of praise ; as, in the temple of the harmless village, all petty foes and adversaries gather round the one sanctuary with one mind. And as often here, on a small scale, the peace of God, will bring about earthly peace, so there, on a larger scale, the same result will frequently ensue. But who can deem it a matter of astonishment, that Catholics should be filled with joy and hope, and enraptured at the view of the beautiful construction of their Church, should contemplate with delight, that grand corporation which they form, since the philosophers of art declare, that the beautiful is only *truth manifested and embodied !* Christ, the eternal truth, hath built the Church: in the communion of the faithful, truth transformed by his spirit into love, is become living among men : how could then the Church fail in the highest degree of beauty ? Hence we can comprehend that indescribable joy, which hath ever filled the Church, when existing contests have been allayed, and schisms have been terminated. In the primitive ages, we may adduce the reunion of the Novatian communities with the Catholic Church, so movingly described by Dionysius of Alexandria and Cyprian of Carthage ; the termination of the Meletian schism, and the rest. From a later period we may cite the event of the reunion of the Western and Eastern Churches which occurred at the Council of Florence. Pope Eugenius IV expresses the feelings which then overflowed all hearts, when he says, ' Rejoice, ye heavens, and exult, O earth : the wall of separation is pulled down, which divided the Eastern and the Western Churches ; peace and concord have returned ; for Christ, the corner-stone, who out of two, hath made one, unites with the strongest bands of love both walls and holds them together in the covenant of eternal unity : and so, after long and melancholy evils, after the dense, cloudy darkness of a protracted schism, the light of long-desired union beams once more upon all. Let our mother, the Church, rejoice, to whom it hath been granted to see her hitherto contending sons return to unity and peace : let her, who, during their division shed such bitter tears, now thank Almighty God for their beautiful concord. All believers over the face of the earth, all who are called after Christ, may now congratulate their mother, the Catholic Church, and rejoice with her, etc.' [1]

II. Yet it is not merely the imagination and the feelings of the Catholic which are contented by this idea of the Church but his reason also is thereby satisfied—and, indeed because the

---

[1] Hard. Acta Concil. tom. ix, fol. 985. Eugenius spoke in the same strain, when he informed the Christian princes and universities of the reconciliation in question : fol. 1000. At the same time, the Armenians and Jacobins, as the documents style them, meaning the Jacobites and Copts, renounced their errors and united with the Latins : fol. 1015-1025.

idea which he has conceived of the Church, alone corresponds to the notion of the Christian Church, and to the end of revelation. It corresponds, in the first place to the notion of the Christian Church, as is clear from what follows. Truth we cannot conceive other than as one, and the same holds good of Christian truth. The Son of God, our Redeemer, is a distinct being: he is what he is, and none other, eternally like unto himself, constantly one and the same. Not in vain do the Holy Scriptures connect all with *His Person:* the more they do this, the more important is it to conceive him exactly as he really was. Certain it is that every error, in relation to his person, exercises a more or less injurious influence on the piety and virtue of its professors; whereas a right knowledge of his person forms the surest and most solid basis of a holy and happy life. In like manner will the pure appropriation of *his work*, by, and in our souls, produce the richest, most substantial, and fairest fruits; while any falsification of that work, in any one respect, is sure to be attended with injurious consequences to practical life. As Christ, therefore, is one, and his work is one in itself, as accordingly there is but one truth, and truth only maketh free, so he can have willed but one Church; for the Church rests on the basis of belief in him, and hath eternally to announce him and his work. On the other hand, the human mind is everywhere the same, and always, and in all places, is created for truth and the one truth. Its essential spiritual wants, amid all the changing relations of time and place, amid all the distinctions of culture and education, remain eternally the same: we are all sinners, and stand in need of grace; and the faith which one has embraced in the filial simplicity of his heart, another cannot outgrow, though he be gifted with the subtlest intellect, and possess all the accumulated wisdom which the genius of man, in every zone, and in every period of his history, may have produced. Thus the oneness of the human spirit, as well as the oneness of truth, which is the food of spirits, justifies, in the views of the reflecting Catholic, *the notion* of the one visible Church.

But secondly, the end of revelation requires a Church, as the Catholic conceives it; that is, a Church one, and necessarily visible. The manifestation of the eternal Word in the flesh, had the acknowledged end to enable man, (who by his own resources was capable neither of obtaining, with full assurance, a true knowledge of God and of his own nature, nor of mastering that knowledge even with the aid of old surviving traditions), to enable man, we say, to penetrate with undoubting certainty into religious truths. For those truths, as we stated above, will then only give a vigorous and lasting impulse to the will in an upward direction, when they have first taken strong hold of the reason, whence they can exert their effects. The words of Archimedes, δός μοί ποῦ στῶ, are here applicable, and in an especial degree. The divine truth, in one word, must be embodied in Christ Jesus, and thereby be bodied forth in an outward and living phenomenon, and accordingly become a deciding authority, in order to seize deeply on the whole man, and to put an end to pagan scepticism—that sinful uncertainty of the mind, which stands on as low a grade as ignorance.[1]

But this object of the divine revelation in Christ Jesus, would, according to the conviction of Catholics, either have wholly failed, or in any case have been very imperfectly attained, if this bodying forth of the divine truth had been only momentary, and the personal manifestation of the Word had to hand sufficient force to give to its sounds the highest degree of intensive movement, and to impart to them the utmost efficacy, or in other words, to breathe into them the breath of life, and call into existence a society, which, in its turn, should be the living exposition of the truth, and remain unto all times a derivative, but adequate authority; that is, should represent Christ himself.

This sense Catholics give to the words of the Lord, ' As the Father hath sent me, so I send you;' 'whoso heareth me, heareth you;' ' I shall remain with you all days, even to the consummation of the world;' ' I will send the Spirit of truth, who will lead you into all truth.' Man is so much a creature of sense, that the interior world—the world of ideas—must be presented to him in the form of an image, to enable him to obtain a consciousness, or to gain a true and clear apprehension of it, and to hold by it firmly as the truth; and, indeed the image must be *permanent*, that, being present to every individual through the whole course of human history, it may constantly renew the prototype. Hence, the authority of the Church is

---

[1] How beautiful are those words in the Preface for the Christmas mass :—
' Vere dignum et justum est, æquum et salutare, nos tibi semper et ubique gratias agere, Domine Sancte, Pater omnipotens, æterne Deus. *Quia per incarnati Verbi mysterium nova mentis nostræ oculis lux tuæ claritatis infulsit ; ut dum visibiliter Deum cognoscimus, per hunc in invisibilium amorem rapiamur,*' etc. etc.

necessary, if Christ is to be a true, determining authority for us. Christ wrought miracles; nay, his whole life was a miracle, not merely to establish the credibility of *his words*, but also *immediately to represent and symbolise* the most exalted truths; to wit, God's omnipotence, wisdom, love, and justice, the immortality of man, and his worth in the eyes of God. If we adopt the idea of an invisible Church, then neither the *incarnation* of the Son of God, nor his *miracles*, nor in general any outward, positive revelation can be conceived; because they comprise *authoritative proofs, outward visible manifestations* of eternal ideas; and accordingly they are by force of an internal necessity there gradually rejected, where it is assumed that Christ has founded a mere invisible Church, since the members of such a Church need only invisible internal proofs to obtain certitude. *On the other hand, the authority of the Church is the medium of all, which in the Christian religion resteth on authority, and is authority, that is to say, the Christian religion itself; so that Christ himself is only in so far an authority, as the Church is an authority.*

We can never arrive at an external authority, like Christ, by *purely spiritual* means. The attempt would involve a contradiction, which could only be disposed of in one or two ways; either we must renounce the idea, that in Christ God manifested himself in history, to the end, that the conduct of mankind might be permanently determined by him, or we must learn the fact through a living, definite, and vouching fact. Thus authority must have authority for its medium. As Christ wished to be the adequate authority for all ages, he created, by virtue of his power, something homogeneous to it, and consequently something *attesting and representing* the same, eternally destined to bring his authority before all generations of men. He established a credible institution, in order to render the true faith in himself perpetually possible. Immediately founded by him, its existence is the *de facto* proof of what he really was; and in the same way as in his life he made, if I may so speak, the higher truths accessible to the senses, so doth his Church; for she hath sprung immediately out of the vivid intuition of these symbolised truths. Thus, as Christ, in his life, represented under a visible typical form the higher order of the world, so the Church doth in like manner; since what he designed in his representation, hath through the Church and in the Church been *realised.* If the Church be not the authority representing Christ, then all again relapses into darkness, uncertainty, doubt, distraction, unbelief, and superstition ; *revelation becomes null and void, fails of its real purpose, and must henceforth be even called in question, and finally denied.*

The truth which the Catholic here expresses, can be, in another way, made evident by occurrences in every-day life, and by great historical facts. The power of society in which man lives, is so great, that it ordinarily stamps its image on him, who comes within its circle. Whether it serve truth, or falsehood ; whether it direct its efforts towards higher objects, or follow ignoble pursuits ; invariably will it be found to fashion the character of its members after its own model. Hence, where scepticism has spread in a community, and has impressed its image on its bosom, it is a work of infinite difficulty for the individual to rise superior to its influence. Faith on the other hand, when man sees it firmly established, like a rock, about him, and the community, which presents a great and lively image of attachment to the Redeemer and of happiness in him—the community, we say, whose imperishable existence is faith in him, and accordingly himself—necessarily seizes and fills up the whole mind of the individual. Accordingly, should the religious man not live in a community, which hath the indestructible consciousness of possessing the truth, and which hath the strongest internal and external grounds for that belief, such an individual would necessarily become a prey to the most distracting doubts, and his faith would either take no root, or soon again wither.

Let us once more recur to the miracles in the history of the Christian religion, but regard the subject from a different point. A certain view of divine things, which has once obtained full consistency among any people, or any number of nations, takes so strong a hold on the individual man, that without some higher extraneous interposition, any *essential* change for the better, that is to say, any transition from falsehood to truth, is utterly impossible. Had Christ not wrought miracles ; had the labours of the apostles not been accompanied with signs ; had the Divine power to work such wonders not been transmitted to their disciples, never would the Gospel have overcome the heathenism of the Greek and Roman world. Error had usurped the rights which belong to truth alone ; and man, who by his very nature is compelled to receive the worship of the social state in which he has been fixed, as the true expression, the faithful image of religious truth, as it is in itself, needed, of course, extraordinary external proofs for the new order of things; and, indeed till such time as this order had been consolidated into a vast social organism. These high attestations, in favour of truth, appear most striking and most frequent in the life of the Redeemer himself; because the yet concentrated power of the old world was first to be burst asunder, and those who were destined to be the first-fruits of the new kingdom of God, were to be torn from its magic circle. In proportion as the boundaries of the Church were extended, and the idea of redemption and the power of the cross were embodied in a more vigorous social form, miracles declined, till at last they had completely fulfilled their destination, and had caused the recognition of the authority that was to supply their place. In this authority, as we said above, they always continue their attestation, because that authority is their own production; and the Church is conscious of owing her very existence to those miracles, and without them cannot at all conceive herself. Hence the fact again, that together with the authority founded by these extraordinary works of God, faith, too, in these works ever simultaneously disappears.

Hence, what a whimsical—we cannot say wonderful—race are the idealists of our time! St Paul, who had such a spiritual but at the same time ecclesiastical conception of all things, instituted so living a relation between his faith and the conviction of the Lord's resurrection, that he expressly declared, 'If Christ be not risen from the dead, then is our faith vain.' And how was it otherwise possible, since in Christianity, which is a divine and positive revelation, the abstract idea and the historical fact—the internal and the external truth are inseparably united? Our idealists and spiritualists have no need of miracles for the confirmation of their faith! *Yes, truly, for that faith is one of their own making, and not the faith in Christ;* and it would be indeed singular if God were to confirm a faith so fabricated by men. No less false and idle is that idealism, which separates the authority of the Church from the authority of Christ. Even in this point of view, the reverence which the Catholic bears for his Church, is fully justified by reason. As from the beginning, the abstract idea and the positive history, doctrine and fact, internal and external truth, inward and outward testimony were organically united; so must religion and Church be conjoined, and this for the reason, *that God became man.* Could Satan succeed in annihilating the Christian Church, then the Christian religion would be at the same time annihilated, and Christ himself would be vanquished by him.

III. The third point in which the Catholic finds his view of the Church so commendable, is the influence which it has exerted on the cultivation and direction of the will, on the religious and moral amelioration of the whole man. We speak here no longer of the influence of a clear and firm belief of the truth on the will—a firmness of belief, which only the recognition of an outward and permanent teaching authority can produce—(of this we have already spoken)—but of a direction given to the will by a living membership with an all-embracing, religious society. An ancient philosopher has, with reason, defined man to be a social animal. However little the peculiarity of man's nature is here defined (for his peculiar kind of sociability is not pointed out), yet a deep trait of what determines the civilisation of man by means of man, is, in this definition, undoubtedly indicated. It is only races which, groaning under the destiny of some heavy curse, have sunk into the savage state, that become from the loss of their civilisation seclusive, and with the most limited foresight fall back on their own resources, feel no want of an intercourse with other nations, or of an exchange of ideas, of which they possess nothing more, or of a communication of the products of their industry and art, that have entirely disappeared. These productions, which are already in themselves symbols of the intellectual character of their authors, flow into foreign countries, dressed, as it were in the mental habits and characteristics of their home. Traces of the spirit of all nations through which these productions pass are impressed upon them in their course; so that they always arrive at the place of their destination with a wealth of a far higher kind, that that which they intrinsically possess. From all these currents of civilisation is the savage withdrawn; for, because he is all-sufficient to himself is he a savage, and because he is a savage, he suffices for himself.[1] When the foreigner (hostis) was synonymous with the enemy; when one's country (Iran) included all that was absolutely good, and abroad (Turan) all that was absolutely evil; when the gods in the east and the west, in the land of the

[1] Persius says, ' With pepper and other productions of the South, science came to the Romans.' A sarcasm undoubtedly, whereby he meant to stigmatise the luxury that was at the same time diffused; *sapientia cum saporis mercibus invecta*. But in this fact lie truths exalted above all satire, although, as in everything great, much that was deplorable, every kind of vice, despotism, etc., were intermingled with this blessing.

Colchians, the Cretans, and the Egyptians, rejoiced in the blood of foreigners; what a gloomy, ferocious existence must have circumscribed nations in this their seclusion and mutual independence! For the divinity of the nation was regaled with such blood, only because the nation itself found therein a horrible gratification, and made its own delight a standard for the joys of its deity. *The maintenance of intercourse and communion with foreigners, and accordingly, the voluntary establishment of relations of dependence on them*, is thus an absolute condition to the general civilisation of man; so that the more this communion and mutual dependence is extended, that is to say the more the notion of what is foreign disappears, the more is humanity exalted. With this general relation of dependence, the dependence of man on the domestic relations of law and government keeps equal pace. The more polished and civilised the members of a state, the more are they bound together by wise ordinances, holy laws, venerable customs and manners, which wisely determine the mutual relations of rights and duties; so that in fact, with every higher degree of internal freedom the outward bonds are proportionably straitened. On the other hand, the greater the state of barbarism, the greater is the external independence; so that the wildest savage is, in a material point of view, the most free.

What do these facts import, but a wonderful, mysterious, inexplicable connection of the individual man with the human race; so that he comprehends himself better, the more he seems to be absorbed in his kind, and it is only in humanity that man is understood? Yet, this internal emancipation by means of outward restraints of which we have hitherto spoken, is not that which is the most interior: and serves only as a similitude or illustration of something higher. The true emancipation from low-mindedness and self-seeking is a problem, which, as is avowed, religion alone can solve. In the same way as civilisation is determined by political life, and by obedience to the institutions of the state, yea, even by the dependence, though naturally looser, on other nations; so is true religiousness promoted by subjection to the Church. For it is an incontrovertible maxim of experience, that the individual who is unconnected with any ecclesiastical community, has either no religion, or a very meagre and scanty one, or is given up to a distempered fancy, and a wild fanaticism; so that in none of the three cases can religion exert her blessed influences. On the other hand, the more stable the ecclesiastical community to which we belong, the more will the true, interior qualities of man expand and bloom forth in freedom ; so that he who will lead a righteous life in the Catholic Church, whereof the very principle is the real unity and vital communion of all believers, he, we say, will attain to the highest degree of moral and religious perfection. It is no inane conception—no idle phantom—no illusion of a diseased mind, which he embraces, and to which he surrenders his obedience ; but it is a reality, and a holy reality, wherein true faith, and love manifesting itself in deeds, coupled with *humility* and *self-denial* in the strongest and most comprehensive sense of the words are nurtured. The more widely diffused the community, to which the Catholic belongs, the more defined and the more manifold are the relations wherein he stands, the more multiplied the bonds wherewith he is encompassed. But, as we said above, those very bonds, which exhibit the reality of the community, produce a result the very reverse of restraint, and establish the internal freedom of man, or promote the purest *humanity ;* for this expression may be used, since God became man. Without external bonds, there is no true spiritual association, so that the idea of a mere invisible universal community, to which we should belong, is an idle, unprofitable phantom of the imagination and of distempered feelings destitute of all influence on mankind. In proportion only as a religious society approximates to the Catholic Church, doth it exert a more efficacious influence on spiritual life. Here, indeed we may observe, as shall be afterwards proved, that it is only according to Catholic principles a Church can be consistently formed ; and where out of her pale anything of the kind exists, the truth of what we assert is confirmed, to wit, that where a ray of true Christian light doth fall, it will have the effect of binding and uniting, whereby all the doctrines tending to schism and division are, practically at least, refuted.

And what the Catholic, in the way described, feels and thinks, wishes and strives for, he finds clearly laid down in Holy Writ. The divine Founder of the Church, in the following important words enlarges, among other things, on the oneness and visibility of the community, into which those, who were to take his name, were to be received :—' And not for them only do I pray *but for them also who through their word shall believe in me*, that they all may be one, as thou Father in me, and I in thee : that they also may be one in us ; *that the world may believe that thou hast sent me.* And the glory which thou hast given me, I have given to them, that they may be one, as we also are one. I in them, and thou in me that they may be made perfection in one: and the world may know that thou hast sent me, and hast loved them, as thou hast also loved me.' (John xvii, 20, 24.) What fulness of thoughts we find here! The Lord putteth up a prayer for the gift of unity, and the union of all who shall believe: and for an unity, too, which finds its model only in the relation existing between the Father and the Son of Man. '*In us* shall they be one:' that is to say, the unity of those believing in me is of so exalted a nature, that it is only by the communication of a higher life, by a divine principle, it can be brought about by the one faith, the same hope, and love, which are of divine institution. In the same way as the living foundation of this unity is divine, so shall it be attended with divine effects: by this unity the world shall recognise the heavenly mission of Christ. The unity must be a visible unity—obvious to the eyes, perceptible by the identity of doctrine, by the real mutual relations and communion of all the followers of Christ with each other; for otherwise the consequences adverted to could not be deduced from it. Thus the true vital communion of all attest the dignity of Christ, as every work vouches for its master. On the other hand, in the schisms and dissensions among believers, the dignity of Christ is lost sight of; strangers are brought not to the faith, and even those already believing are delivered up to doubt and unbelief.

In expressions a little altered, but still more energetic, the Saviour now repeats the same prayer, whose mighty theme are the conditions of the prosperity, the growth, and the duration of God's kingdom upon earth. He saith:—' The glory, which thou hast given me, I have given to them: that they may be one, as we are one. I in them, and thou in me; that they may be made perfect in one.' Or, in other words, he would say:— The glorious destination, the mission which as the Son of Man I received from thee, for the glorification of thy name, to the end that I might enter into the inmost fellowship with thee (I in thee), I have transferred to them also, that I might contract the most living fellowship with them, in order that they might thereby attain unto perfect unity. ' And that the world may know that thou hast sent me, and hast loved them, as thou hast also loved me,' that is to say, their oneness in all things—a oneness not to be brought about by human powers—oneness in belief, thought, and will; and every effort shall be to unbelievers a sign that I have worked according to thy commission, and with divine plenipotence ; and that the believers are thy chosen people, to whom, out of love, thou hast revealed thyself, as out of love thou hast constituted me thine envoy. So speaketh the Lord himself.

Paul the apostle is admirable, when, in simple words, he expounds the relation between the law and grace, between the works of the law and faith ; when he instructs us respecting the series of divine revelations, and the education of the human race by God, and respecting the laws which govern the world's history. But his philosophy, if I may be allowed so to speak, his philosophy on man's social relations generally, and on his ecclesiastical ones in particular, is, in depth, and majestic simplicity, inferior to none of his other expositions. Our reason feels itself irresistibly compelled to accede to his judgments, whether he enlarge in general on the infirmity of the individual man, and the absolute necessity of aiding it, by attachment to a community ; or whether he point to the limited powers of individual reason, and show how they are dilated and improved, preserved, and rescued from destruction by means of society ; or whether he remind us of the one spirit, that should pervade all diversities, or of the diversities that are permitted in the one spirit ; or, lastly, represent the idea, which he spiritually contemplates, under the image of the relations of the members of the body. (1 Cor. xii.) And how doth not our bosom swell, when he calls the attention of his readers to the living foundation, out of which the new community, that had appeared in the world, and was destined to unite all nations, had arisen. It is at times, as if we felt the infinite power stirring within us, which gave existence to that society. (Eph. iv, 16.) In Christ, national distinctions, in a religious point of view, are obliterated (Eph. xi, 15) ; the enmities of people he hath destroyed—he is become our peace, and by ' breaking down the middle wall of partition,' hath made one out of two. All men, in a like degree, have in him access to God ; but as in Christ they all become one, so they are united with each other in one body and one spirit. (Eph. iv, 4.) All invites to this unity ; the one Lord, the one baptism, the one faith, the one God and father of all. (Eph. iv, 5, 6.) The oneness of faith, and of the knowledge of the Son of God, is at once the reality, and the supreme ideal, which should be aimed at ; and without this unity, in which the individual is strong, he is given up to every wind of doctrine, and to the craftiness of men. (Eph. iv, 14.)

These and similar passages are the foundations whereon the Catholic theory of the Church has been constructed. Hence flowed the inspired eloquence of Cyprian ; hence Augustine drew his reflections on the Church, which in depth of feeling and vigour of thought, contain by far the most splendid things that, since the time of the apostles, have been written on this subject. Hence, too, in later times came the glow that warmed the iron bosoms of the chilly north, and melted them into a heat, whereby all the gold and silver of our modern European civilisation were by degrees purified from dross.

To the Catholic, it appears the most trivial proceeding, when such pictures of the Church, as we have attempted to trace, are ridiculed as ideal representations, which have never had in past, nor ever will have in all future times, a perfectly corresponding reality. In fact, little is told him but what he already knows ; to wit, that the idea is not the vulgar reality, and *vice versa*: but he knows, likewise, that where there is no fundamental idea to any reality, there is as little truth as where no reality corresponds to the idea. He feels convinced that if, in the above-mentioned manner, the doctrine of his Church is to be seriously assailed, the gospel itself would be open to the same attacks ; for one might say, ' all is indeed excellent and wonderful, which is there prescribed touching the pious sentiments and holiness of conduct which *should* distinguish Christians : but do these sentiments, and this conduct *really* distinguish them ? This is the question at issue.' Everything must live according to an ideal, to which the vulgar reality is not equal ; for how else could it be vulgar ? The words of the Lord, ' Be ye perfect, as your heavenly Father is perfect,' will not therefore be vain, because no man is like to God. No, woe to him who shall reject the ideal, because he finds it not perfectly represented among men.

Even the fact that at all times, from our Lord and his apostles downwards, in the midst of whom a Judas was found, there has been much evil in the Church, nay, that the evil seemed at times to exceed the good, cannot impair the reverence of Catholics for their Church. The Church, as the institution of Christ, hath never erred, hath never become wicked, and never loses its energy ; which is constantly evinced, though the proof may not always be so obvious to the eye. To exhibit the kingdom of

God on earth, *and also to train mankind for the same*, she has had to deal with men who were all born sinners, and were taken from a more or less corrupt mass. Thus she can never work out of the sphere of evil, nay, her destination requires her to enter into the very midst of evil, and to put her renovating power continually to the test. The Catholic Church has, moreover, experienced a long, and often arduous, history; she has passed through periods of time wherein all the elements of life were unbound, and in wild uproar seemed arrayed one against the other. The anterior civilisation, and the social institutions, under which Christianity had hitherto flourished, were really destroyed by savage and semi-barbarous hordes; and they were not civilised Greeks and Romans, but wild, untamed natures, who now entered into the Church, which henceforth assumed quite another form. As her priests and bishops fall not from the skies; as she must take them out of the description of men that the age can furnish; she could indeed for a succession of centuries boast of no Clemens of Alexandria, no Origen, no Cyprian, no Basil and Gregory of Nazianzen, no Hilary, Jerome, and Augustine, who were trained up in all the art and science of ancient Greece and Rome, before they became priests, or anywise attached themselves to the Church. And yet it is impossible to estimate the great and splendid things which the Church achieved in those troublous times ! Upon the foundation of the same doctrine, which in more flourishing ages had been developed into a systematic form, universally received, the Church displayed her educating power. Nay, all the fulness of energy, which Christianity had manifested in the first centuries, it now again unfolded, though in quite another form; for the matter to be wrought was totally different. Under such circumstances, there sprang up from the twelfth century a variety of sects, born of yesterday, without any historical ancestry, consisting of a small number of elect, to whom was vouchsafed the privilege of dreaming a Church, and who ventured to urge against the existing Church, that had passed through so many storms and revolutions, the reproach that *she* had failed to fulfil her destination : and with the learning which they had received from the Church, they resisted her on account of the ignorance to be found within her. Had these creations of fancy and egotism, which they are certainly to be considered, even if we should, not deny the better elements they contained, borne the burden of ages imposed on the Catholic Church. they would in the first moment have sunk back into the original nothingness, from which they had emerged. Doubtless, examples enough can be alleged of priests, bishops, and popes, who, in the most unconscionable and unjustifiable manner, have failed to discharge their duty, when it was quite in their power to bring about a reform of morals; or who, by their own scandalous conduct and lives, have extinguished the still glimmering torch, which they ought to have kindled. Hell hath swallowed them up. Avowals of this kind Catholics must not shrink from, and never have shrunk from: it would be even idle to attempt to elude them, for the Protestants themselves furnish an irrefragable proof of the state of manifold neglect, into which the people had fallen during the fifteenth century. Never would a system of doctrine like theirs have sprung up, still less have obtained such wide effusion, had individual teachers and priests been faithful to the duties of their calling. Truly, the ignorance could not have been slight, on which a system of faith, like that of the Reformers, was imposed as worthy of acceptance; and thus Protestants may learn to estimate the magnitude of the evil, which then oppressed the Church, by the magnitude of the errors into which they themselves have fallen. This is the point at which Catholics and Protestants will, in great multitudes, one day meet, and stretch a friendly hand one to the other. Both, conscious of guilt, must exclaim, 'We all have erred—it is the Church only which cannot err; we all have sinned—the Church only is spotless on earth.' This open confession of mutual guilt will be followed by the festival of reconciliation. Meanwhile we still smart under the inexpressible pain of the wound which was then inflicted—a pain which can be alleviated only by the consciousness that the wound has become an issue, through which all the impurities have flowed off, that men had introduced into the wide compass of the dominions of the Church; for she herself is ever pure and eternally undefiled.

In thus stating the view which Catholics take of their Church, without pretending to any completeness of detail, we think we have duly prepared our readers for understanding the following section.

§ XXXVIII—THE CHURCH AS TEACHER AND INSTRUCTRESS—TRADITION—THE CHURCH AS JUDGE IN MATTERS OF FAITH

The main question, which we have now to answer, is this: how doth man attain to possession of the true doctrine of Christ; or, to express ourselves in a more general, and at once more accurate manner, how doth man obtain a clear knowledge of the institute of salvation, proffered in Christ Jesus? The Protestant says, by searching Holy Writ, which is infallible: the Catholic, on the other hand, replies, by the Church, in which alone man arrives at the true understanding of Holy Writ. In a more minute exposition of his views, the Catholic continues: doubtless the Sacred Scriptures contain *divine* communications, and consequently, the pure truth: whether they contain *all* the truths, which, in a religious and ecclesiastical point of view are necessary, or at least very useful to be known, is a question which does not yet come under consideration. Thus, the scripture is God's unerring word; but however the predicate of inerrability may belong *to it, we ourselves* are not exempt from error; nay, we only become so when we have unerringly received the word, which is in *itself* inerrable. In this reception of the word, human activity, which is fallible, has necessarily a part. But, in order that, in this transit of the divine contents of the Sacred Scriptures into possession of the human intellect, no gross illusion or general misrepresentation may occur, it is taught, that the Divine Spirit, to which are entrusted the guidance and vivification of the Church, becomes, in its union with the human spirit in the Church, a peculiarly Christian tact, a deep sure-guiding feeling, which, as it abideth in truth, leads also into all truth. By a confiding attachment to the perpetuated Apostleship, by education in the Church, by hearing, learning, and living within her pale, by the reception of the higher principle, which renders her eternally fruitful, a deep interior sense is formed that alone is fitted for the perception and acceptance of the written Word, because it entirely coincides with the sense, in which the Sacred Scriptures themselves were composed. If, with such a sense acquired in the Church, the sacred volume be perused, then its general essential import is conveyed unaltered to the reader's mind. Nay, when instruction through the apostleship, and the ecclesiastical education in the way described, takes place in the individual, the Sacred Scriptures are not even necessary for our acquisition of their general contents.[1]

This is the ordinary and regular course. But errors and misunderstandings, more or less culpable, will never fail to occur; and, as in the times of the apostles, the word of God was combated out of the word of God, so this combat hath been renewed at all times. What, under such circumstances, is the course to be pursued ? How is the Divine Word to be secured against the erroneous conceptions that have arisen ? The general sense decides against particular opinion—the judgment of the Church against that of the individual: *the Church interprets the Sacred Scriptures.* The Church is the body of the Lord: it is, in its universality, his visible form—his permanent, ever-renovated, humanity—his eternal revelation. He dwells in the community; all his promises, all his gifts are bequeathed to the community—but to no individual, as such, since the time of the apostles. This general sense, this ecclesiastical conscious-

---

[1] We can see from Irenæus, adv. Hær. lib. iii, c. 3, how ancient the above laid down doctrine is. With the clearest conviction it was pointed out, in the earliest controversies in the Church: and, in fact, if Christ hath founded a Church, nothing can be more strikingly manifest than this view of the matter. Irenæus says: 'Traditionem apostolerum in toto mundo manifestatam, in omni ecclesia adest perspicere omnibus, qui vera velint audire ; et habemus annumerare eos, qui ab apostolis instituti sunt episcopi in ecclesiis, et successores eorum usque ad nos, qui nihil tale docuerunt, neque cognoverunt, quale deliratur ab his. . . . Tantæ igitur ostensionis quum sint hæc, non oportet adhuc quærere apud alios veriatem, quam facile est ab ecclesia sumere ; quum apostoli quasi in depositorium dives plenissime in eam detulerint omnia quæ sint veritatis ; ut omnis, quicunque velit, sumat ex ea potum vitæ. Hæc est enim vitæ introitus : omnes autem reliqui fures sunt et latrones, propter quod oportet devitare quidem illos : quæ autem sunt ecclesiæ cum summa diligentia diligere, et apprehendere veritatis traditionem. . . . Quid autem, si neque apostoli quidem scripturas reliquissent nobis, nonne oportebat sequi ordinem traditionis, quam tradiderunt iis, quibus committebant ecclesias ? Cui ordinationi assentiunt multæ gentes barbarorum, quorum qui in Christum credunt, sine charta et atramento scriptam habentas per Spiritum Sanctum in cordibus suis salutem, et veterem traditionem diligenter custodientes, in unum Deum credentes. . . . Hanc fidem qui sine literis crediderunt, quantum ad sermonem nostrum, barbari sunt, quantum ad sententiam, et consuetudinem, et conversationem, propter fidem, perquam sapientissimi sunt, et placent Deo, conversantes in omni justitia, et castitate, et sapientia. Quibus si aliquis annuntiaverit ea, quæ ab hereticis adinventa sunt, proprio sermone eorum colloquens, statim, concludentes aures, longius fugient, ne audire quidem sustinentes blasphemum alloquium. Sic per illam veterem apostolorum traditionem ne in conceptionem quidem mentis admittunt, quodcunque eorum ostentiloquium est.'

ness is tradition, in the subjective sense of the word.[1] What then is tradition? The peculiar Christian sense existing in the Church, and transmitted by ecclesiastical education; yet this sense is not to be conceived as detached from its subject-matter—nay, it is formed in, and by this matter, so it may be called a full sense. Tradition is the living word, perpetuated in the hearts of believers. To this sense, as the general sense, the interpretation of Holy Writ is entrusted. The declaration which it pronounces on any controverted subject, is the judgment of the Church; and, therefore, the Church is judge in matters of faith (*judex controversiarum*). Tradition, in the objective sense, is the general faith of the Church through all ages, manifested by outward historical testimonies; in this sense, tradition is usually termed the norma—the standard of Scriptural interpretation—the rule of faith.

Moreover, the Divine Founder of our Church, when he constituted the community of believers, as his permanent organ, had recourse to no other law than that which prevails in every department of human life. Each nation is endowed with a peculiar character, stamped on the deepest, most hidden parts

---

[1] Euseb. Hist. eccles. lib. v, c. 27 : ἐκκλησιαστικὸν φρόνημα ; Commonitor. Vincent. Lirins. c. 2, ed. Klupf. 1809, p. 90. 'Hoc forsitan requirat aliquis: cum sit perfectus scripturarum canon, sibique ad omnia satis superque sufficiat: quid opus est, ut ei *ecclesiasticæ intelligentiæ* jungatur auctoritas? Quia videlicet scripturam sacram, pro ipsa sua altitudine, non uno eodemque sensu universi accipiunt; sed ejusdem eloquia aliter atque aliter alius atque alius interpretatur, ut pene quot homines sunt, tot illinc sententiæ erui posse videantur. . . . Atque idcirco multum necesse est, propter tantos tam varii erroris anfractus, ut propheticæ et apostolicæ interpretationis linea secundum *ecclesiastici et catholici sensus normam* dirigatur.' These words occur immediately after the conclusion of the first chapter, wherein he says, there are two ways whereby the Catholic doctrine can be distinguished from the heretical: 'Primum scilicet divinæ legis auctoritate: tum deinde ecclesiæ Catholicæ traditione.' By the Council of Trent (sess. iii, c. 2) tradition is called, 'Universus ecclesiæ sensus.' Sess. iv, Decret. de editione et usu sacrorum librorum: 'Ut nemo suæ prudentiæ innixus, in rebus fidei et morum ad ædificationem doctrinæ Christianæ pertinentium, sacras scripturas ad suos sensus contorquens, contra eum sensum, quem tenuit et tenet sancta mater ecclesia, cujus est judicare de vero sensu et interpretatione scripturarum sanctarum.' Decret. de. canon. Script: 'Perspiciens hanc veritatem et disciplinam contineri in libris scriptis et sine scripto traditionibus, quæ ipsius Christi ore ab apostolis acceptæ . . . traditiones pisas, tum ad fidem, tum ad mores pertinentes, tanquam vel ore tenus a Christo, vel a Sancto Spiritu dictatas, et continua successione in ecclesia Catholica conservatas, pari pietatis affectu ac reverentia suscipit et veneratur.' Compare Melchior. Cani loc. theol. (lib. iii, c. 3, p. 179 *seq.* ed. Venet.) on Tradition; et lib. iv, c. 4, p. 234, on the authority of the Church.

of its being, which distinguishes it from all other nations and manifests its peculiarity in public and domestic life, in art and science, in short, in every relation. It is, as it were, the tutelary genius; the guiding spirit transmitted from its progenitors; the vivifying breath of the whole community; and, indeed, the nations anterior to Christianity, personified this their peculiar character, revered it as their national divinity, deduced from it their civil and religious laws and customs, and placed all things under its protection.

In every general act of a people, the national spirit is infallibly expressed; and should contests, should selfish factions occur, the element destructive to the vital principle of the whole, will most certainly be detected in them, and the commotion excited by an alien spirit, either miscarries, or is expelled, as long as the community preserves its own self-consciousness, as long as its peculiar genius yet lives, and works within it. If on the other hand, things have come to such an extremity, that the living bond which connects the present with the past is dissevered; that no concurrent national effort can be called forth; that all falls into a state of confusion; that struggle and opposition totally efface the common characteristics of the community, or reveal them only in opposition, which is boasted of as life; then there is no doubt that such a people is near its downfall, that its peculiar plastic principle is already paralysed, and its Divinity has ceased to live—' Pan is dead!' did seamen hear resounded from every quarter, at the period of the birth of Christ.

To confine our attention, more particularly to religious communities, we need only look to the Chinese, and the Parsees, or to the Mohammedans, and we shall be astonished to observe how consistently, throughout the course of their history, the principles, established at the outset, were applied to details, how consistently the latter were conceived and modelled by the standard of the former. Let us investigate the Hellenic Heathenism also, and the most perfect agreement between the various religious phenomena that have risen up in succession, and the primitive fundamental view, cannot escape observation. Lastly, let us contemplate the religious sect founded by Luther himself. The developed doctrines of his Church, consigned as they are in the symbolical books, retain, on the whole, so much of this spirit, that on the first view, they must be recognised by the observer as genuine productions of Luther. With a sure vital instinct, the opinions of the Majorists, the Synergists and others, were rejected as deadly; and, indeed (from Luther's point of view), as untrue, by that community whose soul, whose living principle he was; and the Church, which the Reformer of Wittenberg established, proved herself the unerring interpretess of his word.

Let us now, for a moment, suppose the case, that the progenitors of nations, and the founders of the above-mentioned religions, had been real envoys from above; then must we consider the movement, that emanated from them, as divine, yet as one which, by its transmission to those attracted by its fundamental principle, had become human; and the later collective actions, whereof we said, that they had retained the spirit of the founder, would then be at once divine and human acts and deeds. They would be divine, because they would have only worked out what was originally given, and applied it to occurring relations and circumstances; human because this development would have been carried on through the agency of men; lastly, an unerring standard of thought and action for all those who follow such a founder; for the breath of life, which proceeded from him, guides, like a natural impulse, the movements of the whole community. According to this type hath the infallibility of the Church also, in its interpretation of the Divine Word, been formed, and by this standard we are to judge it. All the developments of its dogmas and its morality, which can be considered as resulting from formal acts of the whole body, are to be revered as the sentences of Christ himself, and in these his spirit ever recurs. Here, indeed, subsists between the Church and the above-named religious communities the great difference which must ever be maintained between Jesus Christ and mere men. The institutions of the latter even after the most consistent expansion of their vital principles, advance to an inevitable end; and their productions, however much they may have worked, according to their original spirit, possess no greater value than that spirit itself, and both, in an equal degree, sink by degrees into nothing.

§ XXXIX—THE CHURCH AS INTERPRETER OF HOLY WRIT, AND THE DOCTRINE ON TRADITION CONTINUED

On these subjects, Scripture and Tradition, and the relation of the Church to both, we must now enter into fuller and clearer explanations.

Undoubtedly, on this most important matter, the records of ecclesiastical history will serve to throw the clearest light. If we accept some Jewish parties, which did not so much spring out of Christianity, as wish to encumber it, in its infancy, with Judæo-national observances, the earliest sect were the Gnostics. Their doctrines on the eternal co-existence of an evil matter with God—on the creation and government of the world, by an inferior spirit, the Demiurgos—their principle of Docetism and the rest, are too well known to be detailed here. However decidedly, in the opinion, perhaps, of all who now profess Christianity, these doctrines are adverse to its nature ; did the Gnostics, on that account, suffer themselves to be convinced, out of Scripture, of the perversity of their views ? So far from it, they preferred to reject the Old Testament, and to declare the Gospels to be falsified ![1] There are certainly few who have studied the Gnostic errors, that are not seized with the deepest astonishment how their partisans could possibly deem their whimsical opinions, the fantastic forms of their demonology, and the rest to be *Christian apostolic* doctrines ; and many among us perhaps believe, that we could in a single hour confute thousands of them by the Bible, and bring them back to pure Christianity. So confident did they feel in their superiority, that they were even disposed to accuse their then opponents of a want of dexterity, because they did not succeed.

But, when once a peculiar system of moral life hath been called into existence, should it even be composed of the most corrupt elements, no ordinary force of external proofs, no con-

[1] Even Tertullian in his work (de Præscript. c. xvii.) against heretics, lays down some remarkable observations, which the experience even of the second century had furnished him. 'Ista hæresis non recipit quasdam scripturas : et si quas recipit, non recipit integras, adjectionibus et detractionibus ad dispositionem instituti sui intervertit, et si aliquatenus integras præstat, nihilominus diversas expositiones commentata convertit. . . . Quid promovebis, exercitatissime scripturarum, quam si quid defenderis, negetur ; ex diverso, si quid negaveris, defendatur ? Et tu quidem nihil perdes nisi vocem in contentione : nihil consequeris, nisi bilem de blasphematione.'

clusions of ratiocination, no eloquence, are able to destroy it : its roots lie mostly too deep to be pervious to mortal eye : it can only perish of itself, become gradually exhausted, spend its rage, and disappear. But, as long as it flourishes, all around is converted into a demonstration in its favour : the earth speaks for it, and the heavens are its warranty. Meanwhile, a new age, with another spirit and other elements of life, springs up : this, without any points of internal contact with the past, is often at a loss to comprehend it, and demands with astonishment how its existence had been possible. But, should divine Grace, which can alone enkindle the opposite *true life*, succeed in delivering one individual from such errors, then he expresses the incomprehensible and inconceivable nature of his former state, by saying, that he had been, as it were, enchanted, and that something, like scales, has fallen from his eyes!

As the impossibility was now manifest of convincing the Gnostics of the truth out of Holy Writ, must the Catholic Church declare, that the questions whether God created the world, whether Christ were a true man, should remain in abeyance, till these doctrines were made evident to them by the testimony of Scripture ? By no means. They were directed to tradition —to the living word ; they were told that, if even a doubt could arise as to the doctrine of Scripture, the announcement of the word perpetuated in the Church, since her first establishment, and the common faith of believers, decided the question clearly enough ; and that to this decision, all who wish to attach themselves to Christ, and choose him for the Shepherd of their souls, ought not to refuse obedience.

The teachers of the Church, indeed, by no means omitted to employ Scripture for the refutation of the Gnostics, and to appeal to its testimony in detailed expositions. But herein, one learned investigation was but opposed to another : man stood against man, and the Bible on both sides.[1] By adherence to Scripture, the individual Christian could undoubtedly convince himself, that the Gnostics were involved in grievous errors. Of this he was subjectively certain : but as the adversary had

[1] This fact misled Dr Lücke, in his writing, ' On the authority of Scripture, and its relation to the rule of faith in the Protestant and the ancient Church ; three theological epistles to Dr Delbrück, from Dr Sack, Dr Nitzch, and Dr Lücke ; ' pp. 125, 141, 142, 145. Not only Irenæus Hippolytus, Novatian, Origen, and others, prove the Catholic dogmas out of *the Bible also*, but in all ages, down to the present day, Catholics adduce the scriptural proof.

the like subjective conviction, that the true Christian view of the world was to be found on his side, the objectivity of Christianity would have necessarily disappeared, if, besides the Bible, there had not been a rule of faith, to wit, universal Tradition.[1] Without this rule, it would ever be impossible to determine with positiveness, safety, and general obligation, the peculiar doctrines of Christianity. The individual, at best, could only hazard the assertion, this is *my* view, *my* interpretation of Scripture, or in other words, without tradition there would be *no doctrine of the Church, and no Church*, but individual Christians only; no certainty and security, but only doubt and probability.

Scarcely had the struggle of the Catholic Church with Gnosticism reached its highest point, when, in the most decided contrast with the latter, the one class of Unitarians arose; for these, and not, as Neander thinks, the Montanists, form the contrary extreme to the Gnostics. If the Gnostics saw in Christianity *nothing but* what was divine, and in Christ recognised *merely* the divine reason, so that they attributed to the Redeemer only an apparent body, represented him as merely putting on an illusive form of man, but not taking the real nature of man, and regarded moreover the visible world as thoroughly evil; these Unitarians on the other hand, discovered in the Saviour a mere man, enlightened by Heaven; and consistently with this doctrine, denied the descent of the Divine Spirit upon the apostles and the Church, and the high supernatural aid of grace; which they the less needed, as they acknowledged the existence of no deeply implanted corruption in human nature. Did the former look upon the Gospel as a plastic impulse, a divine germ of life, a celestial energy; so the latter regarded it as a law of formation, a dead rule, an abstract notion, a pure ethical system,

---

[1] Tertullian, in the work just cited, c. 18, makes the following luminous observations, drawn fresh from life: 'Si quis est, cujus causa in congressum descendis scripturarum, ut eum dubitantem confirmes, ad veritatem, an magis ad hæreses diverget? *Hoc ipso motus, quod te videat nihil promovisse* æquo gradu negandi et defendendi adversa parte, statu certe pari, altercatione incertior discedet, nesciens quam hæresim judicet.'
. . . . C. 19: 'Ergo non ad scripturas provocandum est: *nec in his constituendum certamen*, in quibus aut nulla aut incerta victoria est, aut par incertæ. Nam etsi non ita evaderet collatio scripturarum, ut utrumque partem parem sisteret, ordo rerum desiderabat, prius proponi, quod nunc solum disputandum est: quibus competat fides ipsa? Cujus sint scripturæ? A quo, et per quos, et quando, et quibus sit tradita disciplina, qua fiunt Christiani? Ubi enim apparuerit esse veritatem et disciplinæ et fidei Christianæ, illic erit veritas scripturarum et expositionum et omnium traditionum Christianarum.'

by application whereof the defects to be found in our otherwise excellent moral nature, may be totally eradicated. The Unitarians of this class (after falsifying Holy Writ) appealed to the same, and by the rejection of tradition, relied exclusively on its authority.[1] What course, under these circumstances, was the Church to be advised ? Was she to declare that everyone was provisionally to follow his own views, until results, satisfactory to each individual, could be more surely obtained from the study of Holy Writ ? Most undoubtedly if the Church had been a mere historico-antiquarian association ; if she had had no conception of herself, of her foundation, of her essence, and of her task, and no sense of the power of faith. But, as she enjoyed the possession of these, she acted otherwise, and from her conduct clearly resound the words : ' eternally certain is the doctrine of the Redeemer to his disciples—the written word is one with the living—that which is inscribed on paper and parchment, with that which is engraven on the hearts by the power of the Holy Spirit ; and the doubts, which may arise out of the former, are dispelled by the latter.' The faith existing in the Church, from the beginning throughout all ages, is the infallible standard to determine the true sense of Scripture : and accordingly, it is certain, beyond the shadow of doubt, that the Redeemer is God, and hath filled us even with divine power. In fact, he who grounds his faith on Scripture only, that is, on the result of his exegetical studies, has no faith, can have none, and understands not its very nature. Must he not be always ready to receive better information ; must he not admit the possibility, that by nature study of Scripture, another result may be obtained, than that which has already been arrived at ? The thought of this very possibility precludes the establishment of any decided, perfectly undoubting, and unshaken faith, which, after all, is alone deserving of the name. He who says, ' this is my faith,' hath no faith. Faith, unity of faith, universality of faith, are one and the same ; they are but different expressions of the same notion. He who, if even he should not believe the truth, yet believes truly, believes at the same time that he holds fast the doctrine of Christ, that he shares the faith with the Apostles, and with the Church founded by the Redeemer, that there is but one faith in all ages, and one only true one. This faith is alone rational, and alone worthy of man : every other should be called a

[1] Euseb. Hist. Eccl. lib. v, c. 27.

mere opinion, and, in a practical point of view, is an utter impotency.

Ages passed by, and with them the ancient sects : new times arose, bringing along with them new schisms in the Church. The formal principles of all these productions of egotism were the same ; all asserted that Holy Writ, abstracted from Tradition and from the Church, is at once the sole source of religious truth, and the sole standard of its knowledge for the individual. This formal principle, common to all parties separated from the Church ;—to the Gnostic of the second century, and the Albigensian and Vaudois of the twelfth, to the Sabellian of the third, the Arian of the fourth, and the Nestorian of the fifth century— this principle, we say, led to the most contradictory belief. What indeed can be more opposite to each other, than Gnosticism and Pelagianism, than Sabellianism and Arianism ?[1] The very circumstance, indeed, that one and the same formal principle can be applied to every possible mode of belief ; or rather that this belief, however contradictory it may be in itself, can still make use of that formal principle, should alone convince everyone, that grievous errors must here lie concealed, and that between the individual and the Bible a mediating principle is wanting.

[1] With respect to the Arians, compare Athanasius de Synodo, sect. 13-14, 40, 43, 47 ; Basil de Spiritu Sancto, c. 10. ' Id quod impugnatur fides est, isque scopus est commonis omnibus adversariis et sanæ doctrinæ inimicis, ut soliditatem fidei in Christum concutiant, apostolicam traditionem solo æqualem abolendo. Ea propter, sicut solent, qui bonæ fidei debitores sunt, probationes e Scriptura clamore exigunt. Patrum testimonium, quod scriptum non est, velut nullius momenti rejicientes.' Compare c. 27, Augustin. lib. i, contra Maximin : ' Si quid de divinis protuleris,' says the Arian ; ' quod commune est cum omnibus, necesse est ut audiamus. Hæ vero voces, quæ extra scripturam sunt, nullo casu a nobis suscipiuntur. Præterea quum ipse Dominus moneat nos, et dicat : sine causa colunt me, docentes mandata et præcepta hominum.' In August. de Nat. et grat. c. 39, Pelagius thus expresses himself : ' Credamus igitur quod legimus, et quod non legimus, nefas credamus adstruere.' Eutyches, act. 1, Concil. Chalced. in Hard. Act. Concil. tom. ii, p. 186 : "Ετοιμον γὰρ αὐτὸν εἶναι ἔφασκε ταῖς ἐκθέσεσι τῶν ἁγίων πατέρων, τῶν τε ἐν Νικαίᾳ καὶ ἐν Ἐφέσῳ τὴν σύνοδον ποιησαμένων, συντίθεσθαι, καὶ ὑπογράφειν ταῖς ἑρμηνείαις αὐτῶν ὁμολόγει· εἰ δέ που τύχοι τι παρ' αὐτῶν ἔν τισι λέξεσι ἢ διασφαλθὲν, ἢ διαπλανηθὲν, τοῦτο μήτε διαβάλλειν, μηδὲ καταδέχεσθαι, μόνας δὲ τὰς γραφὰς ἐρευνᾷν, ὡς βεβαιοτέρας οὔσας τῆς τῶν πατέρων ἐκθέσεως κ. τ. λ. ' He said that he was ready to receive the decrees of the holy fathers assembled in the Councils of Nice and Ephesus, and he promises to subscribe to their definitions. But if in their declarations anything by chance should be found either unsound or false, he says that he will neither reject nor approve of it : but search the scripture alone as being more solid than all the decrees of the fathers.'

What is indeed more striking than the fact, that every later religious sect doth not deny that the Catholic Church, in respect to the parties that had previously seceded from her, has in substance right on her side, and even recognises in these cases her dogmatic decisions; while on the other hand, it disputes her formal principles? Would this ecclesiastical doctrine, so formed and so approved of, have been possible, without the peculiar view of the Church entertained of herself? Doth not the one determine the other? With joy the Arian recognises what has been decided by the Church against the Gnostics; but he does not keep in view the manner in which she proceeded against them; and he will not consider that those dogmas on which he agrees with the Church, she would not have saved and handed down to his time, had she acted according to those formal principles which he requires of her, and on which he stands. The Pelagian and the Nestorian embrace also, with the most undoubting faith, the decisions of the Church against the Arians. But as soon as the turn comes to either, he becomes as it were stupified, and is inconsiderate enough to desire the matter of Christian doctrine without the appropriate ecclesiastical form—without that form, consequently, by the very neglect whereof those parties, to which he is most heartily opposed, have fallen on the adoption of their articles of belief. It was the same with Luther and Calvin. The pure Christian dogmas, in opposition to the errors of the Gnostics, Paulicians, Arians, Pelagians, Nestorians, Monophysites and others, they received with the most praiseworthy firmness and fervency of faith. But, when they took a fancy to deliver their theses on the relations between faith and works, between free-will and grace, or however else they may be called, they trod (as to form) quite in the footsteps of those whom they execrated, and when they were able to obtain possession of their persons, even burned.[1]

[1] The observation of Chemnitius (in Exam. Conc. Trident. P. 1, p. 118, and still more further on) is very remarkable. He says, Irenæus and Tertullian, who appealed to tradition, wished only to show that tradition agreed with Scripture. 'Non video, si integra disputatio consideretur, quomodo alia inde possit erui sententia, quam quod ostendat consensum traditionis apostolicæ cum Scriptura, ita ut eadem sit doctrina, quam Scriptura tradit, et quam primitiva ecclesia ex apostolorum traditione acceperat. P. 321. Et omnia sunt sacris Scripturis consona, quæ nos et recipimus et profitemur.' Hence, he draws the conclusion, that testimonies for tradition from the second, third, and fourth centuries, could not be turned against th Perotestants, because they receive all which was then decided through tradition against the heretics. But Chemnitius

This accordingly is the doctrine of Catholics. Thou wilt obtain the knowledge full and entire of the Christian religion only in connection with its essential form, which is the Church. Look at the Scripture in an ecclesiastical spirit, and it will present thee an image perfectly resembling the Church. Contemplate Christ in, and with his creation—the Church—the only adequate authority—the only authority representing him, and thou wilt then stamp his image on thy soul. Should it, however, be stated, in ridicule of this principle, that it were the same as to say—' Look at the Bible through the spectacles of the Church; be not disturbed, for it is better for thee to contemplate the star by the aid of a glass, than to let it escape thy dull organ of vision, and be lost in mist and darkness. Spectacles, besides, thou must always use, but only beware lest thou get them constructed by the first casual glass-grinder, and fixed upon thy nose.'

§ XL—FORMAL DISTINCTION BETWEEN SCRIPTURAL AND ECCLESIASTICAL DOCTRINE

If we have hitherto shown that, conformably to the principles of Catholics, the doctrine of Scripture is one and the same with the doctrine of the Church, since the Church hath to interpret the Scripture, and in this interpretation cannot err; so this unity applies to the substance only, and not to the form. In respect to the latter, a diversity is found inherent in the very essence and object of the Church, so that, indeed if the divine truth must be preserved and propagated by human organs, the diversity we speak of could not possibly be avoided, as will appear

did not place himself in the right point of view. He ought to have considered, that if in the matter under discussion, Catholics appeal to Tertullian and others, the question is not respecting any particular doctrine, but about the *very principle of tradition*. Chemnitius, indeed, for the most part, agrees with Catholics in their doctrinal decisions against the Gnostics; but, as regards tradition, in *a formal* point of view, he stands quite on the side of the latter. He must have learned from the writings of Irenæus and Tertullian, that the most simple and fundamental doctrines of Christianity could not even be established by Scripture. Then he proceeds farther (p. 128): ' Veteres damnaverunt Samosatenum et deinde Arium. Judex erat verbum Dei, id est, testimonia ex Evangelio . . . quæ convincunt non calumniose judicantem.' Certainly, and the judges of doctrine at the Council of Nice were incapable of convincing, out of Holy Writ, the Arians of their error, precisely because these were the ' calumniose judicantes.'

from the following observations. The conduct of the Redeemer, in the announcement of his word, was corresponded to by that of the Apostles, and the Word became immediately in them faith—a human possession—and after his ascension, existed for the world in no other form than in this faith of the Lord's disciples, whose kernel in Peter he therefore called the rock, whereon his Church was, in such a way, to be built, that the powers of hell should never prevail against it. But, after the Divine Word had become human faith, it must be subject to all mere human destinies. It must be constantly received by all the energies of the human mind, and imbibed by the same. The preservation and communication of the Word were, in like manner, attached to a human method. Even with the Evangelists, who only wished to recount what Christ had spoken, wrought, and suffered, the Divine Word appears subject to the law here described; a law which manifests itself in the choice and arrangement of the matter, as well as in the special plan, which each proposed to himself, and in the general conception and execution of his task.

But the Divine Word became still more subject to this law, when the Apostles were fulfilling their mission—executing the divine charge, which they had received; for various questions of dispute arose, the settlement whereof could not be avoided, and on that account claimed human reflection, and required the formation of notions, judgments, and conclusions—things which were not possible to be effected, without tasking the reason and the understanding. The application of the energies of the human mind to the subject matter, received from the Lord, necessarily caused the Divine Word, on the one hand, to be analysed, and, on the other hand, to be reduced to certain leading points; and the multiplicity of objects to be contemplated in their mutual bearings, and resolved into a higher unity, whereby the human mind obtained, on these matters, greater clearness and definiteness of conception. For, everything, that the human mind hath received from an external source, and which is destined to become its property, wherein it must find itself perfectly at home, must be first reproduced by that mind itself. The original doctrine, as the human mind had variously elaborated it, exhibited itself in a much altered form : it remained the original, and yet did not; it was the same in substance, and yet differed as to form. In this process of the development of the Divine Word, during the apostolic age, we may exalt as high, and extend as wide as we please the divine

T

guidance, given to the disciples of Christ; yet certainly, without human co-operation, without the peculiar activity of man, it did not advance of itself. As in the good work of the Christian, free-will and grace pervade each other, and one and the same undivided deed is at once divine and human; so we find this to be the case here.

The same could not fail to hold good, even after the death of the apostles, even after the Gospels and the Epistles had been written, and whatever else we include in the canon of the New Testament, had been already in the hands of the faithful. When, in the manner described, the Church explains and secures the original doctrine of faith against misrepresentations; the apostolic expression is necessarily changed for another, which is the most fitted alike clearly to set forth and reject the particular error of the time. As little as the apostles themselves, in the course of their polemics, could retain the form, wherein the Saviour expounded his divine doctrine; so little was the Church enabled to adhere to the same. If the evangelical doctrine be assailed by a definite theological system, and by a terminology peculiar to itself; the false notions cannot by any means be repelled in a clear, distinct, evident, and intelligible manner, unless the Church have regard to the form of the error, and exhibit its thesis in a shape, qualified by the garb, wherein the adverse doctrine is invested, and thus render itself intelligible to all contemporaries. The origin of the Nicene formula furnishes the best solution to this question. This form is in itself the human, the temporal, the perishable element, and might be exchanged for a hundred others. Accordingly, tradition often hands down to later generations the original deposit in another form, because that deposit hath been entrusted to the care of men, whose conduct must be guided by the circumstances wherein they are placed.

Lastly, in the same manner as in the Apostolic writings, the truths of salvation are laid open with greater clearness, and in all their mutual organic connection; so, in the doctrine of the Church, the doctrine of Scripture is ever progressively unfolded to our view. Dull, therefore, as it is, to find any other than a mere *formal* distinction, between the doctrine of Christ and that of his apostles; no less senseless is it, to discover any other difference, between the primitive and the later tradition of the Church. The blame of this formal difference arises from overlooking the fact, that Christ was a God man, and wished to continue working in a manner conformable to his two-fold nature.

Moreover, the deeper insight of the human mind into the divine revelations in Christ seems determined by the struggles of error against Christian truth. It is to the unenlightened zeal of the Jewish Christians for the law, we owe the expositions of Paul touching faith and the power of the Gospel: and to the schisms in Corinth we are indebted for his explanation of principles, in respect to the Church. The Gnostic and Manichean errors led to a clearer insight into the character of evil, destitute of, and opposed to, all existence as it is, as well as to a maturer knowledge of the value of God's *original* creation (nature and freedom), and its relation to the *new* creation in Christ Jesus. Out of the Pelagian contest arose a fuller and more conscious recognition of human infirmity, in the sphere of true virtue; and so have matters gone on down to our days. It would be ridiculous, on the part of Catholics, to deny as a foolish boast of Protestants (should the latter be inclined to claim any merit in the case), that the former had gained much from the controversy with them. By the fall of the Protestants, the Catholics necessarily rose; and from the obscurity which overclouded the minds of the reformers, a new light was cast upon the truth; and such indeed had ever been the case in all earlier schisms in the Church. Assuredly, in Christian knowledge we stand one degree higher than the period prior to the Reformation; and all the dogmas that were called in question, received such an elucidation and confirmation, that it would require no very diligent or long-continued comparison between the modern theological works, and those written prior to the Council of Trent, to see the important difference which, in this respect, exists between the two epochs.

The fact that the deeper consciousness of Christian truth (in itself eternally one and unchangeable), is the result of contest and struggle, and consequently matter of history, is of too much importance not to detain our attention for some moments. It explains the necessity of a living, visible authority which in every dispute can, with certainty, discern the truth, and separate it from error. Otherwise, we should have *only* the variable—the disputed—and at last Nihilism itself. Hence it happens (and this we may venture to premise), that where Holy Writ, without Tradition and the authority of the Church, is declared to be the sole source and rule for the knowledge of

Gospel truth, all more precise explanations and developments of Christian dogmas are willingly left in utter ignorance, nay, are even absolutely rejected. Guided by this principle, men can find no rational object to connect with the history of believing intelligence in the Christian Church, and must necessarily evince hostility towards everything of this tendency, which hath occurred in the Church. Or, when they lose all confidence and all hope of freeing themselves from the turmoil of opinions, and of seeing a bright, steady light arise out of the dark chaos, they cast, in their despair, upon the Bible the whole mass of opinions, that ages have thrown up ; and of that which is, boldly assert it could not have been otherwise, consequently exists of necessity, and is inherent in the very essence of Christianity. They do not see that, with that complaisance to acknowledge every variety of opinion which, in the course of time, may have gradually been founded on Scripture, a destructive principle, for the solution of all the enigmas of Christian history is laid down—to wit, the principle, that its object is to show that the Scripture, as it includes *every* sense, hath consequently none. But all charges against the Catholic Church are reduced to this, that she has been so absurd, as to suppose the Scriptures to contain one sense and consequently only one, and that definite, whereof the faithful, in the course of history, must ever obtain a clearer and more intuitive knowledge : while, on the other hand, the refutation of the above-mentioned prejudice, which manifested itself soon after the origin of the Church, has been, in the succession of ages, the peculiar task of Christian science.

§ XLI—TRADITION IN A MORE LIMITED SENSE—THE CANON OF THE SCRIPTURES

From that notion of Tradition, which we have hitherto expounded, another is to be distinguished, although both are intimately united with each other. Tradition we have hitherto described as the consciousness of the Church, as the living word of faith, according to which the Scriptures are to be interpreted, and to be understood. The doctrine of tradition contains, in this sense, nothing else than the doctrine of Scripture ; both, as to their contents, are one and the same. But, moreover, it is asserted by the Catholic Church, that many things have been delivered to her by the apostles, which Holy Writ either doth not at all comprise, or at most, but alludes to. This assertion of the Church is of the greatest moment, and partially indeed, includes the foundations of the whole system.[1] Among these oral traditions must be included the doctrine of the canonicity, and the inspiration of the Sacred Scriptures; for, in no part of the Bible do we find the books belonging to it designated; and were such a catalogue contained in it, its authority must first be made matter of inquiry. In like manner, the testimony as to the inspiration of the biblical writings is obtained only through the Church. It is from this point we first discern, in all its magnitude, the vast importance of the doctrine of Church authority, and can form a notion of the infinite multitude of things involved in that doctrine. He can scarcely be a sincere Christian, who will not attribute to a special protection of Divine Providence, the preservation of the works of those apostles, and such of their disciples, who have made a contribution to the biblical canon. But, in taking into consideration this special protection, he cannot set aside the Catholic Church, and must even in despite of deliberate repugnance, admit that it was that Church, which the Saviour employed as a medium for preserving to all ages the writings, that had been penned under his peculiar assistance. Every learned theologian is aware, that the Gnostics, as well as one class of anti-Trinitarians, in the second and third centuries, rejected sometimes this or that gospel, sometimes the Acts of the Apostles, and sometimes the apostolic epistles; nay, even brought forward spurious gospels and acts of the apostles and mutilated, in the most criminal manner the genuine apostolic works, which they retained. And yet no one can refuse to acknowledge that the visible Church, which these heretics assailed, in the same manner as is usual with Protestants—the Church that the former like the latter, continually denounced as the corruptress of pure doctrine, as exerting a tryanny over minds, as wicked beyond conception—that this Church, we say, was selected and deemed worthy by Almighty God, to

---

[1] On that passage from the Council of Trent cited above (sess. iv, c. 2), 'Hanc veritatem et disciplinam contineri in libris scriptis et sine scripto traditionibus,' Pallavicini remarks as follows: ' Duo per illam sanctionem intendit synodus, alterum, palam facere, fidei Catholicæ fundamenta non modo esse divinas literas, quod recentes hæretici pertinaciter contendebant; sed non minus etiam traditiones, a quibus denique dependet, quidquid certi obtinemus de legitima ipsarum scripturarum auctoritate.' —Lib. vi, c. vii, n. 7.

preserve the most precious jewel of Christians! What conclusions may not hence be immediately deduced! On Luther himself, as we shall have occasion later to see, this fact made a deep impression; and he brought it forward at times in a train of ideas, that can scarcely be reconciled with the position which, in other respects, he had taken up against the Catholic Church.

Moreover, in reference to the canon of the sacred writings, some difference exists between Catholics and Protestants. Originally, indeed, it seemed probable as if in this department very important differences would have arisen; as if the melancholy spectacle of the first ages would have been renewed, in which, according to the suggestions of caprice, or the interest of mere individual opinions, sometimes one, sometimes another portion of the Bible was rejected. It is generally known (and indeed in Berthold's and de Wette's Introductions to the Sacred Books, the reader may in part see the passages on this matter cited from Luther), that the Reformer called the Epistle of St James, an Epistle of straw, and was not disposed to acknowledge it as an apostolic production; judged not more favourably of the Revelations of St John, and was wont to say of the first three Gospels, that in them the Gospel was not to be found; whereas, the Gospel of St John, the Acts of the Apostles, and the Epistles of St Paul, he exalted in peculiar strains of eulogy. In this matter the opposition between St James's doctrine on the relation between faith and works, and Luther's exposition of the same subject, exerted an undeniable influence. Luther preferred the rejection of this valuable portion of Holy Writ, to the amendment of his own opinions, and chose rather to question the genuineness of a canonical Scripture, than to doubt the truth of his own theory. Assuredly, if in the otherwise obscure Apocalypse, there had not been found passages of extreme clearness, like the following: 'Happy are they who sleep in the Lord, *for their works follow them;*' Luther would have found less to offend him in this book. The remarkable expression, 'that in the Gospels the Gospel is not contained,' may be explained from what has been said above, respecting the signification, which the old Lutherans attached to the word *Gospel*. Luther's prejudices, however, were not able to obscure the sounder sense of his followers; and so it came to pass, that they, as well as the Calvinists, admitted with the Catholic Church, the entire books of the New Testament to be canonical. But, in regard to the Old Testament, doctrinal prejudices prevailed; and those Scriptures, which the Catholics call the deutero-canonical,[1] were gradually expunged from the Canon, yet more decidedly on the part of the Calvinists, than of the Lutherans. Among the modern Protestants, Clausen, at least, has not denied, that in this matter regard was paid to other considerations, than to those of a merely historical and critical kind.

§ XLII—ON THE RELATION OF THE ECCLESIASTICAL INTERPRETATION OF HOLY WRIT TO THE LEARNED AND SCIENTIFIC EXEGESIS—PATRISTIC AUTHORITY AND FREE INVESTIGATION

As the notion of doctrinal tradition[2] and of the ecclesiastical interpretation of Holy Writ has been now fully unfolded, it is necessary, in order to obviate some singular misconceptions, to state, in a few words, the relation between the learned exegesis as applied to the sacred writings, and that interpretation which emanates from the Church. The interpretation of the Church does not descend to the details, which must claim the attention of the scientific exegetist. Thus, for example, she does not hold it for a duty, nor include it in the compass of her rights, to determine when, by whom, and for what object the Book of Job was written; or what particular inducement engaged St

[1] In the decree of the Council of Trent on the canonical Scriptures, sess. iv, the following is the catalogue of the Old Testament Scriptures: 'Sunt infrascripti: Testamenti veteris, quinque Moysis, id est, Genesis, Exodus, Leviticus, Numeri, Deuteronomium: Josue, Judicum, Ruth, quatuor Regum, duo Paralipomenon, Esdra primus et secundus, qui diciter Nehemias, Tobias, Judith, Hester, Job, Psalterium Davidicum centum quinquaginta psalmorum, Parobolæ, Ecclesiastes, Canticum Canticorum, Sapientia, Ecclesiasticus, Isaias, Hieremias cum Baruch, Ezechiel, Daniel, duodecim Prophetæ minores, id est, Osea, Joel, Amos, Abdias, Jonas, Micheas, Naum, Abacuc, Sophonias, Aggæus, Zacharias, Malachias, duo Machabæorum primus et secundus.' The French Protestant confession of faith, called the Gallic Confession, i. c. p. 111, gives the following canon of the writings of the Old Testament: 'Quinque libri Moysis, nempe. . . . Josue, Judices, Ruth, Samuelis 1, 2, Regum 1, 2, Chronicon, sive Paralipomenon 1, 2, Esdræ lib. 1, Nehemias, Ester, Job, Psalmi, Proverbia, Ecclesiastes, Canticum Canticorum, Esaias, Jeremias cum Lament., Ezechiel, Daniel, Minores Prophetæ 12 nempe.' There are here wanting Tobias, Judith, Baruch, Sapientia, Ecclesiasticus, Machabæorum primus et secundus.
N.B.—The Scriptural canon of the Anglican Church is the same with that of the French Protestants as here given.—*Trans.*

[2] We do not speak here of disciplinary, liturgical, and other kinds of tradition.

John to publish his gospel, or the Apostle Paul to address an epistle to the Romans ; in what order of time the epistles of this messenger of the Lord followed each other, etc. etc. As little doth the Church explain particular words and verses, their bearings one to the other, or the connection existing between larger portions of a sacred book. Antiquities, in the widest sense of the word, fall not within the domain of her interpretation ; in short, that interpretation extends only to doctrines of faith and morals. Thus much as to the extent of her interpretation.

But now as to the nature and mode of the Church's interpretation ; this is not conducted according to the rules and well-known aids of an historical and grammatical exegesis, whereby the individual seeks to obtain scientific insight into the sense of Holy Writ. On the contrary, the doctrinal contents of Scripture she designates in the general spirit of Scripture. Hence the earliest œcumenical councils did not even adduce any particular scriptural texts, in support of their dogmatic decrees ; and Catholic theologians teach with general concurrence, and quite in the spirit of the Church, that even a Scriptural proof in favour of a decree held to be infallible, is not itself infallible, but only the dogma as defined. The deepest reason for this conduct of the Church lies in the indisputable truth, that she was not founded by Holy Writ, but already existed before its several parts appeared. The certainty which she has of the truth of her own doctrines, is an immediate one, for she received her dogmas from the lips of Christ and the apostles ; and by the power of the Divine Spirit, they are indelibly stamped on her consciousness, or as Irenæus expresses it, on her heart. If the Church were to endeavour, by learned investigation, to seek her doctrines, she would fall into the most absurd inconsistency, and annihilate her very self. For, as it would be the Church that should institute the inquiry, her existence would be presupposed ; and yet, as she would have first to find out her own being, the thing whereby and wherein she absolutely consists, namely, Divine Truth, her non-existence must at the same time be presupposed ! She would have to go in search of herself, and this a madman only could do ; she would be like the man, that would examine the papers written by himself, in order to discover whether he really existed ! The essential matter of Holy Writ is eternally present in the Church, because it is her heart's-blood—her breath—her soul—her all. She exists only by Christ, and yet she must have to find him out ! Whoever seriously reflects on the signification of those words of Christ, 'I am with ye even to the consummation of the world,' will be able to conceive at least the view, which the Catholic Church takes of herself.

What we have said involves the limits prescribed to the freedom of the Catholic scholar, in the interpretation of Holy Writ. It is evident, of course, that we speak not here of that general freedom possessed by every man, at the peril of his own soul, like the Jew and the Heathen, to hold the Bible as the work of impostors or dupes, as a medley of truth and error, wisdom and folly. This freedom the Catholic possesses, like the Protestant; but we speak of that freedom only which the Catholic enjoys, when he will not renounce his character as Catholic; for were he to entertain the above-mentioned view of the Sacred Scriptures, he would thereby renounce all connection with our church. As a Catholic, he is freely convinced, that the Church is a divine institution, upheld by supernal aid, 'which leads her into all truth;' that, consequently, no doctrine rejected by her is contained in Scripture; that with the latter, on the contrary, her dogmas perfectly coincide, though many particulars may not be verbally set forth in Holy Writ. Accordingly he has the conviction, that the Scripture, for example, doth not teach that Christ is a mere man; nay, he is certain, that it represents him also as God. Inasmuch as he professes this belief, he is not free to profess the contrary, for he would contradict himself; in the same way as a man, who has resolved to remain chaste, cannot be unchaste, without violating his resolution. To this restriction, which everyone most probably will consider rational, the Catholic Church subjects her members, and consequently, also, the learned exegetists of Scripture. A Church which would authorise anyone to find what he pleased in Scripture, and without any foundation to declare it as unecclesiastical, such a Church would thereby declare, that it believed in nothing, and was devoid of all doctrines; for the mere possession of the Bible no more constitutes a Church, than the possession of the faculty of reason renders anyone really rational. Such a Church would in fact, as a moral entity, exhibit the contradiction just adverted to, which a physical being could not be guilty of. The individual cannot at one and the same time believe, and not believe, a particular point of doctrine. But if a Church, which consists of a union of many individuals, permitted every member, as such, to receive or to reject at his pleasure, any article of faith, it would fall into this very contradiction, and would be a monster of unbelief, indifferent to the most opposite doctrines, which we might indeed, on our behalf, honour with the finest epithets, but certainly not denominate a Church. The Church must train up souls for the kingdom of God, which is founded on definite facts and truths, that are eternally unchangeable; and so a Church, that knows no such immutable dogmas, is like to a teacher, that knows not what he should teach. The Church has to stamp the image of Christ on humanity; but Christ is not sometimes this, and sometimes that, but eternally the same. She has to breathe into the hearts of men the word of God, that came down from heaven: but this word is no vague, empty sound, whereof we can make what we will.

That, accordingly, the principles of the Catholic Church agree with the idea of a positive Church, and the claim is but natural, which she exacts of her members, to recognise in the Bible, when they make it the subject of a learned exegesis, those doctrines of faith and morality, which they themselves acknowledge to be biblical, we trust we have now made sufficiently evident. In other respects, no one belonging to the Catholic Church professes aught else, than her doctrines of faith and morality. For, in this respect, she expresses the sense of Holy Writ, and indeed only in a general way; so that the learned expositor, by the laws of his religious community is bound to nothing more; and a wide field is ever open to him, whereon he may exert his talents, his hermeneutical skill, his philological and archæological learning, and employ them usefully for the advancement of science.

But, if we should be reminded of the decree of the Council of Trent, which directs the Catholic to interpret the Scripture, according to the unanimous testimony of the holy fathers,[1] how can we escape the reproach, that an *absolutely* sacred exegesis hath existed for centuries, and that consequently all idea of progress in the understanding of the Bible must be given up? Before we lay down the Catholic view of this subject, it may be proper to state, with the utmost succinctness, the relation of patristic authority to learned investigation. Whoever takes the pains to study the writings of the holy fathers, may without much penetration discover, that while agreeing perfectly on all

---

[1] Conc. Trid. sess. iv, decret. de edit. et usu sacror. libror. 'Ut nemo . . . contra unanimen consensum Patrum ipsam Scripturam sacram interpretari audeat.'

ecclesiastical dogmas, they yet expatiate most variously on the doctrines of Christian faith and morality. The mode and form wherein they appropriate the one Gospel to themselves, demonstrate its truth to others, develope it in their own interior, and philosophise and speculate upon its doctrines, most strikingly evince the individuality of each writer. One manifests a deeper, the other a clearer and acuter view of his subject ; one turns this, the other that talent to his profit. While now all Catholics gladly profess the same dogmas with the fathers of the Church, the individual opinions, the mere human views of the latter, possess in their estimation no further value, but as they present reasonable grounds for acceptance, or as any peculiar affinity of mind may exist between one father of the Church, and a Catholic of a subsequent age. These principles, at all periods of the Church, were openly professed, and brought into practice. Never did any father, not even the most revered, succeed in imposing his own peculiar opinions on the Church ; as of this fact, St Augustine furnishes a remarkable proof. What writer ever acquired greater authority than he ? Yet, his theory respecting original sin and grace, never became the doctrine of the Church ; and herein precisely he showed himself a good Catholic, that he gave us the permission to examine his private opinions,[1] and to retain only what was sound. Moreover, the

[1] Augustin. contra Faustum Manich. lib. ii, c. 5. ' Id genus literarum, *quæ non præcipiendi auctoritate, sed proficiendi exercitatione* scribuntur a nobis non cum credendi necessitate, sed cum judicandi libertate legendum est ; cui tamen ne intercluderetur locus et adimeretur posteris ad quæstiones difficiles tractandas, atque versandas *linguæ ac stili saluberrimus labor*, Distincta est a posterioribus libris excellentia canonicæ auctoritatis V. et N. Testamenti, quæ apostolorum confirmata temporibus, per successiones episcoporum et propagationes ecclesiarum tanquam in sede quadam sublimiter constituta est, cui serviat omnis fidelis et pius intellectus. Ibi si quid velut absurdum noverit, non licet dicere, auctor hujus libri non tenuit veritatem : sed, aut codex mendosus est, aut interpres erravit, aut tu non intelligis. In opusculis autem posteriorum, quæ libris innumerabilibus continentur, sed nullo modo illi sacratissimæ canonicarum scripturarum excellentiæ coæquantur, etiam in quibuscunque eorum invenitur eadem veritas, longe tamen est impar auctoritas. Itaque in eis, si qua forte propterea dissonare putantur a vero, quia non ut dicta sunt intelliguntur ; tamen liberum ibi habet lector auditorve judicium, quo vel approbet, placuerit, vel improbat quod offenderit. Et ideo cuncta ejusmodi, nisi vel certa ratione, vel ex illa canonica auctoritate defendantur, ut demonstretur sive omnio ita esse, sive fieri potuisse, quod ibi disputatum est, vel narratum : si cui displicuerit, aut credere noluerit, non reprehenditur. In illa vero canonica eminentia ss. literarum, etiamsi **unus** propheta, seu apostolus, aut evangelista, aliquid in suis literis posuisse **ipsa canonis** confirmatione declaratur, non licet dubitare quod verum sit :

expression, 'doctrine of the fathers,' is frequently synonymous with tradition : in this sense they are considered as representatives of *the faith* of antiquity—as channels and witnesses of transmitted doctrine ; but by no means so when, upon a thousand subjects, they lay before us their own peculiar views and speculations. From this point of view, where they do not speak, *but through them the belief of the universal Church is made known*, they possess, undoubtedly, a decisive authority : — an authority, however, which belongs not to their persons but to their tradition, whereby they themselves were regulated, and which they only reflect. In this respect, we must needs agree, with them because one doctrine of faith hath subsisted, and must subsist, through the whole history of the Church. We will not and cannot believe otherwise, than as our fathers have believed ; but as to their peculiarities of opinion, we may adopt them, or not, as we please. Besides, the truth, which we possess in common with them, has, as we have already elsewhere had occasion to observe, by means of the splendid intellects, which devoted their undivided energy

alioquin nulla erit pagina, qua humanæ imperitiæ regatur infirmitas, si librorum saluberrima auctoritas aut contemta penitus aboletur, aut interminata confunditur.' Thomas Aquin. Sum. tot. theolog. P. 1, q. 1, art. 8, edit. Caj. Lugd. 1580, p. 10. 'Auctoritatibus canonicæ scripturæ utitur (sacra doctrina) proprie ex necessitate argumentando : auctoritatibus autem aliorum doctorum ecclesiæ quasi arguendo ex propriis, sed probabiliter. Innititur enim fides nostra revelationi apostolis et prophetis factæ, qui canonicos libros scripsere, non autem revelationi, si qua fuit aliis doctoribus facta.' Unde dicit Augustinus in epistola ad Hieronymum (xix) : 'Solis enim scripturarum libris, qui canonici appellantur, didici hunc honorem deferre, ut nullum auctorem eorum in scribendo errasse aliquid firmissime credam. Alios autem ita lego, ut quantalibet sanctitate doctrinaque præpoleant, non ideo vero putem, quod ipsi ita senserunt vel scripserunt.'

Catholics distinguish very well between the *testimony* of the father of the Church, as to the universal belief in his time, and his own philosophy or theological speculations. In the latter respect, the views of the fathers are considered by us as mere views, and if all were to concur in the same view, that concurrence would never constitute a dogma. Melchior Canus (loc. theol. lib. vii, c. 3, p. 425) observes : ' Sanctorum auctoritas, sive paucorum, sive plurium, cum ad eas facultates affertur, quæ naturali lumine continentur, certa argumenta non suppedidat : sed tantum pollet, quantum ratio naturæ consentanea persuaserit.' P. 432, he continues : 'Omnium etiam sanctorum auctoritas in eo genere quæstionum, quas ad fidem diximus minime pertinere, fidem quidem probabilem facit : certam non facit.' Canus here means, as is clear from the development of his proposition, inquiries which have reference to doctrines of faith. At page 430, he subjoins : ' Auctores *canonici*, ut superni, cœlestes, divini perpetuam stabilemque constantiam servant, reliqui vero scriptores sancti inferiores et humani sunt, deficiuntque interdum ac monstrum quandoque pariunt, præter convenientem ordinem institutumque naturæ.'

to its defence, been often more deeply investigated, or contemplated in all its bearings, and viewed in a more general connection; so that Christian science makes continual progress, and the mysteries of God are ever more clearly unfolded. For this subjective insight into the doctrines of salvation, eternally immutable in themselves, the fathers of the Church have by no means laid down the standard, nor prescribed any pause in the progress of inquiry.[1]

The same principle holds good, with regard to their interpretation of Scripture. Except in the explanation of a very few classical passages, we know not where we shall meet with a general uniformity of Scriptural interpretation among the fathers, further than that all deduce from the sacred writings, the same doctrines of faith and morality, yet each in his own peculiar manner; so that some remain for all times distinguished models of Scriptural exposition, others rise not above

[1] St Vincent Lirinensis expresses himself on this subject with incomparable beauty and truth. ' Esto spiritualis tabernaculi Beseleel (Exod. xxxi, 2) pretiosas divini dogmatis gemmas exsculpe, fideliter coapta, adorna sapienter, adjice splendorem, gratiam, venustatem. Intelligetur, te exponente, illustrius, quod ante obscurius credebatur. Per te posteritas intellectum gratuletur, quod ante vetustas non intellectum venerabatur. Eadem tamen, quæ didicisti, doce: ut, cum dicas nove, non dicas nova.' C. xxviii: ' Sed forsitan dicit aliquis: nullusne ergo in ecclesia Christi profectus? Habeatur plane et maximus. Nam quis ille est tam invidus hominibus, tam exosus Deo, qui illud prohibere conetur? *Sed ita tamen ut vere profectus sit ille fidei, non permutatio. Siquidem ad profectum pertinet, ut in semet ipsa unaquæque res* amplificetur, ad permutationem vero, ut aliquid ex alio in aliud transvertatur. Crescat igitur oportet, et multum vehementereque proficiat tam singulorum, quam omnium tam unius hominis, quam totius ecclesiæ ætatum ac sæculorum gradibus intelligentia, scientia, sapientia; sed in suo duntaxat genere, in eodem scilicet dogmate, eodem sensu, eademque sententia.' C. xxix: ' Imitetur animarum religio rationem corporum; quæ licet annorum processu numeros suos evolvant, et explicent, eadem tamen, quæ erant, permanent. Multum interest intet pueritiæ florem et senectutis maturitatem; sed iidem tamen ipsi fiunt senes, qui fuerant adolescentes; ut quamvis unius ejusdem hominis status habitusque mutetur, una tamen nihilominus, eademque natura, una eademque persona sit,' etc. Commonitorium, ed. Klüpfel, Vienn. 1809, c. xxvii, p. 199: ' This explanation of St Vincent was occasioned by the Manicheans, who, as we gather from St Augustine's works, *De utilitate credendi, De vera religione, Contra Faustum*, etc., brought up the old Gnostic charge against Catholics, that they were under a religious tyranny, that among them was found no independent inquiry into doctrine, and no progress in knowledge. How desirable it were, that we could everywhere find such clear notions of the progressive development of Christian dogmas as are here advanced by Vincentius! Now we think we have made a *progress* in *Christian* knowledge, when we deny Christ to be what He declared himself to be!'

mediocrity, while others again are, merely by their good intentions and love for the Saviour, entitled to veneration. As in this manner, among the fathers themselves, one is superior to the other, and by his exegetical tact, by the acuteness and delicacy of his perceptions, by an intellectual affinity with the writer expounded, by the extent of the philological and historical knowledge brought to the task of interpretation, holds a higher place ; so this may and will be the case in all ages. The same dogmas, the same morality, all like the fathers, will find in Holy Writ ; yet in another way ; we will bring forward the same things, but often not in the same manner. More extensive philological acquirements, and the more abundant aids of every kind, which modern times furnish, enable us, without in the least degree deviating from the unanimous interpretation of the fathers, to explain many things in a better and more solid manner than they did.[1] The better Catholic exegetists since the

[1] Cardinal Cajetan, in the Preface to his Exposition of Genesis, says : ' Non alligavit Deus expositionem scripturarum sacrarum priscorum doctorum sensibus; sed Scripturæ ipsi integræ, sub Catholicæ ecclesiæ censurai ; alioquin spes nobis et posteris tolleretur exponendi scripturam sacram, nisi transferendo, ut aiunt, de libro in quinternum.' The meaning of the cardinal is, that, by a general interpretation of Holy Writ no tenet can be elicited contrary to Catholic doctrine, to the sense of the Church, to the faith unanimously attested by the fathers ; although in details the interpretation may differ from that of the fathers. When, for example, it is said of God, He hardened the heart of Pharaoh, He will raise up false prophets, He hated Esau and loved Jacob before they were born ; so no Catholic exegetist, like Calvin and Beza, would thence infer, that the Bible represents God as the author of evil, and would say the Deity creates a portion of mankind for sin, in order to be afterwards able to damn them ; for such a monstrous assertion would be contrary to the universal testimony of the fathers ; that is to say, to the constant doctrine of the Church. On the other hand, the Catholic interpreter may, in his peculiar mode of explaining those passages by the biblical phraseology, differ, if there be adequate grounds, from all the fathers put together. Melchior Canus was not quite satisfied with the above-mentioned principle, because he deduced from it those fanciful opinions, which are not unfrequently met with in Cajetan's exegetical writings : for what Canus, in the work already cited, says, p. 437, is perfectly true : ' Illud breviter dici potest, Cajetanum summis ecclesiæ ædificatoribus parem esse potuisse, nisi . . . ingenii dexteritate confisus literas demum sacras suo arbitratu exposuisset, felicissime quidem fere, sed in paucis quibusdam locis acutius sane multo, quam felicius.'

Pallavacini, on the other hand (in his Hist. Concil. Trident, lib. vi, c. 18, n. 2, p. 221), takes Cajetan under his protection, and shows that he has not acted contrary to the Council of Trent ; that rather Melchior Canus required from every writer among the Dominicans, an exclusive adoption of the maxims of that Order, to which he himself belonged. ' Equidem in primis affirmo,' says Pallavacini, ' Cajetanum, quamvis a suis (Cajetan

Reformation, from Thomas de Vio, Contareni, Sadoletus, Masius, Maldonado, Giustiniani, Estius, Cornelius, à Lapide down to our own days, furnish a proof of what is here asserted ; and the Biblical researches of several critics, such as Richard Simon, Hug, Jahn, Feilmoser, and others, will certainly not show, that the earlier theologians have left nothing to the later ones, but to edit their works anew. Accordingly, wherein consists the impropriety that we should still revere in the Holy Scriptures, the same miracles of divine wisdom and compassion, which our fathers revered fourteen and eighteen hundred years ago ? Doth the impropriety lie in the shortsightedness of our understanding which is unable to discover, that such simple writings as the Sacred Books, should not have been understood as to their essential import in the times wherein they were published, and in the communities to which they were addressed ? Must we thus look for this impropriety, in our inability to conceive how an age, which was nearest to the composition of the Bible should have been the furthest removed from the true understanding thereof ? Or, doth it consist in our regarding the opinion as singular, that the Christian Church had not penetrated into the sense of her own sacred records at a time when she exerted a truly renovating influence over the world, when

was also a Dominican) in hoc dicto licentiæ nota reprehensum, nunquam protulisse sensa Tridentino decreto in hac parte adversantia. Secundo, concilium neque præscripsisse, neque coarctasse novis legibus rationem intelligendi Dei verbum ; *sed declarasse illicitum et hæreticum quod suapte natura erat* hujusmodi, et prout semper habitum ac declaratum fuerat a patribus, a pontificibus, a conciliis. . . . Prohibet quidem concilium, ne sacris literis aptetur interpretatio repugnans SS. patrum sententiæ, idque in rebus tum fidei, tum morum ; et Cajetanus, utut rem Canus intelligat, de his minime ioquitur, neque unquam declarat, fas esse adversus communes SS. patrum sententias obviam ire, sed fas esse depromere scripturæ expositionem prorsus novam, et ab omnibus eorum expositionibus diversam. Etenim quemadmodum ipsi discreparunt inter se in illius explicatione sententiæ, adeoque singulæ eorum explanationes per se ipsas dubitationi subjacent, ita, quantum conjicio, visum est Cajetano, posse cunctas simul dubitationi subjacere et quandam aliam esse veram quæ ipsis haud in mentem venerit.' Canus himself, however, says, p. 457 : 'Spes inquiunt, nobis et posteris tollitur, exponendi sacras literas nisi transferendo de libro in quinternum. Minime vero gentium. Nam, ut illud præteream, quod in sacris bibliis loci sunt multi, atque adeo libri integri, in quibus interpretum diligentiam ecclesia desiderat, in quibusque proinde juniores possent et eruditionis et ingenii posteris ipsi quoque suis monimenta relinquere, in illis etiam, quæ antiquorum sunt ingenio ac diligentia elaborata, nonnihil nos christiano populo, si volumus, præstare et quidem utilissime possumus. Possumus enim vetustis novitatem dare, obsoletis nitorem, obscuris lucem, fastiditis gratiam, dubiis fidem, omnibus naturam suam et naturæ suæ omnia.'

she conquered Judaism, destroyed Heathenism, and overcame all the powers of darkness ? Or, that we should not be able to convince ourselves, that the night is dispersed by darkness, and illusions by error ? Or, doth the impropriety consist in the opinion, that Holy Writ could not possibly have been destined in the course of every fifteen years, and even under the hand of each of its expositors, to receive, as if by a divine miracle, an essentially different import than in former times.

Lastly (and this is the principal point), since the Catholic Church regards herself as that institution of the Lord, wherein His doctrines of salvation and the knowledge of the same, have, by the immediate instruction of the apostles, and the power of the Divine Spirit, been deposited; her claim to interpret, according to her rule of faith, the sacred writings, in which the same doctrines of salvation, under the guidance of the same Spirit, have been laid down, perfectly agrees with the claims of a genuine historical and grammatical exegesis; and it is precisely the most successful interpretation of this kind, that would of necessity most faithfully reflect her doctrines. From her point of view, it appears accordingly quite unintelligible, how her claim should not be consistent with the laws of a true exegesis, alone deserving of the name; or, how in other respects the able interpreter, when supported by her rule, should not be precisely the most distinguished. The Protestants, on the other hand, starting from the prejudice, that the peculiar doctrines of the Catholic Church are not conformable to Scripture, must consequently regard her principle of interpretation as one outwardly imposed, and therefore arbitrary and unnatural; but this prejudice the Catholic repels as idle, and totally devoid of foundation.

§ XLIII—THE HIERARCHY

It now remains for us to make a few remarks on the Hierarchy. The primary view of the Church, as a divine and human institution, is here evinced in a very striking form. Accordingly, for the exercise of public functions in the Church, for the discharge of the office of teaching, and the administration of the sacraments, a divine internal calling and a higher qualification are, above all things, required. But, as the divine, invisible nature of the Church is connected with a human, visible form; so the calling from above must necessarily be here below first discerned, and then acknowledged; and the heavenly qualification must appear attached to an act obvious to the senses, and executed in the visible Church Or in other words, the authorisation for the public exercise of ecclesiastical functions is imparted by a sacrament—an outward act to be performed by men according to the commission of Christ, and which partly denotes, partly conveys an inward and divine grace.[1] The introduction into an invisible Church, requires only a spiritual baptism: the continuance in the same, needs only an internal nourishment, we cannot say with the body of Christ (because 'body' already reminds us of an *outward* origin of the Church), but with the logos of God. An invisible Church needs only an inward purely spiritual sacrifice, and an universal priesthood.[2] But it is otherwise with a visible Church. *This* requires that the baptism of fire, and of the Spirit, should be likewise a baptism of water; and that the nurture of the soul, which Christ imparts, should be visibly represented by a bodily food. In the very idea of such a Church, an external sacrifice, also, is necessarily involved. The same observation will apply to priestly orders: the internal and outward consecration go together; the heavenly and the earthly unction become one and the same. As the preservation of the doctrines and institutions of Christ, hath been intrusted to the Church, so it is impossible for her to revere as a priest, every individual who declares he hath been inwardly consecrated to the priesthood. On the contrary, as he must previously be carefully and strictly bred up, and instructed in the divine dogmas of the Church, in order to contribute

[1] Concil. Trident. sess. xxiii, cap. 3. 'Cum scripturæ testimonio, Apostolica traditione, et patrum unanimi consensu perspicuum sit, per sacram ordinationem, quæ verbis et signis exterioribus perficitur, gratiam conferri; dubitare nemo debet, ordinem esse vere et proprie unum ex septem Sanctæ Ecclesiæ Sacramentis; inquit enim Apostolus: Admoneo te, ut resuscites gratiam, quæ est in te, per impositionem manuum mearum.'

[2] It is admirably observed by the Council of Trent, cap. i, lib. 1: 'Sacrificium et sacerdotium ita Dei ordinatione conjuncta sunt, ut utrumque in omni lege extiterit. Cum igitur in novo testamento sanctum Eucharistiæ sacrificium visibile ex Domini institutione Catholica ecclesia acceperit; fateri etiam oportet, in ea novum esse visibile et externum sacerdotium, in quod vetus translatum est. Hoc autem ab eodem domino Salvatore nostro institutum esse, atque Apostolis, eorumque successoribus in sacerdotio potestatem traditam consecrandi, offerendi et ministrandi corpus et sanguinem ejus, nec non et peccata dimittendi et retinendi, sacræ literæ ostendunt, et Ecclesiæ Catholicæ traditio semper docuit.' Hence, in an invisible Church only the invisible forgiveness of sins and confession before God are necessary; but it is otherwise in the visible Church.

U

towards their further propagation; so he receives through the Church, through her external consecration, the inward consecration from God; or, in other words, he receives, through the imposition of the hands of *the bishops*, the Holy Ghost. The visibility and the stability of the Church, connected therewith, require, accordingly, an ecclesiastical ordination, originating with Christ, the fountain-head, and perpetuated in uninterrupted succession; so that as the apostles were sent forth by the Saviour, they, in their turn, instituted bishops, and these appointed their successors, and so on, down to our own days.[1] By this episcopal succession, beginning from our Saviour, and continued on without interruption, we can especially recognise, as by an outward mark, which is the true Church founded by him.[2]

The episcopate, the continuation of the apostleship, is accordingly revered as a Divine institution: not less so, and even, on that very account, the Pope, who is the centre of unity, and the head of the episcopate. If the episcopate is to form a corporation, outwardly as well as inwardly bound together, in order to unite all believers into one harmonious life, which the Catholic Church so urgently requires; it stands in need of a centre, whereby all may be held together and firmly connected.

[1] Irenæus says to the heretics of his time (Adv. hæres. lib. iii, c. 3): 'Hac ordinatione et successione, ea quæ est ab apostolis in ecclesia traditio et veritatis præconizatio pervenit usque ad nos. Et est plenissima hæc ostensio unam et eandem vivificatricem fidem esse, quæ in ecclesia ab apostolis usque nunc sit conservata et tradita in veritate.' Lib. iv, c. 43, 'Quapropter eis, qui in ecclesia sunt presbyteris obaudire oportet, his qui successionem habent ab apostolis, qui cum episcopatus successione charisma veritatis certum secundum placitum patris acceperunt.' Tertullian remarks against the same heretics: 'Edant ergo originem ecclesiarum suarum: evolvant ordinem episcoporum suorum ita per successiones ab initio decurrentem, ut primus ille episcopus aliquem ex apostolis, vel apostolicis viris, qui tamen cum apostolis perseveraverint, habuerit auctorem et antecessorem. . . . Hoc enim modo ecclesiæ apostolicæ census suos deferunt. Sicut Smyrnæorum ecclesia habens Polycarpum ab Johanne conlocatum refert: sicut Romanorum Clementem a Petro ordinatum edit; proinde utique et cæteræ exhibent. Confingant tale aliquid hæretici.'

[2] The Council of Florence gives the following definition of the Papal power:—' Item definimus, sanctam apostolicam sedem et Romanum pontificem in universum orbem tenere primatum, et ipsum Pontificem Romanum successorum esse beati Petri principis Apostolorum, et verum Christi vicarium, totiusque ecclesiæ caput, et omnium Christianorum patrem et doctorem existere; et ipsi in beato Petro pascendi, regendi, et gubernandi universalem ecclesiam a domino nostro Jesu Christo plenam potestatem traditam esse, quemadmodum etiam in gestis œcumenicorum conciliorum et in sacris canonibus continetur.' See Hardouin Acta Concil. tom. ix, p. 423.

What a helpless, shapeless mass, incapable of all combined action, would the Catholic Church not have been, spread as she is over all the kingdoms of the earth, over all the parts of the world, had she been possessed of no head, no supreme bishop, revered by all. She would, of necessity, have been split into an incalculable number of particular Churches, devoid of all consistence, had not a strong, mighty bond united all, had not the successor of Peter firmly held them together. Had not the universal Church possessed a head instituted by Christ, and had not this head, *by acknowledged rights and obligations* been enabled to exert an influence over each of its parts; those parts, abandoned to themselves, would soon have taken a course of development, contrary to each other, and absolutely determined by local relations;—a course which would have led to the dissolution of the whole body. No one can be so weak-minded as not to perceive, that then the whole authority of the Church, in matters of faith, would have vanished; since the several Churches opposed to each other could not attest one and the same thing, nay, must stand in mutual contradiction. Without a visible head, the whole view, which the Catholic Church takes of herself, as a visible society representing the place of Christ, would have been lost, or rather, never would have occurred to her. In a visible Church, a visible head is necessarily included. The following instances may serve to evince, more clearly, the truth of what is here asserted. If, in the appointment of bishops to their particular districts, the universal Church exerted no decisive influence, did not possess, for example, the right of confirmation; then views inimical to the interests of the Church would infallibly raise to the episcopal dignity men who, in a short time, would venture to destroy, or, at least, permit the destruction, of the common faith. The same would be the result, if the universal Church did not enjoy the right of deprivation, in case the pastor of a particular church did not fulfil his essential duties, or even acted in open violation of them. But what could the universal Church accomplish without her organ, or the organ itself, if no one were bound to obey it? Yet it is, of course, to be understood, that the rights of the head of the Church are restricted to purely ecclesiastical concerns; and if, in the course of the Middle Ages, this was otherwise, the causes of this occurrence are to be sought for in the peculiar circumstances and necessities of that period. With the visibility of the Church—with the visible, regular, and established reciprocal intercourse of the faithful; with the internal necessity of their very existence to be members of one body, a visible head, with essential and inalienable rights, was, accordingly, ordained. In addition to his essential ecclesiastical rights, whose limits may be found traced out in the canonists, the Pope, according to the different degrees of civilisation in particular ages, and among particular nations, acquired the so-called non-essential rights, admitting of various changes, so that his power appears sometimes more extended, sometimes more contracted. Moreover, it is well-known, that, partly in consequence of the revolutions of time and of disorders in the Church, partly through the internal development of opposite ideas, two systems became prevalent, the episcopal and the papal system; the latter whereof, without questioning the divine institution of bishops, exalted more particularly the central power; while the former, without denying the divine establishment of the Primacy, sought to draw authority more particularly towards the circumference.[1] As each system acknowledged the essence of the other to be divine, they constituted an opposition very beneficial to ecclesiastical life; so that, by their counteraction, the peculiar free development of the several parts was, on the one hand, preserved, and the union of these in one living, indivisible whole, was, on the other, maintained.

The dogmatic decrees of the episcopate (united with the general head and centre), are infallible; for it represents the universal Church, and one doctrine of faith, falsely explained by it, would render the whole a prey to error. Hence, as the institution which Christ hath established for the preservation and the explanation of his doctrines, is subject, in this its function,

[1] The most general maxims of the episcopal system are comprised in the Synods of Constance (1414) and of Basil (1431); they assert the Pope is *subject* to a general Council lawfully convoked, representing the Church militant—a one-sided principle which, when carried out to its legitimate consequences, threatened the Church with annihilation. This coarse opinion may now be considered as obsolete. Concil. Const. Sess. iv, in Hardouin, lib. 1, tom. viii, p. 252: 'Ipsa Synodus in Spiritu Sancto congregata legitime generale Concilium faciens, ecclesiam Catholicam militantem repraesentans, potestatem a Christo immediate habet, cui quilibet cujuscunque status vel dignitatis, etiamsi papalis existat, obedire tenetur in his quæ pertinent ad fidem et extirpationem dicti schismatis, et reformationem generalem ecclesiæ Dei in capite et in membris.' In the fifth session this is repeated, and the like is added. The Council of Basil, also, in its second session, has adopted both decrees verbally. See Hardouin, lib. 1, p. 1121.

to no error; so the organ, through which the Church speaks, is also exempt from error.

The Metropolitans (archbishops) and patriarchs are not, in themselves, essential intermediate grades between the Bishops and the Pope; yet has their jurisdiction, the limits whereof have been determined by general councils, proved very useful for maintaining a closer connection, and a more immediate superintendence over the bishops, subject to their authority.

The priests (taking the word in a more limited sense) are, as it were, a multiplication of the bishop; and as they acknowledge themselves his assistants, they revere in him the visible fountain of their jurisdiction, their head and their centre. In this way, the whole body is bound and joined together in a living organism: and as the tree, the deeper and wider it striketh its roots into the earth, the more goodly a summit of intertwining boughs and branches it beareth aloft unto the sky, it is so with the congregation of the Lord. For the more closely the community of believers is established with him, and is enrooted in him, as the all-fruitful soil; the more vigorous and imposing is its outward manifestation.

As to the remaining non-sacerdotal orders, the deacons were instituted by the apostles, and, as their representatives, were charged more immediately with the affairs of administration, not immediately connected with the apostolic calling. The sub-deaconship, and the four so-called minor orders are restricted to a circle of subordinate, yet indispensable ministrations, and in former times, formed altogether (including the deaconship) a practical school wherein the training for higher ecclesiastical functions was acquired, and a test of qualification for their discharge was afforded. For, in the ancient Church, the pastors as well as believers were formed in, and by the immediate experience of life; as the inferior ministers constantly surrounded the bishop or priest, and attending him in all his sacred functions, imbibed the spirit which animated him, and qualified themselves to become one day his successors. But they rose only slowly and by degrees; and every new ordination was but the recompense of services faithfully performed, and a period of probation for a still more important trust. At present, these orders, from the sub-deaconship downwards, are preserved but as ancient customs; for, the educational system of modern times bears an essentially different character, and follows a decidedly theoretical course. Hence, the duties which the inferior members of the clergy once performed are now nearly everywhere discharged by laymen, such as acolytes, sacristans, and the like.

LUTHERAN DOCTRINE ON THE CHURCH

§ XLIV—THE BIBLE THE ONLY SOURCE AND ARBITRESS IN MATTERS OF FAITH

Great importance has been attached by us to the proposition, that a positive religion, if destined to act with a permanent and decisive authority on mankind, must be ever imparted to successive generations, through the medium of an authority. In the application of this truth, however, an illusion may easily occur. Thus we may imagine that the ordinary mode, in which an historical fact is attested, may here absolutely suffice ; and that thus, if credible eye and ear-witnesses have delivered a written testimony respecting the divine envoy, their evidence should constitute an adequate and lasting authority for all times. In the same way, as Polybius and Livy are our sources of information in respect to the second Punic war, and Herodian in regard to the heroic deeds of the emperor Commodus, so Matthew, Mark, Luke, and John, are the standing authority for those who desire to know Christ, to surrender to him their faith ; and thus the necessary claim, that the authority of Christ should be represented by an authority, is fully satisfied.

But here, several extremely important circumstances are completely overlooked. The sacred historians the Christian, in fact, by no means ranks in the same class with other writers of history, nor, on that account, the readers of the Bible with those of any other historical work. We hold it to be necessary that, under quite special conditions, the evangelical historians should have written down their narratives, in order not to be disturbed by the doubt, whether they had in reality rightly heard, seen, and understood. *For this very reason*, from the foundation of Christianity, it has been deemed a matter of necessity, that only under certain peculiar conditions could the right understanding of the sacred penmen be secured, in order that we might have the decided conviction, that what they recorded without falsification, we apprehended without confusion. As little, nay, from evident reasons still less, can we trust alone to the honest purpose and personal capacity of the authors of the apostolic epistles, when the question at issue is, whether, in the application and further development of what they had learned from and respecting Jesus, they have not erred; but precisely, because we do not wish, and cannot wish to bestow such confidence, we are unable to rest satisfied with those ordinary means, which are employed to discover the sense of an author. And this, because here far other wants are to be satisfied than those which the study of a Greek or Roman classic can gratify; because matters of far graver moment, and unquestionably weightier influence on life, are involved, than in the case of the latter; to wit, the knowledge whereon depends the salvation of immortal souls.

The following circumstance, also, was overlooked, the non-observance whereof was likely to entail important consequences. We have two sources from which we derive our knowledge of God and divine things—the natural and the supernatural revelation: for brevity-sake we will put a part for the whole, and say—the revelation of God within us, and the revelation of God out of us in Christ Jesus. The revelation of God within us, is likewise the organ whereby we apprehend the outward revelation; and it has, therefore, a twofold function, at once to bear testimony unto God, and our relation towards Him, and also to receive the testimony coming from without. Accordingly, in behalf of one and the same object, we are directed to two witnesses, quite distinct one from the other; and the matter of importance is, that the one witness within us should not overvalue the worth of his evidence, and should willingly confess that his declarations stand in a subordinate relation to those of the other; for, otherwise, the necessity of another witness, beside him, would be inexplicable. Precisely as historical criticism decides on the qualities of the witnesses, and seeks to discover, in each particular case, whether they could rightly *apprehend*, and desired faithfully *to recount* what they had learned; so must the witness in our own interior be examined. But this inward witness possesses a very decided advantage over the outward one. *Being the organ for the latter*, he is too inclined, in his narrative, to substitute his own pretended internal perceptions for the testimony of the voucher who stands by his side; and persuades himself that he is but faithfully relating what he had learned from without, when he has been listening only to himself, and in this wise has thrown everything into confusion.

For this simple reason it is evident, that the attestation of the purport of an external revelation can, by no means, be unconditionally ranked with the attestation of any other fact; nor can it be affirmed that the written testimony of credible eye and ear-witnesses is an adequate authority in the one case, as it is in the other. What any informant relates, respecting the events of ordinary life, we can learn only from the testimony of him and his like. That Carthage was taken by Scipio Æmilianus, is known to us only from the ancient historians; and as our own interior suggests not the slightest hint as to such a fact, there is no danger of confounding here our internal voice with the narrative of the historian. Religious truths, on the other hand, are attested in a two-fold manner; and there is an imminent danger that what hath been revealed to us from without, while we are but bringing it home to our own conviction, may take the colour of our minds, and undergo a greater or less change. Hence, besides Holy Writ, which objectively is unerring, the living authority of the Church has been instituted, in order that we may obtain *for ourselves*, subjectively, the divine word, as it is *in itself*. Between *two persons*, moreover, an absolute understanding alone is possible; between a person and a writing, on the other hand, an absolute misunderstanding is but too possible.

Had we no innate, internal testimony of God, so that we were by nature utterly godless; then indeed, provided only we had still the faculty of apprehending Him, a mere book would have availed as sufficient authority. In that case, at least, our own interior, perhaps delusive, testimony could not possibly have been confounded with the outward one; still less, could a tacit preference have been given to the former, if not the slightest tone of a divine voice came forth from our bosoms. No fear then could have been entertained, that we were listening *to ourselves*, instead of to God, when all in man that could point to heaven, were mute. This is the point where Luther's doctrine, on Scripture and the Church, coincides with his other errors that have been previously investigated. His doctrine touching original sin inculcated, that nothing in man intimated and attested the Deity: His doctrine on the absence of human free-will, and the exclusive operation of God in the work of salvation, that the Divine Spirit *alone* engenders faith in man. So next the proposition was advanced, that Holy Writ is the sole fountain-head, standard, and judge in matters of faith.[1] While, therefore, the Catholic Church, in order to guard man against errors, in the reception of Christian truth, and to afford him the certainty that he is in possession of the same, presents herself as the all-sufficient, because divinely appointed, surety; Luther, on the other hand, seeks to obtain the same end, by not only exalting the measure of the communications of the Holy Spirit, but by annihilating all human concurrence, and reserving to the Deity an exclusive agency: he says, the Holy Spirit readeth in the Scriptures, not thou.

As, accordingly, the Reformers represented all human concurrence in the work of salvation, not only as unnecessary, but as impossible, and held that, where human eagerness ventured an intrusion into this work, an abortion was unavoidably engendered; so they indulged in the idea, that whoever addressed himself immediately to Holy Writ, obtained an immediate knowledge of its contents. They rejected the mediating authority of the Church, which guided the intellectual activity of each individual, because they wished to avoid *every* thing human, without apprehending that the subjectivity of the believer would, thereby, be set in the most unrestrained movement, and be confounded with the objective revelation; nay, without fearing, that any human alloy were possible in this work, because such had been discarded from their own imagination.

This view often breaks out with singular naïveté; as for instance, in the oft-repeated assertion that the Bible is the judge in matters of faith. The reader of the Scripture is, unhesitatingly, confounded with the Scripture itself, and the immediate conveyance of its contents to his mind, most childishly assumed. It is one thing to say 'the Bible is the source of the doctrine of salvation;' and another to say, 'it is the judge to determine what is the doctrine of salvation.' The latter it can as little be, as the code of civil law can exercise the functions of the judge: it forms indeed the rule of judgment, but it doth not itself pronounce judgment. But, as Luther originally quite overlooked the concurrence of human energies, and held all man's thoughts, judgments, and conclusions, in regard to the

---

[1] Epitome, Comp. sect. p. 543. 'Credimus, confitemur, et docemus, unicam regulam et normam, ex qua omnia dogmata, omnesque doctores judicare oporteat, nullam omnino aliam esse, quam prophetica et apostolica, tum veteris, tum novi Testamenti Scripta.' Solid. declar. forma dijudic. controv., sect. ii, p. 605.

kingdom of God, to be as much the effects of an exclusive divine operation, as his will in reference to the kingdom of God; so all conceptions of Scripture, and of the readers of Scripture, floated indiscriminately in his mind; and the proposition was then advanced, that the Bible is the judge in controversies of faith.[1] In numerous passages of the writings of the Reformers, as, for example, in the following sentence of Zuinglius, this confusion recurs. In wishing to explain what Church cannot err, and how it cometh that it cannot err, he says, 'The sheep of God follow the word of God alone, which can in nowise deceive: it is accordingly clear, which is the inerrable Church, the one, to wit, which rests on the word of God alone.'[2] In other words, he who holds to the infallible Word of God alone is regarded, in the most unqualified manner, as infallible; just as if it were one and the same thing to read the inerrable Scripture, and to be forthwith inerrable: and as if a vastly important intermediate step were not here overleaped. On the other hand, the Reformers concluded, that Catholics are in error, because they interpret Holy Writ, according to the authority of the Church.

That the union which we have pointed out between the mode wherein, according to the Reformers, man, in his inward sentiments and his powers of will, is converted to God, and the mode wherein the religious thoughts and conceptions of the believer are formed, is based on no arbitrary assumption, may be irrefragably proved by numerous passages from Luther and Zuinglius, when even the general connection of their doctrines did not clearly imply it. In his writing to the Bohemians, on the institution of Church ministers,[3] Luther expressly declares, that

[1] We know indeed that the opinion, the Bible is the judge in doctrinal disputes, is made to signify as much, that the Bible best explains itself; that thus the context, parallel passages, etc., remove obscurities and allay controversies. But this is far from completely meeting the view of the first Reformers, and, abstractedly considered, is historically quite false.

[2] Zuingl. de vera et fals. relig. comment. Opp. tom. ii, fol. 192. 'Hæc tandem sola est ecclesia labi et errare nescia, quæ solam Dei pastoris vocem audit, nam hæc sola ex Deo est. Qui enim ex Deo est, verbum Dei audit; et rursus, vos non auditis, qui ex Deo non estis. Ergo qui audiunt, Dei oves sunt, Dei ecclesia sunt, errare nequeunt: nam solum Dei verbum sequuntur, quod fallere nulla ratione potest. Habes jam, quænam sit ecclesia, quæ errare nequeat, ea nimirum sola, quæ solo Dei verbo nititur.'

[3] Luther de instit. minist. eccles. Opp. tom. ii, fol. 584. 'His et similibus multis locis, tum evangelii, tum totius Scripturæ, quibus admonemur,

the believer is the freest judge of all his teachers, *since he is inwardly instructed by God alone*. Excellently well doth Zuinglius illustrate the sense of his colleague in Wittenberg ; and we may the more confidently summon him, as a witness to Luther's original view, as he nowhere manifests a productive genius, has not, perhaps, in all his writing, expressed one original, pregnant idea, and almost always pushes Luther's opinions to an extreme, albeit he often ridiculously puts in claims to originality. Zuinglius compares, without scruple, the word of Scripture to the word of God, whereby all things were created out of nothing—with that word in virtue whereof light arose when the Lord Spake ; ' Let there be light.'[1] To explain the mode of operation of the Divine word, he appeals, moreover, to that internal word, which came to the prophets of the old covenant, and which, although it exacted what was most extraordinary, and promised what was most marvellous, *yet without the aid of human reflection and mental activity*, took possession of those to whom it was addressed and brought them under subjection.[2] Mingling truth with falsehood, and reducing the latter from the former, he concludes that no man can instruct another, since Christ saith, ' No one cometh to him, unless the Father draw him.' That no man can implant faith in another—that, without the internal attraction of the Father, without the mysterious opening of the internal sense by the Holy Spirit, no one can believe, is undoubtedly quite certain. But the opinion, that on this account, human co-operation is unnecessary, rests on the very same false conclusion, which the Reformers drew, when they represented the conversion of the will, as the exclusive work of God.[3]

ne falsis doctoribus credamus, quid aliud docemur, quam ut nostræ propriæ quisquis pro se salutis rationem habens, certus sit, quid credat et sequatur, ac judex liberrimus sit omnium, qui docent eum, *intus a Deo solo doctus*.' Other passages we shall cite below.

[1] Zuingl. de certitud. et clarit. verbi Dei. c. 11, Opp. tom. i, fol. 165. ' Tanta verbi Dei certitudo et veritas, tanta etiam ejusdem virtus et potentia, ut quæcunque velit mox juxta nutum illius eveniant. Dixit et facta mandavit et creata sunt. . . . Dixit Deus, fiat lux, et facta est lux. Ecce quanta sit Verbi virtus,' etc.

[2] Loc. cit. c. 111, p. 168, seq.

[3] Loc. cit. p. 169. ' Cum Deo docente discant pii, cur non eam doctrinam ; quam divinitus accipiunt, iis liberam permittitis ? Quod vero Deus piorum animos instituat, Christus eodem in loco non obscure innuit, dicens ; omnis qui audiverit a patre et didicerit, ad me venit. Nemo ad Christum pervenit, nisi cognitionem illius a patre acceperit. Jamne ergo videtis et auditis, quis sit magister fidelium ? Non patres, non doctores titulo superbi, non magistri nostri, non pontificum cœtus, **non sedes,**

Here, moreover, we can clearly discern the cause, why the Reformers were originally such decided adversaries to all philosophy and speculation—why Carlstadt, who was a confederate of Luther's in the famous disputation at Leipzig, required the candidates of theology to apply themselves to some handicraft, rather than to study, in order that the human mind might not be filled with things, which only impeded the entrance of the Divine Spirit. Accordingly he himself gave up the scientific investigation of the Scriptures, in order that, from simple artisans, who had not disqualified themselves by indulging in human reflections, he might learn immediately, through God, the mysteries of His kingdom, and be initiated in the true sense of Holy Writ. Melancthon went as an apprentice to a baker, not only to learn how to understand the Bible, but to apply it, when understood in the manner we have mentioned; for, the passage ' by the sweat of thy brow,' etc., he conceived to be a divine precept, imposing the duty of manual labour.

We are, indeed, aware, that Luther himself very much modified this his original view, which, on the part of the Lutherans and Calvinists, had been made to undergo a still greater change. But, when we wish to exhibit to view the internal genesis of the Protestant theory of the Church, we should not hold up the later phase as the earliest, nor, in general, confound one with the other. The later conceptions of Luther, which were meant to be an improvement on his earlier opinions, brought into his system contradictions, which must themselves be accounted for. It was also only outward phenomena, that induced Luther to pursue another course—to wit, the rise of the Anabaptists. As the authors of this sect, like Luther, appealed to the interior teachings of the Divinity, and as he felt utterly incapable of meeting their objections on this ground, he saw himself forced to insist anew on the indispensable necessity of human efforts, for the right understanding of Scripture. In general, the

non scholæ nec concilia, sed pater Domini nostri Jesu Christi. Quid ergo, objicitis, an homo hominem docere non potest ? Nequaquam. Christus enim dicit : nemo venit ad me, nisi pater traxerit eum. . . . Verba spiritus clara sunt, doctrina Dei claia est, docet et hominis animum sine ullo humanæ rationis additamento, de salute certiorem reddit,' etc. In Zuinglius, the doctrine of absolute predestination, and of the exclusive agency of the Deity, evidently exerted a great influence in the framing of this article ; namely, that what man, in the reading of the Bible and so forth, performs by reflection, *he seems* only so to do. Loc. cit. p. 171 : ' Quod vero hac in re opus tamen esse credis, non tuum sed Spiritus sancti est, qui occulte in te et per virtutem suam operatur.'

fanatical commotions, excited by the so-called heavenly prophets, gave a very different turn to Luther's mind, from what he previously had; and this fact, Adolphus Menzel, in his 'Modern History of the Germans,' has observed with great penetration. But, at all events, those are far from duly appreciating Luther's views and spirit, who imagine, that he absolutely believed that he could discover the true sense of Scripture, by an historic-grammatical interpretation. Nothing was more alien to him —nothing more at variance with his whole system: the very notion, that, by human exertions, we can win and appropriate to ourselves the knowledge of divine things, he held to be the acme of ungodliness. Learned interpretation was, by no means, his method for discovering the sense of the Bible, but only for obtaining for himself and others an exegetical explication of the sense, engendered in man by the immediate and exclusive operation of the Deity—an explication, which, according to his principles, should have appeared quite unnecessary. Zwingle's and Luther's original views, may thus, in a certain sense, be compared with the Catholic doctrine. The Catholic Church saith: 'I am immediately certain, wherein the true doctrine of Christ and of the Apostles consists, for, I have been therein instructed, trained up and educated; and what I have learned, hath been, by the Divine Spirit, deeply impressed and confirmed on my heart. The written word of the Apostles can only coincide with their oral communications, and must be interpreted by the same.' On the other hand, the opinion of the two Reformers appears to have been this: 'God, by his own interior word of power, working without human co-operation, hath implanted his doctrine within us, through the vehicle of the Sacred Scriptures. According to this interior word, whose working forms the Christian consciousness, the outward word must, in its details, be then explained.' It is indeed extremely difficult to form a very clear conception of the primitive views of the Reformers: but, we think it vain to attempt to reconcile, in any other manner, the words of Luther, 'The believer is internally taught by God alone,' with the perpetually recurring assertion, that, without the Bible no Christian knowledge is possible. In the sequel, we shall obtain fuller explanations on this matter.

§ XLV — CONTINUATION — INTERNAL ORDINATION — EVERY CHRISTIAN A PRIEST AND TEACHER, AND CONSEQUENTLY INDEPENDENT OF ALL ECCLESIASTICAL COMMUNION — NOTION OF ECCLESIASTICAL FREEDOM

These opinions were attended with the weightiest and most decisive consequences. As each believer was deemed to be instructed by God alone, and capable, without human aid, of attaining to Christian knowledge; so, in the first place, an outward Christian ministry could not even be conceived: God, by means of Scripture, was the sole teacher. In the second place, ordination, as a sacrament, became no longer necessary; since this presupposes the necessity of a continuance of the divine work of salvation, by the mediation of the Church. But then, as God communicates himself, with indubitable certainty, only in an immediate and interior manner, it follows, that as no human teacher is any longer necessary; so an outwardly accredited ministry is equally, and still more unnecessary. The exterior ordination becomes transmuted into a purely internal act, whereby God imparts the consecration of the Spirit, not to this or that individual in a special manner, but to all in an equal degree. In a word, Luther laid hold of the old Christian idea of a universal priesthood, disfigured it, and then applied it to his new scheme. This is a subject to which he often recurs, but he treats it, at full length, in the Writing to the Bohemian Brethren, which we have already had occasion to cite. We must here briefly state the leading ideas of this essay. Quite in the beginning, and still more in the course of this production, Catholic Ordination is exhibited as a mere daubing, shaving, and jugglery, whereby nought but lying and idle fools, true priests of Satan, were made. One could likewise shave the hair of any sow, and put a dress on any block.[1] Luther requires his disciples confidently to reject all those who have been ordained by the beast, as he calls the Pope, that is to say all those who had received ordination in the Catholic Church, in whose place the Pope is named, as being its representative. No one should doubt, he says, that he is justified, nay, obliged to do this, since all believers have received from Christ a priestly dignity, which not only entitles but binds them to exercise the office of teaching, to forgive sins, and to administer all the

[1] Luther de instituendis minist. eccles, opp. tom. ii, fol. 585.

sacraments. *The Holy Spirit with its interior unction, instructs each one in all things*, engenders faith in him, and makes him assured of its possession.¹ Although now all be qualified for, and possess the right of exercising the priestly functions, yet, *in order to avoid disorder* they must delegate to one or more of their body the general right, to be exercised in their place, and in their name, after the more respected members of the community have imposed hands on him, and thereby made him their bishop. (Ordination according to this point of view is nothing more than a mere act of introduction into an ecclesiastical office.)

Before we proceed in this exposition we may be permitted to express the thoughts, which the views of Luther here stated, have excited in our minds. His writing to the Bohemians, in the true democratic tone of the most disgusting popular adulation, ascribes to every Christian a degree of perfection, which is belied by the most casual glance, that an impartial spirit will cast into its own interior. That yearning after communion, which is discernible in every man, and by none is felt more vividly than by the Christian, would be utterly inexplicable, if each man, like to a God, knew everything, possessed all truth and all life within himself, and, in every respect, absolutely sufficed for himself. All communion arises and exists but by the sense, or the clear knowledge of our own wants and deficiencies, and the perception thereby determined, that it is only

---

[1] Loc. cit. fol. 584. ' Christianum esse puto eum, qui Spiritum sanctum habet, qui (ut Christus ait) docebit eum omnia. Et Johannes ait : unctio ejus docebit vos omnia, hoc est, ut in summa dicam : Christianus ita certus est, quid credere et non credere debeat, ut etiam pro ipso moriatur aut saltem mori paratus sit.' (What would Luther *now* say ?) Fol. 585 : 'Deinde cum quilibet sit ad verbi ministerium natus e baptismo, etc. Quodsi exemplum petimus, adest Apollo Act. 18, quem legimus plane sine ulla vocatione et ordinatione Ephesum venisse et ferventer docuisse, Judæosque potenter revicisse.—Aliud exemplum præstant Stephanus et Philippus. . . . Quo jure, rogo, et qua auctoritate ? Certe nusquam nec rogati nec vocati a quopiam, sed proprio motu et generali jure.' (What astonishing proofs !) Then : ' Nova res est, inquiunt, et sine exemplo, sic eligere et creare episcopes. Respondeo : Imo antiquissima et exemples Apostolorum suorumque discipulorum probata, licet per Papistas contrario exemplo et pestilentibus doctrinis abolita et extincta.' (Compare the Acts of the Apostles, c. xiv, 22 ; Titus c. i, 5 ; 11 Tim. ii, 2.) ' Deinde si maxime nova res esset, tamen cum verbum Dei hic luceat et jubeat, simul necessitas animarum cogit, prorsus nihil movere debet rei novitas, sed verbi majestas. Nam quid rogo non est novum, quod fides facit ? Non fuit etiam Apostolorum tempore novum hujusmodi ministerium ? Non fuit novum, quod filii Israel mare transierunt ? ' etc.

in connection with, and in the closest adherence to others, our own capacity and helplessness can be removed. From Luther's view of the rights of a Christian, we cannot even conceive why the latter should at all need a teacher, and wherefore a community of which each individual member possesses sufficient power, to satisfy all his own wants, should be called on to appoint such a teacher. Even the quite material and paltry motive, which he assigns for the necessity of a public teacher, namely, 'the avoidance of disorder,' is, in his scheme, devoid of all consistency.

What need is there of a congregation, for mutual edification or mutual instruction, when each individual is taught to consider himself as an independent, all-sufficient monad? Far other principles than these of Luther's did the Apostle Paul, in his first epistle to the Corinthians (c. xii) unfold on the communion of life in the Church, which he finds established in the distribution of the diverse gifts of the one Spirit among many, yet, in their operations necessary for all believers, who, therefore, like the members of one body, are taught to depend one upon the other. If Luther says, 'each one is born out of baptism for the ministry,' so Paul, on the other hand, saith: 'Are *all* apostles, are *all* prophets, are *all* teachers?' Luther considers the Divine Spirit as so distributed among all, that in each individual it is found in all its forms, whereby the very idea of a common organic life is utterly destroyed. Paul, on the other hand, asserts the various revelation of the One in the many, whereby a living connected whole is produced.[1]

---

[1] Melchior Canus (Loci theologici, lib. iv, c. 4, p. 238, seq.) has already well answered the objection of the Reformers, that Catholics attributed the entire gifts of the Holy Spirit to the body only, and were unwilling to concede to individuals the full measure of such graces, though they need them all. Canus replies, 'As the peculiar functions of every member in the physical body tend to the profit of the whole, and each participates in them all, so it is with the moral body of the Church.' 'Unicuique, ait S. Paulus, nostrum data est gratia secundum mensuram donationis Christi. Et, Ipse dedit quosdam quidem apostolos, etc., ad consummationem sanctorum in opus ministerii, in ædificationem corporis Christi. Et posterius: accrescamus in illo, qui est caput Christus; ex quo totum corpus compactum et connexum secundum operationem, in mensuram uniuscujusque membri, augmentum corporis facit in adificationem sui in charitate.' (Eph. c. iv, 11, 16.) Membrum igitur, quoniam id, quod totius corporis est, nihil sibi vindicat proprium: sed ita in corpus omnia confert, ut magis corporis, quam membri actiones perfectionesque esse videantur. Quocirca illud absurdum est, quod ii scilicet, quibuscum nunc dissertitur, eam curam, quam debent capere, non capiunt. . . . Nos sane, quemadmodum scimus, animam satam et perfectionem esse, maxime

Luther thus considered each individual believer as absolutely independent of a religious community, because standing in need of none, and therefore *ecclesiastically free*. Here we are enabled to explain a phenomenon, the connection whereof with others was impervious to the understanding of a celebrated historian. Schmidt, in his history of the Germans, deemed it strange, on the part of the Lutherans, that they should reject metaphysical freedom, and yet, on the other hand, lay claim to ecclesiastical liberty. It was precisely, however, the denial of the former, which led to the affirmation of the latter. He who believes himself to be guided by God *only*, cannot possibly discover any meaning in a dependence on men; nay, he must reject such as absurd—as, on the one hand, the offspring of arrogance, ambition, and the love of a besotting domination; so on the other, as the effect of spiritual blindness, and of a slavish sense, ignorant of Gospel liberty—the liberty of the children of God. The Catholic, on the other hand, who concedes to man the first-named species of freedom, and pretends not to deny his power of independent action, cannot do otherwise than look on himself as bound by the authority of the Church, and for this reason, because everything human is to be considered as established in manifold relations, and determined by the finite world, in which it lives.[1]

quidem corporis physici organici, secundo autem loco membrorum etiam singulorum, quibus varias licet edat functiones, sed omnes illæ et corporis propriæ sunt, et propter corpus ipsum membris a natura tributæ; ita spiritum veritatis ad corpus primum ecclesiæ referimus, deinde propter ecclesiam ad singulas etiam ecclesiæ partes, non ex æquo sed analogia et proportione quadam juxta mensuram uniuscujusque membri. Unum corpus, inquit, et unus spiritus. Unicuique autem nostrum data est gratia secundum mensuram donationis Christi. Quænam, vero, hæc mensura Christi est? Secundum operationem, ait, in mensuram uniuscujusque membri. Spiritus ergo suo quidem modo singulis promissus est, ut magnos doceat, doceat et parvulos. Ac parvulis lac potum dat, majoribus solidum cibum. Illis Christum loquitur et hunc crucifixum: his loquitur sapientiam in mysterio absconditam. Verum singulis membris sic spiritus veritatis adest, ut non solum corpori universo non desit, sed corpori quam membris prius potiusque intelligatur adesse, etc.

[1] Luther de capt. Babyl. p. 288, b. 'Christianis nihil nullo jure posse imponi legum, sive ab hominibus, sive ab angelis, nisi quantum volunt, *liberi enim sumus ab omnibus*. Decebat enim nos esse, sicut parvuli baptizati, qui nullis studiis, nullis operibus occupati, in omnia sunt liberi, solius gloria baptismi sui securi et salvi. Sumus enim et ipsi parvuli in Christo, assidue baptizati.' P. 288, a: 'Dico itaque: neque papa, neque episcopus, neque ullus hominum habet jus unius syllabæ constituendæ super Christianum hominem, nisi id fiat ejusdem consensu, quidquid aliter fit, tyrannico spiritu fit.' Hence, Melancthon, in further proof of this,

Moreover, in considering the outward relations of things, it is not difficult to conceive how the doctrine we have stated, might, nay must, have arisen in the mind of Luther. As he had against him the authority of the existing Church, he was forced to resort to the immediate power of God working within him ; as the old ecclesiastical spirit became extinct in his breast, he must begin by renouncing all historical and traditionary guidance, and incapable of calling back in person the Apostles themselves, in order to be authorised by them in the name of Christ, he saw no other expedient than an appeal to an invisible, internal authorisation. The consequences were not slow to follow. Scarce had Luther's opinions obtained currency, and begun to be enforced, when men, the most uncalled, deemed themselves to have received the calling of teachers, and universal confusion ensued.[1]

The Augsburg Confession sought to obviate this evil, and hence enjoined, that no one should teach in public who had not received a lawful vocation. An article which, in the Lutheran system, is utterly unintelligible, and to which, therefore, we can assign no place therein ; but must merely rest satisfied with stating its existence, as well as the *extraneous* causes, to which it owed its origin. It is, too, a consequence of the *accidental* character of this article, that it merely asserts, that every teacher is to be called in a lawful manner, without at all determining in what this lawfulness consists.[2] Lawfulness,

asserts that, after Christ, no new law, no ordinance and rite *ought* to be instituted. Loci. p. 6: ' Ademit igitur potestatem, novas leges, novos ritus condendi.'

[1] The congregations elected such men for their preachers, as spoke in a manner the carnal sense was delighted to hear. It was, by such preachers, that the war of the peasants was, in a great degree, enkindled. George Eberlin, a Lutheran pastor, in the year 1526, dissuaded the peasants from joining in the insurrection, and among other things observed : ' Should the people say, why had revolt been preached up to them, the answer is, why did they not let their preachers be tested beforehand, and without advice suffer every loose fisherman to preach ? ' Compare Bucholz : Geschichte der Regierung Ferd. I. (History of the reign of Ferdinand I.) Vienna, 1831, vol. ii, p. 220.

[2] Confess. August. Art. xiv. De ordine ecclesiastico docent, quod nemo debeat in ecclesia publice docere, nisi rite vocatus. Moreover, it was necessary not only to pass this ordinance, but to enjoin, that teachers should generally be procured, and be maintained. The Saxon nobility and peasants took Luther at his word ; and since he had told them, that, by the interior unction, they were made acquainted with all things : and as men divinely illuminated, they stood in need of no human teachers, they were uncommonly flattered by this declaration, and seriously resolved

according to the principles of the Reformers, consisted in this: that nothing external could be lawfully instituted, and that everyone might undertake the office of teacher, who believed himself under the impulse of the Divine Spirit, and could find such singular hearers, as, firmly convinced, they already knew everything, and needed no instruction, yet were, nevertheless, most desirous to learn. That, at a later period, the Consistories reserved to themselves the right of deciding on the qualifications of a candidate for the office of preacher, and permitted the congregation to elect only such as had enlisted the approval of the higher functionaries, is a fact as well known, as the utter inconsistency of such an arrangement with the fundamental dotcrines of Luther, must be evident to every mind. At all events, it is a very remarkable fact, that the Lutherans, nay, Luther himself, in his maturer years, should have practically, at least, rejected his fundamental opinions, and thereby unequivocally demonstrated, that, perfectly adapted as those opinions might be for the destruction of an existing Church, and for the subversion of all established notions, yet were they utterly unserviceable for the building up and consolidation of a new Church. To construct such a Church, they were forced to recur to the old Catholic method, which had been so violently assailed. In the examination of the doctrines of the Anabaptists, we shall first have occasion to furnish the most striking evidences of this retrograde *movement.*

§ XLVI—CONTINUATION—INVISIBLE CHURCH

By the analysis we have followed, we have obtained a tolerably complete insight into the Lutheran theory of the Church. The

to do away with the public ministry. Hence, they withheld from the curates their dues. Luther complains somewhere: 'That if aid be not speedily brought, the Gospel, schools, and parish ministers, are all ruined in this land; the latter must go, for they possess nothing, and wander about, looking like haggard ghosts.' Elsewhere he says: 'The people will no longer give anything, and there is such thanklessness among them for the holy Word of God, that, if I could do it with a safe conscience, I should help to deprive them of pastors or preachers, and let them live like swine, as they already do.' See Plank's History of the Protestant System of Doctrine, vol. ii, p. 342. (In German.) Had not the sovereign power interfered to set restraints on this gospel liberty, never, according to Luther's principles, could an ecclesiastical community have been formed.

believer, according to what has been stated, is, in the first place, instructed by God only, exclusively of all co-operation of human activity, whether it be his own, or that of other men. In the second place, he is on this account infallible, because, having been taught by God, without human concurrence, whereby error can alone arise, he is in himself absolutely inerrable. Thirdly, it cannot hence be discerned, why he should need the supplemental aid of a congregation, invested with authority, from whose centre the Word of God should be announced to him; for, by the assistance of the outward Divine Word, written in the depths of the heart, he hears His voice alone, and without an intermediate organ.[1]

What, after all this, can the Church be other than an invisible community, since no rational object, in the visibility of the Church, can any longer be conceived? So, in fact, Luther defines its notion, when he says, 'As we pray in faith, I believe in a Holy Ghost, in a communion of saints. This means the community or congregation of all those, who live in the right faith, hope and charity; thus, the essence, life and nature of christendom consists not in a bodily assemblage, but in the assemblage of hearts in one faith.'[2] That this one faith will never fail, Luther had not the slightest cause to doubt, for God, whose agency is here represented as exclusive, will everywhere produce the same effects.

But we have already seen how Luther, although, according to him, believers are inwardly taught by God alone, yet all at once (and without its being possible to discover, in his system, any rational ground for such an assumption), admits the establishment of human teachers, and even the lawfulness of their calling. Hereby the Church becomes visible, recognisable, obvious to the eye, so that the ill-connected notions of God, the sole teacher, and of a human teacher declared competent, and

---

[1] We must here for once observe to our readers, that it is not our fault, if, in the words of the text, a contradiction should be apparent. For, the words, 'God alone without any intermediate organ worketh in man,' and those, 'He worketh by the aid of the external, divine, and written Word,' involve a contradiction. It is only in the second part of this work, this contradiction will be fully solved.

[2] Luther 'On the Papacy.' Jena. German edition, vol. i, p. 266. Respons. ad librum Ambros. Cathar. anno. 1521. Opp. tom. ii, fol. 376. In the work on the Papacy, Luther says, ' Furthermore, because communion with the visible Church constitutes no communion with the invisible, and because many non-Christians are found in the visible Church, so no visible Church is at all necessary!'

who cannot yet be dispensed with, meet us again in such a way as to imply, that the invisible is still a visible Church also. In Luther's work against Ambrosius Catharinus, this singular combination of ideas is most decidedly expressed. Luther asks himself the question, which Catharinus had already proposed, ' but those will say, if the Church be *quite in the spirit*, and of a nature thoroughly spiritual, how can we discern where on earth any part of it may be ? ' And he accordingly confesses, that it must be absolutely internal in its nature ; only he replies, ' the necessary mark, whereby we recognise it, and which we possess, is baptism and the Lord's Supper, and above all, the Gospel.'[1] Hereby the Church evidently becomes outwardly manifest, and consequently not entirely, and in every respect spiritual. Still better doth the Augsburg Confession describe the Church as a community of saints, in which the Gospel is rightly taught, and the sacraments are duly administered ;[2] so that, in as far as it consists of saints only, it is absolutely invisible ; for the saints no one knoweth but God alone ; and, inasmuch as the Gospel is there taught, and baptism, and the body of the Lord are therein administered, it cannot avoid being visible. The singularity of the notion, that the Church, which should be only an invisible, because a purely spiritual one, yet must be perceptible to the senses, is still further heightened by the addition, that it is found there, where the Gospel is *rightly* taught, and the sacraments are *rightly* administered. For, this passage supposes that there are false Churches ; and now to distinguish the true from the opposite Churches, the right doctrine set forth by the saints, and the right worship administered by them, is given as a sign. Doubtless, the true Church possesses the pure evangelical Word and sacraments, and lives by them, and consequently possesses saints. Yet, from all this, the true Church of Christ, amid the struggle of various parties, is not to be recognised. 'For, either from the circumstance, that a saint, or, in other words, a man qualified

[1] Luther's Respons. ad libr. Ambros. Cathar. loc. cit. fol. 376, 377. ' Dices autem, si ecclesia tota est in spiritu, et res omnino spiritualis, nemo ergo nosse poterit, ubi sit ulla ejus pars in toto orbe. . . . Quo ergo signo agnoscam ecclesiam ? Respondeo : signum necessarium est, quod et habemus, Baptisma, ac panem et omnium potissimum Evangelium.'

[2] Confess. August. Art. vii. ' Item docent, quod una sancta ecclesia perpetuo mansura sit. Est autem ecclesia congregatio sanctorum in qua Evangelium recte docetur, et recte administrantur sacramenta. Et ad veram unitatem ecclesiæ satis est, consentire de doctrina Evangelii, et administratione sacramentorum.'

by God alone for the ministry preaches, we should conclude his doctrine to be true ; or else, from the truth of his doctrine we infer that he is a saint. The first is not possible, for, from a thing to us uncertain, nothing certain can be deduced. The second presupposes, that he, who wishes to learn the true doctrine of Christ, and consequently demands a characteristic of the same, already possesses the true doctrine, and is certain and assured of its possession, and therefore needs no mark. Yet, everyone inquires after the true Church of Christ, only because he wishes to attain to the possession of Christ's true doctrine, as well as to acquire the certainty and assurance that he possesses it. But, should he receive for answer, the true Church is there, where the true doctrine is found, so a reply is evidently given, which is nought else but the question itself, that is to say, nothing at all is answered.

§ XLVII — CONTINUATION — RISE OF THE VISIBLE CHURCH ACCORDING TO LUTHER—ULTIMATE REASONS FOR THE TRUTH OF AN ARTICLE OF FAITH

But, as yet this reasoning can scarcely be understood ; and its real sense will then only be clearly apprehended, when we have dwelt more at large on the origin of the Church, such as Luther darkly conceived it. His meaning may thus be more accurately expressed as follows. In a man, belief in Christ takes seed ; if this faith come to maturity, then is the disciple of Christ formed. But, as a mere believer, he stands only in one relation to God in Christ ; he is a member of the invisible Church, of the concealed and everywhere scattered worshippers of the Lord. But as soon as he gives utterance to his faith, that which was hidden within him, bursts visibly forth, and he appears an open disciple of the Saviour, perceptible to the eyes of the whole world. If he finds now several with the like views, if they associate with him, and together outwardly set forth the substance of that, which they internally recognise as religious truth : then the invisible community becomes visible. The common faith, which inwardly animated and united all, ere they knew each other's sentiments, becomes, as a common doctrine, an outward bond holding them all together. In the same way it is with the sacraments, and the outward worship, which they acknowledge to be ordained by

Christ. That Luther had this idea, is evident from what follows. In his apology for free-will, Erasmus took occasion to touch on this weak side in the Lutheran doctrine respecting the Church. Luther had then made considerable steps in the way of improvement, and solemnly declared, that he approved not the principles of those who, in all their assertions, constantly appealed to the language of the Spirit in their interior; and expressed his opinion in what manner the Scripture should be judge in matters of faith. He says, an internal certainty of having seized the true sense of Holy Writ, is to be distinguished from the outward certainty; the former (the Christian consciousness) consisting in the testimony of the Holy Spirit, which assures each individual, that he is in possession of the truth; the latter consisting in the Scriptural proofs alleged by the public ministry.[1] In this passage, the clergy are conceived to be the representatives of the Church, which accordingly is of a nature quite visible, and professing the faith of the invisible Church, expressing its consciousness, has a defined system of doctrines, that through the instrumentality of its ministers it defends, and, as the sentence of the saints, holds to be true and inerrable. The visible Church appears, consequently, as the expression and the copy of the invisible.

The following considerations are of great importance, to enable us to form a complete conception of the Lutheran theory of the Church, and of its divergence from the Catholic system. Luther confounded the internal sense of the truth of a pro-

---

[1] Luther de servo arbitrio. Opp. tom. iii, fol. 182. 'Neque illos probo, qui refugium suum ponunt in jactantia spiritus. Nos sic dicimus, duplici judicio spiritus esse explorandos seu improbandos. Uno interiori, quo per Spiritum sanctam vel donum Dei singulare, quilibet pro se, suaque solius salute illustratus, certissime judicat et discernit omnium dogmata et sensus, de quo dicitur 1 Cor. ii, 1. Spiritualis omnia judicat et a nemine judicatur. Hæc ad fidem pertinet, et necessaria est cuilibet etiam privato Christiano. Hanc superius appellavimus interiorem claritatem Scripturæ sacræ. Alterum est judicium externum, quo non modo pro nobis ipsis, sed et pro aliis et propter aliorum salutem, certissime judicamus spiritus et dogmata aliorum. Hoc judicium est publici ministerii in verbo, et officii externi, et maxime pertinet ad duces et præcones verbi. Quo utimur, dum infirmos in fide roboramus (?) et adversarios refutamus. Sic dicimus, judice Scriptura, omnes spiritus in facie Ecclesiæ esse probandos. Nam id oportet apud Christianos esse imprimis ratum atque firmissimum, Scripturas sanctas esse lucem spiritualem, ipso sole longe clariorem: præsertim in iis, quæ pertinent ad salutem vel necessitatem.' Thus he speaks in the year 1525, not when he wrote to the Bohemians. Here we find the source of what was afterwards put forth as a claim of the Lutheran clergy.

position, with its outward testimony, or rather, his view of the purely interior and spiritual nature of the Church, whose members were instructed by the Holy Spirit only, necessarily involved this confusion. After dilating at length on the manner in which the Christian, amid the various views as to the sense of the written Word, can assure himself that his own view is the true one, he lays down the maxim : ' then thou canst be assured of any matter, when thou canst freely and safely assert, this is the pure and genuine truth ; for this will I live and die, and he who teaches otherwise, be he who he will, let him be anathema.' [1] Hereby, Luther made subjective certainty the highest criterion of Gospel truth, without reflecting that, by the very fact, the eternal Word of God had become an *outward teacher ; an external authority* for attesting that that Divine Word had revealed such and such doctrines, was above all things necessary, in order to impart the certainty in question. The passage of St Paul's, ' If an angel from Heaven were to teach another Gospel, let him be anathema,' gave him occasion to make this assertion. But Luther did not consider, that Paul, to whom the Saviour himself appeared, to whom extraordinary revelations had been made, was in a very different situation from an ordinary Christian. Doubtless, the unconquerable firmness of Christian conviction is the mark of a true-believing soul ; yet, unfortunately, the grossest error hath the power to exert the most lamentable fascination over the mind, and bring it by degrees under bondage, as Luther, had he even been unacquainted with earlier examples in history, might have seen in those fanatics,[2] whom he so violently combated.

An expedient, varying in expression, yet the same in substance, is resorted to by Zuinglius, when, in his ' Commentaries on True and False Religion,' he says, the mark of true doctrine, the sign that we have rightly understood the Divine Word, is the unction and testimony of the Holy Spirit. Faith, according to him, is no science, for it is precisely the learned who are often most addicted to error ; and, on this account, faith is no matter for investigation, and is exalted above all strife.[3]

Zuinglius makes here the most perverse application of a truth, which he had found a thousand times repeated in Catholic

---

[1] Luther's Commentary on the Epist. to the Galat. part i, p. 31. In the writing to the Bohemians, this sentiment is often expressed.
[2] The Anabaptists.
[3] Zuingli Comment. de vera et falsa relig. Opp. tom. ii, fol. 195.

writers, especially the mystics. The belief in Jesus Christ must undoubtedly attest itself; in each one, who possesses it in the right way, it will exalt and extend the consciousness of God; it will pervade and transform his whole existence; infuse into his soul the fullest confidence in God, the deepest tranquillity, and the most joyous consolation; and impart to him a power for all good, and the victory over hell and death. In these personal perceptions, the dogmas professed *by the understanding* as the doctrine of Jesus Christ are tested: and we clearly recognise herein the fulfilment of what that doctrine promised, and the truth of its claim to be a power from God. But, the converse of this proposition can, by no means, be affirmed, that a series of religious tenets, which tend to nourish the piety of an individual, or a greater or smaller circle of men, necessarily contain the doctrine of Christ, or even are not at variance with it. There is no doubt but that the opinion, that man in his regeneration worketh nothing, and God alone worketh all things, captivated and strongly excited the religious feelings of Luther. But the inference which he thence drew, that *therefore* that tenet was taught by Christ, cannot be admitted. The writings of Calvin, Beza, Knox, and others show, that, from a belief in the doctrine of an absolute predestination, they and their disciples derived a marvellous ease of mind, a boundless religious enthusiasm (which often even degenerated into a frightful all-destructive fanaticism), and an uncommon energy, activity, and perseverance of conduct. But it thence as little follows, that the doctrine which rendered these Calvinists personally easy, is a Christian and apostolic one, as from the mere circumstance, that in the reception of the sacraments, Zuinglius felt himself impressed, strengthened and solaced by no high Divine power, we could conclude, that, through these channels of salvation, Christ imparts not from the spring, whose waters flow unto eternal life. And if all the three Reformers, together with all their followers, had the personal experience and living conviction of never having performed one good work, what would thence follow? Evidently nought else, than that the state of their souls was most lamentable, and we, if they still lived, would be obliged to require them seriously to amend their lives. But by no means will we draw the inference, that it could not have been otherwise; nay, we will urge against them, as a matter of capital reproach, *that out of themselves, out of their own individual life they have deduced an universal law. Christ is our pattern as well as our lawgiver;* but such no creature is. The Lutheran Church is the incarnate spirit of Luther, and therefore thus one-sided.

§ XLVIII—CONTINUATION—DIVERGENCES IN THE DOCTRINE ON THE CHURCH, SHORTLY EXPRESSED

Now only, can the differences between the Catholic and the Lutheran view, be reduced to a short, accurate, and definite expression. The Catholics teach: the visible Church is first, then comes the invisible; the former gives birth to the latter. On the other hand, the Lutherans say the reverse: from the invisible emerges the visible Church: and the former is the groundwork of the latter. In this apparently very unimportant opposition, a prodigious difference is avowed. When Christ began to preach the kingdom of God, it existed nowhere but in him, and in the Divine idea. It came from without to men, and first of all to the apostles, in whom the divine kingdom was thus founded by the Word of God, speaking from without, and after a human fashion unto them; so that it was conveyed to them from without. When, through external media, the religious consciousness of these had been awakened by the *incarnate* Son of God, and they had, accordingly, received the *outward* calling to announce the Gospel unto others, they went into countries where, in like manner, the kingdom of God *was not*, but the dominion of Satan; and, as instruments of Christ working within them, they impressed, from without, the image of the celestial man on the interior of those, who before had been stamped with the image of the earthly one. And as Christ had done unto them, they also did again unto others: they appointed disciples, who, like them, continued to preach the doctrine of salvation, as the Holy Scripture, in numerous passages, loudly declares, and so on perpetually did the invisible spring out of the visible Church. This order of things is implied in the very notion of an external, historical revelation, whose entire peculiar essence requires a definite, perpetual, and outward ministry, to which each one must adhere, who will learn the dictates of that revelation. By the testimony of this ministry, and so by an outward testimony, the external revelation is preserved in its truth, purity, and integrity.

But according to Luther, it is quite otherwise. First, it is the Christian consciousness (*interior claritas sacræ Scripturæ*); then comes the outward certainty (*exterior claritas sacræ Scripturæ*); the Church is a community of saints, in which the Gospel is rightly announced; saints, above all, are consequently described as existing, whose origin, extraction and rise, are utterly unknown, and then they preach. How then have they become disciples of Christ ? The universal priesthood of all Christians precedes, and out of this grows the special priesthood; but, on the contrary, it is the special which determines the general priesthood, the outward the internal one. If the apostles have not produced the Lord, as little have the disciples of the apostles elected the latter. And wherein, according to Luther, is a man in the last result to find the certainty, that he possesses the truth ? In a purely internal act, in the testimony of the Holy Spirit; just as if the revelation in Christ Jesus were an interior one; as if he had not become man—as if in consequence, the question at issue were not about an external testimony, an outward authority, to impart to us the certainty as to what he taught. Hence, the respect for tradition in the Catholic, and the rejection of it in the Protestant Church. By Luther, the outward authority of the Church is converted into an interior one, and the exterior Word authenticated as divine into the internal voice of Christ and of his Spirit.

Had he wished, from his idea of the Church, to draw a consistent inference in respect to Christ, so he might very well have given up an outward, historical Christ, and an external revelation; nay he would have been compelled to reject the latter as incongruous. But all Christianity rests on the *incarnate* Son of God : hence, by an appeal to the outward, and written Word, Luther attempted to maintain an unison with an external revelation. Yet, the impossibility of clearing his doctrine of all reasonable doubts, and well-founded objections, which might be adduced, even from the Scriptures themselves, urged him, in his controversy with Catholics, to accord the *final* decision, in religious matters, to the internal Word.[1] But, when arguing with the fanatics, who themselves appealed to

---

[1] As a proof of this, we may cite the conference of Ratisbon, in the year 1541, at which the speakers, on both sides, had agreed on the article, that to the Church alone belongeth the interpretation of Scripture. When now the notion of the Church came to be discussed, and the Catholics understood by it the outward, visible Church, Melancthon declared at the end, that by the Church were to be understood, *the saints*, that is to say, those in whom God alone hath begotten faith.

the voice of the Spirit, he then held fast to the outward Word, and even entrenched himself within the authority of the perpetually visible Church.[1] Hence, from this essential perversion of view, sprang the constant vacillation between the adoption of a visible and an invisible Church, an outward and an internal Word, as the ultimate ground for the profession or the rejection of any doctrine; so that, sometimes, the visible Church is made to judge the invisible, sometimes *vice versa*. Hence, in the succeeding history of the Lutherans, the constant uncertainty,

---

[1] Luther, in a letter to Albert, Elector of Prussia, writes as follows:—
'This article,' says he (the real presence of Christ in the sacrament of the altar), 'is not a doctrine or opinion invented by men, but clearly founded and laid down in the Gospel by the plain, evident, undoubted words of Christ, and, from the origin of the Christian Churches, down to the present hour, hath been unanimously believed and held throughout the whole world. This is proved by the dear Fathers, books, and writings, both in the Greek and the Latin tongues; and, moreover, by the daily use and practice of this Institution, down to the present day. This testimony of all the holy Christian Churches (had we even nothing more), should be alone sufficient to make us adhere to this article, and not to listen to, or be led by any fanatical spirit; for, it is dangerous and frightful to hear and believe anything contrary to the unanimous testimony, belief, and doctrine of all the holy Christian Churches, as from the beginning, and with one accord they have now taught, for upwards of fifteen hundred years, throughout the whole world. Had it been a new article, and not from the foundation of the holy Christian Churches; or, had it not been so unanimously held by all Churches, and throughout all Christendom; then it were not dangerous or frightful to doubt it, or to dispute whether it be true. But since it hath been believed from the very origin of the Church, and so far as Christendom extends; whosoever doubts it, doth as much, as if he believed in no Christian Church, and not only condemns the whole Christian Church, as a damned heretic; but condemns even Christ himself, with all the apostles and the prophets, who have laid down this article, which we utter, "I believe in one, holy Christian Church," and have vehemently proclaimed (as Christ himself in Matthew, c. xxviii, 20)—"Behold, I am with ye all days, even to the consummation of the world;" and (as St Paul, in 1 Tim. iii, 15)—"The Church is the pillar and the ground of the truth." If God cannot lie, then the Church cannot err. And let not your highness think that this is my counsel; as if it sprang from me; it is the Counsel of the Holy Ghost, who knoweth all hearts and things better than we do; for, such He hath declared by His chosen instrument, St Paul, when the latter says to Titus (c. iii. 10-11), "An heretical man, thou must know, is subverted, and sinneth, being condemned by his own judgment."'—The following passage, too, from the same Reformer, is well worthy of remark:—'We confess, that under the Papacy there is many a Christian blessing—nay, every Christian blessing—a true baptism—a true sacrament of the altar—true power of the keys for the forgiveness of sins—true office of preaching—a true catechism. I say, that under the Pope there is the true Christianity—yea, the right pattern of Christianity,' etc. Then he goes on to enforce this truth against his opponents.

whether and how far the symbolical books were to be received as binding, and in what relation the Scripture stood to them. Hence, the contest, whether Luther had willed, or not, a visible or an invisible Church : he willed both, and taught what was inconsistent with either. But Luther's true spirit gradually gained, in this respect, the most decided victory, yet only in an inverted course : Luther followed a mystical impulse, and what in the dark, tumultuous, irresistible rush of his feelings, appeared to him as the truth, he firmly maintained ; whereas, his later followers have given themselves up to the *rational* element predominant in man ; and in consequence, whatever seems *rational* to them, whatever they can most easily and most conveniently master by the understanding, they immediately hold to be the Scriptural doctrine. As subjectivity must decide what is matter of history, we see the numberless variations of the doctrine of Christ ; and what seemeth true to each individual, he forthwith places in his Saviour's mouth. So it came, at length, to such a pass, that among Christians themselves, the revelation of God in Christ was doubted, denied, and even ridiculed ; for, a revelation which leaves us in the dark, as to its own purport, and can establish among its own followers no common, settled, and lasting understanding of the same, reveals on that account nothing, and thereby contradicts and refutes itself.

We again repeat it : the meaning of the doctrine, the Word is become flesh, the Word is become man, was never clear to Luther's mind. For, otherwise, he would have seen, in the first place, that it signified far more, than that for thirty years and upwards, the Divine Word had visibly and palpably worked among the Jews in Palestine : secondly, that it intimated far more, than that the Word had therewith ended, that happily before its extinction, it had been recorded on paper. Had Luther been able to rise to the true notion of the *incarnation of the Logos*, he certainly would have conceived the Church to be an institute of education ; but this was never clearly stated by him, and still less from his point of view were it intelligible, had he even most clearly expressed himself on the subject. We cannot perceive in his system, how man really cometh by Holy Writ, nor even indeed, why he needeth instruction and human education to attain *to true knowledge ;* since God alone, and by interior means, teacheth him. As little can we conceive, wherefore human exhortation, menace, and instruction should be necessary, to induce him to *will* what is good, since this God alone worketh.

§ XLIX—THE TRUTH AND THE FALSEHOOD IN LUTHER'S DOCTRINE ON THE CHURCH

Luther's notion of the Church is, however, not false, though it is one-sided. If he found it impossible to conceive the Church as a living institute, wherein man becometh holy; so he still retained the view, that it should consist of saints, whereby its ultimate and highest object is declared. In more than one place, he says he attaches great weight to the definition of the Church, as a community of saints; because each individual can thence infer what he should be. In his system, the interior part of the Church, which is yet the most important, is everywhere put forward; and that no one in the Divine kingdom can enjoy the true rights of citizenship, when he belongs only outwardly to the Church, and hath not entered into the true spirit of Christ, is in a praiseworthy manner pointed out. Moreover, it is not to be doubted, that Christ maintains his Church, in the power of victory, by means of those, who live in his faith, belong to him in heart and spirit, and rejoice in his second coming. It is also not to be doubted, that these are the true supporters of his truth; that without them it would soon be forgotten, turn into pure error, or degenerate into an empty, hollow formalism. Yes, without doubt, these—the invisible, who have been changed and glorified into the image of Christ, are the supporters of the visible Church: the wicked in that Church, the unbelievers, the hypocrites, the dead members in the body of Christ, would be unable for a single day to preserve the Church, even in her exterior forms. Nay, as far as in them lies, they do all to distract the Church, to sacrifice her to base passions, to pollute her, and abandon her to the scorn and mockery of her enemies. With never-failing profusion doth the Lord raise up, in the fulness of His strength, men, through whom he sheds over his Church, light and the newness of life; but, because after a human fashion, they cannot be infallibly recognised as his disciples, and even ought not to be so, in order not to promote confidence in mere man, and because his followers are to be called after no man, be he Athanasius, or Arius, Augustine, Luther, or Calvin, we are by him referred to *his own* institution, wherein the truth can never fail, because he, the truth and the life, ever abideth in it.

Luther, moreover, has rightly seen the necessity of admitting, that a revelation, emanating immediately from God, requireth a divinely instituted Church, and the Christian faith a far higher, than a mere human guarantee. But his fault was, that he did not seriously weigh what was signified by the words, the immediate revelation in Christ is external; for, otherwise he would have understood, that a divinely instituted Church is necessarily visible, founded as it is by the Word of God become visible, and that the warranty of faith must needs be external. Vast were the consequences of this want of perception. In the religious community, which owes its existence to Luther, the so-called invisible revelation in the human mind has since determined the conception of the visible, nay, even the written revelation; and, according as each one believes, God reveals himself to him in his interior, he explains and distorts the outward Word, and against such arbitrary interpretations, no Lutheran can allege any solid objection, *since from the inward emanates the external Church.*

Lastly, the proposition, that the internal Church is to be first established, and then the exterior one, is, in one respect, completely true, and hereby Luther was deceived. We are not *living* members of the external Church, until we belong to the interior one. What hath been imparted to us from without, must be reproduced by and within us; the objective must become subjective, ere we be entitled to consider ourselves true members of the Christian Church. Thus far, certainly, the invisible is to be ranked before the visible Church; and the latter is eternally renovated out of the former. But, this kingdom of God begins, grows, and ripens within us, after it has first externally encountered us, and made the first steps to receive us into its bosom. The act of exterior excitement, instruction, and education, is ever the first condition of life to what is internally excited, taught, and educated; but, as soon as the exterior hath passed into the interior, then the inward becometh, in its turn, the outward; and the image, which from without, was impressed upon the interior, is reflected from the interior on the exterior. But, as Luther wished to break with the existing outward Church, he was obliged to give the *absolute* precedence to the invisible Church, and consider himself as the immediate envoy of God.[1] But, by exalting, into a general principle, his view of the relation of the internal to the external Church, he fell into the greatest embarrassments. On one hand, he desired (and in perfect consistency with the view he entertained of himself, as a divinely inspired evangelist), that the doctrine, which coming forth from his interior as the voice of God, he had announced abroad, should be merely re-echoed by his disciples: and, thus from him, too, the visible should again bring forth and absolutely determine the invisible Church—a condition, which utterly annihilated his own principle.[2] But,

---

[1] After his journey from the Wartburg, Luther, as is well known, wrote from Borna to the elector Frederick, as follows:—'He had received his Gospel,' said he, ' not from men, but from heaven alone, from Jesus Christ; and, therefore is he a Christian and an evangelist, and such he wished to be called in future.' Even Calvin, in his answer to Sadolet's Epistle to the Genevans, appeals to this immediate mission: Opusc. p. 106. 'Ministerium meum, quod Dei vocatione fundatum ac sanctum fuisse non dubito.' P. 107. 'Ministerium meum, quod quidem ut a Christo esse novi,' etc.

[2] In modern times it has often been denied, that Luther had desired to lay down for all future ages dogmatic decisions. But, the sort of proof, which is adduced, would, in all cases, where personal interests were not concerned, be declared to be anything but satisfactory. Men cannot, in the least degree, have transported themselves into the spirit of those ages, and, least of all, have attended to the character of the Reformers, and particularly of Luther, when they advance such a statement. If the doctrinal uncertainty of the greater part of his present worshippers, had been one of Luther's peculiarities, it would be difficult to account for his constancy and perseverance in his career, nay, for the very origin of his reformation. Yet in proof of what has been asserted in the text, we may cite, though briefly, the words of the reformer himself. In his reply to Erasmus (Adv. Erasm. Roterod. lib. 1, p. 182, b.) he lays down the principle, 'fidesi est non falli,' which he applies, in the passage following, to particular articles. Erasmus had said, 'if the doctrine of free-will had been an error, God would certainly not have tolerated it in his Church, nor have revealed it to any saint.' To this Luther answers: 'Primum non dicimus, errorem hunc esse *in ecclesia sua* toleratum a Deo, nec in ullo *suo* sancto; ecclesia enim Spiritu Dei regitur, sancti aguntur Spiritu Dei. Rom. viii. Et Christus cum ecclesia sua manet usque ad consummationem mundi. Matt. xxviii. Et ecclesia est fundamentum et columna veritatis. 2 Tim. iii. Hæc, inquam, novimus, nam sic habet et Symbolum omnium nostrum: credo ecclesiam sanctam Catholicam, ut impossibile sit, *illam errare etiam in minimo articulo*.' Nay, Luther adds: 'Atque si etiam donemus, aliquos electos in errore teneri in tota vita, *tamen ante mortem necesse est, ut redeant in viam*,' etc. In his opinion on the imperial decree of the 22nd September, 1530, he says to the same effect: 'Whoso professeth the Augsburg Confession, will be saved; although its truth should become manifest to him only later: *this confession must endure until the end of the world, and the day of judgment*.' See Bucholz's History of the Reign of Ferdinand I, vol. iii, Vienna, 1832, p. 576 (in German)—a work where the history of the diet at Augsburg, with

if he held to the latter principle, and considered each one like himself, as internally and immediately taught by God alone, then the most opposite doctrines were proclaimed, and the internal voice of God contradicted and belied itself. From this dilemma, his disciples to this day have never been able to extricate themselves.

§ L—NEGATIVE DOCTRINES OF THE LUTHERANS IN REGARD TO THE CHURCH

If we would now point out more accurately, the negative doctrines of the Lutherans in regard to the Church; it is easy in the first place, to conceive wherefore the papal supremacy was, and must necessarily have been, rejected by them. The opinion, that Christ had founded only an invisible Church, is absolutely incompatible with the other, that he had given to it a visible head: the one notion destroys the other. Luther looking on every determination of belief, through human mediation, as equivalent to what was diabolical, the idea of the papal supremacy, wherein the doctrine of the dependence of each member on the whole body is most distinctly expressed, must (independently of the faults of individual pontiffs, which not unfrequently cast a shade on the history of the Papacy), have appeared to his mind as anti-Christian and the Pope himself as anti-Christ. For the Papacy is quite inconsistent with the idea of a purely internal, and invisible, and so far exclusively divine Church, and encroaches, according to this system, on the office of Christ, the sole and invisible head of the Church, who alone and by internal means, teacheth his disciples, and without any intermediate agency, draweth them to himself. When Protestants so often repeat, Christ is alone the head of the Church; the assertion has exactly the same sense, as when Luther says, Christ is the sole teacher, and should accordingly

all the ecclesiastical negotiations, is most copiously and instructively detailed. Hence, we can, by no means, agree with Baumgarten Crusius, when, in his 'Manual of the History of Christian Dogmas,' he thus blames the more precise definitions of the Lutheran doctrine in the formulary of Concord: 'These thoughts were rendered *matters of dogma*, while, at the origin of the Reformation, they had in their higher, more spiritual sense, been opposed to the worldly spirit of the ruling Church, and had been meant to express only the idea of human helplessness, and of the devotion of human life to God.' See his Lehrbuch der Dogmengeschichte, part i, p. 595. Jena, 1832.

Y

be estimated in precisely the same manner. Moreover if the Protestants, of the present day especially, find the idea of the Papacy objectionable, this aversion is still more conceivable. Of what could the Popedom exhibit the unity ? Of the most palpable, decided, and irreconcilable contradictions : this, indeed, would be an utter impossibility :—it could only be the representative of what was in itself a thousand fold and most radically opposed, and this anti-Christ, Satan himself alone could be. Of what body could the Pontiff be the head ? A body, whose members declare themselves independent one of the other : a thing which is inconceivable. The fault of Protestants is this, that what with them is impracticable, what from their point of view may with indisputable consistency be rejected, they would refuse to the Christian Church also, which is anything but a distracted, self-contradictory, self-annihilating self-belying thing, that ever at the same moment utters the affirmative and the negative. If a considerable portion of Protestants, instead of naming Christ their invisible head would designate him as their *unknown* head, concealed from their view, they would at least give utterance to an historical truth. The same judgment, moreover, which Protestants must form of the Papacy, they naturally pass on the Catholic view of Episcopacy.

Lastly, in respect to Tradition, it is sufficiently evident from what has been said, and it has already been explicitly shown, why in the two-fold signification above pointed out, Protestants cannot concede to it the same place, which it occupies in the Catholic system. It has occasionally been said, however, that the Reformers had not rejected Tradition ' in the ideal sense ; ' but only *Traditions*. It is certainly not to be doubted, that still partially subdued by that old ecclesiastical spirit, which, on their secession from the Church, they had unconsciously carried away with them, they believed in the same, and read the Holy Scriptures in its sense. Though *materially* they did not reject every portion of Tradition, yet they did so *formally* For, if indeed, they acknowledged the doctrinal decisions of the Church, as embodied in the first four œcumenical councils, they did so, not on account of their ecclesiastical *objectivity*, but because, according to their own *subjective* views, they found them confirmed by Holy Writ. But the Gospel truth, which hath been delivered over to the Church for preservation and for propagation, remaineth truth, whether, in consequence of a subjective inquiry, or of a pretended internal illumination, it be acknowledged or be rejected. Hence, the ecclesiastical traditionary principle is this : such and such a doctrine—for instance, the divinity of Christ—is a Christian evangelical truth, because the Church, the institution invested with authority from Christ, declares it to be his doctrine ;—not because such or such an individual subjectively holds it, as the result of his Scriptural reading, for a Christian truth. The Bible is ever forced to assume the form of its readers : it becomes little with the little, and great with the great, and is, therefore, made to pass through a thousand transformations, according as it is reflected in each individuality. If that individuality be shallow, flat, and dull, the Scripture is so represented through its medium : it is made to take the colour of the most one-sided and perverse opinions, and is abused to the support of every folly. In itself, therefore, and without any other medium, the Bible cannot be considered by the Church, as a rule of faith : on the contrary, the doctrine of the Church is the rule whereby the Scripture must be investigated. The Reformers failing to acknowledge this great truth, their partial agreement with Tradition was purely *accidental;* as is most clearly evinced by the fact, that, in the sequel, nearly all those positive doctrines of Christianity, which Luther and the first Reformers still maintained, have been cast off by their disciples, without their ever ceasing to profess themselves members of the Protestant Church. On no point did the Reformers recognise Tradition for the sake of its objectivity ; and, therefore, they rejected it, wherever it accorded not with their own subjective caprices. What doctrine doth tradition more clearly attest, than that of free-will ? Yet, this they rejected. In short, they entirely merged the objective, historical Christianity into their own subjectivity, and were consequently *forced* to throw off Tradition.

Accordingly, they refused obedience to the Church—deeming it ignoble and slavish. They forgot that, a divine authority impresses upon the obedience also, which pays homage to it, the stamp of divinity, and exalts it as much above servitude, as the spirit is raised above the flesh. It is remarkable, that no one any longer doubts, but that an outward, fixed, eternally immutable moral law, though not in all its parts first established by Christ, yet hath been by Him confirmed and brought to greater perfection. This rule of will and of action, every Christian recognises ; and, however far short of it he may fall in his own conduct, yet, he never thinks of changing it, according to his subjective moral point of view; nor, in the commission of his faults, of flattering himself, that the standard, according to which he should act, and that according to which he, in reality, doth act, perfectly correspond. But, the necessity of a like fixed and unchangeable standard for the intelligence is disputed. Here each one is to give himself up to the guidance of his own subjective feelings and fancies, and to be certain, that what he feels and thinks, is truly felt and thought; although any individual, who has only attended for some weeks to his own train of thoughts, may easily perceive, that in this field he is not a whit stronger, than in the sphere of morals. That the Bible alone cannot in itself, constitute such a settled, outward rule, nor was ever so intended by Christ, no one surely, after the awful experience, which, in our times especially, has been made, and is still daily made, will feel any longer disposed to deny.

§ LI—DOCTRINE OF THE CALVINISTS ON THE CHURCH

The Calvinists adopted Luther's general views, respecting the Church, without alteration, and solemnly confirmed them in their Symbolical writings.[1] But Calvin is distinguished by many peculiarities, which deserve to be mentioned. The phenomena which in the whole compass of ecclesiastical life from the commencement of the revolution attempted by Luther, down to the flourishing period of Calvin, had presented themselves to the attention of the observer, had not passed by without making the deepest impression upon the mind of the Genevan Reformer. He had observed the boundless tyranny, which had followed in the train of the new principles: nor had he overlooked the fact, that the idea of a Christian put forward by his predecessor,

[1] Zuingl. Commentar. de vera et falsa Relig. Opp. tom. ii, fol. 197, where he comprises, in ten short propositions, his whole doctrine on the Church. Calvin Instit. l. iv, c. i, fol. 190, seq; Confess. Helvet. i, c. xvii, ed. Augs. p. 47; Helvet. ii, Art. xiv; Anglic. Art. xix, p. 133: which, however, very clearly points out the visible character of the Church: 'Ecclesia Christi visibilis est cœtus fidelium, in quo verbum Dei purum prædicatur, et sacramenta, quoad ea, quæ necessario exigantur, juxta Christi institutum recte administrantur.' Very different from this, on the other hand, is the Confessio Scotorum, Art. xvi, p. 156. The Hungarian Confession has nothing to say respecting the Church; but, on the other hand, it has a section *de vestitu pastorum*, p. 251.

as an independent, all-sufficing being, capable, from the fulness of his own spirit, of satisfying all his higher wants, is a mere fiction, which all experience belies.[1] He had been struck with the fact, that the rulers of the new Church were devoid of all influence and respect; that the people, which had been taught to look on them as the mere work of its own hands, denied them frequently the most indispensable obedience; and that, if temporal princes had not interposed their authority, all order and discipline would have been subverted.[2] As at Geneva, the principal scene of Calvin's activity, the ecclesiastical reformation was connected with a civil revolution, the wildest anarchy had broken through the restraints of public morals, and matter for the most earnest reflection was thus offered in abundance.

Hence, Calvin thought it necessary to straiten the bonds, which united the individual with the general body, to excite a new reverence for the Church (of which Luther had always spoken in such terms of disparagement, and whereof, indeed, he had never formed a clear conception), as well as to establish, on a more solid basis, the authority of its rulers. He carefully collected all that had ever been said upon the Church, in anywise good and useful for his object; and did not even hesitate to transplant into his garden, many a flower from the so-much-detested *Corpus Furis canonici;* taking care, however, not to name the place of its extraction. So he preferred to adopt, in his 'Institutes of the Christian Religion,' propositions, which, in the Protestant system, are utterly untenable and baseless than consistently to enforce the principles, that he had inherited from Luther. At the very commencement of his Treatise on the Church he points out the natural ignorance, indolence, and frivolity of man; and the consequent necessity of certain institutions to implant, cherish, and mature the doctrines of faith. In the Church, hath the treasure of the Gospel been

[1] Calvin. Instit. l, iv, c. 1, sect. v, fol. 572. ' Etsi externis mediis alligata non est Dei virtus, tamen ordinario docendi modo alligavit : quem dum recusant tenere fanatici homines, multis se exitialibus laqueis involvunt. Multos impellit vel superbia, vel fastidium, vel æmulatio, ut sibi persuadeant privatim legendo et meditando se posse satis proficere, atque ita contemnant publicos cœtus et prædicationem supervacuam ducant. Quoniam autem sacrum unitatis vinculum, quantum in se est, solvunt vel abrumpunt,' etc.

[2] Loc. cit. sect. ii, fol. 375. ' Ejus (Satanæ) arte factum est, ut pura verbi prædicatio aliquot sæculis evanuerit : et nunc eadem improbitate incumbit ad labefactandum ministerium : quod tamen sic in ecclesia Christus ordinavit, ut illo sublato hujus ædificatio pereat,' etc.

deposited; he proceeds to say, pastors and teachers have been instituted by God, *and been invested with authority* to the end, that preaching might never fail, and a holy concord in Faith, and a right order might constantly obtain.[1]

But when his reason made him the reproach, how, if the Church were really so constituted he could feel himself justified in severing all ties of connection with the one in existence; he then stunned his conscience with the most violent invectives against her; satisfied as he was, that the generation which had once begun to swear by men, and to revere their opinions, as the Word of God, would easily take such sallies of furious passion, as a substitute for solid argument.[2]

After these introductory observations, Calvin speaks first, of the invisible Church, and requires his disciples, in the first place, to be firmly convinced that such a Church doth in reality exist—namely, a host of elect, who, though they do not see each other face to face, yet are united in one faith, in one hope, in one charity, and in the same Holy Spirit, as members under the one Christ, their common head. In the second place, he requires them to believe, with undoubting assurance, that they themselves belong to this invisible Church, which can be only one, since a division of Christ is impossible. Then, he adds: 'though a desolate wilderness on all sides surrounds us, which seemeth to cry out, the Church is vanished; yet, let us be assured, that the death of Jesus is not unprofitable, and that God knows how to preserve his followers even in the obscurest corners.' The reader will not fail to observe, that together with the reasons, which are to be looked for in his doctrine of absolute predestination, there was an especial motive that induced Calvin to enforce on his disciples the conviction, that they belonged to an invisible Church. This was the general demoralisation which he saw prevailing among them, and which threatened to undermine the belief, that the so-called Reformation, had in reality been brought about.[3] So he diverts their view

---

[1] Loc. cit. lib. iv, c. i, fol. 370. 'Quia autem ruditas nostra et segnities (addo etiam ingenii vanitatem) externis subsidiis indigent ... pastores instituit ac doctores (Deus), quorum ore suos doceret: eos auctoritate instruxit; nihil denique omisit, quod ad sanctum fidei consensum et rectum ordinem faceret.'

[2] Loc. cit. c. ii, fol. 381-86.

[3] Loc. cit. sect. xiii, fol. 376. 'Dum enim apud eos, quibus Evangelium annuntiatur, ejus doctrinæ non respondere vitæ fructum vident, nullam illic esse ecclesiam statim judicant. Justissima quidem est offensio, cui plus satis occasionis hoc miserrimo sæculo præbemus; nec excusare licet

from the world of reality, and turns it to the obscurity of the invisible world, in order to afford, to that eternal longing of the Christian soul after communion, a satisfaction which the visible Church evidently denied. He immediately passes over to the latter, to impart to it a more solid and beautiful form, to insure its efficacy and its influence in the training up of believers to make the visible Church appear as the reflection of the invisible, and, in this way, to attempt to reconcile, by degrees, the members of the latter with those of the former.

How salutary, nay, how indispensable, is this view of the nature of the visible Church, says he, is evident alone, from her glorious appellation of ' mother.' There is no coming into life, unless she conceives us in her womb, unless she brings us forth, nourishes us at her breasts, and finally watches over and protects us, until we throw off this mortal coil, and become like unto the angels, For, as long as we live, our weakness will not admit of our being discharged from school. Let us consider, moreover, he continues, that out of the pale of the Church, there is no forgiveness of sins, and no salvation: Isaiah and Joel attest it, and Ezekiel concurs with them. We see from thence, that God's paternal grace, and the especial testimony of the spiritual life, are confined to his flock; so that separation from the Church is ever pernicious.

Calvin appeals to Ephesians, c. iv, 11, where St Paul says, ' that Christ gave some apostles; and some prophets; and some others, evangelists; and some others, pastors and doctors; for the perfecting of the saints, for the work of the ministry, for the edifying of the body of Christ; until we all meet in the unity of the faith, and of the knowledge of the Son of God unto a perfect man, unto the measure of the age of the fulness of Christ : '—a passage which the Catholic Church adduces in support of the view that she takes of herself. After this quotation, the Reformer adds : ' We see that God, *though in one moment he could render His own followers perfect*, yet would have them grow up to maturity only by means of an education by the Church. We see, moreover, the way marked out, wherein

maledictam ignaviam, quam Dominus impunitam non sinet ; uti jam gravibus flagellis castigare incipit. Væ ergo nobis, qui tam dissoluta flagitiorum licentia committimus, ut propter nos vulnerentur imbecilles conscientiæ.—Quia enim non putant esse ecclesiam, ubi non est solida vitæ puritas et integritas, scelerum odio a legitima ecclesia discedunt, dum a factione improborum declinare se putant. Aiunt ecclesiam Christi sanctam esse,' etc.

these plans of God are to be unfolded; for, to the pastors is the preaching of the Divine Word entrusted: all must conform to this precept, so that, with a mild and docile spirit (*mansueto et docili spiritu*) they give themselves up to the guidance of the teachers selected for that purpose. Long before had the prophet Isaiah characterised the Church by this sign, when he said, " The spirit which is in thee, and the words, which I have placed in thy mouth, will never depart from thy mouth nor from the mouth of thy seed's seed, saith the Lord." Hence it follows, that those deserve to perish of hunger and misery, who despise the celestial food of the soul, which is administered from above through the hands of the Church. That we may know that in earthly vessels, an incomparable treasure is presented to our acceptance, God himself appears, and as far as He is the Founder of this order of things, desires to be acknowledged as ever present in his institution. In like manner, as He referred not His chosen people of old to angels, but raised up on earth teachers, who performed truly the office of angels: so He desires now to instruct us after a human fashion. And in like manner, as in ancient times, He was not content with merely revealing His law, but appointed as interpreters of the same, the priests, from whose lips the people were to hear its true sense explained: so it is now His will, that we should not merely be engaged with the reading of Holy Writ; nay, He hath instituted teachers, that we may be supported by their aid. From hence a two-fold advantage springs. On one hand, the Almighty best tries our obedience, when we so hearken to His ministers, as if He spake himself; and, on the other hand, He condescends to our weakness, by choosing rather to address us after a human manner, through the medium of interpreters, in order to draw us to Himself, than to repel us by the voice of His thunders.' Calvin, after remarking, that in all apostasies from the Church, arrogance or jealousy ever lies at the bottom, and that he, who severs the sacred bonds of unity, will not fail to incur the just chastisement for this godless adultery—to wit, spiritual blindness through the most poisonous errors and the most detestable illusions; proceeds to say, ' the more abominable therefore are the apostates who aim at a division in the Church: it is as if they chased the sheep away from the fold, and delivered them up to the jaws of the wolf.' [1]

Calvin is as inexhaustible in his own self-refutation, as he

[1] Loc. cit. c. i. sect. v, fol. 372.

is unshaken in his confidence in the thoughtlessness of the
men, from whom he seriously expects, that the grounds, which
condemn his own disobedience against the Catholic Church,
they will good-naturedly take for proofs that they owe submission to him and to his institutions. As we, he says in
another place, profess an invisible Church, which is seen by the
eye of God alone; so are we bound to revere a Church, which
is perceptible to men, and to persevere in its communion.[1]
He never forgets to point out as a mark of a true Christian
community, its veneration for the ministry, and for the office
of preaching;[2] and, if Luther said the true Church is there to
be found, where the Gospel is rightly announced; so Calvin
adds, it is there to be found where the preaching of the Divine
Word *is heard with obedience*. 'Where,' as he expresses himself,
'the preaching of the Gospel is received with reverence, there
neither a deceptious, nor a doubtful image of the Church is
presented; and no one will go unpunished, who contemns her
authority, or despises her exhortations, or rejects her counsels,
or mocks her chastisements, still less who apostatises from her
and dissolves her unity. For such value doth our Lord attach
to communion with his Church, that he is held for an apostate
and an unbeliever, who obstinately secedes from any [particular
reformed] community, *should it otherwise revere the true ministry
of the Word and of the sacraments*. It is certainly no slight
thing, that is called "the pillar and the ground of the truth,"
as well as the "House of God." Hereby, St Paul means to say,
the Church is the faithful preserver of the truth, that it may
never be lost in the world; for, by her ministry and her aid,
God wished to preserve the pure preaching of His word, and
show himself a kind parent, who nourishes us with spiritual
food, and provides all, which can minister to our salvation.
Even this is no mean praise that the Church is called the "chosen
one," the bride elect, who must be without spot and without
wrinkle, the body of the Lord. Hence, it follows, that
separation from the Church is tantamount to a denial of God
and of Christ; and we should guard the more against the

---

[1] Calvin. lib. iv, c. 1, n. 7, fol. 374. 'Quemadmodum ergo nobis invisi-
bilem, solius Dei oculis conspicuam ecclesiam credere necesse est, ita hanc,
quæ respectu hominum ecclesia dicitur, observare, ejusque communionem
colere jubemur.'

[2] Loc. cit. sect. ix, fol. 374. 'Quæ (multitudo) si ministerium *habet*
verbi, et *honorat*, si sacramentorum administrationem, ecclesia procul
dubio haberi et censeri meretur.'

heinousness of schism, for while, as far as in us lies, we thus labour for the destruction of Divine Truth, we deserve to call down upon ourselves the full weight of God's wrath. And no more detestable crime can be imagined, than by a sacrilegious infidelity to violate the marriage, which the only begotten Son of God hath deigned to contract with the Church.' [1]

Lastly, Calvin, for good reasons, endeavours to enforce on his readers the conviction, that no magnitude of moral corruption can ever deprive the Church of its inherent character,[2] and that those, who, on this point are too rigid, and in consequence incite to defection, are generally swollen with arrogance, and impelled by a pernicious self-complacence. He even adds, that a certain obscuration of the true faith should not be overrated.[3]

From these principles of Calvin, we can understand, why he retained Ordination, and even under the condition, that it should be administered not by the people, but by the presbytery.[4]

---

[1] Loc. cit, sect. x, fol. 374-375.

[2] Loc. cit. c. ii, sect. i, fol. 381. ' Ubicunque integrum exstat et illibatum (verbi et sacramentorum ministerium) nullis morum vitiis aut morbis impediri, quominus ecclesiæ nomen sustineat.' C. i, sect. xvi, fol. 377. ' Hoc tamen reperimus nimiam morositatem ex superbia magis et fastu falsaque sanctitatis opinione, quam ex vera sanctitate veroque ejus studio nasci. Itaque qui ad faciendam ab ecclesia defectionem sunt aliis audaciores, et quasi antesignani, ii ut plurimum nihil aliud causæ habent, nisi ut omnium contemptu ostendant se aliis esse meliores.'

[3] Loc. cit. sect. xii, fol. 374. ' Quin etiam poterit vel in doctrina, vel in sacramentorum administratione vitii quippiam obrepere, quod alienare nos ab ejus communione non debeat.' We could wish that space permitted us to cite some passages from the writings of Theodore Beza upon the Church. What Calvin teaches, Beza excellently applies. We need only peruse Beza's Epistle to a certain Alamannus, ' ecclesiæ Lugdunensis turbatorem,' in order to learn how Calvin's maxims were practically enforced. See Theodori Bezæ Vezelii epist. theolog. liber unus. Genev. 1573, p. 48. May we not consider it as a result of Calvin's deeper conception of the Church surviving to this day, that even now the German Calvinistic theologians have, on this subject, furnished far more excellent matter than the Lutheran ones ? It is Schleiermacher and Marheineke (and the latter, in his book of religious instruction for the Higher Gymnasia, still more than in the Manual of dogmatic Theology, destined for University Lectures), who, among the modern Protestants, have by far the best treated this subject. Marheineke had already written much that was excellent on the Church, before he attached himself to the Hegelian school, from which certainly a better spirit has emanated.

[4] Loc. cit. lib. iv, c. 3, sect. 11-16, fol. 389-392 ; lib. iv, c. 14, sect. 20, fol. 418. ' Sacramenta duo instituta, quibus nunc Christiana ecclesia utitur. *Loquor autem de iis, quæ in usum totius ecclesiæ sunt instituta. Nam impositionem manuum qua ecclesiæ ministri in suum munus initiantur, ut non invitus patior vocari sacramentum, ita inter ordinaria sacramenta*

He even evinced an inclination to acknowledge Holy Orders as a sacrament. Certainly from this point of view, the remarkable fact, that in the English Calvinistic Church episcopacy was retained, finds here its deepest motive; although it is not to be denied, that various other circumstances also concurred to this retention. With Luther's first opinions, no episcopacy could have existed; and the Danish and Swedish episcopal system is essentially different from the Anglican.[1] But, hereby in the Anglican Church, the internal self-contradiction was carried to the extremest pitch. A Catholic hierarchy, and a Protestant system of faith in one and the same community! The Anglican bishops boast, that by means of Catholic ordination, they descend in an unbroken succession from the Apostles; and are, accordingly, in a most intimate and living connection with the ancient Church; and yet, by their participation in the ecclesiastical revolution, they broke off the chain of tradition.

How great, therefore, must be our astonishment, when Calvin makes belief in the divinity of the Scriptures, depend on the testimony of the Holy Spirit in the interior man, and when he could descend to such a pitiable misinterpretation of the true proposition of St Augustine's: 'I would not believe in the Sacred Scriptures, if the authority of the Church did not determine me thereto.'[2] Here again that effort was relaxed, which had so earnestly endeavoured to oppose an objective matter to subjective caprice; and evidently in order to obviate the possible consequences, which, from the undeniable fact, that in and by the Catholic Church, the canon of the Bible had been settled, and its several books preserved in their integrity, might be deduced in favour of that Church.[3]

non numero.' If, by sacramentum ordinarium, Calvin understands, quod in usum totius ecclesiæ (omnium fidelium) institutum est, so the Catholic Church quite agrees with him.

[1] Confess. Anglic. Art. xxxvi.

[2] Calvin. Instit. lib. i, c. 7, sect. 3, fol 15. 'Maneat ergo fixum, quos Spiritus sanctus intus docuit, solide acquiescere in Scriptura, et hanc quidem esse αὐτόπιστον, neque demonstrationibus et rationi subjici eam fas esse: quam tamen meretur apud nos certitudinem spiritus testimonio consequi. Talis ergo est persuasio, quæ rationes non requirat: talis notitia, cui optima ratio constat, nempe in qua securius constantiusque mens acquiescit, quam in ullis rationibus; talis denique sensus, qui nisi ex cœlesti revelatione nasci nequeat.'

[3] Loc. cit. sect. 1, fol. 14. 'Sic enim magno cum ludibrio Spiritus sancti quærunt: ecquis nobis fidem faciat, hæc a Deo prodiisse? Ecquis salva ac intacta ad nostram usque ætatem pervenisse certiores reddat? Ecquis persuadeat, librum hunc reverenter excipiendum, alterum numero

Yet these principles of Calvin emanated from the thoroughly subjective nature of Protestantism; and it must be admitted, that his views on the Church are far more inconsistent with the inmost spirit of the reformation, than his opinion as to the mode of assuring ourselves of the divine origin of any sacred writing, is with his doctrine on the Church. But at all events, it is highly honourable to his perspicacity, as well as to his Christian spirit, that he saw, or at least felt, that by means of mere learned investigation, the believer could obtain no satisfactory result; that on account of the obscurity, which involves the origin of many of the sacred writings, and the formation of the canon itself, and which spreads in general over the first two centuries of the Church, doubts as to the genuineness of one or other canonical Scripture may ever be raised—doubts on the final solution whereof, faith cannot remain suspended: and that accordingly, some higher guarantee must be sought for. Such he found, following out earlier indications; and what he found was not false, but one-sided, unsatisfactory, and cheerless for the Church. That through such principles an opening was made to the desolation of the sanctuary, proceeding from a one-sided culture of the religious spirit, Calvin might have learned from Luther's views touching the Biblical canon. Where the latter 'did not perceive the spirit.'[1] that is to say, did not

expungendum, nisi certam istorum omnium regulam ecclesia præscriberet ? Pendet igitur, inquiunt, ab ecclesiæ determinatione et qua scripturæ reverentia debeatur, et qui libri in ejus catalogo censendi sint. Ita sacrilegi homines, dum sub ecclesiæ prætextu volunt effrænatam tyrannidem evehere, nihil curant, quibus se et alios absurditatibus illaqueent, modo hoc unum extorqueant apud simplices, ecclesiam nihil non posse.' Moreover, no Catholic so expresses himself, that it depends on the Church to determine what veneration be due to the sacred writings, and what books are to be held as canonical; but Catholics have at all times asserted, that the Church is only a witness and a guarantee, that the canonical scriptures are really what they are considered to be. Calvin, however, expresses himself more honestly than Luther, who, in his *Commentary on the Epistle to the Galatians*, c. i, p. 30 (Wittenberg, 1556, part i), says : ' So the Church should have power and authority over Holy Writ : as the canonists and the sententiarii (schoolmen) have written against God, and in the most shameless manner. The ground which some assign for this opinion is, the Church hath not approved of and adopted more than four gospels ; therefore there are only four, and had the Church adopted more, there would have been more. But now, if the Church hath the power, according to her good-will and pleasure, to adopt and to approve of gospels, what and how many she chooses, so it thence follows that the authority of the Church is above the Gospel.' This was now, indeed, easy to be refuted, as even Luther himself refutes his own fiction.

[1] 'Den Geist verspürte.' These are Luther's own words.—*Trans.*

find the reflection of his own spirit, he forthwith believed the suspicion of spuriousness to be well founded. But, who can ultimately decide on this test of the Spirit, which a book of Scripture doth abide or not, when that book is rejected by one party, and defended by another? Neither can be refuted, because each exalts individual sentiment, as the highest and the ultimate criterion of certainty; and will not let its religious faith be moulded according to the objective doctrine of the Bible, but will itself, according to its own pleasure, determine what is, or is not Scripture. Accordingly, from the language of the Spirit, it can never be decided, whether Matthew, Mark, Paul, Peter, and the rest, have written any book; at most, it declares that a Christian is the author of such a writing. But when the question turns on the canonicity of the Scriptures, it is the former, and not merely the latter fact, which we desire to know; for, the apostles only we hold to be unerring, but no one besides.[1]

CHAPTER VI

THE CHURCH IN THE NEXT WORLD AND ITS CONNECTION WITH THE CHURCH MILITANT

§ LII—DOCTRINE OF CATHOLICS ON THIS MATTER

HITHERTO we have considered the Church only in her terrestrial being and essence; and her supermundane part remains still to be described. The faithful, who, summoned away from hence, have quitted their visible communion with us, and have passed into another state of existence, do not (so the Catholic Church teaches) thereby sever the bonds of connection with us. On the contrary, holy love, which was transferred from a higher order of existence to this lower world, perpetually enfolds in her sacred bands all those whom she hath once held in her embraces, (provided only they have not wilfully torn themselves from her), and amid the dissolution of all earthly energies,

---

[1] Confessio Gallica (c. iv, lib. i, p. 111) agrees with Calvin when it says: ' Hos libros agnoscimus esse canonicos, id est, ut fidei nostræ normam et regulam habemus, atque non tantum ex communi ecclesiæ consensu, sed etiam multo magis ex testimonio et intrinseca Spiritus sancti persuasione: quo suggerente docemur, illos ab aliis libris ecclesiasticis discernere, qui ut sint ules (utiles?) non sunt tamen ejusmodi, ut ex iis constitui possit aliquis fidei articulus.'

still retains her eternal power. All now, who, with the hallow of love, have departed hence, as also those higher created spiritual beings, who, though they never lived with us in the relations of space and time ; yet, like us, stand under the same head, Christ Jesus, and are sanctified in the same Holy Spirit, form together one Church—one great and closely united confederacy with us.[1] But, not all believers, who have been members of this terrestrial Church, and have departed from it, with the sign of the covenant of love, enter immediately on their passage into eternity, into those relations of bliss, destined from the beginning, for those who love God in Christ. According as they quit this earthly life, either slightly touched by divine love, or by it effectually freed from the stains of sin, they pass into different forms of a new existence. The former are transferred to a state, suited to the still defective moral and religious life of their souls, and which is destined to bring them to perfection : the latter to a state of happiness, corresponding to their consummate sanctification. The first, like the members of the Church terrestrial, are with reason included in the suffering Church ; for their peculiar existence must be considered as one, not only still passing through the fire of purification,[2] but as also subjected to punishment ; for, it depended only on themselves, by the right use of their free-will, during their earthly career, to have established themselves in a perfect, intimate, and untroubled union with God.[3] Those, however, admitted

---

[1] Cardinal Sadoletus, in his letter to the Genevans, admirably expresses the pith of the doctrine of the Catholic Church : ' Sin mortalis anima sit, edamus, et bibamus, inquit apostolus, paulo enim post moriemur : sin autem sit immortalis, ut certo est, unde, quæso, tantum et tam repente factum est corporis morte dissidium, ut et viventium et mortuorum animæ inter se nihil congruant, nihil communicent, omnis cognationis nobiscum et communis humanæ societatis oblitæ ? Cum præsertim charitas, quæ præcipuum Spiritus sancti in Christiano genere est donum : quæ nunquam non benigna, nunquam non fructuosa est, et in eo, in quo inest, nunquam inutiliter consistit, salva semper et efficax in utraque vita permaneat.—Jacob. Sadolet. Card. opp. tom. ii, p. 181.

[2] In the Missal, one of the prayers for the dead, runs thus : ' Suscipe, Domine, preces nostras pro anima famuli tui N. *ut si quæ ei maculæ de terrenis contagiis adhæserunt,* remissionis tuæ misericordia deleantur. Per Dominum nostrum Jesum Christum.'

[3] In the Florentine formulary of reunion (which expresses the unity of belief of the Greek and Latin Church), it is said : ' Item si vere pœnitentes in Dei caritate decesserint, antequam dignis pœnitentiæ fructibus de commissis satisfecerint et omissis, eorum animas pœnis purgatoriis post mortem purgari (καθαρτικαῖς τιμωρίαις καθαίρεσθαι ἐπὶ θάνατμον): et ut a pœnis hujusmodi releventur, prodesse eis fidelium vivorum suffragia, Missarum

into the ranks of happy spirits, form, together with these, the Church triumphant—a denomination which sufficiently explains itself.

That the doctrine of an ulterior state of purification, of a purgatory in fine, is involved in the Catholic dogma of justification, and is absolutely inseparable from the same, we have already, in a former part of this work, demonstrated. We shall, accordingly, speak here only of the peculiar mode of communion which is kept up between us and the poor souls, that are delivered over to the cleansing fire. We are taught, and are even urged by the strongest impulse of our hearts, to put up for them to God and Jesus Christ, our most earnest supplications. We present to God, more especially, the sacrifice of Christ upon the cross, and beseech him, that for his Son's sake, He would look down with graciousness and compassion upon our suffering brothers and sisters, and deign to quicken their passage into eternal rest.[1] This custom, which we cannot absolutely abandon, for we are impelled to its exercise, by all the power of faith and of love, is not only confirmed by the usages of the most ancient nations, and of the chosen people of God in particular, but may be proved to have been authorised by the practice of the primitive Church; and is, accordingly, revered by us as an apostolic tradition. But, moreover, as to the mode of punishment, and the place, which purgatory occupies, the Church teaches nothing further; for she has, on this point, received no special revelations; and when we use the expression, 'purifying fire,' we employ it only in the usual figurative sense.

Of a different kind is the intercourse subsisting between

scilicet sacrificia, orationes, et eleemosynas, et alia pietatis officia, quæ a fidelibus pro aliis fidelibus fieri consueverunt, secundum ecclesiæ instituta.' Harduin Acta concil. tom. ix, p. 422.

[1] Concil. Trid. Sess. xxv, decret. de Purgator. ' Cum Catholica ecclesia . . . docuerit, purgatorium esse : animasque ibi detentas fidelium suffragiis, potissimum vero acceptabili altaris sacrificio juvari, præcipit sancta synodus episcopis, ut sanam de Purgatorio doctrinam, a sanctis patribus et a sacris conciliis traditam, a Christi fidelibus credi, teneri, doceri, et ubique prædicari diligenter studeant. Apud rudem vero plebem difficiliores ac subtiliores questiones, quæ ad ædificationem non faciunt, et ex quibus nulla fit pietatis accessio, a popularibus concionibus secludantur. Incerta item, vel quæ specie falsi laborant, evulgari ac tractari non permittant. Ea vero, quæ ad curiositatem quandam, aut superstitionem spectant, vel turpe lucrum spectant, tanquam scandala, ac fidelium offendicula prohibeant,' etc. Sess. xxii, c. 11. ' Quare non solum pro fidelium vivorum peccatis . . . sed et pro defunctis in Christo nondum pleniter purgatis offertur.' Sess. vi, can. xxx.

us and the triumphant Church. Let us turn our view, more particularly, to those of its members, who were once incorporated with the Church on earth. Not only do they work among us by the sacred energies, which, during their earthly pilgrimage, they displayed, and whereby they extended God's kingdom, and founded it more deeply in the hearts of men; energies, whose influence, acting at first on those within their immediate sphere, spread thence ever wider and wider, and will extend to all future times. Not only are they permanent models of Christian life, in whom the Saviour hath stamped his own image, in whom he, in a thousand ways, reflects himself, and in whom, exhibiting to us patterns for all the relations of life, he brings vividly before our view, the whole compass of virtues rendered possible through him. But they also minister for us (such is our firm and confident belief) in a still more exalted degree; and this their ministration requires from us a corresponding conduct. The purer their love, and the fuller their share in that ineffable bliss, whereof they have become partakers in Christ, the more they turn their affections towards us, and amid all our efforts and struggles, remain by no means passive spectators. They supplicate God in behalf of their brethren; and we in turn, conscious that the prayer of the righteous man availeth much with God, implore their intercession. The act, whereby we do this, is called invocation (*invocatio*); and that, wherein they respond to this call, is termed intercession (*intercessio*).[1]

The setting up of the saints by the Church, as patterns for religious and moral imitation, connected with the doctrine of their intercession in our behalf with God, and of the corresponding invocation of their aid on our parts, constitutes the principle of the veneration of saints, which is in the same way related to the supreme worship, as the mutual relation existing between creatures, is to the state of dependence of them all on their

---

[1] Concil. Trid. Sess. xxv. ' Mandat sancta synodus omnibus episcopis . . . ut fideles diligenter instruant, docentes eos, Sanctos una cum Christo regnantes, orationes suas pro hominibus offerre, bonum atque utile esse suppliciter eos vocare ; et ob beneficia impetranda a Deo per filium ejus Jesum Christum Dominum nostrum, qui solus noster redemptor et salvator est, ad eorum orationes, opem auxiliumque confugere.' Sess. xxii, c. III. ' Et quamvis in honorem et memoriam sanctorum nonnullus interdum missas ecclesiâ celebrare consueverit ; non tamen illis sacrificium offerre docet, sed Deo soli, qui illos coronavit, unde nec sacerdos dicere solet, offero tibi sacrificium, Petre vel Paule, sed Deo de illorum victoriis gratias agens, eorum patrocinia implorat, ut ipsi pro nobis intercedere dignentur in cœlis, quorum memoriam facimus in terris.'

common *Creator and Lord*. Virtuous creatures look with love and reverence on those of their body, who were eminently endowed by God, and, in virtue of their love implanted within them, they wish each other all good, and lift up their hands in each other's behalf unto God, who, rejoicing in the love that emanates from himself, and binds His creatures together, hears their mutual supplications, in case they be worthy of His favour, and out of the fulness of his power, satisfies them; and this no creature is able to accomplish. Moreover, if we are to worship Christ, we are forced to venerate his saints. Their brightness is nought else than an irradiation from the glory of Christ, and a proof of his infinite power, who, out of dust and sin, is able to raise up eternal spirits of light. He who, therefore, revereth the saints, glorifieth Christ, from whose power they have sprung, and whose true divinity they attest. Hence the festivals of the Lord, whereby the commemoration of the most important events in the Redeemer's history is, in the course of the year, with the most living solemnity renewed, the Church hath encircled with the feasts of the saints, who, through the whole progressive history of the Church, testify the fruitful effects of the coming of the Son of God into this world, of his ministry and his sufferings, his resurrection, and the outpouring of the Spirit; so that, accordingly, in the lives of the saints, the effects of the life of Christ, and its undeniable fruits, are brought home at once to our contemplation, and to our feelings. And with reason may we say, that as God is no God of the dead, but of the living; so Christ is no God of a generation; tarrying in the sleep of death, but of a people truly awakened in the spirit, and growing up to sanctification and to bliss. Lastly, it is to be borne in mind, that the doctrine of the Church does not declare, that the saints *must*, but only that they *can* be invoked; since the Council of Trent, in the passage we have cited, says, ' only that it is *useful and salutary*, to invoke with confidence the intercession of the saints.' Of faith in the divinity of Christ, and in his mediatorial office, or in his sanctifying grace, and the like, the Church by no means teaches that it is merely useful and salutary, but that it is absolutely necessary to salvation.

§ LIII—DOCTRINE OF PROTESTANTS ON THIS SUBJECT

To these principles of the Catholic Church, Protestants oppose but mere empty negations, and a dead criticism. In the first place, as regards purgatory, Luther, at the outset, denied this doctrine, as little as that of prayers for the dead. But, as soon as he obtained a clear apprehension of his own theory of justification, he recognised the necessity of giving way here likewise to the spirit of negation. In the Smalcald Articles, composed by him, he expresses himself in the strongest manner against the doctrine of purgatory, and characterises it as a diabolical invention.[1] Calvin also, with the most furious violence, declares against this dogma, and the symbolical writings of his party coincide with him on this subject.[2] At the same time, with the clearest conviction, they avow the motive, which incited them on to this violent opposition; and disguise *not* the feeling, that the adoption, or even the toleration of the doctrine of purgatory, in their religious system, would admit a principle destructive to the whole. Reconciliation and forgiveness of sins, they allege, is to be sought for only in the blood of Christ. It would be, therefore, a denial of his merits, and of the rights of faith, which alone saveth, if it were to be maintained, that the believer in the other world had still to endure punishment, and were not unconditionally to be admitted into heaven.[3] The miscon-

[1] Artic. Smalcald. p. ii. c. 2, sect. 9. 'Quapropter purgatorium, et quidquid ei solemnitatis, cultus et quæstus adhæret, mera diaboli larva est. Pugnat enim cum primo articulo, qui docet, Christum solum et non hominum opera, animas liberare.'

[2] Calvin. Instit. lib. iii. c. 5, sect. 6, fol. 241. 'Demus tamen illa omnia tolerari aliquantisper potuisse ut res non magni momenti, at ubi peccatorum expiatio alibi, quam in Christi sanguine quæritur, ubi satisfactio alio transfertur, periculosissimum silentium. Clamandum ergo non modo vocis sed gutturis ac laterum contentione, purgatorium exitiale Satanæ esse commentum, quod Christi crucem evacuat, quod contumeliam Dei misericordiæ non ferendam irrogat, quod fidem nostram labefacit et evertit,' etc. Confess. Helvet. i, art. xxvi, p. 86: 'Quod autem quidam tradunt de igne purgatorio, fidei Christianæ: credo remissionem peccatorum et vitam æternam, purgationique plenæ per Christum adversatur.'—Anglic. xxii, p. 134.

[3] The mere attention to the prayers of the Church, for instance, of the following prayer (in die obitus seu depositionis defuncti), might have shown to the Reformers the utter groundlessness of their reproaches. '*Deus, cui proprium est misereri semper et parcere*, te supplices exoramus pro anima famuli tui N. quam hodie de hoc sæculo migrare jussisti: ut non tradas eam in manus inimici, neque obliviscaris in finem; sed jubeas eam a sanctis angelis suspici, et ad patriam paradisi perduci: *ut quia in te speravit et credidit*, non pœnas inferni sustineat, sed gaudia æterna possideat. Per Dominum nostrum Jesum Christum.'

ceptions, which these assertions betray, have been already pointed out elsewhere.

As regards the kingdom of saints made perfect, and our relation to them, the Lutheran opinions on this matter stand in the closest connection with their doctrine on the Church, and are only a transfer of their maxims, respecting the ecclesiastical communion of believers in this world to that of the next. They deny not the communion of believers in the Church militant; but they reject the conditions under which it can become real, living, and effectual. The believers, indeed, stand all in a spiritual communion between each other, but we know not why: the whole doth not govern the individual—there is no mutual action between both, so that the member can well dispense with the body; the idea of communion remains completely idle, powerless, and ineffective. In the same manner they question not the existence of a communion existing between us and the saints, but they rest satisfied with the bare representation of it—a representation devoid of all truth, because it either hath no reality, or, at best, but an imperfect one. The angels must be devils, and the saints wicked demons, if they could only be conceived to be in a state of cold, stiff indifference towards us; and their love of God would be idle in itself, did it not extend to rational creatures, equally susceptible of love, and were not active in our behalf. It was this idea which partly induced the German Reformers not to offer a direct opposition to the Catholic doctrine.

In the first place, they concede that the lives of the saints are worthy of imitation, and that they should be honoured by our imitation. They even deny not that the saints pray for the Church at large; but they assert, that the saints must not be prayed to for their intercession.[1] The reason which they adduce, is the same that brought about the dissolution of the ecclesiastical communion—namely, that Christ is our only Mediator! We must, however, examine the coherency of these

---

[1] Confess. August. xxi. 'De cultu sanctorum docent, quod memoria sanctorum proponi potest, ut imitemur fidem eorum, et bona opera juxta vocationem. . . . Sed Scriptura non docet invocare sanctos, seu petere auxilium a sanctis. Quia unum Christum proponit nobis mediatorem, propitiatorem, pontificem, et intercessorem.' Apolog. ad Art. xxi, sect. 3, 4, p. 201 : ' Præterea et hoc largimur, quod Angeli orent pro nobis. De Sanctis etsi concedimus, quod sicut vivi orant pro ecclesia universa in genere, ita in cœlis orent pro ecclesia in genere.—Porro ut maxime pro ecclesia orent Sancti, tamen non sequitur, quod sint invocandi.'

ideas. It is indeed, passing strange, that the saints should pray to God for us, without apprehending that they encroach on the mediatorial office of Christ; and God and Christ should even permit these, their functions, in our behalf, and, accordingly, find them free from all presumption : and yet, that we on our parts, should not beseech the exercise of these kindly offices, because our prayer would involve an offence, whereas the thing prayed for involves none. But the prayers of the saints must surely be termed culpable, if our requests, for such prayers, be culpable. But should their supplications, in our behalf, be laudable and pleasing unto God, wherefore should not the prayer for such supplications be so likewise ? Accordingly the consciousness of their active intercession necessarily determines an affirmation of the same on our part, and excites a joy, which, when we analyse it, already includes the interior wish and prayer for these their active aids. For all communion is mutual, and to the exertions of one side, the counter-exertions of the other must correspond, and *vice versa*. Certes, our indifference for the intercession of the saints would annihilate the same, and completely destroy all communion existing between the two forms of the one Church. But, if it be impossible for us to be indifferent on this matter, then the doctrine of the Catholic Church remains unshaken.

The intercession of the saints, as well as the corresponding invocation of that intercession on our part, is so far from impairing the merits of Christ, that it is merely an effect of the same ; a fruit of his all-atoning power, that again united heaven and earth. This our ecclesiastical prayers very beautifully and strikingly express; as they all, without exception, even such wherein we petition the benign influence of the celestial inhabitants on our earthly pilgrimage, are addressed in the Redeemer's name. Moreover, if the intercession of the saints interfere with the mediatorial office of Christ, then must all intercession and prayer for intercession, even among the living, be absolutely rejected. It should be borne in mind, that Catholics say of no saint, he hath died for us ; he hath purchased for us redemption in his blood, and hath sent down the Holy Spirit ! But, by communion with Christ, all glorified through him, partake, as well in his righteousness, as in all things connected therewith ; and *hence*, the power of their intercession ; hence also, the right of petitioning for that intercession from the living, as well as from the departed just.

The opinions, which, according to Calvin's examples, his disciples in France, and the Remonstrants in Holland, have formed on this matter, have the merit of entire consistency. They declare the idea of an intercession of saints for mortals to be an absolute imposture and delusion of Satan, since, thereby, the right manner of praying is prevented, and the saints know nothing of us, and are even quite unconcerned as to all that passes under the sun.[1] From this point of view in which it is imagined, that the saints resemble the gods of the Epicureans, and live joyous and contented in heaven, without being, in the least, concerned about our insignificant actions, or suffering themselves to be thereby disturbed in their enjoyments, the prohibition to solicit the suffrage of the saints, is alone tenable. Such an idea of blessed spirits, as only the most obtuse selfishness could imagine, possesses certainly nothing to invite to a friendly intercourse with them : and God forbid, that in heaven a felicity should be reserved for us, to which the condition of any earthly being, in whose breast the spark of a loving sensibility is yet alive, would be infinitely to be preferred !

[1] Confess. Gall. Art. xxiv, p. 191. 'Quidquid homines de mortuorum sanctorum intercessione commenti sunt, nihil aliud esse, quam fraudem et fallacias Satanæ, ut homines a recta precandi forma abduceret.' Remonstrant. Conf. C. xvi, sect. 3 : ' Quippe de quibus (sanctis) Scriptura passim affirmat (!) quod res nostras ignorent, et ea, quæ sub sole fiunt minime curent.' A deeper view into the connection of ideas, which induced the ancient Protestants to hold, here also, a negative course, is afforded us by Theodore Beza, who says of the veneration of saints, that it destroys the unity of God. In his epistle to Andrew Dudith, in order to dispel his doubts, that in the end Catholics might yet be right, he observes, that these had not left a single article of religion unfalsified, and he continues : ' Unum, scilicet Deum reipsa profitentur (verbo enim id eos profiteri ac etiam vociferari non inficior), qui quod unius Dei tam proprium est ac ἀκοινώνητον atque est ipsa Deitas, ad quoscunque suos, quos vocant sanctos, transferunt.'—See his Epist. theol. lib. i, Geneva, 1573, n. 1, p. 15. Certainly ; for Catholics, doubtless, assert that the saints have helped God to create the world ! In his writing on Divine Providence, Zuinglius, as we have in a former part of the work observed, adduces, among other things, this argument against human freedom, that thereby a sort of polytheism would be introduced, and the true God set aside, since the notion of freedom involves independence, and therefore, everyone to whom free-will was attributed, would be converted into a God. The same argument is now alleged against the veneration of saints ; whence we may also see, how closely are interlinked all the doctrines of Protestants.

BOOK II

THE SMALLER PROTESTANT SECTS

§ LIV—INTRODUCTION

WE have, already, often had occasion to observe, that the principles of the German Reformation were not on all points consistently carried out by the German Reformers; nay, that they frequently resisted, with their utmost energy, what comprised nothing more than a very natural inference from their own principles, or a continuance and development of the views laid down by themselves. We here by no means allude to the so-called Rationalist theology, which, in modern times, has been often represented by Catholics as well as by Protestants, as a mere continuance and further prosecution of the work begun by Luther.[1] It is difficult to explain, how the notion could ever have obtained such easy, unqualified, and often implicit credence, that a doctrine, which denies the fall of the human race in Adam, is to be looked upon as a further development of that which asserts that in Adam we are all become incurable; or that a system, which exalts human reason and freedom above all things, must be considered as an ulterior consequence of the doctrine, that human reason and freedom are a mere nothingness; in short, that a system, which stands in the most pointed general contradiction with another, should be admired as its consummation. Regarded from one point of view, the modern Protestant theology must be acknowledged to be the most complete reaction against the elder one. In the modern theology, Reason took a fearful vengeance for the total system of repression

[1] We presume to suggest, that Catholic theologians, in asserting that the modern rationalism is a necessary consequence of the Reformation, mean not to deduce it from *all* the peculiar theological tenets professed by Luther and the first Reformers. They only, thereby, mean to assert, that the doctrine of the Supremacy of Reason in matters of religion proclaimed by Luther and other Reformers, more boldly and unequivocally than by all former heresiarchs, necessarily led to the introduction of rationalism. The doctrine of private judgment is the common parent of all, even the most discordant and opposite heresies.—*Trans.*

practised upon her by the Reformers, and did the work of a most thorough destruction of all the opinions put forth by the latter. There is, however, it cannot be denied, another point of view from which the matter may be considered (see sect. 27); but this we must here pass over unnoticed.

When, accordingly, we speak of an incomplete development of the principles of primitive Protestantism; or, when we say that the consistent development of the same was even rejected and assailed by the Reformers; we advert to those doctrines, which could and must be deduced from their one-sided supernaturalism; if we be justified in supposing, that a doctrine once put forth, being in itself pregnant and important, is sure to fin some souls ready to devote themselves to it with all their energy, and own its sway without reserve. The fundamental principle of the Reformers was, that without any human co-operation, the Divine Spirit penetrates into the soul of the true Christian, and that the latter, in his relation to the former, is with respect to all religious feeling, thought, and will, perfectly passive. If this principle led the Reformers, in the first instance, only to the rejection of Church authority and Tradition, and to the adoption of Scripture as the sole source and rule of faith; it must, when rigidly followed up, be turned against the position and the importance of Holy Writ in the Protestant system itself. Is written tradition not in itself a human means for propagating doctrines and precepts? For the understanding of the Bible, which has come down from ages long gone by, and from a people so utterly different from ourselves, is not very great human exertion requisite, such as the learning of languages, the study of antiquities, the investigation of history? In what connection, therefore, stands the proposition, that Scripture is the only source of faith, with the other proposition, that independently of all human co-operation, the Divine Spirit conducts to God? If such an overruling influence of the Deity on man really exist, wherefore doth God still need the Scripture and the outward word, in order to reveal His will to man? In such a way, and by such an intermediate train of thought, men deduced, from the fundamental principle of the Reformation adverted to, the erroneous opinion, that independently of all human forms of communication, the Deity by immediate interior revelations, makes himself known to each individual, and in such a shape communicates his will to man. From which it follows, that Holy Writ itself must be held as a subordinate source of knowledge for the Divine decrees, or as one that may be entirely dispensed with. If the Christian Religion, by the severance of Scripture from the Church, had been already menaced with an utter absorption into mere individual opinions; so now even the written Word, in the writings of the Evangelists and the Apostles, was no longer asserted to be the first and the only fountain of religious truth; and everything, accordingly, was given up to the most unlimited caprice. Returning from this its extremest point of development (though in an erroneous way), Protestantism passed into a formal system of visions. And this was effected by the instrumentality of Count Swedenborg, who believed himself elected by God, to hold a real intercourse with, and receive real instruction from, celestial spirits, who appeared to him in outward, locally determined forms, to enable him to oppose to vague, mere inward inspirations, and to subjective feelings, a fixed, outward, objective standard, and to prevent the complete dissolution and evaporation of all Christianity. In Swedenborg's system, accordingly the one-sided mysticism became plastic, and false spiritualism took an outward, bodily shape, whereby the fantastic spirit of the Protestant sects was pushed to its farthest extreme; as subjectivity, striving after objectivity, became to itself an outward thing, in order to replace the external, visible Church founded by Christ. In other words, the mere impressions and feelings of the other Protestant sects receive, through the plastic phantasy of Swedenborg, visible forms; about the same as if a man were to take for realities the images of his dreams!

The false spiritualism of these Protestant sects, to which everything imparted from without appeared like death and petrifaction itself, directed its assaults more particularly against ecclesiastical institutions. And a distinct order of sacred ministry, even in the Lutheran and Calvinistic guise, it considered as an abomination, whereby the spirit was fettered; and the forms of outward worship, even the few which the Reformers had retained or new modelled, it looked upon as heathenish idolatry. Thus grew up the conviction of the necessity of reforming the Reformation itself, or rather of consummating it; for this had not yet delivered the spirit from all outward works, nor brought it back to itself, to its own inmost sanctuary.

However, in more than one respect, these new-sprung sects approximated to the Catholic Church, from which they appeared to be still further removed than even the Lutheran and the Calvinistic communities. It was almost always in the doctrine of justification, which, though they made use of unwonted forms of expression, they mostly conceived in the spirit of Christ's Church, this approximation was perceptible. They represented the inward, new life obtained by fellowship with Christ, as a true and real renovation of the whole man, as a true deliverance from sin, and not merely from the debt of sin; and their feelings revolted at the doctrine of a mere imputed righteousness. Even in the Pietism of Spener, which receded the least from the formularies of the orthodox Protestantism, this tendency is manifest. There is no difficulty in discovering the connection of this phenomenon with the ruling fundamental principle of these sects. The stronger the sway of the Divine Spirit over the human heart, as asserted by them, the less could they understand, how its cleansing fire would not consume and destroy all the dross of sin; and hence, in the harshest terms, they often censured the Lutheran and the Calvinistic doctrine of justification by faith alone, which they depicted as a carnal, nay, diabolic principle. This hostility appears most violent in Swedenborgianism, whose author, in conformity with the mode in which he believed he arrived at the knowledge of all his doctrinal peculiarities, sees Calvin descend into hell, and finds Melancthon totally incapable of rising up to heaven; as in the proper place, we shall have occasion to recount this vision in connection with his whole system. Hence, in fine, the very rigid ecclesiastical discipline, and the seriousness of life, which mostly characterise these sects; hence, too, the maxim that even the visible Church should consist only of the pure and the holy; a maxim which connects them with the ancient Montanists, Novatians, and Donatists. With the ecstatic Montanists, especially, they have great affinity.

CHAPTER I

THE ANABAPTISTS OR MENNONITES

FIRST PERIOD OF THE ANABAPTISTS

§ LV—FUNDAMENTAL PRINCIPLE OF THE ANABAPTISTS

THE Reformation had scarcely boasted an existence of five years, when, from the midst of its adherents, men arose who declared it to be insufficient. Luther was at the castle of Wartburg, when from Zwickau, Nicholas Stork, Mark Thomas, Mark Stubner, Thomas Müncer, Martin Cellarius, and others, came to Wittenberg, to enter into a friendly conference with the theologians of that city. They spoke of revelations which had been imparted to them, without, however, at first exciting attention by any singularity of opinion, save the rejection of infant baptism. Writers have occasionally expressed their astonishment, how the above-named men (two only of whom possessed any tincture of learning, the rest belonging to the class of workmen) were able to bestow reflection upon the subject adverted to, which had not then been agitated. This phenomenon, however, can only then afford matter for surprise, when we would call in question the active intercourse between these men and the Reformers of Wittenberg—an intercourse which it is vain to deny; for when Melancthon conversed with them about their faith, he found it in exact conformity with that of the new Saxon school. And why should Luther's maxims and writings not have reached their ears, more especially as the leading preacher at Zwickau was among the number of his confidants? If such be the case, then nothing is easier than to account for their rejection of infant baptism. Luther having, as we observed in a former place, connected the efficacy of the sacraments with faith only, it is not possible to understand why infants should be baptised: and from the Reformer's point of view, it is not difficult for anyone to discover the utter want of an adequate ground for this ecclesiastical rite. From Melancthon's inclination to recognise the gospellers of Zwickau, as well as from the embarrassment Luther experienced in refuting their arguments, without totally abandoning his theory, respecting the mode of sacramental efficacy, men might long ago have inferred the close affinity between the Anabaptists and the Saxon Reformers, and should utterly have disregarded the pretence of any extraction from the Vaudois.

Undeniable as is the original affinity between the Anabaptists and the Lutherans, yet this affinity soon changed into a mutual opposition the most decided. An indescribable confusion prevailed in the minds of the new sectaries, and a fearful fanaticism drove them on to every species of extravagance and violence; and as they had the inmost conviction of doing all things by the impulse of the Divine Spirit, all hope of opposing their errors by rational instruction was utterly fruitless.[1] Müncer was deeply implicated in the war of the peasants; and the very tragic history of Münster, must have, at last, opened the eyes of the most indulgent and impartial observer. From this time forward, especially, the Anabaptists encountered everywhere the most determined adversaries; and hundreds in their community, under Catholics as well as Protestants, had to forfeit their lives for their principles.

In unfolding to view the doctrines of the Anabaptists, we may rightly assign the most prominent place to their Millenarian expectations. After foretelling the utter extirpation of all the ungodly, they announced the kingdom of Christ as immediately thereupon to be established on earth. A new, perfect life, in common among Christians, would then be founded, which was to subsist without external laws, and without magistracy; for in all its members the moral law written on every man's heart would revive, and be powerfully exhibited in life. Even Holy Writ would be abolished; for, the perfect children of God no longer need the same (and its contents would be no longer an outward object, but rather the inmost portion of their being). Then perfect equality among all would be established; and everything would be in common, without any individual calling anything his property, or laying claim to any privilege. Wars and hostilities of every kind would cease to exist. Even marriage

---

[1] Melancthon's History of Thomas Müncer. (In German.) Luther's works, ed. Wittenberg, part ii. p. 473. 'Hereby he imparted to these doctrines an illusive appearance;—he pretended he had received a revelation from heaven, and taught nothing else, commanded nothing else, but what God had approved.'

would no longer be contracted, and without marrying or giving in marriage, 'some pure and holy fruit would yet be produced, without any sinful lust and wicked desire of the flesh.'[1]

Thus it was an ideal state of the Christian Church, that floated before the imagination of the Anabaptists—the confused representation of a joyful kingdom of holy and blessed spirits, which inspired these sectaries with such deep enthusiasm, gave them such power and constancy of endurance under all persecutions, and caused them to exert on all sides so contagious an influence.[2] The more exalted, pure, and innocent, the vital principle of the sect appeared, the more easily could its adherents inflame the souls of their contemporaries. We cannot refuse to these fanatics an infantine originality in their view of human society; and the impetuous desire after a complete realisation of the idea of God's kingdom—the impatient haste which prevented them from awaiting the development of time, and with which they panted for a sudden irruption of the relations of the next world into the present—a sudden unveiling of that state, that only in the course of ages could be gradually revealed, announces something magnanimous, and rejoices the heart amid all the aberrations we encounter in their history, and which were quite inevitable. In fact, they, in part at least, only anticipated a future state of things; and all they strove to realise, was not the mere invention of an unbridled phantasy. Social life rests on a spiritual and bodily community of goods; all the thought and reflection—all the learning and knowledge of the individual become the common property of the social body, to which he belongs; and whatever he acquires for himself, he acquires ultimately for others also. For, an indomitable propensity to communicate his acquirements is inherent in every man; and we think we know nothing, if our knowledge be not for the benefit of those with whom we live. Whoever hath brought forth some original idea, is urged by a mysterious inward impulse to submit it to the judgment of intelligent men;

---

[1] Justus Menius's 'Doctrine of the Anabaptists refuted from Holy Writ,' with a preface by Luther: included in the works of the latter, Wittenberg, ed. part ii, p. 309, b. (In German.)

[2] Melancthon's History of Thomas Müncer, loc. cit. p. 474. 'With such idle talk he made the populace gape; then people ran to him, and everyone desired to hear something new; for, as Homer says, "The new song is ever the favourite with the populace!"' How could Melancthon thus speak against the Anabaptists! As if the song which *he* sung were an old one!

for, the peculiar constitution of our intellectual nature will not permit us to trust our own thoughts, if they meet not with approval. There is, perhaps, no other more certain criterion of madness, than the clinging to some idea, which everyone holds to be a mere idle fancy. In a word, all men form, as it were, but one man; and herein, among other things, consists the truth in the Neo-Platonic doctrine of a universal soul—a doctrine by which the followers of that philosophy even sought to explain the sympathy existing between men. But if a man will have his thoughts and ideas recognised, he must of necessity communicate them to others.

In the Catholic Church, this idea of the community of spiritual life is most fully expressed; since, in what regards *religion*, the inidvidual submits all his productions to the judgment of the whole body, and foregoes the pleasure of having discovered any truth, if his lucubrations be considered, by the community, as containing aught inconsistent with its fundamental principles.

It is nearly the same with corporeal goods. Man enters into civil society, not only with the view of securing his property by the union into which he has entered, but also with the resolution of sacrificing it, in case of necessity, to the exigencies of the commonweal. What are hospitals, poorhouses, infirmaries what are all public establishments for education and instruction, but a special reflection of the idea of the community of goods among all? The greater the progress which social life, under the influence of Christianity, makes, and the greater in consequence the civilisation of the human race; the more do special associations for special objects arise, wherein a multitude of members go security for the individual, in order to guarantee and insure his earthly existence. Insurance establishments become ever more numerous, and more comprehensive in their objects; and these also, we hold to be ever more significant expressions of the idea of a community of goods—an idea, indeed, which, like all others, can never be completely realised in this finite life. Who doth not here, too, recall to mind the first Christian community of Jerusalem? The consummation of the Christian period will doubtless, though in a freer and milder form, lead us back to the state of its primitive age. Moreover, we here stand on ethical ground; for external existence possesses value only as it is the expression of inward life, and the work of spontaneous resolution. But the Anabaptists wished to realise at once and *by violence*, one of the highest moral ideas; and this is ever impossible. Nay, they wished to introduce it among men such as they are, who, by their entire education, are as unsusceptible, as they are unworthy, of such an idea, and they made its introduction into life the prop for their own indolence, yea, for every possible wickedness. The greater the contradictions, accordingly, between the idea of the Anabaptists and the reality of life, the more the difficulties increased, when they wished to realise that idea in society. The more undoubting, amid all these obstacles, their belief in their own divine mission; the more infuriated must they become, and the more convulsive must be all their efforts. Hence, in the first Anabaptists we discern, beside the simplicity of the child, the fury of the wildest demagogue; who, to create a holy and happy world, destroyed in the most unholy and calamitous manner, the actual one; and, as a blind instrument, ministered to the ambition, the avarice, and all the basest passions of the reprobate men, whom we so frequently meet with, in the early history of the sect.[1]

§ LVI—INITIATION INTO THE SECT—SIGNS AND CONFIRMATION OF COVENANT

The Anabaptists believed themselves authorised by an injunction from above, to prepare the way on earth for the ap-

[1] The idea of the absolute community of goods is far more ancient than Plato's Republic, and all the institutions of his time, which he might, perhaps, have had in view. When the Golden age, the period of Saturn's rule, was to be portrayed; when the goddess Justitia (who is something far more than the idea of the *suum cuique*) still dwelt on the earth; the poet connects the words:

'Nondum vesanos rabies nudaverat enses,
Nec consanguineis (such all men are) fuerat discordia nata,
Flumina jam lactis, jam flumina nectaris ibant,

with *Ne signare quidem, aut partiri limite campum.*'

Even the freedom allotted to slaves during the Saturnalia, called to mind the original absence of all distinction among men. But the happy period ceased since ' deseruit propere terras justissima virgo.' Plato, as well as Aratus, Macrobius, and others, drew from the same cycle of sagas. It is worthy of remark, that the idea of the absolute community of goods appears, almost always, connected with that of community of wives. Such is the case in Plato, in Epiphanes, the son of Carpocrates, and very clearly among the Anabaptists, and the elder Gnostic sects; and when the latter are so frequently charged with the *libido promiscua*, this accusation ought not, as often happens, to be so slightly called in question. Hence also it follows, that an absolute community of goods would annihilate the whole civilisation of the human race: because it is incompatible with the existence of marriage and of the family: domestic life absolutely presupposes property.

proaching establishment of the above-described perfect kingdom of God. They travelled about, accordingly, in every direction, to announce the liberty of God's children, and to make a preliminary election of all those whom the Lord would use as instruments for the rooting out of all tares, and the extirpation of all the ungodly. The community about to be gathered together by them, was to consist exclusively of saints, and typically to represent, in every way, the celestial Church, which was expected. Hence, all who wished to be taken into the new community were baptised anew, for they had before received only the powerless, watery baptism of John; whereas they now would be cleansed with Christ's baptism of fire and of the Spirit. By this baptism, they understood the real regeneration of the spirit out of the Spirit—the complete surrender of the whole man unto God—the disengagement of the will from all creatures —the renunciation of every attempt to wish to be anything in oneself—lastly, the being filled with power from above. This notion of the effects of baptism is essentially the same as the Catholic Church has ever set forth. And it was partly the perception, that so many rest satisfied with the mere outward work, and confound the water with the Spirit, and the bodily ablution with the internal purification of the soul; and partly the guilty and wilful ignorance, that such a conceit was condemned by the Church itself, which could have persuaded the Anabaptists that their doctrine on baptism was a new revelation from God. At all events, we clearly see, from this fact, that some lofty idea animated and impelled them.

According to the baptismal formula of Hans Denk, every candidate renounced seven evil spirits, namely: man's fear man's wisdom, man's understanding, man's art, man's counsel, man's strength, and man's ungodliness, and in return received fear of God, wisdom of God, and so forth. Melchior Rink made use of the following formula:—'Art thou a Christian? —Yes. What dost thou believe, then?—I believe in God, my Lord Jesus Christ. For what wilt thou give me thy works? —I will give them for a penny. For what wilt thou give me thy goods; for a penny also?—No. For what wilt thou give then thy life? for a penny also?—No. So then thou seest thou art as yet no Christian, for thou hast not yet the right faith, and art not resigned, but art yet too much attached to creatures and to thyself; therefore thou art not rightly baptised in Christ's baptism with the Holy Spirit, but art only baptised with water in John's baptism.

'But if thou wilt be saved, then thou must truly renounce and give up all thy works, and all creatures, and lastly thy own self, and must believe in God alone.[1] But now I ask thee, dost thou renounce creatures?—Yes. I ask thee again, dost thou renounce thy own self?—Yes. Dost thou believe in God alone?—Yes. Then I baptise thee in the name,'[2] etc. This action the Anabaptists called the sealing and the sign of the covenant.

It must here, however, be observed, that these sectaries by no means connected with the outward act the communication of the Holy Spirit. On the contrary, they accurately distinguished between both, as Calvin from the same motives afterwards did; and they regarded the exterior act in baptism only as the symbol of suffering in general, and of the mortification of wicked lusts in particular.[3] The members of this sect, moreover, did not baptise their new-born children, as not understanding the signification of this holy act; and they administered the sacred rite to them only on their attaining to riper years. Hence, the name of 'Anabaptists,' is characteristic of the proceedings of the sect only in reference to its initiation of strangers, but by no means denotes their principles in relation to their own members; as they never twice baptised those of their own body, who were to be initiated into their Church.

Of the holy eucharist, the Anabaptists taught, in like manner, that it has only a figurative signification. 'Eating and drinking in common,' said they, is throughout the whole world a sign of mutual love: the same holds good of 'the supper' of Christians. As wine, moreover, is extracted from the grape only by the wine-press; so, they taught, it is only by the pressure of sufferings, the Christian is prepared for the kingdom of

---

[1] From these maxims it is clear, that the justifying faith held by the Anabaptists, was the *fides formata* of the Catholic Church.

[2] Justus Menius, loc. cit. p. 309, b.

[3] Philip Melancthon's Instruction against the Anabaptists, in Luther's works. Part ii. p. 292, ed. Wittenberg, 1551. (In German.) 'Baptism is a sign that Christians in the world must let themselves be oppressed, and bear and suffer every kind of danger and persecution. This is signified by the outpouring of water upon them.' Compare p. 299. 'In the third place, baptism is a covenant, exclaim the Anabaptists, whereby man engages to mortify his wicked lusts, and to lead a rigid life, and exercise patience under sufferings; but this infants do not yet understand or practise.'

2 A

God, and the felicity it insures. The corn must first be ground before it can be converted into bread; so man must first be ground down by misfortune, before he can be qualified for entering into the kingdom of heaven. So we see that baptism, and the eucharist, were, in their estimation, rites pre-eminently figurative, denoting the necessity of sufferings, and of unshaken constancy under persecution. Their very afflicted condition forced the sectaries to look out everywhere for a source of solace and of fortitude under their trials; and therefore, in the above-named sacraments, they saw only the properties, whereof they stood in such especial need. Hence, whosoever among them felt himself at any moment not sufficiently strong to stand the combat courageously, was exhorted to abstain from communion; for it was more particularly fear and despondency, which they loved to set forth as those sins, whereby a man 'eateth and drinketh judgment to himself.'[1]

§ LVII—THESE SECTARIES ASSAIL THE PROTESTANT DOCTRINE OF JUSTIFICATION

With peculiar bitterness did the sectarians express themselves against the Lutheran doctrine of Justification, and in this respect, they almost come round to the Catholic point of view. Their notion, respecting the justifying faith of Protestants, is very well expressed in the following passage, from the work of the Lutheran Justus Menius:—'They mightily boast,' says he, 'they have in their doctrine the true power of God, and that ours is an idle, weak, unfruitful husk; that we can do nothing more than cry out, faith, faith alone; but this cry remaineth, in every respect, an idle and dead cry.' It strikes us, at the first glance, that it was only to faith, as united with good works, that the Anabaptists ascribed the power of justification: whereas, however, according to the above-cited formula of baptism, they declared themselves ready to give up their works for a penny. This is, however, only a coarse expression for the great truth, that the Christian should ever think humbly of himself, and not be proud of his moral endeavours—it is only a condemnation of the deadliest foe to all Christian piety—to wit, arrogance and confidence in one's

[1] Melancthon, Instruction, loc. cit. p. 292. Justus Menius, loc. cit. p. 339.

own works. The following reasoning of Justus Menius against the Anabaptist will set this matter in the clearest light; while, at the same time, it is of importance, as determining the notion, which the Lutherans attached to justification by faith alone. He says—'The fanatics cannot here get out of this difficulty; though they often repeat, that we are not to put faith in the merit of works and sufferings; yet they insist, that we ought to have them, however as things necessary to salvation. *That is nonsense, for if works be necessary to salvation, then we cannot certainly obtain salvation without them, and then consequently, faith alone doth not save; but that is false.*'

This memorable passage, in a writing which Luther accompanied with a preface, by no means signifies that the principle, whereby salvation is obtained, consists, in faith and not in the works to be wrought besides; but that faith, even when it should not produce the fruit of good works, yet insures salvation. The Pastor of Eisenach will also discover a contradiction in the doctrine, that on the one hand, works are necessary to salvation; and on the other, that the Christian should not attach importance to the same. But here the self-same objection recurs, which the Lutheran theology also raised against the Catholic doctrine of justification, to wit, that it leads to self-righteousness, and obscures the glory of God. Menius observes, 'Only see how consistent is their system: *man, they say, must renounce his own works, and yet they contend and urge, with all their might, that he must have, together with faith, works also, or he will not be saved.* But what is the meaning of this? Works are necessary to salvation; and yet he, who will be saved, must renounce his works. Ergo he, who will be saved, must himself renounce what is necessary to salvation, and without which he cannot be saved. Make this tally,[1] rebel! Remember, that *mendacem oportet esse memorem*, that is, he who will lie, ought to have a good memory; otherwise, when in what he afterwards says, he shall contradict himself, people will observe, how he hath lied in what he had before spoken; this should make the lying spirit more heedful.'[2]

The theology of the good Justus Menius finds the inculcation of good works absolutely incompatible with the idea of humility.

---

[1] In the German, the word *bundschuch* (a buckled shoe) is used; this Menius employs as a term of reproach, because such was painted on the banners of the rebellious peasants under Müncer.

[2] Justus Menius, loc. cit. p. 319, 320.

And, accordingly, he thinks the doctrine, that we must 'renounce' such works—that is to say, acknowledge ourselves useless servants, even when we have done all, to be perfectly irreconcilable with the other tenet, that works are a necessary condition to salvation. Whereupon, in his opinion, there remains no other alternative, than to believe, that faith, even without ever evincing its efficacy in works, can render us acceptable to God!

§ LVIII—CONTINUATION—CONCURRENCE OF THE MOST VARIOUS ERRORS IN THE SECT

Among the Anabaptists, considered as a sect, we discover not other doctrinal peculiarities, though we find a considerable multitude of errors professed by individuals, or even larger parties among them. Justus Menius had learned, that even original sin was denied by the Anabaptists; probably, it would seem, to give a broader basis to their doctrine respecting the unlawfulness of infant baptism. On this subject, they were wont to appeal to the language and conduct, which the Saviour, on several occasions, had manifested in respect to children. From a misunderstanding, they attached especial importance to the text, wherein children are held up by him as models for adults, if they would enter into the kingdom of heaven.[1] That, however, only a few of the Anabaptists rejected the doctrine of original sin, although Justus Menius charges, without restriction, the whole body with such a denial, is evident from the fact of another accusation being preferred against them; to wit, that they held the body of Christ to have been created by the Holy Spirit, and merely fostered in the womb of the Blessed Virgin; so that, thereby, the Saviour would not have taken flesh and blood from Mary. They feared that, in conceding more, they would have been unable to uphold the sinlessness of Christ. Whereas this error is not even conceivable, except on the supposition of original sin; the kindred doctrine above adverted to respecting the peculiar, sinless sort of generation to take place in Christ's future kingdom on earth, necessarily involved a belief also in an evil transmitted by the present mode of sexual intercourse. And, indeed, that violent antagonism between the human and the divine, which runs through the whole doctrinal

---

[1] Justus Menius, loc. cit. p. 332.

system of these sectaries, were not possible, without the conviction of a deep-rooted corruption tainting humanity in all its relations. Moreover, the doctrine in question, respecting the conception of Christ, appears to have obtained a very wide currency among the Anabaptists—at least, very many adversaries take the trouble of refuting it.[1] The greater the multitude who gave into this error, the smaller must have been the number of those who, to assail infant baptism, denied original sin.

Many Anabaptists rejected the doctrine of Christ's divinity; others taught an ultimate restoration of all things—the ἀποκατάστασις πάντων, and in consequence, the final conversion of Satan; others again, that souls, from the moment of death, sleep until the day of judgment. Even an antinomian tendency was discernible in some individuals among them. These, like the 'brothers and sisters of the free spirit,'[2] and like the libertines,[3] asserted that no one who had once received the Spirit,

[1] Melancthon: Propositions against the doctrine of the Anabaptists, loc. cit. p. 282, b; Urbanus Regius, ibid. p. 402-418; Justus Menius, p. 342. The reader may also consult in the same volume of Luther's works, the dialogues between the Hessian theologians Corvinus and Rymæus, and John of Leyden, Krechtingk, and others, p. 453. It is clear, moreover, from this that the Protestant Church historian, Schröckh, has fallen into an error, in representing this doctrine of Christ's conception as a peculiarity of Menno; for it was taught in the sect, long before Menno joined it.

[2] 'The brothers and sisters of the Free Spirit,' were a fanatical sect of Pantheists, that sprang up in the early part of the thirteenth century. They probably owed their origin to the philosophical school, which Amalrich, of Bena, and David, of Dinant, had founded, and which was, in the year 1209, condemned by a synod at Paris, whose sentence was confirmed by the Pope. They derived their name from the abuse they made of the texts of Scripture in Romans viii, 2-14; and in St John iv, 23, asserting that 'the law of the Spirit of life in Christ Jesus, had freed them from the law of sin;' 'that, being led by the Spirit of God, they had become the sons of God.' Professing a mystical Pantheism, they held, like the Paulicians, that everything is an immediate emanation from the Deity, referring to themselves the words of Christ, 'I and the Father are one.' Whoever attained to their view, belonged no longer to the world of sense (abusing, as they did, the words in John viii, 23, 'I am not of this world'); he could no longer be contaminated by it, and therefore he no longer needed the sacraments. Separating body and mind, they maintained that all sensual debaucheries could not affect the latter; and hence, some among them abandoned themselves without scruple to the grossest vices. In Swabia, particularly, about the middle of the thirteenth century, they went about inciting monks and nuns to abandon their rules, and suffer themselves to be led entirely by God and the 'Free Spirit.' Severe measures were then taken against them. The Apostolicals, a sect founded by Segarelli, of Parma, towards the close of the same century, held tenets very similar to those just described.—*Trans.*

[3] The 'Libertines' were a sect of fanatical Pantheists, that sprang out of the general religious ferment of the sixteenth century. They first

could any longer sin in any work whatsoever ; and that therefore, for them, adultery even was no sin ; and Zwingle refers by name to a member of the sect, who had announced this to him as his personal conviction. For a time, also, the opinion that polygamy is not forbidden to Christians, was very general amongst them.¹

appeared in Flanders, in the year 1547, and thence spread into Holland, France, and Geneva, where they gave Calvin much annoyance. At Rouen a Franciscan monk, who had imbibed the tenets of Calvinism, was the first to inculcate the abominable doctrines of the new sect.—*Trans.*

¹ On the denial of Christ's divinity, see Justus Menius, loc. cit. p. 342 ; and Zwingle's Elenchus contra Catabapt. Op. tom. ii. fol. 38. This account is perfectly credible, as we know of Lewis Hetzer, for instance, that he was at once an Unitarian and an Anabaptist ; and at a later period, as is well known, an Unitarian congregation was formed in Poland, which professed likewise Anabaptist principles. On the opinions which the Anabaptists entertained respecting the ἀποκατάστασις, or final restoration of things, compare Justus Menius, p. 343 ; and Zwingle's Elenchus, loc. cit. p. 38, b. The sleep of souls after death is there also attested, p. 37, b. For the antinomianism of the Anabaptists, see ibid, fol. 16. On the polygamy of John of Leyden, and the defence set up for the same, see Luther's works, part ii, p. 455, ed. Wittenberg. Here we find recorded the above-mentioned dialogue, held by the Hessian theologians, Antonius Corvinus, and John Kymæus, with John of Leyden, and Krechtingk, from which I will take the liberty of extracting the following passage, in order to show at once the extremely meagre and mean view the ancient Lutherans entertained respecting marriage, and the straits into which, by their rejection of tradition, they were necessarily driven. After several questions and answers, wherein, especially, the Old Testament polygamy was discussed, King John of Leyden, in defence of his plurality of wives, observed :—' Paul says of a bishop, he should be the man of one wife. If now a bishop should be the man of one wife, it follows that in the time of St Paul, it was permitted for a man to have two or three wives according to his pleasure.' The Lutheran preachers replied :—' *We have before said, that marriage belongs to civil policy, and is a res politica ; but as the civil policy, on this matter, is now very different from what it was in the time of St Paul, and as it has forbidden, and will not tolerate the plurality of wives, you cannot answer for such an innovation, either before God or man.*' To this King John :— ' Yet I have the hope, that what was permitted to the fathers, will not damn us ; and I will in this case rather hold with the fathers, than with you ; still less allow, that I profess therein any error, or unchristian innovation.' The Lutheran preachers :—' We would in this case much rather obey the civil power, because it is ordained of God, *and in such external matters*, hath the right to command and forbid, than recur to the examples of the fathers ; as for such a course we have not a warrant in God's word, but, on the contrary, know truly, that the Scripture countenances our opinion respecting marriage, rather than your view. For instance, the Scripture saith, " Therefore shall a man leave father and mother, and shall cleave unto his wife." Here we are told, a man shall cleave unto his wife, and not unto many wives. And St Paul saith, " Let each man have his own wife." He saith not, " Let each man have many wives." ' King John : ' It is true, St Paul here doth not speak of all the wives in general, but of each wife in particular : for the first is my wife, I cleave to her ; the

These opinions, however, should not be considered as strictly Anabaptist; for, in part, they were in direct opposition to other maxims of the sect. It is, on the contrary, to be presumed that at the commencement, amid the general religious ferment of the age, a multitude of men joined the Anabaptists without having anything akin to them, save a dark fanaticism and confusion of ideas. But in general the remark holds good that the first Anabaptists had neither a compact system of theology, nor any body of doctrines however ill-connected, which all uniformly professed. If we consider that their sect had not originated in one man as the common centre of all; and that the leading idea, round which all resolved, though powerful enough to inspire enthusiasm, was yet, in a doctrinal point of view, unproductive, if we consider, moreover, that the dark feelings by which all were animated and impelled, had not received a definite expression in any public formulary—a circumstance which gave occasion to a general complaint on the part of their adversaries,[1] we shall feel the less surprised at the fact above-mentioned.

§ LIX—CONTINUATION—RELATION OF SCRIPTURE TO THE INWARD SPIRIT—THE CHURCH

It will be still more easy to conceive the confusion of doctrines in this sect, if we direct our attention more particularly to the opinions which they entertained respecting the office of preaching, and also what was immediately connected with this, the relation of Scripture to the inward motions of the free, living Spirit. It was a principle with this sect, that everyone marked and sealed with the sign of the covenant, was not only able, but was also bound to appear as a prophet and teacher, as soon as

second is my helpmate, I cleave to her likewise, and so on. Thus, the Scripture remains intact in all its dignity, and is not opposed to our opinion. And wherefore should I waste many words? It is better for me to have many wives, than many strumpets.' The king finally proposed to leave to the tribunal of God, the judgment on this matter. Here we discover the origin of the desire, subsequently expressed by Philip, Landgrave of Hesse, to have two wives—a desire which Luther and Melancthon, together with Bucer, however reluctantly, complied with.

[1] Justus Menius, ' Spirit of the Anabaptists,' loc. cit. p. 363. ' If they taught only the right doctrines, they would not prowl about so secretly in the dark, nor their preachers lurk in holes and corners.' See also Zwingle in several passages of his cited work, Elenchus. Also, ' Doctrine of the Anabaptists refuted from Holy Writ,' loc. cit. p. 311.

he felt himself moved by the Divine Spirit, and perceived he was favoured with a revelation. To these inspirations, Holy Writ was made in such a degree subordinate, that the Anabaptists did not long strive to bring them into an even apparent conformity with Scripture, but declared the Bible to be in its present form absolutely falsified.[1] Hereby every standard for the regulation of subjective opinions was rejected; the entire system of Christianity was severed from all external historical basis, and abandoned to the stormy fluctuations of a dreaming fancy. With such errors no distinct order of preachers was at all compatible; for, without settled doctrines, such an institution involves a self-contradiction. Hence also, the Anabaptists strained their utmost efforts to subvert the Protestant preachers to prevent the consolidation of the new, and (in their opinion) too material Church, which depended on these ministers; and then to convert it into a purely spiritual institution.[2]

If some years previously, the Lutherans had urged against the Catholic clergy the ever-recurring reproach, that instead of the doctrine of the Bible they preached up only the ordinances of the Church, so they, in their turn, were now blamed for fettering the living spirit to a dead word of Scripture, and not allowing men to follow the fresh, pure, untroubled impulse from above; 'and, like the Jewish scribes, they were declared to have no Holy Ghost, but to be only conversant with Scripture, and to chase their weariness away with its perusal.'[3] On the

---

[1] Justus Menius 'On the spirit of the Anabaptists,' p. 364. 'For it is undeniable, that Thomas Müncer, and after him his disciple Melchior Rink, together with many other disciples, had no regard at all for Holy Writ, called it a mere dead letter, and clung to special new revelations of the Spirit: nay, they dared even openly to give the lie to Scripture, as I myself heard from the lips of Rink, who had the effrontery to say that all the books of the New Testament in every language, Greek, Latin, German, etc., were altogether false, and that there was no longer a genuine copy on earth.' Hereupon follows a special application of this principle to the passage in Matthew xxvi, 28, where the words, ' which shall be shed for many for the remission of sins,' were according to this doctor, inserted by the devil.

[2] Calvin (instructio adv. Anabapt. opusc. p. 485) accuses them of only asserting that there should be no fixed teachers appointed to any particular place, but that all, like the apostles, should be itinerant preachers. But then he adds: ' Hæc porro philosophia inde manabat, quod serio cuperent, fideles ministros sibi cedere, vacuum que locum sinere, quo liberius venenum suum ubique effundere possent.'

[3] Justus Menius, Doctrine of Anabapt. refuted, etc., p. 310-313. On the spirit of the Anabapt. p. 364, b. In short, it is well known and not to be denied, that the Anabaptists have no more injurious appellation for anyone than to call him a Scribe.

other hand, the Lutherans prove against the Anabaptists, what, as coming from the Catholics, they would never themselves assent to. They point out to them the establishment of an apostleship by Christ himself, and draw from this institution nearly the same conclusions as the Catholics themselves. They allege, with laudable industry, Scriptural texts, whereby the Holy Ghost had instituted teachers, prophets, and administrators, and the disciples of our Lord had appointed bishops and elders, in order that the one true and pure doctrine might be preserved unfalsified; and they repeatedly enjoin that teachers, though chosen by men, are yet ordained by the Holy Ghost.[1] This assertion Melancthon approved even so far as to hold others to be a sacrament. He says, in his Instruction against the Anabaptists: 'That priestly orders should be placed in the number of the sacraments, affords me much satisfaction. Yet so, that by orders be understood the calling to the office of preaching, and of administration of the sacraments, and so the office considered in itself. For it is very necessary that in Christian Churches the function of preachers should be regarded and esteemed as something most precious, venerable, and holy; and that people be instructed, that it is by the hearing of sermons and the reading of God's Word and Holy Writ, God will impart the Holy Spirit, *to the end that no one may seek, out of the regular ministry, for any other revelation and illumination, such as the Anabaptists pretend to.*'[2] The Lutherans were so unkind as to torment the poor fanatics with questions, which, to this day, they have been unable to answer themselves. They asked the Anabaptists who had sent them, and as they could show no ordinary mission, where were the miracles whereby they authenticated their extraordinary mission? The Anabaptists, with reason, retorted the same questions upon them.[3]

Luther had once said, 'Whoever is so firmly convinced of the doctrine he announces, that he can, without hestitation, curse the opposite view, furnishes, in that case, a proof of the verity of his opinions.' In this sort of demonstration, the

---

[1] Justus Menius, Refutation of doctrine of Anabapt. p. 312, b; Spirit of the Anabapt. p. 358, b; Melancthon, Instruction against Anabapt. p. 294.

[2] Melancthon's Instruction, etc., loc. cit. p. 294.

[3] Zwingli Elenchus, loc. cit. fol. 29; Menius Anabapt. refuted, loc. cit. p. 311. 'Also, how will they prove that they have been sent by Christ to gather together the elect, and to seal them? They work no signs to enable us to discern this mission with certainty.'

Anabaptists certainly far surpassed all who lived and flourished in their time.

§ LX — HATRED AGAINST ALL OUTWARD INSTITUTIONS FOR PROMOTING EDIFICATION—ECCLESIASTICAL DISCIPLINE—MANNERS AND CUSTOMS

To the ideas, which the Anabaptists had formed respecting the Church, corresponded their views as to the accidental parts of outward worship, and the arrangements having reference to the same. If Carlstadt in Wittenberg, and Zwingle in Zurich, had broken down images and altars, and the latter even had destroyed organs, the Anabaptists on their part, declared the bared and despoiled temples to be still idol-houses.[1] Of singing, they entertained nearly the same opinion as in former ages Peter de Bruys, who held it to be a worship of Satan. Had their loquacity not been too great, they would, doubtless, have looked down upon the manifestation of the Christian spirit in words, as something too outward and too material; and hereby alone would they have acted with perfect consistency.

As regards their ecclesiastical discipline and their peculiar customs, they perfectly bear the impress of the ruling principle of the sect. The idea of the community of goods, though this was to be completely realised only after the advent of Christ, was in the language at least of the community provisionally applied; and, even prior to the establishment of the millennium, a sort of proximate application of this principle was to be attempted among those, who, in the meantime, professed the doctrines of the sect. The authority which we have already often cited, says among other things : ' They have neither father nor mother, brother nor sister, wife nor children in the flesh, but are mere spiritual brethren and sisters among one another. Each one says, I am not in mine, but in *our* house, I lie not in mine, but in *our* bed, I clothe myself not with mine, but with *our* coat. It is not I and Kate my wife, but I and Kate *our* sister keep house together. In short, no one has anything more of his own, but everything belongs to us the brethren and sisters.' [2]

They rigidly maintained excommunication, for no unholy

---

[1] Menius, Spirit of the Anabaptists, loc. cit. p. 354.
[2] Menius, Doctrine of Anabapt. refuted, loc. cit. p. 309, b.

one was to be in the Church of God.[1] Their prohibition against assuming any function of magistracy, was in close connection with this persuasion. Rulers there were to be none, and universal freedom and equality were to prevail in all the relations of life. But it is observable that we not only find attributed to them the doctrine that the ministers of the gospel should alone be invested with civil authority—a proof that magistracy was not wholly despised—but we see this doctrine carried out into practice. We see, moreover, laymen also at the head of their political government. We need only remind the reader of Thomas Müncer in Orlamünde and Muhlhausen, as also of John of Leyden in Münster, who even called himself king. These facts stand in twofold contradiction with the doctrines of the Anabaptists—first, with their principle that the office of teaching is common to all Christians; secondly, with their just alleged prohibition against undertaking any function of civil power. These facts, moreover, are easily explained by the utter impossibility of their realising such theories in life.

Furthermore, that the Anabaptists should not allow the sword to be wielded, and accordingly, should hold all warfare to be unlawful, was a principle that immediately followed from the fundamental tenet of the sect. Yet again, we are not astonished, when we see them so often, in despite of their principles, with arms in their hands, and hear them vociferate the fearful cry against all princes, nobles, and proprietors: 'Strike Pinkebank on the anvil of Nimrod.' Lastly, they declared all oaths to be illicit; and in fact among perfect Christians, such as the new kingdom to be erected by them presupposed, no oaths need ever be taken.[2]

§ LXI—THE ANABAPTISTS IN THE FORM OF MENNONITES— THEIR SECOND PERIOD

With that bold confidence, which is wont to characterise fanatics, the Anabaptists had announced the near approach

---

[1] Calvin Instruct. adv. Anabapt. opuscul. p. 476. 'Usus excommunicationis,' said the Anabaptists, 'inter omnes esse debet, qui se Christianos profitentur. Qui baptizati noxam aliquam imprudenter aut casu admittunt, non ex industria, ii secreto moneri debent semel atque iterum : tertio publice coram toto cœtu exterminandi sunt. Ut possimus eodem zelo una panem frangere, et calicem bibere.'

[2] Melancthon, 'Refutation of some unchristian doctrines put forward by the Anabaptists,' loc. cit. p. 285. Joannes Calvinus, loc. cit. p. 493.

of the thoroughly holy kingdom of God on earth. But day after day, they saw themselves deceived in their expectations, so that they at last renounced the chimerical hope. They had not even succeeded in uniting the portion of Christians the most important, if not in number, yet in eternal energy, nor in bringing about, as preparatory to Christ's coming, the total abolition of all civil magistracy, and the establishment of a holy theocracy. Nay, they encountered such a mighty opposition, that the most credulous were soon obliged to look upon the hopes they had fondly cherished, even in this respect, as idle and vain. Hereby vanished that idea which had been the inmost, vital principle of the sect, and which had constituted all its importance; and with it accordingly, it lost all historical interest. Its members became more modest and more tranquil, and more reconciled with the social relations. But as the high, practical object of their existence had been given up, and as a real doctrinal interest they had never possessed; the Anabaptists, by degrees, directed the energies that still survived their first mighty excitement, to the settlement and regulation of the insignificant relations of ordinary life, falling into the most whimsical contests on these matters, and thereby exhibiting a striking contrast to their earlier history, where all the attempts at reformation had been conducted on a grand scale. As this second crisis of their existence was approaching, its introduction was accelerated by means of a Catholic priest, Menno Simonis, curate of Wittmarsum, near Franeker in Friesland, who, in the year 1536, went over to the Anabaptists,[1] and who possessed so little intellect and literary culture, as to join a party [2] whose vital object was allowed to be vain, and yet enough of these qualities to pass among his fellow-religionists for a very distinguished personage. He possessed, moreover, a very pious, energetic zeal, and a certain degree of moderation (which, however, was never evinced towards Catholics); so that, by the confidence he had won, he was enabled to appease the contests of the Anabaptists, to unite them together, and to regulate their social relations. They took their name from him, and have since been usually called Mennonites. He died in the year 1561.

[1] Hermanni Schyn, historiæ Mennonitarum plenior deductio. Amstelodami, 1729, c. v, p. 116.
[2] Loc. cit. p. 138, we find a letter of Menno Simonis, wherein he says he had written his treatise on baptism in German, ' nam Litinæ inscitiæ causa non bene possem.'

It is worthy of remark, that the Mennonites call in question their descent from the earlier Anabaptists. When the first intoxication of fanaticism was over, they forgot all they had perpetrated under its influence ; and what they heard recounted of themselves, they conceived to regard some other community. Sometimes they deduce their origin from the first Christians ;[1] sometimes they assert, that quite independently of all outward impulse, Menno Simonis had arrived at his peculiar opinions through the exclusive study of Holy Writ ;[2] and sometimes again they allege that among the first Anabaptists of the sixteenth century, there were men of a calm and moderate tone of thinking, from whom they were themselves the descendants ; and this assertion is not entirely devoid of foundation.[3]

§ LXII—PECULIAR DOCTRINES OF THE MENNONITES—THEIR CHURCH DISCIPLINE

From the later symbolical writings of the Anabaptists, it is at the first sight evident who were their progenitors. We shall now proceed to give the main substance of these Confessions, taking as our standard the Confession of Waterland,[4] composed in the year 1580, by John Ries and Lubbert Gerardi, Mennonite preachers ; without, however, leaving the other unnoticed. After enlarging first on God, the Trinity, and the incarnation of the Logos, the Confession comes to the doctrine of the Fall, and says, that the first man, by his transgression of

---

[1] The good Schyn, in his Historiæ Mennonitarum plenior Deductio, c. i, Amst. 1729. ' Ex primis Christianis, qui ex institutione Domini nostri Jesu Christi exemplisque Apostolorum, per omnia Christiana sæcula in hunc usque diem inter cætera dogmata adultorum baptismum docuerunt, et adhuc docent, descendisse (Mennonitas).' *Immediately* thereupon, it is said : ' Inter hos sæculo undecimo (rather duodecimo) emicuerunt Waldenses.' What a leap from the first to the twelfth century !

[2] Schyn (loc. cit. p. 135) observes, after citing the account which Menno Simonis had given of his going forth out of Babylon : ' Evidentissime constat, ipsum sola sacræ Scripturæ lectione, meditatione, et illuminatione Spiritus Sancti . . . ex Papatu exivisse.' But from the very narrative of Menno adduced by Schyn himself, it appears that the former, even when a Catholic priest, had been in connection with the Anabaptists, though he condemned the extravagances of the Münster fanatics.

[3] Schyn Historia Mennon. p. 263-265 : here he appeals with justice to some favourable testimonies of Erasmus.

[4] This Confession is found in Schyn Hist. Menn. c. vii, p. 172. See in Hist. Menn. c. iv, p. 78, the historical notices on this Confession.

the Divine precept, had incurred the anger of God, yet had been again strengthened by consoling promises, in consequence whereof, none of his descendants are born with the debt of sin, or of penalty.[1] This, in itself, very obscure proposition derives from the following doctrines some degree of light. It might be explained, as if the Mennonites denied original sin. But their opinion is rather, that a sinfulness is transmitted from Adam to all his descendants; but that is attended with no debt; since this is remitted by God's grace. In the fifth article, an explanation is given respecting the faculties which man in his fallen state still possesses; and it is taught with great propriety, that in the same way as Adam, before his fall, had the power of giving or of refusing admittance to the spirit of evil into his soul: so after the fall, he still has the power of perceiving the Divine influences, and accordingly of receiving or rejecting the same;[2] and this doctrine other formularies express to the effect, that fallen man still possesses free-will.[3] Hence it is clear, that the Mennonites considered those born of Adam, to be subject to corruption, and as such, to be incapable of producing and executing anything acceptable to God; yet still they believed them to be possessed of free-will. In consequence of this opinion, they declare themselves explicitly against an absolute grace of election: they even devote a special article to the doctrine of Providence, and combat the Calvinistic opinion, that God worketh evil.

After confessing, moreover, the vicarious atonement of Christ, they declare, in terms the most clear and unequivocal, that saving faith is that which 'worketh by charity,' and that through the same is righteousness acquired. Righteousness they describe as forgiveness of sins, on account of Christ's blood, and accordingly, as a transformation of the whole man; so that, from a wicked, carnal, avaricious and arrogant man, he becometh a good, spiritual, generous, and humble one; in a word, that

---

[1] Art. iv, p. 175. 'Eousque ut nemo posterorum ipsius respectu hujus restitutionis aut peccati aut culpæ reus nascatur.' The fourth formulary of the united Frieslanders and Germans, which is likewise tolerably full, says in Article iii, 'per eam (inobedientiam) sibi omnibusque suis posteris mortem conscivit, atque ita ex præstantissima miserrima factus est creatura.'—See Hist. Menn. p. 90.

[2] Art. v, p. 176, 'Eidem jam lapso et perverso inerat facultas occurrens et a Deo oblatum bonum audiendi, admittendi, aut rejiciendi.'

[3] The fourth Formulary of the United Frieslanders and Germans, Art. iv, p. 90. 'Dominum æque post ac ante lapsum liberam homini reliquisse voluntatem acceptandi vel rejiciendi gratiam oblatam,' etc.

from an unrighteous he becometh a righteous man.¹ What they now inculcate respecting good works, follows as a matter of course. They even teach, that the life of the righteous and regenerated man should be in perfect correspondency with the Divine law; if, on his part, he anxiously looks forward to the future *rewards* so graciously promised.²

Of such righteous and regenerated men, the Church, according to them, exclusively consists.³ In this hath Christ appointed a teaching ministry; for although every believer be a member of Christ, he is not on that account a bishop, priest, or deacon; for the body of Christ, the Church, consists of various members. Moreover, the ministers of the word, though called and elected by the ministers of the same, must be confirmed through imposition of hands on the part of the elders.⁴ Lastly, they must set forth only what coincides with the written word in the Old and New Testament.

Christ, according to them, hath instituted only two sacraments to be administered by the teachers. The sacraments are outward, sensible acts, whereby is represented an inward, divine act, that transforms, justifies, spiritually nourishes and sustains man; while the person receiving the sacrament testifies thereby his religion, his faith, his penitence, and his obedience, and binds himself to the observance of the latter. Here, however, we must remark that in this system, neither by baptism, nor by the Lord's supper, for these are the two sacraments of the Mennonites, is that divine power communicated, which purifies, renovates, and nourishes the spirit of man. They merely typify what perpetually occurs through the power,

[1] Art. xx, de vera fide salvifica. 'Omnibus bonis et beneficiis, quæ Jesus Christus, per merita sua, ad peccatorum salutem acquisivit, fruimur gratiose per veram et vivam fidem, quæ per charitatem operatur.' The third symbolical writing of the united Frieslanders and Germans called the 'Olive Branch,' says: 'Hinc patet, fundamentale certumque filiorum Dei criterium et Jesu Christi membrorum esse veram et salvificam fidem per charitatem operantem.'

[2] Art. xxi. 'Per vivam ejusmodi fidem acquirimus veram justitiam, id est, condonationem sive remissionem omnium tam præteritorum quam præsentium peccatorum, propter sanguinem effusum Jesu Christi, ut et veram justitiam, quæ per Jesum, cooperante Spiritu sancto, abundanter in nos effunditur vel infunditur (let the reader here mark the adoption of Catholic phraseology): adeo us ex malis, carnalibus, avaris, superbis fiamus boni, spirituales, liberales, humiles, atque ita ex injustis, revera justi.'

[3] Art xxiv.

[4] Art. xxv—xxviii. See also formulary of the United Frieslanders and Germans, Art. x, p. 98.

which from Christ and his spirit eternally streams down on all believers, and only symbolise this constant action of the Deity. The Mennonites, moreover, baptise only adults, as these alone are capable of faith and penitence. That their doctrine respecting original sin renders infant baptism in their opinion unnecessary, is clear from what has been above stated.[1] Lastly, Menno Simonis adopted the washing the feet of the travelling brethren as an indispensable ceremony; and the confession of the United Frieslanders and Germans expressly upholds it, and makes mention of it after the article on baptism.[2]

On impenitent sinners, excommunication, after some brotherly exhortations, is rigidly enforced.[3]

Obedience to the civil power is enjoined as a religious duty; yet, singular enough, it is asserted that the exercise of all functions of magistracy is unbecoming to the true Christian (*aut male aut plane non convenire*), and that on this account he should forbear undertaking offices of this kind. The motive assigned is, that Christ instituted no civil authority, and still less did he command his apostles to assume the functions of magistracy. On the contrary, they were invited by him to imitate his defenceless life, and to carry his cross, whereby certainly nothing of earthly grandeur, secular power, or the right of the sword was indicated. Moreover, princes and public functionaries are under the obligation of waging war, of marching against enemies, and depriving them of property and life; but all this is forbidden to the Christian.[4] Finally, the Mennonites absolutely proscribe all oaths; and, in almost all their confessions, declare against polygamy.[5]

§ LXIII—CONCLUSION—SPECIAL CONTROVERSIES

It is beyond all doubt, as is clear from the preceding statement, that the Mennonites in several articles of doctrine differ considerably from the first Anabaptists, and that they have thrown off their more fanatical tenets. The direct revelations from Heaven, communicated to each individual, have here ceased; and we find established a distinct order of ministers, bound by the written word. The violent introduction of God's kingdom upon earth, associated with the annihilation of the

---

[1] Art. xxx-xxxv.　　[2] Art. xiii, p. 101.　　[3] Art. xxxv, xxxvi.
[4] Art. xxxvii.　　[5] Art. xxxviii.

established order of society, and of the rights of property, has given way to the formation of a new inward life, and to a concomitant willingness to assist the indigent according to ability, and to share everything with them in Christian love, without an external community of goods being required. By the setting forth of a common system of doctrines, moreover, very unchristian and demoralising tenets have been excluded. But in other respects, we clearly discern in the Mennonite only the purified Anabaptist. In the view, especially, entertained respecting the civil power, we see the glimmering of that earlier fanaticism, that would fain have doomed it to utter destruction, as totally unsuitable to the Christian. In the prohibition, likewise, to engage in war, and to take oaths, we see ever shadowed forth that ideal kingdom of Christ which, through the mediation of the Anabaptists, was to confer a sudden felicity on the world.

Yet the establishment of a definite system of doctrines, already adverted to, must be so understood only in a very limited sense. This will be apparent from what follows, wherein the opposition between the inhabitants of Waterland and the united Frieslanders and Germans, to which allusion has been made, will be more closely examined.

The Mennonites, likewise, soon broke up into different parties; but as the sect had lost all high importance, most of the controversies that sprang up in its bosom, were utterly insignificant. They divided into the subtle, and the gross party. Those, who rigidly adhere to the ancient rule of manners, received the former epithet; the latter was given to those, who allowed themselves various mitigations of the rule. The latter are called from the district in Holland, which they inhabit, Waterlanders; the former Flemings and Frieslanders. The gross Mennonites soon became by far the most numerous; while the subtle ones disputed among themselves on the questions, whether or not a Mennonite may acquire by purchase a house; whether it be also lawful for him to clothe himself in fine linen, if he wished truly to evince the austere spirit of the sect. These and the like differences fall not within the scope of our inquiries; though the first-mentioned controversy, as a remnant of the doctrine of the community of goods, and of the prohibition to hold property, is deserving of attention, and coincides with the fact, that the rigid Anabaptists frequently wish to be nothing more than mere farmers of lands.

The Ukevallists, called after a preacher of Friesland, who

maintained the proposition, that Judas and the high-priests, who condemned Christ, as they only executed the divine decrees, have been admitted to salvation, can here only receive a passing notice. More important are the differences on the question, whether or not an individual, whatever may be his doctrinal views—should he even be a Socinian—can be received as a member of the community, or can be permanently so considered ? This question was connected with that respecting value and importance of public formularies, to which the Mennonites on the whole, though at different times they published several confessions, were never very favourably disposed. Those, who declared for absolute freedom, were called Remonstrants, and also Galenists, from their leader, a physician of that name at Amsterdam. Their opponents, the Apostools, were likewise called after a physician in their communion of that name, who resided at Amsterdam. But in proportion, as the Mennonites unreflectingly opened a door to foreign influences, their old respectable, though often pedantic, earnestness, and the religious hallow of life by degrees declined. Or rather is not this phenomenon—this aversion to a settled, definite system of doctrine—a remnant of that one-sided practical tendency, which characterised the sect in its very origin ; and in pursuance of which it tolerated in its bosom the most various, and the most opposite views on the most important dogmas of faith ? The original spirit, accordingly, would here have only returned.

So much respecting the Mennonites or Anabaptists. With them the *Baptists* are not to be confounded. Such are those Puritans in England named, who with respect to infant baptism hold opinions similar to those of the Mennonites, without, however, being on other points distinguishable from the English Calvinists of that party. From the year 1633 they have formed a separate community.

CHAPTER II

THE QUAKERS

§ LXIV—SOME HISTORICAL PRELIMINARY REMARKS

WHOEVER would undertake the task of tracing historically the gradual development of Protestant Sectarianism, should after the Anabaptists treat of the Schwenkfeldians, who though they appeared only a few years later than the former, yet as exaggerated spiritualists, stand considerably higher. He would next have to describe some individual enthusiasts, as well as larger communities of this description, that made their appearance in the latter half of the sixteenth, and the former half of the seventeenth century ; and then only could he turn to the Quakers, who went to the farthest verge of the boldest spiritualism, and were to be outdone only by contradictions. Among the first Anabaptists, the effort of a false spiritualism took quite an eccentric course, and the pure spiritual life, which they would fain have introduced, rested on the expectation of an extraordinary marvellous introduction of a higher order of things into this lower world. All the ordinary relations of earthly life were menaced with destruction, and that delicate subtle kingdom of the spirit which they aimed at was in manifold ways troubled by a very gross political spirit ; for earthly bonds cannot be, without violence, suddenly dissevered, nor at once replaced by supermundane things. This spiritual kingdom was founded in a very carnal manner, and the means proved destructive to the end. The supersensual principle also, even where it had attained, in this sect, to any consolidation, was not presented in its purity and integrity ; since the sacrament was retained, not as the channel and conductor, but merely as the emblem of divine graces. Moreover, among the doctrines of this sect, there were some which mere accident had annexed to its stem, or which at least had not naturally grown out of its root.

Far more developed appears the spiritualism of Schwenkfeld, whose peculiarities, however, we shall not be able to point out ; as no remains of his sect have survived down to our days. But in its most complete form doth this false spiritualism manifest itself, as we before said, among the Quakers, who honour as their founder George Fox, a shoemaker and shepherd, born at Drayton in Leicestershire in the year 1624, and who departed this life in the year 1690. Among the Quakers we discover an interior piety, which, when we can succeed in forgetting, now and then, the utter perverseness of the whole system, marvellously cheers and refreshes, and even, at times, deeply moves the mind, though not, by any means, in the same degree as our own better mysticism. Moreover, we find among them a conscious and firm prosecution of the point of view they have once adopted —a consistency extremely pleasing and cheering, which flinches from no consequences, and has given to Quakerism such an advantage over the orthodox Protestantism, where the most crying dissonances are to be found. All parts stand in the most harmonious proportion with each other, forming a fine connected whole, whose architectural perfection leaves little to be desired; and to the Catholic, especially, who is forced by his own religious system to look everywhere for internal keeping and consistency, appears entitled to respect. Consistency is not indeed truth itself, and doth not even supply its place; but a system of doctrine is ever false, which includes parts inconsistent with the whole. In George Fox, the founder of the sect, we doubtless do not find this internal harmony of system, nor the transparent clearness of doctrine determined thereby; but that the system was capable of attaining to this harmony, lay in the very nature of the fundamental idea, out of which it sprang. A very remarkable and amiable trait of Quakerism is that avoidance of every kind of asperity, which so frequently shocks us in the orthodox Protestantism. The manner, too, wherein Quakers treat all the better phenomena of religion and morality in the times anterior to Christianity, evinces great tenderness of feeling; nor is this less manifest in their rejection of the Calvinistic doctrine of absolute predestination. Here, also, the Quaker strives to emulate the Catholic; but the capital error of Quakerism is, that though in itself a fair, deeply conceived and harmonious system, it stands in the most direct opposition to historical Christianity, and as far as in it lies, annihilates the same; for this the following exposition of its principles will clearly show. This task we will now undertake, taking for our guide the Apology by Barclay—the most celebrated writer among the Quakers, and whose book enjoys an almost symbolical authority; for they have not put forth a regular confession of faith.[1]

Before, however, we make our readers acquainted with the system of this remarkable religious community, we must lay before them the motives which induced its first propagators to establish a peculiar sect. Like many other religious parties in the deeply-convulsed age of Cromwell, they particularly missed in the High Church of Enlgand the free expansion of the spirit of piety—religious life, and interior warmth and unction. Everything in this Church appeared to them torpid and petrified. The Divine Spirit, which heretofore had filled the Church, was denied, and out of the living congregation had been banished, and confined to the dead word of Scripture; and the boast of the Reformers that this dead word would infallibly shed a heavenly light over its readers, and enkindle them with a holy fire, was refuted by every day's experience. The established worship appeared void and meaningless in the eyes of the Quakers, and seemed to consist of nothing more than a dry, cheerless repetition of forms and hymns, composed though they were in the vernacular tongue. And, in fact, when the real presence of the Saviour had been rejected, and the sacrifice been abolished, nothing more remained which directly, and by itself, could fill the susceptible soul with devotion and sacred awe, or exalt, solace, and bless it. The act was bereaved of its very soul; it became an earthly thing, and though rational, yet unspiritual and uninspiring. All now depended on the fact, whether the preacher were able to draw words of life from the inmost core of a soul filled with the Divine Spirit, and were enabled to edify by a heavenly power the assembled believers, and by the combined animation, clearness, and depth of his discourses to initiate them more and more in the mysteries of Christ's kingdom. But it was here, precisely, the longings of the Quakers were most cruelly deceived, so that not unfrequently they would interrupt the sermons of the Anglican ministers, and in their revolted feelings would bid ' the man of wood ' descend from the pulpit.

[1] Roberti Barclai Theologiæ vere Christianæ Apologia, edit. sec. Lond. 1729. With Barclay, however, we shall always compare the following work, entitled: ' A Portraiture of Quakerism, taken from a view of the moral education, discipline, peculiar customs, religious principles of the Society of Friends.' By Thomas Clarkson, Esq., in three vols., 3rd edit. Lond. 1807. The author was, for a long time, in habits of intercourse with the Quakers; and finding them vigorous opponents to the slave-trade, to the suppression whereof Clarkson devoted all his energies, he came to entertain a great affection for them. This book must be used with caution.

Even the most spiritual-minded preacher is not master of celestial unction and illumination; days and weeks of internal dryness and desolation will occur, and no human art can supply the gift from above. The majority of preachers, alas! abound neither in divine nor human energy; others possess not even the will, and thus it cannot fail to happen, that the greater part of sermons attain not by one-half their end, and very many fall even far short of it. This the Quakers deeply felt, and in default of an act in the public worship, which by its intrinsic worth could take possession of the soul, they rejected the whole established service as an institution incapable of satisfying the higher wants of the religious man. To this we must add the numberless disputes which then convulsed the Anglican Church. Opinions crowded upon opinions, each seeking its foundation in Holy Writ, yet not one being able to prove by that standard its own truth, or the untenableness of the opposite systems, and no living human authority invested with a divine sanction, was anywhere recognised. It appeared to the Quakers that the truths of Christianity were in imminent danger, and that, if they had no other support than Holy Writ, they must perish in the struggle of parties. Thus they receded from every external institution—not only from the Church and public worship, but in a great degree from Scripture itself; and, for what they held to be vital truths of salvation, they sought an indestructible basis in the *immediate* inspiration of a creative, inward light, which, *without any other medium*, was to be, if not the exclusive, yet the principal source of nurture to the spirit.

§ LXV—RELIGIOUS SYSTEM OF THE QUAKERS—THE INWARD LIGHT

While avoiding all explanation as to the nature of the Paradisaic man,[1] the Quakers hold, that from the fallen Adam, a germ of death, a seed of sin, has been scattered over all his posterity; for the word, 'original sin,' they will not employ, nor indeed any other technical expression unsanctioned by the usage of Scripture. Hereby all men were entirely bereaved of the Divine image, which, however, the Quakers do not particularise; and this bereavement, according to them, must be

[1] Barclaii Apolog. theolog. Christ. p. 70. 'Curiosas illas notiones, quas plerique docent, de statu Adæ ante lapsum, prætereo,' etc.

understood by the menaced death, which they thus conceive to have been only spiritual.¹ So long, however, as the universal seed of death, through a conscious and active culture of the same, beareth no fruits, it constitutes, they continue, no guilt, and therefore by no means entails damnation. On this account, unconscious infants were not subject to eternal punishment.²

In a very remarkable way do these sectaries represent the work of the atonement after Adam's fall. God doth not merely promise a future Redeemer—He not only guideth the general and particular destinies of individuals and nations, in order to prepare them for the great day of the incarnate Deity—He doth not merely vouchsafe to raise up among all nations wise men, teachers of their contemporaries in word and deed, great law-givers and rulers. No ! from the Logos himself, who personally appeareth in the centre of history, and for the sake of whose merits, a creative vital principle emanates through all ages, as from the centre of a circle the rays are emitted to every point of the circumference ; so that the breath of Christ's Spirit blows forward and backward, and leaveth no one untouched. To this they refer the passage in St John's Gospel : ' He is the

---

[1] Loc. cit. ' Hæc mors non fuit externa, seu dissolutio exterioris hominis ; nam quoad hanc non mortuus est, nisi multos post annos. Ita oportet esse mortem quoad spiritualem vitam et communionem cum Deo.' A valid conclusion forsooth ! What a betrayal, too, of ignorance in philology ! On all this Clarkson furnishes us with more details. Of the consequences which Adam's sin produced first in him, and then in all his posterity, Clarkson says as follows : ' In the same manner as distemper occasions animal life to droop, and to lose its powers, and finally to cease ; so unrighteousness, or his rebellion against this Divine Light of the Spirit, that was within him occasioned a dissolution of his Spiritual feelings and perceptions ; for he became dead as it were, in consequence, as to any knowledge of God, or enjoyment of His presence.' See the above-cited work, p. 115.

[2] Barclaius, p. 70. ' Quod Deus hoc malum infantibus non imputat, donec se illi actualiter peccando conjungant, etc.' The whole is thus summed up in p. 80. ' Confitemur igitur, semen peccati ab Adamo ad omnes homines transmitti (licet nemini imputatum, donec peccando sese illi actualiter jungat), in quo semine omnibus occasionem peccandi præbuit, et origo omnium malarum actionum, et cogitationum in cordibus hominum est ; ἐφ' ᾧ nempe θανάτῳ (ut v. ad. Rom. habet) : i.e. in qua morte omnes peccavere. Hoc enim peccati semen frequenter in Scriptura mors dicitur, et corpus mortiferum, quum re vera mors sit ad vitam justitiæ et sanctitatis ; ideoque hoc semen, et quod ex eo fit, dicitur homo vetus, vetus Adam, in quo homnes peccant. Poinde hoc nomine ad significandum peccatum illud utimur, et non originali peccato, cujus phrasis in Scriptura nulla fit mentio, et sub qua excogitata, et ut hoc verbo utar, inscripturali barbarismo, hæc peccati infantibus imputatio inter Christianos intrusa est.'

true Light, which enlighteneth every man, that cometh into the world.'[1]

We must not here think of St Justin's σπέρμα τοῦ λόγου (seed of the Logos) λόγον σπερματικόν; for, by this is understood the germ of rationality, the image of God, the copy of the Logos in every man—in one word, the higher nature of man himself. But, under the aforesaid light, which emanates from Christ to every member of the human race, the Quakers understand a divine energy, to be superadded only to man's higher nature.[2]

Around this vital principle, dispensed by Christ, the eternal friend of man, and pervading the human race, through all the extent of space and of time, revolve all the thoughts and feelings of the Quakers; to this is all piety and devotional awe referred, and hence, we must make ourselves particularly acquainted with the description, which they give of it. They apply to it various denominations, such as 'spiritual, celestial, and invisible principle and organ,' wherein the Father, Son, and Spirit dwell; the body and the blood of Christ, wherewith all the saints are nourished to eternal life; 'the eternal light,' on which account the Quakers are called the Friends of Light, or simply Friends (a title which is the most gratifying to them); 'the inward Christ,' 'the seed of Christ,' 'grace,' 'internal revelation,' and so forth.[3]

---

[1] Barclaius p. 126. ' Hic locus nobis ita favet, ut a quibusdam Quakerorum textus nuncupetur; luculenter enim nostram propositionem demonstrat, ut vix vel consequentia vel deductione egeat.'

[2] Clarkson in the above-cited work, p. 117, differs from Barclay. According to the former, 'God did not entirely cease from bestowing His Spirit upon Adam's posterity.' According to the latter, Christianity is quite a new manifestation of grace on God's part, in order to regenerate man; 'a new visitation of life, the object of which was to restore men, through Jesus Christ, to their original innocence or condition.'

[3] Loc. cit. p. 106. ' Hoc semine, gratia, verbo Dei et lumine, quo unumquemque illuminari dicimus, ejusque mensuram aliquam habere in ordine ad salutem, et quod hominis pertinacia et voluntatis ejus malignitale resisti, extingui, vulnerari, premi, occidi et crucifigi potest, minime intelligimus propriam essentiam et naturam Dei in se præcise sumtam, quæ in partes et mensuras non est divisibilis . . . sed intelligimus spirituale cæleste, et invisibile principium et organum, in quo Deus, ut est Pater, Filius et Spiritus, habitat; cujus divinæ et gloriosæ vitæ mensura omnibus inest, sicut semen, quod ex natura sua omnes ad bonum invitat et inclinat et hoc vocamus vehiculum Dei spirituale Christi corpus, carnem et sanguinem Christi, quæ ex cœlo venere, et de quibus omnes sancti comedunt, et nutriuntur in vitam æternam. Et sicut contra omnia facta mala hoc lumen et semen testatur, ita ab eis etiam crucifigitur, extinguitur, et occiditur; et a malo fugit et abhorret, quod naturæ suæ noxium et contrarium

From the lips of the Quakers, these words ever resounded; but the Anglicans would by no means understand them. Barclay bitterly complains of this, and says, that while formerly those only were held to be Christians, who, as St Paul (in Romans viii, 9) teacheth, had ' the Spirit of Christ,' or, as he expresses himself in the same place (viii, 14), ' those only are the sons of God, who are led by the Spirit of God;' no one now any longer recognises the sovereign necessity of this possession by the Spirit.[1] It was objected to the Quakers, that they held man to be of a divine essence, or every individual to be Christ. Others again interpreted their language, as signifying by the inward light, merely the conscience, the reason, or the religious feeling of man. All these allegations they denied, in replying that the principle in question is not the essence of the Deity itself, but an energy and an organ of God; whereby divine life, as from a grain of seed, is expanded in man. They added, they did not even compare themselves with Christ, as in him the Godhead dwelt bodily; but they stood in the same relation to him, as the vine-branch to the vine-stem, which diffuses vigour through every part. Lastly, the inward light, they said, is not a human faculty, since in quality it is distinct from the nature of man.[2] The real cause of these mistakes, we shall point out below.

§ LXVI—CONTINUATION OF THE SAME SUBJECT—EFFECTS OF THE INWARD LIGHT

We now proceed to describe the workings of this inward light. Every man hath a day of visitation (*diam visitationis*),[3]

est. Et quum hoc nunquam separetur a Deo et Christo, sed ubi est, ibi etiam Deus et Christus est in illo involutus et velatus : eo igitur respectu, ubi illi resistitur, Deus dicitur resisti et deprimi et Christus crucifigi et occidi, et sicut etiam recipitur in corde, et effectum suum naturalem et proprium producere non impeditur, Christus formatur et suscitatur in corde. . . . Hic est Christus ille internus, de quo nos tantum et tam sæpe loqui et declarare audimur, ubique prædicantes illum et omnes hortantes, ut in lumen credant, illique obediant, ut Christum in semetipsis natum et exsuscitatum noscant, ab omni peccato illos liberantem.'

[1] Loc. cit. p. 4.
[2] Loc. cit. p. 107-108.
[3] Loc. cit. p. 102. ' Primo quod Deus, qui ex infinito suo amore filium suum in mundum misit, qui pro omnibus mortem gustavit, *unicuique*, sive Judæo, sive Gentili, sive Turcæ, sive Sythæ, sive Indo, sive Barbaro . . . certum diem et visitationis tempus dederit, quo die et tempore possibile est

on which God graciously approacheth to him, and will awaken and enlighten him, in order to form Christ within his soul. From this no one is excepted, but yet no one is forced (for predestination there is none, nor irresistibly working grace).[1] The instrument which God employs for this end, is the inward revelation, which, without any sort of medium—without outward words or signs—endeavours to implant moral and religious ideas in the soul of man, and hath sufficient power to make them living.[2] This inward light, our authority continues to say, all the ancient philosophers and teachers of nations attest—this all the higher efforts, which we meet with in universal history, avouch (*revelatio objectiva*.)

This inward word, whereby God speaketh to every man, and manifesteth Himself to him, is, through the external revelation and the communication of Holy Writ, not rendered unnecessary, either for mankind in general, or even for such, as are acquainted with God's outward word. That that mysterious language of God is requisite for opening the sense of Scripture, and for admitting its contents into our soul, ought never to be doubted, says Barclay (this is the *revelatio subjectiva*); 'for the

illis servari et beneficii Christi mortis participes fieri. Secundo, quod in eum finem Deus communicaverit et unicuique homini dederit mensuram quandam luminis filii sui mensuram gratiæ, seu manifestationem Spiritus . . . Tertio, quod Deus per hoc lumen et semen invitet omnes, et singulos vocet, sed et arguat, et hortetur illos, cumque illis quasi disceptet in ordine ad salutem.'

[1] Barclay says of Calvin's doctrine, p. 84: 'Quam maxime Deo injuriosa est, quia illum peccati authorem efficit, quo nihil naturæ suæ magis contrarium esse potest. Fateor hujus doctrinæ affirmatores hanc consequentiam negare ; sed hoc nihil est, nisi pura illusio, cum ita diserte ex doctrina sua pendeat, nec minus ridiculum sit, quam si quis pertinaciter negaret, unum et duo facre tria.' Compare Clarkson, vol. ii, c. viii, Relig. p. 216. 'This doctrine is contrary to the doctrines promulgated by the Evangelists and Apostles, and particularly contrary to those of St Paul himself, from whom it is principally taken.'

[2] Loc. cit. p. 19. 'Oportet igitur fateri, hoc esse Sanctorum fidei objectum principale et originale, quod sine hoc nulla certa et firma fides esse potest. Et sæpe *hoc uno* fides et producitur et nutritur absque externis illis et visibilibus supplementis, ut in permultis sacrarum literarum exemplis apparet : ubi solum dicitur, et loquutus est Dominus et verbum Domini tali factum est.' P. 29: 'Sed sunt qui fatentur Spiritum hodie afflare et ducere sanctos, sed hoc esse subjective . . . non autem objective affirmant, *i.e.* exparte subjecti illuminando intellectum ad credendam veritatem in Scriptura declaratam, sed non præstando eam veritatem objective, sibi tanquam objectum. . . . Hæc opinio, licet priori magis tolerabilis, non tamen veritatem attingit : primo quia multæ veritates sunt, quæ ut singulos respiciunt, in Scriptura non omnino invenientur, ut sequenti thesi ostendetur.'

things that are of God, no man knoweth, but the Spirit of God; and, therefore, have we received the Spirit that is of God, that we may know the things that are given us from God' (1 Cor. ii, v, 11, 12).[1] But even in the Christian Church, the objective revelation is indispensable, and is to be considered as the primary source of truth, and Scripture as a revelation of a subordinate kind; for the source, from which Scripture itself flowed, must surely stand higher than the latter. It is by the testimony of the Spirit, Holy Writ itself first acquires authority: and, therefore, is the Spirit the first source of all knowledge and truth. In one word, continue the Quakers, if it be true, that it is through the Spirit alone we are to arrive at the real knowledge of God; that through Him we are to be led into all truth, and are to be taught all things; then it is the Spirit, and not Scripture, which is the foundation, and the source of all knowledge and all truth, and the primary rule of faith.[2]

Moreover, it must be observed, that on very many relations of the spiritual life, and on numerous particulars, which are of great importance, Holy Writ imparts no instruction, and is, in part, incapable of so doing; that very many men are unable to read it even in their native tongue: that at all events, there is not one in a thousand conversant with the original languages, and that there are not three texts on which the interpretations of the learned agree. Under such circumstances, should man be abandoned to himself, or to other men? What doubts doth not even the history of the Biblical text give rise to? And how can a man convince himself from Scripture, that any disputed book—for instance, the epistle of James—is canonical? Be-

[1] Loc. cit. p. 48. 'Licet igitur fateamur, scripturas scripta esse et divina et cœlestia, quorum usus ecclesiæ et solatio plenus et perutilis est, nec non laudemus Deum, quod mira Providentia scripta illa servaverit ita pura et incorrupta . . . nihilominus tamen illas principalem originem omnis veritatis et scientiæ, et primariam adæquatam fidei et morum regulam nominare non possumus, quoniam oportet principalem veritatis originem esse ipsam veritatem, *i.e.* cujus certitudo et authoritas ex alio non pendet. Cum de amnis alicujus vel fluminis aqua dubitamus, ad fontem recurrimus, quo reperto, ibi sistimus, nam ultra progredi non possumus, quia nimirum ille ex visceribus terræ oritur et scaturit, quæ inscrutabilia sunt. Ita scripta et dicta omnium ad æternum verbum adducenda sunt, cui si concordent, ibi sistimus; nam verbum illud semper a Deo procedit, it processit, per quod inscrutabilis Dei sapientia, et concilium non investigandum, in Dei corde conceptum, nobis revelatum est.'

[2] Loc. cit. p. 49. 'Illud, quod non est mihi regula in ipsa scripturas credendo, non est mihi primaria, adæquata fidei et moarum regula: sed scriptura nec est, nec esse potest mihi regula illius fidei, qua ipsi credo: ergo, etc.'

cause, perhaps, it is not in contradiction with other canonical books? Then every essay, which is not opposed to Scripture, may be admitted into the Canon! No alternative remains, but either to return to Rome, and receive, at the hands of her infallible Church, the Scriptural Canon, or to revere the Holy Spirit, as the first and principal fountain of truths.[1]

The Quakers, however, failed not to observe, that the revelations of the inward light, communicated to each individual, are not in contradiction with the outward word of Scripture, and even only an eternally new, immediate manifestation of the same old gospel.[2] By this, however, they would by no means set up the Bible, as a check and a touch-stone to the teaching of the inward light; for this would be again to make Scripture the arbiter of the Spirit, whose work it only is.

§ LXVII—CONTINUATION OF THE SAME SUBJECT—OF JUSTIFICATION AND SANCTIFICATION—PERFECT FULFILMENT OF THE LAW

The workings of this divine and inward light in man, as hitherto described, refer exclusively to the infusion of religious and ethical knowledge into his breast: but this light is also the source of all pious life. The day of visitation, graciously vouchsafed by the Almighty to every man, is to be the turning-point of his *whole* history, is in every respect inwardly to renew him—in a word, is to establish his regeneration. On this matter of regeneration and of justification before God, the Quakers (if we except the different view they take of the relation between the Divine and the human operations in this work, whereof we shall have occasion to speak later), very nearly coincide with the Catholic Church. And yet this coincidence they will not allow; and in virtue of deeply imbibed prejudices, taken in with their mother's milk, they persuade themselves, that it is only

[1] Loc. cit. p. 67. 'Exempli gratia, quomodo potest Protestans alicui neganti Jacobi epistolam esse canonicam per scripturam probare? . . .Ad hanc igitur angustiam necessario res deducta est, vel affirmara, quod novimus eam esse authenticam eodem spiritus testimonio, in cordibus nostris, quo scripta erat: vel Romam reverti dicendo, traditione novimus ecclesiam eam in canonem retulisse, et ecclesiam infallibilem esse; medium, si quis possit, inveniat.'

[2] Loc. cit. pp. 33, 61, 63. 'Distinguimus inter revelationem novi Evangelii, et novam revelationem boni antiqui Evangelii, hanc affirmamus, illam vero negamus.'

in outward works, such as pilgrimages—fasting—the mechanical repetition of forms of prayer—mere outward alms-deeds—the use of the sacraments without any interior emotions—the gaining of indulgences, which the Quakers confound with forgiveness of sins—that Catholics think they render themselves acceptable to God. Under this misconception the Quakers assert, that, by denying the value and meritoriousnes of suchlike pious exercises, Luther has, doubtless, rendered a great service ; but on this, as on other points, they contend he is more to be praised for what he destroyed than for what he built up.[1] For Luther and the Protestants, they say, have gone to the other extreme ; as they have denied the necessity of moral works for justification, and made the latter consist not in internal newness and sanctification, but solely in the belief in the forgiveness of sins.[2]

The Quakers describe Justification as the stamping of Christ on our souls—as the Christ born and engendered within us, from whom good works spring, as fruits from the bearing tree ; as the inward birth within us, which bringeth forth righteousness and sanctification, purifieth and delivereth us from the power of evil, conquers and swallows up corrupt nature, and restores

---

[1] Loc. cit. p. 159. ' Nobis minime dubium est, doctrinam hanc fuisse et adhuc esse in ecclesia Romana magnopere vitiatam ; licet adversarii nostri, quibus, melioribus argumentis carentibus, sæpissime mendacia refugium et asylum sunt, non dubitarunt hoc respectu, nobis, Papismi stigma inurere, sed quam falso postea patebit. . . . Nam in hoc, sicut in multis aliis, magis laudandus est (Lutherus) in iis, quæ ex Babylone evertit, quam quæ ipse ædificavit.'

[2] Loc. cit. p. 164. Barclay distinguishes between a two-fold redemption an objective and a subjective one. By the former he understands the ' redemptio a Christo peracta in corpore suo crucifixo extra nos, et qua homo, prout in lapsu stat, in salutis capacitate ponitur et in se transmissam habet mensuram aliquam efficaciæ, virtute spiritus vitæ, et gratiæ istius, quæ in Christo Jesu erat, quæ quasi donum Dei potens est superare et eradicare malum illud semen, quo naturaliter, ut in lapsu stamus, fermentamur.— Secunda hac cognoscimus potentiam hanc in actum reductam, qua non resistentes, sed recipientes mortis ejus fructum, videlicet lumen spiritum, et gratiam Christi in nobis revelatam, obtinemus et, possidemus veram, realem, et internam redemptionem a potestate et prævalentia iniquitatis, sicque evadimus vere et realiter redempti et justificati, unde ad sensibilem cum Deo unionem et amicitiam venimus.—Per hanc justificationem Jesu Christi minime intelligimus simpliciter bona opera, etiam quatenus a Spiritu Sancto fiunt ; ea enim, ut vere affirmant Protestantes, effectus potius justificationis, quam causa sunt. Sed intelligimus formationem Christi in nobis, Christum natum et productum in nobis, a quo bona opera naturaliter procedunt, sicut fructus ab arbore fructifera : internus iste partus in nobis, justitiam in nobis producens et sanctitatem, ille est qui nos justificat, quocum contraria et corrupta natura . . . remota et separata est.'

us to unity and communion with God. The doctrine of the Friends of Light, who, on this point, were truly enlightened, is, as everyone must perceive, only the Catholic doctrine couched in other language ; yet, when they wish to express themselves with perfect clearness, they make use of precisely the same formulas as the Council of Trent.[1] Even the word, 'merit,' is not unknown to them ; the necessity of good works for salvation is openly asserted, the possibility of the fulfilment of the law is demonstrated, and even the possibility of a total exemption from sin maintained.[2]

---

[1] Loc. cit. p. 165. Barclay here speaks of a ' causa procurans,' instead of a ' causa meritoria ' : then he uses the formula, ' causa formalis ' and ' formaliter justificatus,' whereby he understands the same as Catholics do.

[2] Loc. cit. 1, p. 167. 'Denique, licet remissionem peccatorum collocemus in justitia et obedientia a Christo in carne sua peracta, quod ad causem ejus procurantem attinet, et licet nos ipsos formaliter justificatos reputemus per Jesum Christum intus formatum, et in nobis productum, non possumus tamen, sicut quidam (?). Protestantes incauti fecere, bona opera a justificatione excludere ; nam licet proprie *propter* ea non justificemur, tamen *in* illis justificamur, et necessaria sunt, quasi causa sine qua non ' (by which the Quakers understand something different from the Majorists). P. 168 : ' Cum bona opera necessario et naturaliter procedant a partu hoc, sicut calor ab igne, ideo absolute necessaria sunt ad justificationem, quasi causa sine qua non, licet non illud propter quod, tamen id in quo justificamur, et sine quo non possumus justificari : et quamvis non sint meritoria, neque Deum nobis debitorem reddant, tamen necessario acceptat et remuneratur ea, quia naturæ suæ contrarium est, quod a Spiritu suo provenit, denegare. Et quia opera talia *pura* et *perfecta* esse possunt, cum a puro et sancto partu proveniant, ideoque eorum sententia falsa est, et veritati contraria, qui aiunt, sanctissima sanctorum opera esse polluta, et peccati macula inquinata : nam bona illa opera, de quibus loquimur, non sunt ea opera legis, quæ apostolus a justificatione excludit.' P. 167 : ' Licet non expediat dicere, quod meritoria sint, quia tamen Deus ea remuneratur, patres ecclesiæ non dubitarunt verbo " meritum " uti, quo etiam forte nostrum quidam usi sunt sensu moderato, sed nullatenus Pontificiorum figmentis . . . faventes.' A singular strife, forsooth, with the Papists, when the Quakers so express themselves respecting good works! Compare with this again page 195. Moreover the formula *in illis* justificari, instead of *propter illa*, is very felicitous, for the latter expression is used in respect to the merits of Christ. Yet is the latter also scriptural, and the distinction between *causa meritoria* and *causa formalis* obviates all confusion. The question whether it be possible for a perfect Christian to abstain entirely from all sin, is answered in a special section. The thesis defended, runs as follows :—P. 197 : ' In quibus sancta hæc et immaculata genitura plene producta est, corpus peccati et mortis crucifigitur, et amoritur, cordaque eorum veritati subjecta evadunt et unita : ita ut nullis Diaboli suggestionibus et tentationibus pareant, et liberentur ab actuali peccato et legem Dei transgrediendo, eoque respectu perfecti sunt : ista tamen perfectio semper incrementum admittit, remanetque semper aliqua ex parte possibilitas peccandi, ubi animus non diligentissime et vigilantissime ad Deum attendit.'

Clarkson says, 'The Quakers make but small distinction, and not at all such a one, as many other Christians, between sanctification and justification.' 'Faith and works,' observes Richard Claridge, 'are both included in our complete justification. Whoso is justified, is also in the determined degree sanctified; and in so far as he is sanctified, so far is he justified, and no further. The justification, whereof I speak, rendereth us righteous, or pious and virtuous through the continued aid, working, and activity of the Holy Spirit. With the same yearning as we sigh after the continued assistance of the Divine Spirit, and are prepared to evince the efficacy of His operations within us, shall we inwardly discern that our justification is in proportion to our sanctification. For, as the latter is progressively developed, according to the measure of our confiding obedience to the revelation and the infusion of grace, light, and the Spirit of God, so shall we not fail to perceive and feel the progress of our justification.'[1] In respect to the degree which sanctification in this life can attain to, Clarkson, in full concurrence with Barclay, gives the following as the sentiment of the Quakers: 'The Spirit of God, who redeemeth from the pollutions of the world, and implanteth in man a new heart, is regarded by the Quakers as so powerful in its operations, as to be able to exalt him to perfection. But they would not, on this account, compare this perfection with that of God, because the former is capable of progression. This only would they assert, that in the state of internal newness we can observe the Divine commandments; as Holy Writ relateth of Noah and Moses' (Gen. vi, 9), of Job (i, 8), and of Zachary and Elizabeth (Luke i, 6), 'that they were righteous before God, walking in all the commandments and justifications of the Lord without blame.'[2]

Hence we ought not to be surprised if the same objections are urged against the Quakers, as against the Catholics; that they set up their own righteousness in the room of the

[1] Vol. ii, Rel. c. xiii, p. 319. From Henry Tuke, a Quaker, the following passage is also cited, p. 321: 'By this view of justification, we conceive the apparently different sentiments of the apostles Paul and James, are reconciled. Neither of them says that faith alone, or works alone, are the cause of our being justified; but as one of them asserts the necessity of faith, and the other that of works, for affecting this great object, a clear and convincing proof is afforded, that both contribute to our justification; and that faith without works, and works without faith, are equally dead.'

[2] Vol. ii, c. vii, sect. ii, p. 193. 'This spirit of God . . . is so powerful in its operation, as to be able to lead him to perfection.'

righteousness of Christ. They reply to these objections in the same way also as Catholics are wont to do.

§ LXVIII—CONTINUATION OF THE SAME SUBJECT—DOCTRINE ON THE SACRAMENTS

In the most consistent application of their fundamental principles, the Quakers convert the sacraments of baptism and of the Lord's supper into purely interior and merely spiritual actions and ordinances. The Christian, they contend, needs no other seal to his inheritance (*signatura*)—no other pledge of his sonship but the Spirit. To introduce outward acts of this kind is, in their estimation, entirely to misapprehend the religion of the Spirit, which Christianity undoubtedly is ; to renew a Jewish ceremonial service, and to relapse into Judaism ; nay, to approximate to Heathenism ; for such mere outward things, as we call sacraments, have sprung out of the same spirit as the Heathen worship ; whereas Judaism observed holy rites prescribed by God. Accordingly the Quakers assert that the sacraments are not even to be considered as pledges of Divine promise left by Christ to His Church—nay, not even as emblems and aids to the remembrance of spiritual and historical facts—but as absolute misconceptions of actions and expressions of Christ—misconceptions absolutely inexcusable, for they were the offspring of a Heathenish sense. The baptism which Christ ordained is, in their opinion, merely the inward baptism of fire and the Spirit, whose existence renders utterly superfluous the watery baptism of John. Nay, they were even of opinion, that the water extinguishes the fire—that attention to the external rite draws off the eye from the interior, which is alone necessary. Baptism, accordingly, in their opinion, is nothing more than the ablution and purification of the spirit from the stains of sin, and the walking in newness of life.[1] The Scriptural proof for the proposition that Christ has instituted no outward act of baptism, is managed with uncommon art, and is full of the most striking, singular, and forced constructions. Moreover, the writings of Faustus Socinus were much used by Barclay in

---

[1] Loc. cit. p. 341. ' Sicut unus est Deus, et una fides, ita et unum baptisma, non quo carnis sordes abjiciuntur, sed stipulatio bonæ conscientiæ apud Deum per resurrectionem Jesu Christi, et hoc baptisma est quid sanctum et spirituale, scilicet baptisma Spiritus et ignis, per quod consepulti sumus Christo, ut a peccatis abluti et purgati novam vitam ambulemus.'

this article of doctrine ; although by this remark, I do not wish the reader to conceive it to be my opinion that George Fox, the unlearned founder of the sect, had any knowledge of Socinian writings, and was anywise led by the same to the adoption of his views. Being a shepherd and shoemaker, such literary productions were totally inaccessible, or at least unknown to him ; but his really great, though perverted mind, was led only by the general connection of ideas to his peculiar view, of baptism. But Barclay, who undertook to demonstrate Fox's propositions, made for this end, in the article in question, very evident use of the writings of Socinus.

The body and blood of the Lord is, according to the belief of the Quakers, perfectly identical with the divine and heavenly, the spiritually vivifying seed—with the inward light, whereof we had occasion to speak above.[1] They compare the words in John i, 4, ' In him was the life, and the life was the light of men ; ' with the other text (vi, 50), ' I am the living bread, which came down from heaven, and the bread, which I will give, is my flesh for the life of the world ; ' and they accordingly take ' light,' ' life,' ' bread of life,' and ' flesh of Christ,' and the inward Christ as synonymous terms. The Lord's Supper, therefore, they describe as the inward participation of the interior man, in the inward and spiritual body of Christ, whereby the soul liveth to God, and man is united with the Deity, and remaineth in communion with Him.[2]

§ LXIX—CONTINUATION OF THE SAME SUBJECT—REJECTION OF A DISTINCT ORDER OF MINISTRY — PREACHING — PUBLIC WORSHIP

Carrying out their fundamental principle still further, and gradually drawing into its circle everything else, the Quakers lay down, respecting public worship, the following maxims. No act of divine service is acceptable to God which is produced

---

[1] Loc. cit. p. 380. ' Corpus igitur hoc, et caro et sanguis Christi intelligendus est de divino et cœlesti semine ante dicto.' P. 378 : ' Si quæratur quid sit illud corpus, quid sit ille sanguis ? Respondeo, cœleste illud semen, divina illa et spiritualis substantia, hoc est vehiculum illud, seu spirituale corpus, quo hominibus vitam et salutem communicat.'

[2] Loc. cit. p. 383. ' Ita interna participatio est interioris hominis de hoc interno et spirituali corpore Christi, quo anima Deo vivit, et quo homo Deo unitur, et cum eo societatem et communionem habet.'

and consummated by human activity and importunity: the Divine Spirit—the inward light, must be immediately efficacious, and alone determine, move, and conduct man. Hence prayer and the praise of God, as well as exhortatory, instructive, and solacing discourses, must be the pure result of inspirations, which occur in the right cases, when, and where, and in so far as the utility of man requires.¹ Hence very important consequences ensue.

1. There is no distinct order of ministry, because the members of such an order receive from men the qualification for their functions, whereas this qualification can proceed *only* from the Spirit. By the institution of specific teachers, the human principle in the Church received not only a preponderance over the Divine, but entirely superseded the same. The preaching of the Gospel is degraded into an art—nay, into a trade, which is learned and practised by long preparatory training, though it should be only an outpouring of high inspirations. To enable the preachers of the Church to say but something, they are supplied with a multitude of notices, gathered from the four quarters of the world, and often bearing a Heathenish stamp. And such things are to supply, or to communicate the Spirit of God! Hence the discourses of such preachers are no words of life— no manifestations of higher power; and as they proceed not from a heart filled with God, they are incapable of rousing anyone. It is a dry, dead, unfruitful ministry which we have in the Church.² Even vicious men, deeply plunged in sins,

---

¹ Loc. cit. p. 187. 'Omnis verus cultus, et Deo gratus, oblatus est spiritu suo movente interne, ac immediate ducente, qui nec locis, nec temporibus, nec personis præscriptis limitatur: nam licet semper nobis colendus sit, quod oporteat indesinenter timere coram illo, tamen quoad significationem externam in precibus, elogiis, aut prædicationibus, non licet ea perficere nostra voluntate, ubi et quando nos volumus; sed ubi et quando eo ducimur motu et secretis inspirationibus Spiritus Dei in cordibus nostris; quæ Deus exaudit et acceptat, qui nunquam deest, nos ad precandum movere, quando expedit, cujus ille solus est judex idoneus. Omnis ergo alius cultus, elogia, preces sive prædicationes, quas propria voluntate suaque intempestivitate homines peragunt, quas et ordiri et finire ad libitum possunt, perficere vel non perficere, ut ipsismet videtur, sive formæ præscriptæ sint, sicut Liturgia, etc., sive preces ex tempore per vim facultatemque naturalem conceptæ, omnes ad unum sunt cultus superstitiosus, Græce ἐθελοθρησκεία, et idololatria abominabilis in conspectu Dei, quæ nunc in die spiritualis resurrectionis ejus deneganda et rejicienda sunt.'

² Loc. cit. p. 275. 'Et magna quidem causa est, quod tam aridum, mortuum, siccum, et sterile ministerium, quo populi ea sterilitate fermentantur, hodie tantopere abundat, et in nationibus etiam Protestanibus

can become and remain preachers, provided only they have a human calling! From such men the Spirit cannot come out, because they are void of its influence. Lastly, through the establishment of a separate ministry, the preaching of the doctrine of salvation was debased into an instrument to the meanest ends, since rich revenues and certain advantages of outward rank and social position were connected with it. The Lord will have another kind of preaching; and whosoever, young or old, man or woman, high or low, learned or unlearned, shall be moved by the Spirit, may, and ought to preach, pray, and praise God publicly in the congregation.[1]

2. Another equally natural consequence from the aforesaid premises, is, that all set forms of liturgy are proscribed; as every prayer must spring immediately out of a heart, moved and incited by God. The meetings for divine service are, according to Barclay, solemnised in the following manner. In a plain, unadorned room, filled only with benches, in which no outward object can excite any religious feelings, the Friends of Light sit in the profoundest silence, in order to withdraw the mind from all earthly distractions, to free it from all connection with the relations of everyday life, and by this inward recollectedness, to fit it for hearing the voice of heaven. The spirit, however, in this abstraction from all outward things ought not to strive after independence; nay, it must renounce itself, and act quite passively, in order to receive, in their untroubled purity, the Divine inspirations. The solemn stillness may last a half or whole hour, without experiencing any other interruption, save the sighs or groans of some souls agitated by the Spirit, until, at last, some member shall feel himself moved by heaven to communicate in a discourse or a prayer, according as the

diffunditur, ita ut prædicatio et cultus eorum, sicut et integra conversatio a Pontificia vix discerni possit aliquo vivaci zelo, aut spiritus virtute eos comitante, sed mera differentia quarundam notionum et ceremonarium externarum.' P. 229: 'Vita, vis, ac virtus veræ religionis inter eos multum periit eademque, ut plurimum, quæ in ecclesia Romana mors, sterilitas, siccitas, et acarpia in ministerio eorum reperitur.'

[1] The English Protestants required of the Quakers, that, as they despised the existing ministry of teachers, they should prove their mission by miracles, as, at an early period, the German Protestants had demanded of the Anabaptists. Their answer was the same as that which Luther had given to the Catholics. Barclay, p. 245, 'Yet, in order to preserve the purity of doctrine, the Quakers saw themselves compelled, by degrees, to admit a kind of itinerant teachers, and even to exercise a superintendence over them, by means of *human* ordinances.' See Clarkson, vol. ii, Rel. c. x, xi, p. 217, 276.

Spirit directs, the inward revelations he has received. It may even happen, that the meeting separates, without any individual having been moved to hold a discourse. Yet, nevertheless, the Quakers assure us, that their souls have, in the meantime been saturated, and their hearts filled, with mysterious feelings of the Divine power and the Divine Spirit.[1] It also sometimes happens, that, when the images of this lower world will not depart from a soul, that is looking forward to the manifestation of life (*vitæ apparitionem expectare*), a violent, convulsive struggle ensues, wherein the powers of darkness wrestle with those of light, like Esau and Jacob in the womb of Rebecca. The inward conflict (*prælium*) is outwardly evinced in the heaviest, most deep-felt groans, in tremblings, in the most convulsive movements of the whole body; until at last victory inclines to the side of light, and in the excess of luminous outpourings, manifests itself with holy jubilee. In virtue of the union of all the members of a community in one body, the agitations of an individual, particularly if he be one of the more excited, are frequently imparted to the whole congregation; so that (to use the words of Barclay) 'a most striking, and fearfully sublime scene is displayed, which of itself has irresistibly drawn many over to our society, before they had obtained any clear insight into our peculiar doctrines.' From such trembling and

---

[1] Barclaius, p. 297. ' Imo sæpe accidit integras quasdam conventiones sine verbo transactas fuisse, attamen animæ nostræ magnopere satiatæ, et corda mire secreto divinæ virtutis et Spiritus sensu repleta fuerunt, quæ virtus de vase in vas transmissa fuerit.' Clarkson gives the following account (vol. ii, Rel. c. xxi, p. 279) :—' For this reason (that men are to worship God, only when they feel a right disposition to do it), when they enter into their meetings, they use no liturgy or form of prayer. Such a form would be made up of the words of man's wisdom. Neither do they deliver any sermons that have been previously conceived or written down. Neither do they begin their service immediately after they are seated. But, when they sit down, they wait in silence, as the apostles were commanded to do. They endeavour to be calm and composed. They take no thought as to what they shall say. They endeavour to avoid, on the other hand, all activity of the imagination, and everything that rises from the will of man. The creature is thus brought to be passive, and the spiritual faculty to be disencumbered, so that it can receive and attend to the spiritual language of the Creator. If, during this vacation from all mental activity, no impression should be given to them, they say nothing. If impression should be afforded to them, but no impulse to oral delivery, they remain equally silent. But if, on the other hand, impressions are given to them, with an impulse to utterance, they deliver to the congregation, as faithfully as they can, the copies of the several images, which they conceive to be painted upon their minds.'

quaking, the Quakers have derived their name.[1] In this way, they think to get rid of all superstition in ceremonies, and of all man's wisdom, which might so easily intrude into divine service, to abandon all things to inspiration from heaven, and to establish a pure worship of God in spirit and in truth.[2]

§ LXX—PECULIAR MANNERS AND CUSTOMS OF THE QUAKERS

We must now draw the attention of the reader to certain peculiarities of the Quakers, which have reference merely to civil life, and to certain habits and customs in their social intercourse. They refuse taking oaths to the civil magistrate, (to whom, however, except in matters of religion, they confess they owe obedience); and for conscience' sake, they abstain from all military service. The austere spirit of Quakerism totally interdicts games of hazard, since a being, endowed with the faculty of thinking, should be ashamed of them, and still more, because they are beneath the dignity of a Christian. With equal reason they add that such like games awaken passions, that obstruct the reception of religious impressions, and establish a habit immoral in itself. Not content with this, they declare themselves averse from games of every kind ; a declaration which we should be disposed to praise, did they not condemn, without restriction, all holding a different opinion in this matter. On the other hand, they are much to be censured for banishing, from their society, all music, vocal as well as instrumental. This, indeed, will not surprise us, when we consider that they employ neither kind of music for awakening and cherishing religious emotions (sect. 68) ; and that any regard to the refining of the feelings, and to the culture of the sensibilities in general, still less any appreciation of music as an art, was not of course to be expected from the Quakers. Attendance at all theatrical shows, which on account of their connection with idolatry, and of their gross nature not seldom shocking every tender feeling, were formerly interdicted in the ancient Church during her conflict with

[1] Loc. cit. p. 300. Others give other explanations : Clarkson, for instance (vol. i. Introduct. vii), says with other writers, ' George Fox, on one occasion, called upon a judge *to quake* before the word of God : whereupon the judge called him a Quaker.'

[2] Loc. cit. p. 297. ' Hujus cultus forma ita nuda est et omni mundana et externa gloria expers, ut omnem occasionem abscindat, quo hominis sapientia exerceatur, neque ibi superstitio et idololatria locum habet.'— Compare pp. 293, 304.

Heathenism;[1] and which from their, at all events, equivocal moral tendency, have, in subsequent ages, been ever regarded with a suspicious eye by men of piety; attendance at all theatrical shows, we say, is in the community of Quakers likewise not tolerated. In this particular they were certainly led by a good spirit. With the progress of intellectual cultivation (to view the subject only from a lower point of view), theatrical entertainments will certainly disappear, or at least will be abandoned to those who are not more enlightened than the men, who flatter themselves with being, in our time, the representatives of civilisation. Were dignity and amenity of manners coupled with sincerity—were various knowledge and intellectual conversation more prevalent in the social circles than they really are, many of those, who may now be termed passionate friends and patrons of the theatre, would prefer to derive the enjoyment they so highly value, rather from real life than from the so troublous sphere of fiction, and would leave such entertainments to the uneducated or less educated, who think thereby to raise themselves above the crowd. In fact, nothing is more fit to exhibit, in all its nakedness, the utter insignificancy and void of conversation in cities, than frequent attendance at the theatre. The Quakers will one day be praised as the leaders of those, who, like them, but not precisely from the same motives, renounce the theatre as they would a child's doll, and with indifference abandon its entertainments to the populace.[2] Even

---

[1] Lact. Instit. div. i, lib. vi, c. xx. 'Si homicidium nullo modo facere licet, nec interesse omnino conceditur, ne conscientiam perfundat ullus cruor . . . comicæ fabulæ de stupris virginum loquuntur, aut amoribus meretricum : et quo magis sunt eloquentes, qui flagitia illa finxerunt, eo magis sententiarum elegantia persuadent, et facilius inhærent audientium memoriæ versus numerosi et ornati. Item tragicæ historiæ subjiciunt oculis parricidia, et incesta regum malorum et cothurnata scalera demonstrant. Histrionum quoque impudicissimi motus, quid aliud nisi libidines docent et instigant ? Quorum enervata corpora, et in muliebrem incessum habitumque mollita, impudicas fœminas inhonestis gestibus mentiuntur. Quid de mimis loquar corruptelarum præferentibus disciplinam ? Qui docent adulteria, dum fingunt, et simulatis erudiunt ad vera. Quid juvenes aut virgines faciante cum et fieri sine pudore, et spectari libenter ab omnibus cernunt ? Admonentur utique, quid facere possint, et inflammantur libidine, quæ aspectu maxime concitatur : ac se quisque pro sexu in illis imaginibus præfigurat, probantque illa, dum rident,' etc. When Louis XIV, an admirer of the theatre, once asked Bossuet, whether attendance at the same were permitted, the prelate replied, ' There are incontrovertible reasons against, but great examples for it.'

[2] Clarkson (in Mor. Educ. vol. i, c. i, ix, p. 1-158), sets forth and defends the various customs we have been describing.

dances of every kind and without restriction are, with most undue severity, considered an abomination by the Quakers, and not merely novels and romances of a certain description, but this whole class of poetry is banished from their society. It is easy to perceive that many things which Catholic and Lutheran as well as Calvinistic moralists disapprove of, or even positively forbid, and which an incalculable number of individuals in all these religious communities will not sanction, are made a fundamental maxim in the Quaker sect, and with the more facility; for on one hand it comprehends only a few thousand men, and on the other it is confined almost exclusively to the lower classes of society, to whom many things, condemned by Quakerism, remain naturally inaccessible.

Of a different nature are the following traits, which contain obscure indications of a levelling system of social equality, and evince the strong tinge of democracy, peculiar to this sect. The usual salutations, 'your Majesty,' 'your Lordship,' 'your Reverence,' the Quakers ascribe to an unchristian arrogance, to a vain, worldly spirit. They believe the greeting, 'your obedient servant,' and the like sprang out of hypocrisy, and they firmly act up to this belief in life, as in the same way they hold it to be a sin to take off the hat to anyone, to address him in the plural number, and the like. They demand for all these things proofs from Holy Writ, without which they will not sanction them, especially as the Spirit has never inspired them to doff the hat, to salute the King as Majesty, and the like.[1]

§ LXXI—REMARKS ON THE DOCTRINAL PECULIARITIES OF THE QUAKERS

With the utmost impartiality have we stated the doctrinal system of the Quakers without being in anywise prepossessed against them; nay, we encountered them with a sort of predilection, for their earnest striving after an interior religion of the spirit and the heart, their fearless opposition to the spirit of the world, even where that opposition is petty and pedantic, their longing after the true celestial nourishment and the inward unction by the Divine Spirit, their consciousness that in Christ a power is imparted, powerful enough not only to solace and to tranquillise man, but truly to deliver him from sin, and to

[1] Clarkson, vol. i, Peculiar Customs, ch. i, vii, p. 257-386.

sanctify him—all this has filled us with sentiments of the sincerest respect. We think, therefore, we are in a condition to investigate with an unprejudiced eye, the errors whereon the system of Quakerism is founded.

The view of the Quakers respecting the relation of the Heathens to God, is doubtless far more tender than that of the Lutherans, and the Calvinists; it originated in a purer and less narrow-minded perception of the moral phenomena in the Pagan world. But their peculiar explanation of the better elements in Heathenism proceeded from a desire to set aside the opposition, which many facts in the history of fallen humanity, as well as the dictates of Christian feeling, raise against their views as to the consequences of the fall, without, however, that explanation being at all well-founded in itself, or rising above the level of a mere arbitrary hypothesis. The description which the Quakers give of fallen man, is *in itself* quite the same as that set forth by the Lutheran formularies, and therefore *the history of man* will impose upon them the solution of the same difficulties. But the mode wherein they solved this problem effaced the characteristic distinction between the Christian and the un-christian periods, and, on this account, it was in the very beginning objected to the Quakers, that by ' the Divine seed,' ' the inward light,' they understood merely the light of natural reason, and did not at all believe that the divine image in man had been injured through the fall, and was again renovated in Christ Jesus only. And, in fact, maturer reflection subsequently led many Quakers to such an opinion. The injustice of the reproach made to them consisted only herein that they were charged with an intentional deception of their contemporaries—with a crafty concealment of their real opinion; whereas it should have been only pointed out to them that their views led necessarily to the assumption, that subsequently, as well as prior. to his fall, man enjoyed precisely the same spiritual gifts, so that redemption in Christ was thereby rendered totally unnecessary.

In truth, it would be very difficult, nay, impossible, for the Quakers to give a satisfactory answer to the question, whence it cometh to pass, that since the advent of Christ, the victory of light over all the powers of darkness, hath in all respects been so decisively prominent, if, before his incarnation, Christ had already worked in the souls *of all men* in *the same* mysterious way, as since his ascension into heaven. The reason wherefore the worship of nature hath ceased among Christians, polytheism disappeared, and the whole spiritual life of man become so far other than it is among strangers to their creed, must, according to the view of Quakerism, remain a perpetual enigma. In any change that in the lapse of ages may have occurred in the constitution of human nature, the Quakers cannot look for the cause of this phenomenon; because we can in nowise discover, wherefore human nature, before the incarnation of the Logos, was worse and more unsusceptible of reform than afterwards. But the mysterious, inward divine principle, which in Christ renovated humanity, cannot have brought about the great eventful era in history, because, according to the genuine doctrine of Quakerism, this principle ever evinced its operation before Christ also, and in the same mode as at present.[1] To the knowledge of the incarnation of the Son of God, and of the works he wrought, during his earthly ministry, the Quakers could not be disposed to ascribe the great transformation of the world; for it is precisely to the history of Jesus Christ, and to an acquaintance with the same, that they attach no very great importance. And by the adoption of what they call the objective revelation, they hold preaching and Scripture, considered in themselves, to be everywhere superfluous;[2] since the inward light breaks out of itself, and is described not only as the first, but in case of necessity,

---

[1] Barclay on this matter has a very remarkable passage (p. 145), where he appeals to a Scriptural text. From this we may see how the Quakers applied Scripture to their own views:—' Ad ea argumenta, quibus hactenus probatum est, omnes mensuram salutiferæ gratiæ habere, unum addam, idque observatu dignissimum, quod eximium illud Apostoli Pauli ad Titum dictum est, ii, 11, " Illuxit gratia illa salutifera omnibus hominibus, erudiens nos, ut abnegata impietate et mundanis cupiditatibus, temperanter et juste et pie vivamus in præsenti sæculo "; quo luculentius nihil esse potest, nam utramque controversiæ partem comprehendit. Primo, declarat hanc non esse naturalem gratiam, seu vim, cum plane dicat esse salutiferam. Secundo non ait, paucis illuxisse, sed omnibus. Fructus etiam ejus quam efficax sit, declarat, cum totum hominis officium comprehendat; erudit nos primo abnegare impietatem et mundanas cupiditates; et deinde totum nos docet officium, primo, temperanter vivere, quod comprehendit æquitatem, justitiam, et honestatem, et ea, quæ ad proximum spectant. Et denique, pie, quod comprehendit sanctitatem, pietatem, et devotionem, eaque omnia, quæ ad Dei cultum, et officium hominis erga Deum spectant. Nihil ergo ab homine requiritur, vel ei necessarium est, quod hæc gratia non doceat.'

[2] Barcl. lib. 1, p. 110. ' Credimus enim, quod sicut omnes participes sunt mali fructus Adæ lapsus, cum malo illo semine, quod per eum illis communicatum est, proni et ad malum proclives sint, licet millies mille Adæ sint ignari et quomodo prohibitum fructum ederit, ita multi possint sentire divini hujus et sancti seminis virtutem, eaque a malo ad bonum converti, licet de Christi in terram adventu; per cujus obedientiæ et passionis beneficium hac fruantur, prorsus ignari sint.'

as even the only source of truths, which (in their essence) are the very same, that Jesus outwardly proclaimed, and committed to his Church.[1] The later Quakers appear likewise to feel the obvious difficulty here adverted to; whether it be, that they themselves first observed it, or whether their attention were drawn to it by others. Be this as it may, Clarkson remarks in a note, ' The Quakers believe that this Spirit was more plentifully diffused, and that greater gifts were given to men after Jesus was glorified than before.' To this concession they were driven by the force of evidence; but in their system we cannot find a place where it can possess an organic connection with the whole. It is no ulterior development of what already exists, but an incongruous interpolation.[2]

If, from what has been said, it follows, that the contradictions, wherein the orthodox Protestantism is involved with incontrovertible facts in human history, the Quakers only exchange for other contradictions against that history; we must now demonstrate that their theory is, in itself, perfectly unsatisfactory, and does not even escape those difficulties which they principally aim at avoiding. They wish, as we have already perceived, to escape, in the first place, from the Calvinistic doctrine of absolute predestination, by asserting that to every man the inward light is proffered, and a day of visitation vouchsafed. They would fain, at the same time, escape from Pelagianism and semi-Pelagianism, which they ascribe to the Catholic Church, by deducing all the in anywise laudable acts that the heathen world once achieved, and still achieves, not in any degree from the spiritual nature of man, but solely from the inward word—

[1] Lib. 1, p. 20. ' Quod nunc sub litem venit illud est, quod postremo loco affirmavimus, scil. idem permanere et esse Sanctorum fidei objectum in hanc usque diem.' It is not uninteresting to notice the Scriptural proofs, which Barclay adduces in support of his views. For instance, he says: ' Si fides una est, unum etiam est fidei objectum. Sed fides una est; ergo. Quod fides una sit, ipsa Apostoli verba probant ad. Eph. iv, 5.' Then he goes on: ' Si quis administrationis objiciat diversitatem : Respondeo, hoc nullo modo objectum spectat, nam idem Apostolus, ubi ter hanc varietatem nominat, 1 Co. xii, 4, 5, 6, ad idem objectum semper recurrit. Sic "idem Spiritus, idem Dominus, idem Deus." Præterea nisi idem et nobis et illis erit fidei objectum, tunc Deus aliquo alio modo cognosceretur, quam spiritu; sed hoc absurdum; Ergo.' And so he goes on at considerable length. And the inward Christ again naturally teaches, that these texts must be so interpreted; although, according to all rules of interpretation, they bear quite a different sense.

[2] Clarkson, vol. ii., Rel. ch. vii, sect. 2, p. 187. The Quakers believe, however, that this spirit was more plentifully diffused, and that greater gifts were given to men after Jesus was glorified than before.

the inward light.[1] Thereby they would fain show, that fallen man has every cause for humility ; as he possesses nothing, not the least quality, which, in respect to divine things, can be active or efficacious, as every thing must be accounted for, solely and exclusively, by the inward Christ in each man. Alas ! the Quakers, in wishing to attain one thing, render the other impossible, so that their combination is utterly untenable. Fallen man, according to them, has been so utterly bereaved of all higher faculties and powers, that the good which takes place in him is wrought so *very independently* of him, that not even *in* his will, still less *by means of* his will, doth grace consummate it.[2] The inward light of the Quakers is that sense for Divine things which in Adam all mankind had lost ; yet by this they understood not merely the restoration of a pre-existing, though torpid and paralysed faculty, to its original activity, but the entirely new creation of the faculty itself. In one word, it is the faculty of knowledge and of will in reference to divine things. Hence Barclay calls the inward light a new substance imparted to man, in opposition to an accidental one, and employs the expression, man receives thereby *the aptitude* for righteousness.[3] It must be obvious to every one that the Quakers have

[1] Loc. cit. p. 103. ' Contradicit et enervat falsam Pelagianorum, Semipelagianorum et Socinianorum doctrinam, qui naturæ lumen exaltant et liberum hominis arbitrium ; dum omnino naturalem hominem a vel minima in salute sua parte excludit, ullo opere, actu vel motu suo, quoad primo vivificetur et actuetur spiritu Dei.'

[2] Loc. cit. p. 189. ' Posteriora opera (sc. gratiæ seu evangelii) sunt spiritus gratiæ in corde, quæ secundum internam et spiritualem legem facta sunt : quæ nec in hominis voluntate, nec viribus ejus fiunt, sed per vim spiritus Christi in nobis.' What then does Barclay mean, when he says at times, that Divine grace is designed to resuscitate and excite anew the human faculties ?

[3] Lib. 1, p. 72. ' Quis enim cum aliqua rationis specie autumare potest, tale cor ex se habere potestatem, aut aptitudinem, vel aptum esse hominem ad justitiam perducendi ? ' It is worthy of remark, that the Protestants in their controversy with the Quakers, appealed to the text in Romans (c. xi, 14) in the very same sense, as Catholics had once done in arguing with the Protestants. But Barclay says at p. 530 :—' Respondeo, " hæc natura," intelligi nec debet nec potest de natura propria hominis, sed de natura spirituali, quæ procedit a semine Dei in homine. . . . Ita, ut bene concludamus, naturam, cujus hoc loco meminit Apostolus, qua gentes dicuntur facere ea, quæ legis sunt, non esse communem hominum naturam, sed spiritualem naturam, quæ ex opere spiritualis et justæ legis in corde scriptæ procedit : fateor eos, qui alterum exetremum tenent, quando hoc testimonio a Socinianis et Pelagianis (sicut etiam a nostris, quando hoc testimonio ostendimus, quomodo ex gentibus aliqui lumine Christi in corde salutem adepti sunt) premuntur, et ad augustias reducuntur, respondere, quasdam reliquias cœlestis imaginis in Adamo relictas esse. Sed cum hoc

only here renewed the old Lutheran opinion respecting the divine image—its utter obliteration through the fall, and its restoration in Christ. There is here, as is evident, but this difference—that the Quakers fix the restoration of the divine image immediately after the fall, and ascribe to it a far greater power against sin. Hereby they became involved in the same inextricable difficulties, with which the Lutheran theory had to contend. They set the natural man too low, to enable them to escape from the doctrine of absolute predestination. They say, indeed, like the Lutherans, man is able to resist, or not to resist, divine grace. But if, by his resistance, he is to incur guilt, he must be allowed the faculty of independently *discerning*, by the aid of grace, that a truth presented to him conduces to his salvation : he must, accordingly, embrace this truth with *his own* will. But such faculties the Quakers deny to fallen man ; and therefore they have no alternative, than, either to refer to God *alone* the overcoming of resistance, and thereby to subscribe to the tenet of absolute predestination, which they so strongly condemn in Calvin ; or to impute it to accident alone, when grace triumphs or is resisted. But accident is only another word for fate.[1]

absque probatione affirmatum sit, ita et dictis suis alibi contradicit, quo etiam causam suam amittunt.' P. 108 : ' Non intelligimus hanc gratiam, hoc lumen et semen esse accidens, ut plerique inepte faciunt, sed credimus esse realem, spiritualem substantiam, quam anima hominis apprehendere et sentire potest.'

[1] Clarkson on this, as on other points, differs considerably from Barclay. He endeavours not only to supply the gaps in the system of the Quakers, but to render that system more scriptural, and thereby more rational, than it is in itself ; but in this attempt he introduces not only contradictions into it, but very harsh dissonances into his own productions. He may, nevertheless, record the views of more sensible, yet inconsistent Quakers. Clarkson fills up Barclay's statement in respect to the condition of the Paradisaic Adam ; because to this subject, willingly or unwillingly, men must ever recur. In imitation of Catholics, Clarkson distinguishes a twofold image of God in man—a remoter, and a more proximate one, yet in a different sense from us. The former is the human mind, called ' the mental understanding—the power of Reason.' (Revelation, etc., vol. ii, c. i, p. 114.) This faculty he describes as that, ' by means of which man was enabled to guide himself in *his temporal concerns.*' Thus there would not exist in man, as such, any faculty having reference to God and to the supermundane. The *proper* image of God in man Clarkson then describes, as a spiritual faculty *independent* of human Reason (the words understanding, power of discernment, and the rest, are, in his opinion, synonymous terms. This faculty is a portion of the very life of the Divine Spirit —an emanation from Divine Life, whereby man discerns his relation to God, and keeps up communion with his Creator. ' But he gave to man at the same time, *independently* of his own intellect or understanding, a

Upon the so-called objective Revelation, we have many doubts to suggest; they are chiefly as follows—All outward special Revelations, and even the Incarnation of the Logos, are, by that objective Revelation, rendered not only superfluous, but even inexplicable. For, if God's spirit is to reveal immediately to every man the fit measure of truths—if thus the voice of God is, in this way, to go forth to all men, what end can He still propose in His special Revelations? If all men be prophets, then a distinct prophetic ministry must needs be abolished. And in fact, in order to prove their so-called general objective Revelation, the Quakers appeal, with the greatest boldness, to the particular revelations, which were vouchsafed to the prophets of old.

But it is principally to the self-consciousness of man, and to the laws and conditions under which it is formed and unfolded, the doctrines of Quakerism run counter. It can be

---

spiritual faculty, or a portion of the life of his own spirit, to reside in him. This gift occasioned man to become more immediately, as it is expressed, the image of the Almighty. It set him above the animal and rational part of his nature. It made him spiritually-minded. It enabled him to know his duty to God, and to hold a heavenly intercourse with his Maker. . . . Adam, then, the first man, independently of his rational faculties, received from the Almighty into his own breast, such an emanation from the life of His Spirit.' According to *these* statements, it cannot, in the first place, be *absolutely* asserted, that, through the Fall, man has lost the Divine image; for, even after that catastrophe, he would still retain the mental powers having reference to earthly life—the remoter image of God, and even, according to Clarkson (as above stated), still a part of the likeness unto God, in the strict sense. Secondly, these statements would very well explain the cause, wherefore it is possible for the Quakers to deduce *entirely* from divine inspirations, all true religious instruction—all genuine prayer, etc.: for, according to this system, no human faculty would have any relation whatsoever to supermundane things. Thirdly, this theory would agree very well with that of Barclay; it would, indeed, contain more than the latter had stated; but nothing which he might not have advanced, without introducing any change in his principles. But, among the above-mentioned propositions, expressions like the following occur: 'It (the image of God in the strict sense) made him know things not intelligible *solely* by his reason.' The things of earth, therefore, would not be the only sphere within which reason would have to move; but only it could not, by its unaided efforts, apprehend God. But if the co-operation of reason were necessary to the knowledge of God, then it would be *everywhere* indispensable; and thereby the whole view of the Quakers, respecting preaching and the rest, would fall to the ground; and yet Clarkson puts forward as Quakerish the very same views as Barclay. Lastly, if the activity *of Reason* be unavoidable, when the *knowledge of God* is concerned, so is the *co-operation of the will* equally indispensable when the *love of God* is the question. But this, according to Barclay, the Quakers will by no means admit; while Clarkson asserts the contrary.—Ibid. p. 188.

demonstrated, that without an intellectual excitation, and an extraneous influence, the self-consciousness of man cannot be developed—a law which, so far from being set aside, is directly confirmed, by the historical Revelations of God. Hence, if man is to attain to the true knowledge of the Deity, the inward Divine Light must ever be associated with the outward Light; the external must correspond to the internal Revelation; and the inward inspiration can be understood only by means of the outward communication. Even in respect to the prophets and envoys of God, whom the Christian recognises, it can be proved that their inward illuminations were not without all external media—whether the Spirit revealing Himself to them assumed a sensible shape; or whether He annexed His revelations to long pre-existing doctrines and expectations. It is only the Son of God, whom we must except from this rule; for here the absolute Spirit, exempt from the limitations of mere relative beings, appeared in the world, and conjoined Himself with a human nature in the unity of one consciousness. Yet, it cannot be proved from the Scripture-History, that the human mind of the Redeemer had been developed without any external human influence.

The question now occurs, how have the Quakers come to their remarkable opinion, that the consciousness of God can be formed independently of outward teaching, nay, of all outward influence whatever; and whether this view may not be considered, as a necessary development of the errors of the Reformation. If, in contempt of all the laws of the human mind, Luther taught that, in the regenerated soul of man, new faculties were implanted, through an absolute exercise of divine influences; surely, it was inconsistent to prescribe to these faculties, thus absolutely imparted from within, outward conditions for their insertion. If, in the interior of the human mind, these faculties needed no points of contact—if, in order to become the property of man, they presupposed no kindred qualities—if they worked in the soul, in a manner contrary to the constitution of man—if they were exceptions from the whole order of human nature; with what justice could it be said, that the conditions of *external* excitation and teaching in other respects requisite to the development of the human mind were here necessary? How could those acts of Divine power preserve the assumed character of absoluteness, if they were subjected to limitations? Was it no contradiction to let the

Divine Principle work unconditionally on the one hand, and conditionally on the other? Thus the Lutheran exemption of the Divine influence from all internal conditions, implanted in the human spirit, involved also, by a necessary connection of ideas, an independence of this influence on all outward conditions; and now only could harmony and completeness be introduced into the system. Hence, from this point of view, Quakerism must be denominated the consummation of Lutheranism; and to that expression of the Wittenberg Reformer, 'God teacheth man only inwardly,' it first assigns a true meaning.

We must look at the matter thus. All instruction, which man receives through the instrumentality of man, or which he acquires for himself by reading books, is founded on the supposition that he is endowed with certain still dormant faculties, which, set in motion by those exercises, are resuscitated and become living; so that, what is pre-established—what already exists in man as a prototype—is, through external influence, brought home to his consciousness. But now, the Lutherans deny to fallen man the Divine image—the religious capability. What possible effect preaching, or the reading of Holy Writ, could produce for the awakening of the soul, we are at a loss to understand, since man had nothing more to be awakened. The system, wherein the necessity of outward teaching could be proved, was a far different one from the Lutheran, which, instead of the *training* of the religious faculties, imagined *a new creation* of the same; wherein, therefore, instruction, through reading and writing, could as little find its place, as in the creation of the aforesaid qualities in the first man. By no instruction can the faculty for any kind of knowledge, be infused into the mind of the pupil; as for instance, an aptitude for the mathematical sciences is not given by tuition. Luther's doctrine, accordingly, as to the necessity of outward teaching for regeneration in Christ, had no sort of connection with his propositions respecting the Fall of man. The Quakers understood, or, at least, felt this inconsistency; and while they asserted that, through Adam, fallen man was deprived of all religious faculties, capable of being excited and trained by an external agency, they declared likewise against the necessity of any outward instruction; and, thereby, established the fairest symmetry in the doctrinal edifice laid down by Luther, clearly revealing at the same time, however, the utter hollowness of its foundations.

But, hereby also, the ground was completely cut away from the outward, historical Revelation of God in Christ. The Quakers, indeed, uphold the doctrine, that for the sake of Christ's merits, that inward, supernatural light hath been vouchsafed to man. But the sacrifice, which Christ offered up for the sins of the world, considered in itself, is utterly untenable in the system of the Quakers; and as regards this matter alone, we might just as well say, the Son of God, without its being necessary to make this known to men, might, in some obscure corner of the earth, or in the planets Mars, Uranus, and the rest, have undergone any suffering, and atoned for our guilt. That the love which God evinced in the mission of His Son should be brought to our *knowledge*—that we should be *instructed* in the sentiments of God—that we should be *taught* our own destiny, are things, which indeed, necessarily, appertain to the work of Redemption; but which yet cannot be established by the principles of the Quakers. Hence, they make a reply devoid of all solidity, when, in answer to the objection, that they deny the knowledge of Christ's History to be necessary to our true conversion to God, they declare they hold the same to be not requisite for those only, who are beyond the pale of Christianity, for these are taught all truth by the inward Christ; but that, as to those living within the bosom of the Christian Church, they inculcate the necessity of their making themselves acquainted with the history of Christ,[1] and of believing in the same. This answer, we say, is futile; for it is impossible to discover, wherefore what is absolutely necessary for the one, should be unnecessary to the other, for the attainment of the same object. Hence, a celebrated member of the sect, Keith, was, in several synods, declared devoid of the spirit of the Quakers, and was forbidden to preach; because he could not convince himself that Faith in the death and the resurrection of Christ, was not necessary to salvation. And Spangenberg, the celebrated bishop of the Herrnhutters, in his biography of Count Zinzendorf, thus speaks from a personal knowledge of the

---

[1] Loc. cit. p. 110. 'Sicut credimus, omnino necessarium esse iis historiam externam Christi credere, quibus Deus ejus scientiam voluit aliquo modo communicare; ita ingenue fatemur, hanc externam scientiam esse consolabundam illis, qui subjecti sunt, et hoc interno semine et lumine acti: nam non solum sensu mortis et passionum Christi humiliantur, sed et in fide confirmantur, et ad sequendum præstantissimum ejus exemplum animantur . . . nec non sæpissime reficiuntur et recreantur gratiosissimis sermonibus, qui ex ore ejus procedebant.'

Quakers; 'the doctrine of Christ crucified, and that in his sacrifice alone men can find grace, and deliverance from all sins, is to them, as to all the sages of this world, a mere foolishness, and is beyond their discernment.'[1] We therefore are not surprised, when we are informed, that many American Quakers explain away the whole history of Christ into a mere allegory; and what Barclay so often said, respecting the Christ crucified through sin in every man, respecting the inward Word suffering through the pressure of sin, etc., served to pave the way for the opinion, which sees in the historical Christ, only a philosophical, anthropological, religious Mythos.[2] An historical, visible Christ cannot consist with the invisible, purely spiritual Church of these one-sided spiritualists of Christianity; a Redeemer graciously condescending to the wants and infirmities of our nature, stands in too abrupt a contrast with these high-flying idealists, to allow them to revere him as their Master, in all the fulness of conviction. Hence, as in ecclesiastical history, we often encounter similar deductions from similar principles; they were compelled also to reject the outward, visibly self-manifesting Christ, and to transform him into something purely spiritual—a mere naked idea, in order that the disciples might not be ashamed of their Master, and the foundation might be made to harmonise with the superstructure of their Christianity. Thus was Protestantism, when pushed to its farthest point, formally converted into a species of Gnosticism; so that Christ could be regarded by the Quakers exactly in the same light as by the Jewish Docetæ. The humanity of Christ is the necessary and essential form of his divinity, as the Author of revelation in the new Covenant. In the same way, *and even for that very reason*, the Church, with her fundamental institutions, is the essential form of the Christian Religion: and if we separate

---

[1] But from this it must not be inferred, as has sometimes been done, that the Quakers never believed in Christ's death of atonement. On this point Barclay's language permits no manner of doubt. He says (p. 109): 'Per hoc nullo modo intelligimus, neque volumus minuere, nec derogare a sacrificio et propitiatione Jesu Christi, sed e contra magnificamus et exaltamus illam,' etc. Compare p. 148-164, and other numerous passages. In Clarkson, ibid. p. 320, we find also the following passage, cited from a Quaker, Henry Tuke: 'So far as remission of sins, and capacity to receive salvation, are parts of Justification, we attribute it to the sacrifice of Christ, in whom we have redemption through his blood, the forgiveness of sins according to the riches of his grace.'

[2] A friend of mine, who, a few years ago, met two American Quakers in the West Indies, has assured me, that, in conversing with them on religion, he found they allegorised the whole history of our Lord.—*Trans.*

the form from the substance, then the latter will, in the end, inevitably dissolve into a mere fantastic void, and retroactively, Christ will sink into a mere creature of the brain.

In perfect conformity with its fundamental principles, the false spiritualism of the Quakers manifests the most decided hostility against all theological science; and they are at a loss to find words to express their sentiments of detestation towards it, as well as to testify their regret, that it should have passed from the times of *apostasy* (as they call the ages prior to the Reformation), over to the period of Protestantism. But, herein also, they continue only more violently, and push to the furthest extreme, that condemnation of all severe scientific culture, which, at the commencement of the revolution in the Church, was so often expressed by the Lutherans. Scientific labours are not possible without human exertion; but it is precisely all human activity, which the Quakers wish to banish from the sphere of theology.[1] They are, on that account, averse from all which wears the aspect of a settled, definite religious notion; and, therefore, urged by an instinct, which, according to their views, is perfectly correct, they avoid all the technical expressions of the School and the Church, and only on certain subjects, on which they cannot otherwise make themselves generally intelligible, they permit a deviation from this rule. But hereby it happens that they mostly revolve in vague religious feelings, foster a doctrinal indifferentism; and, as many among them are utterly unconscious of anything deserving the title of real Christianity, so the whole system of Quakerism would, by degrees, dissolve into dull hollow phantasies, were it not, from time to time, brought back to the positive *doctrines* of Christianity, by some extraneous influence, as this appears to have been recently the case.[2]

[1] Clarkson (and the language of Barclay is still stronger) says, loc. cit. p. 249: ' They reject all school divinity, as necessarily connected with the ministry. They believe that if a knowledge of Christianity had been obtainable by the acquisition of the Greek and Roman languages, and through the medium of the Greek and Roman philosophers, the Greek and Romans themselves would have been the best proficients in it; whereas, the Gospel was only foolishness to many of these.' Here we find truth and falsehood intermixed.

[2] Clarkson (loc. cit. p. 313) says in a tone of approval: ' The Quakers have adhered, as strictly as possible, to Scriptural expressions, and thereby they have escaped from many difficulties, and avoided the theological controversies, which have distracted the remainder of the Christian Church.' In the Heathen worships, also, we find no *doctrinal* controversies, precisely because they had no doctrine, and furnished no subject-matter for *thought*,

How little, in fine, their peculiar conceptions of Baptism, the Lord's Supper, and divine worship in general, agree with the essence of an outward, historical Revelation, and with the nature and the wants of the human mind (even overlooking here their, in truth, highly afflicting distortion of Scriptural testimonies), it were almost needless to examine. But the truth to be found in their doctrine on those matters, to wit, that Baptism is no mere bodily ablution, but baptism by fire and the Spirit, and that the Lord's Supper should lead to an inward communion with God, is by no means peculiar to these sectaries. What mortal weariness, vacancy of mind, and dulness; what sickly fancies most of their members labour under, during the silence in their religious meetings, God knows, and every man may infer, who has acquired any knowledge on this subject, from his own personal observation, or the experience of others [1] In order to draw from oneself food for meditation, great extent of knowledge, and great ability, a soul perfectly imbued with faith are requisite. But even this the Quakers will not have—absolute revelations are what they look for during that silence, but only for *fancy* and for *feeling*. Had the primitive Christians been so, like the Quakers, as the latter flatter themselves, Christianity would have long since disappeared. For this depends upon a *doctrine* pronounced by the Supreme Intelligence: *notions* and *ideas* lie at the bottom of its facts; so that, through the former, it calls up genuine feelings and true life. I have, moreover, seldom known anyone, who censured the phraseology of the Church, without discovering, at the same time, that he was tolerably indifferent about dogmas. For it is only in a very few cases, that a reverence for the Bible pushed to superstition, leads to the conduct we condemn, and which would hold the words of *Scripture alone* as holy, and every thing else as profane—a superstition, besides, with which the other views of the Quakers, as to Holy Writ, do not well coincide. They do not, for example, use the words 'Trinity,' 'Persons,' and the rest, when they speak of Father, Son and Holy Ghost, and their mutual relations; but, on that very account, their doctrine on this matter, is so loose and indefinite, that Arians, Sabellians, Photinians, and even disciples of Paul of Samosata, could make use of their formulas of expression. No occasion is, indeed, furnished for disputes; but only because no matter exists for investigations. They say, ' they find the word " Trinity " neither in Justin Martyr, nor in Irenæus, nor in Tertullian, nor in Origen, nor in the Fathers of the first three centuries of the Church,' p. 314. Truly, if they will not read the books of these fathers, they will find nothing in them; for, otherwise, they would have met with the word in question, in Theophilus of Antioch, Tertullian, Novatian, Origen, Dionysius of Rome, and Dionysius of Alexandria.

[1] A writer observes: ' Hence it comes to pass, that in a Quaker meeting, you find a museum of stupid faces; and yet, among the members of that meeting, there are but very few blockheads. Many Quakers appear, like Jacob, to expect heavenly apparitions in sleep; for, in every Quaker meeting, I have found sleepers. Others sit with a countenance, on which weariness herself has evidently fixed her throne.'

The Divine Spirit annexes its inspirations only to what preexists in the soul; and it is a thorough illusion, though easily to be accounted for, when they think that the thoughts and the feelings, which arise during this self-collectedness of the spirit, are pure and immediate creations of the inward Light.[1]

[1] Clarkson (vol. ii, p. 146) has a passage which gives a beautiful and psychological explanation of the manner in which the Quakers arrived at their opinion, that, without any exertion of the human mind, higher thoughts and feelings are implanted within us. The fact, that not seldom man is quite involuntarily raised up to God; that without any conscious preparation on his part, he sinks into religious meditations, and inwardly rejoices in his God and Redeemer, furnished them occasion for their theory As the passage we have in view evinces, at the same time, the tender feelings of the Quakers, we think it expedient to cite it. 'The Society,' says Clarkson, 'considers the Spirit not only as teaching by inward breathings, as it were, made immediately and directly upon the heart, without the intervention of outward circumstances, but, as making the material objects of the universe, and many of the occurrences of life, if it be properly attended to, subservient to the instruction of man, and as enlarging the sphere of his instruction in this manner, in proportion as it is received and encouraged. Thus, the man who is attentive to these divine notices, sees the animal, the vegetable, and the planetary world with spiritual eyes. He cannot stir abroad, but he is taught in his own feelings, without any motion of his will, some lesson for his spiritual advantage; or he perceives so vitally some of the attributes of the Divine Being, that he is called upon to offer some spiritual incense to his Maker. If the lamb frolics and gambols in his presence, as he walks along, he may be made spiritually to see the beauty and the happiness of innocence. If he finds the stately oak laid prostrate by the wind, he may be spiritually taught to discern the emptiness of human power; while the same Spirit may teach him inwardly the advantage of humility, when he looks at the little hawthorn which has survived the storm. When he sees the change and the fall of the autumnal leaf, he may be spiritually admonished of his own change and dissolution, and of the necessity of a holy life. Thus, the Spirit of God may teach men by outward objects and occurrences in the world. But where this Spirit is away, or rather where it is not attended to, no such lesson can be taught. Natural objects, of themselves, can excite only natural ideas; and the natural man, looking at them, can derive only natural pleasure, or draw natural conclusions from them. In looking at the sun, he may be pleased with its warmth, and anticipate its advantage to the vegetable world. In plucking and examining a flower, he may be struck with its beauty, its mechanism, and its fragrant smell. In observing the butterfly, as it wings its way before him, he may smile at its short journeyings from place to place, and admire the splendour upon its wings. But the beauty of Creation is dead to him, as far as it depends on connecting it spiritually with the character of God; for no spiritual impression can arise from any natural objects, so that these should be sanctified to him, but through the intervention of the Spirit of God.'

Great and important, and universally admitted truths are here professed. It is only to him, who is already awakened and illuminated by Divine Grace that Nature truly testifies of God and of all things divine; nay, every particular thought, that springs fresh and joyous up to God, and warms the heart, even if it be occasioned by outward objects only, is

On the contrary, they are only resuscitations of good, by the medium of what has long pre-existed, of what has been communicated from without, and inwardly received and retained by *the human* mind. However much they protest against human agency, they must have it; and, under all forms, it will manifest itself. For the little ones in mind as well as in body, such a religious service will, in every instance, be totally unproductive of fruit; and the illusion that the Divine Spirit here evinces an absolutely creative power, is in this respect most strikingly evident; for, if the Quaker view be correct, what hinders the Spirit from selecting, at times, a child six weeks old for the office of preaching and prayer? If, in the mind of man, nothing pre-exist to which the Spirit can annex its inspirations—if that Spirit be there to create all anew, a child can then surely be its organ as well as an adult.

What the Quakers tell respecting the struggle between the Divine inward Light and the powers of darkness, that during their religious assemblies, seek to entangle and to retain them in worldly distractions, it is not difficult to understand. The human mind can enter far more easily and more deeply into its own interior, and be brought into a more beneficial train of feelings, when it fixes its attention on a matter, presented to it from without, exercises its reflection on the same, and then makes an independent attempt at meditation.

But, according to the method adopted by the Quakers, it is only the minds of very few that can remain free from distractions; whereupon they are naturally thrown into great anguish, terror, and trembling; so that what they take to be a sign of the proximity and visitation of the Divine Spirit subduing the powers of Satan, is an evident symptom of the perversity of the whole sect.

still excited by God's grace. But, without the human spirit and its concurrent activity, no ray, whether it light on us from without or from within, can possibly impregnate: and this truth the Quakers themselves involuntarily admit, since they must annex the condition; ' *who is attentive to these Divine notices, who sees the world with spiritual eyes.*'

Note of the Author.—We see, from the above-cited passage of Clarkson, how on this point also, the tender-thoughted Quakers approximate to our Church; for this habit of making Nature a medium for spiritual contemplations, is one recommended and practised by Catholic ascetic writers. —*Trans.*

CHAPTER III

THE HERRNHUTTERS OR THE COMMUNITY OF BROTHERS, AND THE METHODISTS

§ LXXII—HISTORICAL REMARKS—THE MORAVIAN BRETHREN

THE doctrinal peculiarities of the party, to which we are now to devote our attention, were formed out of the union of the principles of the Moravian brethren, with those of Spener's pietistic school. It will, therefore, be incumbent on us, in the first place, to give a short account of the two last-named religious parties. In despite of all attempts to bring about a union between the Catholics and the Hussites, a considerable number of the latter continued separated from the Church, down to the period of the Reformation, which inspired them with new hopes, and infused fresh life and youthful vigour into their body.

The Hussites and Luther early recognised their spiritual affinity, and entered into a close outward union with each other; in consequence whereof, the former embraced the doctrinal views of the latter, as being the stronger party. The doctrine of the non-united Hussites needed, in fact, a considerable change, to enable them to join with the German reformer; for John Huss and Martin Luther, however they might agree, in their notions of the Church, and of the necessity of a Reformation, that would undermine its fundamental law, were yet, in some essential doctrines, diametrically opposed. We shall now take a brief survey of the mutual relations between Luther and the later Hussites, who under the name of the Bohemian and Moravian Brethren protracted their existence.

The Bohemian Church-Reformer had no idea of that doctrine of justification, put forth by the Saxon; and, accordingly, his view of human works and conduct, was essentially different. Huss laid down the most rigid maxims, in matters of ecclesiastical discipline; of whose impracticable severity we may form an idea, when we recall to mind, that among the four conditions, which his disciples proposed to the Catholics, as a basis for a reunion, there was one, that all mortal sins, under which they included 'gluttony, drunkenness, incontinence, lying, perjury, usury, the receiving of any money for mass and confession, and the like,' should be punished with death ! A party among them even desired that the power of inflicting the penalty of death on anyone, whom he should see polluted with one of the above-mentioned sins, should be conceded to every private individual. Huss, doubtless, had not proceeded to such lengths in his reforming zeal ; yet the excitement he raised, was of a nature necessarily calculated to lead to such unheard-of excesses of fanaticism. That no prince, or prelate guilty of any grievous sin, is entitled to obedience, was even an opinion formally inculcated by Huss. With such passionate exclusiveness, did these sectaries turn to the practical side of Religion, that, not content with the demand just adverted to, they had also the assurance to require of Catholics, to hold as a heathen any man who should let himself be nominated master of the liberal arts, as well as to annihilate all scientific institutions. The soothing influence of time, maturer reflection on the constitution of human nature, and a calmer temper of mind—brought about by want and misery—produced, however, by degrees, many in all respects beneficial changes among the disciples of Huss. On the other hand, those among them, who were known under the name of the Bohemian and Moravian Brethren, adopted, in their intercourse with the Waldenses, doctrinal errors, totally unknown to Huss, as well as to the Calixtines, and their ecclesiastical head, Roxyccana. From the latter, who, by degrees, were to be distinguished from Catholics merely by a ritual difference—the use of the cup in communion—the Bohemian and Moravian Brethren separated in the year 1450, denied (if we may at least so infer from an apology published in the year 1508, and from some earlier documents), not only the doctrine of transubstantiation, but also that of the corporal presence of Christ in the Eucharist, and professed, if any definite meaning is to be drawn from their expressions, nearly the same theory as was afterwards put forth by Calvin on this subject. They retained, moreover, the seven sacraments, yet, as we may conceive, without admitting Catholic ordination, since Christ, according to them, is the immediate source of all ecclesiastical power. Lastly, they rejected purgatory and the veneration of saints. They were ever distinguished for a very rigid moral discipline, and for the vigorous use of excommunication. According to the custom of the old Waldenses, they numbered three classes—the beginners, the advancing, and the perfect, and according to the measure of his spiritual growth, placed the individual in one of these grades. These are now the doctrinal and the disciplinary peculiarities of those Hussites, denominated Bohemian and Moravian Brothers, and at the moment, indeed, when they formed a conjunction with Luther.

Contrary to his usual course, Luther treated with great indulgence the opinion of 'the Brothers' on the Lord's Supper, and thereby served his own ends uncommonly well. For they agreed, in the year 1536, to subscribe to the belief in the presence of Christ's body and blood in the Eucharist,[1] and adopted the fundamental points in the Lutheran doctrine of justification, though, on the necessity of sanctification and of good works, they held a far more distinct and forcible language than Luther.[2] This occurred in a public confession delivered to King Ferdinand. From this time, the league between the Brothers of Wittenberg and of Bohemia was solemnly concluded, and Luther formed a very advantageous opinion of the latter. In the preface which he prefixed to the edition of their symbolical writing just adverted to, he says, ' he had formerly been ashamed of the Picards ' (for so his present friends were once called), ' but now they were much more agreeable—courteous, he might say, sounder, correcter, and better in their conduct.' It by no means redounded to their dishonour that they sent an embassy to Luther, with the purpose of calling his attention to the scandalous morals of his disciples, and of strongly urging on him the necessity of a *reformation in this matter.* ' The Bohemian Brothers ' (these are the words of Francis Buddeus, the Lutheran theologian), ' as they easily perceived *that in the Reformation much importance was not attached to strictness in matters of discipline and conduct*, though they were justified to press, by a new embassy, this subject on Luther's attention.'[3] Even the fact, that the

---

[1] Confess. Bohemica. Art. xiii, in Augusti (loc. cit. part ix, p. 205). 'Item et hic corde credendum ac ore confitendum docent, panem cœnæ dominicæ verum Christi corpus esse, quod pro nobis traditum est, calicemque verum sanguinem ejus, etc. Docent etiam, quod his Christi verbis, quibus ipse panem corpus suum, et vinum speciatim sanguinem suum esse pronunciat, nemo de suo quidquam affingat, admisceat, aut detrahat, sed simpliciter his Christi verbis, neque ad dexteram neque ad sinistram declinando credat.'

[2] Art. vi, p. 284. Compare Art. xi, p. 300.

[3] ' Thoughts on the Constitution of the Moravian Brothers,' by Francis Buddeus, in Count von Zinzendorf's smaller writings. Frankfort on the

Bohemian Brothers constantly retained ecclesiastical celibacy, under the conviction that thereby their ministers could, with less impediment, live up to their calling, did not tend to disturb the harmony of the new associates. Subsequently (in the year 1575) the union between the theologians of Wittenberg and the Bohemian Brothers was renewed, yet without leading to a formal and outward communion between the two Churches.

However courteous and agreeable Luther might find the Picards (their readiness to embrace his doctrine did not certainly a little contribute to produce this favourable impression), the Austrian government did not experience from these sectaries such dispositions towards itself as to induce it to show them any marks of peculiar favour. In the sect, a deep hatred to the Imperial House continued to glow, and, on every occasion, broke out with the most hostile fury. Hence, its members saw themselves compelled, from time to time, to emigrate; they betook themselves to Poland, where they became acquainted with the peculiar errors of the Reformed, and even with those of the Anabaptists. Even so late as the commencement of the eighteenth century, the stream of emigration from Bohemia and Moravia still continued to flow. Several emigrants from the latter country settled, in the year 1722, on the estate of Count von Zinzendorf in Lusatia, and principally at a place called the Hut-berg. Discontented Protestants also, Lutherans, and Calvinists, repaired thither, in order to preserve the freedom of religious worship. The settlement itself was called Herrnhut.

§ LXXIII—CONTINUATION OF THE SAME SUBJECT—SPENER AND THE PIETISTS

We have now reached the point where we have to mention a religious movement among the German Lutherans—a movement with which the Bohemian Brothers came into immediate contact, and which gave a new shape to their existence. Philip James Spener, born at Rappoltsweiler in Alsace, in the year 1635, censured, in the theology of his German fellow-religionists, the want of a scriptural basis—a heartless and spiritless attention to mere dead formulas—the absence of all warmth, unction, and

---

Main, p. 229, 1740. 'The principal work on this period of the Hussites, is Joachimi Camerarii Historica Narratio de fratrum orthodoxorum Ecclesiis in Bohemia, Moravia et Polonia.' Heidelberg, 1605.

interior spirit—and, as a necessary consequence, the most evident sterility in regard to practical life, where he lamented the prevalence of moral laxity and grossness. In the sermons of his day, he found only the successful echo of academical lectures; a polemical violence, a dogmatising dryness, a petrifying coldness; an incapacity so to treat the doctrines of faith, as to move the heart and will; and in the great majority of preachers, men who had never experienced the regenerating power of the Gospel, and who did not even hold such to be necessary, in order to draw down a blessing on their announcement of the Divine word; for, as to the calling of a pastor, they entertained totally mistaken notions.[1] Spener, however, was far from ascribing all these abuses to a mere accidental error of his time. On the contrary, his unprejudiced judgment and acute perception discovered, in the fundamental doctrines of his Church, a strong occasion to such abuses, although he never openly confessed that the former necessarily led to the disorders of his age, and, under a self-delusion, even imagined he was only reviving the original maxims of the Reformation. On the nature of faith and its relation to works; on the reference of both to salvation; on the possibility of fulfilling the Divine commandments; on the moral perfection of man, as required by the Gospel, and on the extent and the depth of the purifying and sanctifying power of the Divine Spirit, in the souls of the Faithful; in like manner, on the relation between nature and grace, and the co-operation of man; on all these subjects, we say, Spener entertained opinions which ran directly counter to the principles of the Symbolical Books, and especially to the errors of Luther.

During his ministry in the cities of Strasburg, Frankfort, Dresden, and Berlin, Spener, in opposition to that dead, heartless course above described, followed up his system with the most abundant success, and in several writings, especially in a work entitled *Pia desideria*, which appeared in the year 1675, he frankly stated his convictions before all Protestant Germany. Many and influential as were the adversaries he found, who took the Lutheran orthodoxy under their protection; honourably and openly as the theological faculty of Wittenberg pointed out the contradictions into which he had fallen, with the funda-

[1] In these and still stronger colours, do Protestants themselves depict those times. Compare the work entitled, 'Philip James Spener and his Times,' an historical narrative by William Hosbach, evangelical preacher at the Jerusalem Church at Berlin. Berlin, 1828. Part. i, p. 1-185.

mental doctrine of his Church, publicly characterising as erroneous the opinion of Spener, that regeneration consisted in the transformation of the whole man, and censuring him for describing faith without holiness of life as a deceptious faith, for representing the good works of the true and living believer as perfect, and for declaring absolution from sins without true and hearty repentance, to be ineffectual, and so forth. In despite of all these censures, Spener won ever more and more on public opinion, and as subsequent events ever more clearly evinced, shook the foundations of Lutheran orthodoxy in Germany.[1] When Doctor Deutschman of Witten-

[1] See Hosbach's 'Spener and his Times.' Part ii, p. 61 (especially p. 221-232), where the differences between the orthodox Lutherans and Spener, on the point of justification, are explained ; but he will not even concede to the former, the merit of having vindicated the orthodox doctrine of the Lutheran Church. Hosbach will pardon us, if, while we pay a just tribute of acknowledgment to his various learning, his historical art, and his deeper religious feelings, we tell him that he does not accurately understand the Lutheran orthodoxy. Almost all the definitions, which he gives of the doctrines here discussed, are wanting in precision ; so that we are not at all surprised, when he asserts, at p. 229, that the whole controversy is a mere strife of words. But the theologians of Wittenberg, as also Schelwig of Leipzig, knew very well that the question turned on things, and not on words. At p. 244, we find, on the question of the necessity of works, a judgment pronounced in favour of Spener, which is expressly condemned by the 'Formulary of Concord.' At p. 240, the author asserts, 'This intemperate zeal led the orthodox theologians to hazard many *strange and utterly untenable* propositions : for instance, as when the Divines of Wittenberg, in contradiction to Spener, said, the Christian cannot at all fulfil the law, and in general, can perform no good works ; whereupon Spener replied, that it was a stigma on the Lutheran Church, to have teachers who could venture on such an assertion, and thus absolutely to contradict Luther, as well as the Symbolical Books (!) ; or when these divines dared to put forth the proposition, that the good works of the regenerate were not so much really good, as only less evil than sin itself ; or when they called on the Pietists, to prove from Scripture and experience, that any regenerated man has constantly kept himself free from all predominant sins, and when they, at the same time, asserted, that to refrain from all deliberate and mortal sins, during his whole life, was an impossibility even for the regenerated man.' These assertions of the orthodox Lutherans are, undoubtedly, when considered from the Scriptural point of view, strange and untenable. But how, on the other hand, within the pale of the Lutheran Church, they can be considered strange and untenable, we are at a loss to understand ; nay, it was Spener's doctrine that was there singular and strange, and contrary to the Symbolical writings, on which the whole dispute hinged. Had Spener shaken off the authority of Luther and of the Symbolical books, then indeed, in his controversy with the orthodox theologians, on the above-mentioned questions, he would have had full right on his side ; but, as in his defence, he rested on the authority of the former, asserting them to be only erroneously understood by his opponents, he was clearly in the wrong. The accounts of the Protestant Church

berg, together with his colleagues, Löscher, Hanneckan, and Neumann, censured in so German (Deutsch) a manner the doctrines of Spener, their conduct should not have been so ill-interpreted. Who was able to show that they had not endeavoured to uphold the pure doctrine of Luther?

Doubtless, Spener, that remarkable and meritorious man, had very great defects. Of the inward nature and importance of the Church, he entertained only very confined views, and promoted in a great degree a spirit of opposition to all ecclesiastical institutions. However much he insisted on a living faith, rooted in the regenerate will, yet he threatened it with utter destruction, by diffusing a certain disgust for all definite and settled religious notions for the enlightenment of the understanding, and by misapprehending the real value of a sound, intellectual culture. Hereby, too, he not only introduced the sickly, trifling, sentimentalising spirit of the Pietists, but also prepared the way for a most pernicious indifference to all dogmas. His views respecting philosophy and speculative theology, were, in like manner, extremely narrow and illiberal. In Spener's mental cultivation we discover, without doubt, a certain universality, which preserved him, personally, from great aberrations,

Historians—Walch, Schrökch, and many others, labour under the same defect, which we here charge on Hosbach.

It was only respecting the Church—the universal priesthood of all believers, and the subjects connected therewith, Spener entertained Luther's earliest principles, as the latter set them forth in his Instruction to the Bohemians. Hence, when the Theological Faculty of Wittenberg, enumerated among Spener's errors the following ones:—namely, ' that he regarded the symbolical books as mere human writings, whose authors God indeed preserved from errors, but in which, however, things not conformable to the Divine Word might be found : that he declared believers free from all human authority in matters of faith ; that he held not the Church, but Holy Writ, to be the sole keeper of God's Word, and asserted, that the Church had done well to frame no new symbolical writings ' ; so it is evident that Spener, in order to justify his own opposition against the Lutheran Church, defended the very same opinions which Luther proclaimed when he unfurled the banner of opposition against the Catholic Church. But, as the Lutheran Church held the system of belief, communicated to it by Luther, as irreformable (which must ever be the case, so long as *any belief*, however erroneous, exists) ; so Spener departed from the faith of the Church *founded* by Luther ; and when the theologians of Wittenberg urged this charge against him, they were decidedly in the right. In short, here too is discernible that inconsistency inherent in the very essence of Protestantism, wherein men are to believe indeed, but at the same time not believe that their belief is infallible ; in other words, that they have absolute and immutable possession of revealed truth. By requiring us to believe in the *fallibility* of our belief, a principle destructive to all faith is conjoined with it.

but the mystical tendency, which in him was by far the most predominant, was rarely transmitted to his disciples with the counteracting qualifications; and so, among the latter, errors of every kind could not fail to ensue. Lastly, a tincture of an arrogant spirit of sectarianism, is undeniably manifest in Spener. However much he might be in the right, when he characterised the whole Protestant Church, as 'the outward, corrupt body,' it did not thence follow, 'that one should leave it and bid it adieu,' and be content with gathering together 'a little Church within a Church.' It was from this presumptuous view, which was mixed up with his well-meant efforts, that in part proceeded his *Collegia Pietatis*, or associations 'of some pious souls' for special edification, which were established in the year 1670, during his abode at Frankfort, and from which the name of *Pietists* has been derived. These form, without absolutely seceding from the Lutheran Church, a closer association among themselves; and are, with all their one-sided views, their manifold pedantry, their hypocrisy, and often hollow, fantastic, and canting piety, the real salt of that Church.

What more especially characterises the Pietists, is the opinion, which Spener himself, however, impugned, that the true believer must be conscious of the moment wherein his justification (the illapse of grace) has taken place. That it is very easy to perceive this moment, they entertain not the slightest doubt, for they are of opinion that every individual must for once be afflicted with the anguish of despair at the Divine judgments, whereupon the solace through faith arises and produces a sense of joy and felicity that gladdens with supermundane fulness the heart of man—a sense whereof, previously, he had no anticipation. This opinion may be attended with the worst spiritual consequences. For those who are not and cannot be conscious of such a moment as having, in childhood, been blessed with a Christian education, the doctrines of the Gospel have made so deep and vivid an impression on their hearts, that, on one hand, they have ever loved God as the all-merciful, and, on the other, have never been guilty of grievous transgressions. These, we say, may on that account be easily precipitated into an agitation of soul bordering on despair, because these terrors of desperation and this frightful torment of the conscience, for the violation of the moral law, will not arise; yet these terrors and this anguish are represented as the universal condition to the true peace of the soul and the joy in God and Christ. Or should anyone, by artificial means, bring on this anguish of the soul, what will be the consequence, but that his whole inward life will be the sport of illusion and self-deception. Who doth not perceive that all these conceptions are only a further development of the course of justification, traced out by Luther ? His individual experience he exalted into an universal law, and in such a way, indeed, that, for instance, he wrote to Wittenberg from the castle of Wartburg, on the subject of the Anabaptists and their new revelations, that they should be examined as to whether they had endured those violent spiritual struggles, and on the result of that investigation, he wished to make the recognition of their divine mission, in part, at least, depend. If we consider, moreover, that Luther maintained that it was only on man's return to God, his spiritual organism became again complete, we shall see that his doctrine necessarily led to the error that *every* believer must be able accurately to mark the day, hour, and minute when his moral renovation took place. With the doctrine of an objective communication of grace through holy baptism, this error is, doubtless, totally incompatible ; for the Divine Spirit once received, cannot, in every instance, remain fruitless in respect to the ulterior progress of man. But it was precisely such an objective communication of the Spirit that Luther originally rejected, when he most spoke of these struggles of desperation.

§ LXXIV — COMBINATION OF THE DOCTRINAL PECULIARITIES OF THE MORAVIANS AND THE PIETISTS

In this Pietistic school, and, indeed, in one of its principal seats—in Halle, where the opinions of Spener had been promulgated from the academic chair—Count Lewis von Zinzendorf,[1] and his friends, Frederick von Watteville and Spangenberg, who were the souls, and successively the Bishops, of the Moravian Brethren assembled in Herrnhut, received, in the leading points at least, their religious education. The one-sided practical spirit and the sectarian arrogance, which the above-named

[1] Respecting Zinzendorf, the reader may consult the very lively, and even impartial sketch of him, which Varnhagen von Ense has traced in his work, entitled Leben des Grafen von Zinzendorf, Berlin, 1830. Spangenberg left behind him a large work on Zinzendorf : smaller ones were composed by Reichel and Duvernoy. He was born at Dresden in the year 1700, and died in 1760.

leaders and partisans brought in an equal degree into the society, formed the element connecting the two parties. The Bohemian Brothers brought a rigid external discipline as their peculiar characteristic, and Zinzendorf, Watteville, and Spangenberg, 'the so-called theology of the cross and blood.' The peculiar doctrines of the Herrnhutters seem to have been composed of these three elements.

In consequence of the one-sided, practical tendency we have described, and which was common to both parties, Count Zinzendorf was enabled to persuade his vassals, who were divided by many differences in matters of faith, especially by the Moravian, Calvinistic, and Lutheran tenets, to disregard the prevailing diversities of opinion, as they yet agreed in 'the fundamental articles,' and to induce the Moravian Brothers to follow his advice. Zinzendorf really entertained the notion that all who merely believed in redemption through the blood of Christ were of one faith, as if this doctrine could even be believed, and maintained unconnected with other dogmas. To remove, however, as far as possible all injurious consequences and injurious reports, he divided his community into three tropes— the Lutheran, the Calvinistic, and the Moravian. With reason did the Lutherans accuse the society of a doctrinal indifferentism, and assail it on all sides.[1]

That Zinzendorf also wished to found the community of Herrnhutters on the basis of sectarian pride, is proved by many incidents in his life, as well as by the strongest declarations on his part. He, too, looked upon the Lutheran Church as, on the whole, irrecoverably, lost; and all his efforts were directed to the planting everywhere branches of the community of Brothers, into which the yet sound portion of Lutherans might be received, while the by far larger incurable remnant might be suffered to perish. 'The Lutheran Church, in his words, was to be so

---

[1] To the well-known judgment of the Faculty of Tübingen on the Herrnhutters, Zinzendorf remarks (p. 205, Collection of his smaller writings): ' He (Melancthon) required unity only on the principal articles, and if these principal articles were but once settled, then the matter might be so arranged, that men could bear and communicate, and unite with each other. *But every man will make his own point, forsooth, a secondary point, when he is charged with heresy, and every hæretifex of his opponent's doctrine will make that a fundamental error.*' How productive this idea might have become, had it been only adhered to! The views expressed by Zinzendorf, in regard to Catholics, on occasion of the persecutions he had to endure from the Lutherans, are well entitled to attention.—See his life by Varnhagen, pp. 49, 143, and elsewhere.

sucked out, unsalted, unspiced, that nothing but a mere skeleton should remain.'[1] Even subscription to the Augsburg Confession he delayed till the year 1748.

In virtue 'of the cross and blood theology' (a favourite expression with the Herrnhutters themselves, but which has been ridiculed by modern Protestants in a very unchristian manner), the disciples of Zinzendorf were, in their public discourses and writings, almost exclusively occupied with the exposition and meditation on the bloody death of our Redeemer on the cross. The death of Jesus Christ being the centre-point of the Christian faith, the religious discourse of Christians, though not always expressly, should certainly, by implication, ever proceed from, and revert to this cardinal mystery. The Herrnhutters, indeed, represent the great sacrifice of atonement offered up for us, too exclusively in its immediate, outward form, and do not sufficiently bring out its idea through the medium of reflection. Wishing to foster sensibility, they strive too exclusively to picture the external fact of the crucifixion to the fancy; and thus if cannot fail to happen that they revolve in a very narrow, uniform circle of expressions, and figurative representations, which frequently produce only undefined, hollow, and empty sentiments. It should never, however, have been denied, that from this theology the Herrnhutters, especially in the first period of their history, which was most obnoxious to censure, derived a moral energy highly deserving of esteem, and which, in their missionary labours, displays itself under the most favourable aspect. But yet there were not wanting among them deeper emotions and beautiful evidences of experience in the interior life; as, to furnish a proof of this, we may appeal to the brief, but very pleasing description, which an uneducated Herrnhutter gives of the inward unction of the spirit.[2] This theology has, moreover, in its moral influence on ordinary life, produced the most beneficial effects. And how could it be otherwise? Who can meditate with love on the passion of the Saviour, without loving him? And he who loveth him, will keep his commandments. The physical part in our Lord's sufferings forms the substratum, and the point of contact for meditation, with which the believer connects his

---

[1] Compare Bengel's Life and Ministry. By Frederick Buck, p. 380, Stuttgart, 1831. From p. 276 to 402, the relation of Bengel to the Community of Brothers, is very well pointed out.

[2] See Zinzendorf's Collected Works, p. 235, et seq.

sorrow for sin, and his sense of gratitude for redemption. Love will not quickly remove from the beloved object, and it dwells, too, with complacency on minute particulars; and, therefore, it argues a profound ignorance of the wants of the human heart, to make it a matter of reproach against the Herrnhutters, that they dwell, with devout contemplation, on the several wounds of the Redeemer, and so forth.[1] The error consists wholly herein, that this devotion is too exclusive—that every member of the sect is trained up to these uniform practices of piety—and that a free development of the peculiarities of different minds is not encouraged—nay, not even permitted. What an inexhaustible fund for contemplation doth not the death of our Lord present to the unlearned, as well as to the learned, to the man of tender sensibility, as well as to the severe thinker! Hence in the Church this wealth reveals itself, according to the different capacities of individuals. But it is a character proper to sectarianism to protrude only one side of a mighty whole.

As regards the ecclesiastical discipline of this religious community—the exclusion of irreformable members from its bosom—the separation of the sexes into bands and choirs, even out of the times of divine service—the washing of feet, which is considered something more than a mere simple function—and other institutions, rites, and customs; the description of these appertains not to this place. But it is worthy of remark, that, in studying the peculiarities of this society, we are often reminded of many phenomena in the early history of the Church. The elections of superintendents by lots, recall to mind the ordeals of the middle age, far more at least than the election of Mathias by the Apostles. The prayers from midnight to midnight, or even during the whole night, once, and perhaps even still practised by them, remind us of the Akoimetæ; and the disgusting and obscene figures of speech which Zinzendorf indulged in, have a parallel in the practice of the Manicheans, who set forth their opinions by images, drawn even from the nuptial relations. It is worthy of remark also, that whereas the sects, which in other countries have grown out of Protestantism, took a far more spiritual course than the elder and orthodox Protestantism itself, the Herrnhutters, on the contrary, the only sect that in Germany remained permanently separated from the Lutheran Church, adopted a very material form, and even,

---

[1] The most singular observation of this kind has been recorded by Varnhagen, in his life of Zinzendorf, p. 283.

in the social relations, so subordinated the individual to the community, that all spontaneous movement was paralysed. The society selected even the bride for the bridegroom! In the Catholic Church, all are, in a like degree, subject to the truth, from which no one can nor may dare to depart. But, in all other respects, there is the desirable freedom restricted by nothing, save the measures which are absolutely necessary for the maintenance of truth and of Christian morals. But, among the Herrnhutters, it is precisely in the department of truth, that a delusive freedom is announced—a department where necessity alone must reign with unlimited sway.

§ LXXV—THE METHODISTS—RELIGIOUS STATE OF ENGLAND AT THE BEGINNING OF THE EIGHTEENTH CENTURY—PROFOUND DEGRADATION OF PUBLIC MORALS—THE METHODISTS WISH TO BRING ABOUT A REFORM—COMPARISON BETWEEN THE REFORMING EFFORTS OF CATHOLICS AND PROTESTANTS, AT SIMILAR EPOCHS

The religious fanaticism of the Grand Rebellion in England, pushed even to frenzy, and to the most atrocious crimes, was followed by a period of general spiritual laxity, which, passing through various grades of transition, sank at last into the most frivolous unbelief. England had seen a Parliament which furnished a proof that an excess of distempered religious feelings can be as deeply revolting to God and to reason, involving even the crime of regicide, as the absence of all religious principles. That Parliament had been succeeded by another, whose illegal convocation Cromwell dared to justify, by the pretended interference of an immediate Divine agency; a Parliament which, to the opening speech of the deceitful fanatic, bore testimony 'that, from the very tone in which it was spoken, it might be inferred, that the Holy Ghost worked within him;' and which opened its deliberations with religious solemnities of its own device, whereat the members confessed that 'they were filled with a peace and joyfulness, and had a sense of the presence of, and an inmost fellowship, with Jesus Christ, such as they had never before experienced.'[1] This period of fanaticism was

[1] Villemain, histoire de Cromwell d'après les mémoires du temps et les recueils Parlémentaires. Bruxelles, 1831, tom. ii, p. 6. Of Cromwell's opening speech to the Parliament of 1655, Villemain says:—' C'est une

followed by a generation, in whose higher circles the principles of a Shaftesbury ever gained ground; and a state of morals prevailed, which Fielding has depicted in his 'Tom Jones.' The populace, which had recruited the Cromwellian army with preachers, enthusiasts, seers, and prophets; that had rejected an established ministry, as totally unnecessary, and as destructive to evangelical freedom; lay now as deeply buried in the mire, as it had previously been exalted into a dizzy elevation. The Anglican clergy, on the one hand, despised, and, therefore, repelled by the blind and excited people, had, on the other hand, learned little from their times of persecution. All enthusiasm, life, activity, deep conviction of the magnitude of their calling, remained, for the most part, ever alien from their minds and habits; so that, on the whole, they looked with a stupid, indifferent eye on the ever-growing depravity.[1]

During the long period of her existence, the Catholic Church has, not unfrequently, had to suffer from like disorders in her clergy. But, it has ever pleased the Lord to raise up men, endued with sufficient courage and energy, to strike terror, and infuse new life, into a torpid priesthood, as well as into a degenerate people. According to the different character of different times, the mode of their rise and action was different; but, the conviction was universal, that mere laws and ordinances under such circumstances were fruitless; and only living, practical energy was capable of infusing new life into an age diseased. On the one hand, we see numerous individuals, at the instigation of the heads of the Church, who were acquainted with their powers of energetic persuasion, travel about as preachers in remote districts, awakening, among high and low, a sense of their misery, and stirring up the desire for deliverance from sin; or, on the other hand, we behold founders of mighty orders arise, whose members made it their duty to undertake the instruction

espèce de sermon, rempli du nom de Dieu, et de citations de l'Ecriture. Il exhorte les deputés à être fidèles avec les Saints, et les félicite d'être avoués par Jesus Christ, et d'avouer Jesus Christ. C'était une adresse assez remarquable d'éluder ainsi l'élection populaire par la vocation divine, et de flatter cette assemblée au nom de ce qu'il avait d'illégal et d'inusité dans sa réunion,' etc. The Appendix to Villemain's first volume (pp. 329-332) will give the reader full insight into Cromwell's artful character.

[1] See Dr Southey's Life of Wesley. In vol. i, p. 261 (German translation), he gives an interesting picture of the times, in order to account for the spread of Methodism. We find there little else to blame, except his ignorance of the history of the Catholic Church, and his vain attempt to exculpate the Anglican.

of the people, or their moral resuscitation (two very different things), or both these offices together, neglected, as they had been, by the ordinary pastors. Happy for the Church, if its episcopacy, misled by a partial feeling of gratitude for the services of such communities, in the time of their bloom and strength, had not prolonged their existence, when they were become morally dead, and were scarcely susceptible of renovation. As new orders sprang up, most of the elder ones were ordinarily forced to disappear.

The end, which several of the smaller Protestant sects, and particularly the Methodists, proposed to themselves, was nearly the same as that, which led to the origin of the monastic institutes adverted to. It appears even, not unworthy of attention, that, precisely at the time when the Pietists were rapidly gaining ground, and Zinzendorf, as well as the founder of Methodism, were flourishing, there arose in the Catholic Church a less celebrated indeed, but not less active, and (as regards the religious life of Italy), not less influential personage—I mean St Alphonsus Liguori, a native of the Neapolitan territory, who took compassion on the neglected people, and devoted himself to their religious and moral culture.[1] The imporatnt distinction, how-

---

[1] See Jeancard, Vie du Bienheureux Alphonse Liguori, évêque de Ste. Agathe de Goths, et fondateur de la Congrégation des Pretres Missionaires du très saint Redempteur. Louvain, 1829. Born in the year 1696, of an old and noble family, Alphonsus Liguori was ordained priest in 1726. Touched with the deepest compassion at the sight of the Lazzaroni, he united himself with other ecclesiastics, in order to devote his energies to the care of this neglected multitude. He founded pious congregations, which still subsist, and at present amount at Naples to the number of seventy-five, each consisting of one hundred and thirty to one hundred and fifty persons. (See p. 47-51.) During a residence in the country, he discovered the rude and utterly neglected condition of the peasantry. ' L'abandon presque général,' says Jeancard, ' dans lequel Alphonse eut alors occasion de reconnoitre que vivaient les habitans des campagnes, le toucha d'un sensible chagrin ; il lui en resta une impression profonde, dont la Providence, qui la lui avait menagée, se servait dans la suite pour l'exécution des grands desseins dont elle voulait que ce digne ouvrier évangélique fut l'instrument.'—P. 82. He now founded an Order, which was destined to meet these crying wants. The idea which led to its establishment, is this : it usually happens that the ordinary ministry of souls, though not conducted badly, is yet carried on after a dull and drowsy fashion. With the priest, the parishes too, slumber. Hence, from time to time, an extraordinary religious excitement and resuscitation are very desirable, which then the local clergy can keep up. This extraordinary religious excitement the missions, undertaken by the Redemptorists, are designed to produce. From the same views, an English Parliament once wished to do away entirely with all stationary clergymen. They were all to be constantly

ever, is not to be overlooked, that such Catholic institutes spring from the conviction, that the spirit of the Church only is to be infused into individuals, or to be carefully awakened and cherished ; while the above-named sects, in a greater or a less degree, ever assailed the fundamental doctrines of the religious community, out of which they arose, and strove to set the same aside. The origin of Protestantism itself is here felt ; for as the Reformers acted against the Catholic Church, so the community, founded by them, was, in turn, treated by its own children in the like manner. The want of reverence towards father and mother (for such is the Church to us in a spiritual relation), is transmitted from generation to generation ; and the wicked spirit, that first raised the son up against his father, goes out of the son as soon as he becomes a parent, and, in turn, goads his offspring on to wreak bloody vengeance upon him.

The man, upon whose heart the spiritual misery of the English people, at the commencement of the eighteenth century, had made a deep impression, was John Wesley, distinguished, beyond doubt, by great talents, classical acquirements, and, (what was still better), by a burning zeal for the kingdom of God. Rightly doth his biographer say, that, in other times and under other circumstances, he would have been the founder of a religious order, or a reforming pope. With his brother Charles, and some others—among whom the eloquent, gentle, kind-hearted, but in every respect far less gifted, Whitfield, soon became eminent—John Wesley, from the year 1729, lived at Oxford, as a student and assistant teacher, devoted to the most rigid ascetic exercises, and careless, as was right, about the remarks of the world. From the strict observance of a pious method of life, which evinced itself in the promotion of an interior spirit, the pious Association obtained, at first in a well-meant sense, and then by way of ridicule, the name of Methodists, which then became generally attached to them.[1]

changing residence in order that the parishes might receive new ones, and thus be kept in a constant state of life and excitement. This was another extreme.

[1] Southey, vol. i, p. 49. 'They were sometimes called, in ridicule, Sacramentarians, Bible-canters, Bible-moths, and even the Holy Club. A certain individual, who by his knowledge and religious feelings, rose superior to the multitude, observed, in reference to the *methodical*, regular mode of life to these despised men, that a new sect of *Methodists* had sprung up.' Allusion was here made to a medical school of that name.

§ LXXVI — PECULIAR DOCTRINES OF THE METHODISTS—MARKS OF DISTINCTION BETWEEN THEM AND THE HERRNHUTTERS—DIVISION OF THE SECT INTO WESLEYANS AND WHITFIELDITES

Still holding to the Thirty-nine Articles of the Anglican Church, and fully retaining its liturgy and constitution, the Methodists at first propagated through smaller circles, out of Oxford, only their ascetic practices, their fasts, their hours of prayer, their Bible-readings, and their frequent communions. Their mode of teaching at first differed from the ordinary one, only by the great stress they laid on moral perfection, which they held to be possible to the regenerated. The energy and enthusiasm of their sermons, delivered, as they were, from the pulpits, of the Anglican Church, attracted, in a very short time, crowds of auditors; so that, encouraged by success, they soon selected the open fields for the theatre of their exertions, and, indeed, principally such places as had been the scene of every sensual excess.

The acquaintance of John Wesley with some Herrnhutters, principally with David Nitschmann, whom, as a fellow-passenger on a voyage out to America, his brother Charles had, in the year 1735, learned to know and esteem; then his connection with Spangenberg—his visit to the Herrnhut communities in Germany and Holland, occasioned a new epoch in the history of his interior life. He became acquainted with the doctrine, that after the previous convulsive feelings, the clearest consciousness of grace before God, accompanied with a heavenly, inward peace, must suddenly arise in the soul; and this doctrine obtained, for a long time at least, his fullest conviction. Yet it was only some years after, he was favoured with such a moment, and (as he himself declares) on the 29th of May, 1739, in Aldersgate Street, London, at a quarter before nine o'clock. How, amid such violent, inward emotions, the time could be so accurately observed, the striking of the clock heard, or the watch attended to, is, indeed, marvellous to conceive! This genuine Lutheran doctrine was, thenceforward, embraced with peculiar ardour, was everywhere preached up, and never failed to be attended with sudden conversions. The impressive eloquence of Whitfield, especially, was very successful in bringing about such momentary changes of life, that were very frequently accompanied with convulsive fits, the natural results of an excessive excitement of the imagination, among a people, for the greater part, totally ignorant, and deeply deluded. Phenomena of this kind were called 'the outward signs of grace,' and were even held to be miracles.[1] The pulpits of the Established Church were refused to the enthusiasts and fanatics, as the Methodists were now called; and, thereby, the occasion was afforded to the latter, to constitute themselves into an independent body. Wesley now raised himself to the episcopal dignity, and ordained priests: a pretended Greek bishop, called Erasmus, then residing in England, was also solicited to impart holy orders. The separation from the Anglican Church was now formally proclaimed, and the most strenuous opposition commenced.[2]

The friendly relations between the Herrnhutters and the Methodists were also soon disturbed. A weighty cause for this, as Southey, justly observes, was, doubtless, to be looked for in the fact, that neither Zinzendorf nor Wesley were disposed to hold a subordinate position, one to the other; and two chiefs could not be honoured in the same community. But there also existed strong internal motives for this opposition, and they were the two following. In the first place, according to the Herrnhutters, all prayer, all Bible-reading, all benevolent actions prior to regeneration—that is to say, prior to the occurrence of the above described turning point in life, are not only fruitless, but even deadly poison; a doctrine, indeed, often put forth by Luther, but which Wesley rightly held to be untrue in itself, and productive of the most fatal consequences. An English Herrnhutter, or Moravian Brother, said that for twenty years he had faithfully observed all the ecclesiastical precepts, but had never found Christ. But hereupon having become disobedient, he immediately contracted as intimate an union with

---

[1] Southey relates, in vol. ii, p. 478 (German translation), that the teachers of a Methodist Latin school at Kingswood, would not permit boys of from seven to eight years of age to have any rest, 'until they had obtained a clear feeling of the pardoning love of God.' The poor children were driven to the verge of insanity; and, at last, the inward despairing contrition arose, and thereupon the full consciousness of Divine grace ensued! Wesley, who was himself present at this act of extreme folly at Kingswood, approved of and encouraged it. Of course, in a very short time, no trace of any such regeneration was any longer to be discerned: and hereupon Wesley testifies his astonishment in the following passage: 'I passed an hour among the children of Kingswood. Strange enough! What is become of the wonderful work of grace, which God, last September, wrought among the boys? It is gone! It is vanished!' etc. etc.

[2] Yet subsequently there were Methodists, again, who adhered to the Established Church.

Christ, as that which joins the arms to the body.[1] The second stumbling-block, in the way of union, was on the part of the Methodists. They taught, that, by the evangelical perfection which the regenerate possess, a moral condition is to be understood, wherein even all the irregular motions of concupiscence —every involuntary impulse of sensuality stimulating to evil, are utterly unknown. Against such a doctrine the Herrnhutters protested with reason; and Spangenberg replied as follows: ' So soon,' says he, ' as we are justified (or taken into favour by God), a new man awakes within us. But the old man abideth, even to the day of our death; and in this old man remaineth the old corrupt heart. But the heart of the new man is clean, and the new man is stronger than the old; so that, albeit corrupt Nature ever continues to struggle, it can never conquer, as long as we can retain our eyes fixed upon Christ.'[2] The form of this reply has undoubtedly much that is objectionable; for we are expressly required to put off the old man, and to put on the new one. The same idea is also expressed by the words, ' new birth,' ' new creation,' and the like; hence, we are to have not two hearts, but only one. But, on the other hand, this reply to the Methodists, is, in substance, perfectly correct; although the degrees in the life of the regenerate are not minutely traced, the setting forth whereof might have rendered possible a reconciliation between the Methodists and the Herrnhutters. That Spangenberg, too, should, in so unqualified a manner, have represented the new man, as being able to conquer, and the regenerated as really triumphant in the struggle against the incentives to grievous sin, proves the great revolution of opinion which Spener had brought about in the Lutheran Church, and wherein the Herrnhutters had also taken part. The controversy adverted to, divided, also, Wesley and Whitfield. The latter, like the Herrnhutters, combated the exaggerated views of the former respecting the perfection of the regenerate, and in this respect chose the better part; but, on another point, Wesley defended the truth against Whitfield. The latter was a partisan of the most rigid predestinarianism, which the former classed among the most abominable opinions, that had ever sprung up in a human head, and which could by no means be tolerated. In this way, not only did the mutual approximation between

[1] Southey, vol. i, p. 309. Compare an equally remarkable passage in p. 313.
[2] Southey, vol. i, p. 317. Zinzendorf's Exaggerations, p. 321.

the Herrnhutters and the Methodists fail of terminating in the desired union, but the one sect of Methodists broke into two, that opposed each other with bitter animosity.

These sectaries, however, by their mode of reasoning with each other, excite in the mind the most painful feelings. It is not without a sense of insuperable disgust that we see Spangenberg appeal against Wesley *to his own experience*, and that of the other Herrnhutters; whence, nothing else could be inferred, than that *they* had such particular experiences, but by no means, that such things must so be. The Wesleyans, in their turn, brought forward men and women, who appealed to *their own* experience, and thence proved that the regenerate no longer perceive, in themselves, the disorderly motions of sensuality, and are in every respect free from sin or even failing.[1] The most egotistical exaltation of oneself, to be a pattern to all, meets us here in its most repulsive, appalling form, against which the slightest spark of shame, we should think, would rise up, and kindle into a flame. Lastly, Whitfield, too, came forward with a shocking arrogance, denominated by him humility, and appealed to his inward experiences, in proof of the theory of absolute predestination.[2]

The prevalence of Antinomian principles, even among the Wesleyan Methodists, was of very important consequence. Wesley distinguished between justification and sanctification, although he allowed both to take place at the same moment. But, in despite of an asserted inward connection between the two things, the mere assumption, that Divine Grace could be annexed to any other principle in our spiritual life, than that whereby man manifests his obedience unto God, necessarily led to a contempt of the law; so that, even here also the doctrine that man is justified by faith only, betrays its essentially Antinomian character. The following account, coming, as it does, from a quarter perfectly friendly to the Methodists, cannot lie

[1] Southey, vol. i, p. 318.
[2] Southey, vol. i, p. 337. 'Pardon me,' wrote Whitfield to Wesley, 'that I exhort you in humility, no longer to resist, with this boldness, the doctrine of election since you yourself confess, that you have not the testimony of the Spirit within you, and are thus no competent judge in this matter. This living testimony, God several years ago granted to me; and I stand up for election. . . . Oh! I have never read a syllable of Calvin's writings; *my* doctrine I have from Christ and His apostles; God himself hath announced it to me; as it pleased him to send *me* out first, and to enlighten me first, so I hope He gives me now also the light.' The separation of the two occurred in the year 1740.

under the suspicion of misrepresentation. Fletcher—a very remarkable, active, and amiable disciple of Wesley—says, in his *Checks to Antinomianism:* ' Antinomian principles have spread like wildfire among our societies. Many persons, speaking in the most glorious manner of Christ, and of their interest in his complete salvation, have been found living in the grossest immoralities. How few of our societies, where cheating, extorting, or some other evil, hath not broke out, and given such shakes to the Ark of the Gospel, that, had not the Lord interposed, it must have been overset! I have seen them, who pass for believers, follow the strain of corrupt nature; and when they should have exclaimed against Antinomianism, I have heard *them cry out against the legality of their wicked hearts*, which, they said, *still suggested, that they were to do something for* their salvation' (that is to say, the voice of their conscience ever cried out against their immoral conduct; but they held that voice to be a temptation of Satan, who wished to derogate from the power of faith). ' How few of our celebrated pulpits,' continues Fletcher, ' where more has not been said *for* sin, than *against* it ! '

Fletcher cites the Methodist Hill in particular, as asserting, ' That even adultery and murder do not hurt the pleasant children, but rather work for their good: God sees no sin in believers, whatever sin they may commit. My sins may displease God, my person is always acceptable to Him. Though I should outsin Manasses, I should not be less a pleasant child, because God always views me in Christ. Hence, in the midst of adulteries, murders, and incests, He can address me with, " thou art all fair, my love, my undefiled; there is no spot in thee." It is a most pernicious error of the schoolmen, to distinguish sins according to the fact, not according to the person. Although I highly blame those who say, " let us sin, that grace may abound," yet adultery, incest, and murder, shall, upon the whole, make me holier on earth, and merrier in heaven ' ; that is to say, the more I need the pardoning grace of God, the stronger becomes my faith, the holier I become.[1]

John Wesley was extremely concerned at the spread of such opinions. He therefore summoned a conference, in the year 1770, which took into deliberation the principles hitherto professed by the Methodists, and justly acknowledged, that all the

[1] See Fletcher's Checks to Antinomianism, vol. ii, pp. 22, 200, 215 Works, vol. iii, p. 50; vol iv. p. 97. Compare Dr Milner's End of Religious Controversy, Letter vi.

evil entirely originated in the opinion, that Christ has abolished the moral law; that believers are thus not bound to its observance; and that Christian liberty dispenses them from keeping the Divine Commandments. The following remarks of Wesley, at the same conference, as to the merit of works, to which he was by necessity urged, are well entitled to attention. 'Take heed to your doctrine! We have leaned too much towards Calvinism. With regard to *man's faithfulness*, our Lord himself taught us to use the expression, and we ought never to be ashamed of it. 2. With regard to *working for life*, this also our Lord has expressly commanded us. Labour, ἐργάζεσθε, literally, *work for the meat that endureth to everlasting life*. 3. We have received it as a maxim that a man is to do nothing *in order to* justification. Nothing can be more false. Whoever desires to find favour with God, should *cease from evil, and learn to do well*. Whoever repents, should do *works meet for repentance*. And if this is not in order to find favour, what does he do them for? Is not this salvation by works? Not by the *merit* of works, but by works as a *condition*. What have we then been disputing about for these thirty years? I am afraid *about words*. As to *merit* itself, of which we have been so dreadfully afraid, we are rewarded *according to our works*, yea, *because of our works*. How does this differ from *for the sake of our works*? And how differs this from *secundum merita operum*, as our works deserve? Can you split this hair? I doubt I cannot.'[1] Wesley was evidently very near the truth. Thus much as to the peculiarities of the Methodists, so far as they fall within the scope of the present inquiry.

We shall conclude with observing that the Methodists have acquired great merit by the instruction, and by the religious and moral reform, of rude and deeply degraded classes of men; as, for instance, the colliers of Kingswood and the negro slaves in America. Their wild way of preaching, which is not entirely the result of *their* doctrines, has evinced its fitness for the obtuse intellect and feelings of auditors, who could only be roused to some sort of life by a violent method of terrifying the imagination. It is worthy of remark that on one occasion, to a minister, who declared it impossible to convert a drunkard, and who said, that at least no example of such a conversion had ever come to his knowledge, Wesley replied that in his society there were many converts of that kind. There are certain moral and

[1] Southey, vol. ii, p. 366.

intellectual capacities and conditions which only a certain style of preaching suits, and on which every other makes no impression. Hence it is to be considered a great misfortune when in any place all things are modelled after a uniform plan. This is to render the Spirit at once inaccessible and inoperative for many preachers, and for many descriptions of people; for the Spirit delighteth at times even in eccentric forms.

CHAPTER IV

THE DOCTRINE OF SWEDENBORG[1]

§ LXXVII—SOME PRELIMINARY HISTORICAL REMARKS

ONE of the most mysterious phenomena in history is the director of mines, Emanuel Swedenborg, the son of a Swedish bishop, and who departed this life in the year 1772. He was, on the one hand, distinguished for acuteness of intellect and for a wide range of knowledge—particularly in the mathematics and the natural sciences, which he cultivated with great success, as is evinced by many writings, highly prized in his day; and on the other hand, he was noted for his full conviction, that he held intercourse with the world of spirits, whereby he believed that he obtained information on all matters in anywise claiming the attention of the religious man. He imagined himself to be transported into heaven, and to be there favoured with oral instructions by the Deity and His angels, as to the Divine Essence—the emanation of the world from God—the purport of the Divine Revelations, and the consummation of the Church—the nature of heaven and hell, and many other things.

Professor von Görres has, in his work, entitled, ' Emanuel Swedenborg, his visions, and his relations to the Church,' and likewise in his Introduction to the writings of Henry Suso, newly edited by Diepenbrock, very convincingly proved that, from the very high character of this visionary, acknowledged by his contemporaries to be pure and blameless, the idea of intentional deceit on his part cannot be at all entertained, and that his ecstasies may best be explained by animal magnetism. As I am unacquainted with the nature of this latter science, I must abstain from offering any opinion on the matter; particularly as the object of this inquiry demands no elucidation of Swedenborg's psychological state. We are here merely engaged with his peculiar doctrinal and ecclesiastical views, and we will leave out of question his theosophistical, cosmogonic, and

---

[1] This article I inserted in the fourth number of the *Quarterly Review of Tübingen*, for the year 1830. It appears here with only a few alterations and additions.

other like theories; for these form no part of the tenets of faith constituting the New Church. These doctrines we shall now set forth, chiefly as they are stated in his last writing, published shortly prior to his death, and entitled, 'True Christian Religion, containing the Universal Theology of the New Church.'[1]

The relation wherein Swedenborg placed himself in regard to the new community he founded, is the first thing which claims our attention. He considers himself not only to be a restorer of primitive Christianity, and to be a divine envoy, in the same comprehensive sense as Luther; but he was under the firm conviction that he had, in the most solemn way, been commissioned by God in heaven, to introduce a new and imperishable era in the Church. The second coming of the Lord, which is promised in the Gospel, was to take place in him. Not that he held himself to be an incarnation of the Deity; on the contrary, he taught that God could no more appear in a human form, and that the foretold second advent of the Lord must be interpreted, as only the general and victorious establishment of His truth and love among men—as His manifestation in the word. This consummation of the Christian Church, he calls the new heaven and the new earth, the new celestial Jerusalem, whereof the Scripture speaketh.[2] This new kingdom of God on earth began, according to Swedenborg, on the 19th June, 1770—precisely the very day after the termination of the work, from which we have taken the above statements, and which was to go forth into all the world and win over the elect. For, as soon as, according to our authority, the last words of this book were written down, Jesus Christ sent his apostles throughout the whole spiritual world, to announce to the same the glad tidings, that henceforth he, whose kingdom hath no end, shall reign for ever and ever; and all this, in order that what stands written in Daniel (vii, 13, 14), and in Revelation (xi, 15), might be fulfilled. The aforesaid mission of the apostles was also foretold in Matthew (xxiv, 31).[3]

---

[1] 'True Christian Religion; containing the Universal Theology of the New Church.' By Emanuel Swedenborg, servant of the Lord Jesus Christ, Translated from the original Latin work, printed at Amsterdam, in the year 1771, vol. ii, 5th edition. London, 1819. The Latin original I have not been able to procure.

[2] Loc. cit. vol. ii, p. 502.

[3] Loc. cit. p. 547. 'After this work was finished, the Lord called together his twelve disciples, who followed him in the world; and the next

§ LXXVIII—PRACTICAL TENDENCY OF SWEDENBORG—HIS JUDGMENT ON THE REFORMERS, AND HIS ACCOUNT OF THEIR DESTINY IN THE NEXT LIFE

The doctrinal system of the Swedish prophet has by no means, as we should be disposed to believe from many of his speculations, a mainly theosophistic tendency, but, on the contrary, an eminently practical one. It sprang out of an opposition to the Protestant principle of justification, and the ulterior doctrines therewith connected; for Swedenborg also held this whole body of Lutheran and Calvinistic tenets to be subversive of morality, and extremely pernicious to practical Christianity. From this polemical spirit, all the virtues and the defects of this sectary are to be deduced. That such is really the case, is manifest from the very great and unwearied attention, which, in lengthened portions of his writings, he devoted to the consideration of the above-mentioned doctrines of the Reformers, as well as from the fact, that on every occasion, and when we least expect, he recurs to the subject, and sets forth the pernicious influence of these errors on moral and religious life. Swedenborg is wont to support his peculiar tenets by an appeal to the immediate teaching of the higher spirits, wherewith he had been favoured. Hence, to the several articles of doctrine he affixes an appendix, wherein he gives a description of these celestial conferences, often with great minuteness, and entering into many subordinate circumstances. But none of his doctrinal views does he uphold by such numerous visions, as that of his hostility to the Protestant doctrine of Justification.[1] Angels inform the visionary, that not faith alone, but together with the same, charity also justifies and saves. In proof of this, he relates the substance of a dialogue heard by him, and which occurred between some angels and several Protestants, who had arrived in the other world. To the most various questions the latter constantly replied, that for them faith must supply the place of all things, and hence they received the final sentence—

day he sent them throughout the whole spiritual world to preach the Gospel, that the Lord Jesus Christ reigneth, whose kingdom shall endure for ever and ever, according to the prophecy in Daniel, c. vii, 13, 14; and in the Revelations, c. xi, 15; and that they are blessed, who come to the marriage supper of the Lamb.'—Revel. xix. 9. This was done on the 19th day of June, in the year 1770.

[1] For instance, vol. i, p. 314, 317, 647, 649; vol. ii, p. 80, 92, 100, 169.

that they were like an artist, who could play but one tune, and therefore showed themselves unworthy of the society of superior spirits. In contrast with this, the following conversation between angels, and some other newcomers from this world, is given. 'What signifies faith? To believe what the Word of God teacheth. What is charity? To practise what that word teacheth. Hast thou believed only what thou hast read in the word, or hast thou acted also according to it? I have also acted according to it. My friend, come with us, and take up thy dwelling in the midst of us.' With Luther and Melancthon, also, Swedenborg, in his celestial travels, made acquaintance, and he gives us the following account of them. Luther (when Swedenborg visited the spiritual kingdom) was not in heaven, but in a sort of purgatory—an intermediate place, where attempts for his improvement were practised on him. When Luther, we are further told, arrived in the next world, he found himself in a locality which Swedenborg honoured with a visit, and which perfectly resembled his domicile in Wittenberg. With the greatest self-complacency, Luther collected around him all his disciples and adherents as they successively entered into the spiritual kingdom, and in proportion as they had evinced more zeal and penetration in defence of his doctrine, he honoured them with a seat nearer to himself, as their leader. With the greatest enthusiasm and firmest confidence, Luther was incessantly setting forth his doctrine of Justification by faith alone, before this circle, when he was suddenly disturbed by the information that that doctrine was thoroughly false, and that if he wished to enter into beatitude, he must utterly renounce it. For a long time he would not yield, until at last he began to doubt whether he were in the truth. Swedenborg, on his departure, received from an angel the consolatory assurance, that Luther seemed really to perceive his errors, and afforded every hope of a thorough amendment. Swedenborg assigns the following reasons for this. Before the beginning of his Reformation, Luther was member of a Church, which exalts charity above faith. Educated in this doctrine from infancy, he was so thoroughly imbued with it, that, though without a clear consciousness of it, it ever regulated his inward spiritual life; and, on this account, even after he had declared war against the Catholic Church, he was enabled to give such excellent instruction in respect to charity. His own doctrine of Justification by faith alone, on the other hand, so little set aside the conviction of his youthful days, that it belonged more to his external, than internal man.¹ It was otherwise with his disciples, who had been confirmed in his doctrine. As an illustrative instance, he recounts the destinies, which, after his death, befell Melancthon. He, too, was no inhabitant of heaven :— on the contrary, he must previously abandon his opinions respecting Justification by faith alone, before he can enter into eternal life. Philip Melancthon was seen by Swedenborg, as he was zealously engaged in the composition of a book; but he was unable to make any progress in his work. He was ever writing down the words : ' Faith alone saves ; ' when the words as often again disappeared. The reason of this phenomenon is, that they are utterly devoid of truth, and in the next world no error can endure. All attempts to bring this Reformer to a better way of thinking, have hitherto failed. On one occasion, indeed, he wrote down the proposition, ' Faith together with charity, justifies ; ' but, as that proposition did not spring out of the inmost feelings of his soul, but had only been taught him, it could be attended with no success. In vain we seek for an assurance, that Melancthon, too, could look forward to a termination of his painful state ; Calvin experiences a still worse fate, because he was always, as Swedenborg says, a sensual man ; and, besides the Lutheran doctrine of Justification, maintained also the revolting error of an absolute and eternal predestination of some to beatitude, and of others, to damnation. Swedenborg saw him on that account thrown down into a pit, filled with the most abominable spirits.

The Catholics, too, according to our seer, must, in many respects, change their convictions, before they can quit the immediate state in the next life and enter into a higher sphere. Strangely prejudiced, however, as Swedenborg is against the Catholic Church—ill as he is wont to speak of popes, bishops, and saints, he yet communicates the information that if Catholics perform works of Charity only in simplicity, and think more

¹ Vol. ii, p. 553. ' I was informed by the examining angels, that this chieftain of the Church is in a state of conversion, far before many others, who have confirmed themselves in the doctrine of Justification by faith alone ; and that, because in his youthful days, before he began his work of Reformation, he had received a strong tincture of the doctrine, which maintains the pre-eminence of charity : this was the reason why, both in his writings and sermons, he gave such excellent instruction in regard to charity ; and hence, it came to pass, that the faith of Justification with him, was implanted in his external natural man, but not rooted in his internal spiritual man.'

of God than of the pope, their transition to pure truth and thereby to eternal felicity is as easy, ' as it is to enter into a temple when the doors are thrown open, or into a palace, by passing between the sentinels who keep guard in the outer courts, when the king enjoins admission ; or, as it is to lift up the countenance and look toward heaven, when angelic voices are heard therein.' [1]

Evident, as it now is, that Swedenborg's reforming zeal was particularly directed against the errors in the Protestant doctrine of Justification : yet his attempts to undermine the same, were conducted with a destructive ignorance ; for he undermined withal, the very foundations of Christianity. Looking for the connection, wherein the notion of faith, as prevalent among his former fellow-religionists, stood with other dogmas, he fell into the error, that the doctrine of the Trinity was the basis of the former opinion, and hence he thought it incumbent upon him to subvert it. Secondly, he observes (and in this instance with perfect justice), that the Lutheran and Calvinistic doctrine of original sin forms the groundwork of the Protestant theory of Justification. He rejected, accordingly, the article of the fall of man in Adam ; and human freedom, which the Reformers had denied, he exalted to the highest pitch. Lastly, he assailed the doctrine of the vicarious death of Christ, in order to cut off the last link, which could connect the notion of Justification by faith alone with other dogmas. A nearer investigation of these three points will, therefore, be our next task.

§ LXXIX — SWEDENBORG'S DOCTRINE ON THE TRINITY — HIS MOTIVE FOR ASSAILING THAT OF THE CHURCH

The connection which Swedenborg established between the dogma of the Trinity, and the Protestant doctrine of Justification, attacked by him with such extreme vehemence, is as follows :—
' After men had discovered three Persons in the Deity, they were forced to allot to each a separate office. The first Person, accordingly, was regarded as the One which had been offended by mankind ; and the second, was considered to be the Mediator. By the establishment of so powerful a mediation, the Father has been involved in the necessity of bestowing unconditional

[1] Vol. ii, p. 578.

pardon; that is to say, without regard to moral worthiness, through faith in the merits of the Son alone.[1] In order to prevent the possibility of the very idea of such an intercession, the new Reformer turned against the doctrine of the Trinity itself, and, indeed, with that decided hostility, which, whenever a dogma is assailed from a practical point of view, is ever wont to arise. Swedenborg says the falsity of the doctrine of three Divine Persons, is clear from the fact, that the angels, with whom he held intercourse, declared to him, that it was impossible for them to designate in words that opinion; and that if anyone approached them, with the intention of giving utterance to it, he was compelled to turn away from them; and that if he really uttered the opinion, he was immediately transformed into a block in human shape. A man, who seriously, and with full conviction professes the Church doctrine of the Trinity, he compares in consequence to a statue with moveable limbs, in whose interior Satan lodges, and speaks by its artificial mouth. The old Christian faith in a Triune God, he, accordingly, places on a level with Atheism; for there is not in fact, he says, a Godhead with three Persons, or, as he expresses himself, there are not three Gods.[2]

He teaches, on his part, that in the Divinity, there is but one Person, the Jehovah God (probably the Jehovah Elohim) of the Old Testament. The same hath in Christ assumed human nature; and the energy of this God-man, that is ever working for our renovation, is the Holy Ghost, whom Swedenborg calls the Divine Truth, and the Divine Power, which worketh the regeneration, renovation, vivification, sanctification, and justification of man. Hence he adopts, indeed, a Trinity of Father, Son, and Holy Spirit; but in his language, he explains it to be three objects of one subject, or three attributes of one Divine

[1] Vol. i, p. 255. 'That this idea concerning redemption and concerning God, pervades the faith which prevails at this day throughout all Christendom, is an acknowledged truth; for that faith requires men to pray to God the Father, that He would remit their sins, for the sake of the cross and the blood of His Son, and to God the Son, that He would pray and intercede for them; and to God the Holy Ghost, that He would justify and sanctify them, etc.' Vol. ii, p. 319: 'Since a mental persuasion of three Gods has been the result, it was impossible for any other system of faith to be conceived or formed, but what was applicable to those three Persons, in their respective stations; as for instance, that God the Father ought to be approached, and implored to impute the righteousness of His Son, or to be merciful for the sake of His Son's suffering on the cross, etc.'

[2] Vol. i, p. 46 . . . p. 339. 'The present faith of the Church . . . is a faith in three Gods.'—Compare p. 45, p. 335.

person.[1] In other words, he conceives the Trinity to be three different manifestations of one and the same Divine Person, who, in the Father, reveals Himself as Creator of the world, in the Son as the Redeemer, and in the Spirit as the Sanctifier. He refers, moreover, the expression, 'Son of God,' to the humanity which Jehovah assumed, and then compares the Father, Son, and Holy Spirit, with the soul and body, and the operations of man, resulting from the union of the two.[2]

Of what is called Scriptural proof, Swedenborg has not the slightest notion. It is a mere accident, if in support of any one, even of his truest propositions, he assigns satisfactory exegetical grounds. He usually heaps passages upon passages, without much troubling himself about usage of speech, the context, parallel passages, or in general, the strict application of hermeneutic rules, although with these he was not unacquainted. It is so in the matter under discussion. Let anyone only read the texts he cites from Isaiah, Jeremiah, Osee, and the Psalms, in order to prove that it was not the Son begotten of the Father from all eternity, but He, whom he calls Jehovah, that became Man and Redeemer; and such a one must be convinced that, with a like course of reasoning, any conceivable fancy of the brain might be supported by Scripture.[3]

Swedenborg's total ignorance of ecclesiastical and dogmatic history, and his presumption, in despite of this ignorance, to allege their testimony in support of his opinion, are particularly afflicting. He ventures on the assertion, that from the time of the Apostles down to the Council of Nice, his notion of the Trinity was the prevailing belief of the Church, till of a sudden in this Council, the true belief was lost! It is remarkable, withal, that elsewhere he includes among the heretics of the first ages the Sabellians; although it is precisely among these that he might have found the most accurate resemblance to his own errors. In truth, had he known that in the second and third centuries the very few persons who professed principles similar to his own were menaced with exclusion from ecclesiastical communion if they refused to renounce their opinions, utterly

---

[1] Loc. cit. p. 327. 'Hence then it is evident, that there is a Divine Trinity, consisting of Father, Son, and Holy Spirit. But in what sense this Trinity is to be understood, whether as consisting of three Gods, who in essence, and consequently in name, are one God, or, as three objects of one subject, and thus that what are so named, are only the qualities, or attributes of one God; human reason, if left to itself, can by no means discern.'

[2] Loc. cit. p. 330.   [3] Loc. cit. p. 163.

repugnant as they were to the universal doctrine of the Church—had he been aware that Praxeas was forced to exhibit a document, wherein he revoked his error; that Beryllus, at the Synod of Bostra, was prevailed upon by the Arabian bishops, as well as by Origen, whom they had summoned to their aid, to take the same step; and that Sabellius excited such great agitation in the Egyptian Church, and became the object of such general abhorrence—how could he have had the hardihood to put forth the assertion, that down to the Council of Nice his opinion was the faith of the Church? If in modern days, many since the time of Souverän have asserted that the ante-Nicene period was addicted to the Arian heresy, a superficial study of authorities, at least, might have led to such a result, but Swedenborg's assertion presupposes the utter absence of all historical inquiry. Yet a book, in which such gross and palpable errors are found, he dares to extol as a work of such Divine contents, that on its completion the Apostles entered upon a mission through the whole spiritual world; that on its publication the very salvation of futurity depends; and that with it commences the new eternal Church!

In respect to the reasoning of Swedenborg, it bears occasionally, in its main features, a striking resemblance to that of the earlier Arians, especially Ætius and Eunomius, except only that these two Arian leaders evince far more acuteness and dexterity. It is equally certain that those Unitarians, in the earliest period of the Church, who bear most affinity to Swedenborg, knew how to allege, in behalf of their tenets, far more plausible and more ingenious Scriptural arguments, as we may perceive from the work of Tertullian against Praxeas, from the fragments of Hippolytus against Noetus, and of the pseudo-Athanasius against the followers of Sabellius. Whosoever, therefore, possesses but the slightest acquaintance with the writings of Athanasius, Hilary, Basil, Gregory Nazianzen, Gregory of Nyssa, and Augustine (who, with such decided superiority, have defended the doctrine of the Church against the earlier and the later Arians, as well as against the Sabellians), must consider with amazement the efforts of Swedenborg, who, with powers immeasurably inferior, attempted to undermine the belief in a dogma, which, in consequence of the defence it had met with on the part of these intellectual giants, had received even a stronger scientific demonstration.

§ LXXX—SWEDENBORG DENIES THE FALL OF MAN IN ADAM— CONTRADICTIONS IN HIS THEORY ON THIS MATTER

We pass now from the most striking peculiarity in Swedenborg's theology [1] to his Anthropology, where, however, it will be only his doctrine on human sinfulness, and particularly original sin, that will engage our attention. The latter, as we remarked above, he denies; but he falls into the most singular self-contradictions. The account in the Bible, respecting the fatal disobedience of our first parents, he explains as an allegory, and regards Adam and Eve, not as real personages, but only (to use his own words), as personifications of the primitive Church.[2] And he adds, that 'if this be well understood, the opinion hitherto received and cherished, that the sin of Adam is the cause of that evil, which is innate in man from his parents, will fall to the ground.'[3] Swedenborg doth not deny, however, that a propensity to sin is transmitted from parents to children; yet, he adds, that it is to be deduced from the parents only, as he says, 'hereditary evil, my friend, is derived solely from a man's parents;' and elsewhere, he even asserts, with great exaggeration, 'that man from his mother's womb is nothing but evil.'[4] If on the one hand, the propagation of an evil by descent be admitted, and on the other, the universality of the evil itself be not called in question, how can we stop at the parents of a child? The question necessarily arises; how then did the parents come by the evil? And if doubtless, it be answered, that they received the bad heritage from their parents, and these again from theirs, we shall certainly, at last, arrive at the first man, called in the Sacred Writings, Adam; and shall be obliged to confess, that the universal phenomenon hath a primary, and withal, universal cause, and, consequently, that sin in the human race, is only the development of sin in Adam. How can we therefore say, that children inherit from their parents a principle of sin, without recurring to the first man? By the allegorical explanation of the Scriptural narrative of the Fall, nothing is gained; for, in the first place, admitting

---

[1] The word *Theology* is here used by the author in a primitive sense, as denoting the doctrines that treat of the nature and the attributes of God.—*Trans.*

[2] Vol. ii, p. 110. 'By Adam and his wife is meant the most ancient Church, that existed on our earth.'

[3] Loc. cit. p. 196.   [4] Loc. cit. p. 195.

even such an explanation, still the sexual propagation of man must have certainly had a beginning ; and, as even according to Swedenborg, the development of sin keeps equal pace with the sexual propagation, we are thus compelled to recur to some beginning—to some first sinner, in whose fall the others were subsequently involved. In the second place, if with Swedenborg, we even take Adam to be a mere collective name, yet it must, at all events, be admitted, that the later race of men have inherited from the earlier a principle of sin, since its sexual transmission our seer does not pretend to deny. To Adam, accordingly, we must ever go back, whether by that name we understand an individual, or a generation of men. But whether Holy Writ teach the former or the latter, no one, who reveres St Paul's epistles as canonical, can for a moment doubt; for in Romans, c. v, 12-14, Adam is very clearly designated as he, by whose fall, the fall of all others has been determined; and he is expressly characterised as one person ($\delta\iota$ $\dot{\epsilon}\nu o\varsigma$ $\dot{\alpha}\nu\theta\rho\dot{\omega}\pi o\nu$). From whatever side, therefore, we contemplate Swedenborg's doctrine, it appears full of obscurities and inconsistencies.

The cause of these contradictions lies, as we said above, in his misguided opposition to the Lutheran doctrine, which regards original sin as a total depravation of man, wherein all free-will is utterly destroyed. Swedenborg now endeavouring, on the one hand, to save free-will, and to discover, in the personal abuse of freedom, the guiltiness of individuals ; and, on the other hand, withheld, by a deeper feeling, from regarding the individual as merely isolated, and possessing evidently a glimpse of the truth, that no man liveth for himself, nor severed from mankind, but is vitally involved in the destinies of the organic whole—Swedenborg, I say, fell into such like inconsistencies, that, in one moment, set up a proposition, and, in the next, subvert it again. He perceives, if we may so speak, an universal flood of sin ; but he dreads to examine it closely, and conceals from himself its source. We cannot, by this theory, understand how sin came into the world ; nor can Reason be satisfied with the doctrine of an evil being inherited by children from their parents, when that evil is considered as a mere accident, and is referred to no primary cause. Or does Swedenborg derive this evil propensity, transmitted by sexual propagation, from the original constitution of man ? Then, undoubtedly, the undeniable fact would not be represented as a mere accident ; but we find in Swedenborg's writings no syllable to justify such a supposition. On the other hand, Gustavus Knös, professor of the oriental languages at the University of Upsal, who died some years ago, and who was by no means a slavish follower of Swedenborg, has, in his soliloquies on God, man, and the world, set forth evil as something *necessarily* connected with the finite nature of man. But the question recurs, whether the other Swedenborgians will subscribe to so perverse a doctrine. Without this tenet, their theory of hereditary evil is the most incoherent rhapsody that can well be imagined.

§ LXXXI—INCARNATION OF THE DIVINITY—OBJECTS OF THE INCARNATION—RELATION BETWEEN GRACE AND FREE-WILL

We must now describe the objects of the Incarnation of the Divinity, as set forth by Swedenborg. The rejection of the great dogma of the atonement, through Christ's bloody sacrifice on the cross, so essentially Christian, so clearly founded in Scripture and Tradition, is intimately connected with the misapprehension of the origin of human sinfulness. The Scriptural opposition between the first and the second Adam, is devoid of sense in the system of Swedenborg. Having once abandoned the Scriptural point of view, he was no longer able to discover, in the condition of mankind, any adequate cause to account for the incarnation of the Logos. He, accordingly, in order to assign sufficient motives for this great event, looked for the causes beyond the sphere of humanity. The human mind is urged by an indomitable instinct, to consider itself an integral member of a great spiritual kingdom extending over all worlds, and to connect the prosperity of the divine institutions established on earth, as well as the disorders and concussions, which interrupt their normal development of life, with occurrences in the next world, and to regard them as a continuance of the vibrations of the latter. Of this fact, the Myths of the Indians, and the religious doctrines of the Parsees, will furnish us with primitive proofs. Christianity, also, points to a connection between the fall of the human race, and the precipitation of higher spirits into the abyss; and speaks, with the utmost clearness, of their continued efforts to maintain and extend the corruption, which, by their means, had been introduced upon our earth. On the other hand, it teaches the active interest, which the spirits, who remained faithful, as well as the souls, who here below died in Communion with Christ, and are glorified in the other world, exert for the diffusion of God's kingdom and its consolidation on earth. But in Scripture and the Tradition of the Church, all this is set forth in a very simple and general outline. But, in the hands of the fantastic Christian Gnostics, particularly the Valentinians, the simple doctrine of the Church was transformed into a vast and connected, but fanciful drama. They taught that the empire of Eons was disturbed by the passionate desire of Sophia—that the latter has been redeemed, and the former renovated; yet, that it was only through the re-establishment in Christ of all the Pneumatic natures, which, in consequence of the aforesaid perturbations, had been transferred into this temporal life, perfect harmony has been restored even in the world of spirits. In the Gnostic, as well as in the Manichean systems, the darker powers are brought into a more or less artificial, and often utterly inconceivable connection with occurrences in the Kingdom of Light, which has to be secured against their strenuous efforts to invade its frontiers, and to conquer it. Now a similar course Swedenborg pursues. He says, ' Redemption consisteth in reducing the hells into subjection, and bringing the heavens into an orderly arrangement, and renewing the Church on earth by this means; and there is no possible method by which the omnipotence of God could effect these purposes than by assuming the humanity; just as there is no possibility for a man to work without hands and arms; wherefore, the humanity is called in the word " the arm of Jehovah " ' [1]—Jos. xi, 10; xiii, 1.

Swedenborg gives the following more detailed description of the disorders, that, in consequence of the invasion of satanic powers, had broken out in the kingdom of happy spirits, and of the deliverance from this danger, by the mediation of the Redeemer. The Church terrestrial, says he, forms, together with the orders of Spirits in the next world, an organic whole, so that both may be compared to a man whose entire members suffer when one only is diseased. The members of God's community on earth, constitute, as it were, the feet of this great body and its thighs; the celestial spirits are the breast, the shoulders, and so forth. The continued growth of moral corruption here below has, accordingly, exerted the most disturbing influence on the whole spiritual world, and placed it in a condition similar

[1] Vol. i, p. 168.

to that of a man obliged to sit on a throne with a broken footstool. The dominion of Satan has, moreover, been so prodigiously enlarged by the very great immigrations from the earth, that his subjects dared to penetrate beyond the frontiers of the blessed, and even threatened to drag these down with them into the abyss. Now the incarnate God delivered the good spirits from this importunity of the demons, as He drove them back within the limits of hell ; for, as beasts of prey retreat into their dens ; as frogs dip under water when their enemies approach ; so fled the demons when the Lord came out against them.[1] We see how Swedenborg here abused the Apostolic doctrine of Christ's descent into hell.

He further observes, that, by this judicial action, by this rigid separation of the good from the wicked, the Lord hath exhibited himself as righteousness itself ; but by no means in rendering perfect obedience, during his earthly life in the room of men, and, in this way, becoming their righteousness. His obedience in general (he continues), and his crucifixion—the last temptation of the Lord in his humanity, especially, have merited for the latter only perfect glorification, that is to say, the perfect union with the Deity. No merit of Christ, therefore, according to Swedenborg, is imputable to man—no vicarious satisfaction can exist. In his opposition against Lutheran orthodoxy, which appeared to him to undermine all vital Christianity, he went so far as even to deny that evangelical dogma, from which the Christian derives an inexhaustible moral strength—that dogma, which hath conquered the world. In the great disfigurement, which that doctrine had, doubtless, experienced in the Confessions of the Lutherans, he could not discover the simple, great, and profound truth—he misapprehended, especially, its psychological importance, and even proceeded so far as to uphold a redemption, in part, at least, depending on the application of mere mechanical powers.[2]

[1] Vol. i, p. 237.
[2] Moehler says, that according to Swedenborg's theory, ' Redemption, in part at least, depended on the application of mere mechanical powers.' How so ? Because the Swedish prophet makes Redemption to consist chiefly in the reducing the hells into subjection, in delivering the blessed spirits from the importunity of demons, and in producing, by this means, the renovation of the Church. The Catholic Church, on the other hand, teaches that the object of the Redemption was the restoration of fallen man, his deliverance from sin, and especially original sin. This is the doctrine clearly inculcated in Holy Writ.—See Luke xix, 10 ; John iii, 14 ; Gal. iv, 4, 5 ; Heb. v, 1, seq. ; John i, 29 ; Rom. v, 12, 15, 21 ; vi, vii, ;

But here Swedenborg could not rest; and the mode wherein he still describes the necessity of the Incarnation of the Deity for the regeneration of mankind, is certainly entitled to the epithet of ingenious. His view is not new and was already unfolded by the Fathers of the Church, and the Schoolmen, and with greater clearness, copiousness, and precision, than by Swedenborg; but, as we have, however, no ground for supposing that he was acquainted with the labours of anterior times on this matter, we ought not to refuse him the merit of an original discovery. He says, without the condescension of God in Christ, faith were comparable to a look cast up towards the heavens, and would be utterly lost in the vague and the immeasurable; but through Christ it hath received its proper object, and is, thereby, become more definite. Some fathers of the Church express this thought in the following manner; to wit, that by his own powers, man is unable to rise above a mere void, meaningless unconscious yearning, and that it is only through revelation this yearning is satisfied, and is blessed with a true object. Swedenborg adds (in common with Cardinal Cusa, who has treated this subject in a most intellectual manner), that, in the relations of man to God, the human and the divine, the earthly and the heavenly must everywhere pervade each other; that by communion with the incarnate Deity, faith and love receive their higher and eternal sanction; but, that as God hath lived among us in a human shape, those virtues have thereby obtained their right foundation, and then only became our own: for the Divine in itself would remain inaccessible to us.[1] The one great work of Divine Mercy we may contemplate from many points of view; and the more comprehensive is our contemplation of that work, the deeper will be our reverence and adoration. But that so important principle in the Incarnation, which is so clearly expressed in Holy Writ, so distinctly asserted through all centuries of the Church, and plastically stamped, if I may so speak, on her public worship—the principle, that the death of the Lord is our life—ought never to be thrown into the background, much less absolutely rejected.

What the northern prophet says as to the duties required

---

1 Cor. xv, 21, 22. Thus according to Swedenborg, Redemption produced, as it were, a mere outward mechanical change in the moral condition of mankind; but, according to Catholic doctrine, it brought about a living, internal, and organic change.—*Trans.*

[1] Vol. i, p. 552.

on the part of man, in order that he should realise, within himself, the regeneration designed for him by God, has much resemblance to the doctrine of the Catholic Church. In Christ, says Swedenborg, Divine truth and love became manifest. Hence, man must approach unto Him, and receive the truth in faith, and walk according to the same in love; faith without love, or love without faith, has no value. Hence, respecting Justification, he has nearly the same idea, which the Catholic Church has ever inculcated; and in his opinion, it is essentially identical with the sanctification, and inward renovation, produced in faith in Christ.[1] But here the great distinction is to be observed, that he deduces not the forgiveness of sins from the merits of Christ. The relation between Grace and Freewill, is pretty well set forth; and in such a way, that he deviates not into Pelagianism, and scarcely into semi-Pelagianism—a circumstance, which from Swedenborg's opposition to Luther's doctrine, must really excite surprise.

But the historian of dogmas will be filled with astonishment when, on these matters, he turns his attention to Swedenborg's historical observations. In order to justify the connection, which he has assumed between the doctrine of the Trinity and that of the vicarious Satisfaction, he asserts that with the Council of Nice the Protestant doctrine of the imputation of Christ's merits has been introduced and maintained.[2] This assertion involves a twofold error; in the first place, because, before the aforesaid council, an imputation of Christ's merits can be proved to have been the universal belief of the Church; and secondly, because, from that council down to the sixteenth century, the peculiar Lutheran theory on this subject, with the exception of some slight and scattered traces, is not to be found. Luther himself never vaunted of this concurrence with the doctrine of the Church, subsequently to the Council of Nice. On the contrary, he made it his glory to have caught a deeper

---

[1] Vol. i, p. 283. 'By means of divine truth originating in good, that is, by means of faith originating in charity, man is reformed and regenerated, and also renewed, quickened, sanctified, justified; and, in proportion to this progress and growth in these graces, is purified from evils; in which purification consists the remission of sins.'

[2] Vol. iii, p. 317. 'That the faith, which is imputative of the merit and righteousness of Christ the Redeemer, first took its rise from the decrees in the Council of Nice, concerning three Divine Persons from eternity; which faith, from that time to the present, has been received by the whole Christian world.' P. 312: 'That imputation and the faith of the present Church, which alone is said to justify, are one thing.'

insight into the meaning of St Paul than all the fathers of the Church. Swedenborg need only have read the commentaries on St Paul's Epistles, which Chrysostom and Theodoret, in the Greek Church, and Ambrosiaster and Jerome, in the Latin, have composed, to see the fallacy of his strange conceit. As to the theologians of the middle age, every page of their writings will refute the assertion of Swedenborg. How then would the opposition between Catholics and Protestants be explicable, if, on the article of belief in question, the former had ever put forth the same doctrine as the latter? Swedenborg does not even adduce a single historical testimony in support of his assertion, and contents himself with mere round assurances, without reflecting that, in matters so important, proofs, and not mere assurances are required. Swedenborg was not aware that we can believe in an imputation of the merits of Christ, without being in the least forced to adopt the peculiar theories of the Reformers of Wittenberg and of Geneva. In other places, where he treats of the separation of Protestants from the Catholic Church, and of their peculiar doctrines in consequence of that schism, he even contradicts himself—forgets, at all events, the broad distinction, which, according to what has been already recounted, he had laid down between Catholics and Protestants as to their capability for embracing in the next world the entire truth, and precisely in regard to the article of Justification.

Upon his doctrine of Free-will also, Swedenborg did not a little pique himself, under the supposition that it was utterly unknown to the whole Christian Church; and his English editor, in all seriousness, points to this notion as to something quite new and unheard of. Truly, if we attend only to the Formulary of Concord, from which Swedenborg makes long extracts, as well as to the writings of Calvin, we should be justified in believing that the doctrine of Free-will is nowhere any longer known. But how much soever Swedenborg descants on Freewill, he gives amid all his images no very clear notion of it, although it is not to be doubted that this idea floated before his mind.[1]

[1] Vol. i, pp. 108-156.

§ LXXXII—SWEDENBORG'S DOCTRINE RELATIVE TO THE SACRAMENTS

Swedenborg's doctrine on the Sacraments has, independently of its peculiar language, nothing very striking, although he thinks the contrary, and opines, that without knowledge of the spiritual sense, that is to say, the mystico-allegorical meaning, and especially of the correspondences between heaven and earth, nothing solid can be adduced even on this article of belief. Moreover, the two sacraments, Baptism and the Lord's Supper (for more he doth not acknowledge), are, in his opinion, very precious, and he strives with all his powers to promote a lively reverence for, and worthy reception of the same. Of baptism, he teaches that through three stages, it is designed to work an inward purification. In the first place, it conducts into the Christian Church; secondly, by its means the Christian is brought to a knowledge and recognition of the Saviour and Redeemer; and thirdly, in it man is born again through the Lord. But these three objects of baptism are in themselves one and the same, and are in the same relation one to the other, as cause and effect and the medium between the two.[1]

But the knowledge of celestial correspondences, above all, serves to initiate Christians into the essence of the holy communion. Flesh and bread are the earthly signs of the Divine love and goodness (holiness); blood and wine the emblem of God's truth and wisdom. Eating is like to appropriation. But now, flesh and bread in the holy communion are the Lord himself, considered in the character of love and goodness. Blood and wine, in like manner, the Lord himself in His truth and wisdom. There accordingly are, as Swedenborg expresses himself, three principles, which, in this sacrament especially, are interwoven into each other—the Lord, his Divine goodness, and his Divine truth; and consequently, it is evident, that in the Lord's Supper, all the blessings of heaven and the Church are, in an especial manner, included and imparted; for, in these three principles, which constitute the universal, all particulars are contained. Thus God, and with Him faith and charity, are the gifts vouchsafed to man in the participation of this sacrament.[2]

[1] Vol. ii, p. 273.
[2] Loc. cit. p. 389. 'In a like manner as a first cause, a middle cause, which is the efficient, and ultimate cause, which is the effect, and the end, for the sake of which the former causes were produced.'

That the glorified humanity is here present, together with the Divinity, Swedenborg, in a special section, very clearly shows, and observes, at the same time, that the Eucharist is a spiritual food, for the very reason that the glorified humanity is there proffered to us.

In order to prove the possibility of such a participation, Swedenborg observes: every sound soul has the faculty to receive from the Lord wisdom, that is to say, truths, and to augment the same to all eternity; in like manner to receive charity, and to increase perpetually in the same. But now, the Lord is charity and wisdom itself; consequently man is able to unite himself to him. It is here evident, that wisdom and charity are regarded by Swedenborg as something substantial—as the subtlest emanations from the Deity, and the Deity itself: in the same way, as in the other world, he beheld God as a sun, from which alone light and heat are emitted, that is to say, wisdom and charity. To avoid probably pantheistic views, the prophet adds, the Divinity itself cannot be *identified*, but only *united* with man; in the same manner as the sun is not conjoined with the eye, nor the air with the ear, but are only adjoined to those organs, in order to render the senses of seeing and of hearing possible.[1]

In the same way, continues Swedenborg, as baptism introduces us into the Church, the holy communion introduces us into heaven. For the Lord and Saviour, who is present in the sacrament, has necessarily heaven also in his train, and opens it to those who worthily partake of the divine repast. It is otherwise with the unworthy communicant. To the worthy, God is, in this feast, inwardly and outwardly present—inwardly, by His love and truth; outwardly, by His omnipresence, which determines the existence of all things. In the wicked is found the mere general omnipresence of God, without the former. To the mere carnal and mere natural men, who withdraw from obedience to God, and only know and speak of the Divine Truth, but never practise it, the Lord, in despite of existence, reveals not heaven. One might feel disposed to conclude from this, that Swedenborg agrees with Calvin, when he teaches, that to the

---

[1] Loc. cit. p. 445. 'Still, however, as man is a finite being, the Lord, divinity itself, cannot be *conjoined* with him, but *adjoined*.' At p. 70, the author says, that '*conjoined*,' signifies an unity like that of the fruit with the tree, but '*adjoined*,' a more external union, as when fruits are bound to tree.'

reprobate, the glorified body of the Lord is not imparted. Swedenborg, however, is utterly opposed to the Genevan Reformer, for according to the latter, the food of eternal life is not imparted to him, who is predestined to eternal death; but, according to the former, it is only not received by the unworthy communicant, that is to say, not imbibed in the inmost life of the spirit, although proffered to him.[1] What Swedenborg teaches, besides, respecting the Eucharist; to wit, that it worketh an union with the Deity, and is the stamp of the sons of God, and so forth, is only a further consequence of what has been hitherto stated. Moreover, in his exposition of the doctrine of the Eucharist, Swedenborg entirely passes over the relation, which the same bears to the death of our Lord, and to the forgiveness of sins, clearly as that relation is pointed out in Holy Writ. The motives, for this his omission, are to be sought for in the above-mentioned view, which he takes of Christ's passion and death.

§ LXXXIII—SWEDENBORG'S REVELATIONS FROM THE OTHER WORLD

With the information which Swedenborg brought from the next world, respecting its state and its relations, and which he has recorded in his writings, we wish not to amuse our readers; though to many, undoubtedly, the investigation of this subject would be, precisely, the most attractive. We shall only communicate so much as appears necessary, partly to complete our knowledge of the Swedenborgian doctrines, and partly to explain much that has been hitherto stated. When souls quit the visible world, they go to a locality hovering between heaven and hell; and feeling themselves by degrees irresistibly attracted to their kindred spirits, they gradually advance into heaven or hell.

The husband, with haste seeks his spouse, and *vice versa;* and in general, each one the companions of his earthly sufferings and joys, among whom alone he finds himself at home. In these descriptions, Swedenborg indisputably displays a very subtle psychology. Those, moreover, who are neither ripe for heaven, nor find joy in hell, are instructed and educated, until, by the use of their freedom, they attain unto pure truth and charity, whereby heaven becomes accessible to them. The

[1] Loc. cit. p. 396.

members of every religion, confession, and sect, receive teachers of their own party, and the Heathen, Jew, and Mohammedan are not excluded from this school. But if they resist all attempts for their improvement or perfection, they are then swallowed up by hell. We do not see why Swedenborg should have manifested such a decided hostility against the Catholic doctrine of purgatory although, undoubtedly, between the latter and the intermediate place of the Swedenborgians, important differences are to be found.

The relations in the next world, according to the depositions of our eye-witness, perfectly resemble those on earth. There also, are houses, and palaces, with rooms and furniture; there, too, mountains and valleys, rivers and lakes. Time, also, and a very substantial space, rule the world of spirits. Nations and individuals retain their peculiarities; hence, in the next world, the Dutch still carry on commerce. The only difference is, that all things are in a more glorified and spiritual shape, than here below, for, the gross body of the present life is thrown off; and even the resurrection of the flesh, according to Swedenborg, does not take place. The new body, however, retains quite the form of the old one, so that many, who pass into the next life, perceive not that they no longer possess their former corporeal integument.

In 1757, the last judgment was held, and Swedenborg, as an amazed spectator, assisted at it. The same is also held from time to time. Even the damned could be delivered, if they wished. Swedenborg saw one of them, who had once been a highway-robber, and had been guilty of adultery, and who, somehow or other, had strayed among the angels. These endeavoured to work on his understanding, and he really understood what they said and wished. But, on their demanding him to love the truth, which he recognised, he replied he would not, and returned to hell. The phenomenon Swedenborg makes use of, in order to prove Freewill. Here the penetrative man evinces his sagacity; for, certainly, there are reprobates, who will not be happy, and therefore cannot be so. This narrative agrees very well with the other doctrines of Swedenborg, that God is perpetually present with man, so long as he lives, and exerts a constant influence over him to procure his conversion; but that those who die in the wickedness of their heart, are irreformable, because the interiors of their minds, says Swedenborg, are fixed and determined.'

§ LXXXIV—BIBLICAL CANON OF SWEDENBORG—ALLEGORICO-MYSTICAL EXEGESIS

With Swedenborg's peculiar views on Holy Writ, we must now make our readers acquainted.[1] On perusing his writings, we are soon very painfully surprised at the fact, that he makes no doctrinal use of St Paul's epistles. At least, we cannot recall to our recollection that we have ever found any notice taken of them, even on those points where such would be indispensable; as in the articles of Justification, and of Faith, and of its relation to Works. This fact we, at last, found cleared up, 'by the chief articles of faith of the New Church,' subscription to which is required, as a condition, from all those who desire to enter into the community founded by Swedenborg. In these 'chief articles,' we find the Holy Scriptures of the Old and New Testament enumerated; but among the component parts of the latter, the four Gospels and the Apocalypse are alone reckoned.[2] The influence which Swedenborg's dogmatic system exerted on the framing of his Biblical Canon, no one can deny. Hence, before we could speak of the latter, it was necessary to set forth his doctrines. The rejection of the dogmas of original sin, of the vicarious satisfaction of Christ, of the resurrection of the flesh, and so forth, led him to expunge, from the catalogue of the sacred writings, the Epistles of St Paul, the Acts of the Apostles, in short, everything which, even by the most forced interpretation, could not be made to harmonise with his own errors. In the Acts of the Apostles, especially, the account of the real descent of the Paraclete, who was to lead the Church into all truth, and to abide with her for ever, must, undoubtedly, have been a great stumbling block in his way. In fact, the Swedenborgians endeavour to represent their master as him, who has at last communicated what originally was inaccessible, or unintelligible, to believers. I have discovered at least, that Swedenborg's disciples, in proof of the divine mission of their teacher, have appealed to those promises of a Paraclete, recorded in St John's Gospel. When, moreover, the apostle saith: 'No eye hath seen, no ear hath heard, nor hath it entered into the heart of man to conceive, what God hath prepared for those

[1] Vol. i, pp. 373-460.
[2] 'Divine Revelations made known by Swedenborg, translated into German by Emanuel Tafels.' Vol. ii. Tübingen, 1824.

who love Him;' he must certainly have appeared not very entitled to credence, in the estimation of one, who, in his own person, had observed the joys of the blessed and in his writings had lifted up, for the edification of mankind, the veil which the apostle had fain have thrown over the realms of eternity. When Swedenborg rejected, also, the Epistle of St James, and other scriptures, as uncanonical, he was driven, for consistency's sake, to this step.

If, together with this arbitrary mode of dealing with the canon, we consider the following hermeneutical principles of Swedenborg, we shall not be surprised, that the most fantastic doctrines should have been propounded by him as Christian. Swedenborg says, that, in the literal sense of Holy Writ, the Divine truth is contained in all its plenitude, holiness and power; and to the demonstration of this truth, he devotes a special treatise. Yet he supposes a mystical sense, which he calls the spiritual one, to be concealed in the letter of Scripture; so that the entire truth is comprised in its every word, nay, often in its every syllable! This doctrine Swedenborg establishes in the closest connection with those correspondences, that, according to him, exist between heaven and earth, and he gives several interpretations of texts from the Apocalypse, whereby he endeavours to render his view more evident. These theories, considered in themselves, are not so very obnoxious to censure; they, on the contrary, are based on a great truth, and, to a certain extent, are justified by those relations, which, according to the most explicit declarations in the New Testament, exist between the Scriptures of the Old and of the New Covenant. To this mode of interpretation, as an exercise for mystical acuteness (if we dare use such an expression), we even cannot entirely deny all value. It is, likewise, a well-known fact, that, according to the character of different ages, and the peculiarities of individual men, it has had great influence in awakening religious feelings, and, at many periods, has guarded Holy Writ against the contempt of arrogant, carnal-minded men, or against the neglect of men, pious indeed, but utterly unacquainted with the laws of a grammatical and historical, yet spiritual, exegesis. But if such a mode of interpretation, when not practised by inspired writers, opens, under all circumstances, boundless scope to the play of an irregular fancy, or to the effusions of mere individual feeling, it is sure to lead to the grossest errors, when it is made the medium for discovering, and establishing articles of doctrine. Dogmas, which by the most unhistorical method, men had perhaps stumbled on, may, by self-delusion and a small portion of wit, be found stated in every text of Scripture. This was now actually the case with Swedenborg, who could discover the strangest things in the Bible. Lastly, the presumptuous ignorance, with which he judges the history of the allegorico-mystical interpretation of Scripture, appears highly censurable. The higher the estimation is, in which he holds the latter, the greater the earnestness wherewith he asserts, that it was all but unknown, as well among the Jews, on account of their carnal sense, as among the Christians of the first three centuries, on account of their too great simplicity, and among those of subsequent ages, from the general corruption. He insists, that it was only by a special revelation he was made attentive to it, or at all events favoured with the true key for its right use. But what is his distinction between the various senses of Holy Writ, other than the Sod (body), the Derusch (soul), and the Phaschüth (spirit) of the Cabala—senses which themselves correspond to the $\sigma\hat{\omega}\mu\alpha$, the $\psi\upsilon\chi\acute{\eta}$, and the $\pi\nu\epsilon\hat{\upsilon}\mu\alpha$, of Philo ?[1] And wherein do the Swedenborgian correspondences between heaven and earth so essentially differ from the celestial and terrestrial Jerusalem (the $\check{\alpha}\nu\omega$ and the $\kappa\acute{\alpha}\tau\omega$ $\text{'}I\epsilon\rho o\upsilon\sigma\alpha\lambda\grave{\eta}\mu$) the carnal and the spiritual Israel (the $\text{'}I\sigma\rho\alpha\grave{\eta}\lambda$ $\sigma\alpha\rho\kappa\iota\kappa\acute{o}\varsigma$ and $\pi\nu\epsilon\upsilon\mu\alpha\tau\iota\kappa\acute{o}\varsigma$), with which the same Philo has made us acquainted? And what shall we say to the astounding assertion that in the first centuries of the Church, the allegorico-mystical exegesis was unknown ! Just as if Basilides Valentinus and Origen had lived in the sixth century ! That Swedenborg should have possessed any acquaintance with the writings of Gregory the Great, of Alcuin, of Richard, of St Victor, or with the description of the three senses given by Thomas Aquinas and others, it would be too much to require of him ; nor should we have even noticed the contradictions, into which he has fallen with well-known historical facts, had he not vaunted himself as an extraordinary divine envoy, and represented his book as one written under God's especial guidance.

Swedenborg shows great pettiness, and even childishness, in making a sort of fire-work out of Holy Writ. In the spiritual world, says he, where the Bible is preserved in holy chests, in

[1] Vol. i, p. 378. 'The spiritual sense doth not appear in the literal sense, being within it, as the soul is in the body ; or as the thought of the understanding is in the eye, or as the affection of love is in the countenance.'

the sanctuary of the Temple, it is regarded with respect by the angels; and it is as radiant as a great star, and at times, like the sun, and its glimmering splendour forms the most magnificent rainbow! If anyone, with his hands or clothes, touch the Bible, he is immediately environed with a brilliant fire, and he appears as if standing in the midst of a star bathed in light! This, adds Swedenborg, he has often seen and admired! But if anyone, entangled in errors, looks into the sacred coffer, then his eyes are overclouded with deep darkness; and if he venture to touch the Word itself, an explosion immediately ensues, which flings him 'into a corner of the room.'[1] Had these descriptions been mere allegorical representations, to point out to sensual men the effulgence of divine light, wherewith a soul is filled, that with feelings hallowed to God draws from Holy Writ life and nurture; and, on the other hand, the profound darkness and appalling night that encompass those, who pervert Scripture to the confirmation of the fancies of their own brain; we should then have commended the aptness of such illustrations. But such is not Swedenborg's meaning; he here designs to state positive facts. For our part, we here discern an idolatry manifested to the dead word of Scripture, which exceeds all that the slavishness to the mere letter has ever exhibited, and has perhaps no parallel in history, except in the controversy among Mohammedans, whether the Koran be created or uncreated. Yet even the rational Moslem will reply, that the ideas, indeed, of the sacred book are eternal, but by no means the form wherein they are set forth.

§ LXXXV—SWEDENBORG'S PLACE IN HISTORY

To form a more comprehensive knowledge of Swedenborgianism, it is necessary to point out more fully the idea which its author entertained of his own historical importance. He divides the history of the world into so many great periods, which he denominates Churches; to wit, the Antediluvian; the Asiatico-African, which attained its term by the introduction of idolatry; the Mosaic; and lastly, the Christian Church. In the latter, he again distinguishes four Churches, the Ante-Nicene, the Greek, the Roman Catholic and the Protestant. The last-named, also, like the preceding Churches, has already reached

[1] Loc. cit. p. 396.

its end: hence, with the New Community, the times revert to the origin of the Church—to primitive Christianity, whose principles can henceforth never more be forsaken. So far Swedenborg, who, as is clear from this, formed no slight estimate of his own historical importance. Let us first take into consideration the view of universal history, prior to Christ, as set forth by him. He says, the four great periods of the world follow each other, according to the type of the four seasons of the year, and the four times of the day; and the same regularity, which, on a small scale, is observed in this succession of times, exists there on a larger scale. On the impropriety of making Christianity fall in with the winter and the night, we will not lay any particular stress, although Christianity expressly declares itself to be the never-setting noonday of ages. But what Christian can tolerate the subordinate position which is assigned to Christ! Instead of representing him, as the great centrepoint of the world's history, he is made to begin a period merely co-ordinate with the other epochs of the world! This would have been, at least, no error of the understanding, had Swedenborg regarded Christ as a mere man; but it becomes the greatest of errors since Christ he considers to be the incarnate God. If the Deity manifests Himself in the flesh, so thereby, it is hoped, an epoch is introduced, to which nothing can be adjoined, but all things should be made subordinate. From this point of view alone Swedenborg might have discerned the essential defects in his system.

The cause of this perverse construction of human history must be looked for in the fact, that Swedenborg would not acknowledge a general fall of the human race, and, in reality, was at a loss how to explain the very evident fact of a radical sinfulness in man. Had Swedenborg deeply considered the scriptural opposition between the first and the second Adam, instead of occupying himself with allegories in respect to the first; had he, in the fall of Adam, deplored with a pious simplicity, at least, the fall of all mankind, though he had been incapable of comprehending the speculative reasons of this fact; then the whole period from Adam to Christ, would have appeared to him as the period of the development of the sinful principle and of an apostasy from God; but, on the other hand, he would have regarded Christ as the great turning-point in history, with whom commenced the unfolding of the principle of sanctification, and of a return to the Deity. This one great period he might then have again, in some manner, subdivided; but should never have placed the period from Adam to Noah, that from Noah to Moses (or what he calls the Asiatico-African Church), and the period from Moses to Christ, on the same level with the Christian epoch. Such a parallel was only possible through a total misapprehension of the Christian view of the moral world. The texts in Romans (c. v, 14-21; xi, 32), and in Galatians (c. iii, 22), might alone have sufficed to teach him the right and the true view, had he not, on that very account, struck out St Paul's Epistles from the catalogue of canonical Scriptures, precisely because they offer so clear a contradiction to his whole conception of religious History.

His main point of view being thus distorted, Swedenborg can give no satisfactory explanation of any great phenomenon in religious history; on the contrary, in his system all is dismembered, unintelligible, and incoherent. The idolatry of Nature he deduces from the accidental circumstance, that the correspondences between the material and the spiritual world had been forgotten. The revelation, which as Swedenborg positively asserts, was made to Enoch, and transmitted to the following generations (namely, that all objects in the lower world had their correlatives in the higher), and the true knowledge of these mutual relations in special, defined cases, were, in the course of ages, according to our prophet, effaced from the memory of nations; earthly things were regarded without connection with the things corresponding to them above; and the veneration, which was due to the latter, was paid to the former. This view of Swedenborg's has much resemblance to the more common, but equally superficial, notion, that out of the confusion of the symbol with the object represented by it, idolatry arose. But the question must ever recur, how could those relations adverted to be forgotten, and where must we look for the cause of this oblivion? Wherefore, also, must the faith in the one, true God have been at the same time abandoned? The consciousness of God was certainly not essentially connected with the knowledge of such correspondences between heavenly and earthly things, since Enoch was the first to be instructed in them; and yet before him, certainly, men had also known the true God. Had Swedenborg acknowledged a general darkening of the human mind through sin, a corruption transmitted from Adam, and with ever-increasing intensity, contaminating all generations, he would not have sought to account for the idolatry of Nature, from such mere external causes. He would have understood, that the soul severed from God by sin, necessarily fell under the dominion of Nature, and chose those powers for the object of its worship, with whom it felt an especial affinity, and by whom it was invincibly attracted. The loss of the essential, internal, and universal correspondences between God and man, led to the ignorance of those external and particular correspondences between the inferior and the higher order of the world. The separation of the soul from God, and its concentration within itself, first produced this conception of Nature, as disconnected from all higher relations.

Let us, once more, recall to mind one of the proofs attempted by Swedenborg, in support of the necessity of the Incarnation of the Deity, in order to bring back men to Himself; for it is only here that proof can be perfectly appreciated. He says, the faith of man, considered in itself, may be compared to a look cast up vaguely towards the sky, but, through the Incarnation, is the same circumscribed, and directed to a definite object. If, hereby, the necessity of an Incarnation of the Divinity be rendered perfectly conceivable; yet this argument offers no reason, wherefore the Divine Word should have become flesh precisely at the commencement of the fourth period of the world. Swedenborg might, just as well, have introduced this Theophany immediately after the creation of the first man. *Nay, he was forced to do this*, unless all the aberrations of the ages prior to Christianity—unless all Heathenism itself be regarded as perfectly guiltless. Did the first men, unfavoured as they were with the descent of the Son of God, cast a less vague look up to Heaven, than those of later times? For this very reason, Swedenborg should have placed the advent of Christ at the very origin of History; and thus the first, and not the fourth period of the world should have begun with him. Had he, on the other hand, kept strictly in view the teaching of the Bible, as to the end of the mission of the Son of God, then he would have understood the epoch of his coming. The whole drama of History as set forth by our prophet, appears without a plan; the members of the great historical organism appear to hang, as if by accident, together, and to mingle in blind confusion. Now we can see wherefore Swedenborg himself seemed to have a sense of the unsatisfactoriness of the cause assigned by him, for the incarnation of the Deity at the particular period wherein it occurred; and wherefore he sought to aid his meagre representation, by a fantastic device as to the relation between heaven and hell. He saw himself forced to the adoption of this device, in order to account by the relations of the next life, for the incarnation of the Deity, which had no foundation in this world's history—a device whereby the error of his whole historical construction is not in the least degree obviated.

When we now come to the Christian period, what a singular view of its history, what an astonishing spectacle, presents itself here! The Church also, as we have already observed, is divided into a cycle of four parts; and yet, says Swedenborg, with the Council of Nice begins the great apostasy from Christian truth, which lasts down to his own time! But the notion of apostasy implies the idea of perversity and disorder. How then would it be possible to find a regular development in the four Christian Churches, the three last members whereof are to be, in the same relation to the first, as summer, autumn, and winter to the spring; or even as youth, manhood, and old age, to infancy! Where a well-ordered development is observed, where a regular transition, from one state to another, is manifest, a rejection of the original vital principle is not conceivable. Where, on the other hand, this is rejected, as Swedenborg accuses the whole Church subsequent to the Council of Nice, of casting off such a principle, there a regular development is not possible. Even our finisher of the Church had a sense of the incoherence of his historical constructions. On this account he endeavours to excuse, in some manner, the apostasy, and speaks of the beneficial variety of religious differences; that mutually enlighten one another, and even lets the remark escape him, that he had been informed, that those Churches, which are in different goods and truths, if only their goods have relation to the love of the Lord, and their truths to faith in him, are like so many precious jewels in a king's crown.'[1] If, hereby, a kind of necessity in the marked out succession of Churches, is acknowledged, so no one, who holds the maxim, that, above all things, a writer should never contradict himself, would expect Swedenborg to designate all the Christian ages, that have elapsed since the Council of Nice, ' as the very night '; ' as the abomination of desolation '; ' as that Church, wherein nothing spiritual is left remaining '; [2]

[1] Loc. cit. p. 515.
[2] Loc. cit. p. 512. 'That the last time of the Christian Church is the very night in which the former Churches have sat, is plain from the Lord's prediction,' etc. Vol. i, p. 253: 'Nothing spiritual is left remaining in it' (the whole Church).

'which in name only is Christian'; [1] or (as the Anglican writer of the preface to the book, from which we have made our extracts, expresses himself), 'as the revelation of the mystery of iniquity'; 'as the man of sin'; or whatever other predicates may please him. A marvellous expansion, truly, of childhood to youth, to manhood, and to age!

After such a confused succession of times and of Churches, Swedenborg fitly follows as the extremest link. In a true development, the continuation and the end are so connected with the beginning, that not only doth the latter follow the preceding in gentle transitions, but it grows out of it, and is in the same relation to it, as the bud, the blossom, and the fruit, are to the seed. Yet Swedenborgianism doth not grow out of the sequence of historical phenomena, but breaks suddenly in upon them. We have already had occasion to observe, that, according to Swedenborg, the corruption of the Church began at once, at a single stroke, as if by some magical interruption to the train of thought of all her members. Equally abrupt and unexpected is the rise of his own religious system. He charges the Church existing before him, with having, by the abuse of free-will, abandoned, and never again returned to, the fundamental principles of Christianity; and asserts, at the same time, that it is impossible to attain to them again, without an intercourse with the spiritual world—without the knowledge of certain truths, which no man before him possessed, because none had been favoured with the like revelations. But, as the revelations were the result of an extraordinary grace of God, and as, in the Church, itself, all elements for a true regeneration had been, since the Nicene Council, utterly lost; how could the Swedenborgian Church follow the preceding Churches in a regular order of development? All sects that had seceded from the Catholic Church could in a certain degree give a plausible justification to their charges against her, inasmuch as they appealed to Scripture, whereby her regeneration were possible. The censure of the Reformers, indeed, must always be termed incomprehensible, since it presupposed the free-will of those against whom it was directed; and this faculty the Reformers denied to men, representing the Deity as the exclusive agent in all spiritual concerns, on whom it entirely depended to set aside, as by a magical stroke, all errors, and who, in consequence, was

[1] Vol. ii, p. 373: 'The former Church being Christian in name only, but not in essence and reality.'

alone obnoxious to any charge, if in His household anything were amiss. These reproaches, nevertheless, might, to men who are not wont to reason with consistency, appear well founded. But Swedenborg boasts that the true spiritual sense of Holy Writ was revealed to him in Heaven only, and, in consequence, quite independently of the ordinary channels furnished through the original institution of the Church; and he therefore denies to the three preceding periods of Christianity the utter possibility of possessing, through the then existing media, any sound doctrine whatsoever. And yet he describes the community he founded as the crown of the Churches following each other 'according to order'! Was then the apostasy of the Nicene Council something conformable to order? Was the darkness of the Greek, the Roman Catholic, and the Protestant Churches founded in the very ordinance of God? In the same way, too, as, according to the theory of our sage, Christ might have appeared in the time of Adam, Noah, and Moses, so he himself, from the destination assigned to him, might have commenced his career in the fourth, fifth, or sixth century of our era. And yet the succession of the Churches was defined and systematic! Not the slightest reference to final causes can be discovered in this contradictory view of History, and its result appears totally unworthy of the Deity.

But here we must draw the attention of the reader to a special circumstance. Wherefore had Christ not power enough to stem by his manifestation the progress of sin, and to ensure the truth he had brought to mankind against the possibility of extinction? Wherefore did the word, which was uttered from his lips, which was preserved and explained by his spirit, lose, so shortly after his ascension, its world-subduing energy? And wherefore doth it work with might and with victory, and become for ever permanent, only when proclaimed by Swedenborg? We should yet be disposed to think that, when God himself speaks, the Word is at least as lasting as when a mortal babbles, though to him all mysteries in heaven should have been disclosed! The work of Christ lasted about three hundred years—a short springtide—till, at last, Swedenborg converts all into eternal spring! Is not this the most evident blasphemy? Swedenborg is really exalted to be the centre-point of all History, and to hold the place of the true Redeemer; with him, and not with Christ, the golden age returns.

§ LXXXVI—CONCLUDING REMARKS

The translations of Swedenborg's writings find, as we hear, a very great sale in and out of Germany, and the number of his followers daily increases. This we can perfectly understand. The unadorned Gospel, the simplicity of the Church's doctrine, are no longer capable of exciting an age so spiritually enervated as our own. Truth must be set forth in glaring colours, and represented in gigantic proportions, if we hope to stimulate and stir the souls of this generation. The infinite void and obtuseness of religious feeling in our time, when it cannot grasp spirits by the hand, and see them pass daily before it, is incapable of believing in a higher spiritual world; and the fancy must be startled by the most terrific images, if the hope of prolonging existence in a future world is not entirely to be extinguished. Long enough was the absurd as well as deplorable endeavour made to banish miracles from the Gospel History; to undermine, with insolent mockery, the belief in the great manifestation of the Son of God; to call in question all living intercourse between the Creator and the creature; and to inundate nations with the most shallow systems of morality—for these followed in the wake of such anti-Christian efforts. But the yearning soul of man is not to be satisfied with such idle talk, and when you take from it true miracles, it will then invent false ones. Our age is doomed to witness the desolate spectacle of a most joyless languor, and impotence of the spiritual life, by the side of the most exaggerated and sickly excitement of the same; and if we do not, with a living and spiritual feeling, return to the doctrine of the Church, we shall soon see the most wretched fanaticism obtain the same ascendancy, as we saw the most frivolous unbelief established on the throne. But by such phenomena will no one be conducted to the faith acceptable unto God; and the answer, which in the Gospel (Luke xvi, 19) that luxurious, hard-hearted, rich man received from Abraham, when he begged him to send Lazarus to his brethren, to the end that they might be converted, may perfectly apply to Swedenborg's followers, when they hold that the world needs a visionary, in order to bring it back to the truth,[1] and will be found to contain a valid testimony against their prophet. We have Moses

---

[1] See the letter from Thomas Hartley, rector of Wenwick, in Northamptonshire, in the preface to the ' True Christian Religion,' p. vii.

and the Prophets, and now also we have Christ, and the Apostles, and the Church; and when we hear not these, we shall give no ear to him who pretends to bring us tidings from the other world. With these words alone hath Christ annihilated all expectations, which might attach to Swedenborg's visions.

CHAPTER V

THE SOCINIANS

§ LXXXVII—RELATION OF THE SOCINIANS TO THE REFORMERS —HISTORICAL REMARKS

IN the Catholic system of doctrine, two elements—the Divine and the human, the natural and the supernatural, the mystical and the rational, or however else we may please to denominate them—move in uniform and harmonious combination; so that the rights of either appear adjusted in a manner that must certainly extort esteem and admiration from every reflecting mind. And whoever unites a pious, Christian, and ecclesiastical spirit to a cultivated intellect, must feel himself impelled to acknowledge, that God's protection hath guarded His Church in an eminent degree. But of the contraries, which in the Church are so beautifully harmonised, the one or the other can easily, in the individual believer, obtain the preponderance. Yet this preponderance will remain innocuous, if the one-sided principle will not proceed to a total misapprehension of its opposite, unduly appreciated as it is; and if the bonds of love, which unite the individual to the body of the Church, be maintained inviolate: for it is these which oppose a beneficial check to the excess of one or other of the aforesaid elements, that both form the life of Christianity. Such one-sided tendencies, existing more or less at all times, were found in the period immediately prior to the Reformation; and the classical studies, which had then once more come into vogue, gave to the rational principle in many a melancholy preponderance; as they may be perceived even in the celebrated, and, in many respects, meritorious Erasmus. Yet the opposite tendency was, by far, more prevalent, as the rapid diffusion of the Reformation itself will prove, wherein the mystical element had predominated, to the utter exclusion of the contrary one. But after this element, exceeding all bounds, had dissevered the bonds of the Church, the one-sided rational principle, in its turn, detached itself from the Church, pursued its own course, and after many unsuccessful attempts, of a Lewis Hetzer of Bischofzeth in Thurgovia,[1] of a John Campanus,[2] of a Michael Servetus,[3] and of a Valentine Gentilis,[4] formed a community which received its name from two Italians of Sienna, Lælius Socinus, who in the year 1562 died at Zurich, and his nephew, Faustus Socinus, who died in 1604, at Luclawicze in Poland.[5]

Socinianism and the old orthodox Protestantism are accordingly, two extremes, whereof the one laid hold of the human, the other of the divine element in Christianity, which is itself one, and so diverged into opposite paths, that Catholicism alone can unite. If, in the Protestant system, the Divinity of Christ be rightly and truly upheld, yet the Humanity of the Redeemer is, by the doctrine of ubiquity, absorbed in his Divinity; but among the Socinians, Christ appears as mere man. If Luther asserted, that the object of the manifestation of the Son of God was solely and exclusively the reconciliation of men with the Deity in the Redeemer's blood; and all the rest, which Jesus taught and wrought, was purely accidental; the Socinians, on the other hand, hold that Christ has offered up no sacrifice for the sins of the world, but wished only to deliver unto men a new doctrine, and be to them a model of virtue. Luther and Calvin could set no bounds to the malignant consequences of Adam's sin, that from him had infected his whole posterity; but the two Socini know absolutely nothing of any moral evil,

[1] Executed at Constance, in 1529.
[2] Born in the territory of Juliers, flourished from the year 1520 till 1580, when he was thrown into prison in his own country.
[3] A Spaniard, who at Calvin's instigation was burned at Geneva in 1553.
[4] A Neapolitan, beheaded at Bern, in 1566.
[5] On the first authors of Socinianism, the Protestant historian, Turretinus (in *Compendium Hist. Eccles.*, p. 373), has the following notice : ' Antitrinitarii hac ætate multi occurrunt ; quorum pars maxima Photinianismum et Sabellianismum ; nonnulli etiam Arianismum renovabant. Tales fuere Itali quidam, numero quadragenarium excedente, qui circa annum 1546 in Veneta ditione prope Vicentiam conventicula et colloquia inter se habebant. In his memorantur Leonardus Abbas Busalis, Lælius Socinus, Senensis Batricius, Bernardinus Ochinus, Nicolaus Paruta, Valentinus Gentilis, Julius Trevisanus, Franciscus de Ruego, Paulus Alciatus, aliique. Sed cum detecti essent, imo et duo, J. Trevisanus et Franciscus de Ruego comprehensi et supplicio affecti, cæteri sibi consulturi in varias oras dispersi sunt.' Of all these, Valentine Gentilis had the most melancholy fate. After having with difficulty escaped the fiery death, destined by Calvin for him, as well as Servetus, he was condemned, by the Zuinglians of Bern, as an anti-Trinitarian, and beheaded.—*Trans.*

that our great progenitor had brought upon his children. According to the former, God alone worketh the deliverance of man from the empire of Satan, and bringeth him into communion with Christ, and man is, in this process, purely passive; according to the latter, man is alone active, and God, after communicating to him His doctrine and His promises respecting a future life, leaves him almost entirely to himself. If the old Protestants speak only of grace, we hear, on the other hand, from the lips of the Socinians, but the word, laws and precepts. If it be the custom of the Wittenberg theologians, constantly to despise reason, and if, at the origin of the Reformation, they were scarcely able to endure its name, it is a maxim with the above-mentioned Italians to consult it in everything, to admit nothing that was impervious to that degree of culture, that it had attained to in their own persons, just as if they had stood at the very summit of all attainable knowledge. If we listen to the Reformers, man has only to take the Bible in hand, and its contents in a magical way will be conveyed, through the Spirit of God, to his mind; but, if we turn to Lælius and Faustus, they will tell us that we must understand all the languages in the world, and all the rules and arts of biblical criticism and interpretation, in order to penetrate into the obscurity of Holy Writ. But if these two species of religious reformers, on the aforesaid and other like points, pursued courses so totally different, they again frequently concur in other matters. Not only did both promise to restore primitive Christianity, and look upon the Bible as the only standard and source from which it was to be drawn, and by which all religious tenets must be tested, but the peculiar starting point of both was also the same. They united in asserting Christianity to have a purely practical tendency, adapted to life; this practical tendency being taken in the narrow and one-sided signification, as opposed to all speculation and high scientific inquiries. In this matter, however, the other differences between the Reformers and Socini exerted, doubtless, a decisive influence; the practical tendency of the former being in its fundamental tone exclusively religious; that of the latter, exclusively moral.

Protestantism and Socinianism have this, too, in common; that as the former checked its own development, and left to the later sects, that sprang out of its bosom, the task of carrying out its own principles, so Socinianism bequeathed to a later period the work of its own consummation—namely, the entire abandonment of those elements of supernaturalism, which, in its origin, it had not wholly rejected.[1]

Having now pointed out the historical connection between the Protestant and the Socinian systems of doctrine, we shall proceed to state a few historical details. Poland, as hinted above, was the first seat of the Socinians. Here, nearly contemporaneously with the Reformation of Luther and of Calvin, the religious system which denied the dogma of the Trinity had penetrated. However much the opponents of the latter doctrine were in hostility with the partisans of the Reformation, they tolerated each other, lived in mutual concord, and formed together one Protestant community, a fact which it is by no means difficult to account for, since the enemies to the fundamental doctrines of Christianity, rendered timid from their small numbers were for a long time cautious in avowing their sentiments. So soon, however, as their numbers were sufficiently increased, and they had assured themselves of the protection of some powerful patrons, they were no longer able to maintain silence or to confine their sentiments to a mere whisper. At the synods of Pinczow and Petricow, the two parties separated from each other in the years 1563 and 1565; and, everywhere held in abhorrence by Catholics and Protestants alike, the Socinians, under the name of Unitarians, formed a separate sect, for the moment undisturbed from without, yet inwardly divided by the most various opinions. Under these circumstances, Faustus Socinus repaired to them, and succeeded by degrees in uniting their discordant views respecting Christ, and in setting aside the anabaptism advocated by the Unitarians. Henceforward the Unitarians exchanged their name for that of Socinians.

In the year 1638, however, their tranquillity was disturbed in Poland also. They saw themselves, partly owing to their own fault, deprived of their school, their church, and their printing-press in Racovia where their chief settlement existed, till at last, chiefly at the instigation of the Jesuits, they were forced to emigrate. The political confederacies of the Unitarians with the Swedes who had penetrated into Poland very much contributed to excite general indignation against them. Under the guidance of their leaders, Schlichting, Wissowatius, Przypkovius, and Lubienisky, they endeavoured now to establish settlements in Transylvania (where already in the sixteenth

[1] Moehler here makes allusion to the Rationalists, who completed the work of destruction, begun by the Socinians.—*Trans.*

century, by means of the Italian physician, Blandrata, Unitarian principles had taken root), and also in Silesia, Prussia, Brandenburg, the Palatinate, and the Netherlands. It was only in Prussia and the March of Brandenburg that they succeeded in founding some unimportant congregations, for the general abhorrence for their principles and for all attempts to propagate them (even, as in Manheim, where they thought themselves secure), opposed great obstacles to their progress. In the Netherlands, though individual Unitarians were tolerated, they were not allowed to form congregations at least. The greater part went over by degrees to the other Christian communities, among which they lived dispersed. It was in Transylvania only that the sect maintained itself.

The chief sources of information for the history of Socinianism are the numerous writings of Faustus Socinus, who made use of the papers bequeathed to him by his uncle, the writings of John Crell, Jonah Schlichting, John Lewis Wollzogen (the works of all these writers are found in the *Bibliotheca Fratrum Polonorum*), and of several others.

Among the Socinian catechisms the larger one of Racovia, edited by Moscorovius and Schmalz in the year 1605, and that by Ostorod, a Socinian preacher at Buscow, near Dantzic, are particularly distinguished. (Rak. 1604.) A regular symbolical writing the Socinians do not recognise; although the Racovian Catechism may pass for such.

§ LXXXVIII—PRINCIPLES OF THE SOCINIANS, AS TO THE RELATION BETWEEN REASON AND REVELATION, AND THE FUNCTIONS OF THE FORMER IN THE INTERPRETATION OF HOLY WRIT

It is our first duty to state the views of the Socinians, as to the sources of all religious and moral knowledge. They assert that, through his own powers, man arriveth at the knowledge and distinction of good and evil;[1] and, on the other hand, they think that the idea of God, and of divine things, is conveyed to man only from without, to wit, by instruction.[2] In accordance with this theory, they represent the Divine image in man, as consisting in the dominion of the latter over animals.

---

[1] Faust. Socin. Prælect. theol. c. 2; Bibliotheca Fr. Pol. tom. i, fol. 537; Volkel. de vera Relig. lib. iv, c. 4.
[2] Faust. Socin. de auct. S. Script. Bibl. Fr. Pol. tom. i, p. 273.

This is avowedly the meanest view, which it is possible to entertain of the affinity to God in man ; a view which renders it utterly inconceivable, how, when God announces Himself, or lets Himself be announced from without, man would be even capable of receiving the doctrine of the Deity. Clearer, and yet withal more frivolous and powerless, the one-sided moralising tendency of Socinianism could not well appear, than in these conceptions, which evidently have in view to represent the ethical principle as the primary and most deeply-seated idea in man ; and the religious principle, on the other hand, as something subordinate, only extraneously annexed to the mind, only to be grasped by the finite understanding, like the geography of Peru, for instance, and therefore, in a manner, accidental. Thus, while Luther assigns to morality a mere temporal, perishable, earthly value, Socinianism, in the most direct opposition, allots the highest place to it. In the sequel, we shall also see, that the religious is made to minister entirely to the ethical principle. Not less do we, here, recognise the instinctive force, which urged Socinianism to carry out that opposition, that it formed against the elder Protestantism ; the latter, in its extreme sects, representing the divine idea in man, (as, for instance, the inward light, the inward Christ of the Quakers), to be so all-powerful as to need no extraneous aid for its rise and development in human consciousness ; while, on the other hand, the Socinians will deduce this divine idea *solely* from an external source. The truth is on neither side. Rational nature, the religious, intellectual, and moral capability, is innate in man ; but, in both respects, it needs the outward excitation, proceeding from a being of a like *spiritual* essence, in order to unfold its own energy, and consummate its own history.

One would be inclined to suppose, that, in virtue of these principles, the Socinians would have adhered literally to the sense of any record of revelation, and have embraced it with unhesitating faith ; since they denied to man the capacity, as it were, for any ulterior criticism of such, or the divine similitude, in the true sense of the word. But in such an expectation we should be totally deceived. There are not, indeed, *wanting* numerous passages, that inculcate an unconditional submission to Holy Writ ;[1] but the very reverse is practised, and the

---

[1] Faust. Socin. Ep. iii, ad Mat. Radec. Bib. Fratrum Pol. tom. i, fol. 386.
' Equidem contra id sentio : Nihil in iis Scriptis legi, quod non verissimum

maxim is not only enforced, but clearly avowed ; that anything contrary to reason, that is to say, to the understanding of the Socinians, must not be considered as a doctrine of our records of revelation. Hence the memorable declaration of some Socinians, that in cases, where a Scripture text does not harmonise with what they denominate reason, they should rather invent a sense, than adopt the simple and literal signification of the words.[1] Hence we find, among them, the first outlines of the subsequent accommodation theory—a theory which is, indeed, closely connected with the conception they had formed of Christ ; for, with the nature of a mere man, an adaptation to errors is perfectly consistent. Yet this point the Socinians did not fully develop. They did not even uphold the theory of inspiration in all its rigour ; and admitted that errors, though only in unimportant matters, might have crept into the Bible.[2] From the analogy of the whole Socinian system, especially from the representation it gives of the Holy Spirit, the higher guidance, under which the sacred Scriptures were composed, was, according to these sectaries, merely confined to a Providential ordinance, which permitted only virtuous, honourable, and well-informed men to write the same. That the followers of Socinus should reject Tradition and the authority of the Church was naturally to be expected.

§ LXXXIX—DOCTRINE OF THE SOCINIANS RESPECTING GOD AND THE PERSON OF CHRIST

Even in the doctrine of the Divine attributes, the opposition, which the Socinians form to the elder Protestants, is very manifest. If the Reformed (and herein the Lutherans had set them

sit. . . . Præstat, mi frater, mihi crede, cum in aliquem Scripturæ locum incidimus, qui nobis falsam sententiam continere videatur, una cum Augustino hac in parte ignorantiam nostram fateri, quam eum, si alioquin indubitatus plane sit, in dubium revocare.' Faustus, after having observed, that if we wish to charge on Holy Writ any untruth, we can do this only through reason, or other grounds, says : ' Ratione vix ullo modo fieri id potest, cum Christiana religio non humanæ rationi ullo pacto innitatur.'

[1] Bengel (in *Suskind's Magazine*, No. xv, p, 128) has excellently proved, that the Socinians, in the interpretation of Holy Writ, adopted as a rule, a negative use of reason. The passage relative hereto, extracted from the writings of Faustus Socinus and Schmalz, may be seen in p. 132 of the above-cited work. See also Marheineke Instit. Symbol. p. 172.

[2] Faust. Socin. de auct. S. Script. Bibl. Fr. Pol. fol. 267.

the example) sacrificed the free-will of man to the Divine omniscience; the Socinians, on the other hand, in order to uphold the capacity of self-determination in man, set limits to God's fore-knowledge. The one party annihilates man, the other disfigures the idea of God. The former represents man as so bound that he can no longer be regarded as an independent being; the latter teaches that God is bound by man and subjects the immutable to extraneous influences.

By all the sects, which we have hitherto described, the doctrine respecting the Person of the Redeemer, as handed down by the Catholic Church—namely, that he is at once God and man—was ever retained. The Socinians, on the other hand, in this article of belief, departed from the ancient truth in such a way, that the errors they adopted in its room determine almost all their own deviations. The Father only of Jesus Christ they hold to be God.[1] They are not, indeed, of opinion that salvation depends on the denial of the doctrine of the Trinity. On the contrary, distinguishing between truths, the knowledge whereof is absolutely necessary to the gaining of eternal life, and such, the adoption of which is only very useful, they asserted that the dogma of the unity of God belongs to the first class; the dogma of the unity of Persons to the second;[2] yet it is singular that, at the same time, the Socinians wished to prove that the unity of person is inseparable from the unity of essence, and, accordingly, from the unity of God.[3] For, hereby, they certainly thought to prove that the Trinity of persons destroys the unity of nature, and, consequently, that the belief in the unity of person is indispensably necessary to salvation.

The Son of God they hold to be a mere man, who was conceived of the Holy Ghost, and therefore called the Son of God. He also enjoyed the distinction (as the Socinians further teach), to have been, prior to entering on his office, admitted into heaven, where he received his commission relative to mankind.

---

[1] Catechism. Racov. qu. 73. 'Quænam est hæc Persona divina ? Resp. Est ille Deus unus Domini nostri Jesu Christi Pater.'

[2] Loc. cit. qu. 53. 'Quænam sunt, quæ ad essentiam pertinent, ad salutem prorsus necessaria ? Resp. Sunt ea, quod Deus sit, quod sit tantum unus,' etc. Qu. 71. 'Expone, quæ ad eam rem vehementer utilia censeas ? Resp. Id quidem est, ut cognoscamus, in essentia Dei unam tantum personam esse.' Christ. Relig. Instit. Bibl. Fr. Pol. tom. i, fol. 652, Col. ii.

[3] Catech. Rac. qu. 74. 'Demonstra hoc ipsum. Resp. Hoc sane vel hinc patere potest : quod essentia Dei sit una numero, quapropter plures numero personæ in ea esse nullo pacto possunt,' etc.

This article of belief the Socinians evidently put forward, not only in order to set aside the difficulties which several Scripture texts presented—difficulties which, on the rejection of Christ's divinity, must have proved very weighty [1]—but also because, from the views they entertained as to the origin of religious ideas, they were unable otherwise to explain, how Christ, even according to the meagre conception they had formed of his doctrines, could have attained to his peculiar religious system. On account of his obedience, they proceed to say, he was, after the consummation of his work of redemption, exalted to divine dignity and honour, and all things were given unto him ; so that Christians may turn with confidence unto him as a God, and one invested with Divine power, and may adore him—nay, are bound to do so.[2] Faustus Socinus was so zealous for the worship of Christ that Blandrata called him to Transylvania, in order to overcome the repugnance of the consistent Unitarians in that country, who, with reason, were unwilling to offer to any creature an act of adoration. Faustus even fell under suspicion of having contributed, with all his power, towards the imprisonment of Simon David, who was particularly zealous in upholding the consistency of his own religious system. Even in the Racovian Catechism, those are declared unworthy of the Christian name who testify not, in the aforesaid manner, their homage to Christ.[3] Once accustomed to admit self-contradictory propositions into their religious system, the Unitarians, who adored Christ, now introduced a distinction in their worship, allotting supreme adoration to God, and an inferior one to Christ.[4] In

---

[1] Catechism. Rac. qu. 194 and 195.
[2] Socin. de Justif. Bibl. Fr. Pol. tom. i, fol. 601, col. i. ' Ipsi Jesu tantam in cœlo et in terra, tanquam obedientæ scilicet usque ad mortem crucis insigne præmium, potestatem dedit, ut,' etc. Catech. Racov. qu. 236. ' Quid præterea Dominus Jesus huic præcepto addidit ? Resp. Id quod etiam Dominum Jesum pro Deo agnoscere tenemur, id est, pro eo, qui in nos potestatum habet divinam, et cui nos divinum exhibere honorem obstricti sumus. Qu. 237. In quo is honor divinus Christo debitus consistit ? Resp. In eo, quod quemadmodum adoratione divina eum prosequi tenemur, ita in omnibus necessitatibus nostris ejus opem implorare possumus. Adoramus vero eum propter ipsius sublimem et divinam ejus potestatem.' Christ. Relig. Instit. fol. 656. Ostorod, Instruction, cap. xix. p. 134.
[3] Catech. Racov. qu. 246. ' Quid vero sentis de iis hominibus, qui Christum non invocant, nec adorandum censent ? Resp. Prorsus non esse Christianos sentio, cum Christum non habeant. Et licet verbis id negare non audeant, reipsa negant tamen.'
[4] Loc. cit. qu. 245. ' Ergo is honor et cultus ad eum modum tribuitur, ut nullum sit inter Christum et Deum hoc in genere discrimen ? Resp.

this way, they who had resolved to maintain so rigidly the unity of the Godhead, admitted, by the side of the one, true, and supreme Deity, a second, unreal, and inferior God, whom, compelled by the clearest texts of Scripture, they resolved to adore; so that they immediately revoked their resolution, as well as enfeebled the doctrine of one God, by the setting up of a second. Had they been acuter thinkers, they must have discerned, that if the Gospel represents the Son as a Person, and at the same time as God (and this the Socinians do not pretend to deny),[1] no other relation between him and the Father is *conceivable*, but that which the Catholic Church hath from the beginning believed. But what strange theology is this, which can teach, that in the course of ages, God permits a change in the government of the world; so that having, down to the time of Christ, conducted that government in His own person, He now resigned it, just as if He had been weary of it, and appointed a vicegerent, to whom He probably communicated omnipotence, certainly, at least, omniscience, and such like attributes; just as if things of this kind could, without any difficulty, be transferred, and, as it were, appended to any individual!

It is remarkable that man, when he has once formed a mean conception of his calling, can rarely rise in speculation, as in will, above the point of elevation, which that conception had fixed. Whoever imagines that he is absolutely incapable of satisfying certain moral claims, will certainly never act up to them in life; and whoever obstinately persists in the prejudice, that his powers are unequal to any speculative problem, will assuredly never solve it Would it not appear that such so-called fancies, at times, at least, determine instinctively the measure of intellectual power in those who possess them? It was so with Socinus. The Divine similitude, the highest faculty in man, that wherein the real man alone consists, he places in the calling to hold dominion over animals. From all the specimens we have given of his religious system, we see a man before

Imo permagnum est. Nam adoramus et colimus Deum, tanquam causam primam salutis nostræ; Christum tanquam causam secundam; aut, ut cum Paulo loquamur, Deum tanquam eum, ex quo omnia, Christum ut eum, per quem omnia.' Compare the letters to Niemojovius (Bibl. Frat. Pol. tom. ii, fol. 466), where we see that to Christ a species of invocation is addressed, bearing some resemblance to the Catholic invocation of saints.

[1] Christ. Relig. Instit. loc. cit. fol. 655. The words of St John's Gospel i, 1 to 20, 21, are here cited.

us who judges of Divine things like a shepherd, a goat-herd, or a cow-herd; but we see no theologian. The following way of dealing with Scriptural texts by Socinus is certainly not calculated to overturn the judgment we have pronounced upon his very narrow-minded views. In order to get rid of the proof, which may be so strictly drawn in favour of the pre-existence of Christ from those words of John (i, 1), 'In the beginning was the Word,' the two Socini thus interpreted this passage: 'In the beginning of John's preaching, Christ already was the envoy of God.' On that text, 'Before Abraham was, I am' (John vi, 58), they foisted the following sense: 'Before Abram becometh Abraham, I am the light of the world.' As the change of name of the aforesaid patriarch was connected with the promise that he should be the father of many nations, but as, before Christ, he was the father only of one nation, and it was only through the latter many nations entered into the relation of sonship to him, so the Saviour wished to say, before Abram, in fact, merits the name of Abraham, 'I will be the light of the world, for I am destined by God to be the mediator of the transformation of the one name into the other.' That Christ is termed by John the Creator of the world, they denied, because the text, 'Through him all things were made,' etc., was to be referred to the new creation occasioned by him [1] Yet it is not here our business to bring forward the exegetical arguments which the Socinians advance in support of their doctrines; we shall therefore return to the exposition of their peculiar tenets.

The Holy Ghost they represent as a power and efficacy of the Deity, but the more exact description they give of this power will claim our attention later.[2] The question has often been proposed, With what ancient heresy doth the Socinian conception of Christ agree? It would be easy to discover

[1] Catech. Rac. qu. 107, 128. Oeder, a Protestant Dean, whose edition of the Racovian Catechism, in the year 1739, I make use of, says, at p. 146, at the question 107, as follows: 'Perversio clarissimi loci (John vi, 58) ita fœda et simul manifesta est, ut fieri non potuisse credam, ut homines sanæ alioquin mentis, in eas cogitationes inciderent, nisi qui ob abjectum amorem veritatis in reprobum sensum traditi sunt.' He is right. Compare Christ. Relig. Instit. Bibl. Frat. Pol. tom. i, fol. 656.

[2] Catech. Racov. qu. 271. 'Spiritum Sanctum non esse in Deitate personam, et hinc discere potes,' etc. Christ. Relig. Instit. ii, fol. 652, Coll. ii. 'Quid, quæro, de Spiritu sancto nunc mihi dicis? Resp. Nempe, illum non esse personam aliquam, a Deo, cujus est Spiritus, distinctam, sed tantummodo ipsius Dei vim et efficaciam quandam,' etc. What an absurd answer, in more than one respect! In general, the whole catechetical exposition is very unsuccessful.

many points of resemblance to ancient sects, but the Socinians are unable to show a perfect concurrence with anyone. With the Arians they doubtless agreed in the veneration and worship of one who became a God—who was a mere creature. But the heretics of the fourth century taught that the Son of God existed before the world, and that through him the universe was created and from the beginning governed—a doctrine which their friends in the sixteenth century called in question, since they represented the existence of the Saviour as, in every respect, commencing with his earthly nativity, and therefore could not teach a creation of the world by him, and even dated from his ascension only, his government of the world, which, even now, according to them, is of a limited nature.

With the Artemonites the Socinians willingly associated themselves: and about the period of their first rise, others (as, for instance, the author of the *Augsburg Confession*), compared the Unitarians with the disciples of Paul of Samosata. The affinity is, doubtless, not to be denied, since all these families of heretics held Christ to be a mere man, who was conceived of the Divine Spirit, and was sent to men with a Divine commission. But if the Socinians denied, that before his birth from Mary, Christ had already existed, and was a secondary lord of the universe (and by this denial they take a position below the Arians); the Artemonites, on the other hand, together with the disciples of Paul of Samosata, rejected even the doctrine, that Christ, after his ascension, was exalted to Divine dignity, and to the government of the world; and hereby fell as far below the Socinians, as these fall below the Arians. Some disciples of Artemon, as well as of Theodotus, rejected, as a later interpolation, the beginning of the Gospel of St John, and were therefore called Alogi; while Artemon himself asserted, that, before Pope Zephyrinus, Christ was not held to be God. Paul of Samosata suppressed the hymns, wherein Christ was addressed as God, and thereby endeavoured to prevent the worship of Christ. The Socinians, accordingly, occupy the middle place between the Arians and the disciples of Artemon, and have something in common with the errors of all these sectaries, without, however, entirely coinciding with them.

They are also wont to be placed in the same category with the Photinians. But as these taught, that in Christ there was an union of the Logos, whom they conceived to be impersonal, with the man Jesus, they herein differed from the doctrine of the Socinians. They preached up, moreover, that the kingdom of the Redeemer would have an end; that the union of the Logos with the man Jesus would again be dissolved, and thereby the dominion of Christ cease; whereas the reverse of this was inculcated by the Socinians.

§ XC—ON THE FALL AND THE REGENERATION OF MAN

With reason the Socinians assert, that by the creation Adam was endowed with free-will, which, in consequence of the Fall, he forfeited neither for himself nor for his posterity; for it is essentially inherent in human nature. Adam, moreover, they say, was created mortal in himself; yet so, that if he had persevered in his obedience to God, he was not under the necessity of dying. Immortality would have been vouchsafed to him as a gratuitous gift. Original sin, they contend, there is none; and the consequences of Adam's fall reach not beyond his person, with the exception of a certain defectiveness, which occasions death to extend to all his posterity. This was a concession, which the undeniable phenomena of ordinary life wrung from the Socinians; but in their religious system, this concession is so isolated as to be utterly untenable.[1]

Corresponding to their notion of the moral malady of mankind, was that of the remedies which they represented Christ to have proffered us against it. These the Socinians make to consist, in the granting of a purer and more perfect legislation, as well as in the opening the prospect of a future life, confirmed as it is by Christ's resurrection, and which, according to them, was not covenanted in the Old Testament, but now is promised only to penitent sinners, and to the observers of the moral precepts.[2] The Socinians saw themselves compelled to circumscribe, as much as was practicable, the ethical and religious knowledge, and the hopes of the ancient world; for otherwise, there would scarcely have remained anything, for which, as Christians, we were bounden in gratitude to God and to Christ. How, otherwise, was Christ to be distinguished from the pro-

---

[1] Catech. Racov. qu. 422, 42, 45.
[2] Catech. Racov. qu. 197. 'Quid vero hoc novum fœdus comprehendit? Resp. Duplex rerum genus, quorum unum Deum, alterum nos respicit. Qu. 198. Sunt perfecta mandata et perfecta Dei promissa,' etc. Socin. de Justif. Bibl. Frat. Pol. tom. i, fol. 601, Col. i, Resp. ad object. Cuteni. Bib. Frat. Pol. tom. ii, fol. 455, n. q.

phets? Hence, they allege even the Lord's Prayer among the especial revelations which, through Christ, the Deity had vouchsafed to men. And had they known that the Saviour found this form of prayer already existing, and only strongly recommended it, then their account of the peculiar services of the envoy of God, would have occupied a totally imperceptible space.[1] The most remarkable, indirect act of Christ must, according to the Socinian system, when we closely investigate the matter, be evidently the abolition of the ritual and legal ordinances of the Mosaic dispensation; an abolition to which they refer the establishment of a more spiritual worship of the Deity. But this is a merit of Christ, which, after all that the prophets of the old law had taught upon the subject, is certainly, in respect to the novelty, at least, of its fundamental idea, not to be so highly estimated.

Thus, admitting no vicarious satisfaction on the part of Christ—no imputation of his merits, which they reject as pernicious to morality—the Socinians know only of a certain meagre communication of Divine power supporting human exertion, and co-operating with it: a power whereof we must, beforehand, form only a very modest idea.[2] The Holy Ghost, whose personality they deny, as was above stated, is, according to them, even in its workings, very far from corresponding to the idea which Scripture, and the perpetual faith of the Church, give of it. They divide his gifts into two classes, into temporal and extraordinary, under which they include the apostolic power of miracles,[3] and into permanent, which they term the Gospel, and the sure hope of eternal life.[4] The former they designate as the outward, the latter as the internal gift of the Holy Ghost. In order that no one might deem the Holy Spirit necessary for the formation of Christian faith, and, consequently, for the beginning of all true virtue in man, the Racovian Catechism devotes a special question and answer to the denial of this opinion.[5] Nay, whether the internal operation of the Divine Spirit be necessary for implanting in the soul a firm

---

[1] Loc. cit. qu. 217. 'Quid vero ad hæc addidit Dominus Jesus?' (Namely, to the commandment in the Old Testament, to worship God alone.) 'Resp. Primum hoc, quod nobis certam orandi rationem præscripsit,' etc.

[2] Socin. de Justif. loc. cit. fol. 601; Relig. Christ. Instit. loc. cit. fol. 665; Catech. Racov. qu. 374.

[3] Catech. Racov. qu. 361.   [4] Loc. cit. qu. 365, *seq.* 430.

[5] Loc. cit. qu. 370.

hope of eternal life, is a matter of doubt to the authors of this Catechism; for they make use of the expression, it *seemeth* that the outward promise afforded us, by the preaching of the Gospel, needs an inward sealing in our hearts.

As regards the fulfilment of the moral law, the above-mentioned inward gift of the Holy Ghost is limited solely to cases of peculiarly grievous temptation.[1] In illustration of this doctrine of the Catechism, the following propositions, taken from a series of answers made by Faustus Socinus to the objections, which a certain Cutenus had proposed to him, deserve to be cited. 'Every man,' says this Reformer, 'in case he be not corrupted by his associates, can live without sin, when the most attractive and stimulating recompense be promised to him, as the reward of his virtues. But, such a recompense is promised in the Gospel; therefore, he can perfectly conform his life to the precepts of Jesus.' To this the still stronger proposition is subjoined: 'Man, not, indeed, by his natural strength, but by the powers afforded to him by God, through the hope of eternal life, can act up to the Divine will.'[2] Hence we see, that the opposition between natural and supernatural powers in the Socinian system, has, in part, quite another signification, than it has ever received in the Church, and still retains among Protestants, as well as Catholics. This phenomenon, moreover, is grounded in the fact, that, according to Socinus, man has no innate sense of religion—not even the slightest sense of the immortality of his own soul: for the doctrine of immortality is represented as one in *every* respect extrinsically communicated —supernaturally revealed; and therefore he denominates even belief in it a supernatural power. Further below, Socinus recurs to the same subject, improving, as it were, on himself. The Christian, according to him, by calling to mind eternal life, can rise again, by his own strength, even from a grievous fall; yet nothing is safer and more praiseworthy,[3] says he, than to turn to God, for one ought not to trust too confidently in one's own powers. But a vicious life, he continues to say, man, without a special favour and grace of God, is not able to reform. The question, however, arises, whether to this grace we are to attach the orthodox notion; or whether, on the contrary, we are not

---

[1] Loc. cit. qu. 368.

[2] No. 6. 'Homo in hac vita non quidem viribus naturalibus, sed viribus sibi a Deo per spem vitæ æternæ tantum subministratis, potest ejusdem voluntatem perficere.'

[3] Laudabilius et securius.'

to understand, by this special favour, the judgments of God ?[1]
How extremely similar the sentiments of the Socinians are to
those of the Pelagians, must be evident to all minds.

Christ also, according to the Socinians, still exerts, after his
ascension, a perpetual influence over our destiny. But the
influence which he exercises they represent as only external.
He protects us, they say, by the fulness of his power; and, in
a *certain degree*, turns away from us the wrath of God, which
is wont to be poured out against sinners: and this it is, we
understand by his intercession. He sets before us, in his own
person, the blessed effects of virtue; but this is to be referred
solely to the reading of the Gospel history, that has been bequeathed to us, and by means whereof he constantly worketh.
Lastly, he purifies from sin by punishments and aids. The
notion of the latter, by being associated with punishments, is
necessarily confined to the granting of earthly prosperity, as an
encouragement to virtue.[2] Hence the Socinians assert, that
Christ discharges his priestly functions solely in heaven, and
his sufferings and ministry on earth have only procured for him
this his celestial influence.

From all we have now stated, the notion which the Socinians
connect with justification, may easily be inferred. That they
would avoid the errors of the Lutherans and the Calvinists on
this matter, may naturally be expected; but it is equally certain
that they rush into the opposite excess. Justification they
conceive to be a judicial act of God, whereby he graciously
absolves from sin and its guilt, all men, who with faith in Christ
fulfil the moral precepts.[3] This definition would be very just,
if the Christian obedience required by them were not, from its
very nature, even in the best case, purely finite; for it usually
is begun only by the natural powers; and to Christ scarcely
any other share is allotted therein, save that of a credible and

---

[1] Bibl. Fr. Pol. tom. ii, fol. 454.
[2] Catech. Rac. qu. 479.
[3] Socin. de Justif. loc. cit. 602, col. ii. ' Justificatio nostra coram Deo, ut uno verbo dicam, nihil est aliud, quam a Deo pro justis haberi. . . . Ratio igitur, qua nobis illa contingit, ad nos respicit. Quod ad Deum attinet, nihil Deum movet ad nos pro justis habendos, nihilne, ut tantum bonum consequamur in Deo esse necesse est, præter gratuitam volun- tatem. . . . Quod vero ad nos pertinet, non aliter reipsa justi coram Deo habemur, et delictorum nostrorum veniam ab ipso consequimur quam si in Jesum Christum credamus. . . . Credere autem in Jesum Christum, nihil aliud est, quam Jesu Christo confidere, et idcirco ex ejus præscripto vitam instituere.' Catech. Racov. qu. 452, an ill-composed article.

trustworthy guide. In other respects, what the Socinians advance touching justifying faith, that it possesses in itself, as an essential form, a power efficacious in works, and can be separated from the same only in thought, is very good, and has been borrowed from the Catholic schools (*fides formata*). It is only to be lamented, that the, in itself, very laudable earnestness, which applied its energy to moral conduct, should have been devoid of the Divine blessing and unction; and we are at a loss to discover how it can attain its ends.[1]

Directed by the truest instinct, the Socinians further assert, that works, or obedience to the Divine precepts, do not, of themselves, merit heaven; for, as in the performance of these, they refer the larger share to human exertion, and therefore admit no truly Divine works, it does honour to their understanding to have allowed no inward relation to eternal bliss, in works founded in such a principle. But if they perceived this, it is then the more inconceivable, how they could deem man capable of future rewards, since with these, according to their system, his earthly feelings and actions possess no true affinity and uniformity. Even from this point of view, they might have discerned the unsatisfactoriness of their own system, and have been brought round to the doctrine of the Church.[2]

In respect to the concurrence of the Socinian view of justification, with the Catholic and the Protestant belief, as well as its divergence from the doctrine of either Church, we shall here make a few brief observations. The Socinians agree with Luther and Calvin, in holding Justification to be a mere judicial act of God. To justify, according to them, signifies only to acquit—to declare men just. But both parties stand in direct hostility one to the other, inasmuch as the former make this Divine declaration to follow upon sanctification; the latter, on the contrary, deduce sanctification only from the belief in this declaration. Catholics reconcile these contrarieties, by teaching, that sanctification and forgiveness of sins concur in the one act

---

[1] Socin. loc. cit. fol. 610, col. ii. 'Fides obedientiam præceptorum Die, non quidem ut effectum suum, sed ut suam substantiam et formam continet atque complectitur. Meminisse enim debemus ejusquod supra recte conclusum est, fidem, hanc scilicet, qua justificamur, Dei obedientiam esse.' Compare de Christo Servatore. Bibl. Frat. Pol. tom. ii. P. i, c. iv, fol. 129; P. iv, c. xi, fol. 234. These passages, as containing the refutation of the Protestant doctrine on faith and works, have an especial importance; and many remarks are, contrary to all expectation, acute and ingenious.

[2] Socin. fragment. de Justific. loc. cit. fol. 620.

of justification. While the Protestants hold, that for the sake of Christ's merits, heaven is thrown open to the believer, in despite of his sins; that not moral worth, but only grace decides our salvation, in order that praise may be rendered unto God alone; while the Socinians, on the other hand, maintain that merit of Christ there is none, but only merits on the part of man, and therefore no *real* grace in Christ, because otherwise moral exertions would be paralysed; the Catholic Church lays hold on the truth in both parties and, at the same time, rejects the errors of either; as she inculcates, that by grace man can and must let himself be moved, exalted, and thoroughly purified in morals; and only inasmuch as he doth this, hath he a living conception of the institution of grace, and doth he place himself in due relation to it. That, however, Protestantism is far more fitted than the system of the two Socini (much as the latter may perpetually exalt morality) to call forth moral exertion, and to found a pure morality, although Protestantism misapprehends its nature, and doth not truly understand its due relation to religion, is a truth which cannot be called in question. Socinianism is utterly wanting in humility, and in all deeper insight into the great necessities of human nature, since in man, even in his present condition, it finds nothing essentially amiss; and accordingly it is deficient in the vivifying and morally inspiring principle. A mere lawgiver, as Christ mainly appears to the Socinians, cannot exert a deep and powerful influence on man. They protest, indeed, against the notion, that they regard Christ exclusively in this light, since they consider the deliverance of the human race as the true object of his mission, and they look upon his legislation as only a means to that higher end.[1] Doubtless it is precisely so; but it is the very one-sided view of the means selected by God which forms the great gulf between Socinian Christianity and the old genuine Christianity. The Socinians went to Emanuel; and, therefore, all which for eighteen hundred years hath wrought the great moral renovation of the world. How weak, how impotent is their legislative Jesus, compared with the Son of God, reconciling, by his self-immolation, the world with his Father! *The Son of God* it is who hath overthrown heathenism and tamed barbarism. And what means the vague expression,

[1] Faust. Socin. Respons. ad object. Cut. loc. cit. ' Nec sane ob id præcipue in mundum venit, ut legem ferret nosterve legislator esset, sed ut nos servaret, in quem etiam finem suam legem dedit.'

'deliver'? From what was he to deliver? From a moral corruption that was unavoidable, since no one before Christ, Jew or Gentile, was, according to the Socinians, instructed in the relations of the present to a future life. At most, by the word 'deliverance,' can here be understood only the liberation from *inculpable* ignorance, and therefore from guiltless immorality also.

§ XCI—ON THE SACRAMENTS

The sacraments of baptism and of the altar the Socinians hold to be mere ceremonies; as, indeed, from their rejection, or at least misapprehension of the inward operations of grace such a view necessarily follows. Baptism is regarded only as a rite of initiation of the carnal Jews and Heathens into the Christian Church; for these needed an outward symbol of the forgiveness of sins and of inward purification. As regards its retention in the Christian Church, this is considered by the Socinians to have arisen out of a misunderstanding of the mere temporary ordinance of Christ. To children, moreover, baptism is inapplicable, for these certainly comprehend not the nature of the act. These sectaries deem it a great concession on their parts when they refrain from damning those who administer baptism to infants; and this, with them, is certainly not surprising, since they deny original sin, and naturally look on the sprinkling with mere water as a ceremony in itself void.[1]

Of the Lord's Supper they believe at least so much, that it hath been instituted for all ages; but, indeed, *only* to announce the death of the Lord.[2]

Lastly, the Socini taught an annihilation of the damned, and accordingly rejected the eternity of hell-torments.

[1] Catech. Rac. qu. 346-351.
[2] Loc. cit. qu. 333. It appears perfectly superfluous to allege any testimonies, on this matter, from the writings of Socinus and others.

CHAPTER VI

THE ARMINIANS, OR REMONSTRANTS

§ XCII—SOME HISTORICAL PRELIMINARY REMARKS

THIS sect, as has been already observed in the Introduction, owes its name and origin to an inhabitant of South Holland, who, in the year 1560, was born in Oudewater. The very solid, and extensive learning, which he had acquired at several learned academies at home and abroad—especially his philosophic studies at Paris and at Padua—certainly made him acquainted with the dogma of free-will, and the doctrines connected therewith; so that, he must have entertained doubts, as to the truth of his own Confession, and the divine origin it laid claim to. Yet he would scarcely have resolved to take up an attitude of formal opposition against the doctrine of his Church, had not, even contrary to his hesitating will, a concurrence of circumstances determined him thereto. The parties of the Supralapsarians and the Infralapsarians already stood opposed to each other in battle array. The former asserted, that, prior to the fall, the predestination to eternal felicity and damnation was already decreed; the latter, that it was so only subsequently to that event. The Supralapsarians alone, as is evident, maintained Calvin's doctrine in all its rigour. Under these circumstances, it happened, unfortunately, that while Arminius was pastor of a congregation, he received the commission to refute some Calvinistic adversaries of the rigid doctrine of predestination; and the investigation which he then undertook, led him to a still more decided rejection of what he had been called upon to defend. As professor of theology at Leyden, he found in his opponents, particularly Gomar, adverse spies, who took offence at anything, which in any, even the slightest, degree betrayed an opposition to the harsh Calvinistic theory of election, and who summoned him, in consequence, to an account. Thus was Arminius led to express his opinions ever more clearly and distinctly; and, in proportion as this occurred, the partisans of his views increased, and, consequently, the fermentation among the Calvinistics of the United States augmented. The civil authorities soon saw themselves forced to take cognisance of the prevailing controversies ; but the attempts at conciliation, which they deemed the most suited to their position, proved abortive.

Arminius died in the year 1609 ; but his principles survived him, and found in Uytenbogart and Simon Episcopius, defenders not less able than courageous. Accused of a departure from the formularies of the national Faith, and of disturbing the peace of the country, they delivered to the States, in the year 1610, a remonstrance, which, in five articles, embodied their principles. From this declaration, they derived the name of Remonstrants. At last, after repeated, but ever ineffectual, attempts on the part of the civil authorities, to bring about a pacific adjustment of these disputes, the adversaries of the Remonstrants, especially after Maurice, Prince of Orange, had declared in their favour, succeeded, in the year 1618, in convoking the Synod of Dort. Condemned by that Synod as heretics, all Arminians were, in consequence, deprived of their places, and even banished the country ; till at length, after the death of Prince Maurice, they came by degrees to be tolerated again, and even, as a separate ecclesiastical community, were insured a legal existence.

We shall describe their doctrinal peculiarities after the Confession, which Simon Episcopius published in the year 1622 under the title *Confessio sive Declaratio sententiæ Pastorum, qui in fæderato Belgio Remonstrantes vocantur*, etc. Its author soon saw himself induced to put forth a defence of his declaration ; for some rigid Calvinistic preachers had published a censure on it. The Apology, termed *Examen Censuræ*, etc., is distinguished for the most dexterous logic, and would well serve to illustrate the Confession of the Remonstrants, had this stood in need of illustration. For the latter is written with the utmost clearness and vigour, and only in respect to certain points, is deficient in that explicitness, which should characterise a public formulary. In these rare cases, the Apology, or *Examen Censuræ*, will be very serviceable, for in it the Arminians were forced to make the most unreserved declarations.

§ XCIII—DOCTRINE OF THE ARMINIANS

The subject of the controversy between the Arminians and the Gomarists, turned, doubtless, more immediately on Calvin's doctrine of predestination. But, as may easily be conceived, a series of other dogmas were soon involved in this dispute; for the aforesaid error doth not stand isolated, but, in part, presupposes, and is grounded on other notions, or rather mistakes; and, in part, has them in its train. But, as the controversy arose on the question of absolute election, we shall commence with the exposition of the Arminian doctrine on that subject; and then set forth the other points, on which it exerted an influence.

Against the rigid Calvinistic theory of predestination the Arminians not only alleged that thereby God was made the author of moral evil, but, they very acutely observed, that by this theory Christ's death of atonement would be deprived of all power and efficacy—nay, become utterly inexplicable. For, they said, if from all eternity the salvation of the elect hath been unconditionally and immutably decreed, it would ensue in virtue of that decree, and not for the sake of Christ's merits; and as to the reprobate, Christ, undoubtedly, could not have appeared on their behalf, since God did not, and could not, seriously wish for their salvation, as this would be in utter contradiction with their eternal destination to misery.[1]

The doctrines of Calvin in respect to the elect and the reprobate, as combated by the Arminians, stood by no means isolated. They changed the idea of a government of the world, and a providential guidance of all things, into the conception of a destiny, whereby all the movements of creatures are absolutely fettered. For there could be no conceivable interest in withdrawing any thing from the circle of necessity, when the felicity and the misery of spirits had once been absolutely decreed; and any conception of final causes, as to what might yet be reserved to Free-will, became utterly impossible. For to deny to man moral liberty, and leave him a so-called political freedom, as the Luther Formularies do, is to betray the most singular levity; as, when once the kernel has been taken away, no interest can attach to the wretched husk; and in the world of man every-

---

[1] Confessio sive Declaratio, etc. Herdewici, 1622-4, p. 31. See the defence in the Examen Censuræ, p. 104, b.

thing hath a moral relation. Accordingly, the Remonstrants in their Confession devoted a particular section to the article on Providence, attaching thereto the notion of a wise, holy, and just guidance (not predetermination) of all things; and, in this way, they conceived they steered the true middle course between the Epicurean system of casualty, and the Stoical and Manichean destiny, or Fatum; for, with the latter, they associated the errors of predestinarianism.[1]

To man, therefore, they ascribe free-will, which is so inherent in his nature that it can never be obliterated.[2] The fall of the first man is, in necessary connection with this, represented not as a mere spontaneous, but as a perfectly free act.[3] As an immediate consequence of the Fall, we see stated the loss of true righteousness, and of the felicity it insured. Adam was doomed to the eternal misery, and the manifold temporal misfortunes, wherewith he had been menaced; and his posterity, in consequence of their ties of relationship with their common progenitor, incurred the same fate. As the Confession adds, that actual sins increase guilt in the sight of God, obscure at first the understanding in spiritual things, then render it by degrees totally blind, and at last, through the habit of sin, entirely corrupt the will, it follows that the Arminians did not conceive original sin in itself had bereaved man of *all* his faculties for good.[4] By such an opinion, in fact, their opposition to the doctrine of absolute predestination would have become utterly untenable.

Redemption in Christ Jesus is, according to the Arminian system, universal. To every man who heareth the Gospel sufficient grace is proffered to enable him to rise from his fall; and where the announcement of the doctrines of salvation is not attended with these effects, man only is to blame. If, on the other hand, grace prevails (*gratia efficax*), then the reason of this is to be sought for, not in its intrinsic nature, but in the reception which it has found in the soul of man. An irresistibly

---

[1] Loc. cit. c. vi, pp. 19-23.
[2] Loc. cit. p. 22. 'Naturalem tamen rerum contingentiam atque innatam arbitrii humani libertatem, olim semel in creatione datam, nunquam per ipsam (providentiam) tollit (Deus), sed rerum naturas ordinario salvas relinquit : atque ita cum hominis voluntate in agendo concurrit, ut ipsam quoque pro suo genio agere, et libere suas partes obire sinat : nec proinde præcisam bene, nedum male, agendi necessitatem eidem unquam imponit.'
[3] Loc. cit. c. viii, sect. 2, p. 24. ' Transgressus est, inquam, non spontanea, tantum, sed prorus libera voluntate.'
[4] Loc. cit. sect. 5, p. 25.

working grace is therefore, according to the Arminian system, totally inadmissible. With reason they assert that its notion is at utter variance with the rewards promised to obedience when rendered, and with the penalties threatened against the refusal of obedience, for God would in that case, extort obedience, and would work exclusively and alone. It were absurd, and contrary to all reason, they add, to promise anyone a recompense, as if he had freely obeyed, and yet wring obedience from him, as from a slave. On the other hand, they finally observe, it were cruel to inflict an eternal punishment on the disobedient, who yet cannot obey; for they want the irresistible Grace, under the condition whereof alone obedience can be rendered.[1]

But if the Remonstrants reject these Calvinistic views of grace, they yet willingly retain those doctrines respecting it, without which the character of Christianity cannot be preserved. The grace of God, according to them, determines the beginning, the progress, and the consummation of all good. Their articles of belief on these points are nearly identical with the Catholic; and therefore, like the Council of Trent, they speak of a resuscitating grace, which only awakens the dormant powers yet existing in fallen man,[2] in opposition to the Lutheran theory, according to which the higher faculties must first be created anew in him.

With the clearest consciousness of their object, and with a genuine scientific insight into, and prosecution of their task, the Remonstrants defined the notion of faith also. As the usual Protestant conception of the same excludes the idea of free-will, and is based on the assumption of the impracticability of the law, the Arminians, having once embraced the true

---

[1] Loc. cit. c. xvii. pp. 55-58, sect. 7. 'Gratiam tamen divinam aspernari et respuere ejusque operationi resistere homo potest, ita ut seipsum, cum divinitus ad fidem et obedientiam vocatur, inidoneum reddere queat ad credendum, et divinæ voluntati obedientum,' etc.

[2] Loc. cit. c. xvii, sect. 16, p. 37. 'Gratiam itaque Dei statuimus esse principium et complementum omnis boni : adeo ut ne ipse quidem regenitus absque præcedente ista, sive præveniente, excitante, prosequente, et cooperante gratia, bonum ullum salutare cogitare, velle aut peragere possit : nedum ullis ad malum trahentibus tentationibus resistere. Ita ud fides, conversio, et bona opera omnia, omnesque actiones piæ et salutares, quas quis cogitando assequi potest, gratiæ Dei in Christo, tanquam causæ suæ principali et primariæ *in solidum* sint adscribendæ.' When the expression ' in solidum ' is here used so, the reader should remember the expression which Dr. Eck employed in the disputation at Leipzic, who very well observed, that the *totum* of regeneration is to be ascribed to God, but only not *totaliter*.

doctrine of free-will, were necessarily compelled to assail the
favourite opinion of the Reformers, as to the saving nature of
Faith without works. He who believeth in a way acceptable to
God is, in their opinion, one who, converted to the precepts of
the Gospel, is filled with contrition for the sins he hath committed, and is inwardly renewed. They observe, as Paul
teacheth, that faith is imputed to man for righteousness; and
James, that 'by works a man is justified, and not by faith
only;' as the Epistle to Timothy promises to godly behaviour,
rewards in this and in the next life; and as the author of the
Epistle to the Hebrews moreover declares, that without being
sanctified, no one shall see God; it follows that the saving faith,
required by the Gospel, is certainly no other, than that which,
from its very essence, includes in itself obedience; is the fruitful
parent of all good works, and the source and the root of all
Christian piety and sanctification. Hence they sum up their
belief in these words—the true saving or salutary faith is that
'which worketh by charity.'[1]

The following five acts of God, according to the Remonstrants, denote the history of the sinner, who hath already
obeyed the Divine call, been converted to faith, and under the
assistance of grace, fulfilleth the Divine precepts. The first
is *election*, whereby the true believers are separated from the
profane multitude of those who perish, and are marked off as
the property of God. Election is followed by *adoption*, whereby
the regenerated are received into the family of God, and fully
admitted to the rights of the celestial heritage, which in its due
time will be awarded. *Justification* is then described as the
gracious absolution from all sin, by means of a faith, ' working
by charity' in Jesus Christ, and in his merits; and *Sanctification* is distinguished from justification as the fourth act of God.
Sanctification the Remonstrants conceive to be a perfect, inward separation of the sons of God from the children of this
world. Lastly, *the Sealing* through the Holy Spirit, as the
fifth act of God, they represent as the firmer and more solid
confirmation in true confidence, in the hope of heavenly glory,
and in the assurance of Divine grace.[2] Of the last periods in
the internal history of the regenerated man the Arminians formed

---

[1] Loc. cit. c. x, xi, pp. 33-38. 'Fides salvifica.' The expression 'fides
justificans' (according to the Examen Censur. p. 107, b), they do not make
use of.

[2] Loc. cit. c. xviii, p. 59.

so high a conception, that they say of him he can no longer sin; for the words in the first Epistle of John iii, 4, and v, 18, they apply to him. Nevertheless, they protest against the notion, that the believer, who is exalted to this high degree of perfection, is no longer guilty of any, even the slightest fault that may be bottomed in error, frailty, and infirmity, especially under grievous temptations.[1]

It was natural to suppose that the Gomarists would charge this doctrine of conversion, with declaring war against the whole Protestant Church, and with being Catholic, or even Socinian; but it can scarcely be conceived, that the Remonstrants would deny the charge.[2] For so soon as we overlook unessential points, and a diversity of expression, the unprejudiced observer must perceive the most striking concurrence with the Catholic doctrine. Against their agreement with Catholics, the Remonstrants appeal principally to the circumstance of their declaring justification to be a judicial act, whereby God releases the sinner from the merited punishments, whereas Catholics regard it as an inward newness of life, wrought by the Deity. But under one act, which they call Justification, Catholics comprehend the Divine forgiveness of sins; whereas the Remonstrants divide this one act into a series of acts, which cannot be defended on scriptural grounds. But their opposition to the Calvinists and Lutherans consists herein, that they assert a true and inward deliverance from sin through regeneration, and do not recognise any imputation of Christ's righteousness through faith only, in opposition to *Christian* works and to *Christian* charity. Next, they place their divergence from Catholics in the difference of ideas, which both attach to faith: for they asserted of themselves, they regarded good works as only the fruits of faith, and this the Catholics were not wont to do. Were then the Arminians ignorant, that Catholics deduce charity from faith, and from both, good works, as their common fruits? In many particular definitions of the Arminians, moreover, the influence of Socinian principles is very manifest; and, on this account, they incurred the charge of Socinianism, which, however, was very unfounded. It was Hugo Grotius, a Remonstrant, who, against the assaults of the Socinians, had defended the doctrine of the vicarious satisfaction!

[1] Loc. cit. c. ii, p. 37.
[2] Examen Censuræ, loc. cit. p. 107, *et seq.*

§ XCIV—DOCTRINE OF THE ARMINIANS ON THE SACRAMENTS

The Remonstrants admit only two sacraments, and consider them as signs of covenant, by means whereof God symbolises His promised blessings, and communicates and seals them *in a certain way*; and the faithful, on their part, publicly declare they will embrace them with a true, firm, and obedient faith, and bear the same in lasting and grateful remembrance.[1] As the expression, 'communicate in a certain way,' is evidently very obscure and indefinite, the Gomarists solicited a fuller explanation, which, after a long and dilatory parley, turned out to be this; that, touching the mode of efficacy in the sacraments, nothing was really known, and no internal communication of grace, connected with their reception, could be admitted. That, moreover, from Holy Writ the notion of a sealing of the Divine promises through the sacraments, can be deduced, was even called in question.[2]

These definitions could not fail to incur strong censure; and they were even charged, as regarded baptism, with bearing perfect resemblance to the maxims of the Anabaptists. In fact, there was, according to these principles, no longer a rational ground for baptising infants; nay, baptism administered to them must needs be regarded as superstitious. Even Episcopius, in his *Examination of the Censure*, could give no other reply, than that infant baptism was not discontinued in his sect, as it was of high antiquity, and its abolition would certainly be attended with great scandal.[3] Yet a rite, which, in itself, was held to be senseless and meaningless, and was retained merely out of respect for custom, could not long endure. And, in fact,

---

[1] Confess. Remonstr. c. xxxiii. p. 70. 'Sacramenta cum dicimus, externas ecclesiæ ceremonias, seu ritus illos sacros et solennes intelligimus quibus fœderalibus signis ac sigillis visibilibus Deus gratiosa beneficia sua in fœdere præsertim evangelico promissa, non modo nobis repræsentat et adumbrat, sed et certo modo exhibet et obsignat: nosque vicissim palam publiceque declaramus ac testamur, nos promissiones omnes divinas vera, firma atque obsequiosa fide amplecti et beneficia ipsius jugi et grata semper memoria celebrare velle.'

[2] Exam. Cens. p. 245, *et seq.*

[3] Exam. Cens. p. 249. 'Eadem ratio est de Prædobaptismo: Remonstrantes ritum baptizandi infantes, ut perantiquum et in ecclesiis Christi, præsertim in Africa, permultis sæculis frequentatum, haud illubenter etiam in cœtibus suis admittunt, adeoque vix sine offensione et scandalo magno intermitti posse statuunt, tantum abest, ut eum seu illicitum aut nefastum improbent ac damnent.'

we find, that the Remonstrants, a portion of them at least, gradually adopted the practice of the Mennonites; as, in general, we discover an interchange of opinions and rites between these two religious communities.

But, in respect to the Lord's Supper, Episcopius, in his *Examination of the Censure*, was forced plainly to admit, that the Remonstrants adhered to the views of Zuinglius, who, in the article of the Sacraments, was to be revered as the best teacher.[1]

From this point a shallow conception of the whole system of Christianity penetrated more and more into the sect, and soon even the dogma of the Saviour's divinity was disputed. Although, in the Confession of the Remonstrants, this dogma, as well as in general, the orthodox doctrine on the Trinity, is expressed with the utmost clearness and correctness;[2] yet Limborch, one of the most eminent Arminian writers, early asserted a relation of subordination in the Trinity. Some of his expressions, nevertheless, may very well coincide with the Catholic exposition of that doctrine; and in so far as they place the Father above the Son, merely because the latter is rooted in the former, and subordinate the Holy Ghost to the two, because in the two He hath the source of His God-head, the expressions are perfectly identical. But Limborch teaches, besides, that, in the strict sense, the Father imparts commands to the Son, and both to the Holy Ghost—a doctrine which is utterly absurd, and subversive of the Trinity. By degrees Socinianism found its way into the Arminian sect—a way, which it cannot be denied, had been long before prepared; so that when the Gomarists, during the first controversies, constantly repeated the charge that Socinian poison had crept in among the Remonstrants, we must not consider this accusation as the mere effect of party hatred. Doubtless this reproach was frequently unfounded, nay, as regards the earlier history of the Arminians, the charge, with the exception of some subordinate definitions in the article of justification, can nowhere, perhaps, be fully *established*. But, nevertheless, many among them must even then have manifested a leaning to the hated system of Socinus; for otherwise the suspicion of the rigid Calvinists could not be at all accounted for, and the sequel has well justified that suspicion. Even

---

[1] Loc. cit. p. 252. ' Et hac in re assentientes sibi habent non paucos Reformatos, inter quos Zuinglius optimus hujus ceremoniæ doctor, princeps est,' etc.

[2] Confessio sive Declar. c. iii, p. 14.

from the very copious treatment, which the doctrine of the Trinity has undergone in the Confession of the Remonstrants, we might feel disposed to look for a confirmation of this suspicion; for, if no special grounds had existed, such detailed exposition would have been quite superfluous. Yet, on the other hand, it may be observed, that as the authors of the formulary seem to have proposed for their object, to give an outline of all the more important doctrines of Christian faith and morality; an important place, without any peculiar or secondary views, was of necessity assigned to the dogma of the Trinity. The well-known exegetical writer, Daniel Brenius, who was an immediate disciple of Episcopius, even at that early period, openly professed Socinian views in respect to the person of Christ, as Sand in his book enumerates him among the Antitrinitarians; [1] and in the subsequent time, such doctrines obtained among the Remonstrants very general diffusion.

[1] Sand Biblioth. Antitrin. p. 135.

APPENDIX

Note A, referred to at page 232

Salig, in his *Complete History of the Augsburg Confession* (book ii, c. 8, sect. 7, p. 297), gives an account of a scene which occurred in the general committee appointed at Augsburg to bring about a reunion of the Churches; from which it will appear that Luther originally, so far from rejecting ecclesiastical punishments, reproached his adversaries with their remissness in imposing them. Salig says: ' I cannot, meanwhile, pass over in silence what Cochlæus has related respecting the transactions of the first and second day, touching the matter of satisfaction in penance. On the first evening, when the difference on this point could not be reconciled, it was agreed that Cochlæus on one side, and Melancthon on the other, should the next morning discover something to bring about an understanding. Cochlæus accordingly adduced a passage, where Luther wrote as follows: " Our mother, the Christian Church, when from kindness of heart she will obviate the chastening hand of God, punishes her children with some penances of satisfaction, lest they fall under the Divine rod. Thus the Ninivites, by their self-imposed works, anticipated the judgment of God. This voluntary punishment is not everything, as the adversaries will have it, yet it is still necessary. For either we, or men, or God, punish sins; but this the adversaries by their indulgences totally set aside. If they were pious pastors, they would rather impose punishments, and, according to the example of the Churches, go before the judgment of God, as did Moses, when, on account of the golden calf, he slew some Israelites [this example is not very relevant]. But the very best thing of all were, if we would chastise ourselves." ' This was an earnest, energetic language on the part of Luther, widely removed from those effeminate maxims subsequently introduced by his doctrine on Faith, which exacts of man nothing disagreeable—I might almost say, nothing incommodious. Salig continues: ' This passage of Luther's, which Colchæus had communicated, Dr Eck read from a schedule before the committee. Cochlæus relates, that the seven Lutheran deputies looked each other in the face, and for a while observed a dead silence. Melancthon, who sat thereby, reddened, and said, " I am aware, indeed, that Luther wrote this." And as he could say nothing more, the Elector, John Frederick, asked, " At what time did Luther write this?" " Perhaps about ten years ago." The Catholics then replied, that it was immaterial when Luther wrote this passage, but it was enough that such was his opinion on this doctrine. Hereupon Brentius and Schnepfius became indignant, and said: " They were there not to defend Luther's writings, but to assert their Confession." Melancthon then delivered his opinion in writing, to the following effect: " We may hold penance to consist of three parts—contrition, confession, *yet so that in this we look in the first place to absolution*, and believe in the same; and next satisfaction, to wit, that worthy fruits of penance follow." In one point all were agreed, that on account of satisfaction, sin was not forgiven as to its guilt. But whether in respect to the penalty, satisfaction were necessary to the forgiveness of sin, still remained matter of dispute. So far Cochlæus. Now I will not entirely call in question his account,' etc. The account cannot be at all called in question. This passage of Luther's is still to be found in the *Assertio* 41 Art. *contra Indulgent.* Art. 5, as Salig himself after Cochlæus has cited them in his work, *de actis et Scriptis Lutheri*, p. 200. That the deputies of the Protestant States should have fallen into some embarrassment, was in the nature of things ; for in Luther's church his variations were never contemplated with pleasure. Melancthon's expressions, however, perfectly coincide with larger passages in the *Apology*, wherein he likewise enumerates three component parts in penance. Art. v : 'Si quis volet addere tertium, videlicet dignos fructus pœnitentiæ, hoc est mutationem totius vitæ ac morum in melius, non refragabimur.'

It is, indeed, surprising that he will *only not be opposed* to what harmonises very well with his doctrine on faith, which will not establish a necessary inward connection between faith and the *mutatio totius vitæ*. From all this it is clear that Melancthon annexed to *his* satisfaction a very different notion from Catholics, as, in the negotiations which took place at that period between the two religious parties, there occurred from laudable motives, though not without reluctance, a sort of mutual self-delusion. In the Catholic Church the purpose of amendment of life is included in contrition, and is the first, not the last, act of the sinner in the sacrament of penance. But as, among the Lutherans, contrition has a very different signification from that which it bears among Catholics, consisting merely in fear—and as from this fear man is liberated through absolution, and then only ensues newness of life, the latter, according to Melancthon, forms the third part of penance, and consequently is not the Catholic satisfaction. This third part the later Lutherans entirely threw aside, because, if amendment of life were made an *integral* portion of penance, the whole Lutheran doctrine on faith would fall to the ground. Here, as on other points, Melancthon became entangled in contradictions, for he always sought to patch up the defects in the doctrines of his Church, without renouncing her fundamental principles. So in this narrative of Cochlæus, after admitting that in penance there were three parts, he turns round and says, that ' we should look *in the first place* to absolution ' ; as if all did not exist, and claim our attention, in a *like* degree.

Note B, *referred to at page* 237

To bring our explanation of the Christian sacrifice more vividly before the minds of our readers, it may be useful to give a few extracts from the liturgies of the eastern and western Churches, and to cite some of the principal forms. In regard to the oriental liturgies, they usually bear the name of the founders of the Churches wherein they were used. So, for instance, the liturgy of the Church of Jerusalem is called the liturgy of St James ; that of the Alexandrine Church, the liturgy of St Mark : or they are entitled after some celebrated bishop, who made use of them, as St Chrysostom, St Basil, St Cyril, and the rest. As to their age, this is a matter which cannot be so accurately determined. Certain it is, that in the fourth century they were already in existence, since the Monophysites of Syria and Egypt, who in part separated from the Catholic Church in the latter half of the fifth age, make use of these liturgies, as well as the orthodox Greeks. Moreover, St Cyril of Jerusalem, in his catechetical discourses, appeals to many passages in the liturgy of St James ; and St Chrysostom, who in his homilies often explains and employs portions of the liturgy, presupposes them to be things of long standing. The latter father lived towards the close, the former about the middle, of the fourth century. In general, there is such a striking conformity between the oriental and the western liturgies, whereof great numbers, through a gracious Providence, have been rendered accessible to us; and this coincidence is so manifest even in the forms, that their formal groundwork indisputably belongs to a period, when all Christians were yet confined within a small space. Already, in the second century, St Irenæus makes mention of the ἐπίκλησις: and the preface with the *Sursum corda*, ἄνω τὸν νοῦν, or τὰς καρδίας, which recurs in every liturgy, St Cyprian speaks of in the middle of the third century. (Compare Bona rer. liturg. tom. ii, c, 10, where several passages of a like kind are brought together.) Respecting the antiquity of the liturgies in general, see the excellent dissertation by Renaudot, *Dissertatio de Liturg. orient. orig. et auctor.* forming an introduction to his *Collectio Liturg. orient.* tom. ii, Paris, 1716. A brief summary of all the investigations pertaining to this subject, the reader may see in *Lienhart de antiquis liturgiis*. Argentorati, 1826.[1]

In the liturgy of St Chrysostom (in Goar's *Euchologium sive Rituale Græcorum*, Paris, 1647, p. 70) the first prayer of the faithful (in the *Missa fidelium*) runs thus:

"Εὐχαριστοῦμέν σοι, κύριε ὁ θεὸς τῶν δυνάμεων, τῷ καταξιώσαντι ἡμᾶς παραστῆναι καὶ νῦν τῷ ἁγίῳ σου θυσιαστηρίῳ, καὶ προσπεσεῖν τοῖς οἰκτιρμοῖς σου ὑπὲρ τῶν ἡμετέρων ἁμαρτημάτων καὶ τοῦ σου λαοῦ ἀγνοημάτων. Πρόσδεξαι ὁ θεὸς τὴν δέησιν ἡμῶν, ποίησον ἡμᾶς ἀξίους γενέσθαι προσφέρειν σοι δεήσεις καὶ ἱκεσίας, καὶ θυσίας ἀναιμάκτους ὑπὲρ παντὸς τοῦ λαοῦ σου, καὶ ἱκάνωσον ἡμᾶς, οὓθ ἔθου εἰς τὴν διακονίαν σου ταύτην, ἐν τῇ δυνάμει τοῦ πνεύματός σου τοῦ ἁγίου ἀκαταγνώστως καὶ ἀπροσκόπτως ἐν κσθαρῷ μαρτυρείῳ τῆς συνειδήσεως ἡμῶν ἐπικαλεῖσθαί σε ἐν παντὶ καιρῷ καὶ τόπῳ, ἵνο εἰσακούων ἡμῶν, ἵλεως ἡμῖν εἴης ἐν τῷ πλήθει τῆς σῆς ἀγαθότητος."

While the seraphic hymn of the *sanctus* is being uttered, the priest, among other things, recites the following prayer (p. 72):—

"Σὺ γὰρ εἶ ὁ προσφέρων καὶ προσφερόμεονς καὶ προσδεχόμενος καὶ διαδιδόμενος, Χριστὲ ὁ θεὸς ἡμῶν, καὶ σοὶ τὴν δόξαν διαπέμπομεν, σὺν τῷ ἀνάρχῳ σου πατρὶ, καὶ τῷ παναγίῳ, καὶ ἀγαθῷ καὶ ζωοποιῷ σου πνεύματι· νῦν καὶ ἀεί, καὶ εἰς τοὺς αἰῶνας τῶν αἰώνων· ἀμὴν."

Further on (p. 75):—

The Priest. Στῶμεν καλῶς, στῶμεν μετὰ φόβου, πρόσχωμεν τὴν ἁγίαν ἀναφορὰν εἰς εἰρήνη (?) προσφέρειν.
The Choir. Ἔλεον εἰρήνης, θυσίαν αἰνέσεως.
The Priest. Ἡ χάρις τοῦ κυρίου ἡμῶν Ἰησοῦ Χριστοῦ, καὶ ἡ ἀγάπη τοῦ θεοῦ, καὶ πατρὸς, καὶ ἡ κοινωνία τοῦ ἁγίου πνεύματος, εἴη μετὰ πάντων ἡμῶν
The Choir. Καὶ μετὰ τοῦ πνεύματός σου.
The Priest. Ἄνω σχῶμεν τὰς καρδίας.
The Choir. Ἔχομεν πρὸς τὸν κύριον.
The Priest. Εὐχαριστήσωμεν τῷ κυρίῳ.
The Choir. Ἄξιόν καὶ δίκαιόν ἐστι προσκυνεῖν πατέρα, υἱόν, καὶ ἅγιον πνεῦμα, τριάδα ὁμοούσιον καὶ ἀχώριστον.
The Priest. Ἄξιον καὶ δίκαιον σὲ ὑμνεῖν, σὲ εὐλογεῖν, σὲ αἰνεῖν, σοὶ εὐχαρι-

---
[1] The translator begs to refer the reader to Dr Rock's learned and interesting work, the *Hierurgia*, where he will find copious information respecting the purport, arrangement and antiquity of the various liturgies.—*Trans.*

στεῖν, σὲ προσκυνεῖν ἐν παντὶ τόπῳ τῆς δεσποτείας σου, σὺ γὰρ εἶ θεὸς ἀνέκφραστος, ἀπερινόητος, ἀόρατος, ἀκατάληπτος, ἀεὶ ὤν, ὡσαύτως ὤν κ. τ. λ.

In the Liturgy of St Basil (in Goar's Euchologium, p. 162) the first prayer of the faithful runs thus :—

"Σὺ κύριε κατέδεξας ἡμῖν τὸ μέγα τοῦτο τῆς σωτηρίας μυστήριον, σὺ κατηξίωσας ἡμᾶς τοὺς ταπεινοὺς καὶ ἀναξίους δούλους σου, γίγνεσθαι λειτούργους τοῦ ἁγίου σου θυσιαστηρίου. Σὺ ἱκάνωσον ἡμᾶς τῇ δυνάμει τοῦ ἁγίου πνεύματος εἰς τὴν διακονίαν ταύτην, ἵνα ἀκατακρίτως στάντες ἐνώπιον τῆς ἁγίας δόξης σου, προσάγωμέν σοι θυσίαν αἰνέσεως. Σὺ γὰρ εἶ ὁ ἐνεργῶν τὰ πάντα ἐν πᾶσι. Δὸς κύριε καὶ ὑπὲρ τῶν ἡμετέρων ἁμαρτημάτων, καὶ τῶν τοῦ λαοῦ ἀγνοημάτων, δεκτὴν γίγνεσθαι τὴν θυσίαν ἡμῶν, καὶ εὐπρόσδεκτον ἐνώπιόν σου."

The Prayer at the Offertory, p. 164 :—

"Κύριε ὁ θεὸς ἡμῶν ὁ κτίσας ἡμᾶς, καὶ ἀγαγὼν εἰς τὴν ζωὴν ταύτην, ὁ ὑποδείξας ἡμῖν ὁδοὺς εἰς σωτηρίαν, ὁ χαρισάμενος ἡμῖν οὐρανίων μυστηρίων ἀποκάλυψιν, σὺ εἶ ὁ θέμενος ἡμᾶς εἰς τὴν διακονίαν ταύτην ἐν τῇ δυνάμει τοῦ πνεύματός σου τοῦ ἁγίου. Εὐδόκησον δὴ κύριε τοῦ γενέσθαι ἡμᾶς διακόνους τῆς καινῆς σου διαθήκης, λειτουργοὺς τῶν ἁγίων σου μυστηρίων· πρόσδεξαι ἡμᾶς προσεγγίζοντας τῷ ἁγίῳ σου θυσιαστηρίῳ, κατὰ τὸ πλῆθος τοῦ ἐλέους σου· ἵνα γενώμεθα ἄξιοι τοῦ προσφέρειν σοι τὴν λογικὴν ταύτην καὶ ἀναίμακτον θυσίαν ὑπὲρ τῶν ἡμετέρων ἁμαρτημάτων καὶ τῶν τοῦ λαοῦ ἀγνοημάτων· ἣν προσδεξάμενος εἰς τὸ ἅγιον καὶ νοερόν σου θυσιαστήριον, εἰς ὀσμὴν εὐωδίας, ἀντικατάπεμψον ἡμῖν τὴν χάριν τοῦ ἁγίου σου πνεύματος· ἐπίβλεψον ἐφ' ἡμᾶς ὁ θεὸς καὶ ἔπιδε ἐπὶ τὴν λατρείαν ἡμῶν ταύτην, καὶ πρόσδεξαι αὐτήν, ὡς προσεδέξω Ἀβὲλ τὰ δῶρα, Νῶε τὰς θυσίας, Ἀβραὰμ τὰς ὁλοκαρπώσεις, Μωσέως καὶ Ἀρὼν τὰς ἱερωσύνας, Σαμουὴλ τὰς εἰρηνικάς· ὡς προσεδέξω ἐκ τῶν ἁγίων σου ἀποστόλων τὴν ἀληθινὴν ταύτην λατρείαν· οὕτω καὶ ἐκ τῶν χειρῶν ἡμῶν τῶν ἁμαρτωλῶν πρόσδεξαι τὰ δῶρα ταῦτα ἐν τῇ χρηστότητί σου κύριε· ἵνα καταξιωθέντες λειτουργεῖν ἀμέμπτως τῷ ἁγίῳ σου θυσιαστηρίῳ, εὑρώμεθα μισθὸν τῶν πιστῶν καὶ φρονίμων οἰκονόμων, ἐν τῇ ἡμέρᾳ τῇ φοβερᾷ τῆς ἀνταποδόσεώς σου τῆς δικαίας."

In the Alexandrine liturgy of St Mark (Renaudot, Liturg. Orient. Coll. t. i, page 145), the priest thus prays at the canon :—

"Πάντα δὲ ἐποίησας διὰ τῆς σῆς σοφίας, τοῦ φωτὸς τοῦ ἀληθινοῦ, τοῦ μονογενοῦς σου υἱοῦ, τοῦ κυρίου καὶ θεοῦ καὶ σωτῆρος ἡμῶν Ἰησοῦ Χριστοῦ· δι' οὗ σοι σὺν αὐτῷ καὶ ἁγίῳ πνεύματι εὐχαριστοῦντες, προσφέρομεν τὴν λογικὴν καὶ ἀναίμακτον λατρείαν ταύτην, ἣν προσφέρει σου κύριε πάντα τὰ ἔθνη, ἀπὸ ἀνατολῶν ἡλίου καὶ μέχρι δυσμῶν· ἀπὸ ἄρκτου καὶ μεσημβρίας· ὅτι μέγα τὸ ὄνομά σου ἐν πᾶσι τοῖς ἔθνεσι, καὶ ἐν παντὶ τόπῳ θυμίαμα προσφέρεται τῷ ὀνόματι ἁγίῳ σου, καὶ θυσία, καὶ προσφορά."

In the liturgy of St James, used by the Jacobites or the Syrian Monophysites, in common with the Church of Jerusalem, the priest says as follows (Renaudot, t. ii, p. 30) :

'Deus pater, qui, propter amorem tuum erga homines magnum et ineffabilem, misisti filium tuum in mundum, ut ovem errantem reduceret, ne avertas faciem tuam a nobis, dum sacrificium hoc spirituale et incruentum celebramus : non enim justitiæ nostræ confidimus, sed misericordiæ tuæ. Deprecamur ergo et obsecramus clementiam tuam, ne in judicium sit populo tuo mysterium hoc, quod institutum nobis est ad salutem ; sed ad veniam peccatorum, remissionem insipientiarum, et ad gratias tibi referendas, per gratiam, misericordiam et amorem erga homines unigeniti Filii tui, per quem et cum quo te decet gloria.'

Further below (p. 32) the priest continues :—

'Memoriam igitur agimus, Domine, mortis, et resurrectionis tuæ e sepulchro post triduum, et ascensionis tuæ in cœlum, et sessionis tuæ ad dexteram Dei patris : rursumque adventus tui secundi, terribilis et gloriosi, quo judicaturus es orbem in justitia, cum unumquemque remuneraturus es secundum opera sua. Offerimus tibi hoc sacrificium terribile et incruentum, ut non secundum peccata nostra agas nobiscum, Domine neque secundum iniquitates nostras retribuas nobis ; sed, secundum mansuetudinem tuam et amorem tuum erga homines magnum et ineffabilem, dele peccata nostra, servorum nempe tuorum tibi supplicantium. Populus enim tuus et hæreditas tua deprecatur te et per te et tecum patrem tuum, dicens,' etc.

In the Gothic Missal (in Mabillon de Liturg. Gallic. Paris, 1729) we read among other things, at p. 210 :—

'Sacrificiis præsentibus, Domine, quæsumus intende placatus ; quibus non jam aurum thus et myrrha profertur, sed quod iisdem muneribus declaratur, offertur, immolatur, sumitur (scil. Christus).'

In the Missal of the Franks, lib. cit. p. 38 :—

'Sacrificium, Domine, quod desiderantur offerimus, etc.—P. 319. Hanc igitur oblationem servitutis nostræ, sed et cunctæ familiæ tuæ, quam tibi offerimus,' etc.

In the old Gallican Missal (lib. cit. p. 334), we read the following prayers :—

'Sacrificium tibi Domine celebrandum placatus intende : quod et nos a vitiis nostræ conditionis emundet, et tuo nomini reddat acceptos : et communicatio præsentis osculi perpetuæ proficiat charitati.—P. 385. Descendat, precamur, omnipotens Deus, super hæc quæ tibi offerimus, verbum tuum sanctum ; descendat inæstimabilis gloriæ tuæ Spiritus ; descendat antiquæ indulgentiæ tuæ donum ; ut fiat oblatio hæc Hostia spiritualis in odorem suavitatis accepta : etiam nos famulos tuos per sanguinem Christi tua manus invicta custodiat. Libera nos ab omni malo, omnipotens, æterne Deus : et quia tibi soli est præstandi potestas, tribue, ut hoc solemne sacrificium sanctificet corda nostra, dum creditur : deleat peccata, dum sumitur.'

Decorum requires us now to cite some forms of prayer from the Roman Liturgy :—

'Suscipe, sancte Pater, omnipotens æterne Deus, hanc immaculatam hostiam, quam ego, indignus famulus tuus, offero tibi Deo meo vivo et vero, pro innumerabilibus peccatis et offensionibus et negligentiis meis, et pro omnibus circumstantibus, sed et pro omnibus fidelibus Christianis, vivis atque defunctis ; ut mihi et illis proficiat ad salutem in vitam æternam.

'Offerimus tibi Domine calicem salutis, tuam deprecantes clementiam ; ut in conspectu divinæ majestatis tuæ pro nostra et totius mundi salute cum odore suavitatis ascendat.

'In spiritu humilitatis et in animo contrito suscipiamur a te Domine : et sic fiat sacrificium nostrum in conspectu tuo hodie, ut placeat tibi Domine Deus.

'Suscipe, sancta Trinitas, hanc oblationem quam tibi offerimus ob memoriam passionis, resurrectionis, et ascensionis Jesu Christi Domini nostri, etc. Suscipiat Dominus hoc sacrificium de manibus tuis ad laudem et gloriam nominis sui, ad utilitatem quoque nostram, totiusque ecclesiæ suæ sanctæ.

'Te igitur, clementissime Pater, per Jesum Christum filium tuum Dominum nostrum, supplices rogamus ac petimus uti accepta habeas et benedicas hæc dona, hæc munera hæc sancta sacrificia illibata, imprimis quæ tibi offerimus pro ecclesia tua sancta catholica, quam pacificare, custodire, adunare, et regere digneris toto orbe terrarum, etc. [This prayer occurs in all the Liturgies.] Memento, Domine, famulorum famularumque tuarum et omnium circumstantium, quorum tibi fides cognita est et nota devotio, pro quibus tibi offerimus, vel qui tibi offerunt, hoc sacrificium laudis pro se suisque omnibus, pro redemptione animarum suarum, pro spe salutis et incolumitatis suæ : tibique reddunt vota sua æterno Deo, vivo et vera.'

More or less detailed representations of the principal actions in the life of Christ, prayers for the living and the dead, and the mention of the saints, occur in every Liturgy from the earliest ages of the Church. But want of space prevents us from citing, in proof of this, any longer passages.

Translation of the Extracts from the Greek Liturgies.

In the liturgy of St Chrysostom (in Goar's Euchologium sive Rituale Græcorum, p. 70, Par. 1647), the first prayer of the faithful in the Missa fidelium runs thus :—

'We give thee thanks, O Lord God of Hosts, who has judged us worthy both to assist now at thy holy altar, and to supplicate thy mercy on account of our own sins, and of the errors of thy people. Receive, O God, our prayers, make us worthy to offer unto thee prayers and supplications and unbloody sacrifices in behalf of all thy people, and make us, whom thou hast ordained for this thy holy ministry, worthy to invoke thee, in all places, and at all times, by the power of thy Holy Spirit, without blame and without offence, and according to the pure testimony of our conscience that thou mayest hear us, and be propitious unto us, according to the multitude of thy mercies.'

While the seraphic hymn of the *sanctus* is being uttered, the priest, among other things, says, as follows (p. 72) : ' Thou art, O Christ our God, the offerer and the offered, the receiver and the distributed, and we render glory to thee, together with thy eternal Father, and with thy most holy, and righteous, and life-giving Spirit, now and for ever, and for ages of ages. Amen.'

Further on, p. 75.

The Priest saith : ' Let us stand up in holiness ; let us stand up with awe ; let us endeavour to offer up in peace the holy oblation.'

The Choir. ' The victim of peace, the sacrifice of praise.'

The Priest. ' May the grace of our Lord Jesus Christ, and the charity of God the Father, and the communion of the Holy Ghost, be with you all.'

Choir. ' And with thy spirit.'
Priest. ' Let us raise up our hearts.'
Choir. ' We have raised them up to the Lord.'
Priest. ' Let us give thanks to the Lord.'
Choir. ' It is most meet and just to worship the Father, the Son, and the Holy Ghost, one consubstantial and undivided Trinity.'
Priest. ' It is meet and just to celebrate thee, to bless thee, to praise thee, to give thee thanks, to worship thee in every place of thy dominion ; for thou art a God ineffable, imperceptible, invisible, incomprehensible, everlasting, and always the same,' etc.

In the liturgy of St Basil, in Goar's Euchologium (p. 162), the first prayer of the faithful runs thus : ' Thou, O Lord, hast revealed to us this great mystery of salvation ; thou hast vouchsafed to make us, humble and unworthy servants as we are, ministers of thy holy altar. Make us, by the power of thy Holy Spirit, worthy of this ministry, that, standing without condemnation in the presence of thy divine glory, we may offer unto thee the sacrifice of praise. Thou art who in all things workest all. Grant, O Lord, that, on account both of our sins and of the errors of thy people, our sacrifice may be received, and become well-pleasing in thy sight.'

The prayer of the Offertory, p. 164 :

' O Lord, our God, who hast created us and hast brought us into this life, who hast shown us the path to salvation, who hast vouchsafed to us the revelation of celestial mysteries ; it is thou who, by the power of the Holy Spirit, hast ordained us for this ministry. Be pleased, O Lord, that we may become ministers of thy New Testament and dispensers of thy holy mysteries. Receive us, O Lord, approaching to thy holy altar, according to the multitude of thy mercies, that we may become worthy to offer unto thee this reasonable and unbloody sacrifice in behalf of our own sins and the errors of thy people. Receive this sacrifice upon thy holy and reasonable altar for a sweet-smelling fragrance, and send us down in return the grace of the Holy Spirit. Look down upon us, O Lord, and regard this our worship, and accept it, as thou didst accept the gifts of Abel, the sacrifices of Noah, the holocausts of Abraham, the sacred oblations of Moses and Aaron, and the peace-offerings of Samuel. As thou didst receive from thy holy apostles this true sacrifice, so also in thy benignity accept, Lord, from our sinful hands these gifts, in order that, being found worthy to minister without offence at thy holy altar, we may meet with the reward of faithful and prudent stewards in the tremendous day of thy just retribution.'

In the Alexandrine liturgy of St Mark (Renaudot Liturg. orient. coll. t. i, p. 145), the priest saith in the offertory : ' Thou hast created all things by thy wisdom, the true light, thy only-begotten Son, our Lord and God and Saviour Jesus Christ, through whom rendering thanks unto Thee, together with him and the Holy Ghost, we offer up this reasonable and unbloody sacrifice, which all the nations offer up to thee, O Lord, from the rising of the sun unto the going down thereof, from the North and from the South ; for thy name is great among all the nations, and in every place, incense, and sacrifice, and oblation, are put up to thy holy name.'

THE END

www.ingramcontent.com/pod-product-compliance
Lightning Source LLC
Chambersburg PA
CBHW020937230426
43666CB00005B/68